Domain-Specific Conceptual Modeling

Dimitris Karagiannis · Heinrich C. Mayr
John Mylopoulos
Editors

Domain-Specific Conceptual Modeling

Concepts, Methods and Tools

Springer

Editors
Dimitris Karagiannis
Universität Wien
Vienna
Austria

John Mylopoulos
University of Trento
Trento
Italy

Heinrich C. Mayr
Alpen-Adria-Universität Klagenfurt
Klagenfurt
Austria

ISBN 978-3-319-81882-5   ISBN 978-3-319-39417-6 (eBook)
DOI 10.1007/978-3-319-39417-6

Printed on acid-free paper

This Springer imprint is published by Springer Nature
The registered company is Springer International Publishing AG Switzerland

Preface

This book represents the result of a community effort and cooperation to create and develop modeling methods and languages, based on the OMiLAB[1] Collaborative Environment.

It aims to increase the visibility of domain-specific conceptual modeling by presenting work of thought leaders who designed and deployed a specific modeling method. Furthermore it provides a hands-on guidance on how to build models in a particular domain, such as requirements in engineering, business process modeling or enterprise architecture. Not only the results are presented, but also the ideas for future developments are communicated.

All this is enriched with any exercises, case studies, papers and updated information the authors deem important. All domain-specific methods described in this volume have also a tool implementation within the OMiLAB. This opens up possibilities to involve a wide community of further developers and users.

The Open Models Laboratory (OMiLAB) is a dedicated research and experimentation space for modeling method engineering. Being both a physical and virtual place, it is equipped with tools to explore method creation and design, experiment with method engineering and deploy software tools for modeling. The laboratory offers also a portal, through which the scientific community can bring in their ideas related to conceptual modeling issues and engage in their exploration process.

We are confident that this book will benefit experts and practitioners from academia and industry, members of the conceptual modeling community as well as lecturers and students.

A large scientific community was involved in creating this book and we would like to extend our gratitude to each and everyone for their contribution. First of all, we thank all the authors who submitted their work and provided their expertise in

[1]www.omilab.org

this field, and reviewers for their helpful feedback. Our special thanks to Ms. Iulia Vaidian for administrative support of the editors, also to Prof. Ovidiu Matiu for language editing. We are thankful for the support received from the team at Springer led by Ralf Gerstner in the publication of this book.

We highly appreciate the efforts from all of those involved!

April 2016

Dimitris Karagiannis
Heinrich C. Mayr
John Mylopoulos

Contents

Part I An Introduction to Modeling Method Conceptualization

Fundamental Conceptual Modeling Languages in OMiLAB 3
Dimitris Karagiannis, Robert Andrei Buchmann, Patrik Burzynski, Ulrich Reimer and Michael Walch

SemCheck: Checking Constraints for Multi-perspective Modeling Languages 31
Manfred A. Jeusfeld

OMiLAB: An Open Collaborative Environment for Modeling Method Engineering 55
David Götzinger, Elena-Teodora Miron and Franz Staffel

Part II Big Data

Design Semantics on Accessibility in Unstructured Data Environments 79
Nicholas Roussopoulos and Wilfrid Utz

Big Data—Integration and Cleansing Environment for Business Analytics with DICE 103
Wilfried Grossmann and Christoph Moser

Part III Business Process Management

Using the Horus Method for Succeeding in Business Process Engineering Projects 127
Andreas Schoknecht, Arthur Vetter, Hans-Georg Fill and Andreas Oberweis

Semantic Evaluation of Business Processes Using SeMFIS 149
Hans-Georg Fill

Business Process Feature Model: An Approach to Deal with Variability of Business Processes 171
Riccardo Cognini, Flavio Corradini, Andrea Polini and Barbara Re

Part IV Business and Process Transformation

Capability-Oriented Enterprise Knowledge Modeling: The CODEK Approach 197
Pericles Loucopoulos and Evangelia Kavakli

Supporting Business Process Improvement Through a Modeling Tool 217
Florian Johannsen and Hans-Georg Fill

Part V Enterprise Information Systems

Multi-perspective Enterprise Modeling—Conceptual Foundation and Implementation with ADO*xx* 241
Alexander Bock and Ulrich Frank

Holistic Conceptual and Logical Database Structure Modeling with ADO*xx* 269
Frank Kramer and Bernhard Thalheim

Tool Support for the Semantic Object Model 291
Otto K. Ferstl, Elmar J. Sinz and Dominik Bork

Part VI Enterprise Strategic Management

Evaluation Chains for Controlling the Evolution of Enterprise Models 313
Frank Wolff

Part VII Internet of Things/Future Internet

Algebraic Method to Model Secure IoT 335
Yeongbok Choe and Moonkun Lee

Security Requirements Engineering for Cloud Computing: The Secure Tropos Approach 357
Haralambos Mouratidis, Nikolaos Argyropoulos and Shaun Shei

Part VIII Knowledge Engineering

MELCA—Customizing Visualizations for Design Thinking 383
Igor Titus Hawryszkiewycz and Christoph Prackwieser

Business Process Flexibility and Decision-Aware Modeling—The Knowledge Work Designer 397
Knut Hinkelmann

Part IX Production Management Systems

Modeling Product-Service Systems for the Internet of Things: The ComVantage Method 417
Robert Andrei Buchmann

User Story Mapping-Based Method for Domain Semantic Modeling 439
Dimitris Kiritsis, Ana Milicic and Apostolos Perdikakis

Product-Service-System Modeling Method 455
Xavier Boucher, Khaled Medini and Hans-Georg Fill

Part X Requirements Engineering

The *i Framework for Goal-Oriented Modeling** 485
Xavier Franch, Lidia López, Carlos Cares and Daniel Colomer

Part XI Service Science: Social Implications

Global Service Enhancement for Japanese Creative Services Based on the Early/Late Binding Concepts 509
Yoshinori Hara and Hisashi Masuda

HCM-L: Domain-Specific Modeling for Active and Assisted Living 527
Heinrich C. Mayr, Fadi Al Machot, Judith Michael, Gert Morak, Suneth Ranasinghe, Vladimir Shekhovtsov and Claudia Steinberger

Part XII Technology Enhanced Learning

Modeling Learning Data for Feedback and Assessment 555
Peter Reimann and Wilfrid Utz

Modeling for Learning in Public Administrations—The Learn PAd Approach 575
Guglielmo De Angelis, Alfonso Pierantonio, Andrea Polini, Barbara Re, Barbara Thönssen and Robert Woitsch

About the Editors

Dimitris Karagiannis holds a full professor position for Business Informatics at the University of Vienna since 1993, leading the Research Group Knowledge Engineering. He earned a PhD degree from the Technical University Berlin in 1987. The same year he joined the Research Institute for Application-oriented Knowledge Processing in Ulm as division head for "Enterprise Information Systems". Karagiannis holds an honorary professorship from the Babes-Bolyai University in Cluj-Napoca, Romania. His research interests include meta-modelling, knowledge engineering, business process management, enterprise architecture management and artificial intelligence. The industrial application of his meta-modelling research was demonstrated within the BOC Group, a European software- and consulting company. In parallel scientific applications of his research are used in the Open Models Laboratory—OMiLAB, http://www.omilab.org, an open collaborative environment for modelling method engineering, which he has established and is currently leading.

Heinrich C. Mayr has been a full professor of Informatics at Universität Klagenfurt since 1990, leading the Application Engineering Research Group. Until then he was an assistant professor at the University of Karlsruhe (today: KIT), visiting professor at several universities, and CEO of a German software company. His research is documented in over 200 publications and includes information system design methodologies, requirements and model engineering, and knowledge management. Amongst other functions, he was President of the Gesellschaft für Informatik (GI), Vice President of the Council of European Professional Informatics Societies (CEPIS), and chairman of the board of trustees of a regional utility company. For 6 years he served as Rector of the University. Currently he is editor in chief of the Lecture Notes in Informatics (LNI), vice-chair of the ER steering committee, chairperson of the council of the Software Internet Cluster SIC, and Member of the TC Wirtschaftsinformatik of the German Accreditation Organisation ASIIN.

John Mylopoulos holds a professor emeritus position at the Universities of Toronto and Trento. He earned a PhD degree from Princeton University in 1970 and joined the faculty of the Department of Computer Science at the University of Toronto the same year. His research interests include conceptual modelling, requirements engineering, data semantics and knowledge management. Mylopoulos is a fellow of the Association for the Advancement of Artificial Intelligence (AAAI) and the Royal Society of Canada (Academy of Applied Sciences). He has served as programme/general chair of international conferences in Artificial Intelligence, Databases and Software Engineering, including IJCAI (1991), Requirements Engineering (1997, 2011), and VLDB (2004). Mylopoulos is currently leading a project titled "Lucretius: Foundations for Software Evolution <http://www.lucretius.eu/>", funded by an advanced grant from the European Research Council.

Part I
An Introduction to Modeling Method Conceptualization

Fundamental Conceptual Modeling Languages in OMiLAB

Dimitris Karagiannis, Robert Andrei Buchmann, Patrik Burzynski, Ulrich Reimer and Michael Walch

Abstract Regardless of the application domain, both the analysis of existing systems and the creation of new systems benefit extensively from having the system modeled from a conceptual point of view in order to capture its behavioral, structural or semantic characteristics, while abstracting away irrelevant details. Depending on which relevant details are assimilated in the modeling language, modeling tools may support different degrees of *domain-specificity*. The boundaries of what *domain-specific* means are as ambiguous as the definition of a *domain*—it may be a business sector, a paradigm, or a narrow application area. However, some patterns and invariants are recurring across domains and this has led to the emergence of commonly used modeling languages that incorporate such fundamental concepts. This chapter focuses on the metamodeling approach for the hybridization of BPMN, ER, EPC, UML and Petri Nets within a single modeling method identified as FCML, with a proof of concept named Bee-Up implemented in OMiLAB.

Keywords Hybrid metamodeling · BPMN · ER · EPC · UML · Petri Nets

---

D. Karagiannis (✉) · P. Burzynski · M. Walch
Research Group Knowledge Engineering, University of Vienna,
1090 Vienna, Austria
e-mail: dk@dke.univie.ac.at

P. Burzynski
e-mail: patrik.burzynski@dke.univie.ac.at

M. Walch
e-mail: michael.walch@dke.univie.ac.at

R.A. Buchmann
Business Information Systems Department, Babes-Bolyai University,
400591 Cluj-Napoca, Romania
e-mail: robert.buchmann@econ.ubbcluj.ro

U. Reimer
Institute for Information and Process Management, University of Applied Sciences
St. Gallen, 9001 St. Gallen, Switzerland
e-mail: ulrich.reimer@fhsg.ch

D. Karagiannis et al. (eds.), *Domain-Specific Conceptual Modeling*,
DOI 10.1007/978-3-319-39417-6_1

1 Introduction

The goal of this chapter is to advocate the hybridization of widely adopted modeling languages. Thereby, the benefit is the availability of conceptualizations which have established foundations that can be specialized or extended in domain-specific modeling languages. The modeling languages under our scrutiny are BPMN [1], ER [2], EPC [3, 4], UML [5] and Petri Nets [6, 7]. Based on them, the FCML (Fundamental Conceptual Modeling Languages) modeling method was derived through a metamodeling approach that allows modeling with these languages within the same tool. The motivation behind FCML is manifold:

1. it is a multi-purpose method whose implementation enables users to model in several commonly used languages, in the same tool, thus defusing the typical decision dilemma in choosing, for example, which business process modeling language should be adopted in a certain enterprise; different modelers in an enterprise may require or have familiarity with different languages (e.g., CEOs preferring EPC, while CTOs favoring UML);
2. it exploits recurring semantics by allowing the user to execute certain mechanisms (e.g., simulations) on different notations that comply to specific patterns (e.g., workflow patterns); at the same time, it also provides language-specific mechanisms and language-independent mechanisms, by exploiting the different layers of abstraction involved in the hybridization of the different incorporated languages;
3. it opens possibilities for domain-specific extensions, semantic linking and lifting of what otherwise have been considered domain agnostic or general purpose languages.

For demonstration purposes, an academic proof of concept of didactic and experimentation interest was developed within the Open Models Laboratory [8] on the ADO*xx* metamodeling platform [9].

Additionally, the chapter discusses the metamodeling approach that is employed in the research environment of the Open Models Laboratory and therefore has enabled the works presented throughout this book.

The chapter is structured as follows: Sect. 2 will discuss the relation of the languages selected for the FCML method to domain-specific modeling and will clarify the OMiLAB assumptions about what domain-specific modeling is. Section 3 will provide background on the modeling languages assimilated under the FCML acronym and will establish the notion of modeling method and its metamodeling framework, as employed by FCML and also by the other OMiLAB projects. Section 4 will detail the FCML conceptualization in relation to the underlying platform's meta^{2}model and Sect. 5 will showcase several key capabilities of the Bee-Up modeling tool, which implements FCML.

2 The Relevance of FCML for Domain-Specific Modeling

When designing languages for domain-specific modeling, a modeling method engineer will, on the one hand, (a) consider the established experience and lessons learned from standard languages or notations and, on the other hand, will (b) consider specializations and/or extensions with respect to *modeling requirements* raised for the addressed domain by the stakeholders who will either benefit from using models or work on the creation of models. Modeling requirements are commonly derived from two kinds of sources [10, 11]:

1. *Directly, from design-time needs* with respect to the capabilities of a required modeling tool. These typically pertain to the functionality that must support decisions regarding the engineering or re-engineering of a "system under study" (e.g., analysis, simulation and evaluation), to intrinsic qualities that models should have (e.g., understandability, semantic richness and consistency; see also existing frameworks for evaluating model quality [12, 13]) or to non-functional qualities that the modeling tool should have (e.g., usability, the ability to generate or reuse certain parts of models);
2. *Indirectly, from run-time needs* with respect to the capabilities of an information system that somehow makes use of the model contents—e.g., process-aware systems or other kinds of model-driven systems [14, 15]. The advocates of the model-driven engineering paradigm have emphasized the role of domain-specific modeling in capturing the domain concepts that are relevant to applications at run-time [16].

Such modeling requirements provide the starting motivation for the development of modeling languages with *domain-specificity*—that is, domain-specific modeling languages. The exact boundary of what "domain-specific" means, and where it differentiates from "cross-domain" or "general purpose", is not fixed in an absolute way. Some languages are more specific than others, and some domains are narrower than others. The notion of *domain* itself may have different interpretations—it could be a business sector, a community-driven paradigm, a narrow application area or even a single (typically virtual) case of an enterprise that is not interested in model interoperability or understanding outside its environment. In this line of argumentation, we cannot argue that languages, such as those included in the proposed FCML method, are truly "general purpose" languages: UML is primarily involved in software engineering, compared to ER which has a narrower focus on data modeling; EPC and BPMN were designed for business process management and can be extended towards the more holistic scope of enterprise modeling. Petri Nets are the most abstract due to the fact that their inherent nature is based on a strong mathematical formalism, but their applicability is also clearly limited to a class of problems pertaining to process dynamics. Therefore, the languages discussed in this chapter, although addressing wider classes of problems than most of the methods described in this book, are also domain-specific in their own right, and some of them are more specific than the others—e.g., for describing a business process,

BPMN has more specificity than UML activity diagrams, as it will be stressed further in this chapter in an attempt to illustrate the generic-to-specific spectrum in the context of conceptual modeling.

The fundamental nature of a process, whose description may be traced back to ancient Greek philosophers and the "ontology of becoming" (and later to state-transition systems), is based on a flow that alternates transitions (changes, actions) with states (outcomes of changes, possibly considering also incidental external events). A conceptualization process led to translating this ontological view to *Transitions* and *Places* in Petri Nets, or to the more business-oriented *Functions* and *Events* in EPC. The reason why both exist, despite the obvious conceptual redundancy, is the different modeling requirements that they satisfy:

1. *on a syntactic level*: minimal notation in Petri Nets, to visualize some formalized behavior, versus color-coded and shape-coded notation in EPC to improve readability and cognitive effectiveness;
2. *on a semantic level*: formal semantics open to grounded interpretation (to enable cross-domain reuse) in Petri Nets, versus business concepts with non-local semantics, limited reuse, but good familiarity for targeted stakeholders, in EPC;
3. *on a functionality level*: focus on dynamic simulation and excitability in Petri Nets, versus focus on understandability and model interoperability in EPC.

Although approaches exist to cover all these classes of requirements, there is an inherent trade-off between machine-oriented executability and human-oriented understandability and this trade-off determines a polarization of requirements.

Modeling requirements also determine how we perceive the quality of models, as enabled by the modeling language. In an absolutist sense, "all models are wrong" [17], since all of them must leave out properties of the system under study (in this sense, domain-specific languages would be "less wrong" the more specific they are). Therefore, completeness, correctness, usefulness and other quality attributes should be judged in a frame that is built on the addressed requirements. While, for some users, model executability is essential (as input for some process automation system), for others, reasoning on model contents or cognitive effectiveness may be much more important. What some modelers would perceive as modeling agility, others may consider as ambiguous semantics. For exemplification, let us consider the following comparison:

- For some users, it is convenient to repurpose the UML activity diagram type as an algorithm flow chart notation in some contexts and for business process diagrams in other contexts. This is perceived as model agility since it allows a loose interpretation of the same notation, based on how the activities are named or based on some a priori understanding of what the model is expected to describe;
- Other users may require a clear distinction between high-level business tasks and low-level algorithm steps, between business decisions and conditional (IF) split nodes. Such a distinction imposes a more constrained use of the modeling tool/language, but also opens possibilities with respect to how models

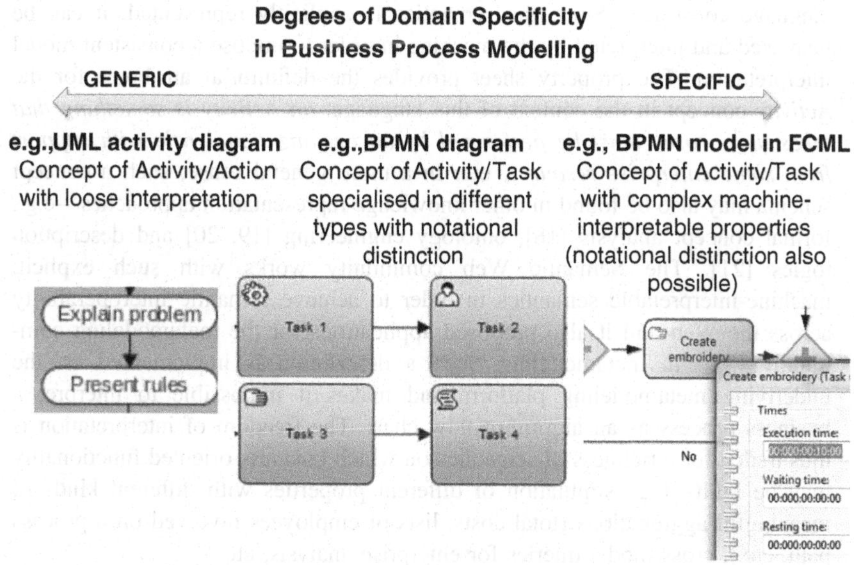

Fig. 1 Degrees of domain-specificity in business process modeling

can be processed by some model-driven functionality. The distinction may be enforced by the language syntax (e.g., subsumptions and notational variants for the same concept) or by the language semantics (i.e., explicitly defined in the language metamodel).

A straightforward example of the varying degrees of domain-specificity is illustrated in Fig. 1. A similar concept (*Activity/Task*) is presented with different notations and different semantics in UML activity diagrams, BPMN diagrams and FCML process models based on BPMN:

- In UML, the loose interpretation is possible by not fixing machine-interpretable semantics (except for the *Activity-Action* granularity distinction), but only a visual distinction from other types of nodes in the diagram. Domain-specificity is assimilated gradually as certain semantic aspects are fixed;
- BPMN adds typing (manual tasks, automated tasks, etc.) which is also reflected in the notation variability. This means that concepts from the application domain (here, business process management) become first-class citizens in the language alphabet, rather than being human interpretations of some generic symbols;
- Further on, the proposal of this chapter, FCML, adds property sheets to each *Activity* element, where the modeler may specify simulation-relevant attributes (e.g., different kinds of costs, times, resource consumptions) or semantic links (e.g., to a responsible role from a related organizational chart). These property sheets are prescribed by an "Activity schema" which is defined in the metamodel of the language as a means to provide semantics for the modeling

language constructs. Since the semantics is explicitly represented, it can be inspected and interpreted by the machine in order to impose a consistent model interpretation. The property sheet provides the definitorial attributes for the *Activity* concept in the context of this language: *an Activity is something that takes time, costs, must be performed by an organizational role with support from some enterprise resource,* etc. In a more general sense, such a concept schema may also be found in other knowledge representation approaches—e.g., formal concept analysis [18], ontology engineering [19, 20] and description logics [21]. The Semantic Web community works with such explicit, machine-interpretable semantics in order to achieve semantic interoperability across the Web and it also proposed applications for the metamodeling community [22]. In metamodeling, such a description is implemented on the underlying metamodeling platform and makes it impossible to interpret a business process as an algorithm flow chart. The freedom of interpretation is thus traded for a richness of semantics on which business-oriented functionality may be built—e.g., simulation of different properties with different kinds of meaningful aggregations (total costs, lists of employees involved on a process path, etc.), cross-model queries for enterprise analysis, etc.

FCML extends both UML and BPMN activities with domain-specific properties that specialize their semantics in an enterprise modeling context. In addition to attributes like costs and times, Fig. 2 shows an example where a BPMN task is assigned to its responsible performer/role not only through the visual means that BPMN provides (e.g., containment in a swimlane/pool) but also through a machine-interpretable semantic link to the organizational chart, as modeled within its own context (an organizational structure model with departments, performers, roles, etc. which may have its own domain-specific elements or editable properties).

These examples show how a modeling language may include concepts of varying domain-specificity even within the same model, or across different implementations. The challenges identified by the paradigm of "multilevel modeling"—see [23] further refine this aspect and contribute to a more flexible view on what the boundaries of a modeling language are. Although a scale from generic to specific may emerge from this discussion (as shown in Fig. 1), it will not hold in the general case. If we add Petri Nets to the discussion, their positioning in the spectrum is unclear (activity diagrams do not have a specialization of the *Place* concept, whereas in FCML the UML activity may have domain-specific semantics).

The goal of this section was to clarify our interpretation on domain-specificity in relation to FCML and with respect to the scope of this book. On the one hand, we tried to defuse the overly simplified traditional dichotomy between *general purpose* and *domain specific* languages, at least in the context of conceptual modeling. On the other hand, we aimed to remove also the simplification that modeling languages should be positioned in a linear range from generic to specific, as they employ different conceptual constructs. Consequently, we assigned the moniker *Fundamental Conceptual Modeling Languages* to the languages selected for hybridization under FCML, due to their quality of established references and starting points for

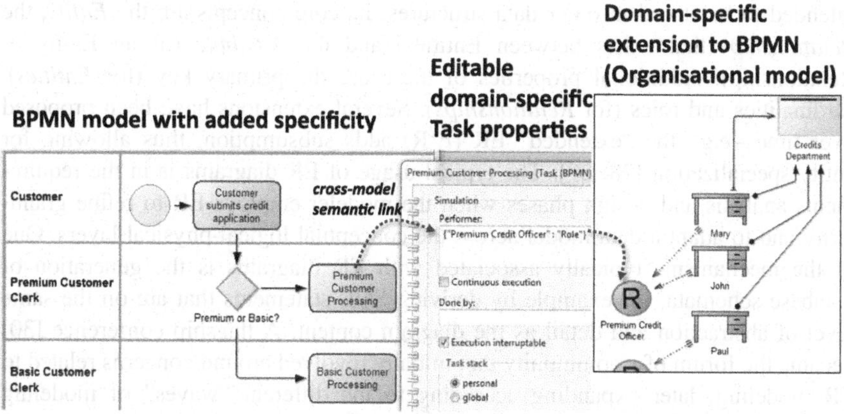

Fig. 2 Extending the domain-specificity of BPMN concepts in the FCML implementation

the concept specialization that is typically required in domain-specific modeling languages. The message of this section is that, when dealing with knowledge representation, any generic-to-specific variation should be discussed on concept level rather than language level, and this conclusion is aimed at extending the previously stated motivation behind FCML.

3 Method Description

3.1 Background on the Fundamental Conceptual Modeling Languages

The FCML modeling method incorporates and extends several modeling languages that gained wide popularity and are supported by communities with the help of a wide array of modeling tools, both commercial and free. This section provides a brief overview on the assimilated languages, to be later illustrated also by the proof of concept implemented in OMiLAB.

Entity–relationship (ER) diagrams have been widely adopted in the conceptual modeling community as the fundamental approach for data modeling, starting with the milestone paper of Peter Chen [2]. ER models have an ontological nature, in the sense that they describe categories of being and their relations, thus having a scope similar to that of UML class diagrams or metamodels. However, the objectives of ER modeling have been traditionally related to data modeling and database design, a prominent use being the generation of data schemata [24] or reverse engineering diagram generation [25]—typically for relational databases, but not necessarily [26, 27]. The ER metamodel is highly abstract, dealing with *Entities* rather than “paradigm-specific” tables/tuples. Therefore, ER diagrams may also describe data intended to be stored in other data structures. Its core concepts are the *Entity*, the *Relationship* (that exists between Entities) and the *Attribute* (of an Entity or Relationship). Additional properties of these are the primary key (for *Entities*), cardinalities and roles (for *Relationships*). Several extensions have been proposed over time—e.g., the "extended" ER (E^2R) adds subsumption, thus allowing for entity specialization [28, 29]. The typical usage of ER diagrams is in the requirements analysis and design phases when the modeler employs ER to refine granularity and to adapt a data model across the conceptual-logical-physical layers. One of the mechanisms typically associated with ER diagrams is the generation of database schemata, for example by deriving SQL statements that are on the same level of abstraction and detail as the diagram content. A flagship conference [30] became the forum of a community that initially revolved around concerns related to ER modeling, later expanding according to the different "waves" of modeling approaches developed over decades, including the one driven by the standardized Object Management Group languages such as UML [5].

Unified Modeling Language (UML) is one of the most prominent standards in software engineering, a language established in the late 1990s to support a unified method for object-oriented software development, by incorporating lessons learned from the large number of modeling languages that had been in use during the 1980s and early 1990s [31]. Therefore, UML may be seen as a natural descendant of the simpler and more focussed ER modeling approach. It covers a much wider scope through a number of diagram types addressing various aspects of a software system, classified into two categories: *static* (structural)—e.g., class diagrams, component diagrams and *dynamic* (behavioral)—e.g., activity diagrams and sequence diagrams. It still shares with ER the desideratum of code generation; however, UML addresses an object-oriented development context (e.g., class definitions derived from class diagrams). Additionally, UML fuelled the model-driven software engineering paradigm, due to some key strengths that are complementary to the modeling language itself: (a) model interoperability through diagram interchange formats—XMI [32]; and (b) a standard constraint definition language—OCL [33]. The notions of *UML profiles* and *stereotypes* were introduced to enable customization of the language alphabet for different development paradigms—e.g., XML-based applications [34]; or even domain-specific extensions—e.g., SysML [35], SoC [36]. Just like ER modeling, UML also ignited research interests and a community aggregated around a long-standing scientific conference—MODELS [37].

Business Process Model and Notation (BPMN) is an OMG standard [1] designed to support the business process management paradigm with a more extensive range of diagrammatic possibilities compared to traditional flowcharting or UML activity diagrams. One of the key benefits of BPMN is the domain-specificity added by typing generic concepts that have been available in traditional flowcharting languages. This specificity (addressing the "domain" of business process management) manifests as a richness of types (*Task* types, *Event* types, *Gateway* types) that provide semantic enrichment for not only human-readable interpretation but also for executability—thus stimulating the rise of business process execution engines. This was possible in tandem with the syntactic interoperability means provided by the XML ecosystem—specifically, the dedicated schemata for capturing a machine-processable serialization of diagrammatic process descriptions: BPEL [38], XPDL [39]. BPMN places a strong focus on the notational level, with the semantic variability being reflected in notational variability, through visual cues added to the shapes that represent tasks, events, gateways, etc.; at the same time, translations between BPMN and BPEL have been proposed [40] to support executability. Limitations of such mappings have been discussed in the sense of a conceptual mismatching between the diagramming standard and the serialization standard [41]. Trade-offs must be made between understandability and the formal rigour required for process executions, and consequently, subsets of the modeling constructs have been proposed in BPMN 2.0, addressing different modeling scopes—see also the analysis of [42]. The overall scope of BPMN being limited to business process descriptions, it provides only minimal support for describing the enterprise context—e.g., swimlanes reflecting organizational responsibilities for different parts of a process. Decision logic was recently separated from BPMN in a complementary modeling language—Decision Model and Notation [43].

Event-driven Process Chain (EPC) diagrams were introduced by the framework of Architecture of Integrated Information Systems (ARIS) and its software tools [3, 4]. EPC shares with BPMN the targeted domain (business process management), although the exact scope is different, due to a different trade-off between understandability and underlying formal rigour and due to how they are contextualized in enterprise architectures—see a comparative analysis at [44]. EPC advocates cognitive effectiveness through color coding and shape coding while removing the rich taxonomical classifications promoted by BPMN (perceived as excessively complicated by certain stakeholders, see [45, 46]). However, EPC formal semantics have been analyzed (with the help of Petri Nets in [47]) and serializations for model-driven systems have been proposed—ARIS was an early adopter of XPDL, attempts at BPEL serialization have been discussed [48] and an EPC-specific XML vocabulary has been proposed [49]. The core concepts of EPC are the *Function* and the *Event*, which can be interpreted as a flow of alternating "changes" and "states", with *Functions* being connected to elements of enterprise context: responsible organization unit, supporting IT system, input and output information. EPC shares with BPMN the basic control flow split and merge nodes of different logical types (XOR, AND and OR). Unlike BPMN, it stresses the need to identify states that emerge from, or trigger the need for the execution of *Functions* (events also exist in BPMN, but quite often they are considered implicit between two consecutive tasks). Another important distinction in general use is that EPC adds elements of the enterprise context (e.g., organizational units responsible for performing a *Function* are a language concept, not only a visual container). Actually, EPC emerged from an integrated way of modeling enterprise architecture, which is out of scope for BPMN.

Petri Nets [6, 7] is one of the longest standing diagrammatic modeling methods, with minimal but powerful semantics based on strong mathematical foundations. The trade-off here is that, on one hand, the method is sufficiently abstract to have cross-domain applicability with respect to process dynamics (especially relevant in the context of distributed systems); on the other hand, the level of abstraction imposes a learning curve that is not typically acceptable for business stakeholders and consequently the method was developed rather for academic concerns or as an underlying abstraction for other languages—see the effort of defining Petri Nets-based semantics for UML activity diagrams [50] or EPC models [47]. The Petri Nets method has a minimal metamodel that includes three highly abstract concepts—*Places* (states), *Transitions* (changes, actions) and *Arcs* (indicating the flow of places/transitions). The behavioral dynamics of a system are captured by a property called *Token*, which may be passed along the flow of places, each passing being triggered by the *firing* of a transition, which signifies an action taken. Simulation mechanisms are employed to monitor the possible states of the system as a whole, based on how the transitions may be fired, on how multiple possibly concurrent tokens are passed along, as well as on token availability in different places during different system states (token availability in a selected place will enable the transitions following that place). Typical simulation goals are the assessment of reachability of certain states, the risk of deadlock, the liveness/deadness of certain transitions. Extensions such as Colored Petri Nets [51] or transfer/reset nets [52] were introduced to enrich expressivity with additional properties (e.g., guarded transitions, token data, reset arcs).

3.2 The Metamodeling Approach

The engineering of a hybrid modeling method such as FCML must follow a *metamodeling approach* to ensure proper semantic coverage, and to ensure that the method is not only bringing different types of diagrams in the same modeling tool, but it also adds the following benefits:

- It extends *diagrams* to the status of *conceptual models* in the following sense: the model is not only a notational construct built with different graphical shapes relying on human interpretation; instead, each shape is instantiated from a higher abstraction concept with explicitly defined, machine-interpretable semantics, based on a concept taxonomy and descriptive properties through which the language terminology is defined. This allows both structural and semantics-driven processing of models, including reasoning on the structure or domain-specific properties of model elements, with rules processed by means that are specific to each metamodeling platform (the FCML implementation in OMiLAB was built on ADO*xx* [9]). The main distinction from other knowledge representation paradigms (e.g., description logics, ontology engineering) is that with metamodeling there was less effort towards interoperability across the popular metamodeling platforms—EMF [53], ConceptBase [54], MetaEdit + [55, 56]—whereas description logics and ontology engineering are following a trend towards the unifying logic envisioned in the Semantic Web "layer cake" and a Web-oriented standardization overlooked by the W3C through several drivers—e.g., RDF for representing facts [57], OWL as an ontology language [20], RIF as a rule interchange format [58]. To stimulate the emergence of a similar unifying abstraction layer, OMiLAB has initiated a cross-platform language for modeling method definition, MM-DSL, with an early draft discussed in [59];

- Furthermore, the metamodeling approach integrates models with meaningful cross-model relations that will act on one hand as semantic relations between concepts of different languages and on the other hand as hyperlinks that support navigation across models (thus improving usability and understandability). This will be showcased in Sect. 5 as a means of making models compliant to cross-notational simulation algorithms, but is not limited to this.

Figure 3 depicts the abstraction layers involved in the metamodeling approach of OMiLAB. A standardized version of a multi-layered conceptual architecture was also defined as a framework for UML, under the name MetaObject Facility [60]. We provide here a brief explanation on these layers:

- On the *Modeling layer*, models are created according to a specific modeling language, with distinctive notation and semantics for each diagrammatic symbol;
- To make modeling possible, on the *Meta layer* the terminology of the language is prescribed by specifying: the concepts that are allowed to be used, their notational manifestations, their semantics (property-based descriptions),

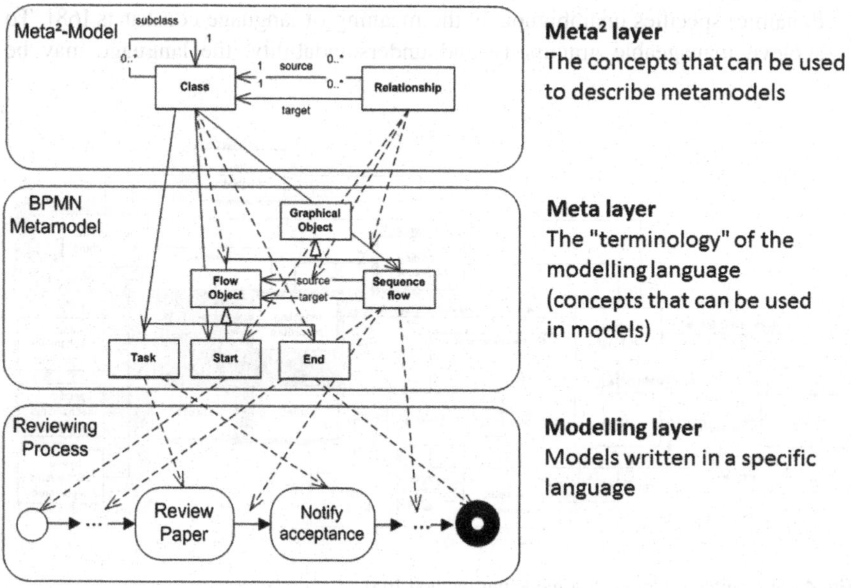

Fig. 3 Abstraction layers in metamodeling—adapted from [65]

syntactic and semantic constraints (e.g., domain or ranges for visual connectors). Without these, a modeling tool is a semantically agnostic diagramming tool. This is where the metamodeling effort and hybridization take place primarily and the result is a terminological structure extended with dynamic visualization and all the properties that are necessary for the required modeling functionality (e.g., simulation);

- The creation of the language terminology requires itself a *Meta² layer*, where several foundational meta-concepts (e.g., class, property) provide invariants that are instantiated in language metamodels. Metamodeling platforms provide these pre-defined invariants: some popular examples are ADO*xx* [9], GOPPRR [61], ECore [62]—see an overview in [63]. Within our metamodeling approach, we investigated current metamodeling approaches and their meta-concepts and proposed meta-concept extensions on Meta² layer for systematic modularization and flexible composition of metamodels, an important aspect of the engineering of hybrid modeling methods [64].

The result of the OMiLAB metamodeling approach is encompassed by the notion of *modeling method*, which extends that of a *modeling language*. The modeling method was defined in [65] and its building blocks are depicted in Fig. 4, with a possible formal view provided in [66]:

1. The *modeling language* provides the set of modeling constructs (their notation, grammar and semantics). The language grammar (syntax) defines fundamental modeling constructs of the language and relationships between them, whereas the notation is concerned with the form of the language [67]. By assigning visual representations to modeling constructs, the semantics (static and dynamic) specifies unambiguously the meaning of language constructs [68]. To achieve manageable granularity and understandability, the language may be

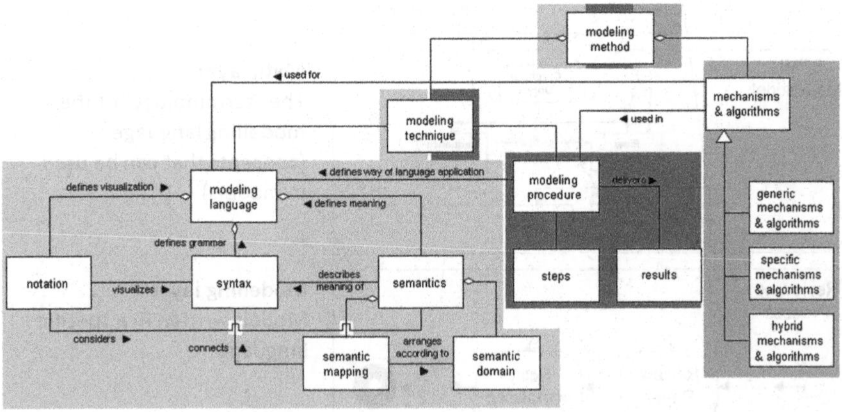

Fig. 4 The building blocks of a modeling method [65]

partitioned in *model types* addressing different facets or dimensions of the modeled system. This partitioning can be motivated as a usability feature (a top-down decomposition approach to avoid visual cluttering) or as a consequence of hybridization (a bottom-up strategy employed to interconnect modeling language fragments). In any case, the model types can be connected with semantic hyperlinks that enable cross-model navigation, as well as cross-model functionality. The work at hand exploits this by semantically extending generic concepts with additional properties that relate them to domain-specific concepts in other model types (e.g., see in Sect. 5 the case of the EPC extension);

2. The *modeling procedure* defines the steps that must be taken by modelers towards their goal. In the simplest case, it advises on the precedence in creating different types of models in order to achieve a coherent set of related models of different types. This includes the preparation of cross-model links to enable specific functionality that relies on certain model patterns, to be highlighted in Sect. 5;
3. The *mechanisms and algorithms* cover functionality that must process model contents for various purposes (simulation, visualization, transformation, evaluation, etc.). In this respect, the work at hand illustrates the generic-to-specific spectrum with respect to modeling functionality:
   - (i) The *SQL generation mechanism* is specific to ER modeling and *token-based simulations* are specific to Petri Nets;
   - (ii) Workflow simulation mechanisms are less specific, as they apply to a wide range of model types, as long as they allow the description of the typical workflow patterns. *Path analysis* or *workload assessment* may aggregate domain-specific properties attached to the control flow model types (BPMN, EPC and UML activity diagrams). Similarly, *reasoning mechanisms* may apply to several model types. For example, querying conceptual models might require reasoning (e.g., to account for inheritance) and can be defined for models represented in UML class diagrams as well as for ER models. Reasoning mechanisms can also provide *inference services* to be utilized by an application that is generated from the model or built on top of it, e.g., for classifying instances into classes. Furthermore, reasoning mechanisms enable *consistency checking* of a model during build time to support the modeler in creating and editing a model [69]. The means for implementing simulation and reasoning mechanisms, as well as other algorithms associated with a modeling language, would be highly dependent on the metamodeling platform. In this respect, ADO*xx* provides the AdoScript scripting language which can be used for programmatic implementations driven by the machine-interpretable model semantics (e.g., the graph rewriting mechanism described in [70]);

(iii) The algorithms that come along with a modeling method (such as the ones mentioned above for generating SQL statements, for simulation, and reasoning mechanisms in general) interpret the constructs of the underlying modeling language in a specific way in order to implement the intended functionality. In other words, the algorithms attribute a specific meaning or semantics to the constructs. Instead of having the semantics local to the algorithms, which introduces the risk of inconsistent interpretations between different algorithms, it is preferable to represent the semantics in an explicit way as part of the modeling language, i.e., in the metamodel. The Semantic Web community achieves such a *machine-interpretable semantics* by formally grounding their modeling languages in description logics [21]. Machine-interpretable semantics opens up new possibilities, such as (semantic) interoperability and (semantic) bridging between models. An example of model mapping, which benefits from such a machine-interpretable semantics is illustrated in Chapter 19 of this book (formally described in [71]), where models regardless of their type are *converted to Linked Data graphs to allow reasoning on model contents* through standardized means using the RDF framework [57]. The metamodeling community has so far been less interested in semantic interoperability across metamodeling platforms and the resulting opportunities—therefore, we mention this challenge here as a current research opportunity.

Based on the definition discussed here, a domain-specific modeling tool must implement a complete method and not only a language. Consequently, the tool should include (a) model-driven functionality that is relevant with respect to the modeling requirements; (b) guidelines and constraints for modeling scenarios with respect to different modeling goals and related functionality. The next sections will emphasize this aspect by using the case of FCML and its Bee-Up implementation.

4 Method Conceptualization: The Underlying Meta^{2}model

To achieve its hybridization goal, FCML makes use of the meta^{2}model foundational constructs provided by the ADO*xx* metamodeling platform [9] whose meta^{2}model was analyzed in detail in [72]. The choice of platform and the implementation followed certain principles, such as: minimizing the workarounds, having the platform-specific metamodels as close as possible to the original ones, having the possibility of restricting metamodels through configuration rather than because of platform restrictions. The ADO*xx* meta^{2}model constructs are shown in Fig. 5 and a mapping of their relevance for each language assimilated in FCML is provided in Table 1.

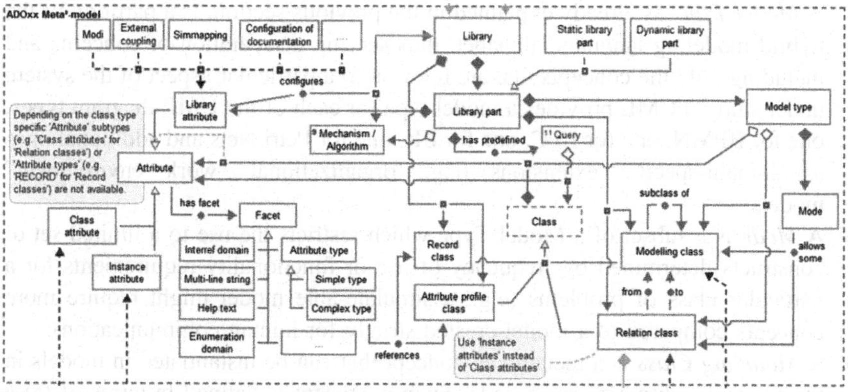

Fig. 5 The underlying ADO*xx* platform meta²model

Table 1 Involvement of different ADO*xx* concepts in the FCML components

Meta²-model Concept	BPMN	EPC	ER	UML	PN
Library	✓	✓	✓	✓	✓
Static Library	≈	≈		≈	
Dynamic Library	✓	✓	✓	✓	✓
Model Type	✓	✓	✓	✓	✓
Mode	✓	✓		✓	
Modelling Class	✓	✓	✓	✓	✓
Relation Class	✓	✓	✓	✓	✓
Record Class				✓	
Attribute Profile Class					
Attribute (Not Platform-specific)	✓	✓	✓	✓	✓
Class Attribute					
Instance Attribute	✓	✓	✓	✓	✓
Inheritance (subclass of)	✓	✓	✓	✓	
Query (Platform-specific)					
Simulation (Platform-specific)	✓	✓		✓	
Custom Algorithms/Mechanisms	≈	≈	✓	≈	✓

- A *Library* contains the ADO*xx* definition for a modeling method, including its language definition, mechanisms and algorithms. It typically has two parts: the *Static* part covering structural model types (e.g., UML class diagrams, ER models, organizational charts, etc.) and the *Dynamic* part covering behavioral model types (e.g., UML activity diagrams, BPMN, EPC and Petri Nets). The table suggests that the Static part is not inherent to BPMN and EPC, but was added as domain-specific extensions in FCML. Several *Library attributes* act as metadata with possible coupling to external systems (e.g., external scripting or system commands);

- A *Model Type*, as already explained in the previous section, is a partition of the hybrid modeling language alphabet, thus serving a separation of concerns and including only the concepts that are relevant to a particular aspect of the system under study. FCML provides a model type for each of the UML diagram types, one for BPMN, one for EPC, one for ER, one for Petri Nets and additional ones as domain-specific extensions (e.g., organizational "work environment" models);
- A *Mode* is a subset of a Model Type which restricts the use to a limited set of constructs determined by frequency of use or functionality requirements for a particular class of problems (e.g., a simulate-able model might require more concepts compared to a model created strictly for human communication);
- A *Modeling Class* is a metamodel concept that can be instantiated in models in the form of a directed graph node. Such a concept is defined in terms of (a) a "schema" prescribing its set of definitorial and descriptive properties and (b) a notation that can be customized according to required visual dynamics (e.g., interaction points as functionality triggers, notation variability determined by instance-level property values);
- A *Relation Class* is another type of metamodel concept, a connecting concept that can be instantiated in models in the form of visual connectors. Connectors have their own schema with their own properties and possibilities for notational customization—however, constraints such as domain, range, cardinality and relational notation must be considered;
- A *Record Class* is a schema for a tabular property that may be included in the prescribed property sets of any modeling concept, to collect property values that are complex and cannot fit a simple property slot. The use of this kind of properties is limited in FCML to only a few of the UML constructs (e.g., class attributes in a class diagram);
- An *Attribute Profile* is a schema for a set of properties that should be reused throughout the metamodel but will not act itself as the schema of a modeling concept. Currently, FCML does not employ this component;
- An *Attribute* is a property attached to the semantic definition of a modeling concept. They can be made visible as editable attributes, in property sheets that are attached to any model element, or they can be used strictly for inheritance purposes at metamodel level. Their *Facets* allow for additional restrictions on their value range, including the possibility of having links (*interrefs*) to elements from different model types;
- The *Inheritance* indicates the possibility of reusing modeling concepts by inheriting their "schema" in more specialized concepts. This is one of the key enablers for extending concept specificity in domain-specific modeling languages and has been extensively used in FCML, with the exception of Petri Nets whose minimal metamodel does not require inheritance;

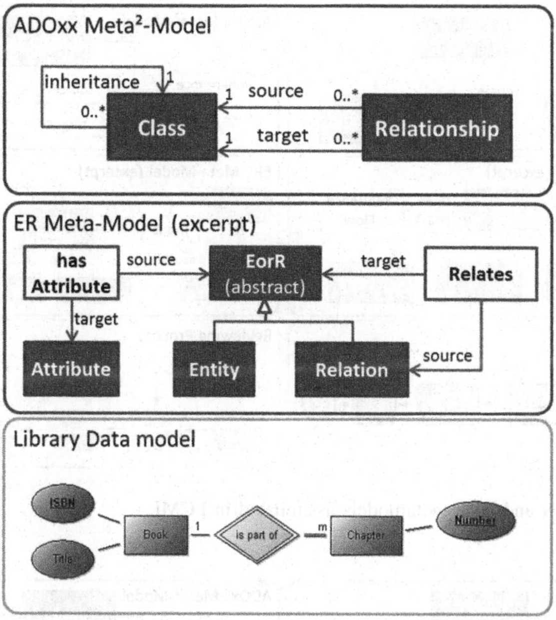

Fig. 6 The ER metamodel assimilated in FCML

- The *Query* indicates the possibility of inheriting an internal query engine built on the generic structure of any model, as well as the customization of pre-defined queries for each specific model type. In the current implementation, FCML does not fully employ this component, although work is underway to design model queries that are relevant to the specificity of each model type;
- The *Simulation* indicates the possibility of inheriting several simulation engines that are applicable on models of various specificities if they comply with certain modeling patterns (e.g., workflow patterns in BPMN, EPC, UML activity diagrams). Section 5 will illustrate how this applies to FCML;
- The *Custom Algorithms/Mechanisms* indicates the possibility of extending model-driven functionality with any customized mechanism (e.g., reasoning, code generation) based on the specific semantics and structure of each model type. These can be programmed in the internal AdoScript language and Sect. 5 will illustrate such possibilities for ER and Petri Nets. The other FCML model types can also make use of the customized mechanism of a more generic nature (e.g., model exporting).

Figures 6, 7 and 8 provide a more detailed view on the core meta²model concepts that are involved in the metamodel for each of the languages assimilated in the FCML (ER, BPMN, EPC, UML—partially depicted, and Petri Nets, respectively).

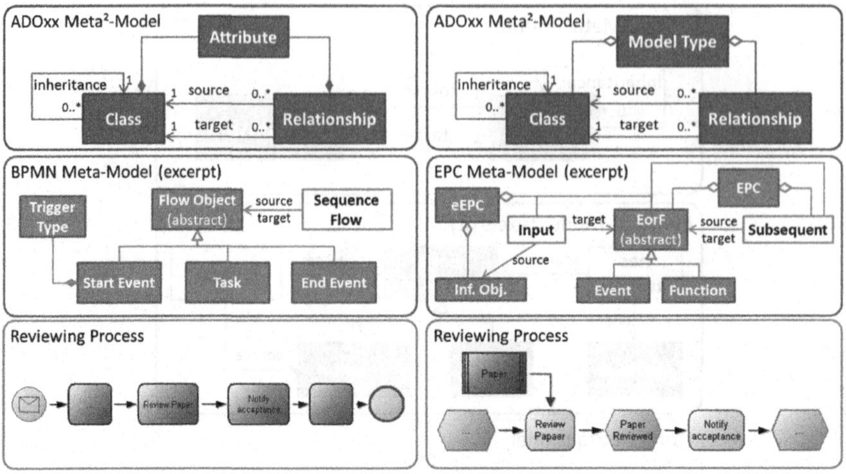

Fig. 7 The BPMN and EPC metamodels assimilated in FCML

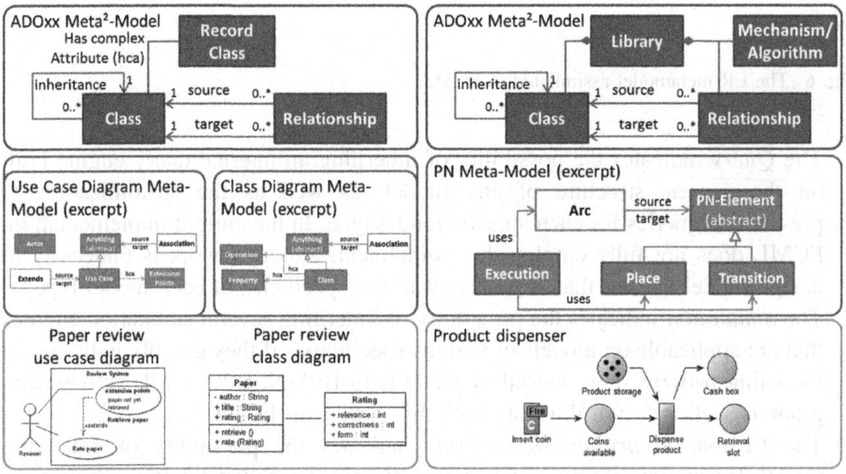

Fig. 8 The UML (fragment) and the Petri nets metamodels assimilated in FCML

5 Proof of Concept: The Bee-up Tool

A proof of concept for FCML was implemented in the OMiLAB environment as the Bee-Up modeling tool [8]. We take the opportunity to showcase in this section how the implementation extends the original specifications of the assimilated languages, due to the added specificity as well as due to method-level integration on the meta²model foundation provided by ADO*xx*.

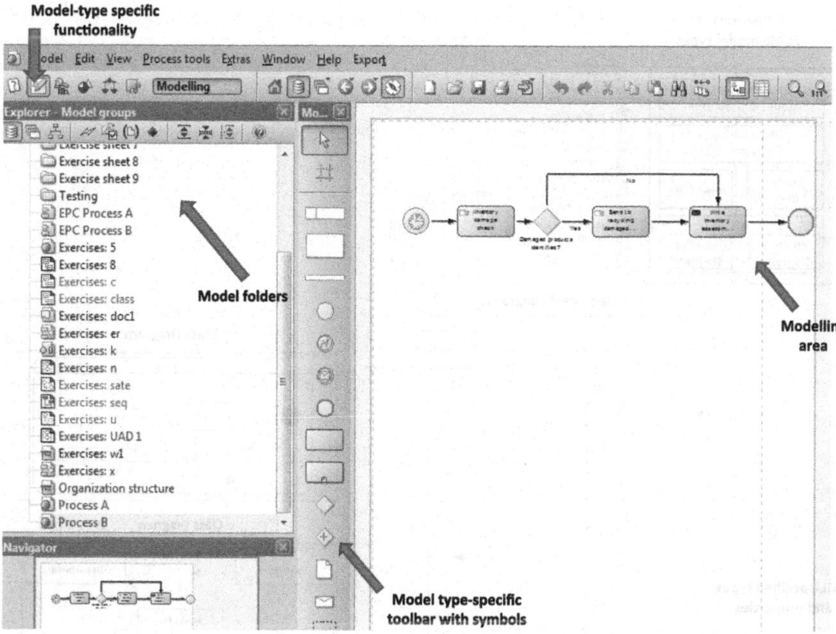

Fig. 9 The Bee-Up user interface

Figure 9 shows an overview of the Bee-Up user interface, with its model management component, the main menu providing implementations of FCML mechanisms and the modeling area providing a Model-Constructs ribbon that is specific for each type of model (determined by its metamodel).

The creation of a model will trigger a panel where the FCML languages are classified according to the categories that may also be found in UML (static or dynamic)—however, we include here all the FCML model types (notice that EPC and BPMN span across the two categories with elements of domain-specificity that are relevant, for example, to simulation mechanisms).

Figure 10 shows this panel and the list of UML model types, as well as several samples of UML models (sequence, class and state diagram). Each diagram element (nodes, containers, connectors) has a sheet of editable properties (bottom-left side of Fig. 10), which includes the possibility of extending the semantic of all the concepts found in the FCML languages with domain-specific properties, additional typing or semantic hyperlinks to related models.

Another model type is Petri Nets. The official notation of Petri Nets is quite minimal, as most languages that have not been designed with enterprise modeling requirements in mind (it provides only the minimal distinctions necessary to grasp

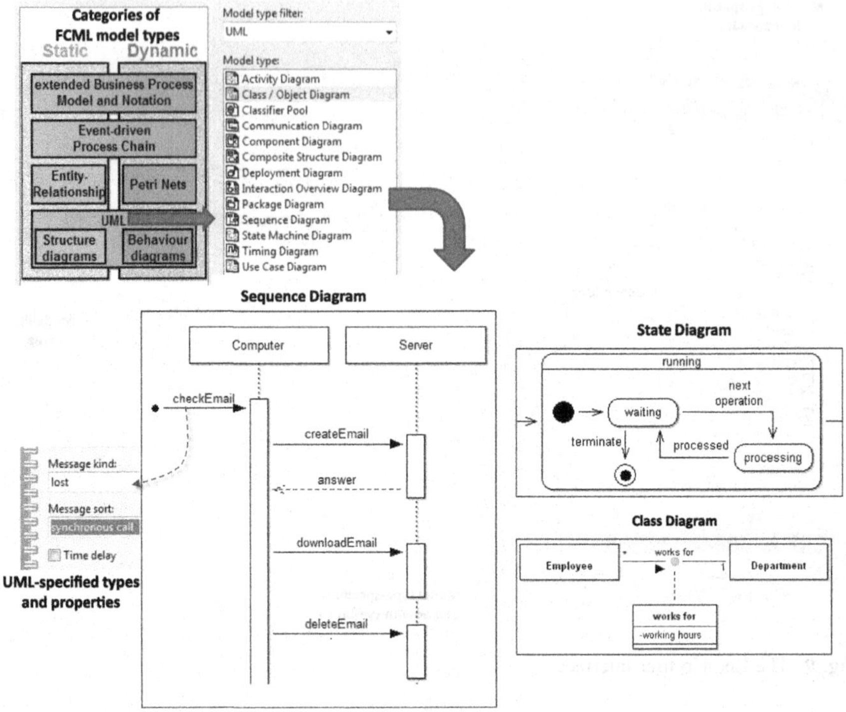

Fig. 10 The UML model types included in FCML

the underlying mathematical formalism). The Bee-Up implementation adds on the notational level several visual cues and visual dynamics to facilitate user interaction in support of Petri Nets-specific simulation mechanisms. Figure 11 shows: (a) interactive visual cues (the *Fire* boxes) that may be used by the modeler to step through the states of the model; (b) a purely functional symbol added to the modeling language to provide simulation triggers with preset parameters (e.g., transition priorities) directly on the modeling canvas; (c) symbols that may store and restore relevant system states described in terms of the number of tokens present in each place.

Figure 12 shows an example of a BPMN process model together with simulated costs for a particular process path (highlighted by the notational dynamics that can be programmed in ADOxx). This is actually a *Path analysis* mechanism that is domain-specific in the following senses: (a) it is applicable only to those models whose structure conforms to workflow-specific patterns (e.g., BPMN, EPC and UML activity diagrams); (b) it aggregates domain-specific properties that were

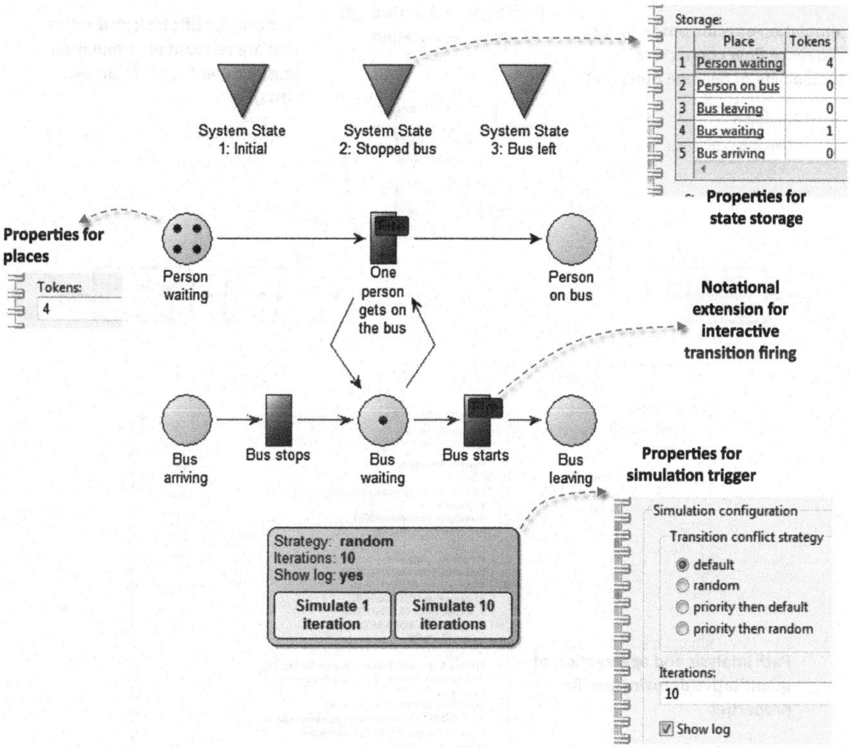

Fig. 11 Petri Nets simulation controlled by interactive visual cues

attached to the process steps along each path (e.g., different kinds of costs, times, domain-specific resource consumptions); these extensions are applied on the metamodel level for the corresponding *Task/Activity* concept in each model type, inheriting some of them from a higher level concept that acts as the hybridization bridge of FCML.

Figure 13 illustrates another domain-specific simulation mechanism, this time applied to EPC models which were semantically extended at metamodel level with hyperlinks between EPC functions and roles or performers from a distinct organizational model. The existence of a separate organizational structure model type allows multiple EPC processes to be linked to the same human resources or responsible units while at the same time avoiding the visual cluttering that would occur by reusing the organizational unit on the modeling canvas of each EPC model. Besides the domain-specific aspects that can be added to the organizational units without affecting the EPC metamodel, the key benefit of this "separation of

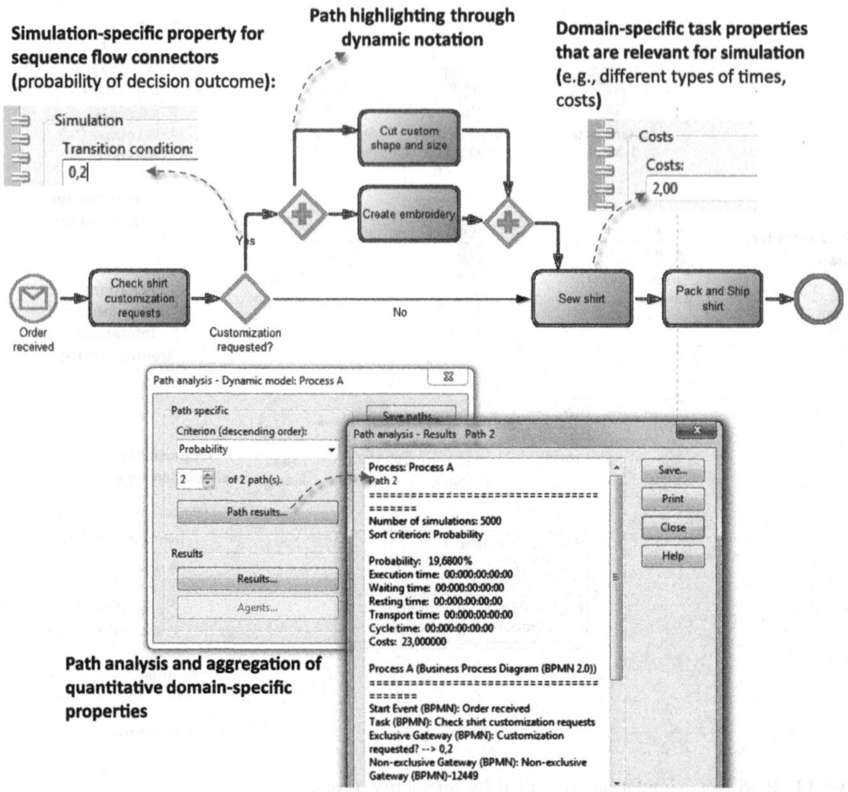

Fig. 12 Path analysis on BPMN model extended with domain-specific task properties

concerns" is the ability to build on it the workload assessment simulation that aggregates relevant properties (e.g., work times) for the organizational unit under scrutiny, as suggested in Fig. 13.

Figure 14 shows an example of a simple ER model and its key mechanism—SQL code generation. The editable property sheets which were used in previous examples to collect domain-specific properties (e.g., for enabling simulation) were tailored here to capture information that is specifically needed for the SQL generation mechanism (e.g., data types or key options for attributes, roles or cardinalities for entity–relationship arcs).

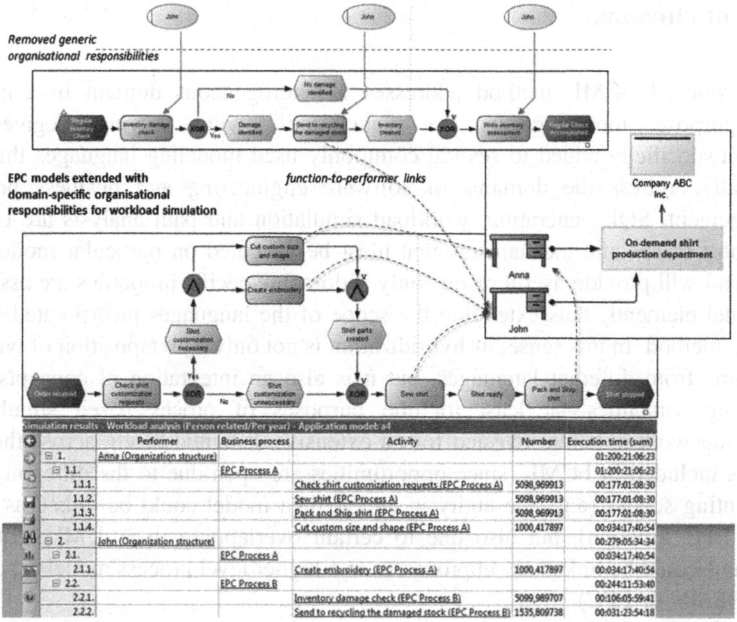

Fig. 13 Workload simulation on multiple extended EPC models in Bee-Up

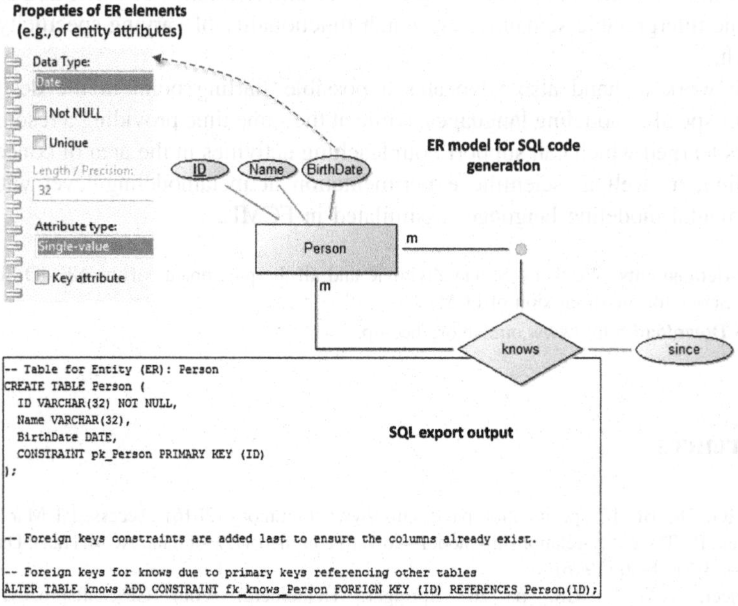

Fig. 14 ER modeling in Bee-Up, with SQL generation mechanism

6 Conclusions

The proposed FCML method addresses a heterogeneous domain by enabling multi-purpose modeling in the same tool, with varying degrees of domain-specificity added to several commonly used modeling languages that traditionally address the domains of software engineering and business process management. SQL generation, workload simulation and path analysis are typical examples of specific mechanisms that must be executed on particular model patterns and will provide useful results only if domain-specific properties are assigned to model elements, thus extending the scope of the languages incorporated in the FCML method. In this sense, its hybridization is not only a juxtaposition of types of diagrams from different languages, but it is also an integration of concepts with recurring semantics—at least for the purposes of process-based simulation. On-going work is being invested for an extensive semantic lifting across the languages included in FCML, since opportunities are open due to the different complementing scopes (e.g., the entity in an ER data model could be linked as input to an EPC function), but also due to certain overlapping (e.g., UML sequence diagrams could be linked as subprocesses to a higher level process model described with BPMN or EPC).

Ultimately, the kind of hybridization proposed by FCML and its proof-of-concept Bee-Up are aimed at being used as a multi-purpose and multi-layered modeling approach, where method agility is manifested by a multitude of notation alternatives in a single tool for different kinds of users, and also by machine-interpretable semantics on which functionality of varying specificity may be built.

The work at hand also advocates a possible starting point in the design of domain-specific modeling languages, while at the same time providing a resource of lessons learned which can support both teaching activities in the area of conceptual modeling, as well as scientific experimentation at metamodeling level with the fundamental modeling languages assimilated in FCML.

Acknowledgements We thank Srdjan Zivkovic and all the participants of the NEMO Summer School Series for the discussion of FCML.

Tool Download http://www.omilab.org/bee-up.

References

1. OMG: The BPMN specification page. http://www.bpmn.org (2016). Accessed 1 Mar 2016
2. Chen, P.: The entity-relationship model—toward a unified view of data. ACM Trans. Database Syst. **1**(1), 9–36 (1976)
3. Scheer, A.W.: ARIS, p. 20. Springer, Heidelberg, Vom Geschäftsprozess zum Anwendungssystem (2002)
4. Software AG: ARIS—the community page. http://www.ariscommunity.com (2016). Accessed 1 Mar 2016

5. OMG: The UML resource page. http://www.uml.org (2016). Accessed 1 Mar 2016
6. Petri, C.A., Reisig, W.: Petri net. Scholarpedia **3**(4), 6477 (2008). doi:10.4249/scholarpedia.6477
7. Reisig, W.: Understanding Petri Nets. Springer, Heidelberg (2013)
8. OMiLAB: The metamodelling page for FCML and the Bee-Up tool. http://www.OMiLAB.org/bee-up (2016). Accessed 1 Mar 2016
9. BOC GmbH: ADO*xx*—official website. https://www.adoxx.org/live/home (2016). Accessed 1 Mar 2016
10. Buchmann, R.A., Karagiannis, D.: Agile modelling method engineering: lessons learned in the ComVantage project. In: Ralyte, J., Espana, S., Pastor, O. (eds.) Proceedings of the 8th IFIP WG 8.1 Conference on the Practice of Enterprise Modelling (PoEM 2015), Valencia, Spain. LNBIP, vol. 235, pp. 356–373. Springer, Heidelberg (2015a)
11. Karagiannis, D.: Agile modeling method engineering. In: Proceedings the 19th Panhellenic Conference on Informatics (PCI 2015), pp. 5–10, Athens, Greece. ACM (2015)
12. Krogstie, J., Sindre, G., Jorgensen, H.: Process models representing knowledge for action: a revised quality framework. Eur. J. Inf. Syst. **15**, 91–102 (2006)
13. Moody, D.: The physics of notations: towards a scientific basis for constructing visual notations in software engineering. IEEE Trans. Software Eng. **35**(5), 756–777 (2009)
14. Bencomo, N., France, R., Cheng, B.H.C., Aßmann, U.: Models@run.time. LNCS, vol. 8378. Springer, Heidelberg (2014)
15. van der Aalst, W.M.P.: Process-aware informations systems: lessons to be learned from process mining. In: Jensen, L., van der Aalst, W.M.P. (eds.) Transactions on Petri Nets and Other Models of Concurrency II. LNCS, vol. 5460, pp. 1–26. Springer, Heidelberg (2009)
16. Schmidt, D.C.: Model-driven engineering. IEEE Comput. **39**(2), 25–31 (2006)
17. Box, G.E.P.: Science and Statistics. J. Amer. Stat. Assoc. **71**, 791–799 (1976)
18. Ganter, B., Stumme, G., Wille, R. (eds.) Formal Concept Analysis: Foundations and Applications. LNAI vol. 3626, Springer (2005)
19. Staab, S., Studer, R.: Handbook on Ontologies. Springer (2004)
20. W3C: OWL 2—the W3C recommendation. https://www.w3.org/TR/owl2-overview. Accessed 1 Mar 2016
21. Baader, F., Calvanese, D., McGuinness, DL., Nardi, D., Patel-Schneider, P.F.: Handbook of Description Logics. Cambridge University Press (2010)
22. Staab, S., Walter, T., Gröner, G., Parreiras, F.S.: Model driven engineering with ontology technologies. In: Aßmann, U., Bartho, A., Wende, C. (eds.) Reasoning Web—Semantic Technologies for Software Engineering, LNCS 6325, pp. 62–98. Springer, Heidelberg (2010)
23. Frank, U.: Multilevel modeling: toward a new paradigm of conceptual modeling and information systems design. Bus. Inf. Syst. Eng. **6**(6), 319–337 (2014)
24. Voultsidis, M.: ER2SQL—the official page. http://www.er2sql.com (2016). Accessed 1 Mar 2016
25. Andersson, M.: Extracting an entity-relationship schema from a relational database through reverse engineering. In: Loucopoulos, P. (ed.) Proceedings of the 13th International Conference on the Entity-Relationship approach, Manchester, England. LNCS, vol. 881, pp. 403–419. Springer, Heidelberg (1994)
26. Della, P.G., Di Marco, A., Intriglia, B., Melatti, I., Pierantonio, A.: Xere: towards a natural interoperability between XML and ER diagrams. In: Pezze, M. (ed.) Proceedings of the 6th International Conference FASE 2003 part of the Joint European Conference on Theory and Practice of Software, Warsaw, Poland. LNCS, vol. 2621, pp 356–371. Springer, Heidelberg (2003)
27. Liu, C., Li, J.: Designing quality XML Schemas from ER diagrams. In: Yu, J.X., Kitsuregawa, M., Leong, H.V. (eds.) Proceedings of the 7th International Conference on Advances in Web-Age Information Management, Hong Kong, China. LNCS 4016, pp 508–519. Springer, Heidelberg (2006)

28. Embley, D.W., Ling, T.W.: Synergistic database design with an extended Entity-Relationship model. In: Lochovsky, F.H. (ed.) Proceedings of the 8th International Conference on Entity-Relationship approach to database design and querying, pp. 111–128. Elsevier, Toronto, Canada (1990)
29. Teorey, T.J., Yang, D., Fry, J.P.: A logical design methodology for relational databases using the extended entity-relationship model. ACM Comput. Surv. **18**(2), 197–222 (1986)
30. Conceptual Modeling conference series. The ER conference series website http://www.conceptualmodeling.org (2016). Accessed 1 Mar 2016
31. Booch, G., Rumbaugh, J., Jacobson, I.: Unified Modeling Language user guidelines, 2nd edn. Addison-Wesley (2005)
32. OMG: The XMI specification page. http://www.omg.org/spec/XMI (2016). Accessed 1 Mar 2016
33. OMG: The OCL resource page. http://www.omg.org/spec/OCL. Accessed 1 Mar 2016
34. Carlson, D.: Modeling XML Applications with UML. Addison-Wesley (2001)
35. OMG: The SysML resource page. http://www.omgsysml.org (2016). Accessed 1 Mar 2016
36. Vanderperren, Y., Mueller, W., He, D., Mischkalla, F., Dehaene, W.: Extending UML for electronic systems design: a code generation perspective. In: Nicolescu, G., O'Connor, I., Piguet, C. (eds.) Design Technology for Heterogeneous Embedded Systems, pp. 13–39. Springer, Netherlands (2012)
37. ACM/IEEE: Official page of the 18th edition of the MODELS International Conference. http://cruise.eecs.uottawa.ca/models2015 (2015). Accessed 1 Mar 2016
38. OASIS: BPEL—the official website. https://www.oasis-open.org/committees/tc_home.php?wg_abbrev=wsbpel (2016). Accessed 1 Mar 2016
39. WfMC XPDL specification—official website (2015). http://www.xpdl.org. Accessed 1 Oct 2015
40. White, S.A.: Using BPMN to model a BPEL process. BPTrends **3**, 1–18 (2005)
41. Recker, J., Mendling, J.: On the translation between BPMN and BPEL: conceptual mismatch between process modeling languages. In: Latour, T., Petit, M. (eds.). Proceedings of Workshops and Doctoral Consortium. The 18th International Conference on Advanced Information Systems Engineering, pp. 521–532. Namur Univ. Press (2006)
42. zur Muehlen, M., Recker, J.: How much language is enough? Theoretical and practical use of the business process management notation. In: Bellahsene, Z., Leonard, M. (eds.) Proceedings of the 20th International Conference on Advanced Information Systems Engineering, Montpellier, France. LNCS vol. 5074, pp. 465–479. Springer, Heildelberg (2008)
43. OMG: The DMN specification page. http://www.omg.org/spec/DMN (2016). Accessed 1 Mar 2016
44. Velitchkov, I.: BPMN versus EPC revisited part 1. http://www.ariscommunity.com/users/ivo/2011-04-11-bpmn-vs-epc-revisited-part-1 (2016). Accessed 1 Mar 2016
45. Burlton, R.: Perspectives on Process Modeling. BPTrends (2009).
46. Swenson, K.: BPMN 2.0: no longer for business professionals. https://social-biz.org/2010/09/01/bpmn-2-0-no-longer-for-business-professionals/ (2016). Accessed 1 Mar 2016
47. van der Aalst, W.M.P.: Formalization and verification of event-driven process chains. Inf. Softw. Technol. **41**(10), 639–650 (1999)
48. Meertens, L.O., Iacob, M.E., Eckartz, S.M.: Feasibility of EPC to BPEL model transformations based on ontology and patterns. In: Rinderle-Ma, S., Sadiq, S., Leymann, F. (eds.) Proceedings of the BPM 2009 workshops, Ulm, Germany. LNBIP, vol. 43, pp. 347–358. Springer, Heildelberg (2010)
49. Mendling, J., Nüttgens, M.: EPC markup language: an XML-based interchange format for event-driven process chains. IseB **4**(3), 245–265 (2006)
50. Störrle, H.: Semantics of control-flow in UML 2.0 activities. In: Bottoni, P., Hundhausen, C., Levialdi, S., Tortora, G. (eds.) Proceedings of the 2004 IEEE Symposium on Visual Languages and Human-Centric Computing, pp. 235–242. IEEE, Rome, Italy (2004)

51. Jensen, K., Kristensen, L.M.: Coloured Petri nets. Springer, Heidelberg (2009)
52. Dufourd, C., Finkel, A., Schnoebelen, P.: Reset nets between decidability and undecidability. In: Larsen, K.G., Skyum, S., Winskel, G. (eds.) Proceedings of the 25th Int Colloquium ICALP98, Aalborg, Denmark. LNCS, vol. 1443, pp. 103–115. Springer, Heidelberg (1998)
53. Eclipse: The Eclipse Modelling Framework official page. https://eclipse.org/modeling/emf/ (2016). Accessed 1 Mar 2016
54. Jeusfeld, M.: Metamodeling and method engineering with ConceptBase. In: Jeusfeld, M., Jarke, M., Mylopoulos, J. (eds.) Metamodeling for Method Engineering, pp. 89–168. The MIT Press, Cambridge, USA (2009)
55. Kelly, S., Lyytinen, K., Rossi, M.: MetaEdit + a fully configurable multi-user and multi-tool CASE and CAME environment. In: Bubenko, J., Krogstie, J., Pastor, O., Pernici, B., Rolland, C., Solvberg, A. (eds.) Seminal Contributions to Information Systems Engineering, pp. 109–129. Springer
56. MetaCase: MetaEdit + tool. http://www.metacase.com/products.html (2016). Accessed 1 Mar 2016
57. W3C: The RDF official resource page. http://www.w3.org/RDF/ (2016). Accessed 1 Mar 2016
58. W3C: The RIF specification page. https://www.w3.org/TR/rif-overview/ (2016). Accessed 1 Mar 2016
59. Visic, N., Fill, H.-G., Buchmann, R., Karagiannis, D.: A domain-specific language for modelling method definition: from requirements to grammar. In: Rolland, C., Anagnostopoulos, D., Loucopoulos, P., Gonzalez-Perez, C. (eds.) Proceedings of the 9th International Conference on Research Challenges in Information Science (RCIS 2015), pp. 286–297. IEEE, Athens, Greece (2015)
60. OMG: The MOF specification page. http://www.omg.org/mof/ (2016). Accessed 1 Mar 2016
61. Kelly, S., Tolvanen, J.P.: Domain-Specific Modeling: Enabling Full Code Generation. Wiley (2008)
62. Budinsky, F., Steinberg, D., Merks, E., Ellersick, R., Grose, T.J.: Eclipse Modeling Framework. Addison Wesley, The Eclipse Series (2004)
63. Kern, H., Hummel, A., Kuhne, S.: Towards a comparative analysis of meta-metamodels. In: The 11th Workshop on Domain-Specific Modeling, Portland, USA (2011). http://www.dsmforum.org/events/DSM11/Papers/kern.pdf. Accessed 1 Oct 2015
64. Zivkovic, S.: Metamodel composition in hybrid modelling—a modular approach. Doctoral thesis, University of Vienna (2016)
65. Karagiannis, D., Kühn, H.: Metamodelling platforms. In: Bauknecht, K., Min Tjoa, A., Quirchmayer, G (eds.) Proceedings of the Third International Conference EC-Web 2002—DEXA 2002, Aix-en-Provence, France. LNCS vol. 2455, p. 182. Springer (2002)
66. Karagiannis, D., Buchmann, R.A.: Model fragment comparison using natural language processing techniques. In: Hess, T. (ed.) Brenner W, pp. 249–269. Wirtschafts-informatik in Wissenschaft und Praxis, Springer (2014)
67. Harel, D., Rumpe, B.: Modeling Languages: Syntax, Semantics and All That Stuff, Part 1: The Basic Stuff (2000)
68. Engels, G., Hausmann, J.H., Heckel, R., Sauer, S.: Dynamic meta modeling: a graphical approach to the operational semantics of behavioral diagrams in UML. In: ≪UML≫ 2000—The Unified Modeling Language, pp. 323–337. Springer, Berlin Heidelberg (2000)
69. Walter, T., Parreiras, F.S., Staab, S.: OntoDSL: an ontology-based framework for domain-specific languages. In: Schürr, A., Selic, B. (eds.) Proceedings of the 12th Inernational. Conference on MODELS, Denver, USA. LNCS vol. 5795, pp. 408–422. Springer, Heidelberg (2009)
70. Buchmann, R.A., Karagiannis, D.: Modelling mobile app requirements for semantic traceability. J. Requirements Eng. (2015). doi:10.1007/s00766-015-0235-1

71. Karagiannis, D., Buchmann, A.: Linked open models: extending linked open data with conceptual model information. Inf. Syst. **56**, 174–197 (2016)
72. Fill, H.G., Karagiannis, D.: On the conceptualisation of modelling methods using the ADO*xx* meta modelling platform. Enterp. Model. Inf. Syst. Architect. **8**(1), 4–25 (2013)

SemCheck: Checking Constraints for Multi-perspective Modeling Languages

Manfred A. Jeusfeld

Abstract Enterprises are complex and dynamic *organizations* that can hardly be understood from a single viewpoint. Enterprise modeling tackles this problem by providing multiple, specialized modeling languages, each designed for representing information about the enterprise from a given viewpoint. The OMiLAB initiative promotes the use of metamodeling to design such domain-specific languages and to provide them by an open repository to the community. In this chapter, we discuss how this metamodeling approach can be combined with the design of integrity constraints that span multiple modeling languages. We propose the services of the ConceptBase system as a constraint checker for modeling languages created by the ADO*xx* platform.

Keywords Modeling language • Consistency • Telos • ConceptBase

1 Introduction

Enterprise modeling environments[1] provide viewpoints for modeling goals, processes, resources, enterprise data, events and more. Each viewpoint may be supported by several modeling languages, e.g., to support alternative representations or to cover different abstraction levels. The resulting enterprise models need to be synchronized since they all make statements about the very same reality, the enterprise. The goal of enterprise modeling is to provide a complete and correct representation of the enterprise, up to the level of detail that is of interest to the modelers. The completeness is rather time-consuming to check since it requires comparing the concepts in the models with observations of the (real) enterprise. The correctness has two aspects

[1]This work was supported in part by the Erasmus + project Open Model Initiative (OMI).

M.A. Jeusfeld (✉)
University of Skövde, IIT, Skövde, Sweden
e-mail: manfred.jeusfeld@his.se

D. Karagiannis et al. (eds.), *Domain-Specific Conceptual Modeling*,
DOI 10.1007/978-3-319-39417-6_2

1. The statements derived from the enterprise models are consistent with the reality. For example, if a process model demands that an activity A always precedes an activity B, then this should hold for all executions of this process in the reality (*external model validity*).
2. The statements in the enterprise models are consistent with each other, or simpler: the statements in the enterprise models do not contradict each other (*internal model validity*).

We focus on the internal model validity in the OMiLAB [1] context. OMiLAB offers a repository, where multiple enterprise modeling languages can be stored and reused. The ADO*xx* platform [2, 3] used in OMiLAB supports both the design of customized modeling languages and their subsequent use. The challenge is to codesign the consistency rules for the new modeling languages. In particular, the constructs of several interrelated modeling languages are subject to consistency checks. For example, if a process model contains a data flow link that retrieves a certain data element from a data store, then the data model of that data store must also define this data element.

The rest of the paper is organized as follows. The next chapter discusses why constraints crossing multiple modeling perspectives occur in enterprise models. We argue for two types of such constraints: one is linking models at the same abstraction level, e.g., the business level. We call them horizontal constraints. The second type links models at different abstraction levels. We call them vertical constraints. After this discussion, we introduce the constraint checking capabilities of the ConceptBase [4, 5] system. ConceptBase allows representing both multiple modeling languages and their models in a uniform data structure. Finally, we propose the architecture to integrate the ADO*xx* platform with ConceptBase. The interaction between the two is described by a simple model exchange interface. The ADO*xx* platform can incrementally submit language and model update to the ConceptBase constraint checker and receives constraint checking results back. New constraints can be added at any time and old ones can be updated or removed at any time. The examples discussed in this chapter are available online at http://conceptbase.cc/nemo2015.

2 Constraints Between Multiple Models

Models describe some real or imagined reality, so enterprise models describe an existing or not yet existing enterprise. A model consists of model elements, which represent some physical or immaterial artefact of the reality. Consider an enterprise that maintains a database DB. This immaterial artefact occurs in multiple models. It may occur in a process model as input or output of some process task. It may also occur in a conceptual data model like an ER diagram defining the schema of the database. And it may occur as logical database design defining the precise datatypes of the database.

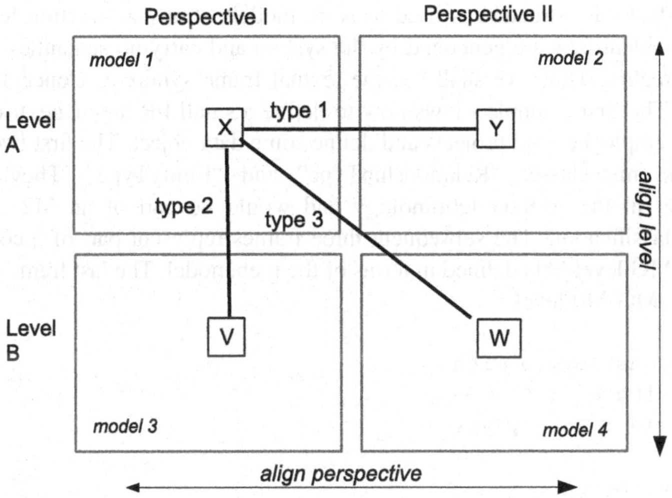

Fig. 1 Links between levels and perspectives

Enterprise models cover multiple perspectives (data, process, goal, …) and abstractions levels (business, applications, technology, …). Links between perspectives relate model elements that are represented in different models but still need to be synchronized. For example, a database model element in a BPMN process model is related to the data model that defines the classes stored in that database (link type 1 in Fig. 1). Link type 2 relates model elements that make statement about the same artefact but uses different levels of detail to do so. This type of link is an "**implementation** link". For example, the relational database schema describes the same database as a UML class diagram but at different level of detail and usually committing to a specific way of implementing. Finally, there may be links of type 3 that change both the perspective and the abstraction level.

Subsequently, we first discuss the constraint language as implemented by ConceptBase. Then, we discuss the types of constraints crossing multiple enterprise models using examples from 4EM [6] and ArchiMate [7].

3 Constraint Checking with ConceptBase

ConceptBase is a deductive database systems specifically designed to manage models and modeling languages. Constructs describing modeling languages are represented in the very same data structure that is used to represent models and even data. The underlying data model of ConceptBase is Telos [8] and the common data structure is the P-fact P(o,x,n,y) ("the statement o establishes a relationship with label n between the statements x and y").

The P-fact data structure is used to store models at any abstraction level. The statements identifiers are generated by the system and carry no semantics from the modeled reality. Thus, we shall use the textual frame syntax of ConceptBase for example. The first example shows how to define a small ER language, use it for a model on employees and projects and define some data object. The first two frames define the metaclasses "RelationshipType" and "EntityType". They form a metamodel in the ADO*xx* terminology and would be part of an M2 model in OMG's classification. The subsequent three frames represent part of a conceptual model (OMG level M1) defined in terms of the metamodel. The last frame on "bill" is at the OMG M0 level.

```
RelationshipType with
  attribute
    role : EntityType
end
EntityType end

Employee in EntityType end
Project in EntityType end
worksFor in RelationshipType with
  role
    toEmp : Employee;
    toProj : Project
end

bill in Employee end
```

Figure 2 displays the example model as a graph. The green links are instantiations. Note that instantiation applies not only two node objects like "bill", "Employee", "EntityType" but also to link objects like the role link of "RelationshipType". The uniform representation of objects, classes and metaclasses allows to specify rules and constraints at any of the abstraction levels. There are no explicit abstraction levels in ConceptBase but rather instantiation relations between objects.

ConceptBase implements a rule and constraint language based on Datalog [9]. Since statements at any abstraction level are represented in the same way, one can also define rules and constraints at any abstraction level. The syntax of the rule and constraint language follows a first-order predicate logic, where variables are bound to class objects, i.e., they range over the instance of the class objects. The most important predicates are

(*x in c*): The object x is an instance of the class object c, for example (bill in Employee)
(*c isA d*): The object c is a specialization of the object d, for example (Manager isA Employee)

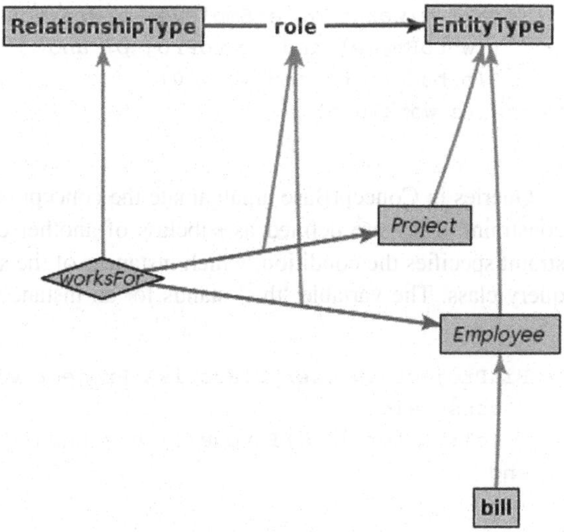

Fig. 2 Example ConceptBase model spanning three abstraction levels

(*x m/n y*): There is a link with label n between x and y and this link has the category m, for example (worksFor role/toEmp Employee)
(*x m y*): There is a link between x and y and this link has the category m, for example (worksFor role Employee); this predicate is derived from the previous one

Links are treated as objects. The expression worksFor!toEmp references the toEmp link of Employee. A complete list of predicates is available from the ConceptBase user manual [10]. To continue the example, we define two constraints, one at modeling language level and the other at model level

```
forall R/RelationshipType exists E/EntityType
    (R role E)

forall e/Employee exists p/Project w/worksFor
    (w toEmp e) and (w toProj p)
```

The two formulas realize multiplicity constraints, however, the constraint language is not restricted to them. Note that the two constraints are syntactically rather similar. They operate at different abstraction levels but ConceptBase does not treat them differently. Abstractions levels are only a user interpretation of the models in ConceptBase.

ConceptBase also supports deductive rules. They are characterized by a single predicate in the conclusion and all variables in the conclusion predicate are for all-quantified, for example

```
forall w/worksFor e/Employee p/Project b/Integer
    (w toEmp e) and (w toProj p) and
    (p budget b) and (b > 0)
==> (e workIn p)
```

Queries in ConceptBase amalgamate the concept of a class and the concept of a constraint. They are defined as subclass of another class and a membership constraint specifies the condition, which instances of the superclass are instances of the query class. The variable 'this' stands for an instance of the superclass 'Project'.

```
BigProject in QueryClass isA Project with
  constraint
    c1: $ forall b/Integer (this budget b) ==> (b > 1000) $
end
```

A class constraint may never be violated by a database, hence any attempt to add objects violating a constraints leads to a rejection of the update. In modeling, this behavior is generally not desired since one starts with incomplete models that may violate certain constraints. Query classes are not constraining the database but returning an answer based on the query class definition. This behavior allows reformulating the original constraints into a negated form that returns all violators. Consider for example the constraint

```
forall this/Employee exists p/Project w/worksFor
     (w toEmp this) and (w toProj p)
```

For the query class reformulation, we decide to return those employees who *violate* the constraint

```
EmployeeWithNoProject in QueryClass isA Employee with
  constraint
   c1: $ not exists p/Project w/worksFor
            (w toEmp this) and (w toProj p) $
end
```

The instances of `EmployeeWithNoProject` are precisely those employees that violate the original constraint.

Attributes of objects are represented in the same way as relationships. Values like integers or strings are objects as well

```
Employee with                    bill in Employee with
 attribute                           age
   age: Integer;                       billsage: 27
   colleague: Employee               colleague
end                                     col1: mary;
                                        col2: anne
                                 end
```

The above frame syntax is closely linked to the base predicates of ConceptBase. The frame for "bill" is equivalents to the predicate facts (bill in Employee), (bill age/billsage 27), (bill colleague/col1 mary), (bill colleague anne). The frame for "Employee" corresponds to the facts (Employee attribute/age Integer), (Employee attribute/colleague Employee). A number of built-in rules and constraints make sure that instantiation and specialization are done in the proper way. For example, the object "27" must be an instance of "Integer", and "mary" and "anne" must be instances of 'Employee'.

ConceptBase also supports active rules that can update the database if certain events (query calls, insertions and deletions) occur. Active rules are more expressive than deductive rules. In particular, they could loop forever if not carefully programmed. Deductive rules, constraints and queries shall always terminate. Another addition is (recursive) functions including arithmetic. Function calls can create new objects on the fly, e.g., 100 + 1 creates the new integer object 101. Like with active rules, functions are beyond the expressiveness of classical deductive rules. We refer to the ConceptBase user manual [10] for more details on active rules and functions. A particular case for using them is the definition of the execution semantics of process models, see end of this chapter.

4 Case 1: Linking STD and DFD

The first case of linking two modeling perspectives is taken from the structured analysis method [11]. It features data flow diagrams (DFD), entity relationship diagrams (ERD), state transition diagrams (STD) and others. The DFD language includes the construct of a control process. A control process is a process that receives events from other processes or the environment and reacts to them by triggering other processes. The inner behavior of a control process in a DFD is specified by an STD. Figure 3 shows the DFD and the STD modeling language as metamodels and below an example DFD and its relation to an example STD.

Like with Fig. 2, the green links are instantiations. The upper level of the figure introduces a cross-notational link (STD attribute/specifies ControlProcess). This link is of type 1 in the classification scheme of Fig. 1. At the lower level, the STD 'AccountsSTD' is linked to the 'ControlAccounts' process

```
(AccountSTD specifies/cp ControlAccounts)
```

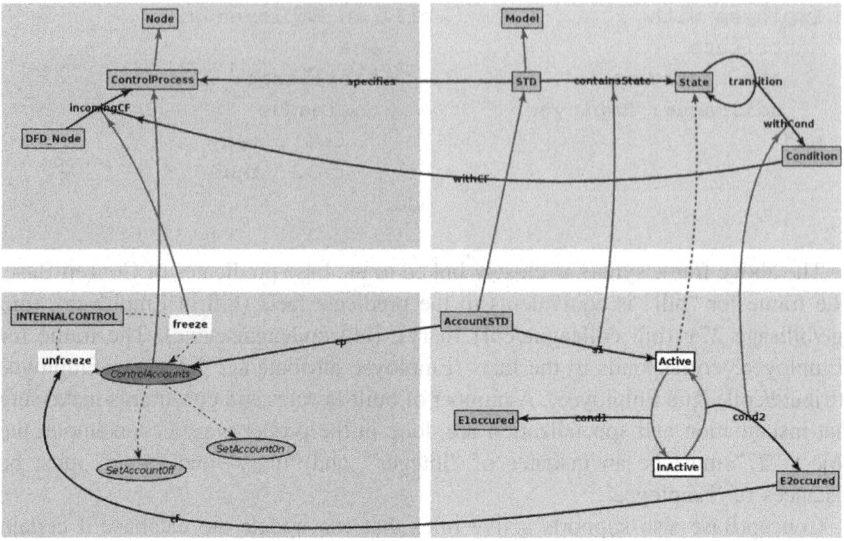

Fig. 3 Linking DFD and STD

The AccountsSTD itself is a model that is decomposed into states (here 'Active' and 'InActive') and the transitions between the states. Such a decomposition is called model explosion in MetaEdit+. So, a model construct from the DFD side is linked to a model on the STD side. A simple constraint crossing the two perspectives is that each control process must have a STD that specifies it. In the negated query class format, we return those control processes that have no STD

```
UnSpecifiedControlProcess in QueryClass
                             isA ControlProcess with
  constraint
    c1 : $ not exists std/STD (std specifies this) $
end
```

A more complex constraint is linking the conditions attached to the STD transitions. They must correspond to incoming control flows on the DFD side. For example, the condition E2 occured on the STD side is linked to the 'unfreeze' control flow on the DFD side. The following query class returns all those incoming control flows on the DFD side that are not matched with a corresponding condition on the STD side

```
UnmatchedIncomingControlFlow in QueryClass
                                   isA DFD_Node!incomingCF with
  constraint c1 : $ exists cp/ControlProcess
         To(this,cp) and
         not exists std/STD s/State
                    c/Condition t/State!transition
         (std specifies cp) and (std containsState s) and
         From(t,s) and (t withCond c) and (c withCF this) $
 end
```

The query class uses two predicates that were not defined yet. The predicate *From*(*p, x*) returns the source object of a relation, and the predicate *To*(*p, y*) returns its destination object.

5 Case 2: Multiple Perspectives in 4EM

4EM is an enterprise modeling language that strongly ties the perspectives by a variant of link type 1. The metamodel of 4EM [ref] heavily uses the specialization construct to define interface classes between the modeling perspectives. Hence the link remains in the same modeling perspective, but classes for other perspectives are integrated via specializing the interface class.

The interface classes are GM_RelatableObject and IM_GoalModivatesEnd. They belong to the goal modeling perspective. The class GM_Goal is linked to GM_RelatableObject. The upper right side of Fig. 4 displays part of the 4EM

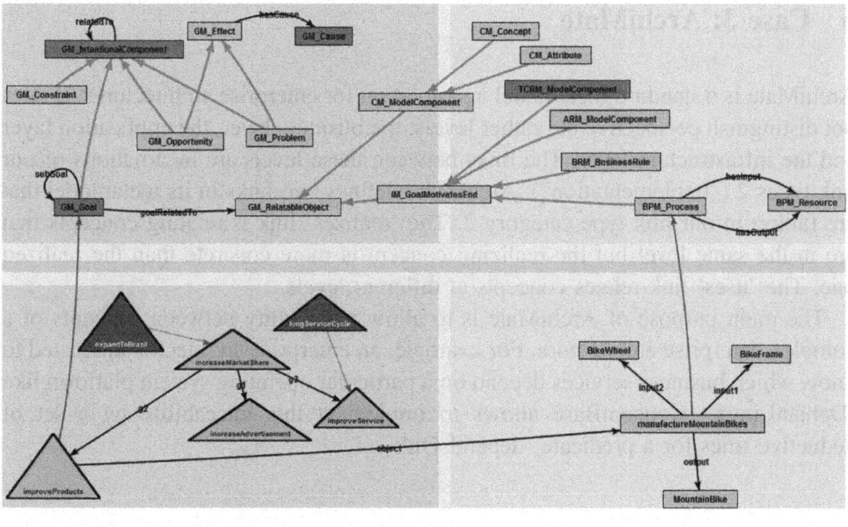

Fig. 4 Linking perspectives in 4EM by interface classes

metamodel for the business process perspective. There, the class BPM_Process is defined as subclass of IM_GoalMotivatesEnd. The high number of subclasses of GM_RelatableObject allows to attach goals to virtually any other 4EM object.

The lower part of Fig. 4 shows an excerpt of a 4EM model, instantiating the metaclasses of the upper part. The process manufactureMountainBikes is related to the goal improveProducts. This link crosses the perspective boundaries between the goal model and the process model.

ConceptBase allows realizing analysis services for 4EM models via query classes. For example, we may want to know to which goals a business process related to

```
ImpactOfGoal in QueryClass isA GM_RelatableObject with
  computed_attribute
    goalElement : GM_IntentionalComponent
  constraint
    hasImpact : $ exists g1,g2/GM_Goal
                (~goalElement relatedTo g1) and
                (g1 subGoal g2) and (g2 goalRelatedTo this) $
end
```

The attribute goalElement is declared as computed attribute. It shall be returned in the answer. The subGoal relation of GB_Goal is defined as transitive and reflexive. These properties are realized by deductive rules, not shown here but easily implemented in ConceptBase. The complete specification is available on the website http://conceptbase.cc/nemo2015.

6 Case 3: ArchiMate

ArchiMate is a standard metamodel and notation for enterprise architectures. It does not distinguish perspective but rather levels: the business layer, the application layer and the infrastructure layer. The links between these levels are incarnations of our link types 2 ("implementation"). ArchiMate defines two links in its metamodel that are falling in our link type category 2. The 'realizes' link is relating concepts that are in the same level but the realizing concept is more concrete than the realized one. The 'uses' link relates concepts at different levels.

The main purpose of ArchiMate is to allow traceability between concepts of a complex enterprise architecture. For example, an enterprise architect is interested to know which business services depend on a particular operating system platform like 'DebianLinux'. ConceptBase allows to implement this traceability by a set of deductive rules for a predicate 'dependsOn':

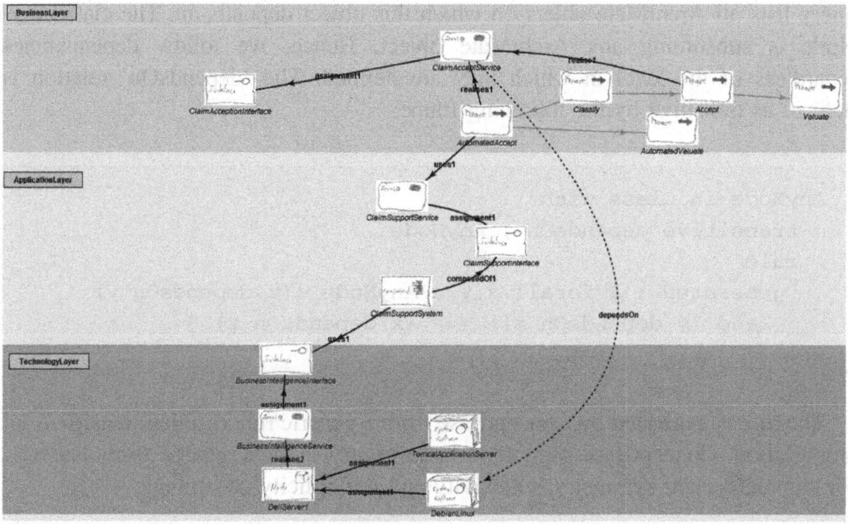

Fig. 5 Tracing dependencies for ArchiMate

```
forall o/AM_Object d/AM_DataObject
   (d realises o) ==> (o dependsOn d)
forall o/AM_Object r/AM_Representation
   (r realises o) ==> (o dependsOn r)
forall b/AM_Behaviour s/AM_BusService
   (b realises s) ==> (s dependsOn b)
...
forall a/AM_AppFunction i/ AM_InfService
   (a uses i) ) ==> (a dependsOn i)
...
```

The rules then allow following dependencies between model elements spanning multiple levels (Fig. 5).

There are in total more than twenty such rules for the 'dependsOn' relation. A generic query computes them all

```
DepService in GenericQueryClass isA AnyNode with
  computed_attribute,parameter
    element : AnyNode
  constraint
    c1 : $ (~element dependsOn ~this) $
end
```

The query has a parameter 'element' that allows to focus on a specific ArchiMate element, e.g., the ClaimAcceptService from the business layer. The answer to the query lists all ArchiMate object on which this object depends on. The class AnyNode is subsuming any ArchiMate object. Hence, we follow dependencies regardless of the level in which they are defined. The 'dependsOn' relation is defined as transitive by the following frame:

```
AnyNode in Class with
  transitive dependsOn : AnyNode
  rule
   generated : $ forall x,y,z/AnyNode ((x dependsOn y)
     and (y dependsOn z)) ==> (x dependsOn z) $
end
```

The rule is generated by ConceptBase from a generic rule defining transitivity of any relation. ConceptBase supports a large library of such generic formulas, e.g., for symmetry, anti-symmetry, reflexivity and multiplicity constraints.

7 SemCheck: Integrity Checking for ADO*xx*

ADO*xx* views a modeling method as combination of several modeling techniques, each coming with a modeling language (represented as a metamodel), a modeling procedure (the workflow of modeling steps that lead to a desired result) and related mechanisms and algorithms (methods that operate on models). Example algorithms are for example discrete event simulation algorithms that take a process model and a configuration of parameters as input and produce performance data such as the average cycle time. The logical language of ConceptBase provides integrity checking services (called SemCheck) both on the generic level (defined for a given modeling language in the ADO*xx* development toolkit) and the specific level (only applicable for specific models defined in the ADO*xx* modeling toolkit).

The dual use in ADO*xx* is possible since ConceptBase uniformly represents models, metamodels and meta^2 models with the same predicates for instantiation, specialization and attribution. The preferred way to realize integrity constraints in ConceptBase is by means of a query class as discussed in the preceding chapters. From the viewpoint of ADO*xx*, a query class is a method that can be called at any time and returns the 'violators' of the integrity constraint that it implements. Most such query classes are defined for a given modeling language, e.g., entity relationship diagrams. An example is the integrity constraint 'RelationshipTypeLacksRoles' that each relationship type must have at least one role link to an entity type (compare section on constraint checking with ConceptBase):

```
RelationshipTypeLacksRoles in QueryClass
                              isA RelationshipType with
  constraint
     c: $ not exists E/EntityType (this role E) $
end
```

The response to calling this query is all relationship types that match the query class. The execution of the query class call can be linked to a specific step of the modeling procedure defined in ADO*xx*. Moving from one modeling state to the next then requires that all query classes defined as postcondition of the current stage return an empty answer.

An example of a model-level constraint is that each employee who works for the R&D department must work on at least one project:

```
RDEmployeeWithoutProject in QueryClass isA Employee with
  constraint
     c: $ (this department R&D) and
          not exists w/worksFor p/Project
             (w toEmp this) and (w toProj p) $
end
```

Such an integrity constraint is specific for a given ER model. The mechanism to call it is the same as for the generic constraint "RelationshipTypeLacksRoles". Note that the above constraint requires as sample data level to be evaluated.

Query classes are subclasses of other classes. The query class 'RelationshipTypeLacksRoles' is a subclass of "RelationshipType" (being part of a metamodel), the class 'RDEmployeeWithoutProject' is a subclass of 'Employee', which is part of a conceptual model expressed in terms of a metamodel. All such query classes of the same superclass form the set of constraints that the superclass must eventually fulfil. Asking the query classes returns the violators, i.e., those instances of the super classes that match the condition of the query class. The use of query classes has the advantage that one can ask them when appropriate. In early modeling stages, the conceptual models are incomplete and possibly violate many conditions expressed in the query classes. One can count the number of instances in the query classes to realize a metric on the degree of inconsistency of a given model, e.g., `COUNT(RelationshipTypeLacksRoles)`. If a class has multiple query classes defined for it, then one can aggregate them into a single query class:

```
FaultyRT in QueryClass isA RelationshipType with
   constraint
       c: $ (this in RelationshipTypeLacksRoles) or
            (this in RelationshipTypeXXX) or …$
end
```

SemCheck is also used for checking the **consistency of a metamodel** (e.g., defining the ER language) against meta^2 models. Consider Fig. 6 (ER metamodel assimilated in FCML) in the chapter "Fundamental Conceptual Modeling Languages in OMiLAB" (FCML). The meta^2 model consists of the concepts 'Class' and 'Relationship'. The latter has two role links 'Class' (labelled 'source' and 'target'). The concept 'Class' has a self-referential link 'inheritance' that is used to specify specialization hierarchies. The semantics of the 'inheritance' link can be specified in ConceptBase by the following definitions

```
CLASS with
  attribute,single,transitive,reflexive,antisymmetric
    inheritance: CLASS
end

InheritanceRule in Class with
  rule r1: $ forall C,D/CLASS x/Proposition
             (C inheritance D) and (x in C) ==> (x in D) $
end
```

The first frame uses a combination of attribute categories 'single', 'transitive', 'reflexive' and 'antisymmetric, which can be imported from a formula repository in ConceptBase. For instance, the definition of 'antisymmetric' is

```
(x M y) and (y M x) ==> (x = y)
```

which translates to

```
(x inheritance y) and (y inheritance x) ==> (x = y)
```

for the 'inheritance link. The other attribute categories are defined in an analogous way. The metamodel instantiated from the meta^2 model uses the 'inheritance link as shown here (see also Fig. 6 in the FCML chapter).

```
ENTITY in CLASS with
  inheritance
    super: EoR
end

RELATION in CLASS with
  inheritance
     super: EoR
end
```

The 'inheritance rule' of the meta^2 model ensures that any instance of 'Entity' is also an instance of 'EoR', the abstract superclass of 'Entity' and 'Relation'. For example, the concept 'Book' is a direct instance of 'Entity' and via generic inheritance rule also an instance of 'EoR'.

The formal specification of rules and constraints at the meta^2 model assists the method engineer in designing compliant modeling languages. Attempts to create metamodels that violate the constraints result in appropriate error messages. For example, a circular specialization hierarchy is detected by the transitivity and anti-symmetry rules of the meta^2 model.

8 Integration Architecture for ADO*xx* and ConceptBase

The three cases discussed above motivate the suitability of ConceptBase as a tool to check constraint and to provide deduction-based analysis services for enterprise modeling frameworks that cover multiple perspectives and levels. ADO*xx* is such a framework. This chapter discusses how to integrate ADO*xx* and ConceptBase.

ADO*xx* offers two toolkits. The development toolkit is used to define a modeling language by means of metamodels. It also assigns a graphical notation of node and link shapes to the elements of the metamodels. Further, the designer of the

Fig. 6 ConceptBase module structure for ADO*xx* integration

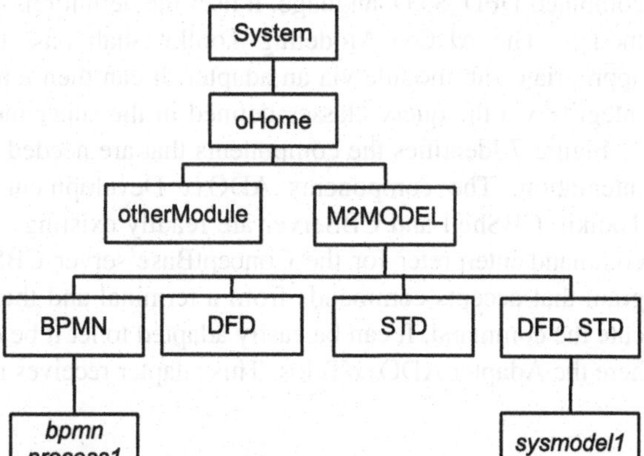

modeling language can associate semantics to the modeling language by linking them to algorithms. For example, a process modeling language is associated to a mapping to simulation models that utilize specific algorithms. The second toolkit is called the modeling toolkit. The development toolkit generates the modeling toolkit for the given modeling language. Hence, this is the environment that is used by an enterprise modeler.

ConceptBase does formally not distinguish between the constructs of a modeling language and the constructs of a model. They are all represented in the very same data structure. Still it makes sense to distinguish the two types of concepts since ADO*xx* distinguishes them. To do so, we propose to use the module system of ConceptBase. Modules in ConceptBase are simply sets of objects. Modules can have sub-modules, in which all objects of the super-modules are visible.

Figure 6 shows the module structure of ConceptBase adapted to the requirements for ADO*xx* integration. Each sub-module 'sees' the definitions made in its super-module hierarchy, i.e., the modules on the path from the sub-module to the top module. The top module 'System' includes the pre-defined objects of ConceptBase. Below is the module 'oHome' which hosts the home modules, one of them being 'M2MODEL'. The 'M2MODEL' module contains definitions of metaclasses that make ConceptBase compatible with ADO*xx*. It also contains a set of generic rules and constraints such as for transitivity and for multiplicity constraints. These constraints can then be reused for all sub-modules of 'M2MODEL'. The sub-modules like 'BPMN' contain the metamodels of the ADO*xx* modeling language to be supported by the SemCheck service of ConceptBase. The definitions are passed from the ADO*xx* Development Toolkit to the suitable sub-module whenever a new modeling language is defined. The translation of the ADO*xx* metamodel to the ConceptBase frame syntax has to be performed by an adapter. Some sub-modules like 'DFD_STD' combine several modeling languages, here DFD and STD. This is achieved by storing the metamodels of both languages in this sub-module. The model DFD_STD shall also include the query classes to check the semantic integrity and to analyse the models, e.g., on dependencies between model elements.

The sub-module 'sysmodel1' is an example for a module storing models in the combined DFD_STD language. It uses the definitions of DFD_STD to represent the models. The ADO*xx* Modeling Toolkit shall pass the model definitions to the appropriate sub-module via an adapter. It can then retrieve reports on the semantic integrity via the query classes defined in the super-module.

Figure 7 identifies the components that are needed for the ADO*xx*/ConceptBase integration. The components ADO*xx* Development Toolkit, ADO*xx* Modeling Toolkit, CBShell and CBServer are readily existing. The CBShell component is a command interpreter for the ConceptBase server CBServer. CBShell is Java program that accepts commands from a terminal and then calls the CBServer to execute the command. It can be easily adapted to let it be called from another program, here the Adapter ADO*xx*/Telos. This adapter receives metamodels and models from

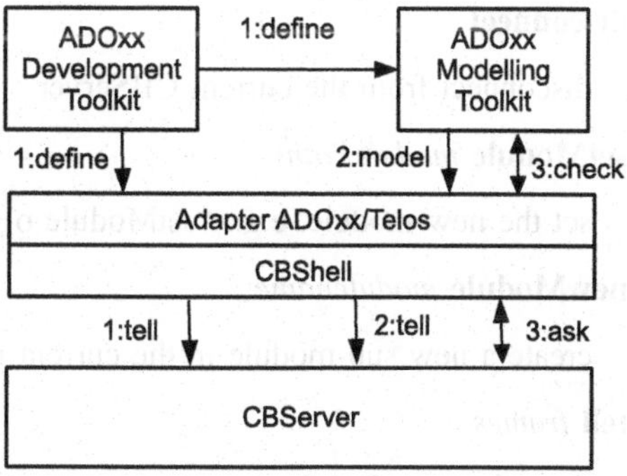

Fig. 7 Integration architecture for ADO*xx* and ConceptBase

the ADO*xx* components and translates them into the ConceptBase frame syntax. This adapter needs to be implemented to get the integration working.

The workflow is starting from the development toolkit. Assume a designer creates a metamodel for DFD_STD. The metamodel is stored in ADO*xx*'s repository and in parallel the definition is passed to the adapter. The adapter transforms the ADO*xx* representation into CBShell commands that store the metamodel in the suitable ConceptBase module, here DFD_STD. The next step is that a modeler uses the modeling toolkit to create an example model. This model is stored in the ADO*xx* repository and then passed it to the CBServer via the adapter and CBShell. The modeling toolkit can then request the consistency checks by calling the query classes implementing them. The answer is a list of 'violators', which can then be highlighted in the modeling toolkit. Depending on the modeling phase, the toolkit could request different consistency checks. For example, the query 'UnmatchedIncomingControlFlow' of the DFD/STD case could be part of the final consistency checks when both the DFD and the STD are regarded as complete.

The commands of CBShell define the interface between the adapter and the CBServer. The following commands are the most relevant ones for the integration:

startServer *serveroptions*

start a new CBServer on localhost. The server options allow among others to specify the database to be used and to specify the port number for TCP/IP connections

connect *host port*

connect to an already running CBServer on host:port

disconnect

disconnect from the current CBServer

setModule *modulePath*

set the new module, e.g., "setModule oHome/ADO*xx*/BPMN"

newModule *modulename*

create a new sub-module in the current module

tell *frames*

store the specified frames (given as text string) to the current module

ask *query options*

ask the specified query given by the name of the query class, possibly including parameters in the query call; the options can be used to specify the answer representation

showAnswer

displays the answer to the query called before

The CBServer stores by default all objects persistently. It can however also be configured to only store them in main memory. Below is a trace of CBShell using the above commands for the DFD_STD example.

```
1. connect localhost 4001
2. setModule ADOxx/DFD_STD/sysmodel1
3. tell "INTERNALCONTROL with
     incomingCF
       reset: ControlAccounts
    end"
4. ask UnmatchedIncomingControlFlow
5. showAnswer
   INTERNALCONTROL!reset
```

It is assumed here that the modules ADO*xx* and DFD_STD have already been defined and that the example model of Fig. 3 has been stored in 'sysmodel1'. The tell command incrementally adds a new model element to the existing model, here a 'reset' link as incoming control flow of the control process 'ControlAccounts'. The query 'UnmatchedIncomingControlFlow' then exposes this new link as being not matched with the STD specifying the control process.

Note that the ask command is typically called after a meaningful sequence of modeling steps in ADO*xx* have been executed. The answer 'INTERNALCONTROL!reset' identifies the 'reset' link of the object 'INTERNALCONTROL' as the violator. The query name 'UnmatchedIncomingControlFlow' tells ADO*xx* how to interpret the answer. In this case, ADO*xx* may present to the modeler that he has link the control flow to some condition in the STD.

Instead of incremental changes, ADO*xx* can also pass the whole model to ConceptBase. ConceptBase will automatically extract only the new objects and then tell only them to the selected module.

There are a number of improvements that the CBServer could offer to support the integration. The most significant one would be to support merging two existing modules. For example, DFD_STD could be defined as sub-module of both DFD and STD and then would see the definitions of both. Currently, one has to duplicate the content of DFD and STD into DFD_STD. A second improvement would be to remove a module, i.e., to delete its content. ConceptBase can handle models with several hundred thousand objects. The query performance for the examples discussed in this chapter are in the range of milliseconds.

9 Inheriting Execution Semantics for Process Models

The ConceptBase module structure discussed in the previous section allows to share metamodels and to separate different modeling environments from each other. In this section, we discuss the uses of so-called active rules and deduction rules to specify the execution semantics for Petri Nets and then to share this semantics as well.

A classical Petri Net consists of places and transitions. Places have a marking being a non-negative integer number. There are flow links between places and transitions. A place is an *input place* for a transition if there is a flow link from the place to the transition, and an output place if there is a flow link from the transition to the place. A transition is enabled if all its input places have a marking greater than zero. In ConceptBase, this can be modeled as follows:

```
GProcessElement with
  attribute flowTo : GProcessElement
end
GPlace isA GProcessElement with
  attribute marks : Integer
end
GTransition isA GProcessElement end
M in Function isA Integer with
  parameter p : GPlace
  constraint c1 : $ (p marks this) $
end
Input in GenericQueryClass isA GPlace with
  parameter t : GTransition
  constraint
    ci : $ (this flowTo t) $
end
ConnectedPlace in GenericQueryClass isA GPlace with
  Parameter trans : GTransition
  constraint
    c : $ (this flowTo trans) or (trans flowTo this) $
end
IM in Function isA Integer with
  parameter p : GPlace; t : GTransition
  constraint
    c1 : $  (t flowTo p) and not (p flowTo t) and (this = 1) or
             (p flowTo t) and not (t flowTo p) and (this = -1) or
            not (p flowTo t) and not (t flowTo p) and (this = 0) $
end
Enabled in QueryClass isA GTransition with
  constraint c : $ forall p/Input[this] (M(p) > 0) $
end
```

The query class 'Enabled' returns the currently enabled transitions. The function M returns the marking of a given place and the function IM realizes the incidence matrix between places and transitions. The firing of a transition can be expressed by an active rule

```
gfire in GenericQueryClass isA YesClass with
  parameter transition : Enabled
end
UpdateConnectedPlaces in ECArule with
  mode m : Deferred
  ecarule
    er : $ t/GTransition p/GPlace m/Integer
           ON Ask gfire[t]
           IFNEW (t in Enabled) and (p in ConnectedPlace[t]) and
           (m = M(p)+IM(p,t))
           DO Retell (p marks m) $
end
```

The active rule is triggered by the command `gfire[t]` for an enabled transition. It will then change the markings of the connected places according to the old state and the incidence matrix IM.

Since the above frames are completely defining the semantics of classical Petri Nets, we can reuse the definition to define semantics to other process modeling languages such as BPMN, state transition diagrams, event-process chains and others just by mapping their constructs into the Petri Net constructs for places and transitions.

Figure 8 shows how the result of the mapping on a sample BPMN model. The figure is an actual screendump of ConceptBase, hence all displayed elements are actually taken from the model definitions stored in ConceptBase. The BPMN tasks are instantiated to GTransition, hence they operate like Petri Net transitions. The start and end events are mapped to GPlace. The connection between two transitions like t1 and t2 is interpreted as a place, and there are corresponding derived flow links from t1 to the link and from the link to t2. The following ConceptBase frames are achieving the mapping:

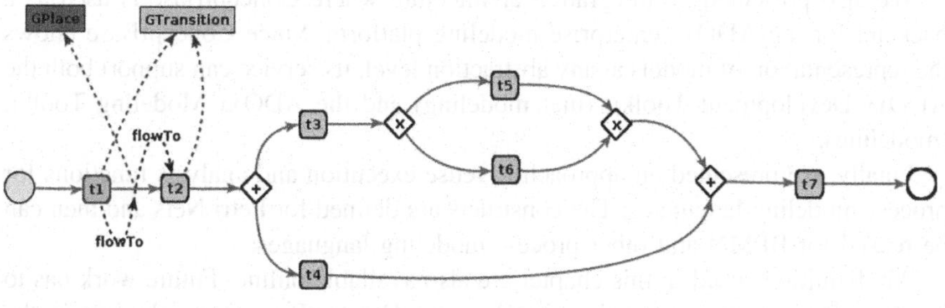

Fig. 8 A BPMN model instantiated to Petri Net constructs

```
TransitionLike isA BPMN_Element,GTransition end
PlaceLike isA BPMN_Element,GPlace end
BPMN_Activity isA TransitionLike end
BPMN_Event isA PlaceLike  end
MapBPMNToGPM in Class with
  rule
    r1 : $ forall a1,a2/TransitionLike link/BPMN_Element!next
           From(link,a1) and To(link,a2) ==> (link in GPlace) $;
    r2 : $ forall a1,a2/TransitionLike link/BPMN_Element!next
           From(link,a1) and To(link,a2) ==> (a1 flowTo link) $;
    r3 : $ forall a1,a2/TransitionLike link/GPlace
              (link in BPMN_Element!next) and
           From(link,a1) and To(link,a2) ==> (link flowTo a2) $
 end
```

This definition allows to directly executing a BPMN process model using the 'gfire' command. The complete definition is available via http://conceptbase.cc/nemo2015. Even if the execution semantics is not needed in the integration with ADO*xx* (since it has more advanced algorithms to specify execution semantics), the query to check enabled tasks on a given state is useful to designers of new process modeling languages.

10 Conclusions

This chapter motivated that enterprise models consist of multiple modeling perspectives and that these perspectives need be synchronized by semantic constraints. We presented the capabilities of the constraint and query language of the ConceptBase system and showed in three cases that it can represent and evaluate typical constraints.

We also presented an integration architecture where ConceptBase is used as a backend for the ADO*xx* enterprise modeling platform. Since ConceptBase allows the representation of models at any abstraction level, its service can support both the ADO*xx* Development Toolkit (metamodeling) and the ADO*xx* Modeling Toolkit (modeling).

Finally, we presented an approach to reuse execution and analysis functions for process modeling languages. The constructs are defined for Petri Nets and then can be reused for BPMN and other process modeling languages.

All definitions used in this chapter are also available online. Future work has to be done for actually integrating ADO*xx* and ConceptBase. One element is the adapter that converts the ADO*xx* models and metamodels into the Telos syntax used by ConceptBase. Since both are based on graphical representations, this should be a rather straightforward step. Second, the semantic constraints have to be declared within ADO*xx* and then passed to ConceptBase. Finally, the error reports returned by ConceptBase need to be displayed in a suitable way by ADO*xx*.

There are some services beyond constraint checking that could be outsourced to ConceptBase. One service is the dependency tracking in large enterprise models, see the case study on ADO*xx*. ConceptBase has a fast Datalog engine to evaluate recursive rules, in particular for following transitive links. A second service is model metrics. The recursive functions in ConceptBase allow the definition of metrics such as for model complexity.

Acknowledgments The ConceptBase models for ArchiMate were created in 2008 by Sander van Arendonk, Niels Colijn, Dirk Janssen and Jeffrey Kramer as part of an assignment for the method engineering course at Tilburg University. Their models are available under a Creative Commons CC-BY-NC 3.0 license. Special thanks to Wilfrid Utz and David Götzinger from the University of Vienna for their help in getting the coupling between ConceptBase and ADO*xx* working.

Tool Download http://www.omilab.org/semcheck.

References

1. Karagiannis, D., Grossmann, W., Höfferer P.: Open model initiative—a feasibility study. Project Study on behalf of the Austrian Federal Ministry for Transport, Innovation and Technology, Vienna (2008)
2. Karagiannis, D., Kühn, H.: Metamodelling platforms. In: Proceedings of the 3rd International Conference EC-Web 2002/Dexa (2002). http://dx.doi.org/10.1007/3-540-45705-4_19
3. Fill, H.-G., Karagiannis, D.: On the conceptualisation of modelling methods using the ADOxx meta modelling platform. Enterp. Model. Inf. Syst. Archit. **8**(1), 4–25 (2013)
4. Jarke, M., Gallersdörfer, R., Jeusfeld, M.A., Staudt, M., Eherer, S.: ConceptBase—a deductive object base for meta data management. J. Intell. Inf. Syst. **4**(2), 167–192 (1995). doi:10.1007/BF00961873
5. Jeusfeld, M.A.: Metamodeling and method engineering with ConceptBase. In: Jeusfeld, M.A., Jarke, M., Mylopoulos, J. (eds.) Metamodelling for Method Engineering, pp. 89–168. The MIT Press, Cambridge (2009). ISBN 978-0262101080
6. Sandkuhl, K., Stirna, J., Persson, A., Wißotzki, M.: Enterprise modeling—tackling business challenges with the 4EM method. The Enterprise Engineering Series. Springer, Berlin (2014). ISBN 978-3-662-43724-7
7. Lankhorst, M., et al.: Enterprise Architecture at Work, 3rd edn. Springer, Berlin (2013). ISBN 978-3-642-29650-5
8. Mylopoulos, J., Borgida, A., Jarke, M., Koubarakis, M.: Telos—representing knowledge about information systems. ACM Trans. Inf. Syst. **8**(4), 325–362 (1990). http://doi.acm.org/10.1145/102675.102676
9. Ceri, S., Gottlob, G., Tanca, L.: What you always wanted to know about Datalog (and never dared to ask). IEEE Trans. Knowl. Data Eng. **1**(1), 146–166 (1989). https://dx.doi.org/10.1109/69.43410
10. Jeusfeld, M.A., Quix, C., Jarke, M.: ConceptBase.cc User Manual. Version 7.8 (2015). http://conceptbase.sourceforge.net/userManual78/
11. Yourdan, E.: Modern Structured Analysis. Prentice Hall, Englewood Cliffs (1989)

OMiLAB: An Open Collaborative Environment for Modeling Method Engineering

David Götzinger, Elena-Teodora Miron and Franz Staffel

Abstract OMiLAB is an open collaborative environment dedicated to modeling method engineering, which employs metamodeling as a technology to manage domain-specific abstraction and complexity. It builds on three pillars: the Collaborative Environment (people, "location" and activities), the Innovation Environment (scope and content) and the Technological Environment (tools and platforms). These three are described here in order to give an overview of the resources offered by OMiLAB to an active multi-disciplinary community of stakeholders interested in the value of models and the possibilities of domain-specific modeling.

Keywords Metamodeling platforms · Open community · Innovation · Modeling method engineering

1 Introduction

When one studies different scientific and industrial communities, one can observe that part of their success is due to some degree to the use of standards[1] and also due to the use of community-shared software platforms.

A practical case is that of architects, civil and structural engineers, landscape architects, etc., in the domain of Building Information Systems. They can all work

[1]OMG, http://www.omg.org; DIN, http://www.din.de, last visit 08.04.2016.

D. Götzinger (✉) · E.-T. Miron · F. Staffel
Research Group Knowledge Engineering, University of Vienna,
1090 Vienna, Austria
e-mail: david.goetzinger@univie.ac.at

E.-T. Miron
e-mail: elena-teodora.miron@univie.ac.at

F. Staffel
e-mail: franz.staffel@univie.ac.at

D. Karagiannis et al. (eds.), *Domain-Specific Conceptual Modeling*,
DOI 10.1007/978-3-319-39417-6_3

with different views, i.e., design, construction and operation of buildings, on common platforms like OpenBIM.[2]

There are similar phenomena in computer science, i.e.,—in Software Engineering with platforms like Eclipse[3] and in mobile computing with Android.[4]

OMiLAB attempts the same for the domain of conceptual modeling. It aims to foster a community [18, 19] that can benefit from access to community-shared platforms, like ADO*xx* and ConceptBase. The audience is a multi-disciplinary community comprising multiple roles, each bringing its requirements or expertise for common benefits, e.g.,:

- experts from different domains, who want to be supported by a modeling tool,
- modeling method engineers who need to consult domain expertise in order to understand the requirements or semantics of a domain,
- modelers seeking an agile modeling tool whose degree of domain-specificity may be customized for different goals,
- scientists who need an experimentation setup that involves models, either as a means to an end or as an artefact under study.

The operationalization is enabled by a complex setting composed of several pillars, namely the:

- Collaborative Environment (people, "location" and activities) which describes the membership types in the community, the infrastructure of the physical and virtual OMiLAB space, the intellectual property and rights management as well as the research and educational activities.
- Innovation Environment (scope and content) which encompasses all content-related matters. It provides concepts and instruments to explore modeling method creation and design, to experiment with modeling method engineering as well as develop and deploy modeling tools.
- Technological Environment (tools and platforms) which provides the tools, services and platforms. It aims to foster interaction in the Collaborative Environment through the OMiLAB Portal and method engineering through the metamodeling platform and development services.

The three pillar structure was developed in order to create a coherent format, which serves the community's needs with innovative content and approaches in conceptual modeling as well as with technological support. The remainder of this paper presents each of the three pillars in detail.

[2]OpenBIM, http://www.graphisoft.at/open-bim/, last visit 08.04.2016.

[3]Eclipse, http://www.eclipse.org, last visit 05.04.2016.

[4]Android, http://www.android.com, last visit 05.04.2016.

2 The OMiLAB Collaborative Environment

Community actions performed in the collaborative environment result in modeling methods/tools in research and in education activities, as well as overall impact. The involvement with OMiLAB benefits community members through:

- dialogue between scientists, educators and innovators,
- access to infrastructure and open-source services,
- strong and sustainable communities, that are active in domain-specific issues,
- amplification instruments which leverage the impact of the activities performed,
- conferences, workshops, seminars,
- common projects,
- exchange and mobility programs and
- publications.

To this end one has to consider the necessary organizational issues, IPR matters and the types of activities which support the community goals.

2.1 Organizational Structure

OMiLAB's idea, environment and tools can be adopted at different levels of cooperation among community members. Independent of their level of involvement, either as an institution or as an individual, all community actors commit to the fundamental principles of openness, participation, sustainability and agile modeling method engineering. Community members perform activities in the OMiLAB Network and in OMiLAB Projects.

2.1.1 OMiLAB Network

The network is formed by all community members of OMiLAB. These may be:

Partners, who are local hubs stimulating the regional impact of the OMiLAB Network. They feature a physical and virtual infrastructure, attract contributors and members from their area of influence and increase the global visibility and impact of the network. Partners may focus on specific research topics within the area of agile modeling method engineering and/or domain-specific modeling. Formal cooperation commences with the signature of a partnership agreement. Current partnerships are located in Europe[5] and Asia.[6]

Associated partners, who are institutions interested in joining the OMiLAB Network. Membership enables them to leverage their activities to the international

[5]OMiLAB Europe, http://europe.omilab.org.

[6]OMiLAB Asia, http://asia.omilab.org.

OMiLAB community and beyond. Benefits include name listing, usage of OMiLAB identity items, free participation in trainings, free use of the online OMiLAB infrastructure, dissemination and communication activities, and participation in networking events. Associated partners include OMiLAB-related actions in their research and educational activities. These may comprise modeling method projects, publications, research projects, various events, courses, the NEMO Summer School and graduation works. Formal cooperation commences with the signature of a cooperation agreement.

Individual members, who are individuals, research groups or communities of practice with no formal organizational structure in relation to OMiLAB and who come together to address a specific problem or domain. They may initiate, lead, participate and contribute in an OMiLAB Project at any stage, in the exploitation of results as well as in advancing research, education or community impact. Cooperation is open.

2.1.2 OMiLAB Project

An 'OMiLAB Project' is a collaborative space where individual engineers and teams can work together in the conceptualization of a new or the further development of an existing modeling method. It includes all contributions concerning a modeling method, starting from creation, to implementation all the way to exploitation. One of the main goals of each OMiLAB Project is to produce a modeling tool. Therefore, the Technological Environment offers functionality with particular regard to development and generates deployable software.

Project members can drive, participate and contribute to the exploitation of results as well as in advancing research, education or community building. Individual contributors may take on different roles in various projects. Cooperation is defined within the project by its members.

2.2 *Physical and Virtual Infrastructure*

OMiLAB is both a physical and virtual collaborative environment. The physical environment is a research laboratory equipped with the infrastructure necessary to carry out the Conceptualization Lifecycle (see Sect. 3.2). It provides at least five working stations, one for each phase of the lifecycle, equipped with the corresponding IT-hardware and the necessary applications. It is equipped with high-speed Internet access and videoconferencing facilities in order to allow access to the virtual part of OMiLAB as well as virtual meetings with other community members. In addition each laboratory should have a meeting area and facilities for collaborative working. OMiLAB identity items make the affiliation of the laboratory to the OMiLAB Network visible. Currently physical environments are located at the University of Vienna in Austria and at the Chonbuk National University in Korea.

The virtual environment replicates the functionalities offered in the physical laboratory and adds services to them. Virtualization platforms can be used as an infrastructure for all services. Suitable platforms are VMWare ESX, Citrix XenServer, Oracle VM or other cloud infrastructure as a service (IaaS) providers. As a base operating system these portal services need a Linux open-source platform that hosts the various software elements. All base elements, e.g., operation systems, databases, web servers, are especially chosen from open source elements, so there are no additionally costs and licensing problems.

2.3 Intellectual Property and Rights Management

OMiLAB claims no ownership rights to the modeling methods, modeling tools, materials, services or any other items produced by community members or institutions independently of the cooperation scenario and level in place. IPRs remain firmly with the creator of the respective work and shall be attributed through corresponding permissions. Artefacts available in OMiLAB must be open source or at least open use for other community members.

2.4 Research Activities

Research questions and activities in the OMiLAB Collaborative Environment are driven by community members and may cover any topic of interest related to conceptual modeling.

Thus research may be primarily directed, for example, towards

1. Individual modeling methods and tools as well as the domains they address,
2. The combination of modeling methods/tools with metamodeling technology,
3. Evolution of agile modeling method engineering and
4. Research on fundamentals about modeling method engineering.

Research activities could address issues such as

- The emergence of a new application domain or the evolution of a specific field,
- The study of new problems and applications within the domain, as well as the identification of requirements for new method constructs/chunks as well as mechanisms and algorithms,
- Creativity concerns in the area of modeling method composition including user-driven innovation, value co-creation, empiric research, (business) ethnography as well as the application of creativity tools in domain-specific modeling method engineering,

- Conceptualization concerns addressing the design of domain-specific methods,
- Technological concerns addressing the creation of a metamodeling domain-specific language (MM-DSL), a platform-independent declarative language that allows code-based editing of modeling method definitions and their compilation for the metamodeling platform of choice,
- Cognitive science aspects pertaining to the understandability and expressivity of models, or the learning curve necessary for a new user to assimilate a new modeling language,
- Formalisms in support of consistently specifying the building blocks of a modeling method.

2.5 *Educational Activities*

The use of modeling tools in education propagates the use of domain-specific modeling methods among students and future researchers. Educational activities within OMiLAB address the pragmatics of modeling for all user groups as well as modeling method engineering. They are offered and driven by the members of the OMiLAB Network.

The openness of tools and materials enables the worldwide uptake/integration of community results in formal and informal educational activities. The primary target groups are universities, training facilities and similar institutions.

The education content in the OMiLAB Portal includes method-specific training materials, tutorials, domain—and the method-related literature, case studies, exercises and all other materials the corresponding community deems useful.

2.5.1 OMiLAB Training Activities

Training activities within the OMiLAB Network address domain-specific modeling methods, method conceptualization and metamodeling. Exemplary items are:

Modeling Method/Tool Trainings and Tutorials aim to transfer knowledge about a domain-specific modeling method and the corresponding tool. Community members may offer modeling method trainings and tutorials on:

1. the respective modeling method/tool and/or domain-specific applications, or
2. a combined approach, introducing parts of the metamodeling technology and demonstrating the implementation of an application scenario or modeling method.

Method Creation Trainings aim to enable method creators to apply collaborative and creativity techniques and instruments. The training focuses mainly on the first two phases of the Conceptualization Lifecycle, as presented in Sect. 3.2.

Metamodeling Technology Trainings aim to enable method engineers to conceptualize their modeling method by applying the metamodeling technology and subsequently transforming it into a modeling tool. Trainings focus either on specific application scenarios or on a modeling method scenario.

In the first case participants in the training session are given a concrete case and its requirements. The training structure guides them along the Conceptualization Lifecycle [4] to understand each step from creation to the implementation of a proof of concept. The training proposes metamodeling with ADO*xx* as it addresses all requirements for a modeling method-based solution.

In the second case participants in the training session already have a modeling method and they work on the implementation of a corresponding modeling tool. Along the same Conceptualization Lifecycle [4], they are guided in the development process with the training proposing ways to address the specific method requirements in the context of the implementation in a specific metamodeling platform.

2.5.2 NEMO Summer School Series

The Next-Generation Enterprise Modeling (NEMO) Summer School Series (http://nemo.omilab.org) is a yearly, international, intensive program addressing the Digital Age. The event focuses on the conceptualization, design and the implementation of modeling methods. It uses the OMiLAB Collaborative Environment as a training space for exercises and practical applications. During a two-week program, graduate and postgraduate students are introduced to a wide array of aspects and application scenarios for conceptual modeling and metamodeling. The course materials and tools used during each summer school remain available for the community at large on the NEMO website.

By inviting every year about 30 internationally renowned experts to provide lectures, to present demonstrators or to discuss research challenges and modeling scenarios, NEMO supports OMiLABs goals to enlarge the community of those actively involved. In addition, it aims to create an international networking environment for peers and a forum for professors and students.

3 The OMiLAB Innovation Environment

The OMiLAB Innovation Environment is based on the

- Agile Modeling Method Engineering (AMME) Methodology, and the
- Conceptualization Lifecycle.

AMME links conceptually agility, as demanded by the rapidly evolving societal and technological advances, and evolution, as provided by domain-specific knowledge and methods. A domain-specific modeling method can be either 'horizontal' or 'vertical'. We define as horizontal all those modeling methods which are general purpose and applicable in multiple domains, while the vertical ones are application domain specific.

The AMME methodology can be operationalized using the phases of the Conceptualization Lifecycle. This can be seen as the 'engine' of AMME. The *Create* and *Design* phases draw upon innovative approaches from social and engineering sciences. *Formalize* uses formal approaches. The conceptual modeling method can be then enriched with a modeling tool by applying the *Development* and *Deployment* phases in the Innovation Environment.

3.1 Agile Modeling Method Engineering

AMME is a domain-independent methodology addressing the interaction between modeling and machine processing of models, including, for example, simulation, analysis and code-generation.

Before describing the methodology in detail, we would like to introduce its defining characteristics with regard to changing requirements, namely [4]:

- Adaptability—the ability to modify existing concepts/properties (to meet new requirements),
- Extensibility—the ability to add new concepts/properties to the existing metamodel,
- Integrability—the ability to add bridging concepts/properties in order to integrate existing building blocks,
- Operability—the ability to provide means (functionality) of operating on models (e.g., simulation, transformation) and
- Usability—the ability to provide satisfying user interaction and model understandability.

The framework of AMME, as depicted in Fig. 1, relies on a methodological core called the Conceptualization Lifecycle which establishes several phases for incrementally deriving modeling tools, from modeling method creation until the technical deployment in the form of usable software. Two types of artefacts, namely "Models that Use Concepts" and "Models of Concepts", facilitate the conceptualization phases in order to (re)use well-established (meta)modeling patterns.

"Models of Concepts" (sometimes also known as "models of the domain") aim to describe categories of being and their relations. Their scope is an ontological one. Knowledge acquisition is done through domain analysis. The concept of "concept" is the main construct (seen as "entity", "class", "set", etc.) [8].

"Models that Use Concepts" (sometimes also known as "models of things in the domain") describe behavioral, structural and intentional elements of an application case. Their scope is an applicative one. Knowledge acquisition is done on a case

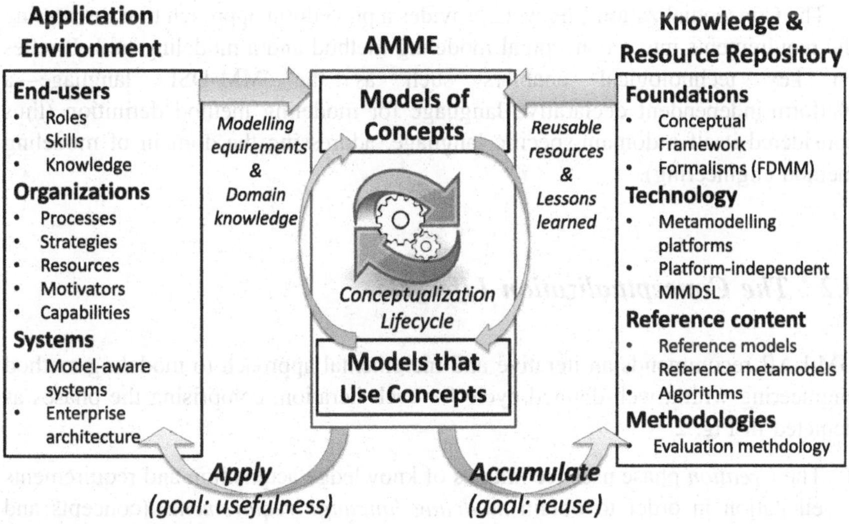

Fig. 1 The AMME framework [4]

basis, implicitly assuming domain understanding. The main constructs used are the concepts designed in the "Models of Concepts" [8].

All other elements of the AMME framework are described in detail in [4]. The management approach used in the AMME Product-Use-Lifecycle follows the principles established by agile software [4]

- Iteration—repeat activities and potentially revisiting the same work products,
- Increment—each successive version is usable and builds upon previous versions,
- Version control—enable for other agile practices and
- Team-oriented—small group of people assigned to the same project with shared accountability.

In the context of the Innovation Environment AMME, as described above, is applied for the realization of domain-specific modeling tools which enable the use of domain-specific modeling languages (DSMLs) [5], i.e., languages dedicated to and restricted by a domain and a specific class of problems [6]. DSMLs ease the specification, design and implementation through appropriate abstractions [7]. Yet, as presented in [4] in the process of language definition one must consider the evolution of requirements towards a DSL over time. Novel requirements might originate from the domain and its understanding itself or from the increasing proficiency of users with the language and their need for more elaborate concepts. In addition to this inwardly focused view, fast changing and volatile environments continually require new languages, new tools and techniques for model development, and (flexible) standards for different collaboration types.

The Conceptualization Lifecycle provides a procedural approach to transforming the requirements into a conceptual modeling method and a modeling tool. It relies on key technological enablers such as the MM-DSL language—a platform-independent declarative language for modeling method definition (thus considered itself a domain-specific language, addressing the domain of modeling method engineering).

3.2 *The Conceptualization Lifecycle*

OMiLAB recommends an iterative and incremental approach to modeling method engineering with a well-defined cycle for each iteration, comprising the phases as depicted in Fig. 2

1. The *Creation* phase uses techniques of knowledge acquisition and requirements elicitation in order to obtain *modeling language requirements* (concepts and relations relevant to the modeling method) and the *modeling functionality requirements* (e.g., competence questions that models should be able to answer; decisions to be supported by model analysis; other functionality pertaining to varying modeling scenarios). Procedural (processes), motivational (goals) and relational (dependencies) knowledge must be extracted during these phases, as well as a common understanding of domain-specific concepts. This phase will potentially benefit also from the analysis of requirements for related run-time systems.
2. The *Design* phase produces specifications for the metamodel, the language grammar, and the recommended graphical representation and functionality. Existing languages commonly used for domain modeling (like class diagrams or ER diagrams) may be used, to specify the structure of the modeling method. In addition, platform-independent or platform-dependent representation of the

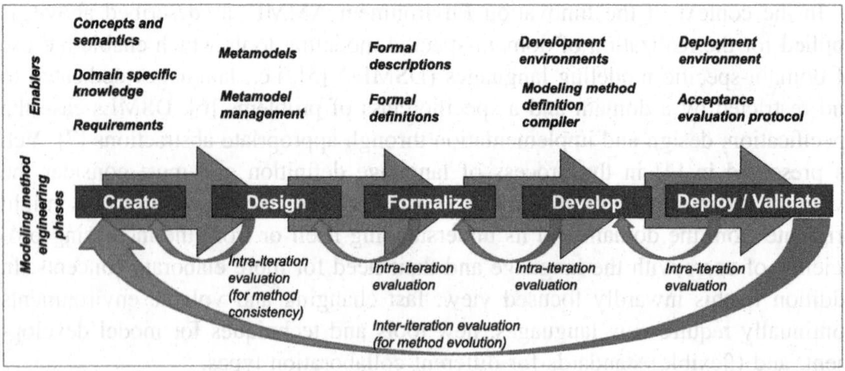

Fig. 2 The OMiLAB Conceptualization Lifecycle [4]

metamodel is required (e.g., MM-DSL [1]). The language grammar of MM-DSL is openly available at [1] and additional details are published [2]. It is constructed as an abstraction of typical meta^2 models provided by popular platforms. Currently a proof of concept compiler is available for the metamodeling platform ADO*xx* [3]. Additional compilers are expected to emerge from community-based efforts.
3. The *Formalization* phase ensures that the outcome of the previous phase has no ambiguity, either with the purpose of sharing specification within a community or in preparation for a platform-specific implementation. A formalism for ADO*xx* method implementations was published in [9]. Other formalisms specific to the method itself may be involved in this phase (e.g., algebra, logic).
4. The *Development* phase will produce a modeling prototype or proof of concept on the targeted metamodeling platform. Various platforms are available [3, 10, 11], each with their own underlying meta^2 model.
5. The *Deployment/Validation* phase deals with packaging and installing the modeling proof of concept and analyzing its user experience and the conformance to modeling requirements. The deployment may take the form of stand-alone or client–server modeling tools as well as cloud-enabled modeling-as-a-service. The feedback is the starting point for the next iteration, including possible changing requirements which might emerge from the first-hand experience of users and their gradual understanding on how the method/tool supports them.

It is, however, important to note that, although the typical outcome of this lifecycle, is a modeling tool, each of its phases produces output that can be relevant and reusable by itself, inside or outside the OMiLAB context—e.g., platform-independent specifications (to be implemented later on different platforms), cross-domain metamodels or other knowledge representations (to be specialized later in languages of varying specificity), generic or hybrid algorithms (to be assimilated later in other modeling methods) etc.

3.3 Selected Scenarios for "Method Engineers"

In order to start a proposal to create a modeling method project a form has to be submitted, stating the main idea of the modeling method and also the community member. After the proposal has been accepted, the project owner is notified and guided through all relevant steps, like filling out information defined in the blueprint. Afterwards the project owner will typically start the method engineering work, by inviting other stakeholders or getting in contact with OMiLAB members already involved—e.g., domain experts, specialists in relevant underlying formalisms, application partners, modelers or knowledge engineers. Each of these roles may take lead as a project owner or fulfil the generic role of "method engineer", depending on the project goals—from practitioner-oriented modeling tools to scientific experimentation and evaluation.

This section presents several selected scenarios within the conceptualization. Their focus is on unstructured, structured and search areas.

Scenario "Get Inspired" A vital point of the OMiLAB Portal (see Sect. 4.1) is to facilitate the exchange of knowledge in the community by means of, for example, events, which inspire other community members. Based on the organizational information, such as time, location, agenda, of the events in the portal a community member may decide to participate. In order to do so, she/he has to register. Upon logging in, user profile information already available in the system, such as name, email address and affiliation, is dynamically pre-filled in the registration form of the event. The registration provides the participant with ongoing interaction with the community.

Scenario "Conceptualize a Method" At its core the OMiLAB Innovation Environment supports the conceptualization of new methods, by giving the "project owner" a space to share the recent development results, and start interaction with the development community. The technical development of the modeling method in itself is supported by the Development Service Library and the metamodeling platform (see Sect. 4).

Scenario "Access Information from Existing Methods" The OMiLAB Innovation Environment facilitates the dissemination of modeling method content by offering a presentation structure for all projects. A common frame for material related to the development of modeling methods, such as research articles, case studies, modeling method manuals and the like are provided. This commented structure facilitates the exchange among users of modeling methods, but also among developers. The focus is on the modeling tool and example models, on material documenting the conceptualization and modeling processes as well as on information about how to apply the modeling tool.

4 The OMiLAB Technological Environment

The Technological Environment provides functionality to enact the Collaborative and the Innovation Environment. The Collaborative Environment is backed by the OMiLAB Portal and the support of the Innovation Environment is comprised of the metamodeling platform, the consistency engine and the development service library.

The OMiLAB Virtual Community Space, depicted in Fig. 3 provides the foundation for the Technological Environment. It is comprised of technology aspects, innovation aspects and collaborative aspects. The former are represented through metamodeling platforms, tools and development services. The collaborative aspects are represented through impact in any form and the innovation aspects, backed by the technology aspects form the base for generating impact.

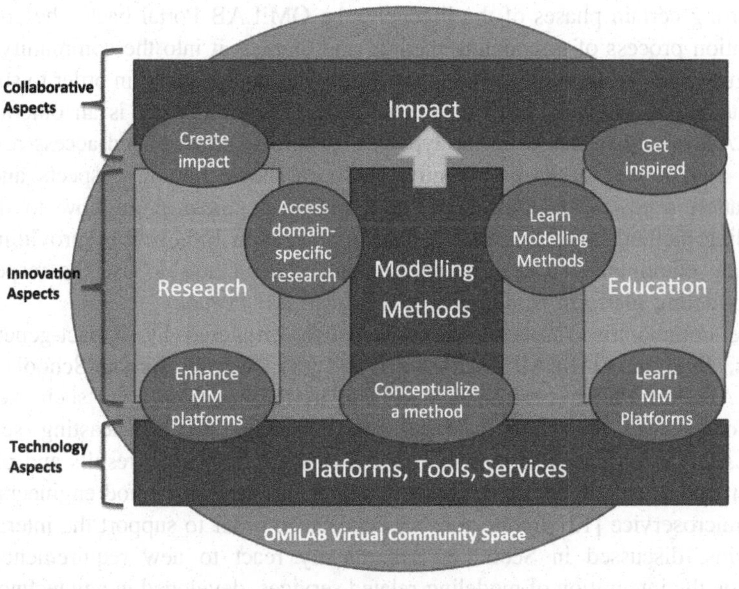

Fig. 3 Key activities supported in the OMiLAB Virtual Community Space

Modeling methods are at the centre of innovation aspects. The conceptualization and development of modeling methods is supported by metamodeling platforms, a consistency engine and development services. Additionally, two different views on the modeling methods are available:

- The research and innovation view, encompasses domain-specific research questions as well as those questions pertaining to metamodeling platforms.
- The education view includes method-specific training material, e.g., case studies, exercises, lectures, as well as training material for metamodeling platforms.

Dissemination spans all three pillars of content and may take the form of events, workshop and seminars.

4.1 The Interaction Approach

The technical support for communication issues is one of the most important requirements, necessary for a sustainable and successful evolution of the community. The OMiLAB Portal supports primarily the collaboration among community members. It deploys an environment that facilitates Agile Modeling Method Engineering by promoting interaction among community members through a microservice architecture [12]. By providing access to information and services, supporting certain phases of the lifecycle, the OMiLAB Portal backs the conceptualization process of a modeling method and embeds it into the community.

Figure 3 shows how the portal functionality has been defined in order to support the interaction and indicates the overlapping. The portal itself is an outcome of OMiLAB, designed based on the types of resources, services and access requirements envisioned for its community. Between the technology aspects and the innovation aspects, the OMiLAB Portal provides guidance on how to design modeling methods and assist in the Conceptualization Lifecycle by providing the adequate community space. The specific material on how to use the respective metamodeling platform is also part of the OMiLAB Portal.

The collaborative aspects are continuously triggered by impact-generating events, like the OMiLAB Workshops and the NEMO SummerSchools. The OMiLAB Portal offers functionality to facilitate the organization of such events.

Another way to create awareness is by using the broadcasting service, OMiLAB TV.[7] It can be employed for disseminating research results and project content and also to show the involvement and diversity of method engineers.

A microservice [12] architecture was chosen in order to support the interaction scenarios, discussed in Sect. 3.3, dynamically react to new requirements and facilitate the integration of modeling-related services, developed in any technology.

This implies that the whole system is partitioned into independent web services that communicate with each other using a standardized interface. By means of this abstraction to a common JSON[8] format, it is effortless to integrate new services. Two building blocks of this infrastructure are essential. On the one hand, there are the services that provide atomic functionality or data set, for a specific use case, required by the OMiLAB Portal, and on the other hand, there is the aggregator which takes care of the arrangement of services by managing the links between the OMiLAB Project and respective service instances.

The other critical component is the aggregator, called Project Structure Manager (PSM). It serves as the main point of interaction for the clients of the end users. All requests are directed to it and, from there, routed to the according service. The service again processes the request, generates the result and returns it to the aggregator. The aggregator in turn embeds this particular result in the overall context of the site.

The communication between these two building blocks is abstracted to a well-defined REST-interface. Hence, the technology of the according service can be freely chosen. This includes especially the programming language, and the according persistence technology, such as SQL, XML, file system or other solutions.

Figure 4 shows the feasibility of the separation of the two components. Due to this separation it is possible to have a single pool of services, providing atomic

[7]OMiLAB TV, http://www.omilab.tv, last visit 05.04.2016.

[8]JSON Data Interchange Format, http://www.ecma-international.org/publications/files/ECMA-ST/ECMA-404.pdf, last visit 05.04.2016.

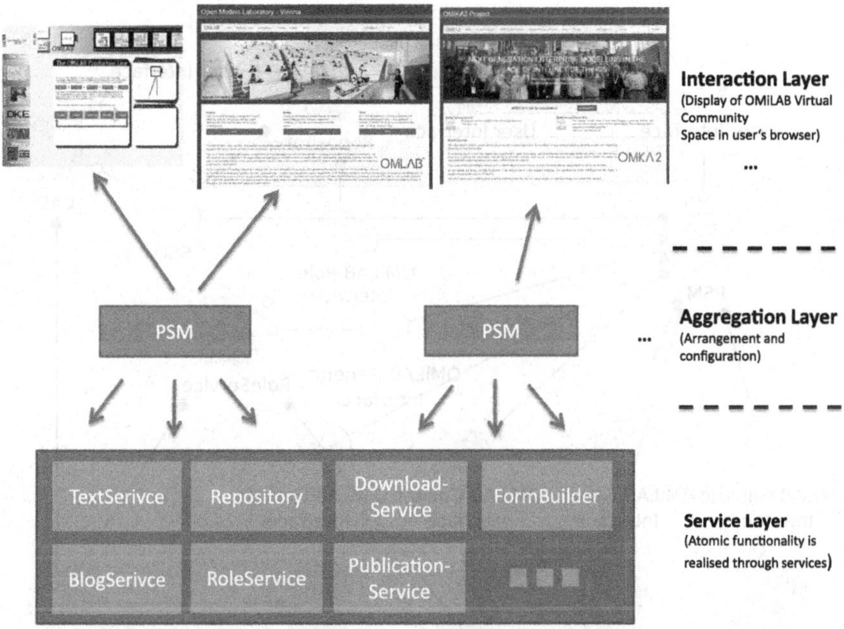

Fig. 4 Elements of the OMiLAB Portal

functionality. The aggregator layer may instantiate the services for their intended use. The PSM will take care of arranging the services in the right context. Multiple PSM, which may have specific configurations and design modifications may access the service pool and thus share the same functionality. The services currently available in the pool and their dependencies are shown in Fig. 5.

The PSM, which aggregates all services, can be seen in the upper left corner of Fig. 5. It accesses the standardized REST interface in order to trigger the related functionality of the respective service. Furthermore, there are a few other interfaces, that are used to provide specialized portal functionality, like logging (OMiLAB Logging Interface) of metadata and which are used to provide a permission system (OMiLAB Role Interface).

The Central Authentication Service[9] (CAS) provides a Single Sign On (SSO) solution for the whole Technological Environment. It accesses the OpenLDAP[10] service, where all OMiLAB user accounts are stored.

Additionally, the OMiLAB project repository [4] has a special position in the infrastructure, as it contains assets from several stages of the Conceptualization Lifecycle [4], that other services may depend on. Furthermore, it acts as "Deployment channel" [4, p. 8] for modeling tools.

[9]CAS, http://jasig.github.io/cas, last visit 05.04.2016.

[10]OpenLDAP, http://www.openldap.org, last visit 05.04.2016.

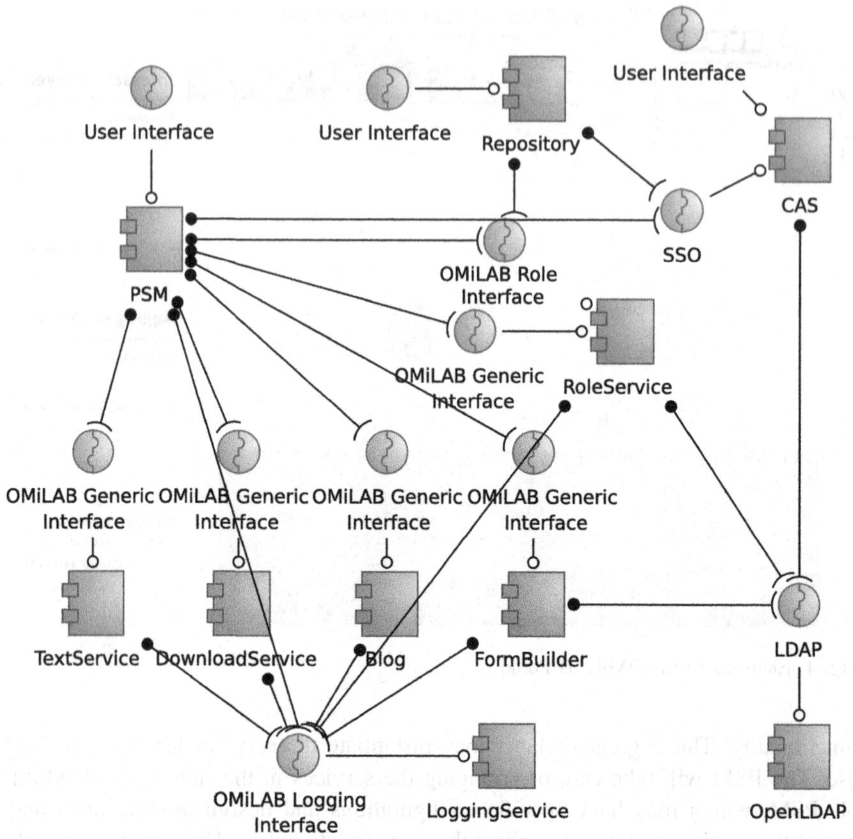

Fig. 5 The OMiLAB Portal Microservice Architecture

All services depicted above were implemented in Java. In order to support the microservice paradigm, Spring Boot[11] was selected as main framework. Additionally, other common Java Frameworks, like Spring Data[12] and Hibernate[13] were used for persistence. The vital part of the infrastructure, the REST interface is backed by Jersey2[14] and Jackson.[15] These technologies were used in order to standardize the technology stack employed within the OMiLAB Portal in order to ease management and maintenance. From a technical point of view, all programming techniques that support the usage of HTTP and JSON can be used to implement additional services or reimplement particular services, whenever new demand arises.

[11]Spring Boot, http://projects.spring.io/spring-boot/, last visit 05.04.2016.

[12]Spring Data, http://projects.spring.io/spring-data/, last visit 05.04.2016.

[13]Hibernate, http://www.hibernate.org, last visit 05.04.2016.

[14]Jersey2, https://jersey.java.net, last visit 05.04.2016.

[15]Jackson, http://wiki.fasterxml.com/JacksonHome, last visit 05.04.2016.

This allows for rapid changes and enables a fast response to new requirements. Also the development and integration of new experimental modeling-related services may happen independently, is uncomplicated and feasible without putting the rest of the infrastructure at risk. As each service is backed by its own data model, a service cannot only evolve independently, but the data, which is better structured, can be reused, i.e., in OMiLAB TV.

4.2 Metamodeling Approach

The metamodeling environment is comprised of the metamodeling platform, the consistency engine and development services, which all aim to support the Conceptualization Lifecycle. Currently ADO*xx* is the metamodeling platform used by the OMiLAB methods.

Metamodeling platforms are an essential component in the OMiLAB Innovation Environment and are an enabler for Agile Modeling Method Engineering. Based on the abstraction capabilities of these platforms, it is possible to address the challenges raised by rapidly changing domains and evolving requirements.

A metamodeling platform offers an abstraction layer between the operating systems interface and other technical interfaces, i.e., SQL and provides an interface to the method engineer, as shown in Fig. 6.

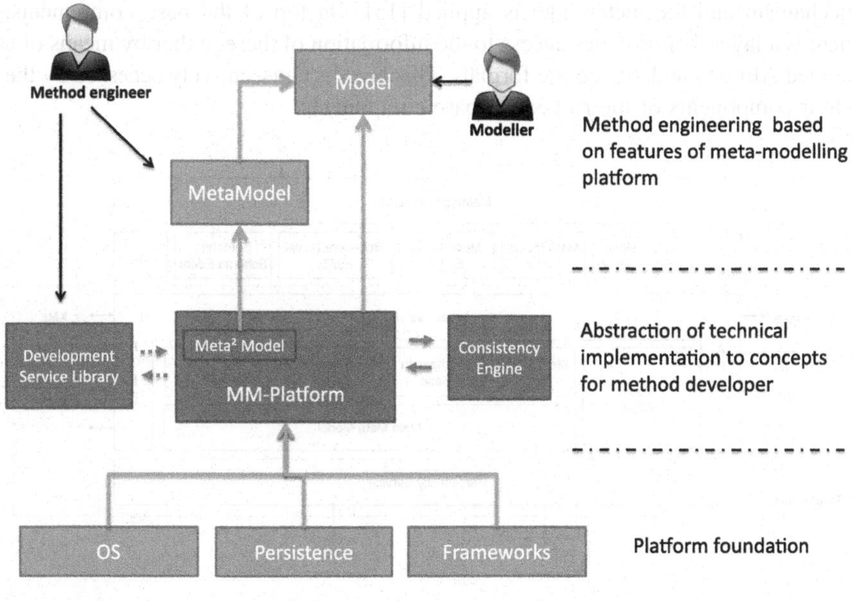

Fig. 6 Interaction layers of technical aspects

The platform abstracts from the technical implementation details of the underlying layers, provided by the operating system, databases and frameworks and enables the user to interact with the system on a higher level, based on the concepts defined in the meta^2 model.

This brings several advantages with regard to the further usage of the platform. Method developers do not need specific technical knowledge about the operating system or database technologies. Their main point of interaction with the platform is the meta^2 model. All further work, like their domain-specific metamodel or concrete models based on these metamodels are built on concepts from the meta^2 model.

A "component-based, distributable and scalable architecture" [13, p. 5] for metamodeling is proposed by [13] and illustrated in Fig. 7. The most important elements in Fig. 7, explaining the components of a generic metamodeling platform are located at the repository level [14]. The bottom layer facilitates the access originating from layers on a higher abstraction level to the data stored in the database.

The critical element, implemented on this persistency service, is the meta^2 model, which contains all concepts provided by the platform [14]. The Meta Model Base contains concrete metamodels based on the meta^2 model and the Model Base contains instantiation of these metamodels [14]. A strong link exists between the meta^2 model and the semantic schemas [15]. The constructs from the metamodel may be classified as a semantic schema, which is assigned unambiguous semantics through an ontology. The mechanism base and procedure model base store mechanism or respectively procedure models, based on the meta^2 model [14]. The mechanism base stores "all mechanisms and algorithms used for evaluation and using models" [14, p. 2] and the procedure model stores information on how this mechanism and the metamodel is applied [15]. On top of the base components, there is a layer that provides access to the information of these, either by means of a defined API or standardized file formats. This layer is consecutively accessed by the editor components of the respective base components.

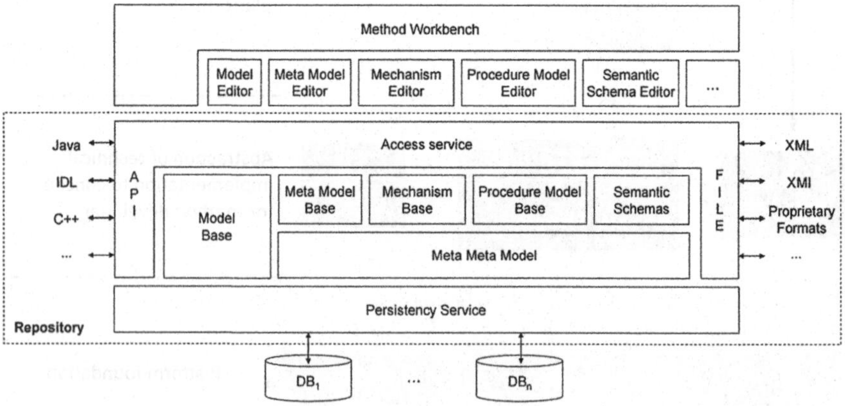

Fig. 7 Components of a metamodeling platform [14]

4.2.1 Metamodeling Platform: ADOxx

ADO*xx*[16] is a metamodeling platform developed at the BOC Group, a spin-off of the University of Vienna and is the metamodeling platform of choice in the current Technological Environment. The tool has been used and tested for over more than 20 years [16] in research and industrial projects and is considered a mature tool for metamodel development with a great variety of features, high scalability and reliability [16].

It develops the above architecture of a metamodeling platform. It features a scripting language, export to XML for external processing and offers the possibility to couple external applications.

ADO*xx* provides two different toolkits, both implementing the ADO*xx* meta^2 model and operating on the same database. The Development Toolkit supports the creation of modeling methods, whereas the Modeling Toolkit allows for the creation of models.

One of the critical components of a metamodeling platform is the respective meta^2 model, as it poses the main point of interaction for the method developer. ADO*xx* implements the concepts as meta^2 model depicted in Fig. 8.

A class is one of the core constituents of the meta^2 model of ADO*xx* [9]. Classes may have attributes and it is possible to create specialized subclasses [9]. Classes can be related with other classes by means of relation classes, where it is possible to specify which class may be connected with which classes by means of the specific relation class [9]. Based on these three concepts and their relations it is already possible to define simple metamodels, which is the prerequisite of deploying modeling toolkits. More details about the ADO*xx* meta^2 model and its concepts can be found in [16].

4.2.2 Consistency Engine: ConceptBase

ConceptBase[17] [17, 20] is the software component that serves as consistency engine in the Technological Environment. Historically, it is developed as a deductive database system, backed by the knowledge representation language Telos [17]. It can be used to store and organize concepts [17].

The logic rules available in ConceptBase will be used for integrity checking between the different layers of modeling languages. In conjunction with ADO*xx*, this can be used to provide assistance for the method developer, by analyzing a metamodel formally, and also in respect to its meta^2 model. Therefore, ConceptBase acts as a consistency engine for method design. A coupling between ADO*xx* and ConceptBase is available, see Chap. 16 of this book.

[16] ADOxx.ORG, http://www.adoxx.org, last visit 05.04.2016.

[17] ConceptBase, http://www.conceptbase.cc, last visit 05.04.2016.

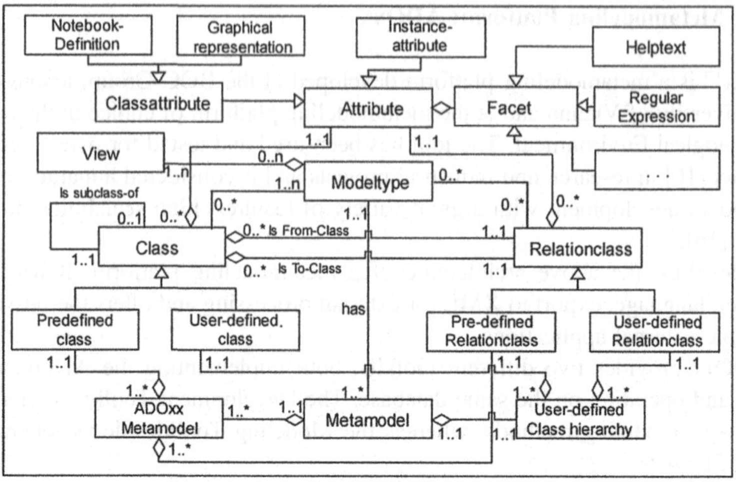

Fig. 8 ADO*xx* meta^2 model [16]

4.2.3 Development Service Library

Services, which are grouped in a library accordingly to their use, support all three OMiLAB Environments. Below, we exemplify some services which support method developers on the implementation level:

- The **GraphRep Generator** allows the user to draw the graphical representation desired for specific constructs in a graphical design application. Upon completion, the graphical construct representation can be automatically translated into the platform-specific code of ADO*xx*.
- The **OMiLAB IDE** is a tool based on the Eclipse Rich Client Platform (RCP) which provides assistance to write platform-specific code for ADO*xx* (i.e., AdoScript, GraphRep and AttrRep). It provides syntax highlighting and code completion for the file types mentioned above, based on the XText Framework.

Additionally, the following services assist in disseminating research results:

- The **ModelAnnotator** is a Java-based web application, which supports the method engineer in assigning meta-information to model elements.
- The **MethodPublisher** enables the export of the modeling method application library in an XML and SGML format.

Other services are provided as reusable plug-ins that can extend the capabilities of a modeling method implementation, for example:

- The **Linked Models serialization** plug-in provides a Java-based mechanism for converting model contents to RDF graphs, by exploiting the underlying graph nature of conceptual models.

In the service library, we manage the software as well as the documentation of these services. Contributors must keep the guidelines of open-source software development and in particular consider updates of the used frameworks and technologies.

5 Conclusion

This chapter presented the OMiLAB as an open, community-driven research environment dedicated to the practice of modeling method engineering through metamodeling. OMiLAB stimulates the sharing of practices, lessons learned, domain requirements, reusable knowledge items and development libraries, while also providing an experimentation setup for evaluating modeling tools which are, ultimately, the end-goal for each OMiLAB Project—regardless of whether they have been created in support of scientific inquiry or for some practitioner goals. The composing elements of the laboratory—the Collaborative Environment, the Innovation Environment and the Technological Environment, as well as their constituents, were presented in detail in this chapter. Exemplary and diverse ways of employing these resources and possibilities for different application domains will be described by the other 26 chapters of this book, which represent also our basis for evaluating the environment provided.

Acknowledgements We thank the international OMiLAB community for participating in this initiative and for inspiring us in the setup of the methodological and technological aspects of this environment. We particularly thank the owners of the on-going projects that are currently listed in OMiLAB, as well as the doctoral, postdoctoral researchers and experts who are active and have been contributing to the repository of tools and associated knowledge currently available in OMiLAB, some of them to be presented within this book. Our thanks go also to Simon Doppler for the technical support for the tools in this book in the OMiLAB Portal.

References

1. Visic, N.: MM-DSL: AN EBNF Specification
2. Visic, N., Fill, H., Buchmann, R., Karagiannis, D.: A domain-specific language for modelling method definition: from requirements to grammar. In: Research Challenges in Information Science (RCIS), pp. 286–297. IEEE (2015)
3. ADOxx.ORG. http://www.adoxx.org. Accessed 07 Apr 2016
4. Karagiannis, D.: Agile modelling method engineering. In: Proceedings of the 19th Panhellenic Conference on Informatics, pp. 5–10. ACM (2015)
5. Frank, U.: Domain-specific modeling languages: requirements analysis and design guidelines. In: Domain Engineering. Springer (2013)
6. van Deursen, A., Klint, P., Visser, J.: Domain-specific languages: an annotated bibliography. ACM Sigplan Notices **35**(6), 26–36 (2000)

7. De Troyer, O., Paret, E.: Challenges in Designing Domain-Specific Modeling Language for Educational Games
8. Karagiannis, D.: Lecture of Agile Modelling Method Engineering (AMME) at NEMO Summerschool 2015. http://nemo2015.dke.univie.ac.at/materials/lectures/mo_13_karagiannis_lecture.pdf. Accessed 07 Apr 2016
9. Fill, H., Redmond, T., Karagiannis, D.: FDMM: A Formalism for Describing ADOxx Meta Models and Models (2012)
10. Eclipse. http://www.eclipse.org. Accessed 07 Apr 2016
11. MetaEdit+. http://www.metacase.com. Accessed 07 Apr 2016
12. Newman, S.: Building Microservices. O'Reilly Media Inc. (2015)
13. Karagiannis, D., Kühn, H.: Metamodelling platforms. In: EC-Web, vol. 2455 (2002)
14. Kühn, H.; Murzek, M.: Interoperability issues in metamodelling platforms. In: Konstantas, D., Bourrières, J.-P., Léonard, M., Boudjlida, N. (eds.) Proceedings of the 1st International Conference on Interoperability of Enterprise Software and Applications (I-ESA'05), Geneva, Switzerland, Feb 2005, pp. 215–226. Springer
15. Kühn, H.: Method Integration in Business Engineering. University of Vienna (2004)
16. Fill, H., Karagiannis, D.: On the conceptualization of modelling methods using the ADOxx meta modelling platform. Enterp. Modell. Inf. Syst. Arch.—Int. J. (2013)
17. Jeusfeld, M.A., Jarke, M., Nissen, H.W., Staudt, M.: ConceptBase—managing conceptual models about information systems. In: Bernus, P., Mertins, K., Schmidt, G. (eds.) Handbook on Architectures of Information Systems, pp. 265–285. Springer (1998)
18. Karagiannis, D., Grossman, W., Höfferer, P.: Open Models Initiative—A Feasibility Study, Project Study on behalf of the Austrian Federal Ministry for Transport, Innovation and Technology (2007)
19. Open Model Laboratory Booklet (2014). ISBN: 978-3-902826-03-9
20. Jarke, M., Eherer, S., Gallersdörfer, R., Jeusfeld, M., Staudt, M.: ConceptBase—a deductive object base manager, https://www.cs.ubc.ca/~rap/teaching/534a/readings/conceptbase.pdf. Accessed 08 Apr 2016

Part II
Big Data

Design Semantics on Accessibility in Unstructured Data Environments

Nicholas Roussopoulos and Wilfrid Utz

Abstract In the dynamic world of the internet and web service, the need to access data in a transparent and flexible way becomes increasingly important. Technological advances on infrastructure level allow us to store and process larger volumes of data, with a higher complexity/variety and modification speed on structure as well as content level close to real-time. In this paper, the concept of "Data Service" is introduced as a novel methodology to match the data needs of services with existing, unstructured data environments. The approach is conceptualized as a domain-independent modeling method enabling developers to semantically design access mechanisms and algorithms, combine available data services according to functionality requirements and enrich retrieved data with metadata and provenance information.

Keywords Big data • Data service • Accessibility • Semantics

1 Introduction

The design of data access and processing mechanisms in the implementation of services and applications is traditionally driven by the assumption that the underlying schema is well defined and known to the developer during the design of the software architecture and implementation phases. Structured queries can be defined, optimized and embedded into various programming languages to access the data source, process and combine result-sets and use it in the logic of the service. For data combination and integration level in the relational world, foundations were described by Codd in 1970 [1], who defined primitive operators with well-founded

N. Roussopoulos (✉)
Department of Computer Science, University of Maryland, College Park
MD 20742, USA
e-mail: nick@cs.umd.edu

W. Utz
Department of Knowledge Engineering, University of Vienna, 1090 Vienna, Austria
e-mail: wifrid.utz@univie.ac.at

D. Karagiannis et al. (eds.), *Domain-Specific Conceptual Modeling*,
DOI 10.1007/978-3-319-39417-6_4

semantics to operate on structured sources as the schema is known in advance. Since then, 45 years of research and development resulted in a mature field in database design and data management.

In the dynamic world of the internet, any device, application or service deployed online is potentially a data source that could be used as input to implement business/application functionality. Data is not hand-crafted anymore but continuously generated by computers, devices, sensors, search results [2, 3]. The related schema has evolved over time. When realizing business logic/functionality using such sources, a dynamic and flexible approach is needed to continuously adapt access and processing mechanisms compare [4].

1.1 Data Services as a Concept

The concept of "Data Services" is described below as a model-based approach for handling dynamic schema evolution and performing a continuous adaptation of access and processing mechanisms using conceptual models as a baseline. This concept builds on thoughts and considerations articulated as "Schema-During (SD)" in [2] resulting in primitives to operate on evolving, unstructured data sources. The concept was developed as the modeling method "Big Data–Data Service (BD-DS)" used to semantically map data sources of different kinds, formats and representations with data demands on application level (see Fig. 1). The modeling method enables the user to (a) model the access and Extract-Transform-Load (ETL) of unstructured (and structured) data, (b) flexibly adapt to schema changes using conceptual models and (c) result in the formation of novel aggregate data services.

The concept shown in Fig. 1 builds on the assumption that data is produced and made accessible by all different kind of devices and infrastructures. Metadata from these sources can be analyzed during the design task. This task aims to map domain demands/queries specified on functionality level to these sources by applying operations categorized in three layers from Access via Query to Result serialization and persistence. The outcome of the design process is another, dynamically composed data source. These three levels cover the following aspects:

- *Access*: on this level, the base sources are made accessible. We distinguish between physical access mechanisms on data and metadata level, on protocol and media level, on access techniques to retrieve data ranging from basic bulk loading techniques to complex ones such as natural language analysis and text/data mining.
- *Query*: for this category, operations were identified to manage and transform sources in line with the requirements. These operations are structured hierarchically allowing the combination and composition of different operations.

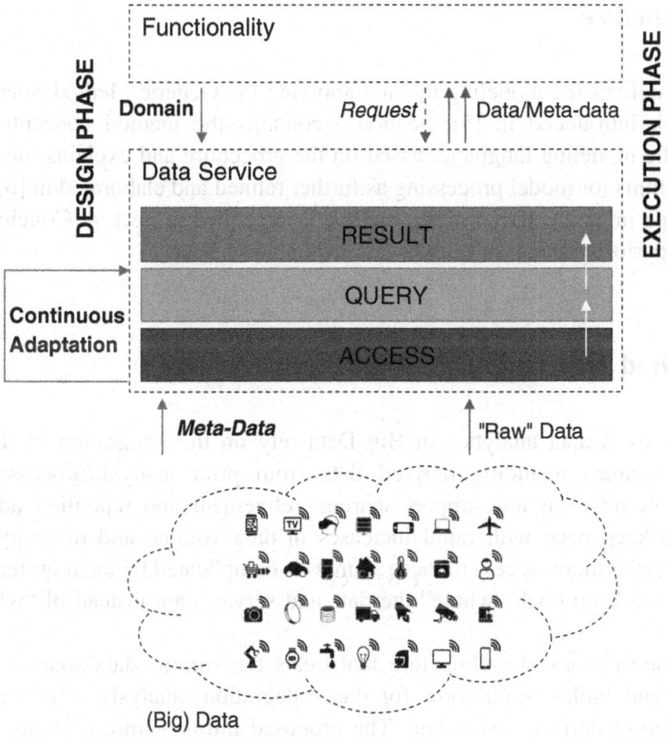

Fig. 1 Concept: data services using BD-DS

- *Result*: the result level triggers the exposition of the newly designed service for further use. This included serialization of result datasets in different formats, standard access protocols such as SOAP or ReST, persistency and reuse of resulting services and operations as well as usage techniques (push of results/notifications vs. pull requests).

As the composition on access, query and result level is performed using conceptual models, adaptation to new base sources and evolution of base source schemas become analysable, hence manageable.

During runtime (shown on the right in Fig. 1), the composed service is exposed and made accessible using the conceptual model for configuration. The service is enhanced by all meta-information from the design level as well as runtime level (e.g., provenance, quality aspects). A meta-mechanism helps traversing the hierarchical definition of the data service and invokes the available operations and returns data.

1.2 Structure

Section 2 defines the modeling method applying the Generic Method Specification Framework introduced in [5]. Section 3 contains the method conceptualization defining the modeling language, based on the procedure and explains mechanisms and algorithms for model processing as further refined and elaborated in [6] and [7]. A prototype implementation of the method is described in Sect. 4. Conclusions on the work performed and an outlook are available in Sect. 5.

2 Method Description: BD-DS

Discovery from data analytics in Big Data rely on the integration of data from disparate sources including derived data from prior analysis/processing. Yet, computer systems do not support sharing, refinement and repetition adequately enough to keep pace with rapid increases in data volume and diversity of data sources. Furthermore, access to these sources is complicated by the requirement that users have to keep track "where" the data and services are instead of "what" they are.

We propose a novel architecture that treats the various data sources as "data services" and builds a platform for data integration, analysis, aggregation and preservation of derived result data. The proposed infrastructure provides a stable, secure and reliable data network with first-class primitives for managing heterogeneous data services, for filtering, curating, aggregating, annotating and naming collections of data from multiple data services. Derived results are captured and become first-class data products that can serve as new data services available for further processing/analysis. Data is decoupled from location, storage, security and retrieval low-level primitives. Instead, it is accessed, exchanged and shared by "name" or by "semantic attributes" that are meaningful to the users. This proposal shares some of the principles of Content-Centric Networking [8], although the emphasis there is on the networking part, rather than data.

2.1 Guiding Example: "End-of-Lifetime (EOL) Assessment for Enterprise Architectures"

We illustrate the concepts of the methodology using an example case from enterprise architecture. The method itself and the implemented prototype are domain independent and not restricted to this particular application domain. Figure 2 shows an instance of a data service for the application case presented below, based on the characteristics introduced above. With reference to functionality, the business logic and the interactions are also defined. In our methodology, this level represents the

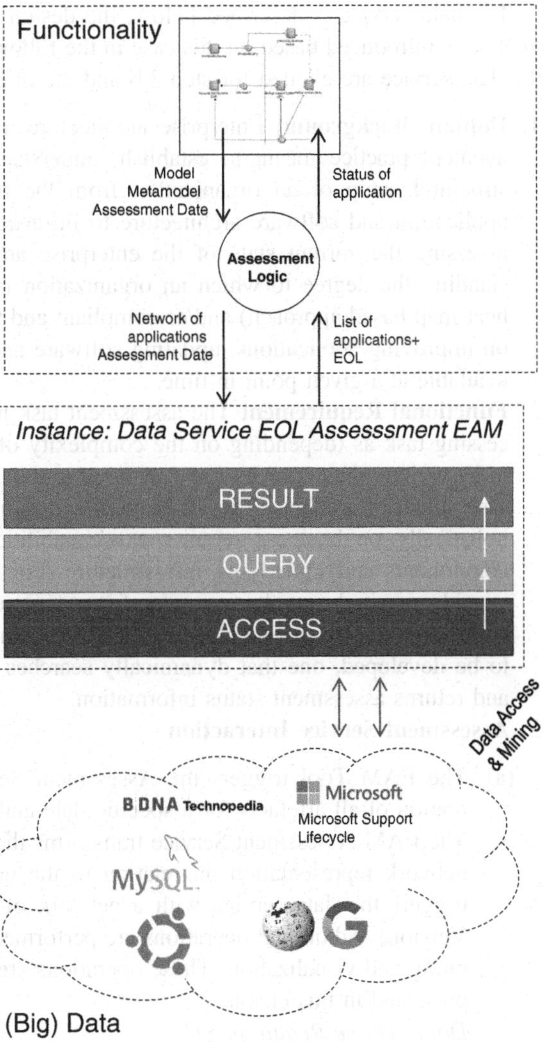

Fig. 2 Enterprise architecture assessment service

domain to be considered and the requirements on data level. The concrete data service defined below returns the required result-set, for further processing on functional level.

For this case, we focus only on the interaction steps in the EAM Assessment Application (in step 3.b and 3.c see below). On the data level, we assume that the sources, as shown in Fig. 2, are accessible online and returns from the sources can be parsed and aligned. Access techniques (e.g., text mining, web crawling, log mining, etc.) are considered on conceptual level only.

The data service is described below; the design and enactment by the BD-DS method is introduced based on this case in the following section. Requirements for the data service are elicited for step 3.b and 3.c in detail.

1. **Domain Background** Enterprise architecture management (EAM) is a management practice meant to establish, understand, maintain and improve the structural setup of an organization from the business capabilities level via application and software architecture to infrastructure elements. Continuously assessing the current state of the enterprise architecture is crucial to understanding the degree to which an organization is technology-fit (see [9] for a heat-map based approach) and/or compliant and to making conscious decisions on improving applications, updating software and modifying the infrastructure available at a given point in time.
2. **Functional Requirement** The assessment task in EAM is a difficult data processing task as (depending on the complexity of the organization's infrastructure) various data sources have to be scanned for parameters that enable an assessment of artefacts. The assessment and rating itself have to be performed holistically on business requirements/capabilities, applications and software components and underlying infrastructure. For this simplified case, we only consider a single result parameter for assessment, the "End-of-Lifetime" of applications, software and infrastructure. An automatic assessment service needs to be developed, one that dynamically searches for evidence data, aggregates and returns assessment status information.
3. **Assessment Service Interaction**

   (a) The EAM Tool triggers the Assessment Service to retrieve status information of all artefacts for a specific date and location.
   (b) The EAM Assessment Service transforms the domain input received into a network representation, in relation to the underlying EAM metamodel it triggers the data service with a network of components (Name, Vendor, Version). Additional operations are performed in the assessment service for rating and visualization. These operations are not within scope of the work presented in this chapter.
   Data Service Requirements

      i. Design of data input and output for representation and format (affects serialization, e.g., XML, JSON, etc.), and semantic (input and output message schema); for the case, the underlying metamodel of EAM tools is used (see ArchiMate [10], ADO*it* [11])
      ii. Define management functionality for persistence of results and revision tracking
      iii. Specify metadata to be collected and annotated along the operations performed as provenance information.

   (c) The Data Service performs a look-up in the data sources for each component, retrieves/parses the sources and performs a combination to add the

End-Of-Lifetime (EOL) date for the given timestamp to the network representation and annotates the result-set items with respective metadata (e.g., provenance information, data quality).
Data Service Requirements

i. Enable definition of logic operations (conditions, looping)
ii. Develop schema, structure, representation recognition for access operation to interactively perform the mapping task. The user can define sources and access techniques; the implementation dynamically retrieves meta-information and constructs a data source model.
iii. Define operations and mapping logic on different layers (Access, Query, Result)
iv. Support verification and validation of conceptual models to provide procedure for evolution of schema on source and target level.

(d) The EAM Assessment Service performs a rating/scoring and returns the score back to the EAM Tool. This is not part of the considerations for data services but represents domain-specific business logic.

2.2 BD-DS Method

The objective of the method is to enable an architecture for integrating a semantic layer to operate on arbitrary sources applying service-oriented techniques for composition and orchestration. This layer allows for efficient adaptation in case of schema changes, updates or modification as the functionality's endpoint is kept stable; a new implementation of the data service is accomplished by updating the model used to specify access, query and result operations. Currently, when using data from the internet, access techniques are hardwired; the user has to keep track of any changes in Access Programming Interface (API), structural or semantical changes at the same time generating updates on code-level. Using BD-DS, these updates can be performed at the model level, whereas the interaction between functionality and data service remains stable and migration strategies are manageable, mediating changes along the three categories of design. Figure 1 shows the interaction logic between functionality and data using the BD-DS approach.

This concept was developed in two stages, which are also reflected the specification of the method.

1. **BD-DS Design Phase** (blue arrows in Fig. 1) as input for the design of a data service, domain semantics and contextual information are needed to trigger the design; on the other hand, meta-information on available services is retrieved. The design method performs the mapping of data requirements with data available.
2. **BD-DS Execution Phase** (green arrows in Fig. 1) the design is verified and deployed. During operation, the endpoint of the data service is exposed and can

be invoked. Management functionality (concurrency, consistency) supports operation (as an interpretation of the conceptual model and enacting it) and improvement iterations (SD approach, schema evolution).

2.3 *Related Work*

Different approaches have been developed and evaluated to make unstructured data accessible for processing. On access level, these techniques build upon mining techniques such as natural language processing (NLP), text analytics in different forms, pattern recognition or clustering; they have in common that (a) they operate on a specific format and (b) the output representation facilitates the application of traditional query mechanisms (e.g., graph-based queries in unstructured data [12]). This implies that for a specific technique used, a format and representation of unstructured data is assumed. On integration level, a model-driven approach to organize data between services has been discussed and evaluated initially in the domain of technology-enhanced learning [13]. Building on a model-driven approach, data providing and consuming services are wrapped and dynamically added to a metamodel to enable end-users to define data flows. In this case, the recognition of runtime services schemas is wrapped into standard interface for get, push and transform operations.

For the definition of our methodology, a broad definition of unstructured data is taken into consideration. Unstructured data is understood as data where the format, representation and semantic is unknown at design time. The data model is therefore not pre-defined in a formal manner but is dynamically assessed and developed using conceptual modeling as a means for personalization and adaptation (see [2]). Structure in such data can still be implied, it might even be highly structured (also relational) but in ways that are unanticipated or unannounced [14] during the design of functionality. Building upon the concept of sibling data (sibdata for short) [2] as a data-network infrastructure, we aim to enable manageability of data by providing efficient operations to construct new, stable and useable data services build upon existing sources.

3 Method Conceptualization

The BD-DS method is conceptualized in accordance with the Generic Method Specification Framework. The conceptualization is performed using the modeling procedure as a starting point (tasks and results), identifying the constructs of the modeling language and relating them to mechanisms and algorithms on model processing level.

3.1 Modeling Procedure

The modeling procedure identifies the tasks of the modeler and results achieved as a result of applying the method. The procedure is structured as a top–down approach with feedback loops and iterations across and within phases (see Fig. 3). The construction of this procedure considers the "Adaptable Methodology for Database Design" in [15] and extends it to include both data service aspects and unstructured data in the sources.

Step 1: Domain/Environment Analysis The initial step in Fig. 3 for the method deals with understanding the functionality and mapping the required structure/schema, representation and semantics for input of the data service and its output. The modeler has to understand what the data consuming functionality needs, defines the interaction format and describes the semantics. Data service management aspects (concurrency, consistency, notification, update intervals) are identified and mapped using the result concept.

This step is performed manually by the modeler; during deployment, a web service with the format, structure and message schema is exposed by the system.

Step 2: Data Source Specification Sources are specified based on the result definition. This specification task builds on the business understanding [16]

Fig. 3 BD-DS modelling procedure

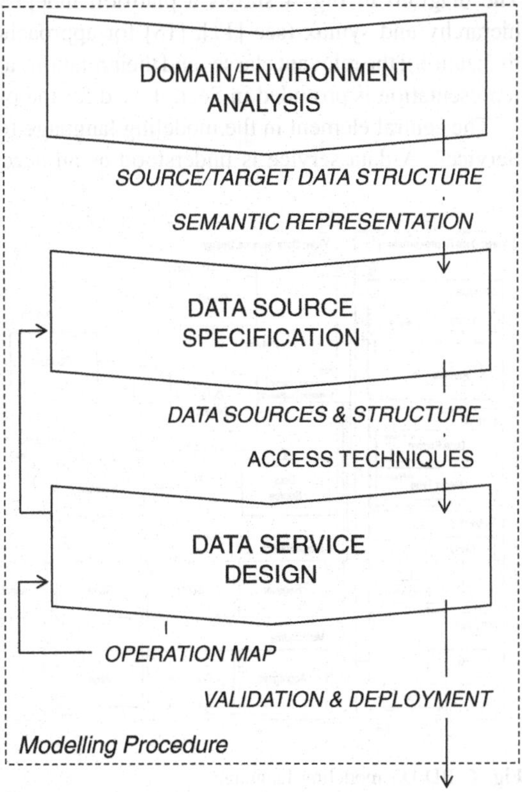

resulting from step 1. The modeler uses the access concept to define all necessary sources to cover the data requirements. This specification is not limited to structural or representational consideration but aims to cover all needed schema requirements.

This step is performed interactively. The modeler maps the logical access mechanisms and interactively retrieves the schema from the underlying data source.

Step 3: Data Service Design The actual design phase aims to map source and required target schema. Various operations as initially defined in [2] build the basis for this design tasks. The design is performed hierarchically; each operation results in another extended, combined, composed data source that can be further refined. As a structuring element, we distinguish between operation on Access (data, metadata retrieval), Query (filtering, aligning, composing, retrieving) and Result (return/serialization, persisting, updating and publication).

This step is also performed iteratively. Each iteration is a refinement of previous models, further closing the gap between source and result specification.

3.2 Modeling Language

The modeling language represents the structural perspective of the modeling method. The diagram in Fig. 4 shows a platform independent representation of the class hierarchy and syntax (see [17], [18] for approaches on conceptualization and formalization); the relevant classes and their relations are mapped. A platform-dependent representation is provided in Sect. 4 used for the proof-of-concept implementation.

The central element in the modeling language for BD-DS is the concept of "Data Service". A data service is understood as an accessing or transforming operation.

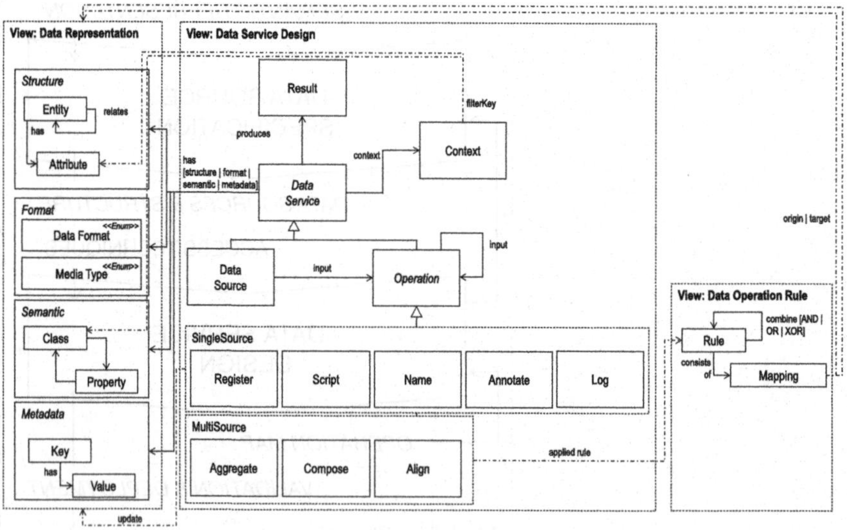

Fig. 4 BD-DS modeling language

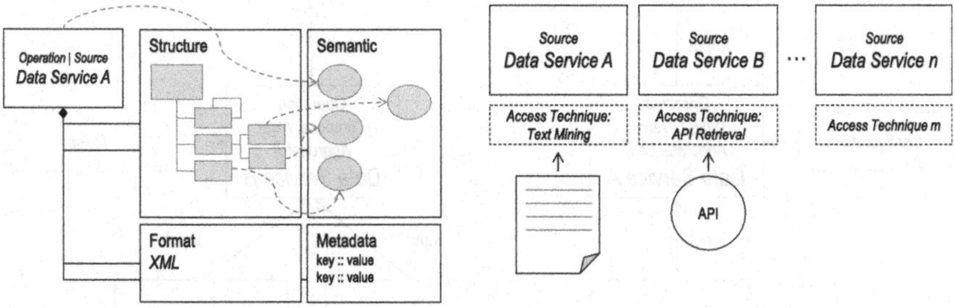

(a) (b)

Fig. 5 Example **a** *DataRepresentation* and **b** *DataSource*

Instances of the service are *DataSource* and the abstract class *Operation*. Each data service considers three elements: source, operation and result as their internal organization. A reflexive association in the metamodel provides the possibility that any operation can be input for another one. The produced output is either further processed by other data operations or consumed by the *Result* element.

The service's data characteristics are constructed through four elements on output level, exemplified in Fig. 5a

1. *Structure*: as a representation of the data elements recognized within a service. The structure (e.g., abstract data type/schema of the input/output). Data structure diagrams are used to represent the structure. [19]
2. *Semantic*: defines the meaning of the data. For BD-DS a lightweight approach is foreseen using annotation concepts as described in [20] from an application domain perspective and [21] from a service-oriented technique. As a technology, a graphical representation of RDF [22] is used as backbone, where the service and the structural representation are subjects, the predicate is defined on the relation and the objects/facts are stored within a common representation of a model.
3. Format: the representation format that the service requires and produces. This attribute is a classification according to Internet Media Types [23]
4. (Management) metadata such as access time, quality and the like of the data service itself. In case of composed services, metadata is also a composition of the related services' metadata.

A *DataSource* class, as a special operation that does not consume other services, defines a data providing entity/system (e.g., internet device, database, web service API, documents). Access mechanisms and techniques are specified. The actual technique used to retrieve data is transparent in the model and can be selected from a pre-defined set of possibilities. This selection possibility can be dynamically extended using wrapper implementation patterns as described in [13]. An example of different data sources and their relation to access techniques is shown in Fig. 5b.

For Operations, a classification is made between SingleSourceOperation and MultipleSourceOperation based on the number of input arguments required to

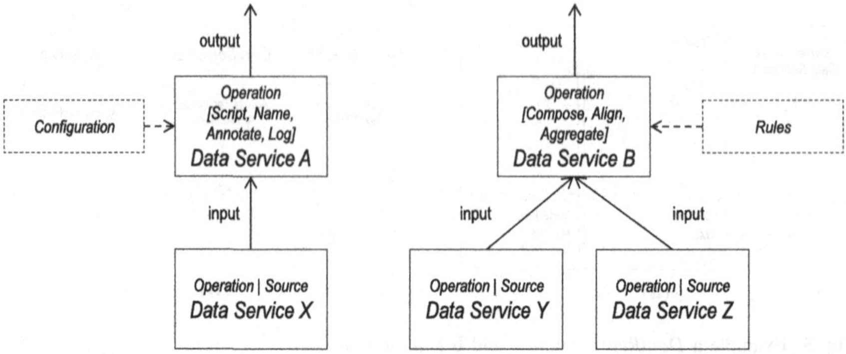

Fig. 6 Example *Operation* hierarchy

perform the operation (see Fig. 6 for an example of a single source and multi-source operation). For MultipleSourceOperation transformation rules for Aggregate, Compose and Align are defined. These operations modify the data representation of the source to correspond to the target representation. SingleSourceOperation enhance the metadata/data of the source through Script, Name, Annotate and Log operations. Operations are configurable (static values, files, rules) and correspond to the data representation.

As *Operation* is an instance of *DataService,* operation trees can be constructed (an operation can provide input to another operation).

- **Naming**: Allows a collection of data (results) returned by one or more data services to be born and become identified by a name. Although a lot of data can be accessed through data services, it stays in a temporary workspace and is lost unless a subset of it is named, and thus it is given permanent status. Because results may be obtained from several diversified data services, we are referring to these collections of results by sibling data. User defined names are mapped to a Globally Unique Identifier (GUI) that is registered along with metadata about the creation of such a sibdata, including the source data services used to obtain the data, including the creator's name, time of creation, and other provenance attributes which are associated with the result name and become integral part of it. Ownership, access rights and security aspects are specified through some capability mechanism [24].
- **Annotating**: Allows a user to annotate data obtained from a data service. Annotation adds and/or updates the key/value set of the data service. This annotation can also relate to the semantic representation of the service.
- **Filtering**: Allows the filtering of data that is not wanted. This can be done manually or by applying a predicate that removes data not satisfying the predicate. In the modeling language representation in Fig. 4, the Context class is regarded as an operation that can filter any source or operation by defining the predicate as a reference to the services' structure/semantic, to their scope and applicability (see Fig. 7a. Example context types are geolocation (e.g., only

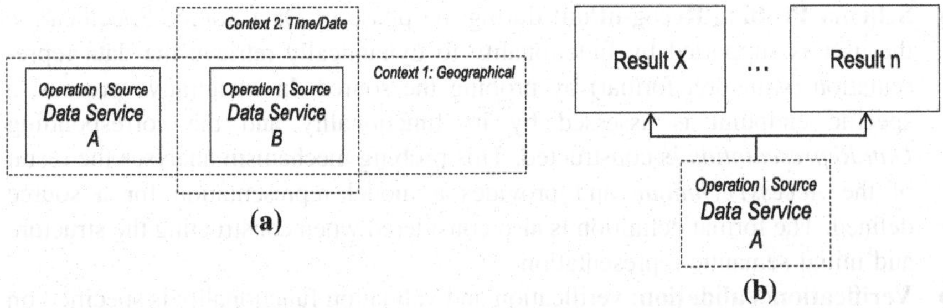

Fig. 7 Example for **a** *Context* (Geographical and Time Filter) and **b** *Result*

retrieve data for a specific geographical context), device (e.g., only data applicable for a device type), time/duration (e.g., only data for a specific point in time, duration). This contextualization of data services acts as a global filter operation.

- **Aggregating/Aligning**: Results obtained from different data services can be aggregated to form a new data service. These results can be grouped together without any order or can be aligned to a specific order of the data. Aligning can be either done manually by selecting the layout of the various data results, or by a program that aligns these data results in compliance with some logical and/or spatiotemporal predicate in a manner analogous to a generalized join operator in relational algebra. Synchronization of data streams is a typical alignment e.g., video, audio and subtitle streams from various source environments
- **Scripting/Logging**: A scripting language provides the mechanism for displaying, aligning, synchronizing and other aggregating operations. The control primitives of the scripting language deal only with the data flow and arrangement or positioning of the data components and not with the control and access paths of the data sources. Therefore, such scripts are data independent.
- **Registering**: as an operation to register the designed service in the infrastructure and make it available to the user

The modeling language as depicted above allows the definition of new operations.

Result is used to define the serialization of results, specify management functionality and persistency techniques to guarantee revision safety and fail-over control. An instance of *Result* per operation tree for deployment purposes is needed, but multiple are possible (see Fig. 7b. A single data service can potentially result in multiple results; different serialization of management techniques might apply.

3.3 Mechanisms and Algorithms

Mechanisms and algorithms that operate on the modeling language are defined to support tasks and result creation of the modeling procedure. Based on the modeling procedure, the following algorithms/mechanisms were conceptualized:

- **Schema Probing/Recognition**: during the phase of Data Source Specification the user is supported by functionality to dynamically retrieve the data representation (structure, format) by probing the source. In an iterative process, a specific endpoint is assessed by its functionality and the corresponding *DataRepresentation* is constructed. This probing mechanism analyses the result of the *AccessTechnique* and provides a model representation for a source defined. The format definition is also considered when constructing the structure and initial semantic representation.
- **Verification/Validation**: verification and validation functionality is specified on different levels, ranging from cardinality checks (are all conditions/constraints of the modeling language satisfied) as syntactical checks to source–target validation. These checks build upon the formal definition of operators. The objective of this mechanism is to support the structural and format transformation design of an Operation Diagram.
- **Animation/Simulation**: model animation functionality is provided to allow for validation of the modeler's results in an interactive format. Similarly, as in the debug mode of current integrated development environments (IDE), the modeler can step through the operation map, running specific operations and validating their results, also from a semantical viewpoint.
- **Deployment**: The model developed by the user is deployable as a service in standard service containers. The implementation of this algorithm is triggered by the user, the model set is package and interpretation logic on runtime level constructs a) the service endpoints (based on the *DataRepresentation*), operations and management functionality (source fail-over, revisions, persistence).

4 Proof-of-Concept

The evaluation of the above conceptualization was done by implementing a proof-of-concept solution using the ADO*xx* [25] metamodeling platform. The implementation focuses on the development of the modeling language as the structural aspect, enhanced by model-support functionalities and related model processing algorithms. The runtime aspect of the concept developed in the prototype using the Apache Axis Web Service Container [26]. Deployment functionality is available as an implementation of the *Register operation* during the deployment to make the models of data services available via the web-service container acting as the registration and execution server of data services.

The following section is focused on the implementation details for the BD-DS Design Environment. Design decision taken during implementation of the modeling language and model processing mechanism of the prototype are documented below. The implementation of the execution environment is rudimentary available as interpretation logic of the models providing interface for browsing the data service store, invoking data services and its operations. The proof-of-concept section

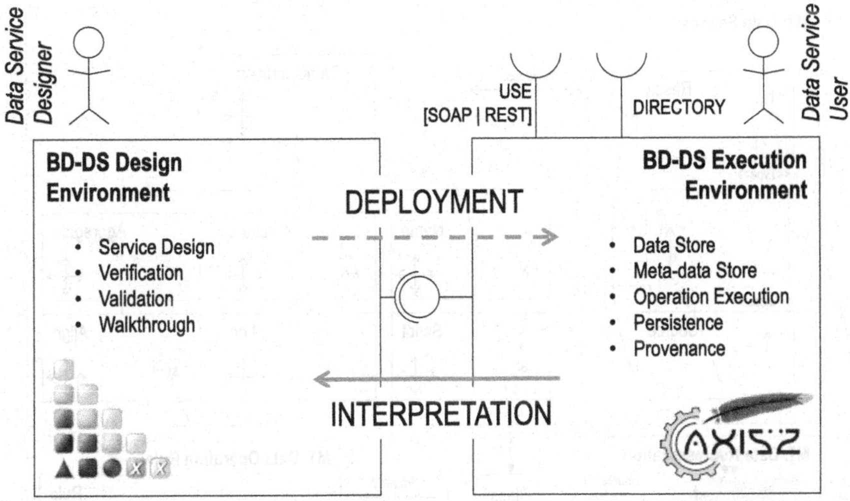

Fig. 8 BD-DS deployment architecture

concludes with the example case modeled in ADO*xx* and made operational in the web-service container (see Fig. 8 for the deployment architecture of the implementation).

4.1 Implementation of the Modeling Language

The implementation of the design environment is performed by mapping the generic concepts introduced in the conceptualization section to platform-specific functionalities and configuration features resulting in an application library on the platform level.

Modeltype Stack and Class Hierarchy The views and related classes/concepts per view are mapped to the concept of Model type (MT) as an aggregation of concrete modeling classes/subviews, and the abstract class hierarchy available in the platform. The BD-DS modeling language consists of the main model type *Data Service* and two supporting model types *Data Representation* (including two filter views) and *Data Operation Rule*.

An instance of model type Data Service is created to represent the design of a new data service according to the concept introduced. This data service is constructed using the operations defined and is exposed through one or more instances of class Result connected to the operation via the produces relation. Figure 9 provides an indication of the modeltypes, their contained classes and graphical representation as well as their relation across modeltypes. Relations within each modeltype are constructed as explicit relation classes or implicit containment links.

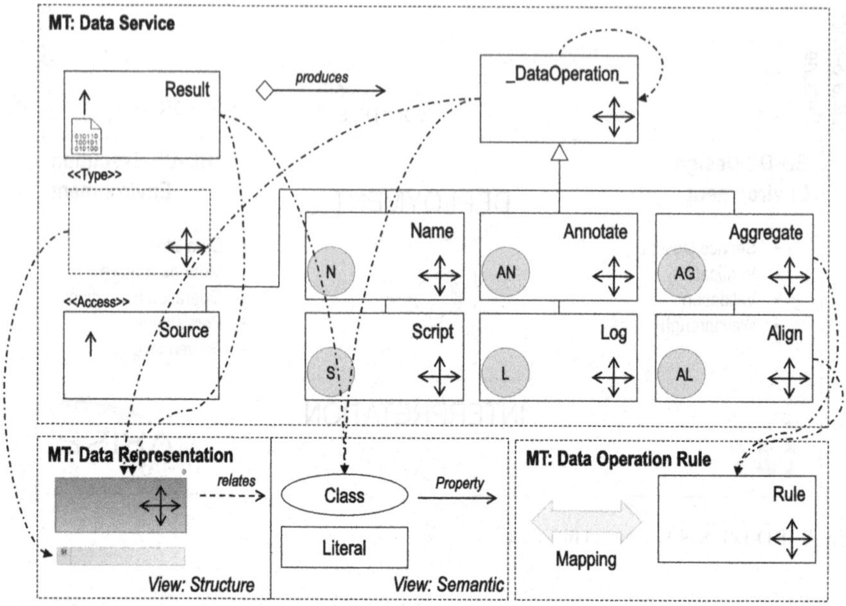

Fig. 9 BD-DS modeltypes and class hierarchy in ADO*xx*

Graphical Representation of a Data Service The graphical modeling in BD-DS for the *Data Service* model type is implemented following a box-in-the-box approach to represent the hierarchical structure of the data service components. This is accomplished using the ADO*xx* container functionality and the implicit and automatically created "Is inside" relation between container elements. This design decision results in the ability of the modeling tool to define hierarchical structures without the need to explicitly model connectors between objects, additionally verifying constraints as cardinalities per operation type.

The prerequisites for generating such a behavior in a graphical modeling environment are (a) objects are resizable on a horizontal and vertical axis; the sizing of the object considers the contained objects and is determined dynamically and (b) containment relations are accessible and can be verified through constraints/cardinalities configured on platform level.

Data Service Bundle The design environment supports the creation of multiple service bundles containing all support information and cross-referenced information. Cross-referenced are on one hand created automatically using model processing mechanisms (e.g., schema probing) or created manually by the service designer (input/output references in mapping rules on semantic and/or structural level).

Figure 10 shows the guiding example designed using the prototype. Following the modeling procedure, in an initial step the result is specified using the *Result* class. For the example case, two result items are defined using the same structure with varying serialization formats (XML, JSON). Next, the *Source* elements are identified. For our case, five sources are used–four individual calls to the Technopedia [27]

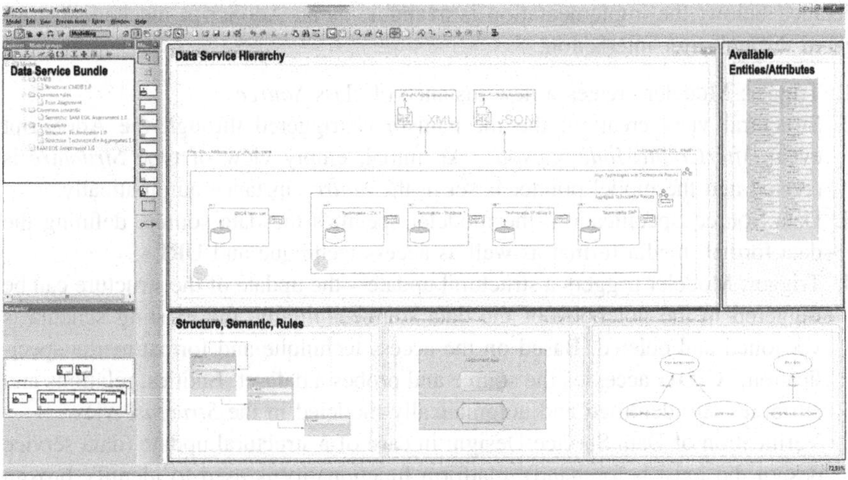

Fig. 10 BD-DS modeling language in ADO*xx*: example case

API for specific technologies and the enterprise architecture-related source on configuration items in the organization.

The transformation from source to target is implemented in a hierarchical way, initially the Technopedia sources (as they are individual requests for a specific technology) are aggregated into a common list. This aggregation is defined in aggregation mapping rules on the *Aggregate* instance, containing all sources. The resulting list is then aligned with the EAM data using alignment rules on structural as well as semantic level. The structural rules are modeled as input–output relations whereas the semantic rule is defined through mapping structural elements into a common vocabulary. This aggregation can be considered as a generic join operation between two datasets. As a final cleaning step, before serialization a *Context* filter is applied to remove unnecessary information resulting from the aggregation.

4.2 Implementation of Mechanisms and Algorithms

The implementation of model processing mechanisms and algorithms is done by configuring platform functionality and by extending functionality/add-on programming using the AdoScript language in ADO*xx*. The objective of these functionalities in the modeling environment is to support the modeling procedure and simplify user interaction. For the prototype, we focused on two aspects of the method, namely Schema Probing/Recognition and Deployment Support.

Schema Probing/Recognition This mechanism supports the second phase of the modeling procedure and allows to derive *Structure* representations through a probing approach of elementary data sources. The phases of the mechanism are detailed below; the implementation is available as an AdoScript mechanism triggered through user interaction.

1. Trigger: Modeler creates a new instance of class *Source*.
2. Structural view creation: the mechanism is triggered through the AdoScript event *AfterCreateModelingNode*. An initial, empty view of type *Structure* is created and the model pointer is set in the *Source* instance automatically.
3. Data Source Specification: the modeler specifies the data source, defining the data format, media format as well as access technique and URI.
4. Trigger: Modeler triggers a structural update—the update of the structure can be triggered in the notebook of the data source. Initially, the existing schema is versioned and deleted. Based on the access technique and format/media specification, ADO*xx* accesses the source and probes a dataset. Entities, relations and attributes are identified and automatically modeled in the *Structure* view.
5. Verification of Data Service Design: in case of a structural update (data service design did exist beforehand), platform functionality is used to identify broken links and missing entities/attributes. The modeler can manually adapt the service design to new structure.

```
set sources to GET_BASE_DATA_SOURCES
for i=0 to source.size
  set format to GET_DATA_SOURCE_FORMAT (source(i))
  set referencedStructure to GET_REF_STRUCTURE
  if (referencedStructure is null)
    set structureModelID to CREATE_NEW_STRUCTURE
    CREATE_REFERENCE (source(i), structureModelID)
  else
    DELETE_ALL_CONTENT (referencedStructure.modelid)
  endif
  if (format is "JSON")
    set probe to GET_DATA_PROBE (source(i))
    set root to GET_ROOT_JSON_ELEMENT (probe)
    set rootobjid to CREATE_ENTITY (root)
    RECURSIVE_CHILD_ITERATE (root)
  elseif (format is "...")
  ...
  endif
endfor

procedure RECURSIVE_CHILD_ITERATE (root)
  for j=0 to root.children.size
    if (root.children(j).isleaf
      CREATE_ATTRIBUTE (rootobjid, root.children(j))
    else
      set childrenobjid to CREATE_ENTITY (root.children(j))
      CREATE_RELATION (rootobjid, childrenobjid)
      RECURSIVE_CHILD_ITERATE (root.children(j))
  endfor
endprocedure
```

[Probing procedure and its application in the context of BD-DS].

The pseudo-code snippet above shows the logic for creating the structural models assuming JSON as the format returned by the operation/source (other formats are supported in the actual implementation such as CSV and XML). The mechanism iterates through all sources and operations, retrieves a probe using the access technique and mechanism, cleans pre-existing content in the structural view and cross-links the operation with the structure. A recursive call on the probe creates entities, relations and attributes. Figure 11 shows the result for the Technopedia source from the guiding example.

A similar logic is also applied for the probing of semantic representations. For semantics, only a global view for all operations and its outputs is constructed. This view is further refined by the modeler to define same concepts in different sources and operations, therefore semantically enriching the design.

Deployment Support Deployment of data service design bundles uses the web-service interface of ADO*xx* to retrieve the bundle as input. Deployment is done by the user (after verification and validation of the design) by releasing the model bundle. This step is done by using the platforms functionality to mark models as released, enhanced by changing this flag for a whole bundle and write-protecting the content.

Actual operation is controlled by the execution environment. The model repository is continuously analyzed and released bundles, not yet deployed, are requested. The execution environment interprets the model bundle, deploys the bundle and enables the interfaces defined dynamically. This interpretation takes place in three consecutive steps:

1. *Tree Construction and Traversal*: Initially, the box-in-a-box representation is transformed into a tree representation using model rewriting functionality

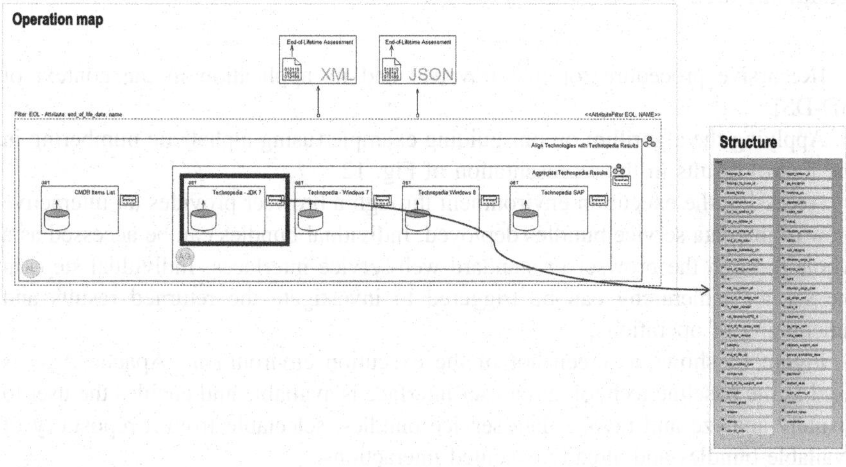

Fig. 11 Probing of the data source technopedia

internally. This tree is needed for traversing the operation using a Depth-first, post-order algorithm [28]. This traversal is used to invoke the operation in the appropriate order, as contained sources/operation need to execute before the container operation is run.

2. *Invocation*: The operations are invoked using generic template implementations available in the Axis container, configured and refined by the model content/configuration.
3. *Result Preparation*: as a concluding step, the root nodes output is serialized and preserved for further use or fail-over. According to the mechanism defined in the *Result* instance, the output is made available.

The algorithm for performing the three steps above is outlined in pseudo-code below.

```
set operations to GET_ALL_OPERATIONS
for i=0 to operations.size
  # identify container, no parents available
  if (operations(i).parent == null and operations(i).hasResult)
    POST_ORDER_HIERARCHY (operations(i))
    for j=0 to operations(i).results
      set result to PREPARE_RESULT(operations(i).results(j))
      PERSIST_RESULT(result)
    endfor
  endif
endfor

#recursive function to traverse the tree
procedure POST_ORDER_HIERARCHY(node)
  if node == null then return
    foreach sibling in node.siblings
      POST_ORDER_HIERARCHY (sibling)
      INVOKE_OPERATION(node)
    endforeach
  endif
endprocedure
```

[Recursive procedure for tree traversal and its application in the context of BD-DS].

Applying the algorithm on our guiding example (using alphabetic numbering in the figure) results in the representation of Fig. 12

Accessing the execution environment through a browser provides an interactive view of the data service bundles deployed. Individual bundles can be accessed as a whole through the browser or standard web-service interfaces. Individual steps in the service's hierarchy can be triggered to investigate the returned results and functioning of operations.

Figure 13 shows a screenshot of the execution environment. Apache Axis is used as the baseline technology, a user interface is available and enables the user to visually analyze and invoke data service bundles, selectable from a repository of available bundles and already executed interactions.

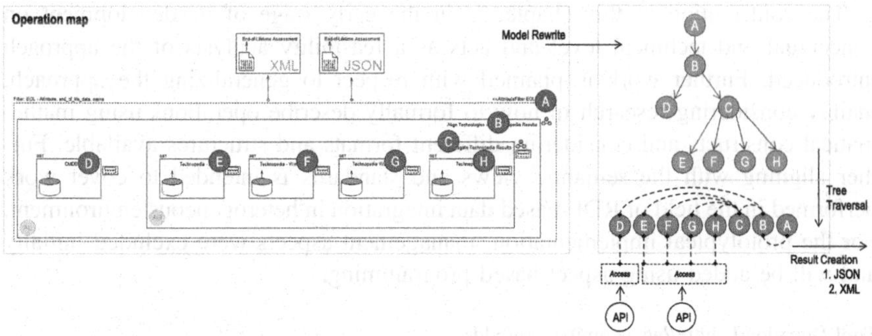

Fig. 12 Deployment algorithm

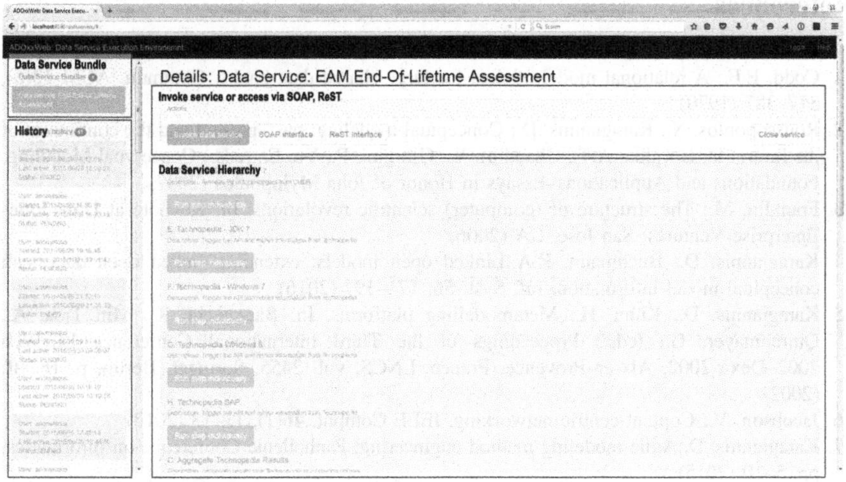

Fig. 13 Browser-based execution environment

5 Conclusion and Outlook

The infrastructure we propose in this chapter aims to contribute to areas such as domain-independent data integration and accessibility. Using conceptual modeling as a baseline for the integration task, the integration into current analysis pipelines and practices becomes feasible, providing data users with additional benefits: The data service composed is within a container and can be easily accessed, tracked and shared on a conceptual level, rather than on actual data level. In distributed environments, the designer shares a graphical model with his co-workers (knowledge management aspects) and enables all users to retrieve the same results through rerunning the query and/or assessing past invocations.

The contribution in this chapter is in the early stage of its development on conceptual and technical level and acts as a feasibility analysis of the approach introduced. Further work is planned with respect to generalizing the approach, mainly considering research in how to formally describe operations using mathematical constructs and considering different formats and structures available. Further aligning with the semantic views and standards is intended to cover work performed in the field of RDF-based data integration in heterogeneous environment. For the prototypical implementation, management aspects were excluded initially and will be added using aspect-based programming.

Tool Download http://www.omilab.org/bdds.

References

1. Codd, E.F.: A relational model of data for large shared data banks. Commun. ACM **13**(6), 377–387 (1970)
2. Roussopoulos, N., Karagiannis, D.: Conceptual modeling: past, present and the continuum of the future. In: Borgida, A.T., Chaudhri, V., Giorgini, P., Yu, E., (eds.) Conceptual Modeling: Foundations and Applications–Essays in Honor of John Mylopoulos (2009)
3. Franklin, M.: The structure of (computer) scientific revolutions. In: Keynote at Dow Jones Enterprise Ventures, San Jose, CA (2006)
4. Karagiannis, D., Buchmann, R.A.:Linked open models: extending linked open data with conceptual model information. Inf. Syst. **56**: 174–197 (2016)
5. Karagiannis, D., Kühn, H.: Metamodelling platforms. In: Bauknecht, K., Min Tjoa, A., Quirchmayer, G., (eds.) Proceedings of the Third International Conference EC-Web 2002–Dexa 2002, Aix-en-Provence, France, LNCS, vol. 2455, Springer, Berlin, p. 182 ff. (2002)
6. Jacobson, V.: Content-centric networking. IEEE Comput. **46**(1), 11–13 (2013)
7. Karagiannis, D.:Agile modeling method engineering. Panhellenic Conference on Informatics, pp. 5–10 (2015)
8. Karagiannis, D.:Meta-Modeling as a Concept: The Conceptualization of Modeling Methods. GI-Jahrestagung 2013: 152
9. Karagiannis, D., Moser, C., Mostashari, A.: Compliance evaluation featuring heat maps (CE-HM): a meta-modeling-based approach. In: 24th International Conference Proceedings of Advanced Information Systems Engineering, Springer Lecture Notes in Computer Science, CAiSE 25–29 June 2012, Gdansk, Poland (2012)
10. The Open Group: ArchiMate 2.1 Specification Dec. 2013. https://www2.opengroup.org/ogsys/catalog/C13L. Access 25 Feb. 2016
11. BOC Group: ADOit Method Manual http://www.adoit-community.com/wp-content/uploads/ADOit_MethodManual_Digital-VersionCompressed_EN.pdf. Accessed 25 Feb 2016
12. Buneman, P., Davidson, S., Fernandez, M., Suciu, D.: Adding structure to unstructured data. In: 6th International Conference on Database Theory (ICDT '97), LNCS, vol. 1186, pp. 336–350
13. Utz, W., Reimann, R., Karagiannis, D.: Capturing learning activities in heterogeneous environments: a model-based approach for data marshalling. ICALT **2014**, 624–626 (2014)
14. Greer, K.: Concept trees: building dynamic concepts from semi-structured data using nature-inspired methods. In: Zhu, Q., Azar, A.T., (eds.) Complex System Modelling and Control through Intelligent Soft Computations, Studies in Fuzziness and Soft Computing. Springer (2015)

15. Roussopoulos, N., Yeh, R.T.: An adaptable methodology for database design. IEEE Comput. **17**(5), 64–80 (1984)
16. Chapman, P., et al.: CRISP-DM 1.0 Step-by-step data mining guides (2000)
17. Fill, Timothy Redmond, T., Karagiannis, D.:Formalizing Meta Models with FDMM: The ADOxx Case. ICEIS 2012: 429-451
18. On the Conceptualisation of Modelling Methods Using the ADOxx Meta Modelling Platform. Enterprise Modelling and Information Systems Architectures **8**(1): 4–25 (2013)
19. Bachman, C.W.: Data structure diagrams. Data Base **1**(2), 4–10 (1969)
20. Karagiannis, D., Hrgovcic, V., Woitsch, R.: Conceptual modeling of the organisational aspects for distributed applications: the semantic lifting approach. In: 2nd IEEE Workshop on Modeling and Verifying Distributed Applications, 22–26 July 2013, Kyoto, Japan (2013)
21. Meyer, H., Weske, M.: Light-weight semantic service annotations through tagging. In: Dan, A., Lamersorf, W. (eds.) Proceedings of 4th International Conference on Service-Oriented Computing–ISOC 2006, Chicago, USA (2006)
22. W3C Resource Description Framework (RDF): http://www.w3.org/RDF/. Accessed 25 Feb 2016
23. W3C Internet Media Type registration: http://www.w3.org/2001/tag/2002/0129-mime. Accessed 25 Feb 2016
24. Keleher, P.J., Spring, N., Bhattacharjee, B.: Chit-based access control. In: Technical Report CS-TR-4878, University of Maryland at College Park (2007)
25. ADOxx Metamodelling Platform: https://www.adoxx.org. Accessed 25 Feb 2016
26. Apache Axis: https://axis.apache.org/. Accessed 25 Feb 2016
27. B|DNATechnopedia: http://lookup.technopedia.com/browse/. Accessed 25 Feb 2016
28. Drozdek, A.: Data Structures and Algorithms in C++, 2nd edn. Brook/Cole. Pacific Grove, CA (2001)

Big Data—Integration and Cleansing Environment for Business Analytics with DICE

Wilfried Grossmann and Christoph Moser

Abstract The paper presents the **D**ata **I**ntegration and **C**leansing **E**nvironment—DICE. Its embedded modeling method supports the data understanding and data preparation phases for business analytics endeavours and subsequently decision-making in business process activities. A prototypical implementation is presented by using an example in the field of campaign management which uses traditional customer data in combination with (big) data about customer sentiments from microblogging platforms.

Keywords Business analytics · Data integration · Data cleansing · Big data · Statistical metadata

1 Introduction

All business activities of organizations, such as marketing, customer relationship management, and risk management rely on meaningful data. Organizations have implemented management approaches, such as business process design, adaptive case management, and business process analysis to ensure effective management of their business activities. Let us consider these typical examples of management approaches. In their work, Laursen and Thorlund [1] explore business processes from different angles, namely from a producer perspective, from a customer perspective and from an organizational point of view. From the producers' point of view, business process modeling (BPM) is an essential activity. Successful process modeling builds upon reliable information about the business environment, which is today often readily available on the Internet, as well as upon knowledge about the resources available, which can be used during the execution of the business process.

W. Grossmann (✉) · C. Moser
Faculty of Computer Science, University of Vienna, 1090 Vienna, Austria
e-mail: wilfried.grossmann@univie.ac.at

C. Moser
e-mail: christoph.moser@univie.ac.at

D. Karagiannis et al. (eds.), *Domain-Specific Conceptual Modeling*,
DOI 10.1007/978-3-319-39417-6_5

Typically, a business process model contains a number of decision points for the determination of upcoming activities and appropriate process variants. Past behavior of process instances is often valuable information for supporting future decision-making. Using this kind of data is known as "decision point analysis", which combines the concepts of business process modeling and data mining methods (cf. for example [2]).

A management approach which goes one step further in this direction is adaptive case management (ACM), which can be understood as a data centred approach for managing individual business cases described by events and outcomes. This approach is of particular interest in the case of modeling administrative processes where the path of execution cannot be predefined. It relaxes the assumption that the individual process tasks are known in advance, but human judgement utilizing the information available about the application domain is required, in order to determine the upcoming process tasks to be performed. For a short introduction, we refer to the work of Hinkelmann and Pierfranceschi [3].

A third example to consider is business process analysis regarding the performance of an instance of a business process. Such an analysis can be done from different perspectives. From the producer perspective, this type of analysis is based on data collected during the run-time of the processes and ideally the performance is summarized by key performance indicators (KPIs). If one takes a customer perspective the analysis of business performance is usually done under the heading of customer relationship management based on data about customer characteristics and the interactions of the customers with the business process. In this case, data is usually taken from different sources like databases for customer characteristics, transactional databases, or data sources capturing the opinion of the customers.

These examples of management approaches show that there is a need to combine BPM ideas with knowledge discovery from databases (KDD) ideas. As shown in Fig. 1, rather independently from the application domain, for example, Crime prevention, Marketing/CRM, or Fraud detection, the data analyst uses a KDD approach for preparing the necessary data for the decision-maker in his management approaches. A first and important step in KDD is the integration of different data sources in such a way so as to ensure that the required information extracted is of high data quality.

DICE offers a method for data integration and cleansing which supports the decision-maker and data analysts in their modeling activities. Starting from internal and external data sources for a certain application domain, a data integration and cleansing process model is formulated which fits into the modeling framework developed by Karagiannis and Kühn [4]. The basic ideas of the DICE method are based on the Cross Industry Standard Process for Data Mining (commonly known by its acronym CRISP-DM) [5] which is the leading data mining framework [6] combined with a conceptual model for metadata which facilitates the assessment of data quality. This method is described in Sect. 2. Section 3 presents the conceptualization of the model and Sect. 4 gives a proof-of-concept using an example from the field of marketing.

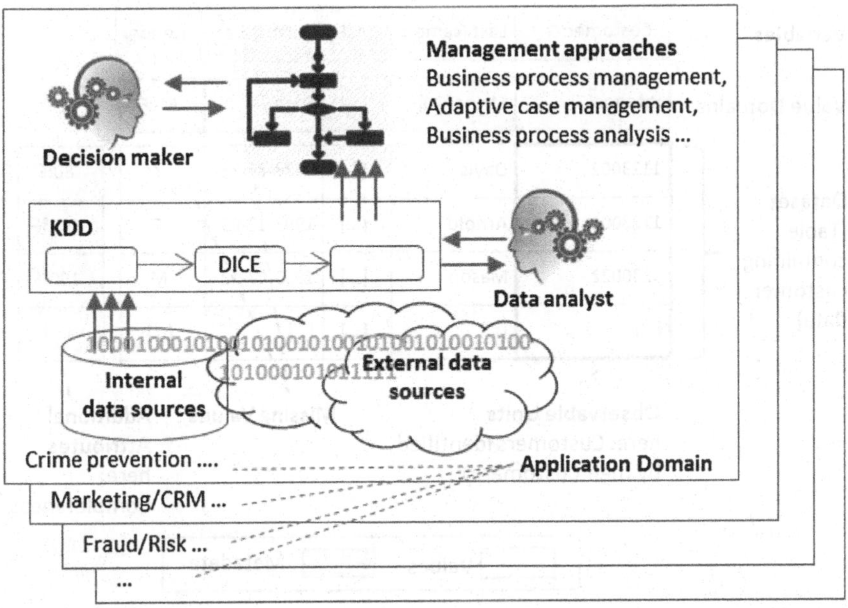

Fig. 1 Positioning of DICE

2 Method Description

Using data in business activities requires a proper understanding of the data involved and proper data quality assessment. This implies that not only a conceptual model for data representation is required, but also an explicit model for the description of the data. Such data descriptions are known as metadata models. In DICE, a metadata model inspired from statistical metadata modeling as described in [7] is used. The starting point of this model is the idea to consider the datasets as essential parts of a composite analysis object

$$O_A = [(\Omega_A, U_A), (V_A, R_A), D_A].$$

Here, U_A represents the observational units for which empirical information is available, Ω_A represents the population to which the observational units belong. In the case of BPM, such units may be enterprises, customers or products and services. The information is represented by attributes V_A which are measured by an appropriate value domain R_A. The dataset itself is denoted by D_A and usually only contains information for a subset of the entire population. The standard representation of such datasets is a table with information for the individual values and describes the characteristics of the entire population. Figure 2 gives an example of such a composite analysis object. It depicts a subset of collected customer data (dataset) and its metadata such as the variables, and their value domains. The

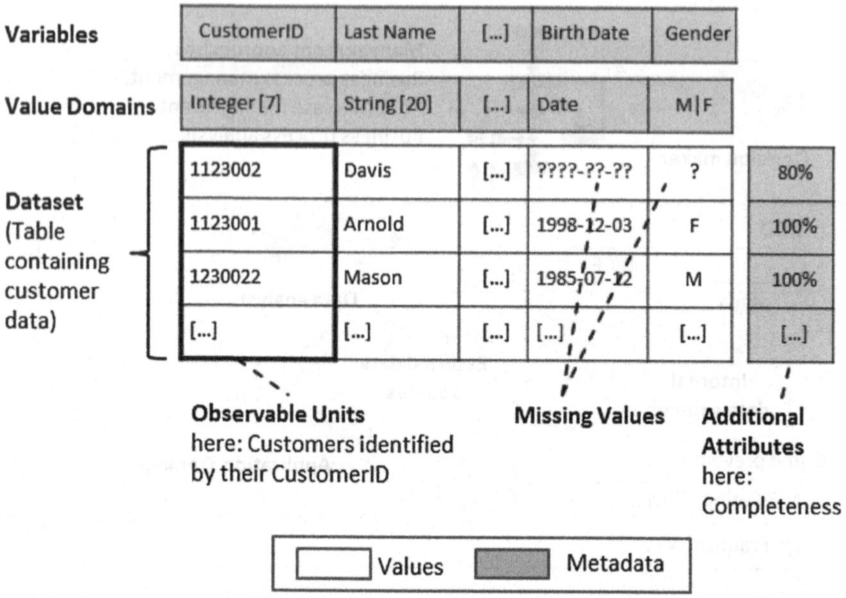
Variables
CustomerID
Last Name
[...]
Birth Date
Gender
Value Domains
Integer [7]
String [20]
[...]
Date
M|F
Dataset (Table containing customer data)
1123002
Davis
[...]
????-??-??
?
80%
1123001
Arnold
[...]
1998-12-03
F
100%
1230022
Mason
[...]
1985-07-12
M
100%
[...]
Observable Units here: Customers identified by their CustomerID
Missing Values
Additional Attributes here: Completeness
Values
Metadata

Fig. 2 Example of a composite analysis object: customer data of an organization

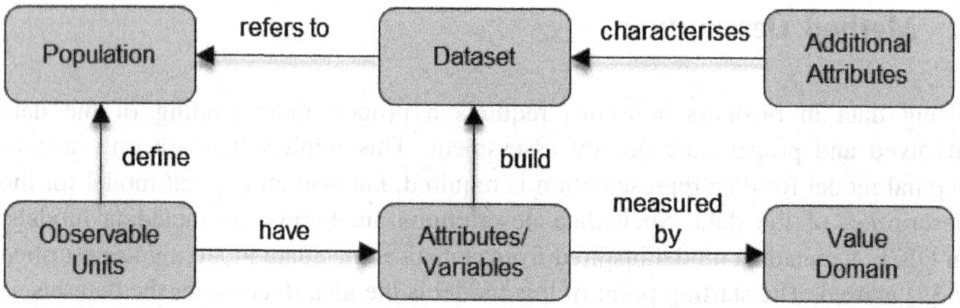

Fig. 3 Schematic representation of a metadata object

customer ID represents the unique identifier for the observable units, which are the customers in this example. The population is the set of all customers of the organization. In order to perform the analysis, the data analyst might face the need to adapt the given dataset. An example is to apply data imputation mechanisms to fill in missing values or to combine the existing data with data derived from other sources (e.g., data from social media). These transformations will obviously have an impact on the dataset, but also on its metadata.

For a proper understanding of the data and the impact of data transformation, we need an associated composite metadata object schematically represented in Fig. 3.

$$O_M = [(\Omega_M, U_M), (V_M, R_M), D_M, I_M].$$

The metadata object (Ω_M, U_M) contains the subject matter definition of the observation units and the specification of the population boundaries, for example, validity period and spatial validity. Furthermore, it is often of interest to use similar populations and observable units to describe this object information metadata; for example, a population of enterprises usually has a connection to establishments. The metadata object (V_M, R_M) informs about definitions of the variables and the admissible value domains. Also, in this case, it is of utmost importance to have reference to related variables. For the dataset D_A, the metadata in D_M have to inform about the type of the dataset, the variables used in the dataset, the part of the population which is represented, and the method used to collect the data. An additional metadata object I_A is necessary for keeping summary descriptions of the data, for example, information well-known as data profiling, administrative information like ways for assessing the data, or information about authorization and security of the data.

Based on the metadata description, one can give an assessment of the quality of the data by extracting the meta-information for different quality dimensions. There are many different proposals for the definition of data quality and numerous dimensions have been defined. For example, the German institute of data quality has identified 15 main dimensions for data quality [8]. Usage of these dimensions and the efforts for measuring different quality criteria obviously depends on the application domain. Let us only mention briefly how the different metadata objects can contribute to some of the most important dimensions relevance, completeness, accuracy and consistency in the context of business modeling activities.

- For accessing the relevance of the information we have to look mainly at the definition of the population (are the observable units the appropriate ones for the application?), and the definition of the variables (are the variables defined and measured in an appropriate way?).
- For accuracy, the most important information is contained in the description of the measurement process.
- If one is interested in the completeness of the information, valuable information can be found in the description of the production of the data set and stated in the metadata object D_M and in the object for additional attributes I_M which contain summaries for missing values.
- For consistency considerations, one has to look at the used value domains R_M.

A quality dimension can refer to different levels of a dataset. It may be a quality indicator for single values of a variable, a quality measure for a certain attribute, or a quality statement for the entire dataset. For a unified representation of the different quality dimensions, one can use a scheme as shown in Fig. 4.

The representation described above of the data objects and the associated metadata objects is the main structure for the DICE method, which supports the manipulation of the data objects in connection with all business modeling activities.

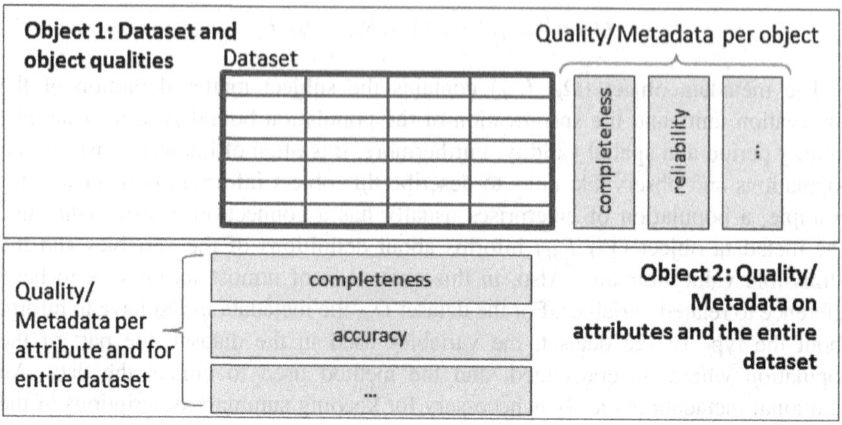

Fig. 4 Augmentation of a dataset object for quality dimensions

Typical manipulations for the datasets are the generation of new attributes, the calculation of various summary measures like sums or means, improvement of the quality of sum attributes by data editing, or integration of a number of datasets into one dataset. Formally, we can represent these manipulations as transformations of the number of input objects $O_A^{(i)}$, $1 \leq i \leq k$ into a number of output objects $O_A^{(o)}$, $1 \leq o \leq p$:

$$T_A\colon\ [(\Omega_A^{(i)}, U_A^{(i)}), (V_A^{(i)}, R_A^{(i)}), D_A^{(i)}] \mapsto [(\Omega_A^{(o)}, U_A^{(o)}), (V_A^{(o)}, R_A^{(o)}), D_A^{(o)}].$$

Different components of the objects may be involved in a transformation. An example involving only one input object and one output object is the calculation of a summary measure. In this case, a new data object with new attributes is generated, which refers to the population of the input object and the variables for which the summary measures were computed.

An example of a transformation involving two input objects is data integration. The input objects are defined by the two data sets which are integrated. The structure of the output object depends on the type of integration: in the case of adding variables by integration, the population and the units remain unchanged but the structure of the variables and the dataset has to be defined as the union of the two input components; in the case of adding new observations by integration, the variables and the structure of the dataset remain unchanged but the population has to be defined as the union of the two populations.

The transformations engage the metadata by describing the analysis objects in different ways. The easy case is that the metadata of the output object are obtained by simple augmentation of the metadata of the input object. An example of that type is a transformation which creates a new variable. Another possible scenario is that some metadata of the input object become data in the output object. This occurs frequently in the case of computation of summary measures where metadata like the size of the data set carried in the additional information will be part of the resulting data object.

More frequently the transformation depends on the existing metadata. A typical example is data editing. Here the edit rules are metadata describing constraints for the admissible values of an attribute and the decision about editing is done according to these rules. The more complex case of interference is that computation at the metadata level is necessary for the computation at the data level. An example of such a computation can occur in data integration if the different datasets show contradictory information and the decision about the most plausible values depends on the analysis of the metadata.

These examples show that we cannot separate data processing from metadata processing in the analysis. Hence, DICE uses a model for data transformations which process the data and the metadata objects simultaneously. Formally, the metadata operations can be denoted as transformations

$$T_M\colon [(\Omega_M^{(i)}, U_M^{(i)}), (V_M^{(i)}, R_M^{(i)}), D_M^{(i)}, I_M^{(i)}]$$
$$\mapsto [(\Omega_M^{(o)}, U_M^{(o)}), (V_M^{(o)}, R_M^{(o)}), D_M^{(o)}, I_M^{(o)}].$$

Figure 5 shows a visualization of this idea for the case of a sequence of three transformations for one data object. The composite data object O1 is first transformed by the transformation task T1 into the data object O2 and afterwards in the data object O3. The corresponding transformations for the metadata objects are shown above the data transformations using the iconic representation of Fig. 3. Note that this approach has the advantage that we can immediately access the data quality of the final object from the metadata description.

The DICE method can be used in various ways. One way is to embed it in a data mining (DM) and knowledge discovery (KD) process, acting as the guardrails of the method. An overview of the DMKD reference models and frameworks is given in [9]. The Cross Industry Standard Process for Data Mining (commonly known by its acronym CRISP-DM) [5] is the leading data mining framework [6]. It focuses on the tasks, inputs and outputs of a data mining endeavour. It comprises the business understanding, data understanding, data preparation, modeling, and model evaluation of the phase. Each of these phases is detailed in generic tasks and corresponding outputs. DICE must be positioned in the data understanding and data preparation phase. Its ultimate goal is to construct final datasets from given raw

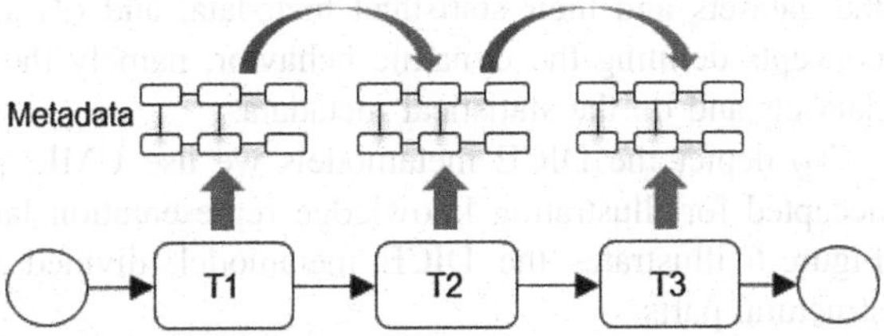

Fig. 5 Simultaneous transformations for data and metadata objects

data. These datasets serve as input for the subsequent modeling phase, which actually extracts knowledge from data based on data mining approaches.

Modeling a DICE workflow—a sequential order of the required data transformation tasks—must be understood as analytical and creative work. The DICE workflow represents the third level propagated in CRISP-DM, namely the specialized task level. As early as the first transformation task of the workflow is specified, the workflow can be executed. Simultaneously to the processing of the input datasets, a set of profiling data—metadata including quality indicators—is generated. Based on these quality indicators (see e.g., [10]), the workflow designer scrutinizes a contacted task, sequences of tasks, or the entire workflow to find the optimum DICE workflow design. Thus, during workflow design, it will often be necessary to repeatedly backtrack to points in the process, and to change the workflow design until a sufficient result is achieved [5].

3 Method Conceptualization

This section below presents the DICE metamodel, including its comprised modeling and relation classes, as well as its dynamic capabilities. The concepts are grounded in the notion of a modeling method, which has been initially presented in [4]. Following this framework, the DICE modeling method is composed of three main building blocks: (1) a modeling language, comprising syntax, semantics, and notation, (2) a modeling procedure, defining the modeling approach for creating and using the models, and (3) mechanisms and algorithms, representing the model-processing functionality. This paper focuses on the modeling language as well as the mechanisms and algorithms building on the modeling language. Both building blocks are discussed in detail in the following sections. The building block 'modeling procedure' has been sketched in the previous section and due to limitations in space is not detailed in the subsequent chapters.

3.1 The DICE Modeling Language

Inspired by UML [11], the concepts of the DICE modeling language, namely the disposable modeling classes and the relation classes that connect them, are grouped into two categories: (1) a structural part, namely the concepts required to describe the datasets and their statistical metadata, and (2) a behavioral part, comprising concepts defining the dynamic behavior, namely the workflows operating on the datasets and on the statistical metadata.

To depict the DICE metamodels we use UML, a modeling language widely accepted for illustrating knowledge representation languages (see, e.g., [12–14]). Figure 6 illustrates the DICE metamodel, divided into the behavioral and the structural parts.

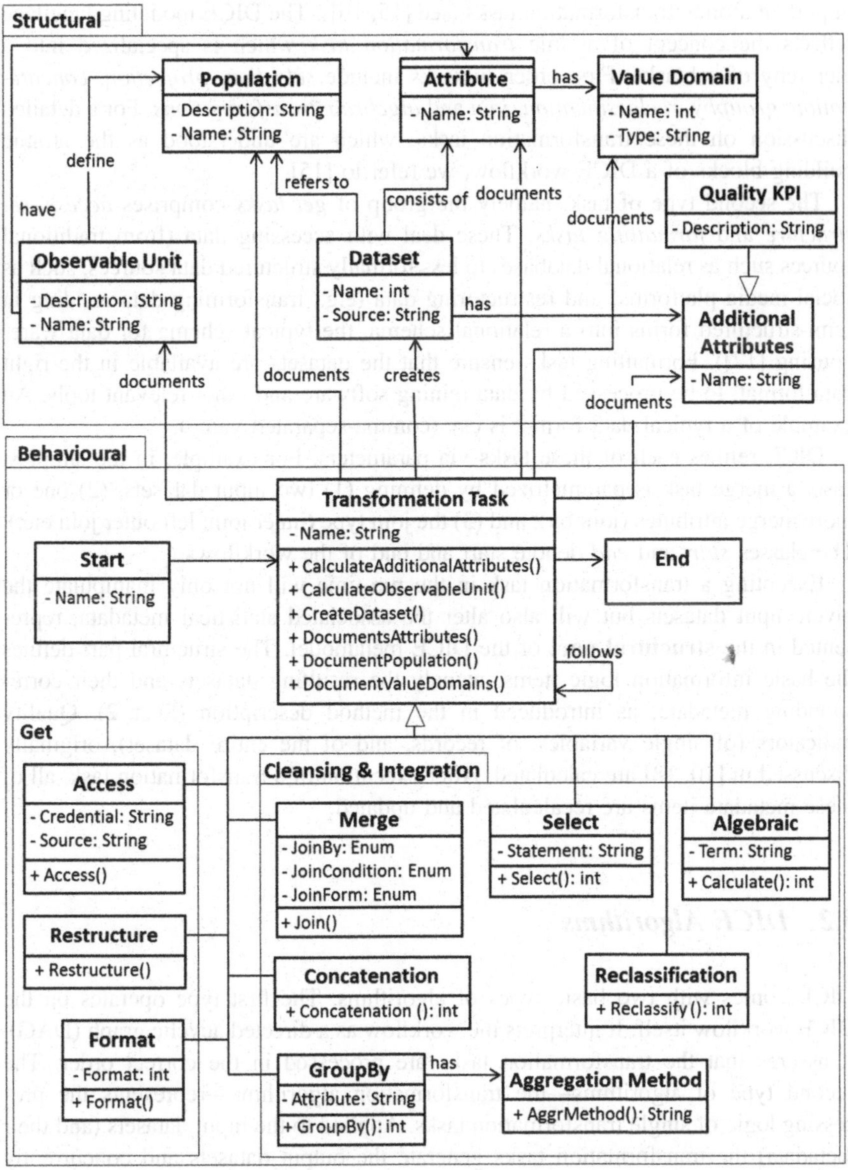

Fig. 6 The conceptual metamodels of DICE

The **behavioral part** defines the processing information of the output datasets. It ensures the traceability of the conducted transformations by recording the processing history of the datasets. It provides the means to define the required transformations while their impact on the datasets and their metadata becomes transparent. In their work, Papageorgiou et al. identify the set of the seven most important atomic transformation tasks (see [15, 16]). The DICE modeling language reflects the concept of atomic *transformation task* which is specialized into a hierarchy of subtasks. First order subtasks include *selection, projection, concatenation, groupby, reclassification, join* and *algebraic transformations*. For a detailed discussion on these transformation tasks, which are understood as the atomic building blocks of a DICE workflow, we refer to [15].

The second type of task, namely the group of *get tasks* comprises *access, restructure* and *formatting tasks*. These deal with accessing data (from traditional sources such as relational databases to less formally structured data sources, such as social media platforms) and restructuring data (e.g., transforming data residing in semi-structured forms into a relational schema, the typical schema for data warehousing [17]). Formatting tasks ensure that the datasets are available in the right data format, to be processed by data mining software and other relevant tools. An example of a typical data format is csv (comma-separated value).

DICE refines each of these tasks via parameters. For example, in the simplest case, a merge task is parametrized by defining (1) two input datasets, (2) one or more merge attributes (join by), and (3) the join type (inner join, left outer join etc.). The classes *start* and *end* denote start and end of the workflows.

Executing a transformation task in the run-time will not only manipulate the given input datasets but will also alter the associated statistical metadata, represented in the **structural part** of the DICE metamodel. The structural part defines the basic information logic items, namely the resulting datasets and their corresponding metadata, as introduced in the method description (Sect. 2). Quality indicators (of single variables, of records, and of the entire dataset), originally discussed in [10, 18] are calculated. After execution of a transformation task, all of these metadata items are recalculated and updated.

3.2 DICE Algorithms

DICE comes with two basic types of algorithms. The first type operates on the DICE workflow itself. It interprets the workflow as a directed acyclic graph (DAG). It assures that the transformation tasks are processed in the correct order. The second type of algorithms—the transformation algorithms—represents the processing logic of single transformation tasks. Applied to the input datasets (and their metadata) the transformation tasks generate the output datasets and concurrently deliver metadata alterations based on the transformation algorithms.

To execute the DICE workflow, an algorithm for topological sorting [19], which operates on the DAG, is applied. Each transformation task is interpreted as vertex and the relation "follows" (connecting the transformation tasks) represents the directed edges. The modeling classes "start" and "end" indicate the start and end nodes of the workflow. They facilitate the readability of the graph but are irrelevant for execution. There exist algorithms for topological sorting. An overview can be

```
L ← List that will contain the sorted transf. tasks
S ← Set of all transf. tasks with no predeceasing tasks
while S is non-empty do
    remove a task n from S
    add n to tail of L
    for each task m with a relation e from n to m do
        remove task e from the graph
        if m has no other incoming relations from
        predecessing tasks then
            insert m into S
if graph has tasks then
    return error (the workflow has at least one cycle)
else
    return L (tasks in topologically sorted order)
```

Fig. 7 Topological sort performed on the DICE workflow

found in [20]. Figure 7 exemplarily illustrates a topological sort algorithm prescribed by Kahn, who documented it as early as in the 1960s [21]:

By applying the topological sort algorithm to a DICE workflow, the required transformation tasks are performed in their logical order. The relation "follows" constitutes the constraint that one transformation task must be performed before another.

Processing a single transformation task is done by applying the second type of algorithms—the transformation algorithms. A transformation task delivers the tuple of an output dataset and its corresponding metadata.

Consider a transformation task of type "merge" as an example. There exist numerous merge algorithms. For example, overviews can be found in [22, 23]. In essence, the advantages and disadvantages to be balanced when choosing an appropriate merge algorithm are performance and proffered join conditions. Figure 8 exemplarily depicts the popular Nested Loop Join, which can handle any kind of join predicates, as compared to other more specialized join algorithms like the sort-merge join and the hash join [24]. Disadvantages are seen in its low performance when executing large size datasets.

On the level of metadata, the transformation tasks are controlled by quality criteria such as completeness ratio and accuracy thresholds. DICE extends the transformation algorithms to calculate these metadata.

Let us consider the calculation of a more elaborate quality criterion for merge transformations: approximate string matching for record linkage. Such methods are used if rows from two records that are believed to relate to the same entity (observation) are merged [25]. There exist a number of record linkage algorithms. For

Fig. 8 Merge algorithm on data level

```
for each ObservableUnit r in R do
    for each ObservableUnit s in S do
        if r and s satisfy the join condition
            then output the ObservableUnit <r,s>
```

Fig. 9 Merge algorithm incl. metadata calculation

```
for each ObservableUnit r in R do
   for each ObservableUnit s in S do
      if r and s satisfy the join condition
        then
          calculate edit distance <r,s>
          output the ObservableUnit <r,s>
for each attribute a in MergedDataset do
    calculate completeness <a>
```

an overview, see [26]. All these methods are based on the calculation of a so-called *edit distance* which defines a similarity measure for strings.

Figure 9 exemplarily extends the presented join algorithm by means to calculate the quality indicator "data completeness" per attribute, and the edit distance per observable unit.

4 Proof of Concept

The hereby presented modeling method was evaluated with respect to feasibility by a prototypical implementation based on a metamodeling platform and a data mining suite. This section describes its architecture. Subsequently, a practical case study is presented, to demonstrate the capabilities of DICE based on the proof-of-concept implementation.

4.1 The Architecture of the DICE Prototype

The DICE 1.0 prototype (which can be downloaded from www.omilab.org) has a three-layer architecture. The top-most level of DICE is the *modeling environment*. The main functions of the modeling environment are, (1) to provide graphical means to design the DICE workflows, (2) to trigger and control the execution of the DICE workflows, and (3) to record and visualize the generated metadata. Prior to the implementation, the DICE modeling language and the algorithms were formalized, based on the approach discussed in [27]. The syntax of the modeling language and its graphical notation were derived from the conceptual metamodels discussed above. Due to limitations of space, the formalized (platform-specific) metamodel is not discussed here.

From this specification, a visual model editor enriched with the required mechanisms and algorithms was implemented on ADO*xx*, a metamodeling platform provided by the Open Models Laboratory (www.omilab.org). The "DICE workflow" model type is central to the implemented modeling method. It contains all relevant modeling classes, relation classes, and attributes to (1) design the DICE

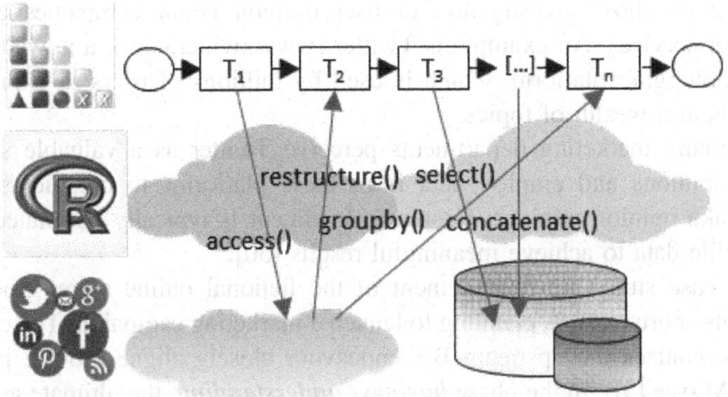

Fig. 10 The DICE architecture

workflow, (2) to specify the required data transformations, and (3) to visualize the generated metadata. A code generator was implemented by using the ADO*xx* macro-language AdoScript and the concept of ADO*xx* expressions (comparable to the concept of formulas in spreadsheet software). During run-time, it delivers the (platform-specific) code to be executed on the second tier, namely the BI-tier.

The modeling environment communicates via a web service API with the BI-tier which is based on R, a programming language and environment for statistical computing and graphical display (see https://www.r-project.org/). R receives the executable code (automatically created through interpretation of the DICE workflow models) and performs the required transformations/calculations. Basically, two object types are created by execution of a single transformation task: a first, namely the output dataset, and a second, holding the corresponding metadata. Whereas the metadata and supporting graphical charts are stored in the modeling environment (returned via API from R), the output datasets are stored on the third layer, the data-tier. The data-tier of DICE encapsulates the data persistence mechanisms (database servers, file shares etc.). Via its access functions, the DICE prototype is capable of accessing data from social media platforms (e.g., from twitter, see www.twitter.com), from cloud storages like Google drive (https://www.google.com/intl/de/drive/), or from local shares. Figure 10 illustrates the three-tier architecture of DICE.

4.2 Case Study

"Successful marketing requires building a data advantage by pulling in relevant data sets from both within and outside the company." [28] Web 2.0 platforms such as blogs, discussion forums, and peer-to-peer networks nowadays motivate consumers to share their brand experiences and opinions on products and service [29].

These sources allow investigation of user opinion about companies and their products or services. An example is Twitter (www.twitter.com), a nowadays popular microblogging platform, which is used by millions of users to express their opinion about a wealth of topics.

Thus, many marketing departments perceive Twitter as a valuable source of people's opinions and employ data from these platforms to conduct sentiment analysis (aka opinion mining). Customer sentiment is typically correlated to customer profile data to achieve meaningful results [30].

In our case study the management of the fictional online store "SportsCX", which deals sportswear, is planning to launch a marketing campaign. The campaign manager organizes the upstream BA endeavour closely aligned to the phases of CRISP-DM (see [5]). In the phase ***business understanding,*** the ultimate goal of the endeavour is determined. That goal is to support decision-making on the target groups of the planned campaign. In this regard two types of data are of interest:

- Data from inside the company (customer profile data): Which are our clients' favored brands?
- Data from outside the company (customer sentiment data): Which potential customers (suspects) expressed interest in our products on social networks?

In the second phase ***data understanding***, the available data is collected and reviewed. Customer data, transaction data and article data are extracted from the IT systems of the organization. Furthermore, Twitter accounts are set up in order to access social media information (in the case of Twitter, the so-called tweets). Figure 11 depicts the structure of the exemplary input datasets.

After reviewing the data, the high quality of the internal data is attested. Although organized in different files, all datasets share global unique IDs. Of course, this is not the case with the external data retrieved from Twitter. Integrating these records is a challenging task, as there are no means to clearly identify the persons. There is no direct match of attributes. Even worse, Twitter followers might not use their full name, so a direct match of name attributes will not work either.

In the phase ***data preparation***, the relevant data is selected and cleaned where required. In the case of missing records or attributes, the missing data is created (e.g., via data imputation mechanisms, see [31]). Finally, the data is integrated as needed. All these steps are planned and designed by modeling a DICE workflow. Figure 12 depicts an exemplary DICE workflow, modelled on the DICE prototype.

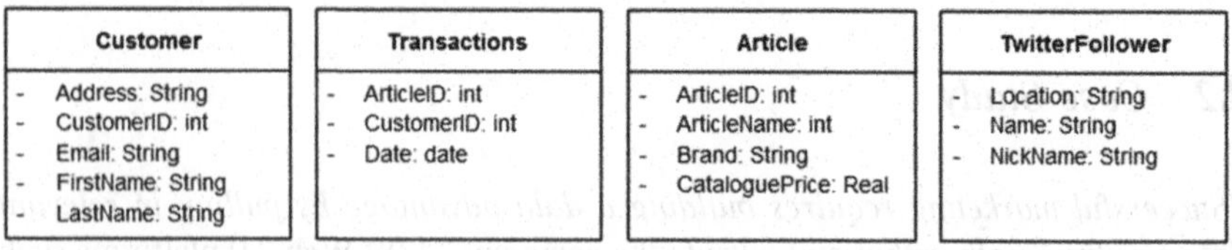

Fig. 11 Structure of input datasets

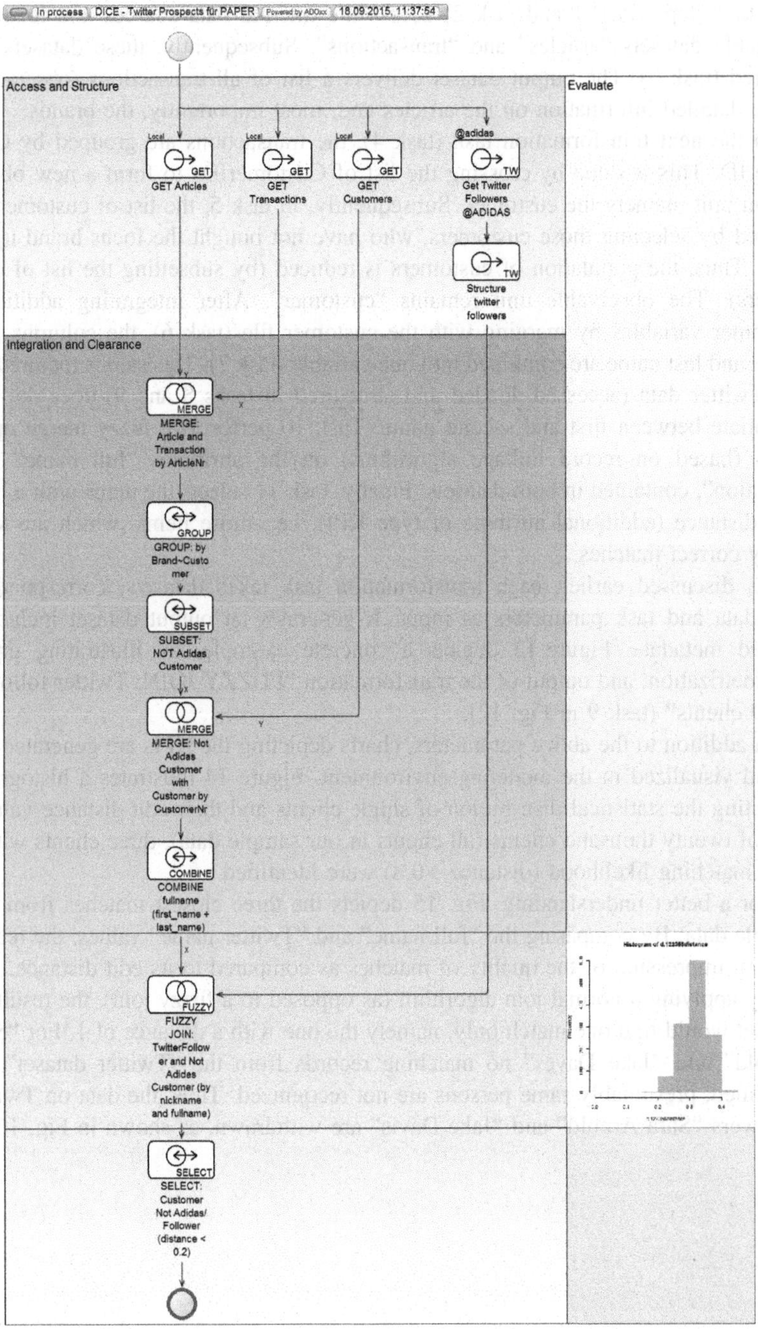

Fig. 12 Example of a DICE process

The first steps (task 1 and task 2) access the internal data sources and load the available datasets "articles" and "transactions". Subsequently, these datasets are merged (task 3). The output dataset delivers a list of all transactions (observable unit), detailed information on the articles and, most importantly, the brands.

In the next transformation task (task 4), the transactions are grouped by CustomerID. This is done by crossing the list of CustomerIDs to form a new observation unit, namely the customer. Subsequently, in task 5, the list of customers is filtered by selecting those customers, who have not bought the focus-brand up to now. Thus, the population of customers is reduced (by subsetting the list of customers). The observable unit remains "customer". After integrating additional customer variables by merging with the customer file (task 6), the columns first name and last name are combined into one variable (task 7). This step is required, as the Twitter data (accessed, loaded and structured in tasks 8 and 9) does not differentiate between first and second name. Task 10 performs a fuzzy merge operation (based on record linkage algorithms) on the attributes "full name" and "location", contained in both datasets. Finally, task 11 selects the items with a high edit distance (additional attribute of type KPI), i.e., those items, which are very likely correct matches.

As discussed earlier, each transformation task takes datasets, corresponding metadata and task parameters as input. It generates an output dataset including altered metadata. Figure 13 depicts a concrete example, by illustrating input, parametrization, and output of the transformation "FUZZY JOIN: Twitter follower AND clients" (task 9 in Fig. 12).

In addition to the above parameters, charts depicting the KPIs are generated via R and visualized in the modeling environment. Figure 14 illustrates a histogram, depicting the statistical distribution of single clients and their edit distance values. Out of twenty thousand clients (all clients in our sample data), three clients with a high matching likelihood (distance >0.8) were identified.

For a better understanding, Fig. 15 depicts the three closest matches from our sample data. By comparing the "full name" and "Twitter name" values, the reader gets an impression of the quality of matches as compared to its edit distance.

By applying a normal join algorithm (as opposed to a fuzzy join), the resulting dataset would find one match only, namely the one with a distance of 1. For "Sara Arnold" and "Jake Daves" no matching records from the "Twitter dataset" are identified, presumably same persons are not recognized. Thus, the data on Twitter followers "Sara Arnold" and "Jake Davis" are withdrawn, as shown in Fig. 16.

Name:
FUZZY JOIN: Twitter follower AND clients

Input datasets:
The fuzzy join requires two input datasets. These are delivered from its direct predecessor tasks. The first table contains the client data (left table), the second table (right table) contains the list of Twitter followers of the chosen brand.

Initial population:
All customers which placed an order in the given time period (right table).

Initial observable unit:
Customer

Parameter - Join type:
The ANSI-standard SQL specifies five types of join: inner, left outer, right outer, full outer and cross [32].
The join type "left outer join" is applied to this task. It selects all rows from the first table (left table), regardless whether there is a matching row in the second (right) table. Non-matching rows of the second table are withdrawn.

Parameter - Join condition:
This argument denotes all those attributes that are mapped through the join operation. For the task at hand, the "full name" and "location" attributes are chosen.

Parameter - Join form:
DICE considers two join forms: regular (equi joins and non-equi joins) and fuzzy joins. In the example, a fuzzy join is applied, as it is unlikely to identify many 100% matches.

There is a vast number of fuzzy join algorithms. Examples available in the DICE prototype are Hamming, Levenshtein, Jaro, and Jaro-Winkler. The set of algorithms is supplied by the R package "stringdist", see [33]. In our example, we use the Jaro-Winkler-Distance.

Generated code (platform-specific):
The DICE modelling environment automatically generates the following R code from the specified input parameters:

```
# conduct merge via record linkage and calculate edit
distance
library(stringdist)
d.12235 <- fuzzy_join(d.12322, d.12166, fuzzy =
c("fullname", "nickname"))
# calculate completeness
d.12235_columns$complete <- colSums(!is.na(d.12235))
d.12235_columns$CompletePercentage <-
(colSums(!is.na(d.12235))/nrow(d.12235)*100)
```

d.12322, d.12166 and d.12235 are the IDs of the processed datasets. These are generated and assigned automatically via the implemented algorithms.

Resulting dataset:
The output dataset contains all attributes of both input datasets. Besides customer profile data like first name, last name and address, it now contains the twitter-related data.

Resulting population:
All clients who placed an order within the given time period. Non-matching Twitter followers (right table) are withdrawn, and thus, the population remains unchanged.

Additional attribute - distance:
For each observation, the KPI "edit distance" is automatically calculated. The chosen record linkage algorithm was the Jaro-Winkler-Distance. The measurement scale is 0.0 to 1.0, where 0.0 is the least likely and 1.0 is a positive match.

Additional attribute - completeness:
For each attribute of the output dataset, the completeness is recalculated. As we are mainly interested in the matchable entities, and the merging did not alter the attributes of internal client data (left table), the resulting KPI is irrelevant in this case.

Fig. 13 Example: fuzzy join

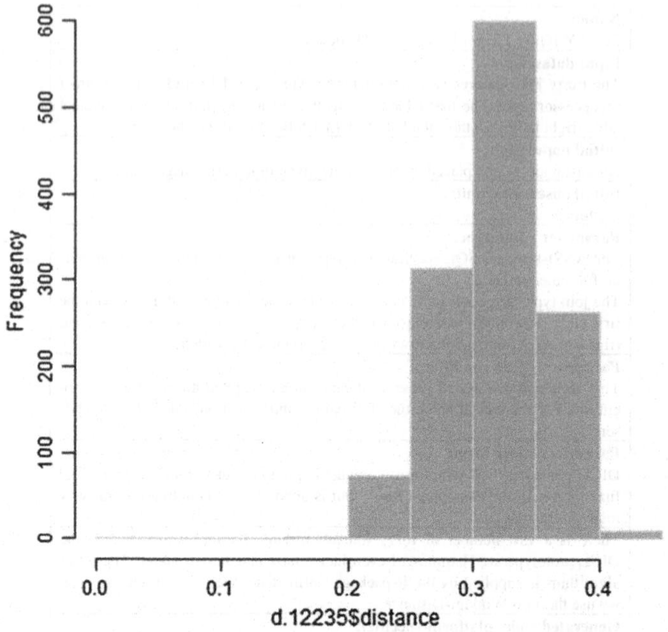

Fig. 14 Histogram on additional attribute "Edit distance"

Distance (rounded)	**Full name (company data)**	**Follower name (twitter)**	**[...]**
1	Jose Mason	Jose Mason	[...]
0,98	Sara Arnold	Sara Arnold	[...]
0,96	Jake Daves	Jake Davis	[...]

Fig. 15 Example: resulting dataset after fuzzy join

Distance (rounded)	**Full name (company data)**	**Follower name (twitter)**	**[...]**
1	Jose Mason	Jose Mason	[...]
--	Sara Arnold	<NULL>	[...]
--	Jake Daves	<NULL>	[...]

Fig. 16 Example: resulting dataset after applying a "normal" join

5 Conclusions and Outlook

The DICE modeling method for data integration and data cleansing was successfully implemented on the metamodeling platform ADO*xx* and the data mining platform R. The presented proof-of-concept implementation shows the key capabilities of DICE, namely a means to simultaneous manipulation of data and metadata. The paper discusses the methods underlying modeling language, and the algorithms required to process the models. The DICE modeling procedure is sketched and embedded in CRISP, one of the most prominent KDD frameworks. Leveraging a concrete showcase in the fields of customer sentiment and big data, the features of DICE are discussed in detail. The following SWOT evaluation points out strengths, weaknesses, opportunities and threats of the DICE method.

According to Starbuck [34], SWOT analyses are nowadays not solely used for strategic planning purposes (e.g., to decide which direction will be the most effective) but are also an effective approach for post hoc rationalization and evaluation. We present below the outcome of the conducted SWOT evaluation performed in order to reveal the possibilities and limitations of the DICE method.

Strengths: DICE allows manipulation of data and metadata at the same time. The prototypical implementation proves that metadata can be automatically generated to a wide extent, relieving data analysts from the burden of traceable documentation of the performed transformations. Moreover, the user can define the required transformation tasks and the entire workflow without any programming skills.

Weaknesses: Up until now the focus of the DICE implementation has been on implementing atomic transformation tasks. The wide range of specialized techniques used to gather, provide access to and analyze data has not been subject to our studies. Not all typical statistical metadata (as e.g., defined by Papageorgiou et al. [15]) are calculated at the moment. The set of metadata in DICE is not complete but can be extended according to user needs. Furthermore, the access transformation tasks need to be extended to react to recent challenges, to integrate data from arbitrary sources, to reshape the oftentimes semi-structured data, and to automatically generate the related metadata.

Opportunities: Business Analytics is a fast-growing management domain and also, besides cloud computing, mobile and security, an often-quoted megatrend. BIaaS (Business Intelligence as a Service), offering business analytics services to BI and non-BI specialists, as claimed for example in [35], will gain more and more importance. Treating each transformation task or sequences of transformation tasks as micro-services, complex KDD processes could be defined and orchestrated, even by non-BI experts. A possible solution could build on the concepts discussed in [36], by building on the synergies of PaaS (Platform as a Service) and metamodeling platforms. By widening the focus on all phases of the KDD process, the DICE can be extended, to cover the entire KDD process.

Threats: A wide range of transformation task templates will be required to support all kinds of BA problems. This might make the orchestration of DICE workflows a complex venture, with negative influence on the goal to provide a BA platform for the wide spectrum of non-BA experts.

Tool Download http://www.omilab.org/dice.

References

1. Laursen, G., Thorlund, J.: Business Analytics For Managers: Taking Business Intelligence Beyond Reporting, vol. 40. Wiley (2010)
2. Dunkl, R., Rinderle-Ma, S., Grossmann, W., Fröschl, K.A.: A method for analyzing time series data in process mining: application and extension of decision point analysis. In: Information Systems Engineering in Complex Environments, pp. 68–84. Springer (2014)
3. Hinkelmann, K., Pierfranceschi, A.: Combining process modelling and case modeling. In: 8th International Conference Methodologies Technologies Tools Enabling E-Government MeTTeG14 (2014)
4. Karagiannis, D., Kühn, H.: Metamodelling platforms, presented at the EC-Web, vol. 2455, p. 182 (2002)
5. Chapman, P., Clinton, J., Kerber, R., Khabaza, T., Reinartz, T., Shearer, C., Wirth, R.: CRISP-DM 1.0, CRISP-DM Consort (2000)
6. Piatetsky-Shapiro, G.: KDnuggets Methodology Poll (2014)
7. Grossmann, W.: Metadata, Wiley StatsRef Stat. Ref. Online (2015)
8. DGIQ: Deutsche Gesellschaft für Informations- und Datenqualität—Graphische Übersicht der 15 IQ-Dimensionen (2007)
9. Marbán, Ó., Mariscal, G., Segovia, J.: A data mining & knowledge discovery process model. Data Min. Knowl. Discov. Real Life Appl. Tech **2009**, 8 (2009)
10. Fröschl, K.A., Grossmann, W.: Deciding Statistical Data Quality. New Tech. Technol. Stat. Technol. Know- Pre-Proc, no. 1 (2001)
11. Rumbaugh, J., Jacobson, I., Booch, G.: Unified Modeling Language Reference Manual, The. Pearson Higher Education (2004)
12. Brockmans, S., Haase, P., Studer, R.: A MOF-based Metamodel and UML Syntax for Networked Ontologies. In: Presented at the International Semantic Web Conference Georgia, US (2006)
13. Buckl, S., Ernst, A.M., Lankes, J., Schneider, K., Schweda, C.M.: A pattern based approach for constructing enterprise architecture management information models. Wirtsch. Proc. **2007**, 65 (2007)
14. Fischer, R., Winter, R.: Ein hierarchischer, architekturbasierter Ansatz zur Unterstützung des IT/Business Alignment. Wirtsch. Proc. **2007**, 66 (2007)
15. Papageorgiou, H., Pentaris, F., Theodorou, E., Vardaki, M., Petrakos, M.: A statistical metadata model for simultaneous manipulation of both data and metadata. J. Intell. Inf. Syst. **17**(2–3), 169–192 (2001)
16. Papageorgiou, H., Vardaki, M., Pentaris, F.: Data and metadata transformations. Res. Off. Stat. **3**(2), 27–43 (2000)
17. Rahm, E., Do, H.H.: Data cleaning: problems and current approaches. IEEE Data Eng Bull **23** (4), 3–13 (2000)
18. Grossmann, W.: A conceptual approach for data integration in business analytics. Int. J. Softw. Inf. **4**, 53–68 (2009)
19. Pearce, D.J., Kelly, P.H.: A dynamic topological sort algorithm for directed acyclic graphs. J. Exp. Algorithmics JEA **11**, 1–7 (2007)
20. Pieterse, V., Black, P.E.: Dictionary of Algorithms and Data Structures (2015)
21. Kahn, A.B.: Topological sorting of large networks. Commun. ACM **5**(11), 558–562 (1962)
22. Mishra, P., Eich, M.H.: Join processing in relational databases. ACM Comput. Surv. CSUR **24** (1), 63–113 (1992)
23. DeWitt, D.J., Naughton, J.F., Schneider, D.A.: An evaluation of non-equijoin algorithms. In: Presented at the Proceedings of the 17th International Conference on Very Large Data Bases, pp. 443–452 (1991)
24. Zhou, J.: Nested Loop Join. In: Encyclopedia of Database Systems, p. 1895 Springer (2009)
25. Herzog, T.H., Scheuren, F., Winkler, W.E.: Record linkage. Wiley Interdiscip. Rev. Comput. Stat. **2**(5), 535–543 (2010)

26. Cohen, W., Ravikumar, P., Fienberg, S.: A comparison of string metrics for matching names and records. In: Presented at the Kdd workshop on data cleaning and object consolidation, vol. 3, pp. 73–78 (2003)
27. Fill, H.-G., Redmond, T., Karagiannis, D.: FDMM: A Formalism for Describing ADOxx Meta Models and Models (2012)
28. Gordon, J., Perrey, J., Spillecke, D.: Big data, analytics and the future of marketing and sales. Forbes Com (2013)
29. Pang, B., Lee, L.: Opinion mining and sentiment analysis. Found. Trends Inf. Retr. **2**(1–2), 1–135 (2008)
30. Yu, Y., Dang, J.: Semantic mining on customer survey. In: Presented at the Proceedings of the 8th International Conference on Semantic Systems, pp. 72–79 (2012)
31. Yuan, Y.C., Multiple imputation for missing data: Concepts and new development (Version 9.0). SAS Inst. Inc Rockv. MD, vol. 49 (2010)
32. ISO/IEC 9075-1.2008: Information technology—Database design—SQL—Part 1: Framework (SQL/Framework). ISO/IEC (2008)
33. Van der Loo, M.P.: The stringdist package for approximate string matching. The R (2014)
34. Starbuck, W.H.: Organizations as action generators. Am. Sociol. Rev. pp. 91–102, 1983
35. Delen, D., Demirkan, H.: Data, information and analytics as services. Decis. Support Syst. **55** (1), 359–363 (2013)
36. Karagiannis, D., Visic, N.: Platform-as-a-Service (PaaS): The ADOxx Metamodelling Platform (2011)

Part III
Business Process Management

Using the Horus Method for Succeeding in Business Process Engineering Projects

Andreas Schoknecht, Arthur Vetter, Hans-Georg Fill and Andreas Oberweis

Abstract This chapter presents the Horus Method for business process engineering, which is divided into four phases. These four phases consist of (1) an initial project preparation phase; (2) a strategy and architecture phase for the definition of strategic aspects as well as enterprise and system architecture; (3) a business process analysis phase; and (4) an application phase for the actual usage of models, thereby covering essential aspects of business process engineering. A formal conceptualization of the Horus Method is provided using the FDMM formalism, which is used for tool specification for the ADO*xx* platform. Thereby, the focus is on the formalization of XML nets, a special variant of high-level Petri Nets, for the modeling of interorganizational business processes in the field of e-commerce. Finally, a real-life case study is described which highlights the capabilities of the Horus Method for successful business process engineering projects.

Keywords Business process management · Business process engineering · Horus method · FDMM formalism

---

A. Schoknecht (✉) · A. Oberweis
Karlsruhe Institute of Technology (KIT), Karlsruhe, Germany
e-mail: andreas.schoknecht@kit.edu

A. Oberweis
e-mail: andreas.oberweis@kit.edu

A. Vetter
PROMATIS Software GmbH, Ettlingen, Germany
e-mail: arthur.vetter@promatis.de

H.-G. Fill
Faculty of Computer Science, University of Vienna, Vienna, Austria
e-mail: hans-georg.fill@univie.ac.at

D. Karagiannis et al. (eds.), *Domain-Specific Conceptual Modeling*,
DOI 10.1007/978-3-319-39417-6_6

1 Introduction

The modeling of business processes is typically regarded as a time-consuming and error prone endeavor [3]. Especially when considering not only the modeling of a business process itself, but also the modeling of related aspects like the context of a business process, risks, or key performance indicators associated to processes. Therefore, a structured procedure might help to mitigate the complexities of such modeling tasks. The *Horus Method* [13] is one such modeling method, which does not only involve the modeling of business processes but also of related aspects. This method was developed for business process engineering, which is also the focus of the case study description.

The term business process engineering thereby refers to two aspects. On the one hand, the detection of inefficiencies in processes and the subsequent mitigation of those is addressed. Such improvements can range from "clean slate" to "incremental improvements." In this context, clean slate means that dramatic improvements should be achieved by fundamentally rethinking and redesigning business processes, whereas incremental improvement refers to the identification and mitigation of local inefficiencies in business processes [2]. On the other hand, the structured approach of the Horus Method is also applicable when no pre-existing processes are available.

This chapter presents an extension of the contents presented in [4] by providing a more elaborate example and by focusing on the Horus Method itself showing its capabilities through a detailed case study instead of focusing on technical aspects of tool implementation. The case study describes experiences from an actual business process reengineering project conducted on the basis of the Horus Method. Thereby it is shown how this method can, for example, be used to detect misunderstandings. Besides that, it is demonstrated how test cases can be created from the process models, which helps in establishing a process working correctly.

The structure of the chapter is: Sect. 2 gives an overview of the Horus Method and the modeling possibilities it contains. Besides, work related to the engineering of business processes is introduced. Subsequently, Sect. 3 describes the corresponding conceptualization of the metamodel and models, while Sect. 4 presents a tool supporting the Horus Method as well as a case study from the industry describing how test cases can be generated with this method. Finally, Sect. 5 concludes the chapter.

2 The Horus Method

The Horus Method described by Schönthaler et al. is a method for business process engineering and can be seen as a recipe which guides the user through different defined steps of a modeling procedure [13]. It is not a project procedure model like Scrum, but can be used additionally for the modeling tasks in a project. Moreover, other aspects related to a project procedure should be considered, such as project management, quality assurance, and documentation.

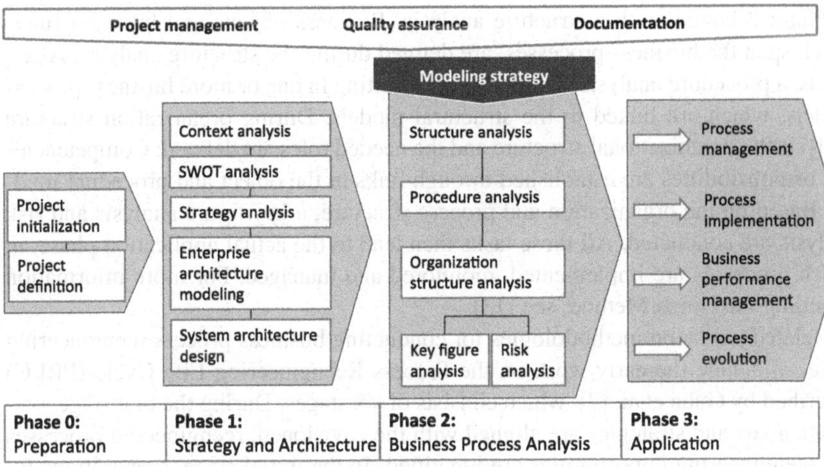

Fig. 1 Overview of the Horus method (adapted from [13])

The method makes heavy use of abstraction and structuring principles and is structured in four phases: the preparation phase, the strategy and architecture phase, the business process analysis phase and the application phase. The preparation phase includes the initialization and definition of the project. The strategy and architecture phase emphasizes strategic aspects and analysis of the enterprise and system architecture. The business process analysis phase is about modeling roles, objects, key figures, risks and processes. The application phase describes the usage of the created models, like the implementation and management of the processes. Figure 1 gives an overview of the different modeling phases and the tasks conducted in those phases. As the Horus Method emphasizes the strategy and architecture phase as well as the business process analysis phase, those two phases will be described in detail.

Before the actual business process analysis is done, the corporate strategy and architecture have to be analyzed. The reason is more practical than theoretical, because practical experience shows that involving decision makers into a modeling project helps to increase the acceptance of the project. In phase 1, a context analysis is conducted to describe the environment, the aims and the supply and services model of the project. The next step is a SWOT analysis [1] to address the strengths, weaknesses, opportunities and threats in the given context of the project. After the SWOT analysis the strategy analysis follows to identify strategies, risks and key figures to measure the corporate goals and strategy implementations. The strategy analysis is followed by the enterprise architecture model. The enterprise architecture model describes all the decision makers, who will detail the different enterprise processes. The core of the enterprise architecture is the business process architecture, linking business objects, business units and business rules together. If the modeling project aims at the development of an information system, phase 1 ends with the system architecture design, which is a high-level representation of the system architecture. It will be detailed in phase 2.

Phase 2 begins with a structure analysis. Business objects and business rules, which span the business processes, are defined during the structure analysis. Afterwards, a procedure analysis is undertaken, resulting in one or more business process models, which are linked to the structural models. During organization structure analysis the organizational structure and the needed roles are defined. Competencies and responsibilities are established through links to the object and procedure models. Based on the organization and process structure, a key figure analysis and risk analysis are conducted. All these tasks then lead to the actual application phase, in which processes are implemented, monitored and managed. For more information regarding the Horus Method, see [13].

Related works on methodologies for conducting business process reengineering projects include the early work on the Process Reengineering Life Cycle (PRLC) described by Guha et al. [7], which consists of six stages. During the first stage, corporate goals and strategies are aligned with the envisioned, reengineered processes and reengineering opportunities are identified. In the initial stage, preparations for the actual changes are made by organizing the reengineering team and setting performance goals, while in the third stage, the processes to be reengineered are investigated for their optimization potential. In the subsequent redesign stage, new processes are designed considering alternative designs, organizational structure, IT platforms, and experiences from prototyping, which are then implemented in the fifth phase. Finally, the sixth stage is dedicated to performance measurement and quality improvement of the redesigned processes. While these six stages are described more from an abstract perspective, the Horus Method provides more detailed guidelines, e.g., on how to actually model different views on a process.

Another related work describes a framework for business process reengineering projects, including principles, a process and different methods and tools [11]. In comparison to the principles of Horus, abstraction and structuring, which are quite general and can be applied for different kind of projects, the principles of that framework are more specific to business process reengineering projects and include goal orientation, value-focus, paradigm-shift, virtual-resources, process-orientation, concurrency, modularity and non-redundancy. The procedure to execute such a project starts with the definition of a vision and mission, followed by an analysis of the as-is system and the identification of improvement opportunities. Afterwards, the to-be system is designed and a trade-off to the as-is system is performed. After the development of a transition plan for the to-be system, it will be implemented and maintained. The methods and tools of the framework support that process and include for example simulations or model-based application generation.

Additionally, Scheer et al. provided another method in [12]. They describe a House of Business Engineering, which resembles a life-cycle model of business process management and consists of four tiers. In tier 1, the design of processes is addressed, while tier 2 is concerned with process monitoring and improvement. Thereby, processes are viewed and modeled from different perspectives: namely the organization, data, function, control and output perspectives. Tier 3 addresses technical processing support, which is controlled by a work-flow system. Finally, tier 4 stands for the application system, which provides functional support for tier 3.

A further related methodology is described in [14]. In the first phase, called *Strategy and Organization*, the organizational prerequisites are defined including setting up project management, conducting an analysis of the organization's strength and weaknesses, and identifying processes to be redesigned. The dependencies between processes to identify supplier-consumer relationships between process outcomes are analyzed during the next phase, *Process Landscape Design*. Afterwards, each process is modeled accompanied by the definition of performance metrics in the *Process Design* phase. Technical as well as organizational aspects regarding process implementation are addressed in the subsequent *Process Implementation* phase. Finally, the newly implemented processes are monitored in the *Operations and Controlling* phase. The performance measurement of the executed processes, which can be used to repeatedly enter the *Process Design* phase, is also included in final phase.

3 Formal Specification of Metamodels for the Horus Method

The section below presents a formal specification of metamodels for a selected set of aspects of the Horus Method, which are based on the FDMM formalizm [5]. This will illustrate some of the core aspects of applying metamodeling concepts to the Horus Method with FDMM. In the next section, we will shortly discuss an implementation on the ADO*xx* platform. However, we will first introduce some background information on the FDMM formalizm. Then, we will describe the actual specification of the metamodels for the Horus Method. This section contains content from [4] to provide some background for the specification of the models used in the Horus Method.

3.1 The FDMM Formalism

In the following, we will focus on the aspects of the modeling language and, in particular, on the description of its syntax by using metamodels and models. In FDMM, a metamodel *MM* contains the following parts:

$$MM = \langle MT, \preceq, domain, range, card \rangle \tag{1}$$

Thereby, the set *MT* comprises the set of model types specified for this metamodel

$$MT = \{MT_1, MT_2, \ldots, MT_n\} \tag{2}$$

Each model type MT_i is a tuple of a set of object types O_i^T, a set of data types D_i^T and a set of attributes A_i

$$MT_i = \langle O_i^T, D_i^T, A_i \rangle \tag{3}$$

All object types, data types, and attributes of the model types are parts of the sets O^T, D^T and A, whereby object types may also exist independent of model types

$$O^T = \cup_j O_j^T, D^T = \cup D_j^T, A = \cup A_i. \tag{4}$$

$\preceq$ is an ordering on the set of object types, O^T. That is, if $o_1{}^t \preceq o_2{}^t$ then we denote object type $o_1{}^t$ as a "subtype" of object type $o_2{}^t$. For assigning attributes to object types the domain function maps attributes to the power set of object types

$$domain : A \to P(\cup_j O_j^T). \tag{5}$$

Similarly, the range function maps attributes to the power set of all pairs of object types and model types, to data types, and to model types. It thus constrains what values an attribute can take in the model instances. Apart from the assignment of data types, e.g., for strings and integers, this mapping also permits to link to object types of the same or other model types and to model types

$$range : A \to P(\cup_j (O_j^T \times \{MT_j\}) \cup D^T \cup MT). \tag{6}$$

The card function constrains the number of attribute values an object may have:

$$card : O^T \times A \to P(\mathbb{N}_0 \times (\mathbb{N}_0 \cup \{\infty\})). \tag{7}$$

The sets O^T, D^T and A are pairwise disjoint. For any attribute it is defined that a corresponding domain function must point to an object type of the same model type. The instantiation of a metamodel MM is then a tuple

$$\langle \mu_{mt}, \mu_O, \mu_D, \tau, \beta \rangle . \tag{8}$$

Thereby, μ_{mt} is a mapping from model types MT to the power set of model instances mt with the set mt being the union of all mappings of model types to model instances so that every element of the set of model instances mt has to be derived from a model type. The function μ_O maps object types of a particular model type to the power set of object instances O, whereby O is the union of all object instances so that there is no object instance without a mapping to an object type and a model type. The function μ_D maps the data types to the power set of data objects. The data objects themselves are not further defined or constrained. The FDMM formalism thus leaves it to the user to further specify the nature and valid content of a data type. For describing the model instances, FDMM uses triple statements τ defined as:

$$\tau \subseteq O \times A \times (D \cup O \cup mt). \tag{9}$$

The function β is then used to map the set of model instances mt to the power set of these triple statements and thus assigns triple statements to the model instances. In this context, a correctness constraint is defined by FDMM so that τ is the disjoint union of $\beta(mt_i)$ with $mt_i \in mt$, meaning that every triple is contained in exactly one model instance. Additionally, FDMM defines a number of disjointness and partitioning constraints for the instantiation of metamodels. For further details on such constraints, the reader is referred to [5].

3.2 Specification of Metamodels

As outlined in Sect. 2, the Horus Method is composed of a large number of model types that are all tightly interconnected. For illustrating the application of the FDMM formalism, we selected four core model types that are used in the Horus Method to describe XML nets [10]. The model types we will discuss below are: the procedure model MT_{PM}, the employee pool model MT_{EM}, the role pool model MT_{RM}, and the object model MT_{OM}

$$MT_{PM} = \left\langle O^T_{PM}, D^T_{PM}, A_{PM} \right\rangle, \tag{10}$$

$$MT_{EM} = \left\langle O^T_{EM}, D^T_{EM}, A_{EM} \right\rangle, \tag{11}$$

$$MT_{RM} = \left\langle O^T_{RM}, D^T_{RM}, A_{RM} \right\rangle, \tag{12}$$

$$MT_{PM} = \left\langle O^T_{OM}, D^T_{OM}, A_{OM} \right\rangle. \tag{13}$$

To illustrate how a model type is detailed by its object types, data types and attributes, we show here the case of the procedure model type. The object types of the procedure model are defined as

$$\begin{aligned} O^T_{PM} =\{ & AbstractProcedureClass,\ ObjectStore,\ Activity, \\ & Connection,\ HumanResourceRequirements\}. \end{aligned} \tag{14}$$

We can then define inheritance relationships between the object types by

$$ObjectStore \preceq AbstractProcedureClass, \tag{15}$$

$$Activity \preceq AbstractProcedureClass. \tag{16}$$

Thereby, the object types "ObjectStore" and "Activity" are defined as subtypes of the object type "AbstractProcedureClass" that is defined as abstract. This makes it easier to assign attributes to the subtypes and also simplifies the specification of relationships between all subtypes of an object type. Next, we define the data types for the procedure model type by:

$$D_{PM}^{T} = \{String,\ Integer,\ Float,\ File,\ Enum_{WF},\ Enum_{AT}\}. \tag{17}$$

As FDMM does not further define the data types that can be used, we are free to use either common types such as *String*, *Integer* or *Float* or custom ones such as *File* that have to be specified during the implementation based on the used implementation platform. By using another set as a data type as it is shown by the $Enum_{WF}$ and $Enum_{AT}$ types for example, we can also express data types with predefined, fixed values

$$Enum_{WF} = \{yes,\ no\}, \tag{18}$$

$$Enum_{AT} = \{executing,\ checking,\ responsible,\ informing\}. \tag{19}$$

Subsequently, we can define the attributes necessary for the object types. In the set A_{PM}, we only present an excerpt of the attributes that were actually defined for this model type for reasons of brevity. For example, the "Activity" object type also requires a number of additional attributes for specifying time properties and simulation parameters. The attribute set also comprises elements that will later be used to specify the start- and endpoint of relation-classes, e.g., the "ConnectionFrom" and the "ConnectionTo" attributes

$$\begin{aligned} A_{PM} = \{&Name,\ ObjectType,\ ObjectNumber,\ Documents,\ ConnectionTo,\\ &ConnectionFrom,\ SubDiagram,\ HRReq,\ RoleRef,\ AssignmentType,\\ &Quantity,\ Percentage,\ XQueryTransitionCondition\}. \end{aligned} \tag{20}$$

In the current formalization of the Horus modeling language, the employee pool model and the role pool model only contain a small number of object types, data types and attributes, e.g., for the employee pool model

$$O_{EM}^{T} = \{Employee\}, \tag{21}$$

$$D_{EM}^{T} = \{String,\ File,\ Calendar\}, \tag{22}$$

$$A_{EM} = \{Name,\ Availability,\ Documents\}. \tag{23}$$

And similarly the definitions for the role pool model

$$O_{RM}^{T} = \{Role,\ Employees\}, \tag{24}$$

$$D_{RM}^{T} = \{String,\ Float,\ File\}, \tag{25}$$

$$A_{RM} = \{Name,\ Quality,\ AssignedEmp,\ Documents,\ Employee\}. \tag{26}$$

In contrast to these simple model types, the definition of the object model type requires more constructs as it constitutes a way of representing actual XML schemas. The object types of this model type are therefore defined as follows:

$$O^T_{OM} = \{Object,\ ObjectCopy,\ ObjectAggregation,\ CollectiveConstraint,\ Relationship,\ Inheritance,\ ConstraintConnection,\ Keys,\ Attributes,\ Constraints\}. \quad (27)$$

For the data types of this model type, we again use the possibility of referring to predefined sets of attribute values

$$D^T_{OM} = \{String,\ Float,\ File,\ Enum_{DT},\ Enum_{OPT},\ Enum_{CT},\ Enum_{CARD}\}, \quad (28)$$

$$Enum_{DT} = \{Unspecified,\ String,\ Integer,\ Float,\ Date,\ Enumeration\}, \quad (29)$$

$$Enum_{OPT} = \{yes,\ no\}, \quad (30)$$

$$Enum_{CT} = \{XOR,\ OR,\ SIM\}, \quad (31)$$

$$Enum_{CARD} = \{< 0..n >,\ < 1..1 >,\ < 1..n >\}. \quad (32)$$

The set of attributes for the object model type are then defined as follows:

$$A_{OM} = \{Name,\ IsRoot,\ XMLSchema,\ KeyAttributes,\ Attributes,\ Constraints,\ ConstraintType, RelationshipFrom,\ RelationshipTo,\ InheritanceFrom,\ InheritanceTo,\ ConstraintConnectionFrom,\ ConstraintConnectionTo,\ IsInside\}. \quad (33)$$

Finally, we can conclude the formal specification by adding domain, range and cardinality definitions for the attributes. Again, we selected some of the attributes and object types defined above to illustrate this. By assigning an attribute to a supertype, all subtypes automatically inherit the attribute definition as, e.g., shown for the "AbstractProcedureClass" object type and the name attribute

$$domain(Name) = \{AbstractProcedureClass\},\quad range(Name) = \{String\},\quad card(Name) =< 1, 1 > . \quad (34)$$

For the specification of references between object instances and model instances, two different directions can be applied in FDMM: the first is to directly reference another object type or model type and the second is to use an intermediary object type that has references to the object and/or model types that shall be connected. The references are in all cases expressed by attributes whose range contains other object types or model types. At first, we illustrate a direct reference to other object types by the example of assigning an object type to an attribute of "ObjectStore"

$$domain(ObjectType) = \{ObjectStore\},$$
$$range(ObjectType) = \{Object,\ ObjectAggregation\},$$
$$card(Name) =< 0, 1 > . \quad (35)$$

A core feature of the tool to represent XML nets is therefore specified. The attribute "ObjectType" that is attached to the "ObjectStore" object type can thus be used to reference object instances of the types "Object" and "ObjectAggregation" that are part of the object model type. As this reference points directly to another object type, no further information can be assigned to the reference itself. An intermediary object type has to be used in order to enable more complex references where the reference itself can be further specified.

We illustrate this below for the specification of edges in the procedure model type, which are denoted as "Connections" in the Horus modeling language. For this purpose, the two attributes "ConnectionTo" and "ConnectionFrom" are assigned to the "Connection" object type with the range definition pointing to the "AbstractProcedureClass". The cardinalities of the from and to attributes are set to $< 1,1 >$ as edges can only occur with exactly two object instances attached to them:

$$domain(ConnectionTo) = \{Connection\},$$
$$range(ConnectionTo) = \{AbstractProcedureClass\},$$
$$card(ConnectionTo) =< 1, 1 > . \quad (36)$$

$$domain(ConnectionFrom) = \{Connection\},$$
$$range(ConnectionFrom) = \{AbstractProcedureClass\},$$
$$card(ConnectionFrom) =< 1, 1 > . \quad (37)$$

When instantiating the object type "Connection", it becomes possible to connect these instances to instances of the type "AbstractProcedureClass" and to treat this relation separately from the objects it connects to. At the same time, further attributes may be assigned to "Connection". This is, for example, necessary to define transition conditions in XML nets that can be specified via XQuery strings

$$domain(XQueryTransitionCondition) = \{Connection\},$$
$$range(XQueryTransitionCondition) = \{String\},$$
$$card(XQueryTransitionCondition) =< 1, 1 > . \quad (38)$$

When a separate treatment of the relationship between object types is not required but the relation should still be detailed by additional attributes, we can express this in FDMM in the following way. The "Activity" objects have to be detailed by their requirements in terms of human resources. Therefore, they are linked to "Role" objects in the role pool model. However, it should be possible to detail for each role if the role is just executing or checking the activity, or is responsible for it, or has to inform someone. First, we specify the attribute "HRReq" that can point to any number of "HumanResourceRequirements" objects.

$$\begin{aligned} domain(HRReq) &= \{Activity\}, \\ range(HRReq) &= \{HumanResourceRequirements\}, \\ card(HRReq) &=< 0, \infty > . \end{aligned} \tag{39}$$

Then, we specify the attribute "RoleRef" for the object type "HumanResource-Requirements"

$$\begin{aligned} domain(RoleRef) &= \{HumanResourceRequirements\}, \\ range(RoleRef) &= \{Role\}, \\ card(RoleRef) &=< 1, 1 > . \end{aligned} \tag{40}$$

As the target reference is now also an object type, we can add further attributes to detail it—for example by reverting to the previously defined $Enum_{AT}$ data type:

$$\begin{aligned} domain(AssignmentType) &= \{HumanResourceRequirements\}, \\ range(AssignmentType) &= \{Enum_{AT}\}, \\ card(AssignmentType) &=< 1, 1 > . \end{aligned} \tag{41}$$

Another important feature in procedure models is the use of refinements for individual activities [13]. Thereby the amount of details which should be displayed on each level is controlled. In FDMM, these refinements can be expressed by references to other model instances of the same type. We show this for the refinement attribute "SubDiagram" whose range encompasses model instances of the type MT_{PM}:

$$\begin{aligned} domain(SubDiagram) &= \{Activity\}, \\ range(SubDiagram) &= \{MT_{PM}\}, \\ card(SubDiagram) &=< 0, 1 > . \end{aligned} \tag{42}$$

4 Horus Modeling Tool and Case Study

In this section, two aspects related to the Horus Method are described: first, we present a free tool supporting the application of the Horus Method through the description of an exemplary instantiation of the formalization described in the previous section. Second, we show the capabilities of the Horus Method when applied in a business process engineering project through a real life case study.

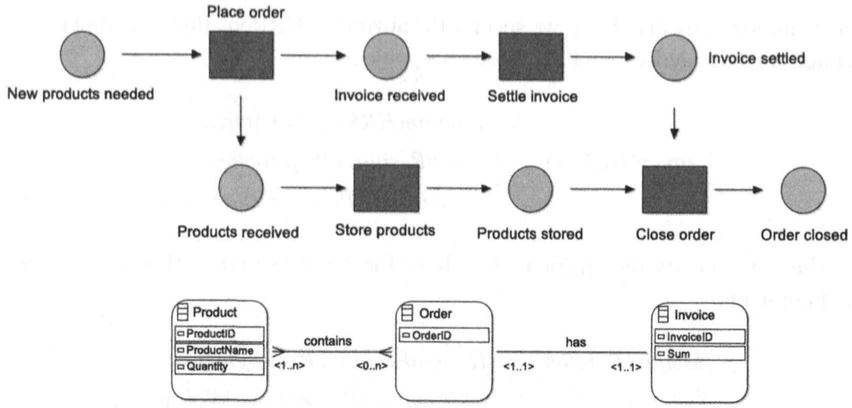

Fig. 2 Examples for procedure and object models

4.1 Modeling Processes and Objects with the ADOxx Horus Modeling Tool

The Horus Method is supported by two free software tools.[1] In the following, the one based on the ADO*xx* metamodeling platform[2] for modeling the various aspects incorporated into the Horus Method [6] is demonstrated in more detail. As the FDMM formalizm not only permits to formally specify metamodels but also the instantiation of metamodels, we will illustrate below how the definitions of the previous section can be applied. We show the instantiation by using a procedure model of a buyer process as well as an object model describing objects referenced in the procedure model. These models are depicted in Fig. 2, while Fig. 3 shows a screen shot of the actual modeling tool.

The procedure model shows an abbreviated version of a process for buying products. When new products are needed, an order is placed. Afterwards, the products and an invoice are received, which leads to the storage of products and the settlement of the invoice. After that the order is closed and the buying process finished. In the object model, three objects are depicted which represent the documents and objects used in the buying process. These objects from the object model can be associated to corresponding object stores (the circles) in the procedure model. The instantiation of these model types is specified by

$$\mu_{MT}(MT_{PM}) = \{mt_{pm}\},$$
$$\mu_{MT}(MT_{OM}) = \{mt_{om}\}. \quad (43)$$

[1]Can be downloaded from http://www.omilab.org/web/adoxx-horus-method/download or http://www.horus.biz/de/produkte/horus-enterprise/horus-business-modeler/.

[2]More information on the project can be found under http://www.omilab.org/web/adoxx-horus-method/home.

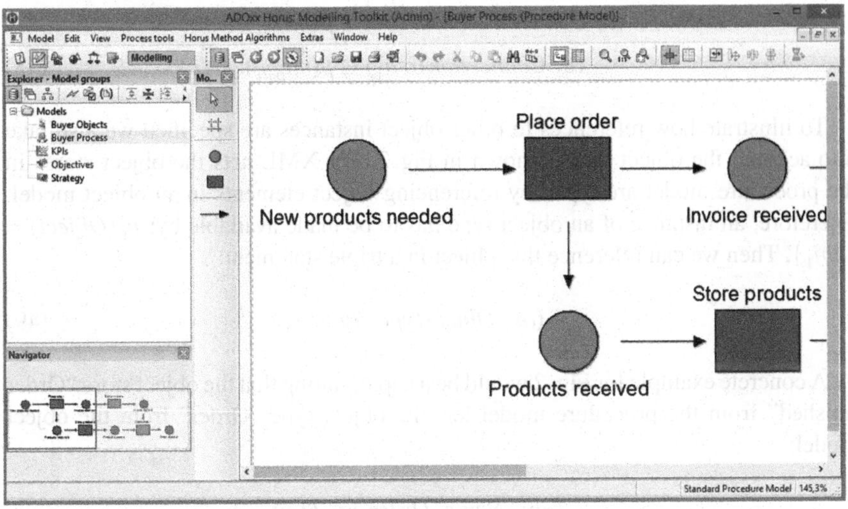

Fig. 3 Screen shot from the ADOxx Horus modeling tool

In the next step, we illustrate the instantiation of object types for these two model types. We show this for the object stores that are represented by circles and the activities that are represented by rectangles in Fig. 2.

$$\mu_0(ObjectStore, MT_{PM}) = \{os_1,\ os_2,\ \ldots,\ os_6\},$$
$$\mu_0(Activity, MT_{PM}) = \{a_1,\ a_2,\ \ldots,\ a_4\}. \tag{44}$$

For the assignment of textual information as shown in the form of labels for the elements in Fig. 2—we first have to instantiate attribute values of the corresponding data types, for example by:

$$\mu_D(String) = \{'New\ products\ needed',\ 'Place\ order',\ \ldots\}. \tag{45}$$

These data objects can then be used in triple statements to assign them to the object instances via their attributes, e.g.,

$$(os_1\ Name\ 'New\ products\ needed') \in \beta(mt_{pm1}),$$
$$(a_1\ Name\ 'Place\ order') \in \beta(mt_{pm1}). \tag{46}$$

For the specification of the edges in the procedure model we first have to instantiate an object of type "Connection" in (47) and can then use two triple statements for defining the start and endpoint in (48)

$$\mu_0(Connection, MT_{PM}) = \{c_1,\ c_2,\ \ldots,\ c_{10}\} \tag{47}$$

$$(c_1\ ConnectionFrom\ os_1) \in \beta(mt_{pm1}),$$
$$(c_1\ ConnectionTo\ a_1) \in \beta(mt_{pm1}). \tag{48}$$

To illustrate how references to other object instances are specified we also take into account the object model shown in Fig. 2. For XML nets the object stores in the procedure model are typed by referencing object elements in an object model. Therefore, an instance of an object type has to be made available by: $\mu_0(Object) = \{obj_1\}$. Then we can reference this object in a triple statement:

$$(os_1\ ObjectType\ obj_1) \tag{49}$$

A concrete example for Fig. 2 would be a triple, stating that the object store "Order finished" from the procedure model has the object type "Order" from the object model:

$$(obj_1\ Name\ 'Order') \in \beta(mt_{om1}),$$
$$(os_6\ Name\ 'Order\ finished') \in \beta(mt_{pm1}),$$
$$(os_6\ ObjectType\ obj_1). \tag{50}$$

4.2 Case Study: Turning an Almost Failed Software Project into a Successfull One

The following case study describes the application of the Horus Method and the corresponding software tool in a software supported business process reengineering project. First of all, the project setting is described, followed by the challenges the project team was facing and the application of the Horus Method to solve the project challenges.

4.2.1 Project Setting and Challenges

PROMATIS software GmbH was consulted by a German wide operating company for mobile services. For two and a half years, the company had been trying to introduce an IT scheduling system for scheduling their mobile services. The system they employed was a widely used standard software in the company which scheduled jobs for field staff considering different parameters like distance from field staff to customer, needed material, time, working time regulations, and many more.

The software was customized and introduced in two pilot regions. During the pilot phase, an increasing number of change requests popped up and the performance of the system got worse, so that the management decided to consult PROMATIS software GmbH to turn around the project from failing to succeeding.

Arriving at the customer, the PROMATIS consultants started analyzing the project and studied the barely existing documentation. Reconstructing the configuration of the system and the changes which were made was impossible because of the missing documentation. Additionally, it was unclear why changes were made at all, because of missing or poorly defined requirements. Changes were made to the system without challenging the need and the overall business requirement of the change.

Apart from that, many changes were needed, because the business process for scheduling jobs of field staff was unclear, not documented and standardized before the project started. The introduction of the scheduling system forced the business to think about the underlying business processes, but that happened in a stage of the project when the software already started to be rolled out and changes were difficult to perform and expensive.

At this stage of the project, changes were made to fire fighting problems which were caused by unclear or even unknown requirements which should have been defined in an earlier stage of the project. But even at a later stage of the project, the business had difficulties to define and structure business requirements. Reasons for that were on the one hand a missing business case, but also the delayed involvement of third parties like the work council, who had also requirements regarding work time regulations. The objectives of the project were unclear, so it was difficult to define requirements, which support the business case.

On the other hand, because of the missing business process definition and documentation, it was unclear which parts of the business process had to be changed and influenced to achieve the objectives. The result were ad hoc changes to the scheduling system without knowing if they positively influenced the business of the customer and which impact they had on other process steps.

All those factors led to an unstructured, scattered, and unfocused development of the scheduling system. The results were, besides customer dissatisfaction and a lot of burned money, performance issues of a scheduling system after being rolled out in two regions of Germany, which was meant to be rolled out nationally.

4.2.2 Application of the Horus Method

In this phase of the project, two consultants of PROMATIS software GmbH joined the project and started to apply the Horus Method to shed light on it. Because of the poor documentation and the impossibility to reconstruct all changes made to the system, it was unclear which requirements the business actually had and which of them were implemented. So the consultants started almost from scratch defining the business case and analyzing what the problems of the customer were, why the customer actually started the project and what he wanted to achieve with the project.

Because phase zero of the Horus Method was already done, phase one was the starting point of the project analysis. Missing a proper business case, aligned to the Horus Method, the consultants started to conduct a context analysis with the aim of creating a model which, on the one hand, could be used to justify the project and the related costs, respectively, the expected cost savings after finishing the project. On the other hand, it was used as a reference point for the requirements workshop with the managerial staff and to challenge every single requirement regarding to what extent it supports the business case. The advantage of the context analysis was also the involvement of interests of third parties like the work council.

After creating the model, a strategy analysis was made to find out with which strategies the customer could achieve his objectives. When analyzing the possible strategies, it came out that just by introducing the scheduling system to automate the planning of the field jobs the objectives could not be reached. First of all, the business process had to be defined and standardized, because in every region of Germany the business process was operated differently. The output of that standardization would not only be a to-be process, but also the guarantee of having a compliant business process to the work council's requirements as well as to the working time regulations of Germany.

After defining the objectives and strategies for the project, key performance indicators (KPI) were modeled to measure the effectiveness of the strategies and the achievement of the objectives. Using the modeling tool various models were created which included objectives, linked strategies and KPIs to present and discuss the first results with the management, who were the sponsors of the project. Figure 4

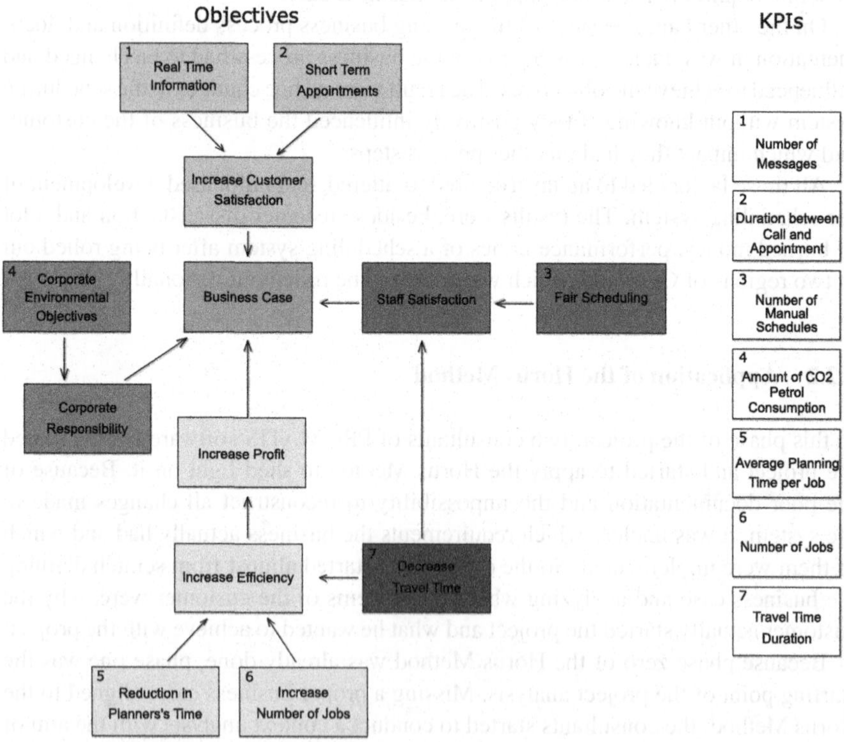

Fig. 4 Exemplary business case

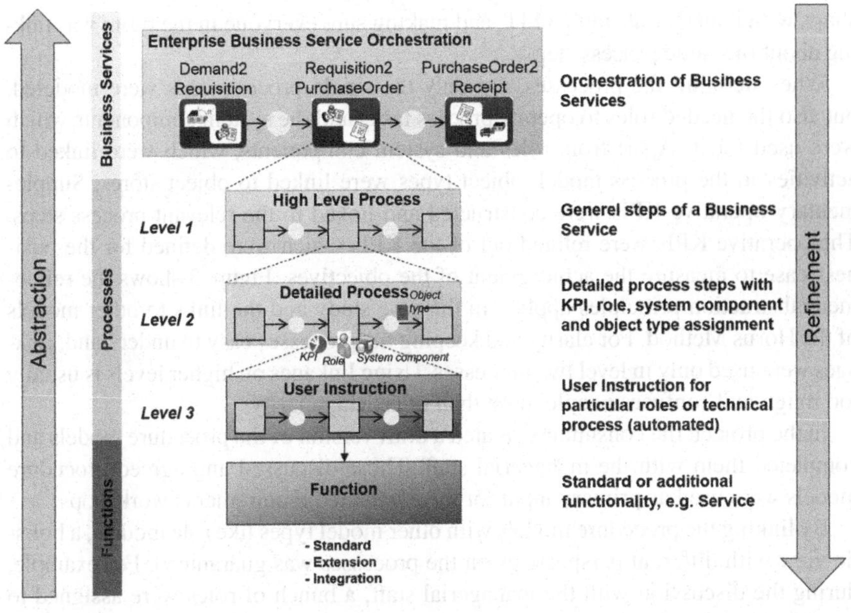

Fig. 5 Used process structure in the case study (adapted from [8])

shows an exemplary business case model representing objectives and linked KPIs. The linkage between objectives and KPIs is represented by the numbers.

The next step was the standardization of the scheduling process. Therefore, a to-be process had to be defined with the management. With the experience of many projects, the consultants used the suggested "abstraction" and "structuring" principles of the Horus Method (see also Fig. 5). First of all, the consultants modeled the relevant business services and refined them afterwards in three more detailed processes, following a top-down modeling approach. On the highest level only the business services were modeled, which represent the purpose of a specific business process. The first refinement level, called level one, shows the abstract high level view of the business process. On level two, the process was detailed and linked to other models. In addition to the links, process steps were colored to show whether the process step could be implemented in the proposed standard software solution or the solution had to be customized. Refining the level two process had the aim to model user instructions. On this level of the process, each single step a role had to undertake was modeled.

The advantage of a refinement up to level three was that the process models could be used to create test cases, training documentation and system documentation quite easily. Another advantage of this approach was that the management could understand the modeled processes easily and the project team did not get lost in, at this stage of the project, unnecessary details during workshops with the managerial staff. The created business processes were also used to structure the requirements workshops with managerial staff and IT, and making sure everyone in the room was talking about the same process step.

When defining the processes, not only the single process steps were modeled, but also the needed roles to operate process tasks and the system components which were used for it. Apart from roles and system components, which were linked to activities in the process model, object types were linked to object stores. Supplementary operative KPIs were constructed and linked to the relevant process steps. The operative KPIs were refined out of the KPIs which were defined for the business case to measure the achievement of the objectives. Figure 5 shows the refinement/abstraction principles applied in the case study and the links to other models of the Horus Method. For clarity and keeping the processes easy to understand, linkages were used only in level two processes. Using linkages on higher levels is usually too rough and confuses people more than improving clarity.

In the project, the consultants created a draft version of the procedure models and completed them with the managerial staff. Those discussed and agreed procedure models were used as primary input for the conducted requirements workshops.

By linking the procedure models with other model types like role models, a holistic view with different perspectives on the processes was guaranteed. For example, during the discussion with the managerial staff, a bunch of roles were assigned to a process step, executing all the same process step, despite different job roles and responsibilities. That aspect was recognized as a serious security issue and could have led to a decrease of service quality. By linking the system component to the process step it was easy to uncover the system, whose access rights had to be clarified.

Another perspective which was handled adequately during the requirement workshops was a more technical one. Because systems were linked to process steps, needed future technical interfaces could be identified as well as the necessary functional information specified during the workshops. Those interfaces were modeled as object types and linked to the specific object store in the procedure model. All functional requirements were defined during the conducted workshops and modeled as services according to the service model of the Horus Method. Finally, all requirements were assigned to the specific process steps.

The result of a couple of workshops were standardized to-be processes with clear roles, the underlying systems, the functional interfaces between those systems, and the specific requirements which were linked to the processes. With the specific tool support, a documentation including all those models and descriptions could be created and used for approval. Tools like Horus[3] provide such a functionality following a model-to-text approach.

At the next stage of the project, the implementation of the scheduling system and integration of third party systems started. Additionally, implementation test cases

[3]For more information visit www.horus.biz.

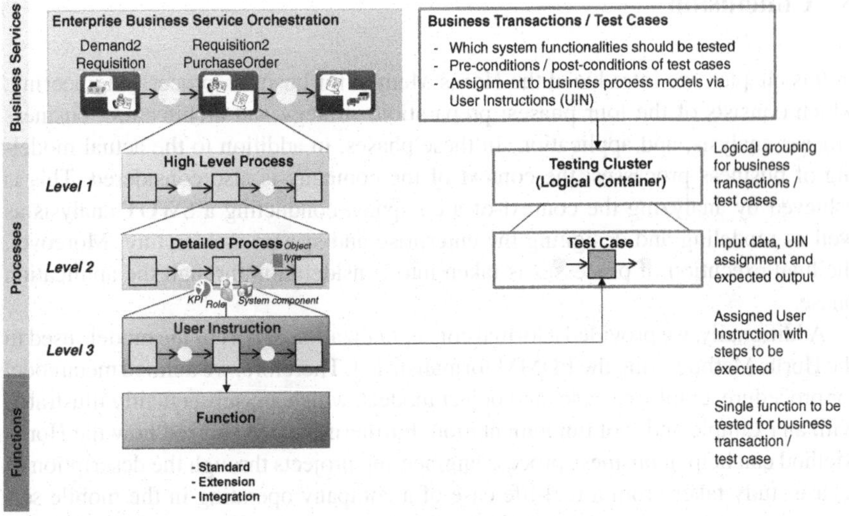

Fig. 6 Relationship between procedure model and test case (adapted from [9])

had to be defined. The modeled processes were also used in this context. As shown above, processes were defined up to level three. On level three, user instructions were modeled. For every step, which needed user interaction, the corresponding application mask was attached as screen-shot to the process step with a detailed description what users have to do, e.g., which button has to be clicked. Because of their detailed description, level three processes were also used as training material to train users before rolling out the system. In addition, a model of that granularity has the advantage that it can be used for the creation of test cases. Because of the detailed description what users have to do, process activity descriptions just have to be completed with the expected result in order to have well-defined test cases. It has to be mentioned that the process models were just used to describe the test cases, and not to document the actual test execution. For that purpose, a test management tool should be used, which is able to import test case descriptions in a text format like CSV. Figure 6 shows the relationship between procedure model and test cases.

The described case study shows how the Horus Method can be applied effectively in business process reengineering projects for structuring the problem as well as the solution. The Horus Method is not only a powerful method to model business processes, but also very useful to define a business case for a project by providing different models like objective and KPI models. With a proper tool support the Horus Method can also be used to create different documents directly out of the models, following a model-to-text approach, which can be used for example for approval, training documents, or the description of test cases.

5 Conclusion

In this chapter, we introduced the Horus Method for business process engineering, which consists of the four phases: preparation, strategy and architecture, business process analysis, and application. In these phases, in addition to the actual modeling of business processes, the context of the company is also considered. This is achieved by analyzing the context of a company, conducting a SWOT analysis as well as modeling and designing the enterprise and system architecture. Moreover, the final execution of processes is taken into consideration through the application phase.

Additionally, we provided a formal conceptualization of part of the models used in the Horus Method using the FDMM formalism [5]. Therefore, we defined metamodels for procedure, employee, role, and object models, which are subsequently illustrated with an example and tool implementation. Furthermore, we showed how the Horus Method can help in business process engineering projects through the description of a case study taken from a real-life case of a company operating in the mobile service industry. This case study highlighted that misunderstandings could be detected through the structured procedure introduced by the Horus Method while also allowing the derivation of test cases for the implemented process.

Tool Download http://www.omilab.org/adoxx-horus.

References

1. Andrews, K.R.: The Concept of Corporate Strategy, 2nd edn. R.D. Irwin (1980)
2. Antón, A., McCracken, W., Potts, C.: Goal decomposition and scenario analysis in business process reengineering. In: Wijers, G., Brinkkemper, S., Wasserman, T. (eds.) Advanced Information Systems Engineering. Lecture Notes in Computer Science (LNCS), vol. 811, pp. 94–104. Springer, Berlin (1994)
3. Becker, J., Rosemann, M., von Uthmann, C.: Guidelines of business process modeling. In: van der Aalst, W., Desel, J., Oberweis, A. (eds.) Business Process Management—Models, Techniques, and Empirical Studies. Lecture Notes in Computer Science (LNCS), vol. 1806, pp. 30–49. Springer, berlin (2000)
4. Fill, H., Hickl, S., Karagiannis, D., Oberweis, A., Schoknecht, A.: A formal specification of the horus modeling language using FDMM. In: 11th Internationale Tagung Wirtschaftsinformatik (WI), pp. 1165–1180. AIS Electronic Library (AISeL), Leipzig, Germany (2013)
5. Fill, H., Redmond, T., Karagiannis, D.: FDMM: a formalism for describing ADOxx meta models and models. In: Maciaszek, L.A., Cuzzocrea, A., Cordeiro, J. (eds.) 14th International Conference on Enterprise Information Systems (ICEIS), vol. 3, pp. 133–144. SciTePress, Wroclaw, Poland (2012)
6. Fill, H.G., Karagiannis, D.: On the conceptualisation of modelling methods using the ADOxx meta modelling platform. Enter. Model. Inf. Syst. Archit. **8**(1), 4–25 (2013)
7. Guha, S., Kettinger, W.J., Teng, J.T.: Business process reengineering. Inf. Syst. Manag. **10**(3), 13–22 (1993)

8. Herfurth, M., Karle, T., Schönthaler, F.: Reference Model for Service-oriented Business Software Based on Web Service Nets. In: Hesse, W., Oberweis, A. (eds.) 3rd AIS SIGSAND European Symposium on Analysis, Design, Use and Societal Impact of Information. Lecture Notes in Informatics (LNI), vol. 129, pp. 55–70. Gesellschaft für Informatik (GI), Marburg, Germany (2008)
9. Karle, T., Teichenthaler, K.: Kollaborative Geschäftsprozess-Umsetzung bei Unternehmensfusionen und ERP-Rollouts. DOAG Bus. News **2**, 5–10 (2015)
10. Lenz, K., Oberweis, A.: Modeling interorganizational workflows with XML nets. In: 34th Annual Hawaii International Conference on System Sciences (HICSS-34). IEEE Computer Society, Maui, Hawaii, USA (2001)
11. Mayer, R.J., DeWitte, P.S.: Delivering results: evolving BPR from art to engineering. In: Elzinga, D., Gulledge, T., Lee, C.Y. (eds.) Business Process Engineering—Advancing the State of the Art, pp. 83–129. Springer, US (1999)
12. Scheer, A.W., Abolhassan, F., Jost, W., Kirchmer, M. (eds.): Business Process Excellence—ARIS in Practice. Springer, Berlin (2002)
13. Schönthaler, F., Vossen, G., Oberweis, A., Karle, T.: Business Processes for Business Communities—Modeling Languages, Methods, Tools, 2nd edn. Springer, Berlin (2012)
14. Weske, M.: Business Process Management—Concepts, Languages, Architectures. Springer, Berlin (2012)

Semantic Evaluation of Business Processes Using SeMFIS

Hans-Georg Fill

Abstract This chapter discusses the evaluation of business processes in terms of semantics. For this purpose, a method providing a set of semantic process evaluation patterns is described. In order to make these patterns operational, the SeMFIS platform for engineering semantic annotations of conceptual models is used as a foundation. SeMFIS not only features a software platform based on the ADO*xx* metamodeling platform but also an open framework for the development of semantic information systems. SeMFIS is thus able to support the semantic process evaluation patterns on a technical level. In particular, the querying and scripting functionality contained in SeMFIS as well as its semantic annotation facilities are used together with business process models in BPMN notation, which are part of the SeMFIS standard distribution. As a proof of concept, a case study from the area of risk management is described in order to illustrate the practical application of SeMFIS when working with the semantic process evaluation patterns.

Keywords Semantic process evaluation • Business process management • SeMFIS

1 Introduction

The systematic management of an organization's business processes is today a well-established function in many enterprises [20]. Particularly large enterprises with a huge number of processes often use some kind of business process management (BPM) approach that enables them to systematically identify, analyze, and optimize their processes. In this context, the use of modeling methods has a long tradition [18]. It has recently been acknowledged that the complexity involved in business processes requires methods that enable decision-makers to abstract from the details of particular process instances and derive more abstract representations for effectively gaining

H.-G. Fill (✉)
University of Vienna, Vienna, Austria
e-mail: hans-georg.fill@univie.ac.at

D. Karagiannis et al. (eds.), *Domain-Specific Conceptual Modeling*,
DOI 10.1007/978-3-319-39417-6_7

insights into the processes they are responsible for. These insights encompass information such as the steps that are being physically and technically executed in a process, which resources are consumed, or which costs are caused thereby.

Typically, this information is today encoded in visual models using one of the many business process modeling languages [5, 27]. Well-known examples for such modeling languages include the business process modeling notation (BPMN) as today's most widely used standard, event-driven process chains, Petri nets, IDEF notation, or some kind of flowchart-based languages. A common characteristic of all these modeling languages is that they are based on a predefined metamodel. The metamodel specifies the syntax of the modeling language [19]. More specifically, the classes and relation classes that are contained in the metamodel can be instantiated when using the modeling language and thus a basic meaning can be assigned to the elements in business process models. Besides the classes, a label containing a name is usually assigned to the instances of types. Furthermore, most business process modeling languages offer additional attributes for describing their elements. For example, classes in business process modeling languages that represent tasks or activities often carry attributes for specifying: *durations*, e.g., the execution, transport, or resting time, *costs*, detailed textual *descriptions*, or *organizational assignments*, e.g., regarding responsibilities or necessary skills.

Apart from their representation function, e.g., to support communication between the various stakeholders in an enterprise about the structure and contents of a process [28], business process models are particularly beneficial for conducting algorithmic analyses [7, 31]. Through the formal definition of the models that is established via the underlying modeling language, algorithms can directly access and process the contained information [4]. Whereas numeric attributes can be easily processed by algorithms, attributes containing natural language are not directly accessible [23]. However, such attributes may also carry considerable semantic information. To make this implicit semantics processable by machines, either techniques of natural language processing have to be applied or the necessary information has to be additionally provided to the machines in a formal, i.e., processable format. Furthermore, also information that is not a priori provided through attributes of the modeling languages may need to be added in a formal way for conducting analyses. This concerns for example information that needs to be added ex-post to process models without having the ability to modify the modeling language. One reason for this may be that other systems and their algorithms already access the information contained in the models and may be affected by changes in the modeling language.

The following section presents a method for the semantic evaluation of business processes. The method provides a set of patterns for choosing the necessary level of semantic evaluation based on a user's information requirements. The method uses the semantic-based modeling framework for information systems (SeMFIS).[1] SeMFIS offers a metamodel for specifying semantic annotations of conceptual models via ontologies as well as a range of analysis, simulation, and import/export functionalities. It has been implemented on the ADO*xx* metamodeling platform and can thus

[1] See http://www.omilab.org/web/semfis/.

be directly added to arbitrary modeling languages based on ADO*xx*. For the purpose of this chapter, SeMFIS will be used in its standard configuration that also contains an implementation of the BPMN modeling language.

The remainder of the chapter is structured as follows. Section 2 will describe the method for the semantic evaluation of business processes, which will then be conceptualized in Sect. 3 based on the SeMFIS approach. In Sect. 4 a solution for a case study will be described based on the SeMFIS ADO*xx* implementation. The paper is concluded in Sect. 5 with an outlook on further research issues in the context of semantic evaluation.

2 Description of the Semantic Process Evaluation Method

The method for the semantic evaluation of business processes described below consists of two parts. The first part concerns the conceptual design of the method for conducting semantic process evaluations. The second part concerns the operational development of the method on the SeMFIS software platform, which is based on the ADO*xx* metamodeling platform [14].

In order to see what makes *semantic* evaluations of business processes distinct from other types of process evaluations, we started from the assumption that representations of business processes are available in the form of business process models, which means that, at this point, their analysis is already started. This may be the case when someone builds a common business process model starting from concrete instances of business processes, or when someone develops from scratch a new business process model that can be used as a template for the execution of processes. These differences are similar to a certain extent to what has been termed in the field of information modeling as the *mapping-oriented* and the *construction-oriented* notions of models [32]. Whereas the mapping-oriented notion focuses on parts of reality for a specific purpose, the construction-oriented notion emphasizes the cognitive performance of the modeler when creating a model. Both directions are today being supported directly by technology. For example, using workflow mining techniques [22], process models are automatically inferred from logs of executed business processes. Similarly, business process models may be manually inferred through interview and workshop techniques for making the relevant knowledge explicit. In order to support this manual derivation or the creation of process models from scratch, business process modeling tools facilitate the specification of models by means of visual editors.[2]

The models created as shown above may subsequently be analyzed, either by people or through algorithms based on the specification of the modeling language employed. This specification may be semiformal or formal, depending on whether it has only a formally defined syntax or whether both syntax and semantics of the

[2]A comprehensive and regularly updated list of tools that can be used for this purpose is provided at http://www.bptrends.com/resources/vendors/ last accessed 10-09-2015.

language have been rigorously defined [4, 16]. As an example for a semiformal modeling language, consider flowchart diagrams. Although the types of elements and the constraints on the relations are well-specified, statements about the operational semantics are typically not given. By contrast, Petri nets offer both an exact specification of their elements and relations as well as about their execution semantics [13, 29]. Thus, the level of formality has a direct influence on the range of possibilities for subsequent analyses. Whereas detailed information about the execution of the model is required for analyses that take into account the dynamic flow of information or resources in business processes, e.g., for conducting simulations of process flows using discrete-event simulation algorithms [21], for analyses that only operate on the level of syntax, semi-formal specifications are sufficient.

This chapter focuses on analyses based on the formal syntax of the modeling language. The reason is that such types of analyses can be applied in a generic way to a multitude of business process modeling languages. By contrast, analyses focusing on the execution of process models need to take into account as well the particular execution rules for a certain modeling language, which are typically not generic enough to be applicable to several process modeling languages. For example, the execution rules for passing tokens in Petri nets would require different analysis designs than the execution rules for handling the various types of events in BPMN models. However, the rules of execution for a modeling language are not the only part of semantics that is relevant for the interpretation of models. An equally large part of semantics is implicitly encoded through the attributes assigned to the elements of the language's grammar. This concerns numerical, textual, as well as reference attributes. Although this information may not be directly accessible through algorithms—e.g., in the case of textual attributes that contain natural language descriptions—a considerable part of meaning of business process models is thus encoded and also needs to be interpreted.

The procedure for the semantic process evaluation method is depicted in Fig. 1. The procedure starts with an initialization through setting the scope of the semantic evaluation. In this stage, it should be ascertained which results the semantic process evaluation shall yield and how this can be achieved. Subsequently, in the preparation phase, models of the business processes to be evaluated are prepared. This can be accomplished by either creating the models from scratch or by retrieving them from a model repository. Subsequently, the models can either be used as they are or enhanced through semantic annotations. These semantic annotations can be added manually if further knowledge needs to be supplied for the evaluation—e.g., if the used modeling language does not offer constructs for representing this knowledge formally. Or, the annotations can be added based on automated analyses, e.g., through natural language processing. The preparation phase is followed by the configuration phase. Based on the goals set for the semantic evaluation, the user now chooses suitable semantic evaluation patterns. In the actual evaluation phase, the chosen patterns are applied to the business process models and, if required, in conjunction with the semantic annotations. Finally, the retrieved results are interpreted by the user.

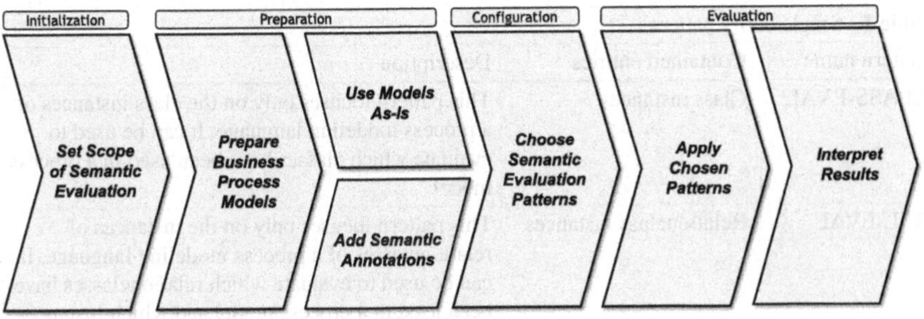

Fig. 1 Phases of the semantic process evaluation method

The semantic evaluations of process models discussed below focus on the semantics encoded by the classes, relationclasses, and attributes of a process modeling language. In particular, we will show how combinations of algorithmic and human-based analyses can lead to evaluations of the content of process models. The aim of these kinds of evaluations is to discover how the content of business process models influences the performance of the process, how implicitly encoded information can be made explicit, and how semantic information can be added to existing process models without affecting the underlying modeling language. The evaluations will be described in the form of patterns that specify which entities of a modeling language are taken into account and what results the analysis returns. This approach is similar to previous attempts for realizing semantic process analyses. For example, Baacke et al. proposed a method for using semantic process evaluation patterns by reverting to semantic web technologies [1]. However, in their approach, they rely on standardized process building blocks and their transformation to RDF triple statements. Becker et al. propose a very similar approach to analyzing weaknesses in business processes [2]. Again, a specifically designed process modeling language is used for the analysis.

2.1 Semantic Process Evaluation Patterns

The semantic process evaluation patterns described below are a first attempt to structure possible semantic process analyses. They are not intended to be complete at this stage and could be extended if required. The typical questions that shall be answered through semantic process analysis thereby comprise aspects like: how are process models structured? how do the different entities in process models connect to each other and which kind of information is exchanged between different steps in the process? or, what additional information on processes can be analyzed based on the models and through additional encoding?

Table 1 Single entity patterns

Pattern name	Contained entities	Description
CLASS-EVAL	Class instances	This pattern focuses only on the class instances of a process modeling language. It can be used to evaluate which classes have been used in a process model
REL-EVAL	Relationclass instances	This pattern focuses only on the instances of relationclasses of a process modeling language. It can be used to evaluate which relationclasses have been used in a process model and which instances of the classes the relationclasses connect
ATTR-EVAL	Attribute values	This pattern regards the attribute values attached to class, relationclass, and model instances in process models. Thereby, the types of the attributes and the attribute values can be evaluated

The patterns were divided into three groups: single entity patterns, composite patterns, and annotation patterns. Thereby, the single entity patterns comprise the most basic forms of semantic evaluations that contain only either classes, relationclasses, or attributes of a process modeling language. For achieving more complex types of semantic evaluations, the composite patterns combine one or more of the basic entities. Finally, the annotation patterns make use of semantic annotations of elements of a process modeling language to perform even more comprehensive types of evaluations.

The single entity patterns comprise three patterns—see Table 1. The *CLASS-EVAL* pattern contains only the classes defined in the modeling language. Regarding a semantic evaluation on this level, it can be assessed which classes were used in process models, which gives information about the semantic complexity of the models. For example, in the case of BPMN with a large number of classes and relationclasses it may be beneficial to restrict these for specifying process models. By means of the CLASS-EVAL pattern, we can ascertain whether such restrictions were correctly performed. Furthermore, the pattern can be used to make calculations on the quantities of class instances, e.g., to evaluate the ratio between the number of class instances for activities and tasks versus the number of class instances for events or decisions. Thus, this is how the first assessments of the complexity and semantic scope of process models can be performed.

The *REL-EVAL* pattern takes the same approach as the CLASS-EVAL pattern in the sense that it only regards one entity. In contrast with the CLASS-EVAL pattern, it is thereby focused only on instances of relationclasses defined for a modeling language. This enables the user to analyze which instances of classes are connected through which relations and also investigate the quantities of instances of a particular relationclass that exist in a model instance. Similarly to the CLASS-EVAL pattern, this pattern may be used to check whether restrictions on certain relationclasses are met, which instances of classes are connected through which relations, and give estimations on the complexity of the model instances.

The third of the single entity patterns is the *ATTR-EVAL* pattern. It focuses on the attributes and the types of attributes of class, relationclass, and model instances. Its purpose is to solely regard the attributes in business process models. This can be useful for analyzing the distribution of attribute data, for example for calculating the average execution time assigned to activities in processes or to check whether all attribute values are contained with previously defined value range constraints.

The composite patterns regard compositions of several entities. They thus allow more complex evaluations by defining dependencies between the entities (Table 2).

The *CLASS-ATTR* pattern takes into account the instances of classes and values of attributes assigned to these instances. This permits the user to analyze which attribute values have been assigned to specific class instances. For example, it may be used to investigate which instances of activity classes in process models exceed a certain threshold in their execution time. Thereby, also multiple attributes may be combined, e.g., for retrieving instances of activity classes whose execution time is longer than their waiting time. This extends of course to textual attributes where, for example, activities with particular strings in their names may be analyzed or the occurrence of textually expressed conditions may be investigated.

The *REL-ATTR* pattern regards the instances of relationclasses and their attributes. In addition to the REL-EVAL pattern, also attributes of relations can thus be analyzed. Relations in process models typically contain attributes for expressing information for transition conditions or transition probabilities. With this pattern, it can thus be checked for example where certain transition conditions occur in a process model or for calculating probabilities for different paths. As this pattern regards instances of relationclasses, the involved classes are thereby only implicitly considered, i.e., based on the constraints set for the relationclass instances in the metamodel.

With the *CLASS-REL* pattern this limitation is partially resolved. In this pattern, instances of classes and relationclasses are explicitly considered. This is particularly useful for analyzing combinations of class and relationclass instances where the involved relations may connect more than one class or where several classes and relationclasses are considered. For example, with this pattern it can be evaluated which instances of activity classes in a process model are connected to instances of certain resource, event or data classes. By combining multiple classes and relationclasses, this pattern allows very complex semantic evaluations of process models.

A further extension is given with the *CLASS-REL-ATTR* pattern. In addition to the CLASS-REL pattern, this pattern also considers attributes, allowing further restrictions to be set. For example, the user can determine which instances of activity classes in a process model are executed by a specific actor which is connected to that activity and who possesses certain skills expressed as an attribute attached to an actor class.

In some cases, the information contained in process models is not sufficient for conducting semantic analyses. It has therefore been proposed to use annotations with concepts from ontologies [6–8]. The notion of ontologies is thereby understood in a very broad sense, encompassing all levels of formalization and not restricted for example to those expressed in logic-based languages [30]. The annotations feature three core characteristics. First, they can be added to a modeling method *ex-post*,

Table 2 Composite patterns

Pattern name	Contained entities	Description
CLASS-ATTR	Class instances and attributes	This pattern focuses on class instances together with their attributes. It can be used to evaluate which attribute values are assigned to specific class instances
REL-ATTR	Relationclass instances and attributes	This pattern focuses on relationclass instances together with their attributes. It can be used to evaluate which attribute values are assigned to specific instances of relationclasses that connect class instances
CLASS-REL	Class instances and relations	This pattern focuses on instances of classes and relationclasses. It can be used to evaluate which instances of relationclasses connect which instances of classes
CLASS-REL-ATTR	Class instances, Relationclass instances, attributes	This pattern focuses on instances of classes and relationclasses, and attributes. It can be used to evaluate complex combinations of class and relationclass instances together with their attribute values

i.e., they do not have to be part of the design of a modeling method but can be added to arbitrary modeling methods after their design and deployment. Second, they are *loosely coupled* with the models to be annotated and the ontologies involved. This means that only the references from the semantic annotations to the models and the ontologies exist, so that neither the models nor the ontologies have to be altered. Third, they are specified in a *formal* way. The main advantage of this approach is that they can be processed by algorithms, thereby extending the algorithmic processing space for the annotated models similar to the way it is done today in programming, cf. [26].

The fundamental relations involved in semantic annotations of business process models are depicted in Fig. 2. Thereby, it is important to note that the references point from the semantic annotation outwards to an instance of a business process model and to an instance of ontology.

Based on these semantic annotations, we can define three further semantic process evaluation patterns—see Table 3. These comprise the *CLASS-ANNOT*, the *REL-ANNOT*, and the *ALL-ANNOT* pattern. The *CLASS-ANNOT* and the *REL-ANNOT* patterns regard instances of classes and relationclasses that are annotated with concepts from ontology. The evaluations that can be conducted with these patterns are manifold. First, the additional meaning added to the class and relationclass instances via the ontology concepts can be used to conduct semantic inferences. This can either be done manually or using machine processing depending on the level of formality

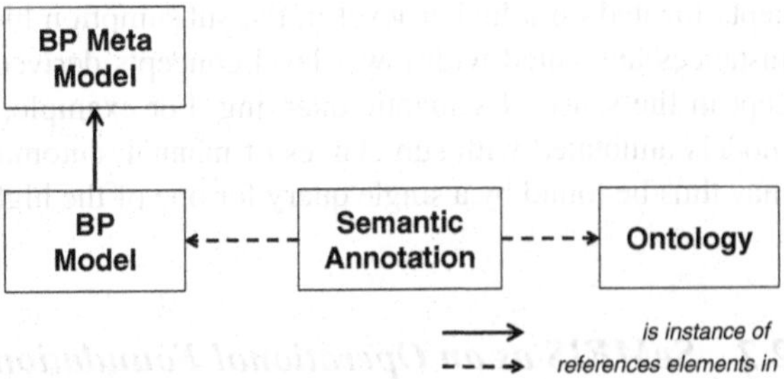

Fig. 2 Fundamental relations for semantic annotation of business process models

Table 3 Annotation patterns

Pattern name	Contained entities	Description
CLASS-ANNOT	Classes and annotations	This pattern focuses on instances of classes that have been annotated with concepts from ontology. It can be used to evaluate which class instances correspond to certain ontology concepts
REL-ANNOT	Relationclasses and annotations	This pattern focuses on instances of relationclasses that have been annnotated with concepts from ontology. It can be used to evaluate which relationclass instances correspond to certain ontology concepts
ALL-ANNOT	Classes, Relationclasses and annotations	This pattern focuses on instances of classes and relationclasses that have been annnotated with concepts from ontology. It can be used to evaluate complex annotation patterns

of the used ontology. For example, when using ontology in the common OWL format, inferences based on the subsumption hierarchy and the constraint specifications of OWL ontologies can be made. Furthermore, the use of ontologies in logic-based formats permits the application of rule-based languages to the information received through the annotations. For example, using ontologies in frames format together with rule specifications in the JESS format, the annotated class and relationclass instances may be processed using rules. This has been shown for example in [8] where parts of a business process model were annotated with concepts from a risk ontology. These annotations were then processed using rules to define the impact and probabilities of the risks during simulations of the business processes.

The third annotation pattern is the *ALL-ANNOT* pattern. It combines semantic annotations of class and relationclass instances. Complex combinations of annotations can be evaluated in this way. This pattern may be used to evaluate which labels of certain class instances have been annotated with an ontology concept embedded in a subsumption hierarchy. This permits the user to issue queries on ontology concepts located on a higher level in the subsumption hierarchy and retrieve all class instances annotated with lower-level concepts derived from this higher level concept in the sense of semantic querying. For example, activity elements in process models annotated with sub classes of manual, automatic, and semiautomatic tasks may thus be found by a single query for one of the higher level ontology concepts.

2.2 *SeMFIS as an Operational Foundation*

The semantic-based modeling framework for information systems (SeMFIS) is used as a foundation for the practical application of the semantic process evaluation patterns. SeMFIS consists of a *metamodel, mechanisms and algorithms*, and *support tools and services* and it was implemented as a *software platform* for engineering semantic annotation of conceptual models and for supporting semantic analyses on a technical level [9].

The SeMFIS metamodel, as shown in Fig. 3, contains at its core the *semantic annotation model type* which links elements of a conceptual modeling language to elements in an ontology. Semantic annotation models are composed of elements for referencing model and ontology elements and for linking them via *annotator* elements. An annotation type can be specified for these annotators to add semantic meaning to the annotation if necessary. For representing ontologies, the base con-

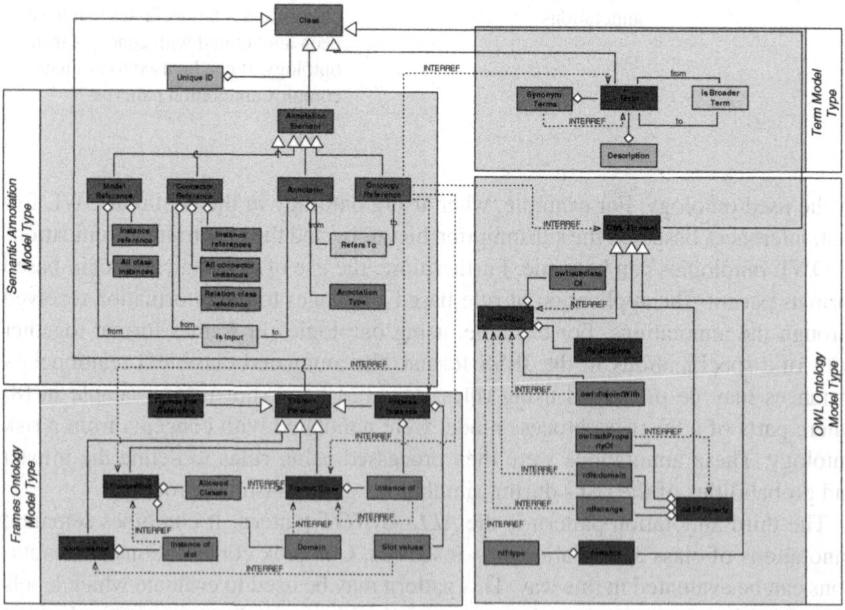

Fig. 3 SeMFIS metamodel

figuration of SeMFIS provides three model types: the *ontology model type* for representing ontologies in OWL format, the *frames ontology model type* for ontologies based on the OKBC frames format as used also in Protégé, and the *term model type* for representing controlled vocabularies.

In terms of mechanisms and algorithms SeMFIS provides in particular *import and export* mechanisms for exchanging models in XML format, a *query language* based on AQL for querying model content, and a *scripting language* based on ADOscript for interacting with the platform programmatically. Based on these mechanisms and algorithms, a variety of additional functionalities can be developed. Examples from past applications include the exchange and further processing of information from ontologies via ontology platforms and rule engines [8] or the integration in a service-oriented web architecture [15]. For supporting the interaction with ontologies, SeMFIS includes an interface to the Protégé platform via a *plugin* [12, 17]. This plugin can be added to Protégé and allows the OWL ontologies to be exported in a SeMFIS-compatible format.

The architecture of SeMFIS is based on the ADO*xx* metamodeling platform [14]. As shown in Fig. 4, the architecture is divided into a user interface layer, a layer of application components and a repository layer. The platform is designed as a Microsoft Windows application. The *modeling* component enables the user to interact with visual models and automatically generates model editors based on the SeMFIS metamodel—see Fig. 5. The *analysis* component is responsible for executing queries and the *simulation* component provides a number of simulation algorithms for simulating business processes. The *web service interface* is a SOAP endpoint that takes requests in the scripting language based on ADOscript, executes them on the platform and returns the results as SOAP messages. It thus directly supports the integration of the SeMFIS platform in web-based environments. The *XML/ADL Import/Export* component is responsible for exchanging model informa-

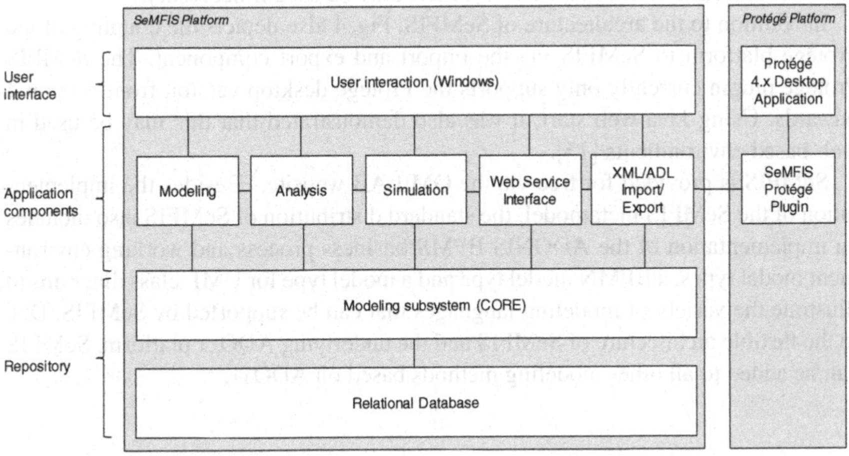

Fig. 4 SeMFIS architecture

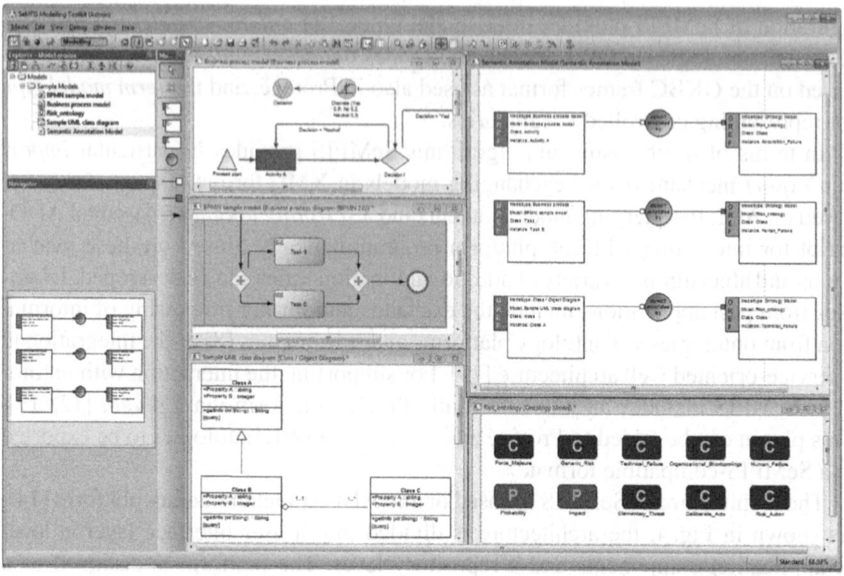

Fig. 5 Screenshot of the SeMFIS user interface showing on the far *right* an instance of a semantic annotation model and below an ontology model and next to them an instance of a model in ADONIS BPMS, BPMN, and the UML class diagram modeling language from *top* to *bottom*

tion in XML format or the proprietary ADL format. The *modeling subsystem* translates between the application components and the repository. It is also responsible for the mapping of the model and the metamodel information to the relational format. All model and metamodel information is stored in a *relational database*. For SeMFIS standard installations the relational database is an MS SQL server but also other databases such as IBM DB2 or Oracle may be used if necessary.

In addition to the architecture of SeMFIS, Fig. 4 also depicts the coupling of the Protégé platform to SeMFIS via the import and export component. The SeMFIS Protégé plugin currently only supports the Protégé desktop version from version 4 onwards. Using Java web start, it was also demonstrated that this may be used in web-based environments [15].

SeMFIS is provided for free via the OMiLAB website.[3] Besides the implementation of the SeMFIS metamodel, the standard distribution of SeMFIS also includes an implementation of the ADONIS BPMS business process and working environment model types, a BPMN model type and a model type for UML class diagrams to illustrate the variety of modeling languages that can be supported by SeMFIS. Due to the flexible architecture of SeMFIS and the underlying ADO*xx* platform, SeMFIS can be added to all other modeling methods based on ADO*xx*.

[3] http://www.omilab.org/web/semfis.

3 The Technical Development of the Method

For the technical development of the semantic process evaluation method we resorted to the standard distribution of SeMFIS. In particular, we assume the usage of the BPMN model type, the semantic annotation model type and the ontology model type for representing OWL ontologies. Based on these information structures we will illustrate below how the semantic process evaluation patterns can be developed using the SeMFIS analysis component for querying model content and the scripting functionalities for more complex evaluations.

As a basis for describing the development of the semantic process analysis we used three sample models as shown in Fig. 6. These depict a BPMN model, an OWL ontology model, and a semantic annotation model. The BPMN model shows a very simple business process for receiving a document, entering the document information in some IT system, checking the information and storing it or correcting it if the entered information is invalid. It consists of an instance of the *start event* class, four instances of the *task* class, an instance of the *exclusive gateway* class, and an instance of the *end event* class. The flow between these elements is modeled using instances of the *subsequent* relationclass. In addition, an instance of the *variable* class and an instance of the *random generator* class have been added. These are required for using the business process simulation capabilities in SeMFIS. Based on this information, transition conditions accessing the variable *Information* were added to two instances of the subsequent relationclass.

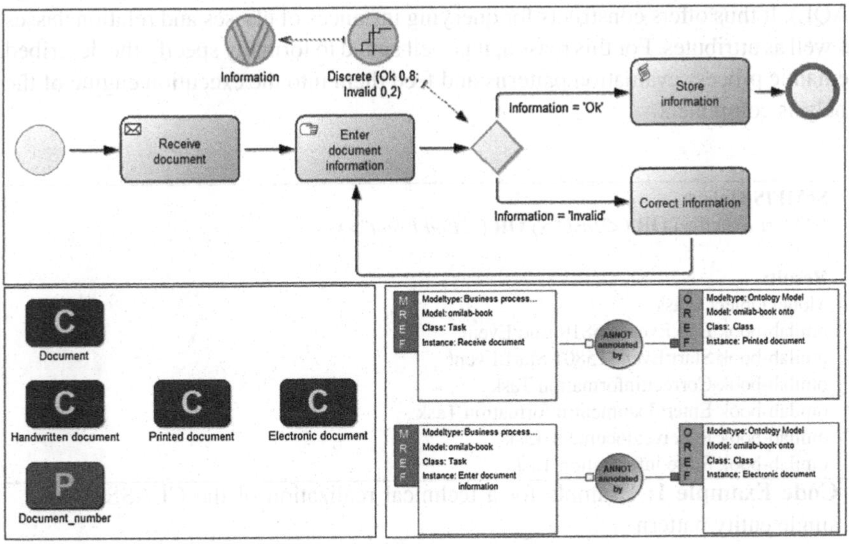

Fig. 6 Sample models for illustrating the technical realization showing a BPMN model, an OWL ontology model, and a semantic annotation model (*top* to *bottom*, *left* to *right*)

On the left side of Fig. 6, an instance of an OWL ontology model is shown. It contains four instances of the *OWL-class* class and one instance of the *property* class. The OWL classes named '*Handwritten document*,' '*Printed document,*' and '*Electronic document*' were defined as subclasses of the '*Document*' class. Because of the visualization used in SeMFIS, these relations are not shown in the graphical representation of the model. On the right side, an instance of a semantic annotation model is shown. It contains two annotations. The first annotation is composed of an instance of the *model reference* class, which is linked to the '*Receive document'* task in the BPMN model, an annotator element of type '*annotated by*', and an instance of the ontology reference class, which is linked to the '*Printed document*' OWL class in the ontology model. Similarly, a second annotation is defined and specifies a linkage between the '*Enter document information*' task in the BPMN model and the '*Electronic document*' OWL class in the ontology model.

Using these models as an example, we can now describe how the semantic process evaluation patterns can be technically developed. This will be done first using the SeMFIS analysis component and subsequently using the scripting language.

3.1 Using the Analysis Component to Develop Semantic Process Evaluation Patterns

The SeMFIS analysis component is used via a domain-specific query language. This query language conforms to the syntax and semantics of the ADO*xx* Query Language (AQL). It thus offers constructs for querying instances of classes and relationclasses as well as attributes. For this reason, it is well suited to formally specify the described semantic process evaluation patterns and feed them into the execution engine of the analysis component.

SeMFIS Query:
(<"*Start Event*">) **OR** (<"*Task*">) **OR** (<"*End Event*">)

Result:
Model Object Class
omilab-book End:Event-15810 End:Event
omilab-book Start:Event-15801 Start:Event
omilab-book Correct:information Task
omilab-book Enter:document:information Task
omilab-book Receive:document Task
omilab-book Store:information Task

Code Example 1: Example for a technical realization of the CLASS-EVAL single entity pattern

In order to make the translation of the semantic evaluation patterns into easily graspable statements in AQL, we will illustrate it using some examples. First, we consider the single entity patterns. The Code example 1, conforms to an implementation of the single entity pattern CLASS-EVAL. When executing this code via the SeMFIS analysis engine on the BPMN model shown above, it retrieves instances of the classes *Start Event*, *Task* or *End Event*. The results of the execution are shown below the query. They contain the name of the queried model, the name of the retrieved class instance and its class name. A reason for this query may be to assess all entry and exit points of a given business process including its contained tasks to get an overview of the overall nature of a process without having to deal in detail with its information and control flows. A direct example for such approaches has for example been discussed in the area of business process improvement where such simplified process structures are used for analyses, cf. [24, 25].

In the next step, we advance to the composite patterns. The Code example 2 illustrates how a CLASS-REL-ATTR pattern can be used to evaluate combinations of class, relationclass instances and attributes. The example specifies a query that searches for all instances of the class *Task* whose attribute value for the attribute *Task type* is "*Manual*" and which are connected to another instance of the class task with a task type attribute set to "*Receive*" via an instance of the relationclass *Subsequent*. The result of this query is shown below and returns a single instance of the class *Task* with the name "*Enter document information*". An interpretation of this query would be to investigate all manual tasks in a business process that immediately follow tasks that receive information or messages. This may be relevant for detecting possible areas of improvement, e.g., by finding ways how these manual tasks can be automated so that the information can be processed faster than using manual interaction.

```
SeMFIS Query:
(<"Task">)[?" Task type" = " Receive"]->" Subsequent")
 AND (<"Task">[?" Task type" = " Manual"])

Result:
Model Object Class Task:type
omilab-book Enter:document:information Task Manual
```

Code Example 2: Example for a technical realization of the CLASS-REL-ATTR composite entity pattern

The third query presented in Code example 3 is an implementation of the ALL-ANNOT annotation pattern. It is applied on the semantic annotation model shown in Fig. 6. The query performs the operations described below. First, it retrieves all instances of the class *Model reference* that have a reference to the task *Enter document information* in the BPMN model named *omilab-book*.

Subsequently, all instances that are connected to these instances via *is input for* and *Refers to* relations of the semantic annotation model are retrieved as a final result. As shown above in the code example, the query is thus able to return the names and references of the ontology concepts that have been used to annotate the given task instance in the BPMN model. It therefore enables a fundamental analysis used in semantic business process management by evaluating how concepts in business process models were semantically enriched through annotations with concepts from ontology. Based on this information, further semantic evaluations may be conducted, e.g., by taking into account the axioms used for linking the ontology concepts and thus developing a semantic search via upper-level ontology concepts that reference lower-level concepts in the subsumption hierarchy that were used for annotating concepts in business process models.

```
SeMFIS Query:
(<'Model reference">
  [?" Instance reference" = "REF mt:\" Business process diagram (BPMN 2.0)
  \"m:\" omilab-book\"c:\" Task\"i:\" Enter document information\"
  ])
  ->" is input for" -> " Refers to"

Result:
Model Object Class Ontology:reference
Semantic:Annotation:Model:-:new
  Ontology:reference-15871 Ontology:reference
  Electronic:document:(Class):-:omilab-book:onto:(Ontology:Model)
```

Code Example 3: Example of a technical development of the ALL-ANNOT annotation pattern

3.2 *Using Scripting to Develop Semantic Process Evaluation Patterns*

Although the technical methods for developing semantic evaluation patterns shown above are already capable of addressing a wide number of semantic evaluation instances, they are limited by the expressiveness of the underlying AQL constructs. For example, the current version of the AQL grammar does not offer joins or groupings as users who are familiar with SQL-like query languages may expect. However, to perform even more powerful queries that are not constrained by these limitations, the queries can be combined with the SeMFIS scripting functionalities. These functionalities enable the user to define algorithms in the SeMFIS scripting language that corresponds to the ADOscript syntax used for the ADO*xx* platform.

The code example 4 shows how the scripting language can be used to combine queries and algorithmic expressions. The sample conducts a semantic evaluation that forms the basis for analyzing the media breaks in business processes based on semantic annotations. It first retrieves the id of the used semantic annotation model in line 1. Then, the statement in line 3 gets all instances of the class *Model reference* in the semantic annotation model. This is an alternative way of using an AQL query.

```
1  CC "Core" GET_MODEL_ID modelname: "Semantic Annotation Model -
     new" modeltype: "Semantic Annotation Model"
2  SET semannot:(modelid)
3  CC "Core" GET_ALL_OBJS_OF_CLASSNAME modelid: (semannot)
     classname: "Model reference"
4  SET allmref:(objids)
5  CC "Modeling" GET_ACT_MODEL
6  SET query:"(<\"Task\">) -> \"Subsequent\" AND (<\"Task\">)"
7  CC "AQL" EVAL_AQL_EXPRESSION expr: (query) modelid: (modelid)
8  FOR o in: (objids) {
9      CC "Core" EVAL_EXPRESSION (objirsobjs(VAL objids))
       modelid: (semannot)
10     SET mref:(tokisect(result, allmref))
11     FOR q in: (mref) {
12         CC "Core" EVAL_EXPRESSION (ctobjs(VAL q, "is input for"))
           modelid: (semannot)
13         FOR a in: (result) {
14             CC "Core" EVAL_EXPRESSION (ctobjs(VAL a, "Refers
               to")) modelid: (semannot)
15             FOR on in: (result) {
16                 CC "Core" EVAL_EXPRESSION (aval(VAL
                   irtobjs(VAL on, "Ontology reference"), "Name"))
                   modelid: (semannot)
17                 CC "AdoScript" INFOBOX (result)
               }
           }
       }
   }
```

Code Example 4: Example for a technical realization of the ALL-ANNOT annotation pattern using the SeMFIS scripting language in ADOscript syntax

The active model is retrieved with the statement in line 5. For the sample it is assumed that the user has opened the BPMN model from Fig. 6. In line 6, a query in AQL syntax is composed to retrieve all BPMN *task* instances that immediately follow another *task* via the *subsequent* relation. This would be used to compare the media used for the task at hand with the media used for the preceding task. Next, in line 7, the query is executed. Subsequently, it is stepped through the retrieved objects via a *FOR* loop. For each task found, all objects referencing this task are retrieved in line 9. This is accomplished using a core expression. To retrieve only instances of the *Model reference* class in the chosen semantic annotation model, the resulting set is intersected with the previously collected model reference instances in line 10. Finally, for all model references the connected annotations are retrieved via the *is input for* and *Refers to* relations in lines 12 and 14. Each of these is processed using *FOR* loops. The identified ontology references are resolved to the referenced ontology concepts in line 16 and displayed to the user in an info box in line 17. Therefore, the user can detect where changes in media occur via the displayed semantic annotations. The example could be further extended, e.g., to automatically detect changes in annotations based on subclasses of the *Document* class in the ontology.

4 Case Study as a Proof of Concept

To show the feasibility of the proposed method and the related implementation we briefly discuss its application to a case study. The case study is positioned in the area of risk management and is provided for free on the web [11]. It describes the business process for opening a bank account and gives information for the contained activities and decisions as well as quantitative data such as execution times and decision probabilities. The goal set by the case study is to analyze the risks that occur during the execution of the business process. This shall be accomplished via a representation of the risks for the purpose of communication. Furthermore, the risks shall be made processable by algorithms in order to analyze their impact, e.g., using simulation algorithms. Therefore, a semantic evaluation of the business process regarding its associated risks is necessary.

Following the steps of the semantic process evaluation method as shown in Fig. 1, at first the scope of the semantic evaluation needs to be set. Based on the aforementioned requirements, the scope is set to the formal evaluation of risks related to tasks in business processes. In the next step, the business process models need to be prepared. For the solution presented here, we used the BPMN modeling language for representing the business process. Due to the fact that BPMN does not provide support for representing risks, it has been further chosen to use semantic annotations. This is accomplished using the semantic annotation model provided by SeMFIS together with the OWL ontology model. An ontology representing risks is specified in the OWL ontology model. This includes different categories of risks as well as data properties such as the impact of the risk and the probability of the impact. All this information can be formally represented using OWL constructs such as classes, subclass relationships and data type properties. Finally, the semantic annotation model is used to link task instances in the BPMN model to instances of risks in the OWL ontology. An excerpt of the resulting models is shown in Fig. 7. The semantic annotation shown in this figure links the task "Create a new customer profile in Bank-ERP application" to an instance of the "Technical Failure" OWL class. This OWL class in turn is a sub-class of "Generic Risk." The instance of the risk is named "ERP system overloaded" and stands for the risk that at a certain time too many request are made to the ERP system at the same time.

After the preparation of the business process model and the addition of the semantic annotations, we continue with the next step of the method by choosing suitable semantic evaluation patterns. In our case, we would like to take into account the information stored in the BPMN model as well as in the semantic annotations. Therefore, we have to select one of the annotation patterns as defined in Table 3. As we are only interested in the risks related to the tasks in the business process, it is sufficient to regard the CLASS-ANNOT pattern. We thus take into account the task instances in the BPMN model and the corresponding semantic annotations. Finally, we apply the chosen pattern to conduct the semantic evaluation. We accomplish this using a combination of queries and scripting as shown by the excerpt in Code example 5.

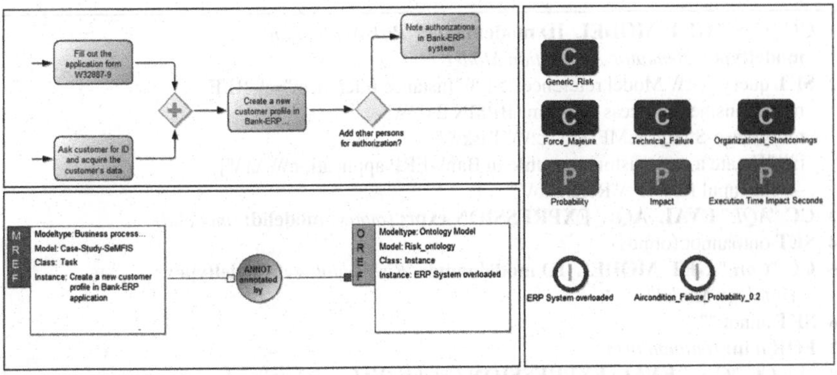

Fig. 7 Excerpt of the BPMN model, the OWL ontology model and the semantic annotation model for the case study

The goal of the shown semantic evaluation is to identify risks of technical failures associated to a given task in the BPMN model. The selected task is "Create a new customer profile in Bank-ERP application". In the query defined in line 2, we first retrieve all model references in the semantic annotation model that reference the given task. From each model reference instance the connected relations *is input for* and *Refers to* are followed to retrieve the linked ontology reference instances. These ontology references are subsequently stored in the variable *ontoannot* in line 4.

For each of the ontology reference instances, the referenced ontology concepts are retrieved and stored in the variable *annot* in lines 7 to 9. Next, all OWL instances of technical failures are retrieved from the OWL ontology model and stored in the variable *techfail* in lines 10 to 12. To retrieve all ontology instances that were used for the annotation of the respective BPMN task instance and that are of the type "Technical_Failure", the intersection between the two sets is calculated in line 13 and stored in the variable *risks*. Finally, all the names of the identified risks are presented to the user via an infobox in lines 14 to 16.

5 Conclusion

In this paper, we presented a method for conducting semantic evaluations of business processes by using the SeMFIS approach. The method is based on a six-phase model and it uses the concept of semantic evaluation patterns to choose suitable formal representation and analysis mechanisms. A particular feature of the presented approach is the use of semantic annotations of business process models. These are developed by means of the annotation approach provided by the SeMFIS, which builds upon a loosely coupled semantic annotation model that links concepts in business process models with concepts in ontologies. As shown above, the technical development of the method can be accomplished using the ADO*xx*-based SeMFIS tool. In particular, several examples for the use of the contained query and scripting functionalities

```
CC "Core" GET_MODEL_ID modelname: "Risk Annotation"
  modeltype: "Semantic Annotation Model"
SET query:"(<\\"Model reference\">[?\\"Instance reference\"= \"REF
  mt:\\\"Business process diagram (BPMN 2.0)\\\"
  m:\\\"Case-Study-SeMFIS\\\" c:\\\"Task\\\"
  i:\\\"Create a new customer profile in Bank-ERP application\\\"\n \"])
  ->\"is input for\"-> \"Refers to\""
CC "AQL" EVAL_AQL_EXPRESSION expr: (query) modelid: (modelid)
SET ontoannot:(objids)
CC "Core" GET_MODEL_ID modelname: "Risk_ontology" modeltype:
  "Ontology Model"
SET annot:""
FOR a in: (ontoannot) {
  | CC "Core" EVAL_EXPRESSION (irtobjs (VAL a, "Ontology
  |   reference" )) modelid: (modelid)
  | SET annot:(tokunion(annot, result))
}
SET query:"(<\"Instance\">[?\"Type\"= \"REF mt:\\\"Ontology Model\\\"
  m:\\\"Risk_ontology\\\" c:\\\"Class\\\" i:\\\"Technical_Failure\\\"\n \"])"
CC "AQL" EVAL_AQL_EXPRESSION expr: (query) modelid: (modelid)
SET techfail:(objids)
SET risks:(tokisect(annot, techfail))
FOR r in: (risks) {
  | CC "Core" GET_ATTR_VAL objid: (VAL r) attrname: "Name"
  | CC "AdoScript" INFOBOX (val)
}
```

Code Example 5: Sample code for the application of the CLASS-ANNOT pattern for identifying risks in a BPMN model via semantic annotations

were given. Finally, the concepts were applied to a case study in the area of risk management. Further research will be focused on extending the approach of SeMFIS by integrating additional semantic technologies. Potential candidates that are currently being evaluated include the use of natural language processing techniques [3] and information from social networks [10] for enhancing user experience and optimizing the process of creating and evaluating semantic annotations, in order to further improve the semantic evaluation patterns.

Tool Download http://www.omilab.org/semfis.

References

1. Baacke, L., Fitterer, R., Rohner, P., Stroh, F.: Using semantically annotated models for pattern-based process analysis. Arbeitsberichte des Instituts für Wirtschaftsinformatik der Universitaet St. Gallen, BE IWI/HNE/03 (2010)
2. Becker, J., Bergener, P., Raeckers, M., Weiss, B., Winkelmann, A.: Pattern-Based semi-automatic analysis of weaknesses in semantic business process models in the banking sector. In: ECIS'2010. AIS (2010)

3. Bergner, M.: Integrating natural language processing with semantic-based modeling. Master's thesis, University of Vienna (2015)
4. Bork, D., Fill, H.G.: Formal aspects of enterprise modeling methods: a comparison framework. In: Proceedings of the 2014 47th International Conference on System Sciences. IEEE (2014)
5. Fill, H.G.: Design of semantic information systems using a model-based approach. In: AAAI Spring Symposium. AAAI (2009)
6. Fill, H.G.: On the conceptualization of a modeling language for semantic model annotations. In: LNBIP, vol. 83, pp. 134–148. Springer, London, UK (2011)
7. Fill, H.G.: Using semantically annotated models for supporting business process benchmarking. In: Grabis, J., Kirikova, M. (eds.) 10th International Conference on Perspectives in Business Informatics Research. LNBIP, vol. 90, pp. 29–43. Springer (2011)
8. Fill, H.G.: An approach for analyzing the effects of risks on business processes using semantic annotations. In: European Conference on Information Systems 2012. AIS (2012)
9. Fill, H.G.: SeMFIS: a tool for managing semantic conceptual models. In: Kern, H., Tolvanen, J.P., Bottoni, P. (eds.) Workshop on Graphical Modeling Language Development (2012)
10. Fill, H.G.: On the social network based semantic annotation of conceptual models. In: Buchmann, R., Kifor, C., Yu, J. (eds.) 7th International Conference on Knowledge Science, Engineering and Management, pp. 138–149. Springer (2014)
11. Fill, H.G.: Enabling risk analysis in conceptual models by using semantic annotations - case study for semantic-based modeling (2015). http://homepage.dke.univie.ac.at/fill/semfis/SeMFIS_Case_Study.pdf. Accessed 21 Aug 2015
12. Fill, H.G., Burzynski, P.: Integrating ontology models and conceptual models using a meta modeling approach. In: 11th International Protégé Conference (2009)
13. Fill, H.G., Hickl, S., Karagiannis, D., Oberweis, A., Schoknecht, A.: A formal specification of the horus modeling language using FDMM. In: International Conference on Business Informatics 2013. AIS (2013)
14. Fill, H.G., Karagiannis, D.: On the conceptualisation of modelling methods using the ADOxx meta modelling platform. Enterp. Model. Inf. Syst. Architect. **8**(1), 4–25 (2013)
15. Fill, H.G., Schremser, D., Karagiannis, D.: A generic approach for the semantic annotation of conceptual models using a service-oriented architecture. Int. J. Knowl. Manage. **9**(1), 76–88 (2013)
16. Fraser, M., Kumar, K., Vaishnavi, V.: Strategies for incorporating formal specifications in software development. Commun. ACM **37**(10), 74–86 (1994)
17. Gennari, J., Musen, M.A., Fergerson, R., Grosso, W., Crubezy, M., Eriksson, H., Noy, N., Tu, S.: The evolution of protege: an environment for knowledge-based systems development. Int. J. Hum Comput Stud. **58**, 89–123 (2003)
18. Giaglis, G.: A taxonomy of business process modeling and information systems modeling techniques. Int. J. Flex. Manuf. Syst. (2001)
19. Harel, D., Rumpe, B.: Modeling languages: syntax, semantics and all that stuff—part i: the basic stuff. Technical report MCS00-16, The Weizmann Institute of Science (2000)
20. Harmon, P., Wolf, C.: The state of business process management 2014. BP Trends Report, p. 54 (2014)
21. Herbst, J., Junginger, S., Kühn, H.: Simulation in financial services with the business process management system ADONIS. Society for Computer Simulation (1997)
22. Herbst, J., Karagiannis, D.: Integrating machine learning and workflow management to support acquisition and adaptation of workflow models. In: Proceedings of the 9th International Workshop on Database and Expert Systems Applications, pp. 745–752. IEEE (1998)
23. Höferer, P.: Achieving business process model interoperability using metamodels and ontologies. In: Oesterle, H., Schelp, J., Winter, R. (eds.) 15th European Conference on Information Systems (ECIS2007), pp. 1620–1631. University of St. Gallen (2007)
24. Johannsen, F., Fill, H.G.: Codification of knowledge in business process improvement projects. In: European Conference on Information Systems (ECIS'2014). AIS (2014)
25. Johannsen, F., Fill, H.G.: Supporting Knowledge elicitation and analysis for business process improvement through a modeling tool. In: International Conference on Business Informatics 2015. AIS (2015)

26. Krahn, H., Rumpe, B.: Towards enabling architectural refactorings through source code annotations. In: Mayr, H., Breu, R. (eds.) Modellierung 2006, vol. 82, pp. 203–212. GI-LNI (2006)
27. List, B., Korherr, B.: An Evaluation of Conceptual Business Process Modelling Languages. ACM, Dijon, France (2006)
28. Mylopoulos, J.: Conceptual Modeling and Telos, pp. 49–68. Wiley (1992)
29. Oberweis, A., Sander, P.: Information system behavior specification by high level Petri nets. ACM Trans. Inf. Syst. **14**(4), 380–420 (1996)
30. Obrst, L.: Ontologies for semantically interoperable systems. In: Proceedings of the 12th International Conference on Information and Knowledge Management. ACM Press (2003)
31. Pedrinaci, C., Domingue, J.: Ontology-Based metrics computation for business process analysis. In: Hepp, M., Hinkelmann, K., Stojanovic, N. (eds.) 4th International Workshop on Semantic Business Process Management (SBPM2009). ACM (2009)
32. Schütte, R., Becker, J.: Subjektivitätsmanagement bei Informationsmodellen (German: Management of subjectivity for information models). In: Pohl, K., Schürr, A., Vossen, G. (eds.) Modellierung 98, vol. 9. GI-Workshop (1998)

Business Process Feature Model: An Approach to Deal with Variability of Business Processes

Riccardo Cognini, Flavio Corradini, Andrea Polini and Barbara Re

Abstract In order to help organizations in providing similar services without the need to structure each of them separately, this chapter presents a modeling notation that supports variability for Business Process modeling. Variability is particularly relevant for Public Administration institutions where different offices organize the provisioning of services to citizens following similar rules, and adapting them to the characteristics of the different offices. The notation and the approach are inspired to feature modeling techniques, whereas in this case features are used to represent activities of a process family that can be differently implemented and connected. The proposed approach facilitates the development of a partially specified process model in terms of a set of fragments that in a subsequent step can be connected in order to fully specify the desired control flow. The notation and the approach were implemented on the the ADO*xx* platform.

Keywords Feature model · Variability · Business processes · Modeling environment

1 Introduction

In the context of BP modeling, variability refers to the ability of expressing and deriving different Business Process (BP) variants from a configurable BP model [14]. This is a generic model integrating all the possible BP variations eliminat-

R. Cognini (✉) · F. Corradini · A. Polini · B. Re
Computer Science Department, University of Camerino,
62032 Camerino, MC, Italy
e-mail: riccardo.cognini@unicam.it

F. Corradini
e-mail: flavio.corradini@unicam.it

A. Polini
e-mail: andrea.polini@unicam.it

B. Re
e-mail: barbara.re@unicam.it

D. Karagiannis et al. (eds.), *Domain-Specific Conceptual Modeling*,
DOI 10.1007/978-3-319-39417-6_8

ing model redundancies by representing variants commonalities only once [4]. Furthermore, given the possibility to explicitly express variability, the approach fosters model reuse increasing the number of possible target organizations for the model. Given a configurable BP model, particularly relevant are the steps used to derive the BP variants through the configuration of the generic model. Individualization (selection) is the activity performed in order to derive a specific BP variant from the configurable BP model. Finally, each supported BP variant acts as a blueprint for a set of BP instances that can be executed. This means that a configurable BP model guides the users to a solution that better fits a specific working context [13].

The possibility of representing variation of BPs is particularly relevant for Public Administrations. In fact, at a certain level of abstraction, and with respect to a specific process, all the departments of a PA share the same abstract process. Nevertheless for concrete situations, the process models differ because of specific department characteristics. For instance, it is possible that in a big municipality different activities related to a residence move request are carried out by different offices, while in a small municipality they are carried out within a single office.

In this chapter, we present the Business Process Feature Model (BPFM) notation that combines concepts coming both from feature modeling and from BP modeling. Feature modeling is an approach which emerged in the context of Software Product Lines (SPL) to support the development of a product family from a common platform. Through the definition of a single configurable model, representing the family, it aims at lowering both production costs and time in the development of single products, that overall share some common characteristic while differ on others, for instance to serve different markets [12]. A Feature Model (FM) is a graphical model that using a tree representation permits to express different relationships among features, and in which the root of the tree represents the generic product (the family).

We extend the notion of product family to BP family, which is a set of related business processes. The BPFM notation is an extension of Feature Models incorporating aspects of BP, enabling the user to represent: activity building blocks, such as atomic task and complex sub-process from which BP models can be composed (functional perspective); the dynamic behavior of an executable BP model (behavioral perspective); data objects involved in the BP (information perspective) and details related to the implementation of the BP activities (operational perspective). The main contributions of the notation can be referred to the mentioned perspectives. With respect to the behavioral perspective, the notation includes new constraints that differentiate between the static inclusion and the dynamic occurrence of an activity. With reference to the information perspective, the notation supports the part-of relation in data object modeling, while some data objects are primitives, others can be decomposed into more fine-grained objects. Finally, if the operational perspective is considered, the approach enables the specification of different possible types of activities.

A BPFM model collects all the possible BP variants in a BP family, and via a configuration step it is possible to derive the most suitable one for the specific organization. Then, using a set of mapping rules the BP manager can derive a set of BP fragments. Fragments can be further enriched with control flow information considering specific characteristics of the organization. This “two stage” procedure seems particularly suitable in a context in which all variability dimensions cannot be fully defined a priori. This is the case for instance of organizational aspects that can impact on the structure of a BP to be deployed, and for which variability aspects cannot be easily enumerated a priori.

Using the ADO*xx* development platform we implemented a modeling environment supporting the usage of the BPFM notation and variants configuration.

The paper is organized as follows. Section 2 reports the description of the method, while Sect. 3 discusses the method conceptualization. Section 4 introduces the modeling environment describing the tool developed for the purpose, and the validation scenario. Finally, Sect. 5 reports the conclusions.

2 Method Description

In order to describe variable BPs, several approaches have been proposed in the literature, in some cases, extending already available notations with the possibility to express variability aspects. Relevant examples are certainly languages such as C-EPC [15], Configurable integrated EPC (C-iEPC) [8], vBPMN [2] or C-YAWL [5]. Language-independent approaches have also been proposed. Among others, PROVOP [7] and PESOA [16] are probably the most used ones.

Such modeling languages enable the user to derive variants for which the control flow is fully determined. The configurable model includes all the possible control flow relations and a subset of them are included in a derived variant. These approaches cannot be easily applied when the characteristics to consider in order to derive the variant are not known a priori. For instance, this is the case when they depend on specific characteristics of the organization in which the BP will be finally deployed. On the contrary, our approach enables the user to derive variants for which the flow can be further refined after a configuration step, thus allowing the user to take into account information, which is dependent from the deployment context.

For a further discussion on the need to introduce BP variability in PA, see also [6, 9]. They do not consider the variability at the level of organization structure and they assume to have a fully structured control flow at the level of the configurable BP model, which cannot be easily defined. Moreover, these works use the C-YAWL approach which does not allow the representation of input–output data objects.

Alternative approaches are those based on the declarative paradigm such as CMMN [10] and Declare [11]. In contrast to our proposal, such approaches do not intend to provide variants with a fully specified control flow, and they typically defer the definition of a precise order between the activities until their execution. Therefore, they are mainly meant to support knowledge-intensive processes.

Inputs of the BPFM approach are regulatory frameworks, as well as available reference manuals related to the provision of a service. The output instead is a BP variant that can be deployed according to the characteristics of the service under analysis, and the organizational model of the PA delivering the service. The proposed approach is structured on four main steps (Fig. 1).

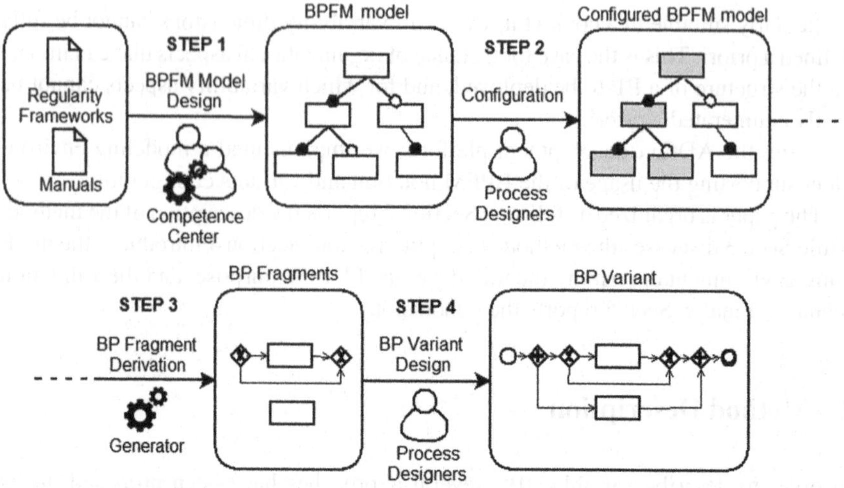

Fig. 1 Steps of the BPFM approach

- **BPFM model design**—The first step aims at manually defining a configurable BP model using the BPFM notation presented in Sect. 3. At this level, a BPFM model may be used to directly express variability aspects related to functional, information, behavioral and operational perspectives. This step includes knowledge acquisition through the study of legal and regulatory frameworks governing the delivery of the service under study. A focus group or a competence centre, including domain experts, BP designers and domain experts, performs the step for each service only once, and for all the offices of the organization that will successively deploy the BP.
- **Configuration**—The second step foresees the definition of a BPFM configuration according to a specific organization. The configuration may be used to define which activities and data objects need to be included in the BP variant. Configuration is defined respecting the activities constraints specified in the BPFM model, and it is guided by include/exclude relationships. This step is typically done manually involving BP designers working in the specific office.
- **BP Fragments Derivation**—The third step takes as input the BPFM configuration defined in the previous step, and then, through the application of the predefined mapping rules presented in Sect. 3, automatically derives BP fragments representing portions of the behavior, to be composed to fully deliver the service under analysis.
- **BP Variant Design**—The last step concerns the derivation of the fully specified BP variant(s) starting from the generated BP fragments, and according to a more detailed view on the organization perspective. At this stage, BP designers compose fragments manually adding sequence flow, parallel execution constraints, events and organization details (swimlanes) among the generated BP fragments, in order to derive a fully specified BP variant. It is worth mentioning that the same fragment (and activity) could be associated to different roles in different BP variants.

3 Method Conceptualization

3.1 BPFM Notation and the Related Metamodel

A BPFM model is constituted by a set of activities organized in a tree, where the root identifies the BP family that is described. Going up and down on the tree, BPFM introduces different levels of detail in the BP specification. In particular, each internal (non-leaf) activity denotes a sub-process, whereas the leaves represent atomic activities (tasks). In order to better specify operational details, the BPFM enables the user to specify atomic activities using the same meaning and symbols used by BPMN 2.0 for the task type. Connections between activities at different levels of the tree are called constraints (such as in standard FM). Constraints may be used to represent variability in two dimensions, (i) if each child activity must be inserted in each BP variant (it means the activity is selected in the configuration phase) and, in the case the activity is inserted, (ii) if it must or can be executed at run-time. This is how both the static and dynamic (execution-time) inclusion of activities can be specified. Constraints can be binary or multiple depending on the number of child activities connected to a parent activity, they also specify a partial execution order of the activities. BPFM binary constraints are reported in the following:

- A *Mandatory Constraint* requires that the connected child activity must be inserted in each BP variant, and it has also to be included in each execution path (Fig. 2a).
- A *Optional Constraint* specifies that the connected child activity can be inserted (or not) in each BP variant, and when included it is not necessary to include it in each execution path (Fig. 2c).
- A *Domain Constraint* requires that the connected child activity must be inserted in each BP variant but it is not necessary to include it in each execution path (Fig. 2b).
- A *Special Case Constraint* specifies that the connected child activity can be inserted (or not) in each BP variant. Nevertheless, if selected, it has to be included in each execution path (Fig. 2d).

The following one is the list of multiple BPFM constraints.

- An *Inclusive Constraint* requires that at least one of the connected child activities must be inserted in each BP variant, and at least one of them has to be included in each execution path (Fig. 2e).

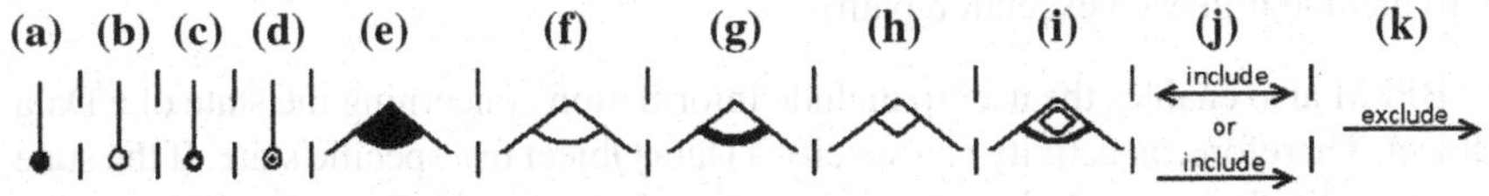

Fig. 2 BPFM constraints

- A *One Optional Constraint* requires that exactly one of the connected child activities has to be inserted in each BP variant, and it is not necessary to include it in each execution path (Fig. 2f).
- A *One Selection Constraint* specifies that exactly one of the connected child activities has to be inserted in each BP variant, moreover it has to be included in each execution path (Fig. 2g).
- An *XOR Constraint* requires that all connected child activities must be inserted in each BP variant, and exactly one of them has to be included in each execution path (Fig. 2h).
- An *XOR Selection Constraint* requires that at least one of the connected child activities has to be inserted in each BP variant, and exactly one of them has to be included in each execution path (Fig. 2i).

Finally, as in "traditional" Feature Model, it is possible to specify *Include* and *Exclude* relationships between activities (Fig. 2j, k).

The BPFM notation gives also the possibility to model Data Objects since each BP variant could include completely different sets of Data Objects. BPFM manages all types of Data Objects introduced by BPMN 2.0, and it uses the same graphical representation. As in BPMN 2.0, Data Objects can be connected as inputs and outputs to one or more activities. To successively execute an activity all the input Data Objects must be available, and as soon as all the output Data Objects are generated the activity can be terminated [1]. A Data Object inherits the characteristics and constraints of the activities to which they are connected. For instance, referring to the BPFM model in Fig. 3a, we can represent the following scenario:

- Data Input X and Data Store Y are optional in terms of their presence in a variant. Moreover, when included in a variant, they may not be instantiated since they are input/output to Activity 1 that is connected to the parent node with an *Optional Constraint* (i.e., the activity can be inserted (or not) in each BP variant and it is not necessary to include it in each execution path).
- Data Object Z is mandatory both in term of presence in a variant and their instantiation at execution time since it is provided as input to Activity 2 that is connected to the parent node with a *Mandatory Constraint* (i.e., the activity must be inserted in each BP variant, and it has also to be included in each execution path).
- Data Object Collection A and Data Output B are mandatory in terms of their presence in a variant, although they will not be necessarily instantiated since they are related to Activity 3 that is connected to the parent node using a *Domain Constraint* (i.e., the activity must be inserted in each BP variant but it is not necessary to include it in each execution path).

BPFM also enables the user to include information concerning the state of a Data Object. Therefore, an activity can specify a Data Object in a specific state. If the state is not explicitly reported, the activity is state independent. A Data Object cannot be in two different states at the same time (Fig. 3b). In case two different states of the same Data Object are indicated as input to the same activity, the modeler will have to manually select just one of them.

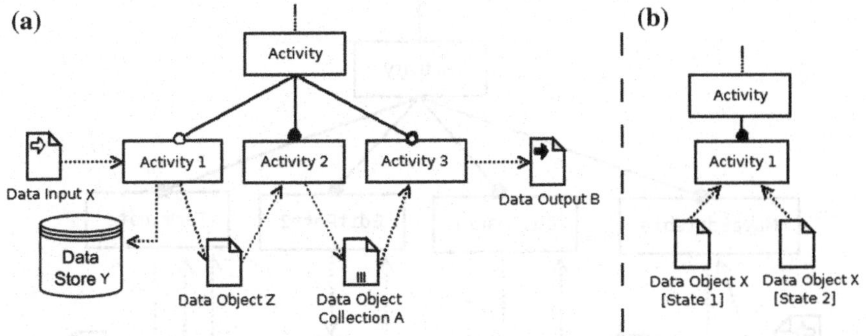

Fig. 3 Data object in BPFM

Finally, BPFM supports the notion of composite and *Part-of* Data Objects that can be used for each type of BPMN 2.0 Data Objects. The possibility of using this characterization for data objects is particularly useful to represent data in BP related to PA domain where documents are generally quite complex and can be decomposed in simpler parts.

- A composed Data Object includes a set of specific block of data, and it is marked with the letter *C*.
- A *Part-of* Data Object is contained in a specific block of data, and it is marked with the letter *P*. It also explicitly refers to the Data Object of which it is part, reporting the name of it inside curly brackets.

Figure 4 reports a simple example where a Data Object named *Composed DO* is composed by two parts *Part1* and *Part2*. The notion of *Part-of* gives the possibility to manage separately the data object parts, such as the filling of different section of the same document.

The *Part-of* notion can also be extended to the state of a Data Object. Nevertheless the state of a composed Data Object cannot be directly deduced from the state of the parts composing it. For instance, Fig. 5 shows that the Data Object *Document* is composed of *Part 1* and *Part 2* that result as output of filling activities. As soon as the filling activities are fulfilled, the state of *Document* is changed in *Filled*, then its state can change again in *Sent* without impacts on the states of *Part 1* and *Part 2*.

Considering the BPFM elements and their relations, we designed the BPFM metamodel (Fig. 6). *Activity* represents atomic or composed tasks. *Constraint* expresses the relationships between activities. Constraints can be *Binary Constraint* or *Multiple Constraint*. Then *Binary Constraint* is further specialized in four sub-classes that are *Mandatory*, *Optional*, *Domain* and *Special Case*. *Multiple Constraint* is specialized in five sub-classes that are *XOR Selection*, *XOR*, *Inclusive*, *Alternative* and *One Optional*. *Data Object* introduces input output data for activities they can be specialized in three sub-classes, they are *Data Input*, *Data Output* and *Data Store*. *Data Object Connector* representing the relationships between activity and Data Object that can be *Input Data Object Connector* or *Output Data Object Connector*.

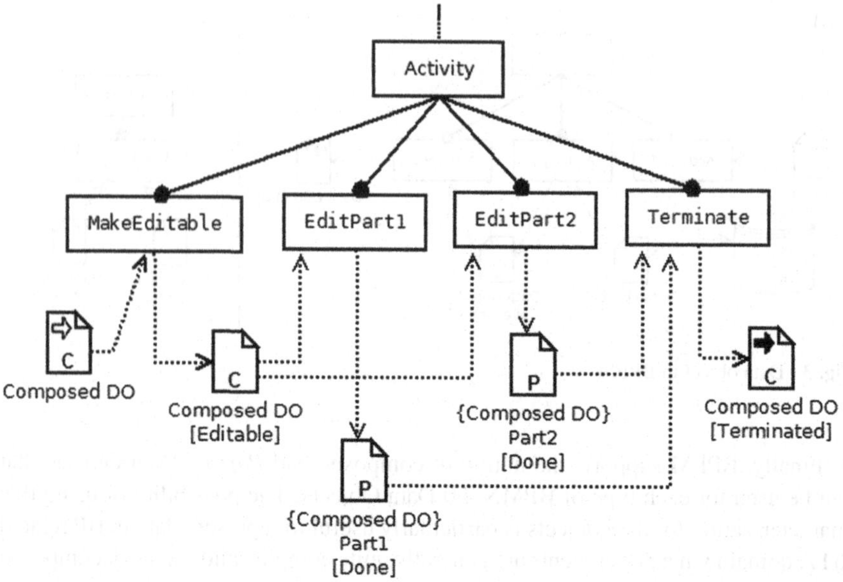

Fig. 4 Composed data object in BPFM

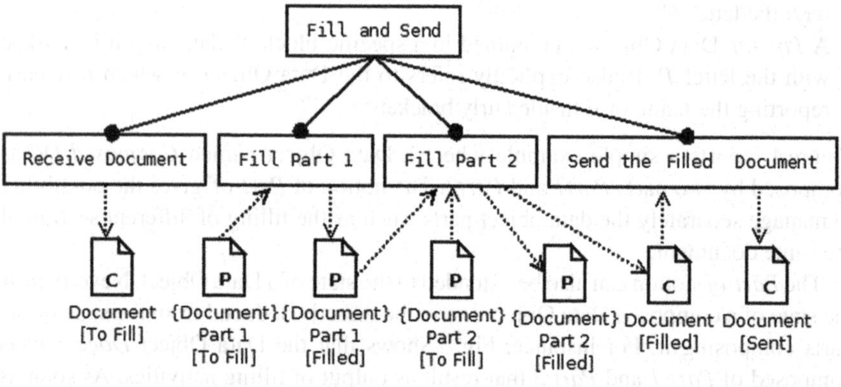

Fig. 5 Composed data object and states

Activity can be specified using the attribute *type* that can have the following values: standard, service, send, receive, manual, user, script, or business rules. These values come from BPMN task types. Relationships between an *Activity* and *Constraint*, and vice versa, are exclusively characterized as binary, or multiple. Regarding the constraints, each activity can take as input zero or one binary constraint or one multiple constraint. There is one special activity, named root, which has zero input constraints. In output, the activity can have zero or more binary constraints, or one multiple constraint. Relationship between activities can also be expressed

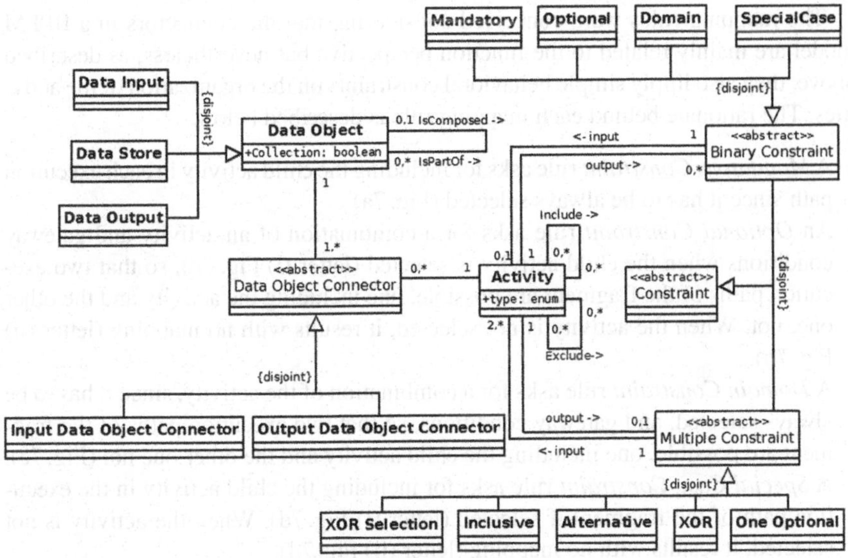

Fig. 6 Business process feature model metamodel

via *Include* or *Exclude* relationship. Each *Activity* can include/exclude zero or more *Activities*. From the other side, each *Activity* can be included/excluded by zero or more *Activity*.

Regarding *Data Object* the attribute *Collection* specifies if the *Data Object* is a collection or not. *Data Object* has a self-relationship to represent the notion of composition. Each *Data Object* can be part of zero or one Data Object. On the other side each *Data Object* can be composed of zero or more parts. Focusing on the *Data Object* relationship with *Data Object Connector*, each *Data Object* must be connected to at least one *Data Object Connector*. For each *Data Object Connector* there is just one connected *Data Object*. Finally, *Data Object Connector* must be connected to an *Activity*, and an *Activity* can be in relationship to zero or more *Data Object Connector*.

3.2 Deriving BP Fragments and BP Variants

As soon as the BPFM model is designed, it is possible to define a configuration of the model in order to derive a BP variant (step 2 of the approach). The BPFM model is configured selecting the activities to include (represented in grey in the following figures). A set of fragments is obtained (step 3 of the approach) from the configuration. The generation phase takes the root of the tree and maps it as a BP variant model, and then applies the defined rules from the first level to the leaves according to the configuration and the rules of the various constraints.

The mapping rules were conceived considering that the connectors in a BPFM model are mainly related to the function perspective but nevertheless, as described above, they also imply simple behavioral constraints on the organization of the activities. The rationale behind each mapping rule is described below.

- A *Mandatory Constraint* rule asks for including the child activity in each execution path since it has to be always selected (Fig. 7a).
- An *Optional Constraint* rule asks for a combination of an activity and gateway conditions when the child activity is selected (letter (i) Fig. 7b), so that two execution paths of the fragment are possible, one including the activity and the other one, not. When the activity is not selected, it results with no mapping (letter (ii) Fig. 7b).
- A *Domain Constraint* rule asks for a combination of the activity, since it has to be always selected, and gateway conditions, so that two execution paths of the fragment are possible, one including the child activity and the other one not (Fig. 7c).
- A *Special Case Constraint* rule asks for including the child activity in the execution path of the fragment if selected (letter (i) Fig. 7d). When the activity is not selected, it results with no mapping (letter (ii) Fig. 7d).
- A *Inclusive Constraint* rule asks for a combination of the selected child activities and inclusive gateway conditions with a default path, so that multiple paths in the fragment are supported. In case only one activity is selected, it is mapped as an activity in the execution path of the fragment (letter (i) Fig. 9e), otherwise if two (letter (ii) Fig. 9e) or more activities are selected, all of them are included in the fragment. Finally, all the activities in the BPFM may be selected (letter (iii) Fig. 9e). Then all of them are included in the fragment.
- A *One Optional Constraint* rule asks for a combination of an activity and gateway condition. When the child activity is selected (assuming that exactly one activity has to be selected), then two execution paths of the fragment are possible one including the activity and the other one not (Fig. 8f).
- A *One Selection Constraint* rule asks for including the selected activity in the execution path of the fragment, since at least one child activity has to be selected (Fig. 8g).
- An *XOR Constraint* rule asks for a combination of the selected child activities and exclusive gateway conditions, so that alternative paths are supported in the execution path of the fragment (Fig. 8h).
- An *XOR Selection Constraint* rule asks for a combination of the selected activities and exclusive gateway conditions, so that alternative paths are supported; in case only one child activity is selected, the rule asks for an activity in the execution path of the fragment (letter (i) Fig. 9i). Otherwise, if two (letter (ii) Fig. 9i) or more activities are selected, all of them are included in the fragment. Finally, it could be possible that all the activities in the BPFM are selected (letter (iii) Fig. 9i), then all of them are included in the fragment.

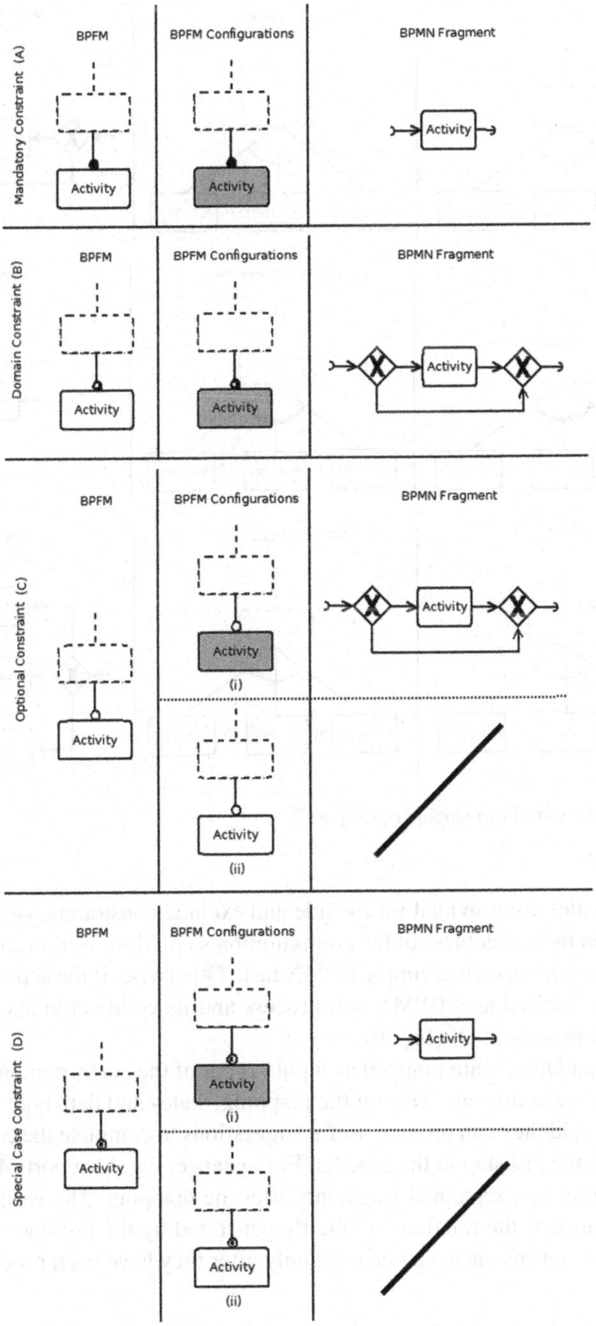

Fig. 7 Binary constraints mapping rules

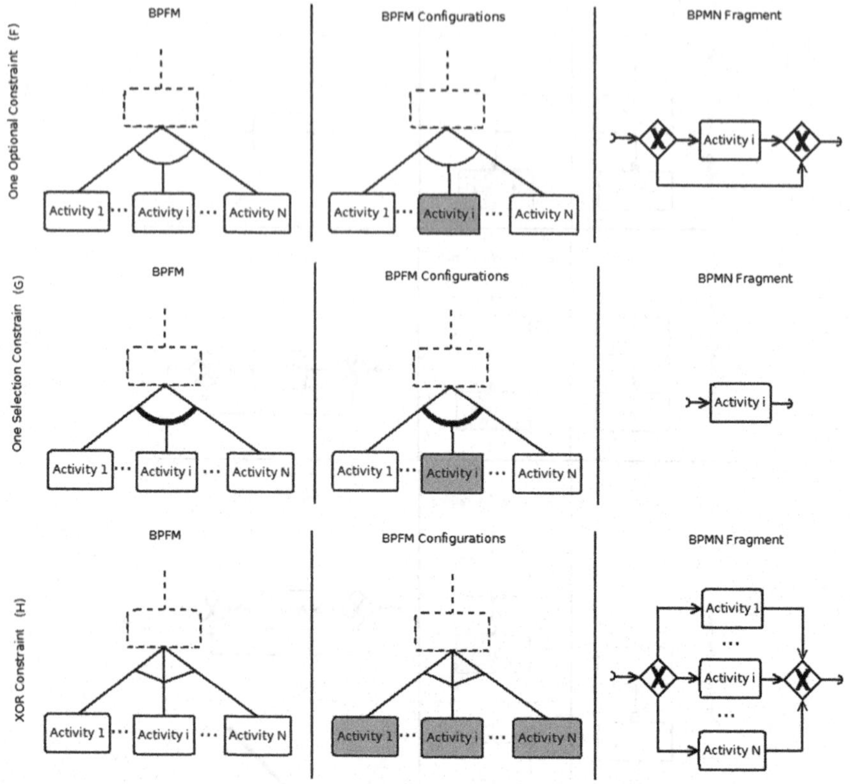

Fig. 8 Multiple constraints mapping rules (part I)

No mapping rules are provided for include and exclude constraints, since they only have impact on the correctness of the configuration step. Moreover, in case the activity is atomic, it is mapped to a simple BPMN task. Otherwise, if the activity is a complex one, it is mapped as a BPMN sub-process and its child activities are mapped inside the sub-process itself (Fig. 10).

Finally, Data Objects are mapped as input/output of the corresponding activities, be they atomic or composite. During the mapping, states and data type information are preserved, and they can provide useful suggestions to complete the configuration as foreseen by the last step in the process. For instance, Fig. 11 reports 4 mandatory activities leading to 4 separated fragments after the mapping. The variant designer then has to consider the relations implicitly generated by the presence of the Data Objects, which, for instance, can be used only after they have been produced.

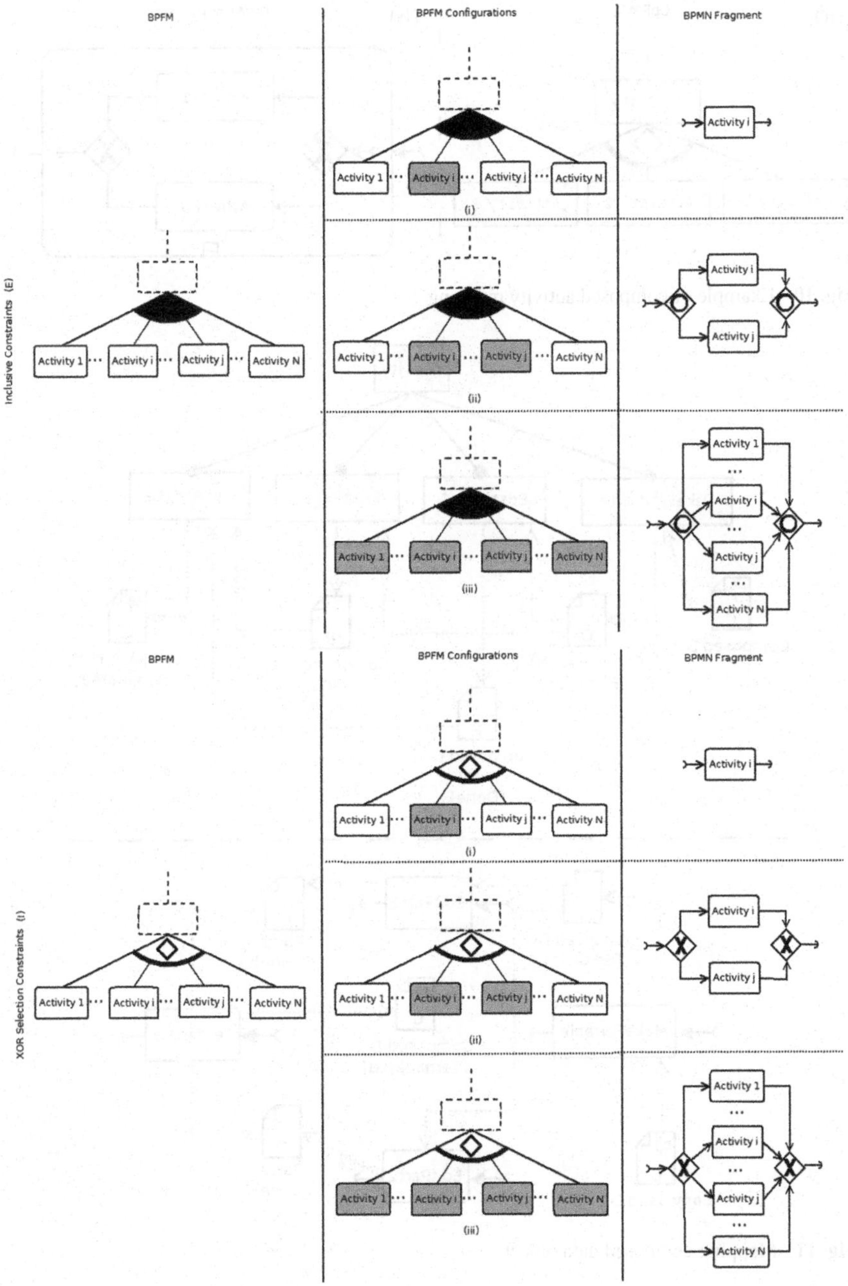

Fig. 9 Multiple constraints mapping rules (part II)

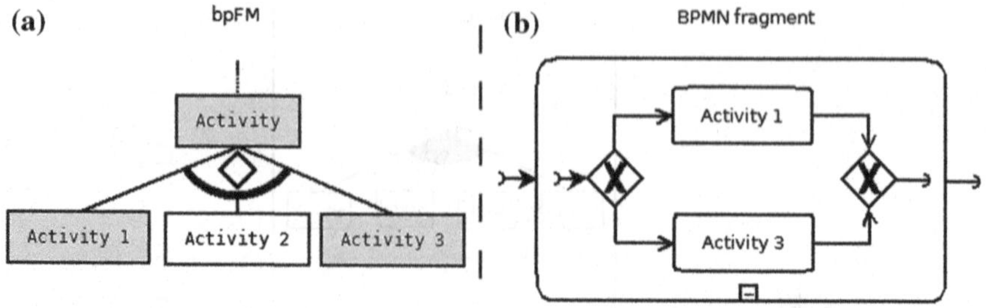

Fig. 10 Example of composed activity mapping

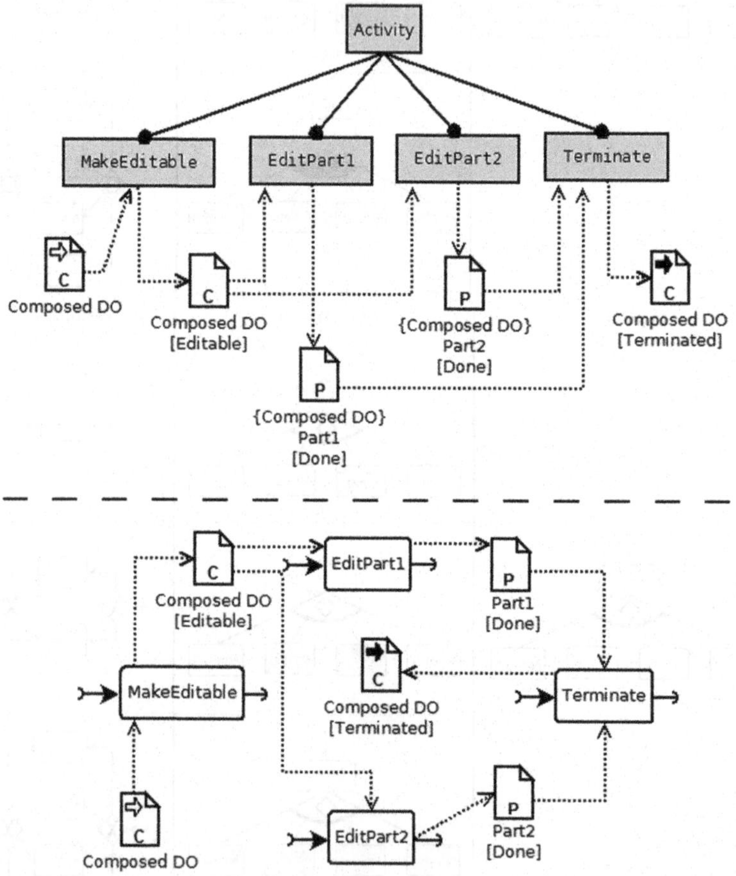

Fig. 11 Mapping composed data object

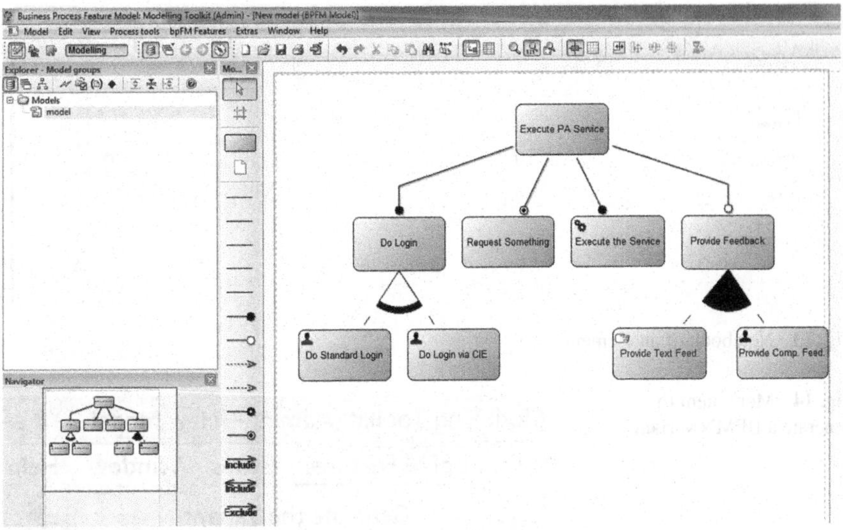

Fig. 12 A BPFM model created via the BPFM tool

4 Proof of Concept

The BPFM notation and approach are supported by a modeling environment that can be freely downloaded from the BPFM web page.[1] The tool was developed using the ADO*xx* platform[2] [3]. The BPFM tool implementation and its functionalities are presented below via a case study.

4.1 BPFM Tool Implementation

To derive the implementation, we started from the already available BPMN 2.0 library and created all the BPFM elements and constraints, as well as the BPFM model-type including all the BPFM elements. Finally, we implemented the mapping rules so that BP designers could directly generate BPMN 2.0 models starting from a configured BPFM model.

The BPFM Modeling Environment is the result of the ADO*xx* validation step (Fig. 12). The user interface is composed of four windows, (1) the models explorer in which models are listed, (2) the palette in which all the notation elements are available, (3) the editing window in which elements can be added in order to create BPFM models and (4) the navigator showing the active part of the editing window.

[1]http://www.omilab.org/web/bpfm.
[2]http://www.adoxx.org.

Fig. 13 Notebook of an element

Fig. 14 Menu item to generate a BPMN variant

In order to generate a BP variant, the modeler has to manually configure the created BPFM model. To do that, the modeler has to double-click on the activities he/she wants to include in the configuration in order to open the notebook of the element. In the notebook, he/she has to look for the attribute *Selection* and choose the *Selected* value (Fig. 13).

When the configuration is defined, the modeler can open the menu item *BPFM Features* and then click on the function *Generate the Variant* in order to run the generation function (Fig. 14). This function checks the correctness of the configuration. In case there is a mistake, the algorithm will stop and will return the reason why the configuration is not correct. Otherwise, the root of the BPFM tree is found and it is pushed in an array (variable *nodes*), in which all activities to be analyzed are inserted. The step is repeated until there are activities in the array and an activity is checked in each iteration. If the activity under analysis is composed, a new BPMN model is created and its child activities are inserted considering the specific mapping rules. They are also pushed in the array since they have to be checked. In the case the activity under analysis is not composed, the algorithm goes ahead to the next iteration since the activity is already inserted into a BPMN model (it is a task). When the loop terminates, a set of BPMN models have already been created. For example, referring to a possible configuration of a BPFM model (in Fig. 12), the folder structure in Fig. 15a is generated.

A main folder (*generated_BPFM_model*) and sub-folders for each level of the BPFM tree are hierarchically generated. In the example, there are two sub-folders

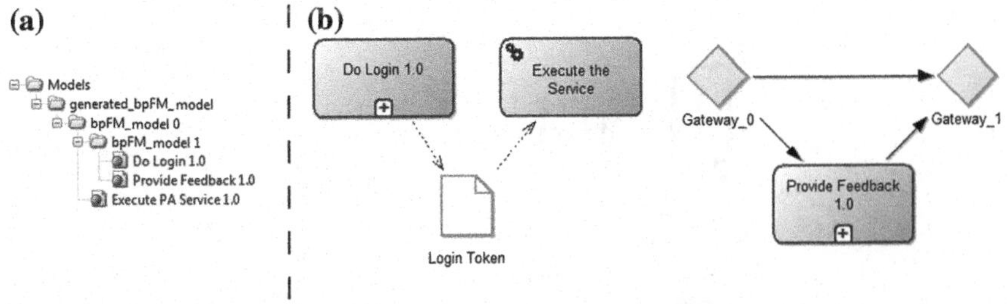

Fig. 15 Folder structure and first level BPMN model

(*BPFM_model 0* and *BPFM_model 1*). They contain the BP fragments of the sub-processes of the referring level. Of course, the first level folder contains the fragments of the main BP (Fig. 15b). They are two tasks such as "Do Login 1.0" and "Execute the Service" and one gateway structure considering the possibility to execute or not the "Provide Feedback 1.0" task. When clicking on a sub-process in the main BP, the tool opens a new window with the referring model. The designer can then model the flow in each of the generated BPMN model.

4.2 Case Study

The modeling environment and the approach presented here were successfully validated considering several Public Administration scenarios. We will consider here the European Project Budget Report case study, which is one of the demonstrators used by the Learn PAd project (http://www.learnpad.eu/). Further details for this case study are discussed in Part XII, the second Chapter, i.e., "Modeling for Learning in Public Administrations—The LearnPAd Approach". We will consider the scenario focusing on the variability perspective.

The participation in an EU financed project requires the beneficiary to perform grant management and related budget reporting activities, as evidence of the tasks carried out as part of the project. The European Commission itself recognized the complexity of the reporting procedures for FP, and has now simplified it in the new research framework program, "Horizon 2020". We will discuss here only a small portion of the overall *periodic budget reporting* BP, focusing on the sub-processes related to the reporting of different projects according to different founding schemes. The BP under analysis contains activities that a specific organization has to put in place in order to report on work done and related costs with reference to a specific project.

The description of the BPFM model resulting from the application of the notation to the *periodic budget reporting* is introduced below. In particular, we refer to the reporting activities of Public Administrations in Italy (e.g., regions, municipalities, universities). The resulting BPFM model has four levels. It includes 4 sub-processes and 12 atomic tasks. Many data objects are also represented. Figure 16 reports the

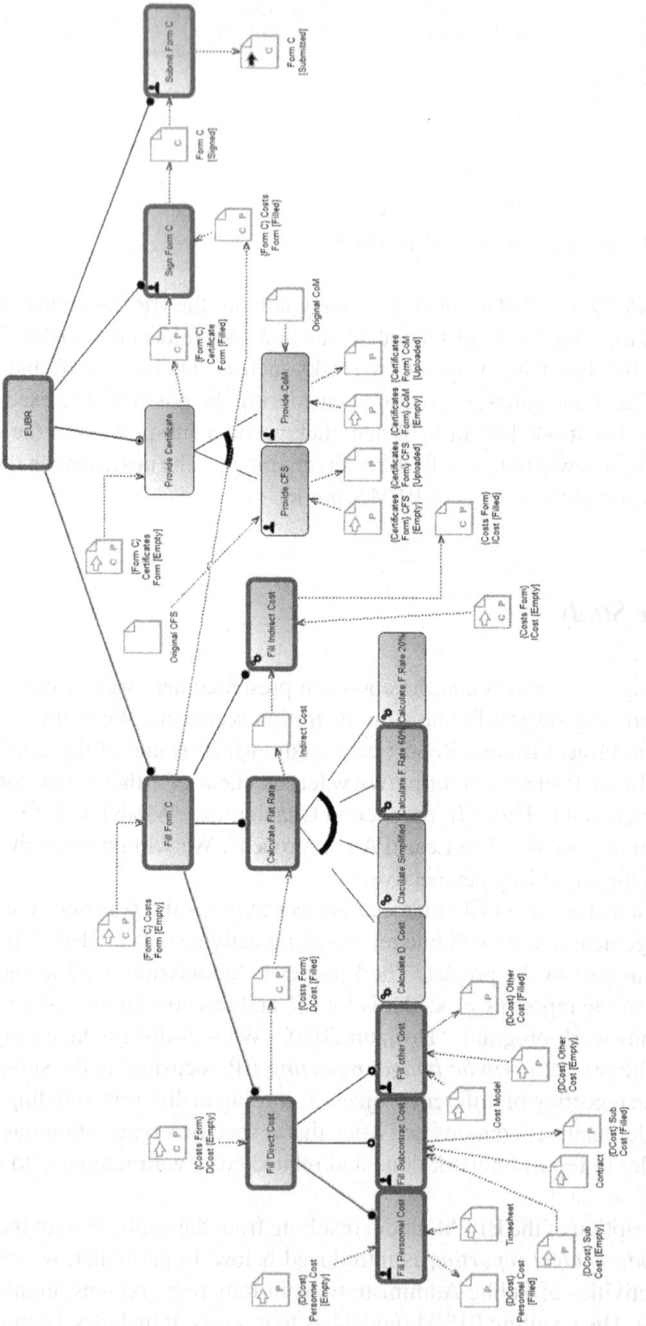

Fig. 16 EU participant periodic report BPFM model—configured

BPFM model we consider here for illustrative purposes. The first level activities are *Fill Form C*, *Provide Certificate*, *Sign Form C* and *Submit to Coordinator*.

In detail *Fill Form C* refers to the need to fill the cost form. It is an activity connected to the root via a *Mandatory Constraint* since it has to be inserted in each BP variant and it has to be always executed. It requires as input the data object *Costs Form* in the state *Empty* and it returns as output the same data object in the state *Filled*. The sub-process is composed of three sub-activities.

- *Fill Direct Cost Model* refers to the need to calculate and then fill the direct cost model; it is an activity connected to the parent via a *Mandatory Constraint*. It needs in input the data object *DCost* in the state *Empty* and it generates the same data object in the state *Filled*. It is composed by the sub-activities *Fill Personnel Cost*, *Fill Subcontracting* and *Fill Other Direct Cost*. They are related to the different parts of the direct cost model. *Fill Personnel Cost* is connected via a *Mandatory Constraint* since in many cases there are personnel costs to be reported, and *Fill Subcontracting* and *Fill Other Direct Cost* are connected via two *Domain Constraints* since they have to be included in the different variant but in some cases they are not reported.
- *Calculate Flat Rate* refers to the need to calculate the flat rate; it is an activity connected to the parent via a *Mandatory Constraint*. The activity requires in input the data object *DCost* in the state *Filled* and it generates the data object *Indirect Cost*. Indirect costs can be calculated considering four different flat rates depending on the specific organization. They are represented as sub-activities connected via a *One Selection Constraint* and they are *Calculate Actual Indirect Cost*, *Calculated Simplified Indirect Cost*, *Calculate Flat Rate 60 %* and *Calculate Flat Rate 20 %*.
- *Fill Indirect Cost Model* is an activity connected to the parent via a *Mandatory Constraint*. The activity requires the data objects *Indirect Cost* and *ICost* in the state *Empty* in input and it generates the data object *ICost* in the state *Filled*.

Provide Certificate is an activity connected to the root via a *Special Case Constraint* since it has to be inserted only in some BP variants. Nevertheless, in case it is included, it has to be executed. The activity requires the data object *Certificates Form* in the state *Empty* in input and it generates the same data object in the state *Filled*. In this activity, the beneficiary has to provide its CFS, or its CoM. Two different sub-activities connected via a *One Selection Constraint* are modeled in order to provide the certificates (*Provide CFS* and *Provide CoM*).

Sign Form C is an activity connected to the root node via a *Mandatory Constraint* since it has to be inserted in each BP variant and it has to be executed. In this activity, the Beneficiary has to fill the periodic report. The activity requires the data objects *Certificates Form* in the state *Filled* and *Costs Form* in input and it generates the data object *Form C* in the state *Signed*.

Submit to Coordinator is an activity connected to the root via a *Mandatory Constraint* since it has to be inserted in each BP variant and it has to be executed. In this activity, the Beneficiary has to submit the periodic report to the project coordinator. The activity requires the data objects *Form C* in the state *Signed* as input and it generates the data object *Form C* in the state *Submitted*.

As soon as the BPFM is provided, several organizations can take advantage of it to define different configurations so as to derive variants better shaped to the organization needs. We will discuss below the application of the proposed approach on the premises of the University of Camerino.

Considering the Configuration **Step 2** starting from the given BPFM, the BP designer, that in our case was the head of the research and technology transfer Macro-Sector, has to define a novel configuration with reference to an EU project recently funded. He selected the activities and the Data Objects that are needed to define the reporting BP variant according to the specific characteristics of the internal organization of University of Camerino. The configuration includes all the mandatory activities as well as some optional activities taking into account that the needed flat rate is 60 % and certificates are not needed, since the defined budget for the specific project is less than 375,000 EUR (Fig. 16).

Then, considering the fragment derivation **Step 3**, the selected configuration is automatically mapped into a set of BP fragments (Fig. 17). The first level activity *Fill the Form C* is mapped as a sub-process using composed activity mapping rules, *Sign Form C* and *Submit to Coordinator* are mapped as tasks using the mandatory constraint rule. The *Fill the Form C* sub-process contains *Fill Indirect Cost Model* and *Fill Direct Cost Model* that are mapped as sub-processes using the composed activity mapping rule and *Calculate Flat Rate* is mapped as tasks using the mandatory constraint rule. *Fill Direct Cost Model* contains: *Fill Personnel Cost* that is mapped using the mandatory constraint rule and *Fill Subcontracting Cost* and *Fill Other Direct Cost* that are mapped using the domain constraint rule. Finally, *Calculate Flat Rate* sub-process contains the activity *Calculate Flat Rate 60 %* that is mapped using one selection constraint mapping rule.

Finally, we derive the variant **Step 4**. At this stage, the BP designer needs to further refine the process introducing missing sequence flows, parallel execution constraints and events among the generated BP fragments, finally resulting in a fully specified BP variant. This step enables the user to introduce more details taking into account the possibility to allocate activities to different participants and roles. A possible variant generated to support reporting activities from the BPFM model and configuration is provided (Fig. 18). The derived BP has three main phases, all of them performed by the research and technology transfer Macro-Sector area of University of Camerino; the first and the last referring to the filling form C and submitted form C are done by the Industrial and International Liaison Office, whereas the signature of the Form C is provided by the head of the Industrial and International Liaison Office that is delegated by the Rector as the official university's legal representative.

To summarize, as expected, the application of the approach allowed the organization to reason on different aspects of the process at different times, and to reuse previous modeling decisions to build a more specific BP models for a given organizational context.

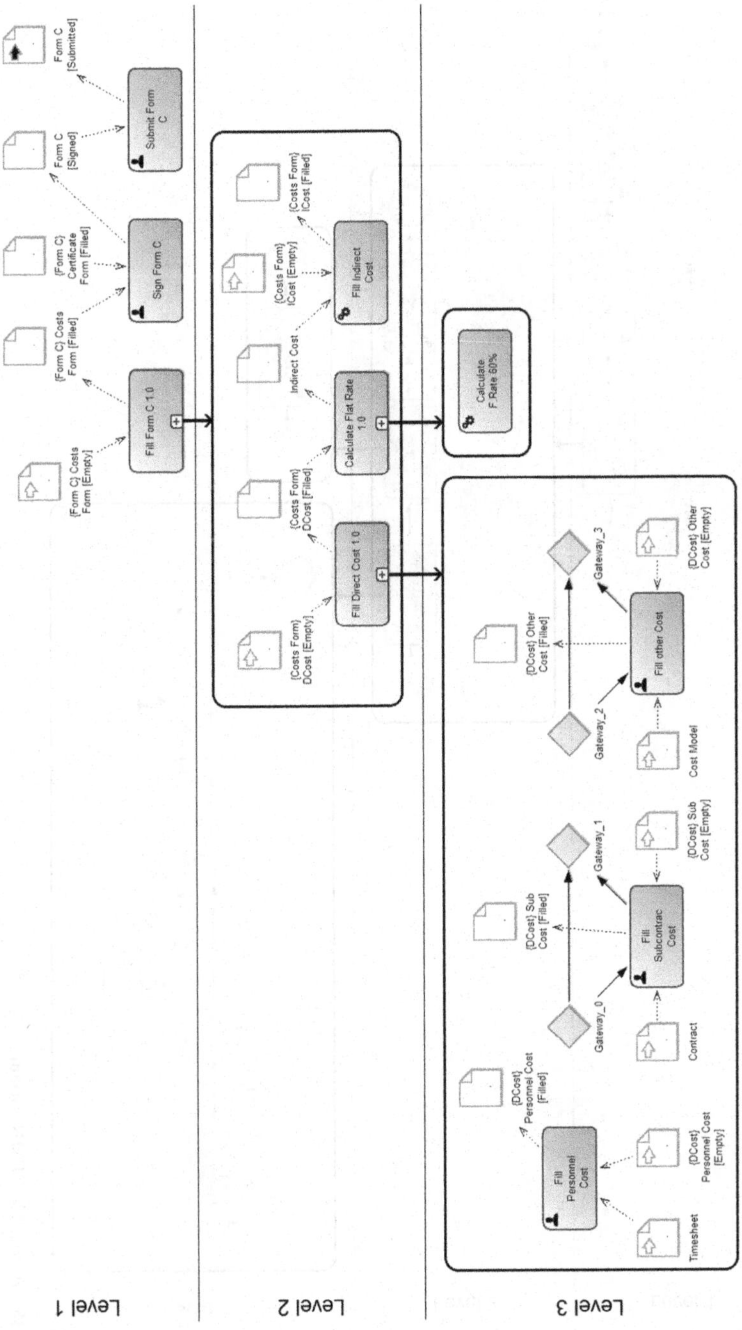

Fig. 17 Fragments generated

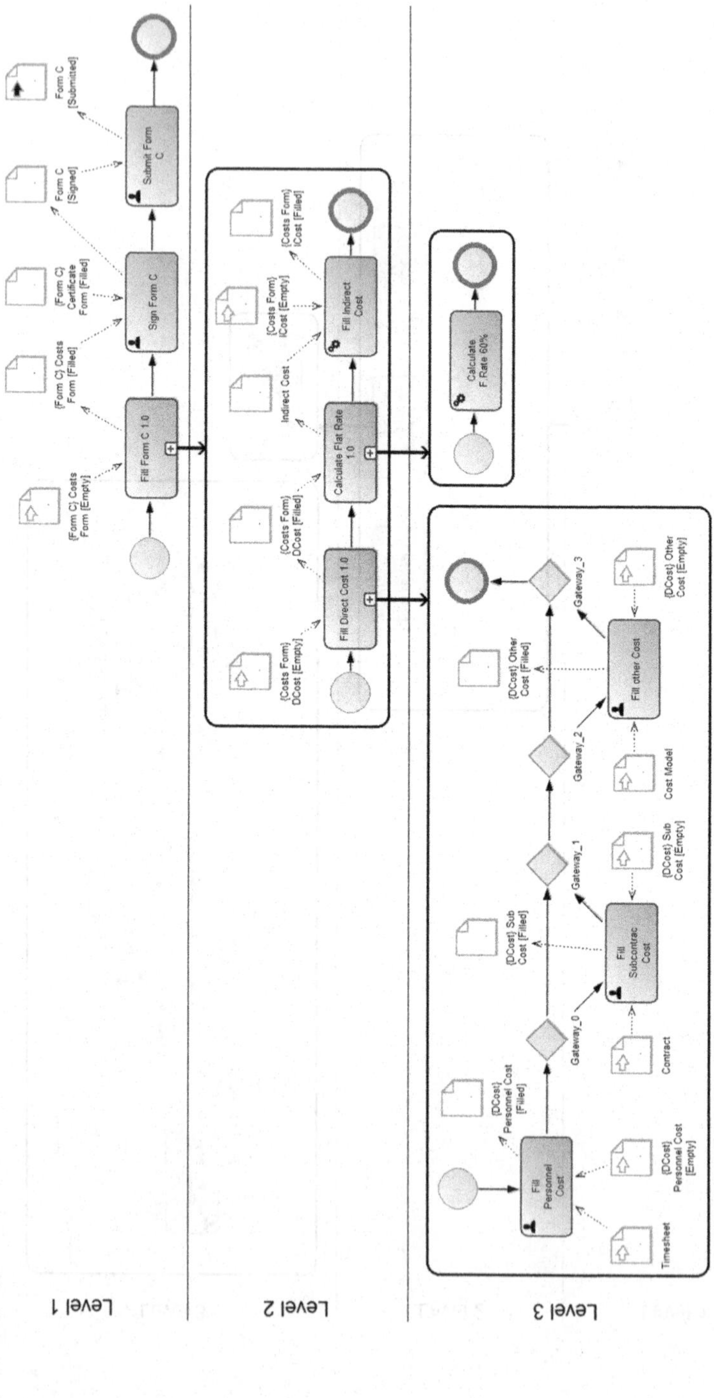

Fig. 18 A possible BPMN variant

5 Conclusion

A novel notation and approach as well as a modeling tool were described in this chapter. They jointly support the modeling of variability aspects for BPs, so as to permit the inclusion of many different variants in a single model. The proposed approach was conceived for situations in which activities composing the configurable BP model have to be successively refined to consider characteristics of the deployment context, such as the different arrangement of the organization supporting the BP itself. In such a case, objectives and activities constituting the configurable BP model are general and independent from the specific characteristics of the organization delivering the service itself. Nevertheless, the precise definition of the BPs, in terms of availability, ordering of the activities and managed documents, depends on deployment related aspects and in particular relates to the organizational model. The approach seems then particularly suitable in those contexts in which complex organizations, such as the PA, deliver the same service in many different ways, and with procedures partially depending on the specific organization.

A modeling environment supporting the usage of the notation and approach was made available thanks to the ADO*xx* platform and made openly accessible through the OMiLAB.

Tool Download http://www.omilab.org/bpfm.

References

1. Awad, A., Decker, G., Lohmann, N.: Diagnosing and repairing data anomalies in process models. In: BP Management Workshops, pp. 5–16. Springer (2010)
2. Döhring, M., Zimmermann, B.: vBPMN: event-aware workflow variants by weaving BPMN2 and business rules. In: Enterprise, Business-Process and Information Systems Modeling, pp. 332–341. Springer (2011)
3. Fill, H.-G., Karagiannis, D.: On the conceptualisation of modelling methods using the ADOxx meta modelling platform. Enterp. Model. Inf. Syst. Architect. **8**(1), 4–25 (2013)
4. Gottschalk, F., van der Aalst, W.M.P., Jansen-Vullers, M.H.: Configurable process models a foundational approach. In: *Reference Modeling*, pp. 59–77. Springer (2007)
5. Gottschalk, F., Van Der Aalst, W.M.P., Jansen-Vullers, M.H., La Rosa, M.: Configurable workflow models. Int. J. Coop. Inf. Syst. **17**(02), 177–221 (2008)
6. Gottschalk, F., Wagemakers, T.A.C., Jansen-Vullers, M.H., van der Aalst, W.M.P., La Rosa, M.: Configurable process models: experiences from a municipality case study. In: Advanced Information Systems Engineering, pp. 486–500. Springer (2009)
7. Hallerbach, A., Bauer, T., Reichert, M.: Capturing variability in business process models: the provop approach. J. Softw. Maintenance Evolution: Res. Pract. **22**(6–7), 519–546 (2010)
8. La Rosa, M., Dumas, M., ter Hofstede, A.H.M., Mendling, J., Gottschalk, F.: Beyond control-flow: extending business process configuration to roles and objects. In: Conceptual Modeling-ER 2008, pp. 199–215. Springer (2008)
9. Lönn, C.-M., Uppström, E., Wohed, P., Juell-Skielse, G.: Configurable process models for the swedish public sector. In: Advanced Information Systems Engineering, pp. 190–205. Springer (2012)
10. OMG. Case Management Model and Notation, Version 1.0, May 2014

11. Pesic, M., Schonenberg, H., van der Aalst, W.M.P.: Declare: full support for loosely-structured processes. In: 11th IEEE International Enterprise Distributed Object Computing Conference, 2007, EDOC 2007, p. 287. IEEE (2007)
12. Pohl, K., Böckle, G., van der Linden, F.J.: Software Product Line Engineering: Foundations. Principles and Techniques. Springer-Verlag, New York Inc., Secaucus, NJ, USA (2005)
13. Recker, J., Rosemann, M., Van Der Aalst, W., Jansen-Vullers, M., Dreiling, A.: Configurable reference modeling languages. Ref. Model. Bus. Syst. Anal. 22–46 (2006)
14. Reichert, M., Weber, B.: Enabling Flexibility in Process-Aware Information Systems: Challenges, Methods, Technologies. Springer (2012)
15. Rosemann, M., van der Aalst, W.M.P.: A configurable reference modelling language. Inf. Syst. **32**(1), 1–23 (2007)
16. Schnieders, A., Puhlmann, F.: Variability mechanisms in e-business process families. BIS **85**, 583–601 (2006)

Part IV
Business and Process Transformation

Capability Oriented Enterprise Knowledge Modeling: The CODEK Approach

Pericles Loucopoulos and Evangelia Kavakli

Abstract Enterprise modeling has been defined as the 'art of externalizing enterprise knowledge'. Traditional approaches to enterprise modeling rely on 'blueprint thinking' that focuses on the formal structure and organization of the enterprise, with business processes being the fundamental components of the enterprise operation. Such approaches generally assume enterprises as deterministic, top-down managed entities, with a well-defined group of processes that develop and maintain products or services for their customers. However, the prevalence and volatility of digital enterprises shifts enterprise modeling towards a more dynamic enterprise configuration, to embrace the idea of dynamic adaptation according to the internal and external influences that constantly (re-)shape the business environment. To this end, enterprise modeling research has adopted model-driven development methods and service-oriented architectures originating from the software development domain, as a means to achieve flexible service delivery and the notion of dynamic capability from the strategic management domain in order to address adaptation to the dynamic business context. This chapter will outline emergent trends in the field, introduce a conceptual framework for the capability-driven development of enterprise knowledge and discuss how this can be used to enable the design of capabilities and services using examples from an eGovernment case study.

Keywords Capability • Enterprise modeling • CODEK • ADO*xx*

P. Loucopoulos (✉)
The University of Manchester, Manchester M15 6PB, UK
e-mail: pericles.loucopoulos@manchester.ac.uk

E. Kavakli
Department of Cultural Technology and Communication,
University of the Aegean, 811 00 Mytilene, Greece
e-mail: kavakli@aegean.gr

D. Karagiannis et al. (eds.), *Domain-Specific Conceptual Modeling*,
DOI 10.1007/978-3-319-39417-6_9

1 Introduction

Enterprise agility is the ability to respond quickly to changes in a business environment, adapting products and services, taking advantage of human and technological resources. The most notable characteristic of agile enterprises is the ability of dynamic decision-making. To achieve this, enterprises need to develop a digital infrastructure, providing the means for quickly supplying valuable information to the people who need it [1].

Information systems (ISs) are the most effective enablers of this digital transformation [2, 3]. They improve information access and coordination across organizational units. A key to effective digital transformation is, therefore, understanding the relationship between business and its ISs.

Enterprise models, present a conceptual map necessary for building an integrated business/IS model, incorporating information about the organization from a number of perspectives (strategy, process, information, organization, etc.). Enterprise Modeling (EM) is an interdisciplinary field, which combines complex areas of research such as IS Engineering, Strategic Management and Socio-cognitive Theory, each providing insights into the enterprise structure, and behavior.

Although, the IDEFØ method based on the Structured Analysis and Design Technique (SADT) [4] can be considered as one of the first enterprise modeling techniques in the early 1980s, EM practically started in the early 1990s as a technique for describing various aspects of an enterprise, especially for the purpose of analysis, design, optimization and more importantly business process reengineering. A variety of frameworks for enterprise integration, particularly in the manufacturing sector [5, 6] such as CIM-OSA [7], paved the way in this field by promoting a process-based modeling approach. The business process approach as practiced throughout the 1990s introduced a natural and horizontal way in organising business systems as opposed to previous vertical function-centric approaches.

Since then, EM has evolved and has been constantly enriched with new constructs in order to cover additional aspects with goal-oriented and agent-oriented approaches being the most prominent. Goal-oriented approaches such as the Knowledge Acquisition in autOmated Specification (KAOS) method [8], the Enterprise Knowledge Development (EKD) framework [9] state that enterprises are purposefully designed and implemented systems. As a consequence, enterprise goals are recognized as the primary factors that govern/explain the current and potential enterprise configuration. Agent-oriented approaches such as the Intentional STrategic Actor Relationships modeling (*i**) framework [10, 11] claim that enterprises are social systems and therefore, the essence of an enterprise's operation lies in the interaction between involved social agents.

Methodological issues relating to development methods, i.e., roadmaps for creating enterprise models were also considered, e.g., the Architecture Development Method part of The Open Group Architecture Framework ADM-TOGAF [12]. Commercial tools were also developed in order to support the development of enterprise models.

Important progress in the EM field in the 2000s consists in the development of open modeling languages (in the spirit of open software) that can be supported by different tool vendors and consulting firms (e.g., ArchiMate [13]), as well as the development of metatools (e.g., ADO*xx* [14]) able to support different modeling languages.

These advances were followed by the introduction of Service-Oriented Architecture (SOA) [15, 16]. From a business perspective, a service is a self-contained piece of functionality that will return a result (i.e., provide a service to a client) under the conditions defined in its service-level agreement (SLA). Service orientation better describes the requirements of enterprise networks and Collaborative Networked Organizations (CNOs), which are made of collaborating entities from different partner companies working together in order to deliver services to customers.

In the line of EM evolution, there has been a change in focus. In the past decades, enterprises were thought of as relatively stable, deterministic, top-down managed static structures. However, as internal and external influences create a turbulent business environment, enterprises need to become more dynamic [17]. Pure top-down directed enterprises become obsolete, being replaced by ad hoc partnerships/networks enabled by IT solutions (e.g., cloud computing) that facilitate easy sharing of data, applications, even business processes. Deterministic processes are being replaced by dynamic processes assembled on-the-fly using available internal and external services, thus adapting to the dynamic business requirements.

The response to the research community has initiated a number of investigative trends, one of which is that of capability-driven enterprise modeling, which is the subject matter of this chapter. This approach uses 'business capabilities' as the fundamental abstraction to describe the business requirements, and then to map from capabilities to services and/or systems [18]. This chapter introduces the key ideas and the main concepts of an approach based on capability modeling known as CODEK (**C**apability-**O**riented **D**esigns with **E**nterprise **K**nowledge). The CODEK modeling framework builds upon earlier foundational work [9] and can be considered as a synergistic exploiter of a set of necessary and desirable modeling views for the design of dynamic enterprise systems.

The objectives of this chapter are to introduce the reader to the notion of 'capability' in EM and to demonstrate how a capability-oriented approach can support the task of co-designing enterprise systems. Obviously, EM for the design of enterprise systems would involve different but complementary viewpoints many of which have been studied and practiced during the past two decades. Coverage of the entire methodological spectrum, which considers all these other viewpoints, is beyond the scope of a single chapter. It is assumed that the reader is familiar with these and the value of this chapter resides in the way in which, in CODEK, the notion of capability is exploited to conflate all these views into a systematic design paradigm.

2 On the Notion of Enterprise Capability

The notion of capability has been exploited in several fields. However, the definition, role and the usage of the capability concept in the context of EM are still unclear and open to different interpretations. In this section, the underlying characteristics of 'enterprise capability' are examined.

The Oxford English Dictionary gives the following definitions of capability: 'The quality of being capable in various senses', 'forces or resources giving an entity the ability to undertake a particular kind of action'.

The Department of Defence defines capability as follows [19]: 'The confluence of capacity and ability to achieve a desired goal under specified standards and conditions through a combination of ways and means to perform a set of tasks'.

It seems that key characteristics of 'capability' are those of *capacity* (i.e., having the resources) and *ability* (i.e., having the know-how) to deliver something of use. Unfortunately, a definition based on natural language becomes a little fuzzy as the terms of 'capability', 'ability' and 'capacity' are often used interchangeably. In the next section, an ontological definition of capability is given in the context of EM.

The notion of 'capability' has been studied in the field of Strategic Management as a means to understand competitive advantage.

Historically, the notion of capability has been studied in distinct fields as shown by the map of Fig. 1.

Of particular relevance to this chapter is the work carried out in Management Science and specifically on the Resource Based View (RBV) and Dynamic Capability Theory (DCT) and in Information Systems, specifically in Service Orientation.

In the field of Strategic Management capability has been studied as a means to understand competitive advantage. In RBV, a resource refers to 'an asset or input to production (tangible or intangible) that an organization owns, controls, or has access to on a semi-permanent basis and an organizational capability refers to the ability of an organization to perform a coordinated set of tasks, utilizing organizational resources, for the purpose of achieving a particular end result' [20].

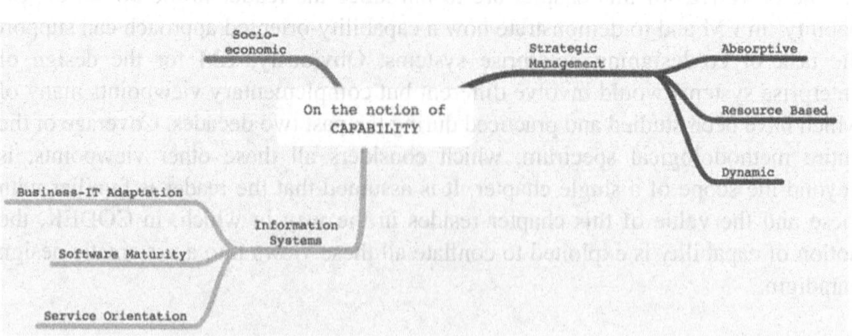

Fig. 1 A map of capability-oriented views in different fields

In DCT, dynamic capabilities are defined as 'the firm's ability to integrate, build, and reconfigure internal and external competences to address rapidly changing environments' [21]. In RBV, researchers focus their attention on identifying possession of valuable, rare, inimitable and non-substitutable resources of the enterprise as a source of sustainable advantage [22, 23]. In contrast, researchers in DCT focus on the dynamic aspect of enterprise and propose (i) sensing mechanisms that identify dynamic and changing requirements within the enterprise ecosystem, (ii) promotes shared vision and adoption of appropriate business models to seize opportunities and (iii) reconfigures the resource base through collaborative and complementary capabilities to transform the enterprise into a new desirable state [23].

In the field of Information Systems, capability has been considered as a means of dealing with agility, flexibility and business/IT alignment. Researchers and practitioners concur that capability, as the fundamental abstraction concept, focuses on stable business components and that business capability modeling and SOA complement each other, thus facilitating the alignment between technical and business architecture [24, 25]. The general consensus is that a business capability is, at a higher level than a business process [26, 27]. It represents a conceptual service that a group of processes and people, supported by the relevant application, information and underlying technology, will perform. The capability represents the *what*, whereas the process and people represent the *how*. Business processes describe the methods an organization employs in order to provide and leverage business capabilities [28].

Modeling enterprise capabilities have been proposed by both academia [29, 30] and practice [28], as the lynchpin to connect strategic objectives and high-level organizational requirements to technological artefacts. A business capability describes what an enterprise does for the purpose of achieving the desired end, or delivering the desired outcome [31]. The main objective of capability-oriented modeling is to describe enterprise agility in terms of the dynamic configuration of enterprise behavior. This, in turn, requires the facility to evaluate the capabilities of the enterprise (capability awareness), with regard to the contextual parameters affecting their delivery (contextual awareness) [32].

The use of capability as the representative of what the business does and needs rather than focusing on the technical implementation (how) serves as a powerful communication tool among technology and business specialists. To realise the benefits of modeling enterprise capabilities, one should carefully consider its relation and dependencies on other design artefacts such as services and processes as well as organizational requirements and settings such as its strategic objectives, social relationships and business context.

In [33] the authors propose a metamodel that relates enterprise capabilities to the context of the domain, business processes and enterprise objectives. Modeling the context of the capabilities of the enterprise allows the design of adjustable services that can adapt to changes in parameters of the capability context. In [30] the authors propose an extension to ARCHIMATE metamodel with the notion of capabilities, resources and value to enable strategic alignment of technical projects. Building upon this work, Azevedo et al. [34] argue that the subjective nature and usage flexibility of the notion of capability can result in multiple interpretations of the dependencies between capability-related concepts and other elements of the enterprise architecture and stress the need for a more rigorous conceptualization of capability. To this end, they discuss the semantics of the capability-related concepts proposed in [30] in terms of the Unified Foundation Ontology (UFO) [35] and reveal a number of additional relationships between capability and the structural and behavioral elements of the enterprise architecture.

From a service orientation perspective, a business capability is defined in [31] as: 'A particular ability or capacity that a business may possess or exchange to achieve a specific purpose or outcome. A capability describes what the business does (outcomes and service levels) that creates value for customers; for example, pay employee or ship product. A business capability abstracts and encapsulates the people, process/procedures, technology, and information into the essential building blocks needed to facilitate performance improvement and redesign analysis'.

In [36], the authors argue that the EM is currently facing a challenge of semantic integration across multiple levels of abstraction and of detail. While traditionally EM emerged from bottom-up approaches, by applying semantic extensions to some core concern (e.g., business process models extended with information about the organizational responsibilities), new technological development necessitates a rethinking on how EM may be practiced in a holistic manner to support the representation and analysis of many factors that could lead to a redesign of the very same business model under which an organization operates. A case at hand is the use of cloud services [37] that demands the consideration of the business model of the cloud service provider as well as compliance to potentially multiple service collaborators.

3 Method Description

3.1 Overall View and Way of Working

The overall capability-centric scheme proposed in this chapter adopts a conceptual modeling paradigm [33], which is partly influenced by previously developed schemes in Enterprise Modeling, e.g., [9, 38–42], and extended with new features which provide opportunities for a greater level of analysis [33]. The modeling framework considers five interrelated viewpoints as shown in Fig. 2.

The teleological view describes an enterprise's goals and objectives that drive its strategy. The service view encapsulates enterprise operation as atomic and composite business or system services that contribute to the achievement of enterprise goals. The social view describes the enterprise organizational structure in terms of interdependent actors that participate in service provision. The contextual view describes the enterprise's ecosystem in terms of the internal and external parameters

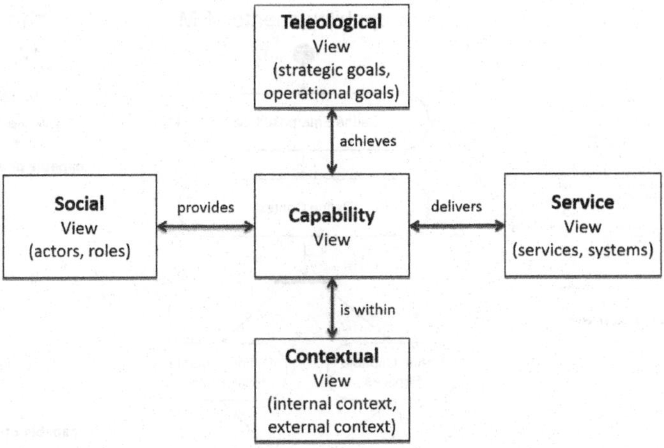

Fig. 2 Conceptual modeling views

that affect its strategic choices. Finally, capabilities represent the relations within the organizational structure required for an enterprise to satisfy its objectives and explore functional alternatives in a given context and become the fifth view.

Modeling within each viewpoint would be done through well-established conceptual modeling languages [9, 11, 43–45].

Capability-oriented application development using the intertwined viewpoints includes the following steps depicted in Fig. 3: define enterprise goals, define contextual parameters, define implementation alternatives and calculate the capability of alternative implementations.

Enterprise models of different views play different roles in the capability analysis process: the goal model acts as the teleological viewpoint that provides the rationale for the designing process, the service and actor models are the basis for describing alternative capabilities for achieving enterprise goals, the context model is the basis for evaluating alternatives and the actor-role model defines the social dimension.

For example, in an eGovernment application (referred to as eGov henceforth) the strategic goal 'increase efficiency' can be decomposed in terms of 'decrease maintaining costs', 'improving the use of existing infrastructure' and 'facilitating content delivery among interested parties'. To decrease maintaining costs, alternative implementations might be considered using different Cloud services. However, different Cloud services might be more suitable in different contexts. For example, in the context of sensitive citizen data, the private Cloud storage might be more suitable whereas in the context of open government data a public Cloud solution is more appropriate.

These different options need to be placed in the context of the level of service to be provided to citizens and central to this is the degree of quality of the future system in its different functionalities [46]. This type of analysis based on capabilities results in more dynamic descriptions of the enterprise.

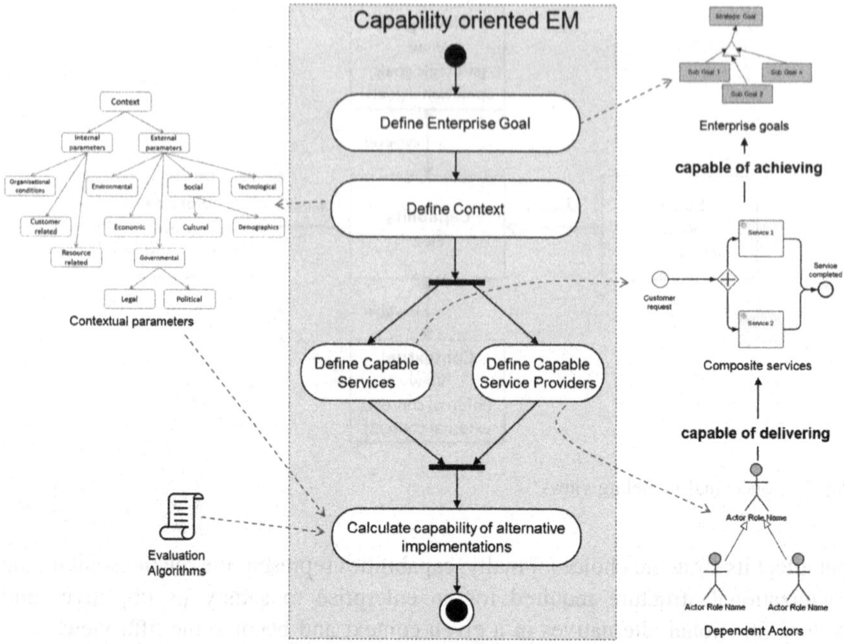

Fig. 3 Demonstration of roles of different enterprise models in capability-oriented EM

3.2 *Main Capability Concepts*

Although a universally accepted definition of an enterprise capability has been elusive, there are some common features of existing enterprise capability definitions that provide guidance as to how enterprise capabilities should be described. In brief, capability demonstrates the following characteristics:

- A capability *is* associated with a certain *owner* (a business entity such as a department, an organization, a person, a system).
- A capability denotes the fitness of its owner for achieving certain *end result* (business goal, customer need, project objective, etc.).
- A capability encapsulates the *resources* (processes, people, technology, assets) required by the capability owner.
- A capability is *context*-specific, its application depends on specific parameters within the enterprise environment (social context, economic context, cultural context, etc.)

It becomes obvious that the notion of capability bears a resemblance to that of *service* since both concepts are used to describe behavior without revealing the internal structure and operations that take place. In fact, both concepts act as the bridge between intentions and behavior, but from a different viewpoint. Services couple intentions to specific behavior, whilst capabilities measure the fitness of a service in a specific context. Fitness relates both to the capacity of the provider to provide the service in the particular context (service provision capability), as well as the ability of the service to satisfy a specific need in a particular context (goal achievement capability). Often a service may compete with another service within the same enterprise. Capabilities can drive the dynamic service provision depending on the context.

Consider as an example the provision of a public service by a local tax office. A goal of the tax office is 'To provide tax clearance information to taxpayers'. In order to achieve this goal, there are two available services (shown in Fig. 4a, b). The first is the 'in-person certificate request' service provided by the office's citizen centre. The second is the 'online certification' service provided by the eTax application. In the first case, the request is processed and the certificate is sent to the taxpayer by paper mail or email. In the second case, the certificate is issued directly and the taxpayer can either save it or print it.

Whilst both services aim at the same goal, their capability depends on several contextual parameters both technological, for example, the taxpayer's location and Internet access, as well as social such as the taxpayer's computer literacy or trust to technology. For instance, if we consider an elder individual with poor computer skills, then the goal achievement capability of the online certification service is low due to the fact that age is negatively correlated with the use of Internet. The situation changes when the same service is provided to a business firm, which has integrated Internet into its daily operation.

Similarly, the service provision capability of an actor is affected by the visitors' context. For example, the service provision capability of the citizen centre to service a certificate request is different depending on the tax payer's location, being at its highest when there is a citizen centre close to the tax payer's location, and decreasing when the citizen centre is far from the tax payer's location.

In the latter case, the tax office may decide to combine the existing capability of the citizen centre's to service certificate requests with an electronic application capability provided by the citizen centre website. The collaboration of the two capabilities brings forward a new e-application service, which requires the collaboration of the two actors (citizen centre and citizen centre website), which enhances the overall goal achievement capability in the context of remote taxpayers (see Fig. 4c).

Therefore, capability modeling can be seen as the process of synthesising enterprise competencies to create a satisfying result, while considering dynamic conditions of the enterprise environment. As such, it explicitly addresses adaptability and evolvability.

From a methodological perspective, it is important to evaluate capabilities. We can distinguish between two capability measures: *efficiency* and *effectiveness*. Efficiency measures the cost associated with service delivery. It might refer to the amount of resources (time, money, people, etc.) that must be used (operational cost), or the cost of buying or renting an external service, as well as intangible costs such as social cost, environmental costs associated with the delivery of a service. Effectiveness measures the value of a service in terms of utility (degree of goal

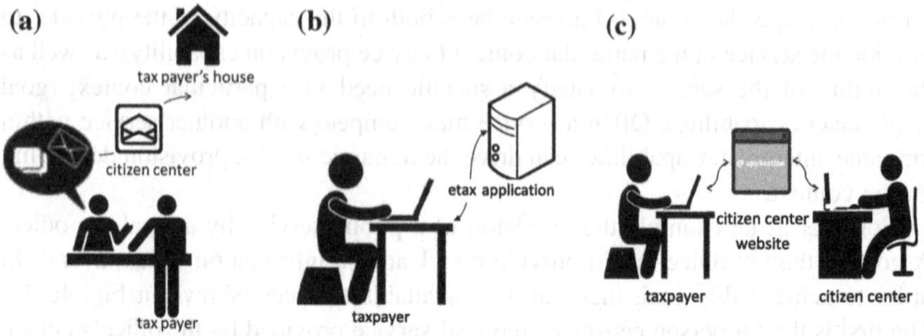

Fig. 4 Three scenarios of eGovernment service provision. **a** In-person certificate request. **b** Online certification. **c** e-application

achievement), quality, customer satisfaction and so on. Once again, capability efficiency and effectiveness vary depending on the context. In order to be able to evaluate the capability effectiveness and capability efficiency in each context, we might employ a combination of different methods including customer satisfaction surveys, scenario analysis, cost analysis, etc.

The aim is to be able to answer questions like 'how capable is an actor to provide a service?' or 'how capable is a service to achieve a goal?' It might be that an actor may be well capable in providing a service but the cost of required resources is very high. Alternatively, two services may be equally capable of achieving a goal but one creates more value and, therefore, is more preferable.

The above requirements are addressed by the metamodel fragment shown in Fig. 5, which provides an overview of the key capability components. Capability is defined as a ternary association class between a Goal that denotes an end the enterprise wants to achieve, the Service(s) capable of achieving this end (goal achievement capability) and the Actor(s) capable of providing the service (service provision capability). The evaluation of the capability efficiency and effectiveness depends on the context.

A capability model can be conceptualized as a directed, acyclic AND/OR graph (capability graph). The root node of the capability graph represents the goal that the enterprise wishes to accomplish within a certain context. The services that are

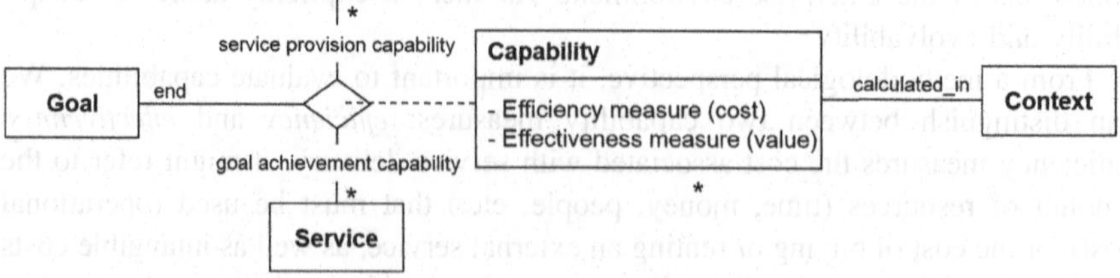

Fig. 5 The key capability concepts

capable of achieving the goal are modeled as intermediary nodes and the actors capable of providing a service are modeled as terminal nodes. A connector (edge) between a goal and a service denotes the goal achievement capability of the service. A connector between a service and an actor denotes the service provision capability of the actor. Collaborating capabilities (either in terms of collaborating services achieving a goal, or in terms of actors collaborating for the provision of a service), are modeled as AND connectors. A solution tree in a capability graph represents a specific goal realization alternative (capability tree).

Each capability connector has two weights, v and c corresponding to the capability effectiveness and efficiency measures accordingly. To calculate these measures one should take into consideration the context within which the capability modeling takes place. The weight of each capability tree represents the overall capability of a specific implementation in the given context and is calculated based on the average weights of all connectors in the tree. Therefore, capability analysis can be formally defined in terms of a search algorithm for identifying an optimum capability tree of a capability AND/OR graph. The above is summarized in Table 1, which provides an overview of the capability model concepts and notation.

Table 1 Notation and semantics of capability concepts

Concept	Notation	Description
Goal	G	A state of affairs (end) that an enterprise wants to achieve/maintain/avoid. A goal might be achieved by alternative behaviors (services)
Context	C	Describes a composition of internal or external elements that may have an impact on the achievement of a goal or the delivery of a service
Service	S	An interface through which internal actor behavior is externalized. It may aggregate other services jointly achieving a goal
Actor	A	Active enterprise entity that performs behavior. Can be a person, an organizational unit, a role or an automated system. Can be internal or external to the enterprise
Capability	– v/c →	A measure of an enterprise's ability and capacity to achieve an end, (provide a service or accomplish a business goal), within a specific context. A capability is defined as the effectiveness (value)/efficiency (cost) which are defined by the user considering the context in which the capability is measured
Collaborating capability	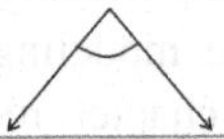	A capability that results from the collaboration of different enterprise actors or services
Capability tree	(g, S, A, C)	A way of achieving a goal in a given context. It contains the starting goal (g), the set of service nodes (S) that are capable of achieving this goal, the set of actor nodes (A) that are capable of providing the above services and the set of capability connectors (C). The overall capability of a capability tree with *n* connectors is defined as the function $f(c_1, c_2, \ldots, c_n)$ of all capability connectors in C

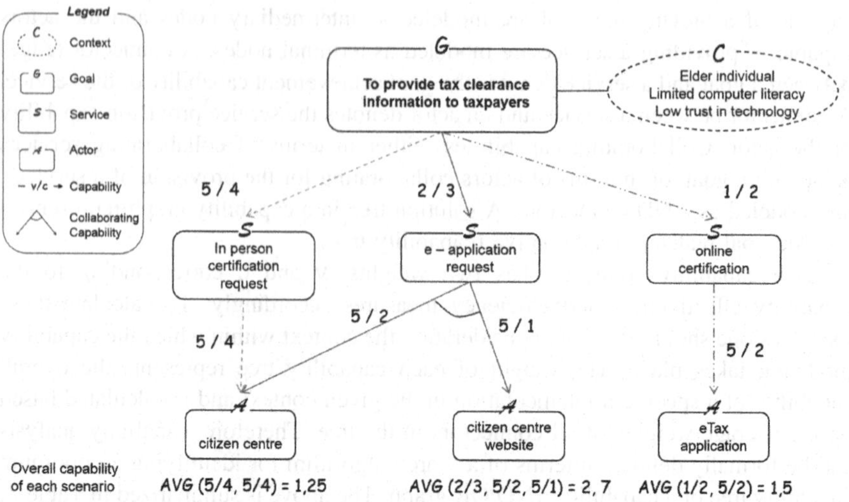

Fig. 6 Capability model example for eGovernment service provision

Returning to the local tax office example, in order to 'Provide tax clearance information to taxpayers' we considered three alternative scenarios, described in Fig. 4. These can be modeled as a capability AND/OR graph shown in Fig. 6, representing the alternative services capable of achieving the above goal and the actors who are capable of providing each service. Capabilities are shown as connectors. Next to each connector, the capability value and cost measures are displayed, as they were defined in the context of an 'Elder individual with limited computer literacy and low trust in technology'. Each scenario corresponds to an alternative capability tree, shown using different colors in Fig. 6. To calculate the overall capability of each scenario an average function is used. This indicates that the second alternative corresponding to the e-application request service collaboratively provided by the citizen centre personnel and the citizen centre website has the greatest average capability.

4 Proof of Concept

The successful handling of the complementary enterprise modeling views comprising the capability-oriented framework proposed in this chapter, requires the use of a modeling tool that will allow the use of different conceptual models within a holistic platform whereby each viewpoint is implemented as a distinct metamodel and the overall enterprise model is obtained as synthesis of the information carried by the different viewpoints, ensuring consistency between the views. In addition, it should allow for different visualizations of the model concepts to align with the stakeholders the view it is designed for. Finally, it should enable the definition of different algorithms and mechanisms for supporting the capability-oriented way of working. To this end, we have used the ADO*xx* metamodeling platform in order to develop a prototype capability-oriented modeling language, currently incorporating two modeling views (capability and service).

For the conceptualization of the modeling method on ADO*xx*, each enterprise modeling view was assigned to a different model type. The capability view concepts were described with classes assigned to a capability model type, whilst for the enterprise service view concepts, we used the BPMN model type, already implemented in ADO*xx*. Inter-model references intertwine the different views.

Since all models in ADO*xx* can be interpreted as graphs, graph-based algorithms can be applied. In particular, in order to support capability analysis, a capability graph search algorithm was defined in ADOscript, the ADO*xx* specific scripting language, based on a general recursive procedure for searching AND/OR graphs defined in [47]. Furthermore, an additional mechanism for assisting the user in calculating average capability was defined as an expression. Additional mechanisms, for example for assisting the user in defining appropriate capability metrics depending on the specific application context could also be defined in the spirit of the GQM approach [48]. Figure 7 presents an excerpt of the capability-oriented enterprise modeling method showing the model types, classes, relation classes, attributes and mechanisms and algorithms that are relevant for the capability-oriented analysis.

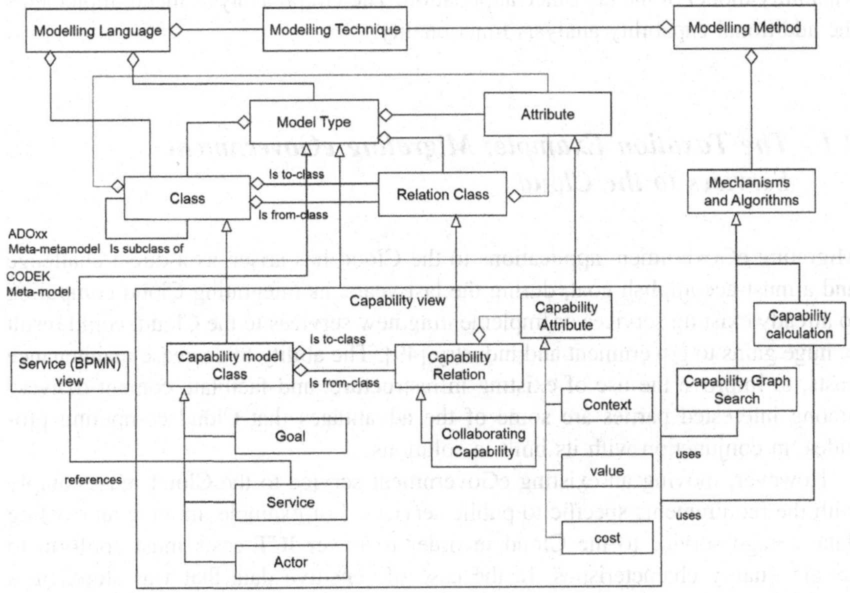

Fig. 7 Excerpt of the capability-oriented enterprise modeling method

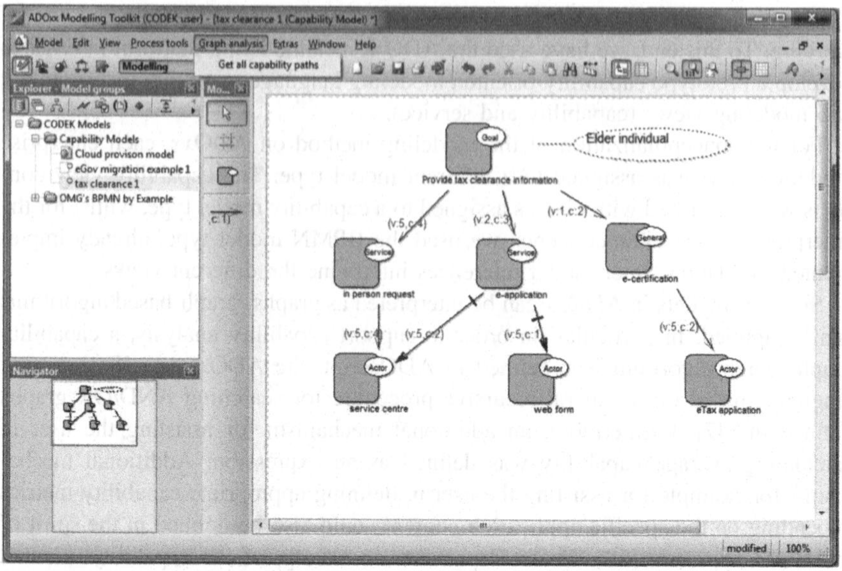

Fig. 8 Excerpt of the capability-oriented enterprise modeling method

Figure 8 depicts the ADO*xx* Modeling environment. In particular, it shows the capability model of the tax office application. The Graph analysis menu implements the additional capability analysis functionality.

4.1 *The Taxation Example: Migrating eGovernment Services to the Cloud*

Migrating eGovernment applications to the Cloud has arisen as a direct challenge and a must-accomplish goal, during the last years, as integrating Cloud computing to already existing services or implementing new services to the Cloud, could result in huge gains to government and industry [49]. The ability to decrease maintenance costs, to improve the use of existing infrastructure, and facilitate content delivery among interested parties are some of the advantages that Cloud computing provides, in conjunction with its built-in solutions.

However, moving an existing eGovernment service to the Cloud must comply with the requirements specific to public services. For example, moving an existing data storage service to the Cloud in order to lower ICT costs must conform to certain quality characteristics. In the case of sensitive data that was stored in a specific encrypted format in the traditional system, the new service must be capable to integrate the existing encryption mechanism in the Cloud storage infrastructure thus complying with the quality requirements relating to the use of 'standards/prototypes' and 'proper use of citizen data'.

It could also be possible that different Cloud services might be more suitable in different contexts. For example, in the context of sensitive citizen data, the private Cloud storage service might be more suitable whereas in the context of open government data a public Cloud solution is more effective.

Capability-oriented design can assist stakeholders to measure the fitness of alternative service models and service providers in a certain context, through comparing their respective capability effectiveness and efficiency. In this way, it can assist them to make informed decisions in order to maximize the benefits of the Cloud.

Revisiting the tax office example, let us consider that aiming to reduce ICT spending (goal) the government is considering migrating the online certification service to the Cloud. First, we need to identify the contextual parameters that affect the migration of this service. Tax clearance certificate provision is a Government to Citizen service (context), which includes sensitive personal and financial data (context) and as such moving of the data to a location in another country is not allowed (context) according to the national data protection law (context). The migration is reinforced by the decreased public funding (context) as well as the national strategy defined in the National eGovernment Action Plan (context).

Two different cloud service models can be defined in this context. In the first implementation, online certification is provided as Software as a Service over the private Cloud. In the second case, online certification is once again provided as Software as a Service but, this time, deploying a public Cloud. With respect to service providers, we can identify two alternatives: The Government Cloud provider (National Gov Cloud) and a Multinational CSP.

Thus, the capability model consists of three alternative scenarios, shown in Fig. 9a as the three branches of the graph.

In order to make an informed decision, we need to calculate the capability of each alternative in terms of the two measures, efficiency and effectiveness. In this example, efficiency can be defined in terms of the operational cost related to service provision, whilst effectiveness in this context can be measured in terms of compliance with the quality requirement of proper use of citizen data [50]. Proper use of citizen data is related to data confidentiality and depends both on protective measures built in the service as well as on the legislation that a service follows.

Having built the capability model the user has to calculate the overall capability of each alternative by defining the capability measures of each capability relation.

In particular, regarding cost efficiency implementation SaaS public cloud service is more efficient since public clouds have higher cost benefits compared to private clouds. With respect to compliance with proper use of citizen data, though implementation of a public cloud service is considered less effective since in public clouds resources are shared between multiple users and thus the risk of data leak is greater. With respect to service provision capability, the cost efficiency of Government Cloud is lower, however, in terms of effectiveness the Multinational cloud service provider is considered lower since he might store data in different jurisdictions.

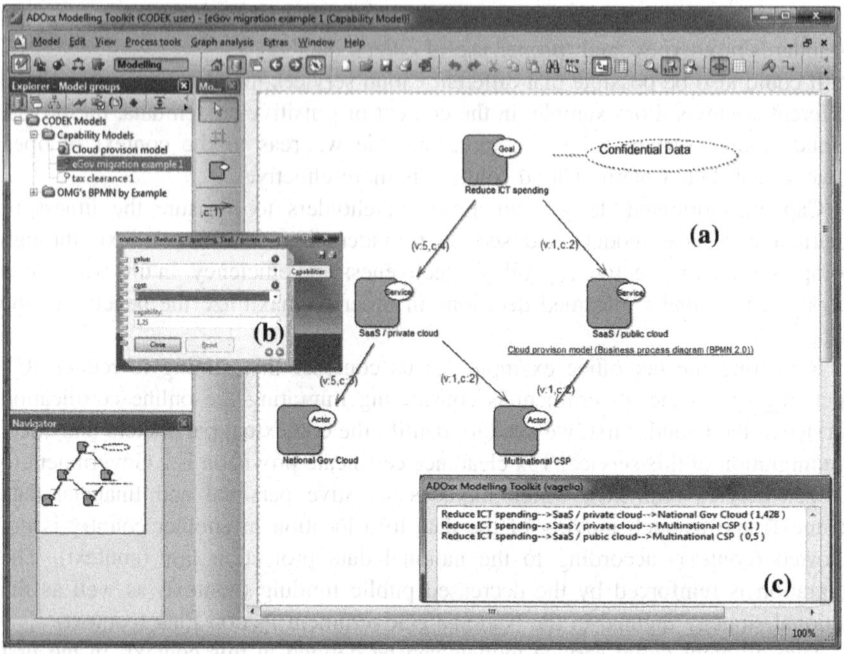

Fig. 9 Migrating an eGovernment service to the cloud using capabilities

Based on this reasoning, the measures of each capability are added (see Fig. 9b). The last step includes the identification of alternative capability trees and the calculation of the average capability of each tree. This is done through the graph analysis menu which implements the graph search algorithm (Fig. 9c). As shown in this figure, the first alternative has the optimum average capability. This type of analysis based on capabilities, though it does not provide a definite migration plan, provides the knowledge required by decision makers in order to make rational and justified design decisions.

5 Conclusion

Enterprise modeling is concerned with the description of key components of both the business and its IT infrastructure in order to achieve alignment of business and IT. There are many different viewpoints that are relevant in coding (representing) and decoding (analyzing) these key components and, indeed, there are various schemes and frameworks to support these activities.

To address dynamic requirements of today's business environments, one should go beyond the static design of services that are aligned with organizational objectives and business requirements. This chapter postulates that existing efforts need to be complemented by a higher level, more strategic-oriented viewpoint namely that of capability modeling. Such a strategic viewpoint would offer designers the opportunity to dynamically configure enterprise services depending on the requirements that arise as a result of changes in the enterprise domain and its ecosystem. The notion of enterprise capability can be used as a conceptual conduit that can integrate the contextual, service, operational and teleological views of the organizations and enable integrated reasoning on enterprise requirements and evolutionary decisions.

Furthermore, this chapter argues that there is a need for the development of a methodology and support software tools, for the design and evaluation of alternative enterprise models that meet the challenges of alignment and agility and, to this end, we described a prototype implementation using the ADO*xx* metamodeling platform. A methodology based on three interrelated conceptual viewpoints, namely those of descriptive, relational and evaluative, would provide for a systematic and holistic approach to designing enterprises processes and IT support systems. Descriptive capability modeling provides the means for expressing functional and non-functional requirements for IT systems and situating these in the context of the corresponding enterprise setting. Relational capability modeling provides an insight into the dependencies between enterprise capabilities and thus supports the analysis of causal effects of change and the impact of this change on the social dimension of the enterprise. Evaluative capability modeling provides the means by which a systemic analysis of the effects of different alternative implementations may have on the dynamics of the enterprise (including unintended consequences) together with an evaluation of the economic impact of each alternative.

Tool Download http://www.omilab.org/codek.

References

1. Gates, B.: Buisness @ the Speed of Thought. Grant Central Publishing (2009)
2. Rouse, W.B.: A theory of enterprise transformation. Syst. Eng. **8**(4) (2005)
3. Sanz, J.: Customer experience and front-office transformation enabled by business process engineering. In: International Conference on Business Informatics, 2013, IEEE, Vienna (2013)
4. Ross, D.: Applications and extensions of SADT. IEEE Comput. **18**(4), 25–34 (1985)
5. Goranson, H.T.: Dimensions of enterprise integration. In: Proceedings of the 1st International Conference on 'Enterprise Integration Modeling', 1992, pp. 101–113. MIT Press (1992)
6. Petrie, C.J. (ed.): Proceedings of the 1st Conference on 'Enterprise Integration Modeling'. Scientific and Engineering Computation Series, 1992. MIT Press, Cambridge, Massachusetts & London, UK (1992)
7. Kosanke, K., Vlietstra, J.: CIM-OSA—its goals, scope, contents and achievements. In: ESPRIT'89, 1989, pp. 661–673, Brussels (1989)
8. Lamsweerde, A.V.: Goal-oriented requirements engineering: a guided tour. In: Proceedings of the Fifth IEEE International Symposium on Requirements Engineering, 2001, p. 249. IEEE Computer Society (2001)

9. Kavakli, V., Loucopoulos, P.: Modelling of Organisational Change Using the EKD Framework. Communications of the Association for Information Systems. (1999)
10. Yu, E.: Modelling Strategic Relationships for Process Reengineering. Department of Computer Science, University of Toronto, Toronto, Canada (1995)
11. Yu, E., Mylopoulos, J.: From ER to "AR"—modelling strategic actor relationships for business process reengineering. In: Entity-Relationship Approach—ER'94 Business Modelling and Re-Engineering, 1994, pp. 548–565 (1994)
12. OPENGROUP: TOGAF—Enterprise Architecture Methodology, Version 9.1. http://www.opengroup.org/togaf/ (2012)
13. OPENGROUP: ArchiMate—Modelling Language for Enterprise Architecture, V2.0. https://www2.opengroup.org/ogsys/catalog/c118 (2012)
14. Karagiannis, D., Niksa, N.: Platform-as-a-Service (PaaS): The ADOxx Metamodelling Platform, Information Technologies—A Strategic Priority for the Knowledge Economy, 2011, 14–15 Oct 2011, Shvistov, Bulgaria (2011)
15. OPEN-GROUP: SOA Reference Architecture. The Open Group (2009)
16. OPEN-GROUP: Service Oriented Architecture: What is SOA? 2012. http://www.opengroup.org/soa/source-book/soa/soa.htm (2012)
17. Molnar, W.A., Korhonen, J.J.: Research Paradigms and Topics in Enterprise Engineering: Analysis of Recent Conferences and Workshops, IEEE Eighth International Conference on Research Challenges in Information Science, 28–30 May 2014, Marrakesh, Morocco (2014)
18. Danesh, M.H., Loucopoulos, P., Yu, E.: Dynamic capabilities for sustainable enterprise IT—a modeling framework. In: 34th International Conference on Conceptual Modeling (ER 2015), Stockholm, Sweden (2015)
19. DoD: Systems Engineering Guide for Systems of Systems, Aug 2008, Washington DC (2008)
20. Helfat, C.E., Peteraf, M.A.: The dynamic resource-based view: capability lifecycles. Strateg. Manage. J. **24**(997–1010) (2003)
21. Teece, D.J.: Dynamic Capabilities and Strategic Management. Oxford University Press, United States, New York (2009)
22. Barney, J.: Firm resources and sustained competitive advantage. J. Manage. **17**, 99–120 (1991)
23. Teece, D.J.: Explicating dynamic capabilities: the nature and microfoundations of (sustainable) enterprise performance. Strateg. Manag. J. **28**, 1319–1350 (2007)
24. Cook, D.:, Business-Capability Mapping: Staying Ahead of the Joneses (2007)
25. Greski, L.: Business Capability modeling: theory and practice. Arch. Gov. (2014)
26. Danesh, M.H., Yu, E.: Modeling enterprise capabilities with i*: reasoning on alternatives. In: International Workshop on Advances in Services DEsign based on the Notion of CApabiliy (ASDENCA'14), pp. 112–123. Springer, Thessaloniki, Greece (2014)
27. Rosen, M.: *Business Processes Start with Capabilities*. BP Trends 2010
28. Ulrich, W., Rosen, M.: The business capability map: the "Rosetta Stone" of Business/IT alignment. Enterp. Arch. **14**(2) (2014)
29. Stirna, J., Grabis, J., Henkel, M., Zdravkovic, J.: Capability driven development—an approach to support evolving organizations. In: Sandkuhl, K., Seigerroth, U., Stirna, J. (eds.) The Practice of Enterprise Modeling, Lecture Notes in Business Information Processing, 2012, pp. 117–131. Springer, Berlin, Heidelberg (2012)
30. Iacob, M.-E., Quartel, D., Jonkers, H.: Capturing business strategy and value in enterprise architecture to support portfolio valuation. In: 16th International Enterprise Distributed Object Computing Conference (EDOC 2012), 2012, pp. 11–20. IEEE (2012)
31. Homann, U.: A Business-Oriented Foundation for Service Orientation. Microsoft Developer Network (2006)
32. Teece, D.J., Pisano, G., Shuen, A.: Dynamic capabilities and strategic management. Strateg. Manage. J. **18**(7), 509–533 (1997)
33. Bērziša, S., Bravos, G., Gonzalez, T., Czubayko, U., España, S., Grabis, J., Henkel, M., Jokste, L., Kampars, J., Koc, H., Kuhr, J.-C., Llorca, C., Loucopoulos, P., Juanes, R., Pastor, O., Sandkuhl, K., Simic, H., Stirna, J., Zdravkovic, J.: Capability driven development: an approach to designing digital enterprises. Bus. Inf. Syst. Eng. **57**(1), 15–25 (2015)

34. Azevedo, C.L.B., Iacob, M.-E., Almeida, J.P.A., Sinderen, Mv, Pires, L.F., Guizzardi, G.: Modeling resources and capabilities in enterprise architecture: a well-founded ontology-based proposal for ArchiMate. Inf. Syst. **2015**(54), 235–262 (2015)
35. Guizzardi, G., Wagner, G., Almeida, J.o.P.A., Guizzardi, R.S.S.: Towards ontological foundations for conceptual modeling: the Unified Foundational Ontology (UFO) story. Appl. Ontol. **10**(3–4) (2015)
36. Loucopoulos, P., Stratigaki, C., Danesh, M.H., Bravos, G., Anagnostopoulos, D., Dimitrakopoulos, G.: Enterprise capability modeling: concepts, method and application. In: 3rd International Conference on Enterprise Systems, 2015. Basel, Switzerland (2015)
37. Zikra, I., Stirna, J., Zdravkovic, J.: Bringing enterprise modeling closer to model-driven development. Pract. Enterp. Model. **2011**, 268–282 (2011)
38. Kardasis, P., Loucopoulos, P.: A roadmap for the elicitation of business rules in information systems projects. Bus. Process Manage. J. **11**(4), 316–348 (2005)
39. Kavakli, E., Loucopoulos, P.: Experiences with goal-oriented modelling of organisational change. IEEE Trans. Syst. Man Cybern.—Part C **36**(2), 221–235 (2006)
40. Loucopoulos, P.: Experiences with modelling early requirements. In: Soderstrom, P.J.E. (ed.) Information Systems Engineering. IGI Publishing (2008)
41. Loucopoulos, P., Katsouli, E.: Modelling business rules in an office environment. SIGOIS Bull. **13**(2), 28–37 (1992)
42. Loucopoulos, P., Kavakli, V.: Enterprise knowledge management and conceptual modelling. In: Goos, G., et al. (eds.) Conceptual Modeling: Current Issues and Future Directions, pp. 123–143. Springer (1999)
43. OMG: Business Process Modeling Notation (BPMN) Version 2.1. Object Management Group (2009)
44. Kavakli, P., Loucopoulos, E.: Enterprise modelling and the teleological approach to requirements engineering. Int. J. Intell. Coop. Inf. Syst. **4**(1), 45–79 (1995)
45. Kavakli, V., Loucopoulos, P.: Goal-driven business process analysis—application in electricity deregulation. Inf. Syst. **24**(3), 187–207 (1999)
46. Heidari, F., Loucopoulos, P.: Quality Evaluation Framework (QEF): modeling and evaluating quality of business processes. Int. J. Account. Inf. Syst. **15**(3), 193–223 (2014)
47. Ghosh, P., Sharma, A., Chakrabarti, P.P., Dasgupta, P.: Algorithms for generating ordered solutions for explicit AND/OR structures. J. Artif. Intell. Res. **2012**(44), 275–333 (2012)
48. Basili, V.R., Caldiera, G., Rombach, H.D., Marciniak, J.: The goal question metric approach. In: Encyclopedia of Software Engineering, pp. 528–532. Wiley, New York, NY, USA (1994)
49. James, A., Chung, J.-Y.: Business and industry specific cloud: challenges and opportunities. Future Gener. Comput. Syst. **48**(C), 39–45 (2015)
50. Gongolidis, E., Kalloniatis, C., Kavakli, E.: Requirements identification for migrating eGovernment applications to the cloud. In: Proceedings of the 2nd IFIP TC5/8 International Conference (ICT-EurAsia), pp. 150–158. Springer (2014)

Supporting Business Process Improvement Through a Modeling Tool

Florian Johannsen and Hans-Georg Fill

Abstract Business process improvement (BPI) ranks among the topics of highest priority in modern organizations. However, considering the rapidly changing customer requirements in times of high market transparency and the increasing collaboration between organizations, the development of BPI projects has become very challenging. Implicit process knowledge from diverse process participants needs to be elicited and transformed into improvement opportunities. In this context, the results achieved need to be properly documented, communicated and processed throughout a company. To face these challenges, we introduce the so-called BPI roadmap which is a concept for systematically performing BPI initiatives based on a set of easy-to-use and proven BPI techniques. Further, tool support is established allowing the efficient codification of results via conceptual model types, the easy sharing of the outcomes and the automatic generation of reports.

Keywords Business process improvement • Metamodeling • Roadmap

1 Introduction

The improvement of business processes is a highly prioritized topic in modern enterprises [8, 45]. The foremost aims of corresponding BPI initiatives are to establish customer satisfaction, to elevate process performance and to achieve consumer loyalty (cf. [45]). At the same time, business process execution should become more efficient as cost reduction is seen as a decisive factor for staying

F. Johannsen (✉)
Department Management of Information Systems,
University of Regensburg, 93053 Regensburg, Germany
e-mail: florian.johannsen@wiwi.uni-regensburg.de

H.-G. Fill
Research Group Knowledge Engineering, University of Vienna,
1090 Vienna, Austria
e-mail: hans-georg.fill@univie.ac.at

D. Karagiannis et al. (eds.), *Domain-Specific Conceptual Modeling*,
DOI 10.1007/978-3-319-39417-6_10

competitive [8, 22]. However, in today's markets, the conduction of business process improvement (BPI) initiatives has become challenging.

At first, customer expectations on products and services are rapidly changing these days [17]. A major reason for that is the increasing market transparency fostered by the dissemination of Web 2.0 technologies (cf. [4, 44]). In that context, there are a variety of platforms (e.g., Price Grabber, Google Shopping) that allow consumers to share product and service experiences, compare prices and find the cheapest provider amongst others. As a result, information asymmetries between sellers and buyers are reduced, making it difficult to keep pace with continuously shifting consumer expectations [32].

Second, more and more firms are engaged in cross-organizational cooperation [36]. In such settings, "value" [46] is created by executing cross-organizational business processes with process participants geographically acting from various sites (cf. [32]). Regarding the conduction of BPI projects, one should make sure that employees from all cooperating partners are involved [26]. Moreover, the results produced in the BPI projects need to be properly documented and shared with the partners across company borders.

Third, the selection of adequate methods and techniques for performing BPI initiatives is challenging [29] Literature offers a huge variety of holistic methods (e.g., Six Sigma, Lean Management, TQM) as well as single techniques (e.g., value-stream-map) suitable for being applied in BPI projects (cf. [25, 39, 46]). Regarding this multitude of approaches, companies are usually overstrained in choosing specific BPI techniques and methods to be used for achieving the aspired project goals [29]. Additionally, extensive methods such as Six Sigma or TQM are often believed to be "over-dimensioned" and complex to handle in terms of BPI projects with a limited scope (cf. [8]). This shows practitioners' need for a pre-defined and manageable set of well-established BPI techniques, to be used for systematically conducting projects with different goals (e.g., cost reduction, increase of service quality) [26].

What is needed is a set of proven and commonly known BPI techniques that support the systematic transformation (cf. [38]) of employees' implicit process knowledge (e.g., on customer requirements, process weaknesses) into explicit solutions to improve a business process [26]. Furthermore, adequate means to codify the generated results, e.g., by conceptual models (cf. [2]), and to share them with all project participants are required. Thereby, the documentation and communication of results can be efficiently supported by tools which ideally enable the automatic processing and analysis of the results and as well the generation of beneficial reports [27, 47].

We addressed these issues by first developing the so-called "BPI roadmap". Generally, the concept of "roadmaps" is established in knowledge management, while a roadmap can be understood as a "guided" process to solve problems occurring in an enterprise's day-to-day business [6]. In our context, the BPI roadmap is a set of logically arranged and easy-to-use BPI techniques eliciting employees' implicit process knowledge for the purpose of developing process improvement opportunities [28]. In this regard, conceptual model types are used to codify the results generated, an approach that has proven beneficial in practice for structuring emerging knowledge [2, 7]. Contrary to business process modeling, which focuses on a business process and the visualization of its single working activities (cf. [20]), our method codifies outcomes and partial results created by applying the BPI techniques of the BPI roadmap. This can be customer requirements or performance indicators for measuring process performance for instance. The modeling method introduced hereafter provides constructs to codify such results and their relation to one another by corresponding model types. For example, it is documented which performance indicators are suitable for measuring the degree of fulfilling particular customer requirements.

Second, the tool "RUPERT (*R*egensburg *U*niversity *P*rocess *E*xcellence and *R*eengineering *T*oolkit)" was implemented. RUPERT supports employees in using the BPI roadmap, documents the results produced in BPI initiatives as conceptual model types, allows to purposefully analyze them by means of automatically generated reports and user-defined queries, and thereby facilitates the efficient communication of the outcomes [27].

The present paper shows how the BPI roadmap and the RUPERT tool were conceptualized and developed. Moreover, the applicability is demonstrated by a practical use case. The paper unfolds as follows: in the subsequent section theoretical foundations are described and the BPI roadmap is explained. Section 3 highlights the development process of the RUPERT tool and presents key results during the implementation. The applicability of the tool is demonstrated in Sect. 4. The paper ends with a conclusion and an outlook on future research.

2 Method Description

2.1 Business Process Improvement

In the last couple of years, many different BPI methods were developed. An often cited work is Harrington's BPI method (1991). It builds on a five-step procedure model comprising the phases: "organizing for improvement", "understanding the process", "streamlining", "measurements and controls" and "continuous improvement" [21]. Another approach, called the "SUPER methodology", was introduced by [33]. It builds on a procedure model consisting of five phases and incorporates ideas from business process reengineering (BPR), continuous process improvement (CPI) and business process benchmarking (BPB) (Lee and Chuah 2001). Adesola and Baines [1] derive a BPI method that integrates diverse established approaches (cf. [21, 31]) and is characterized by a seven-step procedure model.

Besides, approaches such as Six Sigma (cf. [39]), Total Quality Management (TQM) (cf. [9]) or Lean Management (cf. [46]), that are attributed to the discipline of "(process-oriented) quality management" (cf. [41]), are applied for improving business processes in practice (cf. [8, 45]).

However, the use of such methods often is accompanied by complications. First, many of the aforementioned approaches have methodological flaws (e.g., lack of supporting BPI techniques) which hamper their application in BPI initiatives (cf. [48]). Whereas the methods as introduced put a strong emphasis on the procedure model, corresponding techniques to operationalize single activities (e.g., activity "analyse the as-is process") are neglected in several cases for example (cf. [48]). Second, practitioners increasingly shrink back from using holistic methods as they are often judged as being too complex for improvement projects with a limited scope (cf. [8]).

In addition to these comprising methods, literature introduces many BPI techniques that may be applied in projects (cf. [18, 37]). A technique can be understood as some sort of guideline for a particular task leading to a specific result [19]. For example, the *"Ishikawa Diagram"* (cf. [24]) supports the structuring and collection of causes for lacking process performance in BPI initiatives (e.g., long cycle times). In this context, the Six Sigma "7 × 7-toolbox" represents a collection of 49 techniques supporting process improvement efforts [35]. These are classified into seven clusters, such as "quality control techniques" or "customer techniques" amongst others (cf. [35]). Further, [18] analyze and compare 36 BPI techniques focusing on the so-called "act of improvement" [13] in special. Kettinger et al. [31] provides a list of more than 72 BPI techniques and assign them to different phases of project conduction.

However, this large number of existing BPI techniques poses the challenge of selecting those few to be applied in a BPI project (cf. [29]). This is a complex task, as profound knowledge on the BPI techniques is required which cannot be automatically assumed (cf. [16]). Further, practitioners usually neither have the time nor the motivation to become acquainted with a large variety of different BPI techniques [16]. Much more, they prefer a manageable and limited set of easy-to-use BPI techniques (cf. [8]).

What has been missing yet is an integration of commonly established BPI techniques in the form of a "roadmap" to provide means for the systematic support of BPI projects in the service as well as production industries. For that purpose, we developed the so-called "BPI roadmap", which is a logical arrangement of proven and easy-to-use BPI techniques that supports all stages of an improvement project (i.e., definition of project goals, measurement of process performance, analysis of problem causes, etc.) (cf. [26]). In the following, the development of the BPI roadmap is described and its functioning is introduced.

2.2 *The BPI Roadmap*

The BPI roadmap was developed in cooperation with an automotive bank and followed a five-step procedure based on the design science approach (cf. [23, 26]).

In a first step, requirements on the BPI roadmap (representing the artefact) and the corresponding BPI techniques were derived by analyzing literature sources

Table 1 Requirements on the BPI roadmap [26]

Requirements (Rq)	Explanation
Rq1: Support of all stages of the DMAIC cycle	The roadmap should consider BPI techniques to create results for all DMAIC phases
Rq2: Manageable set of BPI techniques	The roadmap should only provide a limited set of BPI techniques (approx. 10–15)
Rq3: Consideration of team-oriented BPI techniques	The techniques must be suitable to stimulate group discussions and visualize the results generated
Rq4: High understandability and learnability of the roadmap	The techniques of the roadmap must be easy to learn and directly usable in workshops, without extra training
Rq5: Flexible handling	The BPI techniques should be adaptable for specific user groups
Rq6: Autonomy of BPI techniques	Each technique should produce results directly (e.g., identified customer requirements)
Rq7: Operational character	The techniques should focus and work on the business process itself
Rq8: Complementary interdependencies	The techniques of the roadmap should be logically dependent so that the output of a technique serves as input to another technique
Rq9: Successive sequencing of techniques	A clear order of techniques should be given

(e.g., [4, 5, 40, 42]). The general applicability of the artefact was supposed to be assured by means of the focus on the literature [26]. In total, nine requirements emerged guiding the design and the development of the BPI roadmap. Table 1 provides an overview of the requirements. For a more detailed description, the reader is referred to [26].

In a second step, BPI techniques were collected (e.g., [15, 18, 31, 37]) and systematically described regarding "purpose", "steps during application", "pros" and "cons". All in all, a list comprising 107 BPI techniques was created that way.

Afterward (step 3), the 107 BPI techniques were discussed against the background of the requirements as they were expressed. This was done in collaboration with six BPI experts of the aforementioned automotive bank. As a result of the discussion, 16 BPI techniques were judged as being potential candidates for the BPI roadmap. Thereby, the techniques covered all phases of the DMAIC cycle (*D*efine, *M*easure, *I*mprove, *A*nalyze, *C*ontrol) (cf. [39]) which was used as a base for structuring BPI projects. The techniques chosen were applied at the automotive bank in diverse BPI initiatives (cf. [26]). Feedback was gathered from project participants to see whether they perceived the techniques to be beneficial regarding the project goals or not. Then, participants were supposed to report aspects they liked or disliked about the BPI techniques. Finally, eleven BPI techniques were chosen to form the BPI roadmap.

In a fourth step, the techniques were logically arranged and complementary and conditional interdependencies were considered [4], i.e., the results delivered by a technique were taken up as input by the subsequent technique. Finally (step 5), the

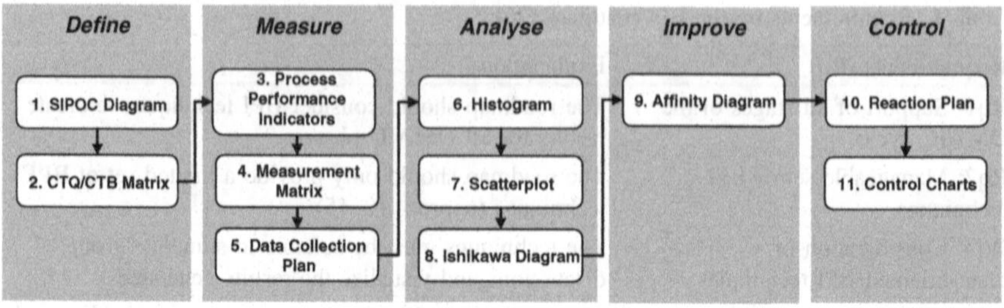

Fig. 1 The BPI roadmap [26]

BPI roadmap was evaluated at the automotive bank in several BPI projects with different scope and various project goals. The main purpose was to validate, whether the logical arrangement of BPI techniques (as defined in step 4) was applicable or whether modifications were necessary.

Figure 1 shows the BPI roadmap as it resulted from the above procedure. It functions as follows (cf. [26]): at first, the *SIPOC Diagram* (*S*upplier, *I*nput, *P*rocess, *O*utput and *C*ustomer Diagram) generates an abstract visualization of the business process under consideration. Requirements on the business process from the customer side (Voice of Customer—VOC) as well as employees' expectations (Voice of Business—VOB) are gathered using the *CTQ/CTB Matrix*. Based on these, "Critical-to-Customer (CTQ)" and "Critical-to-Business (CTB)" factors are derived subsequently. These are the project goals of the BPI initiative. To measure the degree of goal achievement in an objective manner, the so-called *Process Performance Indicators* are defined. These are then prioritized regarding the CTQs and CTBs via the *Measurement Matrix*. After that, a *Data Collection Plan* is established to organize the gathering of measurement data. The measurement data is analyzed using *Histograms* and *Scatterplots*, and problem causes are identified by means of the *Ishikawa Diagram*. Via the *Affinity Diagram*, the solutions for overcoming the problem causes (as identified in the prior step) are worked out. Finally, the *Reaction Plan* and the *Control Charts* are used to constantly monitor the process performance and to define actions in case of unexpected performance deviations.

2.3 The ADOxx Metamodeling Platform

Considering the technical development of the BPI roadmap in the form of a modeling method, the most comprising support is currently offered by metamodeling platforms (cf. [28]). They allow to drastically shorten development cycles as little programming effort is required only and a vast array of additional functionalities (e.g., coupling to other software) is offered [30]. For the work at hand, we used the ADO*xx* metamodeling platform which is freely available at http://www.adoxx.org and was successfully applied in manifold industry projects for more than 20 years [10]. Besides a user interface and a repository, the ADO*xx* architecture also introduces eight components to realize modeling methods, ranging from components providing visual model editors to those enabling the querying of data captured in model instances for example (cf. [10]). More, the C++-based ADO*xx* metamodeling platform offers a set of domain specific languages enabling the specification of modeling languages, their graphical representations, mechanisms and algorithms [10]. In this regard, *ADOxx Library Language* (ALL) is applied for the specification of classes, relationclasses, attributes and model types. The graphical representation of classes and relationclasses is done via the GRAPHREP language whereas the ATTRREP language is used to define attribute visibilities [10]. Finally, mechanisms and algorithms are specified by reverting to the AdoScript language [10].

3 Method Conceptualization and Development

In the following section, the development of the tool RUPERT is described. Therefore, the development procedure is shown at first. Then, each stage of the development procedure is presented in more detail.

3.1 The Development Procedure for the Tool RUPERT

The procedure shown in Fig. 2 was used to develop RUPERT. The procedure is similar to the model-based and incremental knowledge engineering (MIKE) approach (cf. [3]) and follows the principles of design science (cf. [23, 34]). The MIKE approach was initially developed for the implementation of knowledge-based systems and uses semiformal and formal specifications to capture knowledge on a problem domain and transfer it into a running software [3]. The discipline of design science creates and evaluates artefacts that are proposed as solutions to organizational problems [23]. Building on these methodical foundations, the procedure as shown in Fig. 2 smoothly transformed the BPI roadmap—which represents a conceptual problem-solving approach in the BPI field—into a

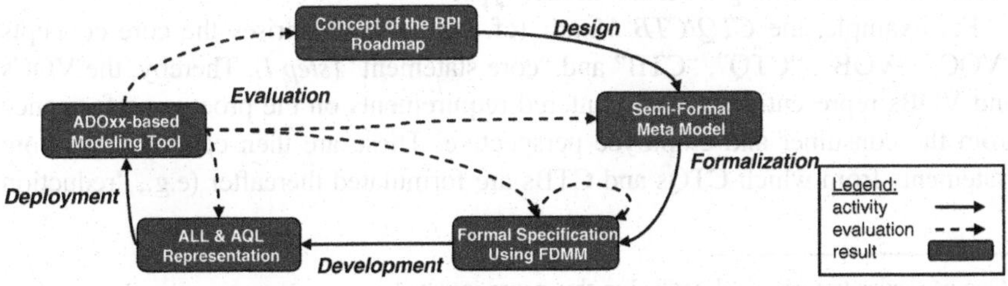

Fig. 2 Development procedure for RUPERT [28]

running software prototype. Thereby, semiformal (e.g., metamodels) and formal specifications were used throughout the development (cf. [28]).

The concept of the BPI roadmap, as introduced in Sect. 2.2, was the starting point for the depicted development procedure (see Fig. 2). In the activity ***"design"*** the BPI techniques of the roadmap were transformed into conceptual model types and an integrated semiformal metamodel was created. Subsequently, the metamodel was formalized to prepare the ground for the implementation (activity ***"formalization"***). Based on the formalization, an implementation-oriented representation could be derived (activity ***"development"***) which was then deployed on the ADO*xx* metamodeling platform to receive a running software prototype (activity ***"deployment"***). The applicability and usability of the software were then evaluated by means of the project data stemming several practical use cases.[1] Then, a usability test based on the SUMI questionnaire is currently performed (*S*oftware *U*sability *M*easurement *I*nventory).[2]

In the remainder of this section, the steps "design" to "deployment" will be described in more detail.

3.2 Design of the BPI Roadmap as an Integrated Semiformal Metamodel

As described, the BPI roadmap was created as a solution to systematically conduct BPI projects and thus to satisfy practitioners' demand for more manageable and operational BPI approaches. In this context, an important topic was the codification (cf. [6]) of the results produced by applying the roadmap. For that purpose, conceptual model types and corresponding metamodels (cf. [2]) were developed, that exactly captured the functionality of the underlying BPI techniques as proposed by the roadmap. By the model types, the documentation, communication and processing of results is facilitated in BPI initiatives (cf. [26]).

A three-step procedure was performed in order to obtain the metamodels for the BPI roadmap (cf. [26]): (I) at first, the core concepts of a BPI technique were recognized; (II) afterwards, the relations between the core concepts were identified, defining how these affect each other; (III) finally, the core concepts and relations were transformed into corresponding classes, respectively, relationclasses of a metamodel determining a certain model type.

For example, the *CTQ/CTB Matrix* (cf. [15, 37]) comprises the core concepts "VOC", "VOB", "CTQ", "CTB" and "core statement" *(step I)*. Thereby, the VOCs and VOBs represent the verbally uttered requirements on the process performance from the consumer and employee perspective. These are then condensed to core statements from which CTQs and CTBs are formulated thereafter (e.g., "reduction

[1]One particular use case is described in this paper in detail.

[2]Service provided by the Human Factors Research Group: http://sumi.ucc.ie/.

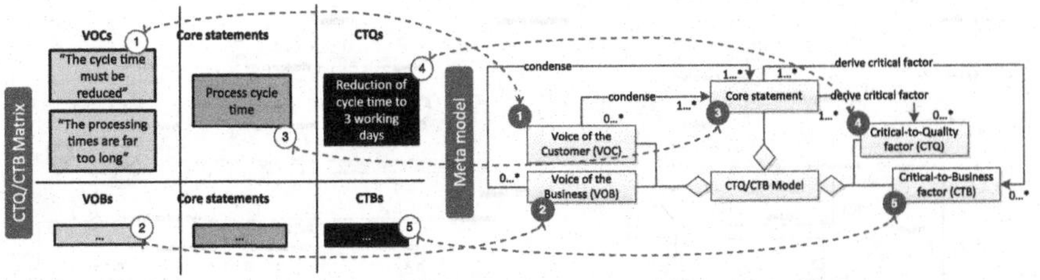

Fig. 3 Example for the design of metamodels reverting to the CTQ/CTB Model

of cycle time to 3 working days"). Therefore, the VOCs and VOBs must be connected to one core statement at least. Additionally, each CTQ and CTB is related to one or more core statements as well *(step II)*. Accordingly, the classes "Voice of the Customer (VOC)", "Voice of the Business (VOB)", "core statement", "Critical-to-Quality factor (CTQ)" and "Critical-to-Business factor (CTB)" were derived for the metamodel. Further, the relationclasses "condense" and "derive critical factor" emerged. Figure 3 visualizes the example once again.

In total, nine model types were developed that way. The statistical techniques of the roadmap (e.g., histograms, control charts, etc.) were covered by the *Statistic Interface Model*. Figure 4 presents the integrated metamodel of the BPI roadmap.

As the techniques of the roadmap logically build on each other (see Sect. 2.2) there are interrelationships between classes across model types. This means that the results captured by a model instance are referenced in an instance of another model type. For example, the CTQs and CTBs as defined in the *CTQ/CTB Model* are used by the *Measurement Matrix Model* to prioritize the process performance indicators later on. In Fig. 4, these interrelationships become obvious by the dotted arrows indicating references (INTERREFs) between model types (cf. [26]).

To analyze the results captured in the conceptual model types, reports were defined that provide the user with beneficial insights on the outcomes emerging in a BPI initiative. In total, 12 reports were specified for the BPI roadmap. For a detailed overview, the reader is referred to [26].

3.3 Formalization of the Integrated Metamodel

To prepare the ground for the implementation of the BPI roadmap as a tool, the integrated metamodel (see Fig. 4) was formalized. This served two major purposes (cf. [28]): at first, the formal specification of the BPI roadmap was the prerequisite to straightforwardly map it to an implementation-oriented presentation directly executable by the ADO*xx* platform. Second, the formalization helped to uncover potential misconceptions, to clarify ambiguous user requirements and thus served as a validation of the semiformal metamodel before its implementation (cf. Fraser et al. 1994). For example, based on the formal specification, it became obvious whether

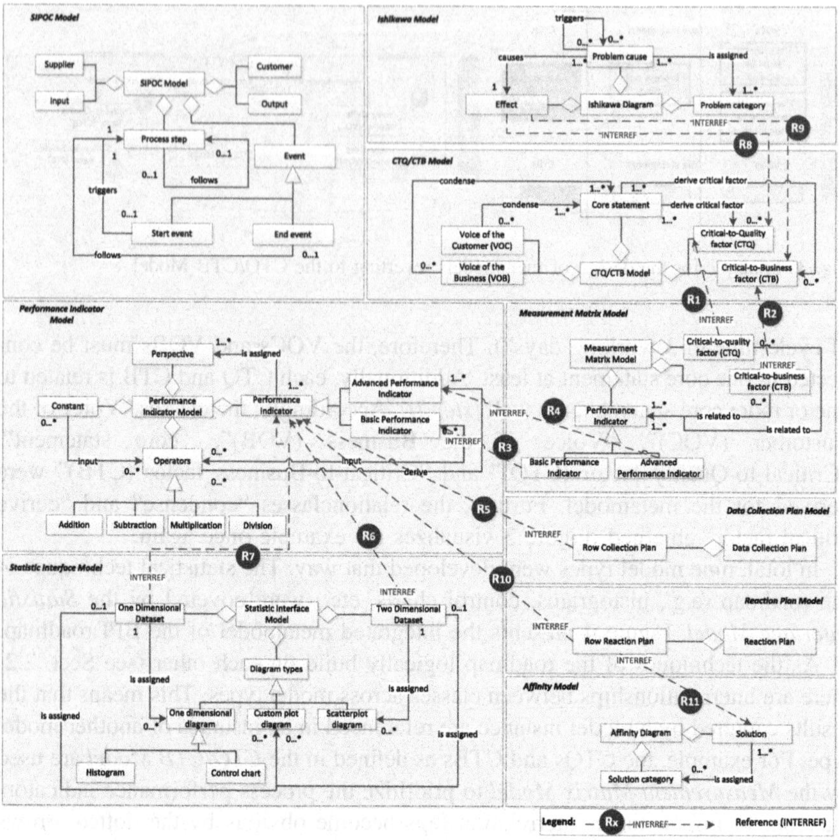

Fig. 4 Integrated metamodel of the BPI roadmap [26]

the value ranges for certain attributes (e.g., values "quality", "time", "flexibility" and "costs" for the attribute "quality dimension" of the class "Critical-to-Quality factor (CTQ)") were sufficient considering the users' requirements and possible project constellations or not [28].

In the work at hand, the FDMM formalism (*F*ormalism for *D*escribing ADO*xx* *M*etaModels and *M*odels) was used (cf. [11]). FDMM is an easy-to-use formalism that builds on set theory and first-order-logic and allows to specify metamodels for different application domains without requiring specific mathematical skills [12, 28].

The functioning of the FDMM formalism is exemplarily shown on the formalization of the *SIPOC Model*. As mentioned in Sect. 2.2, the model type gives an abstract visualization of the business process to be improved (cf. [37]). In that context, the core activities, the process input and output, the suppliers providing the input and the process customers are to be documented (cf. [15, 37]).

The metamodel of the *SIPOC Model* as shown in Fig. 4 was formalized as follows: at first, the model type (MT_{SIPOC}) was specified in FDMM as a tuple of a set of object types (O^T_{SIPOC}), a set of data types (D^T_{SIPOC}) and a set of attributes (A_{SIPOC}):

$$MT_{SIPOC} = \langle O^T_{SIPOC}, D^T_{SIPOC}, A_{SIPOC} \rangle \tag{1}$$

The following object types were defined for the *SIPOC Model*:

$$O^T_{SIPOC} = \begin{array}{l}\{\text{Process step, Input, Output, Supplier, Customer,}\\ \text{Event, Start event, End event, triggers follows}\}\end{array} \tag{2}$$

Then, inheritance relationships were specified. For example, the object types "Start event" and "End event" were subtypes of the object type "Event" that was declared as an abstract object type (see Fig. 4). These inheritance relationships strongly facilitated the assignment of attributes to the subtypes "Start event" and "End Event":

$$\begin{array}{c}\text{Start Event} \preccurlyeq \textit{Event}\\ \text{End Event} \preccurlyeq \text{Event}\end{array} \tag{3}$$

Considering the data types, the *SIPOC Model* mainly built on the type "String":

$$D^T_{SIPOC} = \{\text{String}\} \tag{4}$$

Afterward, the attributes for the object types were specified. This comprised attributes for the names of the object types but also attributes to describe the object types more profoundly. Further, several attributes to express the relatedness between the elements by references had to be considered:

$$A_{SIPOC} = \begin{array}{l}\{\text{Name, Description, provides} - \text{input, receives} - \text{output,}\\ \text{referenced} - \text{document, referenced} - \text{business} - \text{process}\}\end{array} \tag{5}$$

Finally, the attributes were to be refined by information on domain, range and cardinalities. Attributes that were assigned to an abstract type were automatically inherited by all subtypes. For example, the attribute "Description" which was assigned to the abstract type "Event" could be found in the according subtypes "Start event" and "End Event" as well. By this attribute, events in a model instance could be precisely specified via textual descriptions. Though, the cardinality $\langle 0, 1\rangle$ indicates that a user is not forced to add a corresponding description:

$$\begin{array}{c}\text{domain(Description)} = \{\text{Event}\}\\ \text{range(Description)} = \{\text{String}\}\\ \text{card(Description)} = \langle 0, 1\rangle\end{array} \tag{6}$$

As mentioned above, the elements of the *SIPOC Model* are interrelated which was expressed by references accordingly (see Fig. 4). For example, an instance of the object type "Customer" could reference a certain process output (instance of the object type "Output"):

$$\begin{aligned} \text{domain}(\text{receives} - \text{output}) &= \{\text{Customer}\} \\ \text{range}(\text{receives} - \text{output}) &= \{(\text{Output}, \text{MT}_{SIPOC})\} \\ \text{card}(\text{receives} - \text{output}) &= \langle 0, \text{n} \rangle \end{aligned} \tag{7}$$

Such formal specifications were derived for all model types of the BPI roadmap as shown in Fig. 4. Additionally, besides the model types, the queries to generate the above-mentioned reports (see Sect. 3.2) were also formalized via FDMM. Details on that can be found in [28].

3.4 Development and Deployment of the RUPERT Software

The constructs of the FDMM formalism could be directly mapped to the ADO*xx* Library Language (ALL), an implementation-oriented specification directly executable on the ADO*xx* metamodeling platform [10, 12]. In this regard, the ALL representation contained all the information captured in the FDMM formalization of the BPI roadmap but enhanced it by data required for the execution as a software tool, e.g., algorithms (cf. [3]).

For demonstration purposes, the mapping procedure from the FDMM representation to ALL is partially shown for the aforementioned *SIPOC Model*: therefore, the object type "Start Event" was transferred to a corresponding class in ALL (see marker "1" in Fig. 5). Generally, depending on its graphical representation, an object type in FDMM is either mapped to a class or a relationclass [12]. Furthermore, the attributes in FDMM are either transferred to class attributes (e.g., "GraphRep") or user-defined attributes (e.g., the "receives-output" attribute of the object type "Customer"—see Eq. (5) in Sect. 3.3). In Fig. 5, the class attribute

```
MODELTYPE  \"SIPOC\"   from:none  plural:  \"SIPOC\"  pos:1  not-
simulateable bitmap: \"db:\\SIPOC.bmp\"
        INCL \"Process Step\"
        INCL \"Input\"
        INCL \"Output\"
        INCL \"Start Event\"
...
CLASS <Start Event> : <Event>                                    1
...
   CLASSATTRIBUTE <GraphRep>
        VALUE "GRAPHREP                                          2
        PEN color:$000000 w:1pt
        FILL color:$ffaaaa
...
```

Fig. 5 ALL excerpt for the SIPOC Model

"GrapRep" is exemplarily shown which was predefined by the ADO*xx* platform and captured information on the graphical representation of the object type under consideration (see marker "2").

However, some challenges had to be dealt with during the mapping process (cf. [12, 28]). For example, it needed to be decided in ALL whether a relation between object types was to be expressed by a graphical relation, with the GRAPHREP grammar defining the visualization (cf. [10]), or by reference attributes [28].

The FDMM specification of the BPI roadmap strongly facilitated the derivation of an ALL representation, as ambiguities of the semiformal metamodel specification (e.g., unclear attributes with lacking value ranges) (cf. [14]) could be systematically eliminated [28]. After that, the formalized reports defined regarding the BPI roadmap (cf. [26]) were transferred to the ADO*xx* Query Language (AQL) [28]. This enabled to query model instances and thus allowed users to purposefully analyze the results created in BPI projects [28].

The implementation-oriented representations of the BPI roadmap (ALL and AQL) were then deployed on the ADO*xx* platform, leading to a runnable software prototype [28]. Summarizing, the development procedure (see Fig. 2) guided the smooth transfer of the BPI roadmap as a concept to an executable prototype.[3] The applicability of the prototype is dealt with in the subsequent section.

4 Proof of Concept

This section demonstrates the applicability of the tool RUPERT by using it to process data from a real BPI project. The BPI project considered was the optimization of the "document management process" at a German automotive bank. The product portfolio of the automotive bank comprised individual solutions for the mobility of private and business clients, financing and leasing, car insurance, dealer financing as well as fleet management [48]. There was no branch network and the majority of business deals concerned leasing and financing issues for new cars [48].

In the context of a large and global quality initiative, the automotive bank defined strategic target agreements for the document management process which were also explicated in the company's strategy map. These comprised the increased customer orientation by processing incoming documents (letter, fax, email) within two working days, the reduction of monetary and human resources during process execution and a higher degree of process automation. Therefore, a BPI project was triggered to improve the current process performance.

The document management process worked as follows: after receiving the mail, it was first sorted by the postal service of the automotive bank. Next, a fine screening of the documents was performed in the operational departments. The documents were then processed by the corresponding employees and solutions were

[3]Prototype available at: http://www.omilab.org/web/rupert/home.

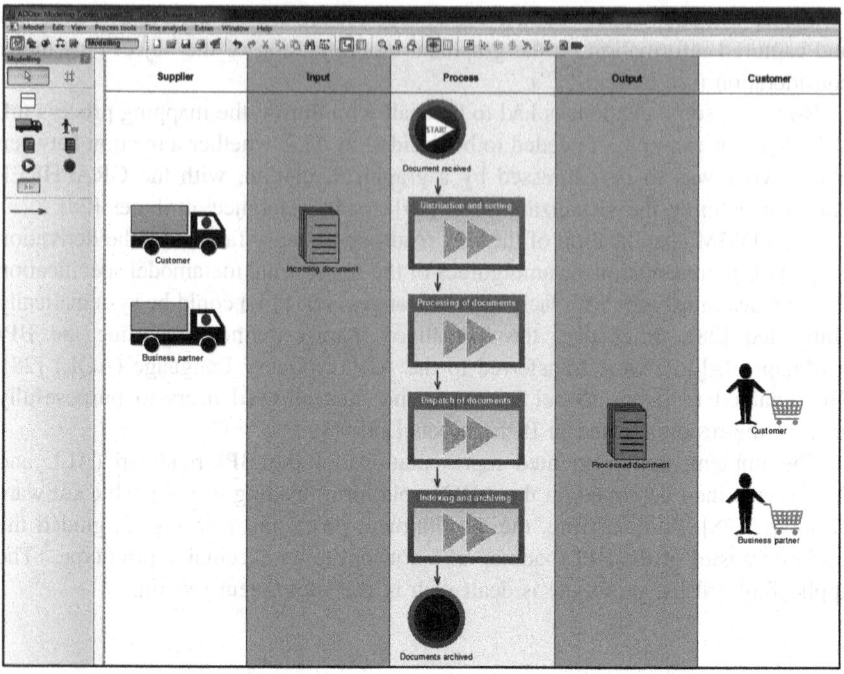

Fig. 6 Screenshot from RUPERT showing the SIPOC Model for the document management process

created as outgoing mail. Afterward, the documents were prepared for being indexed. The process ended with archiving the aforementioned documents.

The BPI project was organized in form of a workshop with process participants from different operating departments being involved. Additionally, a core project team was formed for performing data analysis—prior to starting the project as a pre-analysis of existing performance data (cf. [43]) and during the initiative—for documenting the project results and for managing all organizational tasks (e.g., project management). For conducting the project, the BPI roadmap was applied.

In preparation for the workshop, a *SIPOC Model* of the document management process was created by the core project team, which was meant to provide all project participants with a common understanding of the process. Figure 6 shows a screenshot of the RUPERT tool with the corresponding *SIPOC Model*. The lane "process" presents the major process activities. Accordingly, the remaining lanes are used for visualizing the process customers and suppliers as well as the key process input and output.

According to data analyzed prior to the first workshop (data pre-analysis), the process execution costs amounted to several million € each year. Further, it was estimated by employees, that the indexing of the documents was a time-consuming task severely impacting the process cycle times.

At the beginning of the workshop with process participants from the automotive bank, the project goals (namely CTQs and CTBs) were specified based on the targets as defined in the strategy map. Therefore, it was decided to focus on two major goals to keep the scope of the BPI project manageable. Based on a collection of employee and customer requirements (VOCs and VOBs) that were drawn from personal interviews with the workforce, managers and the CRM system it became evident that the document sorting procedures were error-prone, took a long time and the process was lacking transparency in general. The last aspect led to delays in routing documents to employees responsible for dealing with requests from customers and business clients alike.

Because of that, the first goal of the project was defined as reducing the process cycle time from the stage of document receipt (at the automotive bank) to sending a reply (as outgoing mail) including the archiving of all documents to two working days. A second goal was to reduce process execution costs. For the formulation of these goals, the *CTQ/CTB Matrix* was used. An excerpt of the corresponding *CTQ/CTB Model* is shown in Fig. 7. The VOC requirements as well as the VOB statements were listed and then summarized to core statements. These were the foundation for defining project goals, represented as CTQ factors and CTB factors.

Several *process performance indicators (PPIs)* were formulated to measure the degree of goal achievement. These referred to the categories "costs", "cycle times" and "quality". Regarding "costs", the PPIs (1) "costs for office supplies", (2) "costs for operating IT systems" and (3) "personnel costs" were defined. These were supposed to assess the current process execution costs more precisely. To measure the process cycle times, the (1) "waiting time", (2) "processing time", (3) "sorting time", (4) "time for transportation" of documents as well as (5) the "overall cycle time from the receipt of ingoing documents to dispatch as outgoing mail" were of particular interest and specified as corresponding PPIs. Finally, the (1) "number of errors in archiving" and (2) the "number of errors in dispatching outgoing mail" were defined as PPIs regarding "quality". The performance indicators were documented and further specified by attributes (e.g., "operational definition", "data responsible"). The results are visualized in Fig. 8 in excerpts using the *Performance Indicator Model*.

The collection of the corresponding measurement data, as well as the data analyses, were performed by the core project team right after the workshop. To keep the efforts for the measurement phase manageable, the focus was directed at the following document types for assessing the process cycle times: "account closure", "payment order", "marriage documents", "credit card closure" and "administration of estates". For collecting the data, a questionnaire was attached to the corresponding documents by the post service as soon as such documents were received by the automotive bank. The questionnaire contained fields to document the processing times for the corresponding document and to note the exact time when the document was obtained by an employee in charge. That way, all steps of the document management process were covered by the questionnaire. In total, more than a hundred questionnaires were issued over a period of two weeks. The filled out questionnaires were then screened by the core project team for

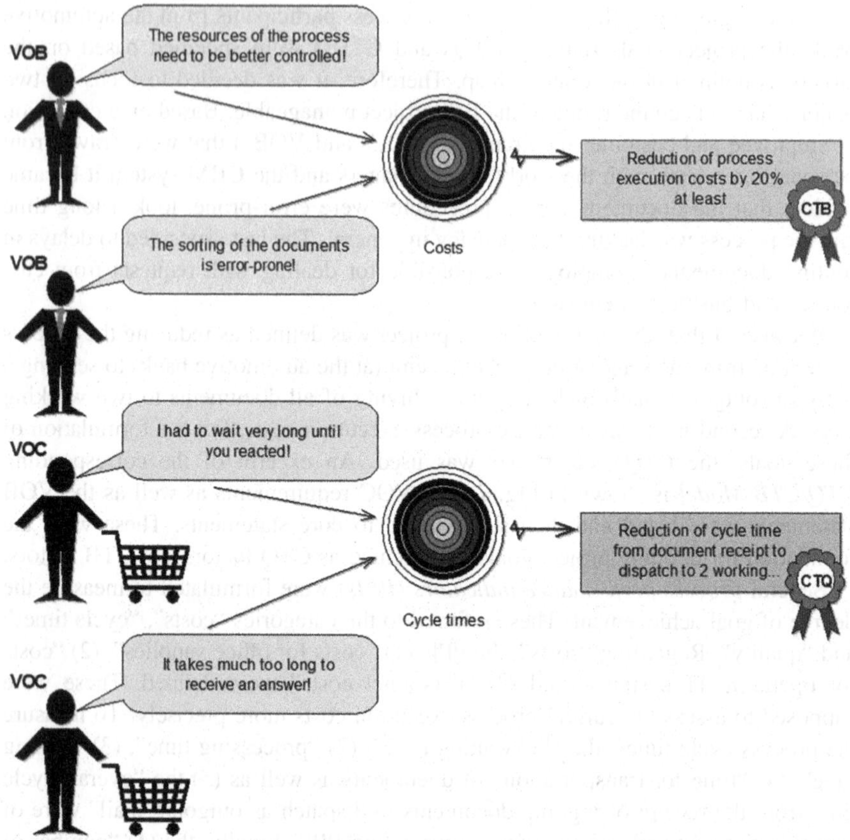

Fig. 7 Excerpts of the CTQ/CTB Model documenting the customer and employee requirements as well as the project goals

completeness as only those were to be further considered for the data analyses. Finally, 68 questionnaires were used for determining the PPIs regarding process cycle times.

For demonstrating the applicability of the RUPERT tool, the data from the questionnaires was entered into a CSV-file. This could be automatically imported into the RUPERT prototype and analyzed by an interface of the statistic software R.[4] In summary, it turned out that almost all documents (92 %) were processed by the operational departments within one working day only. The documents were usually transferred to the post service as outgoing mail the same day their processing was completed by employees. However, there were delays in indexing the documents. This led to the circumstance that the overall cycle time from receiving a document until it was accessible in the document archive took more than ten

[4]https://www.r-project.org/ (access: 30.09.2015).

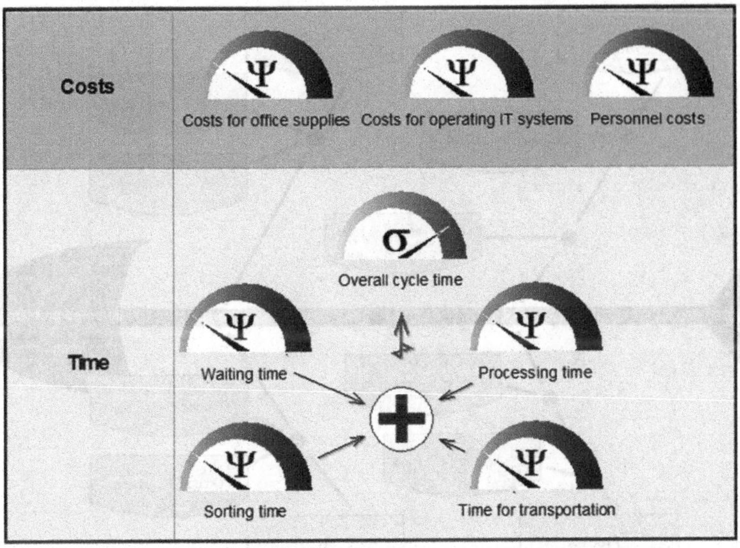

Fig. 8 Excerpts from the Performance Indicator Model showing the cost-related and time-related performance indicators as defined in the project

working days. The existing calculations and reports were used (secondary data) for the assessment of costs. The office supplies costs amounted to approximately half a million Euros per year. The costs of operating the IT systems for document management turned out to be about a million Euros and the personnel costs approximately half a million Euros per year.

Afterward, problem causes for this insufficient process performance were worked out by help of the *Ishikawa Diagram*. The main reasons were lacking communication with customers or the suboptimal process transparency for instance. An excerpt of the results is shown in Fig. 9.

Solutions to overcome these weaknesses were developed and categorized by means of the *Affinity Diagram*. These comprised suggestions on the introduction of supporting IT as well as the redesign of process activities. An example was the proposal to integrate the diverse fax servers or to modify the scanning procedures for the documents. Then, the communication between the participants in the process was to be improved by organizing working parties with regular, scheduled meetings to screen the process performance.

Whereas the impact of these improvement suggestions on costs was to be expected to become evident in the year to follow at the earliest, a positive development of the processing times required for indexing documents could already be observed shortly after finishing the project. In total, it was estimated that the project would lead to a cost reduction of 30 % for the process execution costs at least and tremendously increase customer and employee satisfaction in the near future.

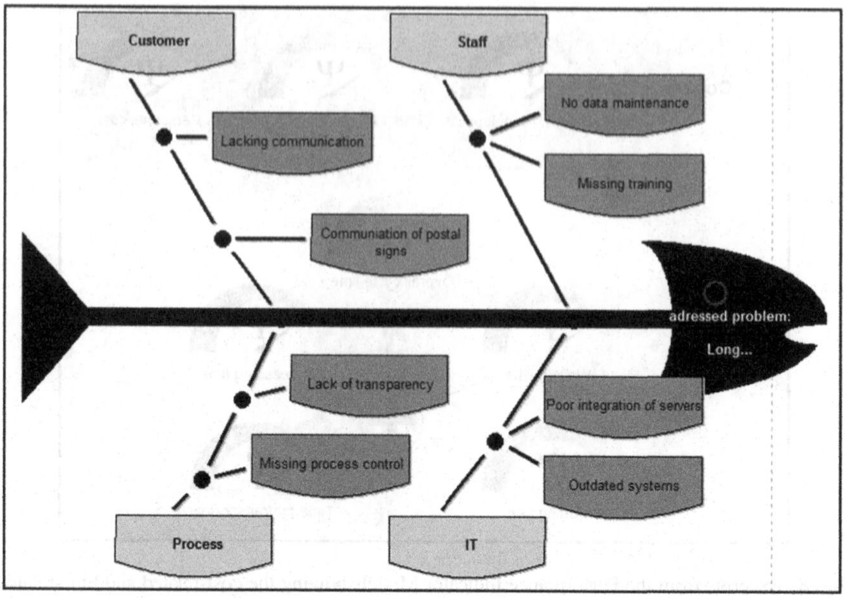

Fig. 9 Excerpts from the Ishikawa Model showing the four problem categories "customer", "staff", "process", and "IT" and relevant problem causes

The use of RUPERT to process the project data proved its applicability regarding the described real-life BPI project. The information stemming from the project could be easily structured and analyzed by the model types, supporting the systematic development of BPI initiatives.

5 Conclusion and Outlook

This paper described the development of a modeling tool to purposefully assist employees in performing BPI initiatives. A major challenge of BPI projects lies in the selection of adequate BPI techniques as well as the documentation, communication and processing of results achieved [26]. To face these problems, we proposed the BPI roadmap and implemented the corresponding RUPERT prototype. By the BPI roadmap, practitioners are offered a solution to systematically conduct BPI projects in the service as well as the production industry [26]. Thereby, RUPERT was implemented to support the user in applying the BPI roadmap and to elicit the project participants' knowledge of the process to be later transformed into improvement opportunities. The research strongly contributes to current BPI research and the question of how projects can be purposefully performed considering the challenges described in the introduction. It became evident that metamodels are suitable for identifying interrelationships between BPI techniques and strongly facilitate their logical arrangement in the form of a roadmap enabling their goal-oriented and coordinated application. Furthermore, the research transferred concepts of knowledge management, such as "roadmaps" and conceptual models (cf. [2, 6]), to the BPI field and thus revealed beneficial synergies between the disciplines providing practitioner-adapted solutions.

However, there are limitations: currently, the application of the BPI roadmap was only done in BPI projects at the automotive bank yet. Further applications with goods-producing industries are to be implemented. Additionally, the selection of techniques for the BPI roadmap was performed in cooperation with six BPI experts in the industry. Subjectivity in the selection procedure thus cannot be excluded completely.

In future work, the RUPERT software will be used in BPI projects with companies of different sizes and from various branches. Thereby, the prototype is to be further developed to better match practitioners' and users' requirements. For that purpose, a usability study based on the SUMI approach is currently performed.

Tool Download http://www.omilab.og/rupert.

References

1. Adesola, S., Baines, T.: Developing and evaluating a methodology for business process improvement. Bus. Process Manag. J. **11**(1), 37–46 (2005)
2. Anaby-Tavor, A., Amid, D., Fisher, A., Bercovici, A., Ossher, H., Callery, M., Desmond, M., Krasikov, S., Simmonds, I.: Insights into enterprise conceptual modeling. Data Knowl. Eng. **69**(12), 1302–1318 (2010)
3. Angele, J., Fensel, D., Landes, D., Studer, R.: Developing knowledge-based systems with MIKE. Autom. Softw. Eng. **5**(4), 389–418 (1998)
4. Bruhn, M.: Qualitätsmanagement für Dienstleistungen, 9th edn. Springer, Berlin et al. (2013)
5. Dale, B.G., McQuater, R.: Managing Business Improvement & Quality: Implementing Key Tools and Techniques. Blackwell Business, Oxford (1998)
6. Dalkir, K.: Knowledge Management in Theory and Practice. McGill University
7. Davies, I., Green, P., Rosemann, M., Indulska, M., Gallo, S.: How do practitioners use conceptual modeling in practice? Data Knowl. Eng. **58**(3), 358–380 (2006)
8. Davis, D.: 3rd Biennial PEX Network Report: State of the Industry—Trends and Success Factors in Business Process Excellence (2013)
9. Feigenbaum, A.V.: Total Quality Control. 3rd edn. McGraw-Hill, New York (1983)
10. Fill, H.-G., Karagiannis, D.: On the conceptualisation of modelling methods using the ADOxx meta modelling platform. Enterp. Model. Inf. Syst. Archit.-An Int. J. **8**(1) (2013)
11. Fill, H-G., Redmond, T., Karagiannis, D.: FDMM: a formalism for describing ADOxx meta models and models. In: ICEIS 2012, Poland (2012)
12. Fill, H.-G., Redmond, T., Karagiannis, D.: Formalizing meta models with FDMM: the ADOxx case. In: Cordeiro, J., Maciaszek, L., Filipe, J. (eds.) Enterprise Information Systems, 2013. Springer, pp. 429–451 (2013)
13. Forster, F.: The idea behind business process improvement: toward a business process improvement pattern framework. BPTrends 1–13 (2006)
14. Fraser, M.D., Kumar, K., Vaishnavi, V.K.: Strategies for incorporating formal specifications in software development. Commun. ACM **37**(10), 74–86 (1994)

15. George, M.L., Rowlands, D., Price, M., Maxey, J.: Lean Six Sigma Pocket Toolbox. McGraw-Hill, New York (2005)
16. Gijo, E.V., Rao, T.S.: Six sigma implementation—hurdles and more hurdles. Total Qual. Manag. Bus. Excellence **16**(6), 721–725 (2005)
17. Greenberg, P.: The impact of CRM 2.0 on customer insight. J. Bus. Ind. Mark. **25**(6), 410–419 (2010)
18. Griesberger, P., Leist, S., Zellner, G.: Analysis of techniques for business process improvement. In: 19th European Conference on Information Systems (ECIS 2011), Helsinki, Finland (2011)
19. Gutzwiller, T.A.: Das CC RIM-Referenzmodell für den Entwurf von betrieblichen, transaktionsorientierten Informationssystemen. Physica-Verlag, Heidelberg (1994)
20. Hammer, M.: What is business process management? In: vom Brocke, J., Rosemann, M. (eds.) Handbook on Business Process Management 1, 2nd edn, pp 3–16. Springer, Berlin (2015)
21. Harrington, H.J.: Business Process Improvement—The Breakthrough Strategy for Total Quality, Productivity and Competitiveness. McGraw-Hill, New York (1991)
22. Heckl, D., Moormann, J., Rosemann, M.: Uptake and success factors of Six Sigma in the financial services industry. Bus. Process Manag. J. **16**(3), 436–472 (2010)
23. Hevner, A.R., March, S.T., Park, J., Ram, S.: Design science in information systems research. MIS Q. **28**(1), 75–105 (2004)
24. Ishikawa, K.: Guide to Quality Control. Tokyo (1980)
25. Johannsen, F.: State of the art concerning the integration of methods and techniques in quality management—literature review and an agenda for research. In: 19th European Conference on Information Systems (ECIS 2011), Helsinki, Finland (2011)
26. Johannsen F, Fill H.-G.: Codification of knowledge in business process improvement projects. In: 22nd European Conference on Information Systems (ECIS 2014), Tel Aviv, Israel (2014a)
27. Johannsen, F., Fill, H.-G.: RUPERT: a modelling tool for supporting business process improvement initiatives. In: Tremblay, M.C., Van der Meer, D., Rothenberger, M., Gupta, A., Yoon, V. (eds.) 9th International Conference on Design Science Research in Information Systems and Technology (DESRIST), pp. 418–422. Springer, Miami (2014b)
28. Johannsen, F., Fill, H.-G.: Supporting knowledge elicitation and analysis for business process improvement through a modeling tool. In: 12. Internationale Tagung Wirtschaftsinformatik, Osnabrück (2015)
29. Johannsen, F., Leist, S., Zellner, G.: Implementing Six Sigma for improving business processes at an automotive bank. In: vom Brocke, J., Rosemann, M. (eds.) Handbook on Business Process Management 1. 2nd edn., pp 361–382. Springer, Berlin (2015)
30. Kern H, Hummel A, Kühne S (2011) Towards a comparative analysis of meta-metamodels. In: Proceedings of the compilation of the co-located workshops on DSM'11, TMC'11, AGERE!'11, AOOPES'11, NEAT'11, & VMIL'11, 2011. ACM, pp 7–12
31. Kettinger, W.J., Teng, J.T.C., Guha, S.: Business process change: a study of methodologies, techniques, and tools. MIS Q. **21**(1), 55–80 (1997)
32. Laudon KC, Laudon JP (2014) Essentials of MIS. Pearson Education Limited
33. Lee, K.T., Chuah, K.B.: A SUPER methodology for business process improvement. Int. J. Oper. Prod. Manag. **21**(5/6), 687–706 (2001)
34. Lipton, P.: Engineering and Truth. In: The Royal Academy of Engineering: Philosophy of Engineering—Volume 1 of the Proceedings of a Series of Seminars Held at The Royal Academy of Engineering, pp 7–13 (2010)
35. Magnusson K, Kroslid D, Bergman B (2004) Six Sigma the pragmatic approach. Professional Pub Serv
36. Mellat-Parast, M.: Supply chain quality management: an inter-organizational learning perspective. Int. J. Qual. Reliab. Manag. **30**(5), 511–529 (2013)
37. Meran, R., John, A., Roenpage, O., Staudter, C.: Six Sigma + Lean Toolset. Springer, Berlin et al. (2013)
38. Nonaka, I.: The knowledge-creating company. Harvard Bus. Rev. **85**(7–8), 162–171 (2007)

39. Pande, P., Neumann, R., Cavanagh, R.: The Six Sigma Way—How GE, Motorola and other top companies are honing their performance. Mc Graw Hill, New York et al (2000)
40. Shamsuddin, A., Masjuki, H.: Survey and case investigations on application of quality management tools and techniques in SMIs. Int. J. Qual. Reliab. Manag. **20**(7), 795–826 (2003)
41. Stracke, C.: Process-oriented quality management. In: Ehlers, U.-D., Pawlowski, J.M. (eds.) Handbook on Quality and Standardisation in E-Learning, pp. 79–96. Springer, Heidelberg (2006)
42. Thia, C., Chai, K.H., Bauly, J., Xin, Y.: An exploratory study of the use of quality tools and techniques in product development. TQM Mag. **17**(5), 406–424 (2005)
43. Ulrich, D., Kerr, S., Ashkenas, R.: The GE Work-Out. McGraw-Hill, New York et al (2002)
44. Wirtz, B.W., Mory, L., Piehler, R.: Web 2.0 and Digital Business Models. In: Handbook of Strategic e-Business Management, pp 751–766. Springer (2014)
45. Wolf, C., Harmon, P.: The state of business process management—2014. BPTrends (2014)
46. Womack, J.P., Jones, D.T.: Lean Thinking. Simon & Schuster, New York (1996)
47. Xu, Y., Bernard, A., Perry, N., Lian, L.: Managing knowledge management tools: a systematic classification and comparison. In: International Conference on Management and Service Science (MASS), 2011, pp 1–4. IEEE (2011)
48. Zellner, G., Leist, S., Johannsen, F.: Selecting critical processes for a Six Sigma project—experiences from an automotive bank. In: 18th European Conference on Information Systems (ECIS 2010), Pretoria, South Africa (2010)

Part V
Enterprise Information Systems

Multi-perspective Enterprise Modeling—Conceptual Foundation and Implementation with ADO*xx*

Alexander Bock and Ulrich Frank

Abstract This chapter describes a method for multi-perspective enterprise modeling (MEMO) and a prototypical implementation of a selected part of the method with ADOxx, called MEMO4ADO. MEMO has been developed during a period of more than twenty years and is still a subject of ongoing research. MEMO includes a set of integrated domain-specific modeling languages to describe organizational action systems as well as information systems. MEMO4ADO implements a subset of MEMO languages specifically tailored for educational purposes. The chapter summarizes the background and evolution of MEMO, illustrates the implementation and functionalities of MEMO4ADO, and outlines future developments.

Keywords Multi-perspective enterprise modeling · Domain-specific modeling language (DSML) · Metamodeling · Modeling tool

1 Introduction

1.1 Motivation

Software is a linguistic artifact. On the one hand, this means that it is ultimately made of some form of machine language. On the other hand, it means that we can use it, i.e., *make sense of* it, only if it is supplemented with a linguistic representation that corresponds to a language with which prospective users are familiar. The better this correspondence, the more convenient it will be to use the software. Furthermore, when it comes to the design of enterprise software, it is generally recommended to involve different stakeholders, such as managers, prospective users, and IT experts.

A. Bock · U. Frank (✉)
Research Group Information Systems and Enterprise Modelling, University of Duisburg-Essen, Essen, Germany
e-mail: alexander.bock@uni-due.de

U. Frank
e-mail: ulrich.frank@uni-due.de

D. Karagiannis et al. (eds.), *Domain-Specific Conceptual Modeling*,
DOI 10.1007/978-3-319-39417-6_11

Analyzing and designing enterprise software require communicating with people who have different professional backgrounds, and who therefore speak different languages. Conceptual modeling has been advanced to help cope with some of these issues. A conceptual model in the traditional sense is an abstraction of a software system that represents the intended meaning of the system using concepts that are supposed to be known in the target domain. These domain-specific concepts, in turn, are conventionally built with generic modeling languages that consist of basic linguistic constructs (one could also call them ontological constructs) such as "entity type" or "attribute".

Building on the notion of conceptual modeling, the idea of enterprise modeling goes one step further. It emphasizes the need to model not only software systems but also the context in which these systems are sought to be deployed. This is for two reasons. First, enterprise software does not work autonomously. It has to be aligned with the operations of an enterprise and needs to account for the tasks it should support. Second, taking advantage of the potential benefits offered by IT will often require to reorganize the organizational action system, e.g., to redesign business processes, tasks, and maybe even the entire business model. As a consequence, the analysis and design of software systems and the surrounding organizational action system should preferably be done in conjunction. Enterprise models are intended to support this kind of conjoint analysis and design. A minimal enterprise model integrates at least one model of an enterprise software system (e.g., an object model) with at least one model of the related action system (e.g., a business process model). The integration of models is intended not only to foster a better understanding of dependencies between business and IT, but also to help avoid inconsistencies.

An enterprise model is usually, though not necessarily, presented in the form of graphical diagrams. While diagrams could be created manually, for economic reasons it is advisable to employ software-based modeling tools to develop and utilize enterprise models. Modeling tools promise to help protect the integrity of enterprise models, to enable navigation through multiple integrated models, and to improve the reuse of models. They may further enable various kinds of model analysis and transformations (e.g., model-based code generation). To sum up, research on enterprise modeling needs to consider the construction of modeling tools alongside the development of enterprise modeling methods.

With this in mind, this chapter has two purposes. First, it presents a method for multi-perspective enterprise modeling (MEMO) [9, 15]. Second, it describes a prototypical implementation of a selected part of the method with ADO*xx* [8]. The implemented tool is called MEMO4ADO. To begin, the next section summarizes historical developments which led to the method in its current state, considering both conceptual foundations and different tool development platforms. Section 2 provides an overview of the major components of MEMO. Section 3 illustrates particular modeling languages and ways of using MEMO. In Sect. 4, the modeling tool MEMO4ADO is presented. The chapter concludes in Sect. 5.

1.2 Historical Background

The development of the method presented here started in the German National Research Centre for Computer Science in 1989. The centre's chairman felt inspired by the vision of fully automated factories and decided to make it the subject of a project in the business informatics research group. The project's mission was to develop a conceptual foundation for promoting the level of automation in organizations. Very soon, the group members agreed that integrative enterprise models would be required as a tool to support the joint reorganization of an enterprise and the design of corresponding information systems. A conceptual high-level framework for multi-perspective enterprise modeling (MEMO) was created and further developed in a habilitation thesis [9]. The framework included modeling languages for various domains such as business processes, organizational structures, corporate strategies, and object models. Instead of specifying metamodels, the languages were directly implemented in model editors. The first integrated enterprise modeling environment was implemented in 1992 with Smalltalk. The screenshot in Fig. 1 shows an editor for process models, integrated with parts of role models, object models, and models of documents.

In the following years, research on the method continued at the University of Koblenz. A metamodeling language (MEMO MML) was created [10] and subse-

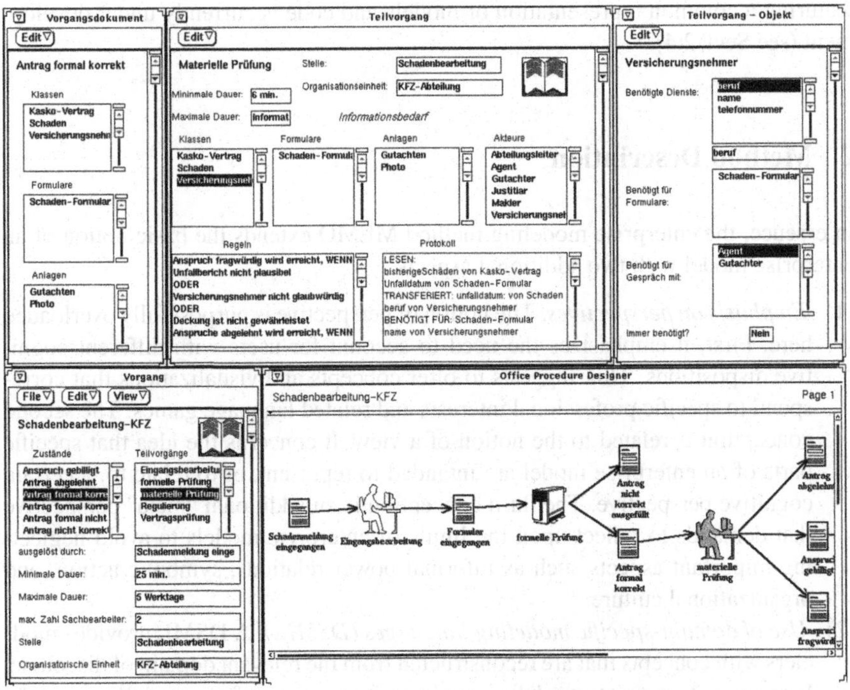

Fig. 1 Screenshot of the first MEMO modeling environment from 1992

quently used to specify metamodels of various languages. Based on this foundation, an entirely new version of the tool environment, called MEMO Center, was developed in 1997. Despite the undisputed benefits of Smalltalk, it was decided in 2003, then at the University of Duisburg-Essen, to use Eclipse as the development platform and Java as a programming language. This decision was based on two assumptions. First, the Smalltalk community seemed to shrink and Smalltalk environments were not developed much further. Second, we recognized the need for a metamodeling component. For this purpose, the Eclipse Modeling Framework [34] and the Eclipse Graphical Modeling Framework [21] were chosen as a foundation. The existing metamodels were represented as Ecore instances. Later, the environment, which we then called MEMO NG ("next generation"), was supplemented with a metamodeling facility that allowed the definition of metamodels with the MEMO MML. The metamodels were transparently transformed into Ecore instances and could be used, after some manual extensions, to generate model editors [22].

In parallel to the tool development, our research on modeling languages identified substantial challenges that concerned the representation of abstraction concepts. It turned out that these problems were related to principal limitations not only of our metamodeling language and the OMG Meta Object Facility (MOF) [27] language architecture, but also of mainstream object-oriented programming languages. To overcome these obstacles, we decided for a radical change, both with respect to the language architecture and the implementation language. A new recursive language architecture has been designed and a corresponding modeling environment featuring a common representation of models and code is currently under development (see Sect. 2.4).

2 Method Description

In essence, the enterprise modeling method MEMO extends the basic notion of an enterprise model with two additional aspects.

(1) *Emphasis on perspectives*: The notion of perspective is purposefully overloaded here. First, it emphasizes the need to account for users with different cognitive dispositions. This suggests to offer concepts and visualizations that correspond to specific professional interests and related language games. The second conception is related to the notion of a view. It concerns the idea that specific parts of an enterprise model are intended to represent, or to relate to, a certain cognitive perspective. The third conception is an additional "meta" perspective that demands to reflect upon the limits of enterprise models to avoid neglecting important aspects such as informal power relations, symbolic action, and organizational culture.

(2) *Use of domain-specific modeling languages (DSMLs)*: A DSML provides modelers with concepts that are reconstructed from the relevant domain of discourse. It promises to promote modeling productivity because it frees modelers from the

need to reconstruct domain-specific concepts from basic linguistic constructs. It also promises to foster model quality because ideally the concepts of a DSML have been carefully developed by domain experts. Finally, domain-specific language specifications can include (domain-specific) constraints that prevent, to a certain extent, the construction of inappropriate models.

The construction of MEMO reflects these general considerations. MEMO comprises four major components. First, the *language architecture* includes the metamodeling language and defines the relationship between models on different levels of classification. Second, an *extensible set of DSMLs* provides the basic instruments for users of MEMO. Third, a *method for designing DSMLs* guides the creation of new modeling languages and the modification of existing languages. Fourth, users are supported by various *modeling methods* that are essentially composed of DSMLs and corresponding process models. Advanced users who want to create their own methods are guided by a (meta) method for method construction. The following description (Sect. 2.1–2.3) refers to the original language architecture of MEMO, as the new recursive language architecture, considered in Sect. 2.4, cannot be represented within ADO*xx*.

2.1 Language Architecture and Metamodeling Language

The original MEMO language architecture corresponds to the three tier architecture that is also proposed by the OMG Meta Object Facility [27]. Figure 2 illustrates its basic structure. The meta-metamodel (see Fig. 3), which defines the abstract syntax and semantics of the metamodeling language MEMO MML, forms the lin-

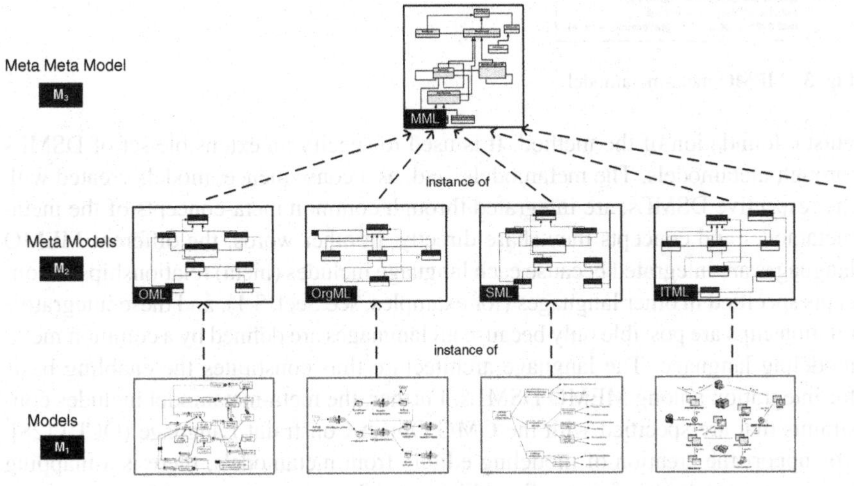

Fig. 2 MEMO language architecture

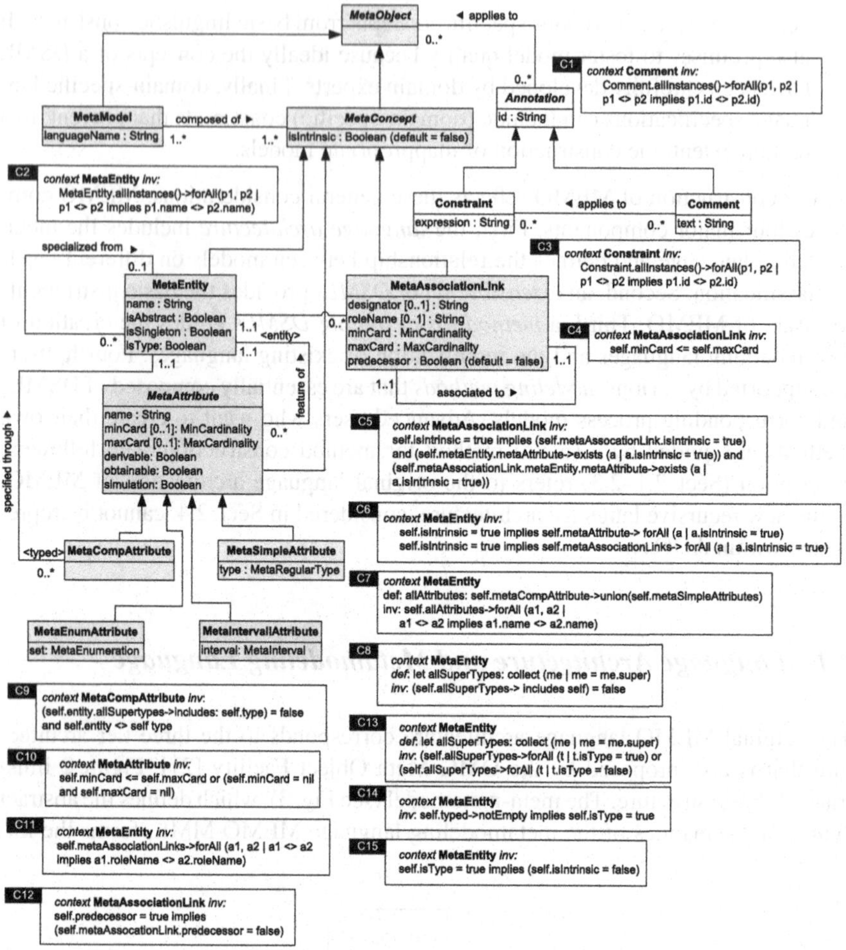

Fig. 3 MEMO meta-metamodel

guistic foundation of the method. It is used to specify an extensible set of DSMLs through metamodels. The metamodels, and, as a consequence, models created with the respective DSMLs, are integrated through common meta-concepts of the meta-metamodel and concepts they share directly. In other words, the different MEMO languages are integrated because each language includes (meta) relationships to concepts specified in other languages (for examples, see Sect. 3.1), and these integrative relationships are possible only because all languages are defined by a common meta-modeling language. The language architecture thus constitutes the enabling basis for integration among MEMO DSMLs. Further, the meta-metamodel includes constraints that are specified with the OMG Object Constraint Language (OCL) [28]. To support the creation of modeling editors from metamodels, there is a mapping from metamodels to corresponding object models.

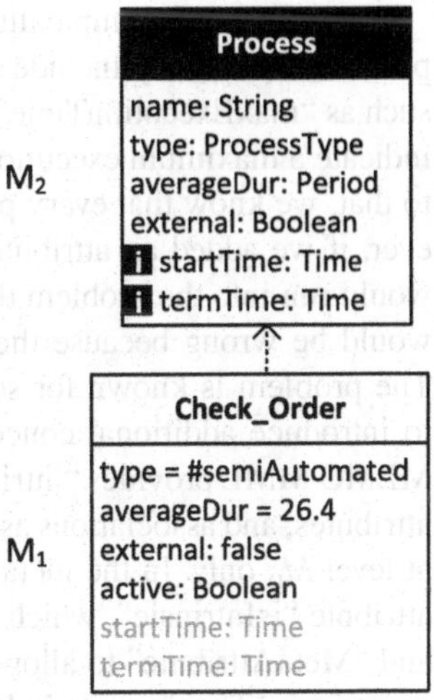

Fig. 4 Illustration of intrinsic features

The latest version of the MEMO MML (see Fig. 3) for the three tier architecture was introduced in 2011 [13]. Some concepts of the MEMO MML are similar to concepts of other metamodeling languages. This mainly concerns basic concepts to specify meta types with attributes and associations. In addition, the MEMO MML also features concepts which address advanced metamodeling issues. These are explained in the following subsection. Lastly, the MML includes a graphical notation that enables the visual distinction between metamodels at level M_2 and object or data models at level M_1 (see example in Fig. 4).

2.2 Advanced Metamodeling Concepts

While the clear separation of classification levels and the restriction to a fixed number of classification levels (up to M_3) together seem to provide a solid foundation for (meta) modeling, there are relevant cases that cannot be handled within such a language architecture. The MEMO MML accounts for these cases with two additional concepts, *intrinsic features* and *language level types*, which are explained below.

Intrinsic features. When we create a conceptual model, we aim at a certain level of abstraction. This means that we intentionally fade out aspects that may become relevant only at lower levels of abstractions. On the other hand, when we design a conceptual model, we would like to create a specification which is as comprehensive as possible at the chosen level of abstraction. This means that we would like to express everything we know at this level, even though it may apply to lower levels only. Failing to do so would prevent the reuse of existing knowledge and jeopardize the integrity of models at lower levels of classification.

The following example illustrates the problem. A language for modeling business processes (M_2) may include a concept “Process”, which could include an attribute such as “maxExecutionTime” that is instantiated at the type level (M_1) and serves to indicate a maximum execution time that applies to all process instances. In addition to that, we know that every process instance has a certain start and end time. However, if we added an attribute such as “startTime” to the meta type “Process”, we would run into the problem that it would be instantiated at the type level (M_1). This would be wrong because the attribute clearly pertains to the instance level (M_0). The problem is known for some time [1, 29], and the only way to deal with it is to introduce additional concepts in the metamodeling language. Accordingly, the MEMO MML provides “intrinsic features”. These can be used to declare meta types, attributes, and associations as ‘intrinsic’, which means that they are to be instantiated at level M_0 only. In the meta-metamodel, the concept “MetaConcept” includes the attribute “isIntrinsic”, which is inherited to “MetaEntity”, “MetaAssociationLink”, and “MetaAttribute” to allow entity types, attributes and associations to be marked as intrinsic. The example in Fig. 4 illustrates how intrinsic attributes are represented in metamodels (see the black and white ‘i’ symbol), and it also shows that they are not instantiated in classes at level M_1.

Language level types. A further problem caused by MOF-like architectures concerns the fact that objects of different classification levels may not coexist at the same level of the architecture. For example, it is not possible that one particular model simultaneously contains objects from level M_1 and M_0. While this constraint is for a good reason, it can prevent the construction of perfectly useful models. Take, for example, a model of a logistic chain. A related DSML might include a concept such as “MeansOfTransport”, which could be instantiated into types such as “Truck” or “Boat”. Further, to model a logistic chain, it is essential to include locations. But modeling a location *type* such as “City” will usually not be satisfactory. Instead, a particular location, such as “Vienna”, will be needed. Different from other objects in a logistic model (which would be located at level M_1), however, a location should be represented as an instance at level M_0. But traditional MOF-like architectures do not permit to mix objects from level M_1 (e.g., “Truck”) and M_0 (e.g., “Vienna”) in one model. To overcome this limitation, MEMO allows to mark concepts in a metamodel (M_2) as representing *types* rather than meta types (using the attribute “isType”). As a result, these types will be instantiated into instances at the model level (M_1) already. For a corresponding example model, see [13, pp. 23–24].

2.3 A Method for Designing DSMLs

While MEMO is intended to cover relevant domains of an enterprise, it would be presumptuous to claim that the MEMO languages are sufficient in all cases. On the one hand, it may happen that a particular DSML needs to be modified. On the other hand, it may turn out that additional DSMLs are needed. A number of tools support the specification of DSMLs and the realization of corresponding model editors.

However, these tools provide little guidance for the conceptual design of a language for a specific purpose. This is even more problematic as many prospective users will not be familiar with the concept of a DSML, which makes requirements analysis for modeling languages especially challenging.

For these reasons, MEMO was supplemented with a method for designing DSMLs [14]. It features a macro-level process model that includes eight phases. Each phase is structured by a specific micro-level process. To support requirements analysis, the method suggests the use of scenarios. A use scenario is characterized by a problem situation, related questions, and a specific technical language. Use scenarios can be identified based on relevant past decision and modeling scenarios. The method further advises to use preliminary diagrams to help prospective users understand what they can expect from a DSML. In order to understand what information could be represented in certain diagram types, it is suggested to start with a rudimentary graphical representation and then develop a list of questions related to the diagram. Analyzing these questions can support the systematic identification of concepts to be included in the target DSML. Further guidelines relate to frequent design decisions to be made during the specification of metamodels (see [14]).

2.4 Next Generation

Even though intrinsic features and type level concepts enable the construction of more expressive models, their representation in the meta-metamodel suffers from the problem that it is almost impossible to implement them satisfactorily with mainstream object-oriented programming languages. Furthermore, a language architecture that consists of two levels of classification only does not support the refinement, and, hence, the reuse, of DSMLs on higher levels. For example, a DSML concept such as "Printer" at level M_2 could be specified as an instance of "PeripheralDevice" at level M_3, which in turn could be part of a higher-level DSML. Finally, mainstream object-oriented programming languages require overloading the M_0 layer: Types or even meta types are represented as objects at level M_0. As a result, it is necessary to maintain two distinct representations of models and code, which causes the notorious problem of synchronization. The only way to overcome these obstacles is to abandon the traditional language architecture, both with respect to modeling languages and programming languages.

A few years ago, we decided to pursue such an approach. It led to a radical modification of the MEMO language architecture. The MOF-like architecture was replaced by a recursive "golden braid" architecture that enables an arbitrary number of classification levels [16]. Furthermore, Eclipse and Java were replaced by XMF (eXecutable Metamodeling Facility), which includes a (meta) programming language that is also based on a recursive architecture [4, 5]. By integrating the MEMO meta-metamodel with the meta-metamodel of XMF, both models and code share a common representation. This architecture enables to build enterprise systems that are integrated with conceptual models of themselves as well as models of the environment in which they operate [19]. Such "self-referential" systems can be represented by interactive models that, when required, may be changed by authorized users—and changing the model, in turn, would mean changing the system [17].

3 Method Conceptualization

The previous section gave an outline of the core modeling facilities provided by MEMO, including its language architecture and metamodeling language. This section presents selected DSMLs, ways of using and constructing related modeling methods, as well as examples to illustrate the use of MEMO.

3.1 Domain-Specific Modeling Languages

MEMO includes three main languages to model the organizational action system. The Goal Modeling Language (GoalML) [26, 30] supports the design and analysis of corporate goal systems. The Organisation Modeling Language (MEMO OrgML) allows to model organizational structures [11] and business processes [12]. Furthermore, MEMO includes a language to model IT infrastructures (ITML) [24]. The ITML is integrated with detailed concepts to model (IT-related) costs and assigns them to cost units [23]. Another language is aimed to support knowledge management [32]. Recently, a variety of further concepts have been developed, which either enrich or build on existing languages. These enable to describe organizational decision processes [2], to model performance indicator systems [35], and to supplement models of IT infrastructures with IT security aspects [20].

Figure 5 shows metamodel excerpts for different MEMO DSMLs and demonstrates how they are integrated through common concepts. On the basis of these modeling languages, numerous diagram types can be created. Furthermore, because the MEMO DSMLs are integrated through shared concepts, diagrams may also be created using several DSMLs at once. For example, a diagram may include parts of a business process model referring to goals from a goal model and to IT resources from an IT infrastructure model (for illustrations, see Sects. 3.2 and 4.4.1).

The MEMO DSMLs resulted from research projects that aimed at developing elaborate and comprehensive languages. As a consequence, most of the metamodels are voluminous and include many constraints. Especially for teaching purposes, some of the languages turned out to be too heavyweight, which suggests to either supplement them with light versions or to provide tool functionality that allows to hide concepts which are not required for certain scenarios (see Sect. 4 for a discussion of the related implementation).

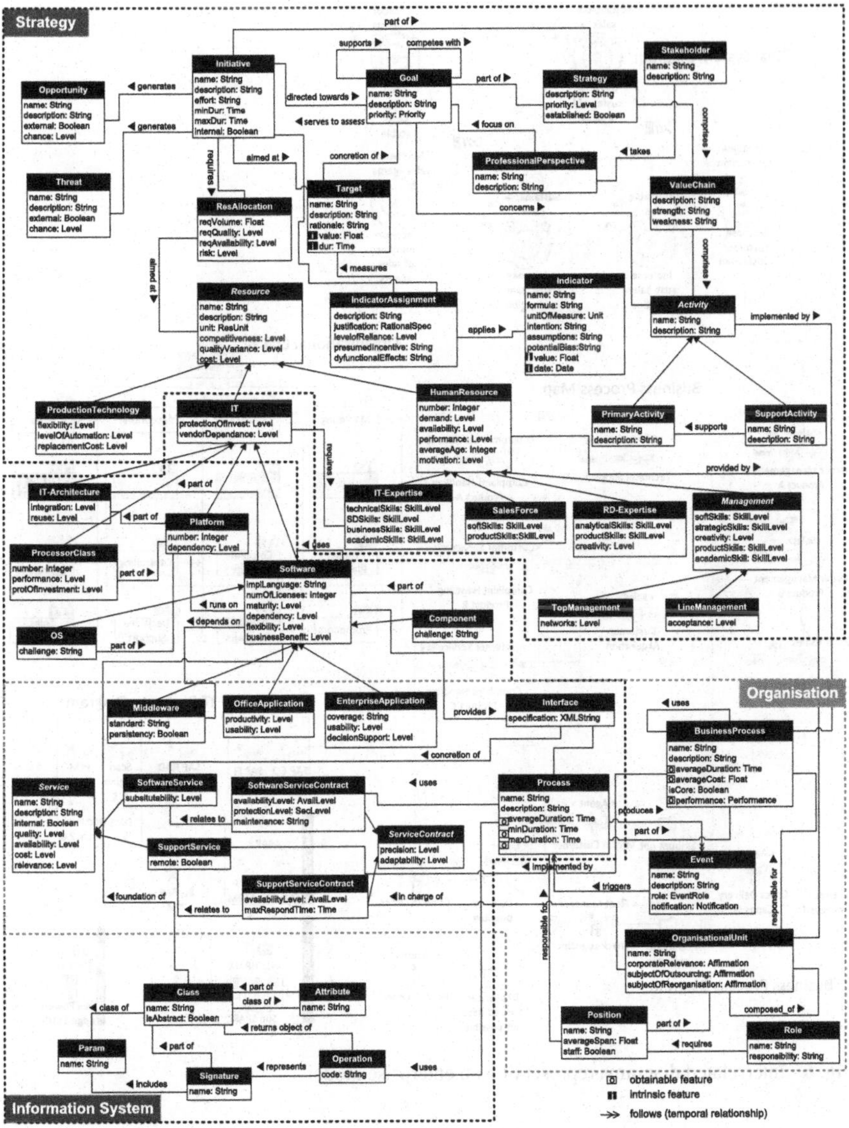

Fig. 5 Excerpt of various integrated metamodels

3.2 Examples

The following examples aim to give an overview of MEMO DSMLs and the construction of modeling methods (further examples indicating the wide range of possible use scenarios are found in Sect. 4.4.1). Figure 6 shows the representation of an

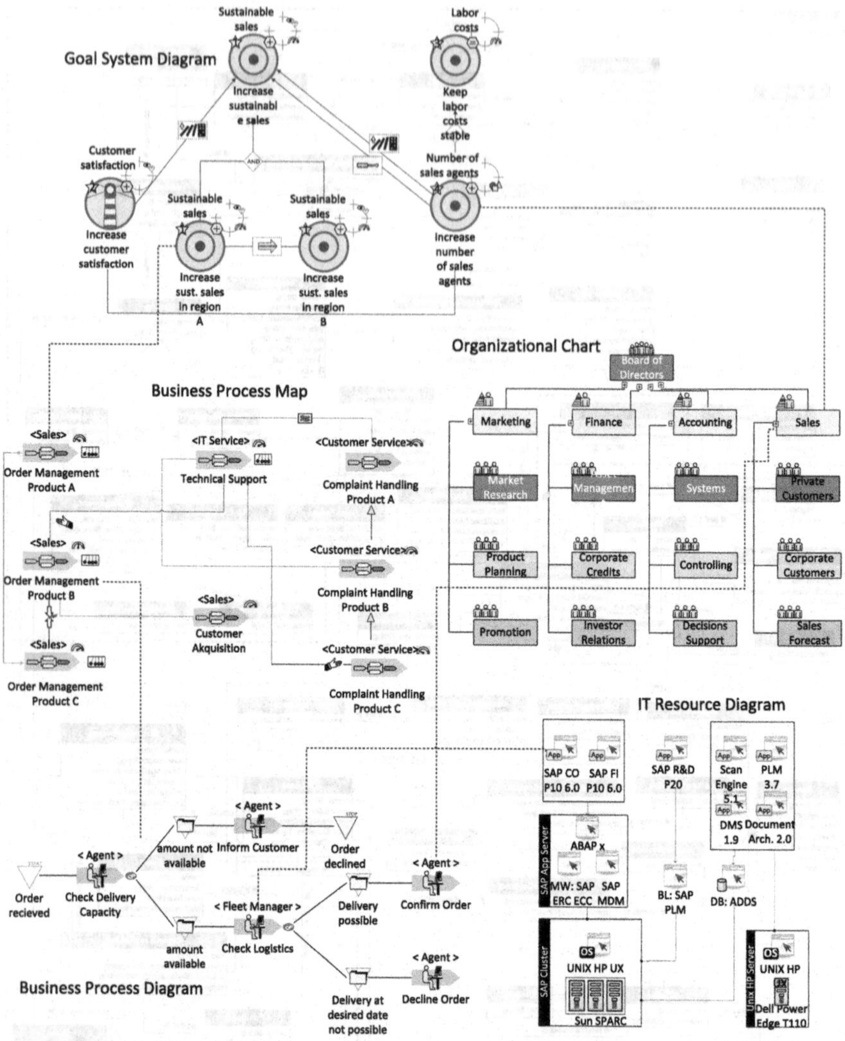

Fig. 6 Interrelated diagrams representing an enterprise model

enterprise model in the form of various diagrams and selected associations between them. A goal system diagram represents various types of goals and their interrelationships. As shown above, the goal "increase number of sales agents" is related to a department in the organizational chart which is responsible for reaching that goal. At the same time, this department is in charge of a particular subprocess within a business process diagram. A business process diagram shows the control flow of a particular process type. An overview of different business process types of the enterprise, in turn, is provided by the business process map. The association between the

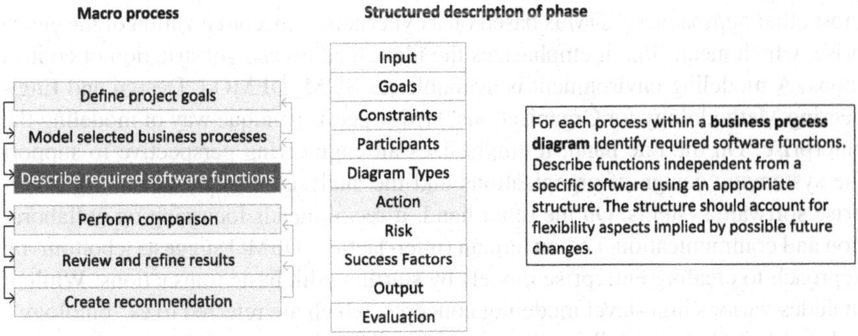

Fig. 7 Example structure of a process within a MEMO modeling method

subprocess "Check Logistics" and the application system "SAP CO P10 6.0" is used to indicate that this application system is required to run the subprocess. Finally, to illustrate how the creation and use of such models can be supported, Fig. 7 shows an excerpt of the representation of an example modeling method that deals with the selection of software systems. MEMO includes a metamodel that supports the construction of further modeling methods (see [15, pp. 950–954]).

3.3 Related Work

A variety of enterprise modeling methods are available. An in-depth comparison would go beyond the scope of this chapter. Therefore, the following overview aims to point out specific particularities of selected approaches.

Zachman's framework for enterprise architecture [38] suggests the enterprise models should be regarded as integrated conceptual models of data, functions, processes, and other basic aspects. The framework remains on a high level of abstraction and does not include specific modeling languages. The "Architecture of Integrated Information Systems" (ARIS) [33] offers a high-level framework ("House of Business Engineering") together with example diagrams. It provides one original modeling language, the "event-driven process chain", and refers to existing modeling languages such as the ERM or DFDs. The method is supported by a comprehensive commercial toolset. CIM-OSA ("Computer Integrated Manufacturing, Open Systems Architecture") [3] was aimed at modeling manufacturing firms. In addition to a high-level framework that covers three dimensions, CIM-OSA includes various templates that serve to collect data at different levels of abstraction. The completed templates are considered to represent an enterprise model.

SOM ("Semantic Object Model") is primarily aimed at supporting system design and implementation [7]. It combines object-oriented concepts with economic concepts such as "business transaction". SOM includes a few modeling languages, mainly for modeling business processes, transactions, and objects. Different from most other approaches, SOM is based on a cybernetic conceptualization of the enterprise, which means that it emphasizes the identification and construction of control loops. A modeling environment is available for SOM. DEMO ("Design and Engineering Methodology for Organisations") [6] suggests a unique way of modeling the enterprise. On the one hand, it emphasizes an engineering perspective to support the systematic design of organizations and the analysis of requirements for enterprise software systems. On the other hand, it recommends focussing on collaboration and communication, i.e., on human (inter-)action. DEMO suggests a bottom–up approach to creating enterprise models by starting with basic transactions. While it includes various high-level modeling concepts, which are referred to as "ontology", it does not include the full specification of modeling languages. Tools are available that cover certain aspects of DEMO, but there seems to be no comprehensive tool environment. The "4EM" ("For Enterprise modeling") method [31] provides basic concepts to model goals, business processes, resources, and related aspects. 4EM particularly promotes enterprise modeling as a participatory process. To describe the languages, the authors mainly refer to example models and place less emphasis on detailed specifications of the abstract syntax and semantics.

TOGAF [36] uses the term "enterprise architecture", which is related to, but not identical with, the notion of an enterprise model. TOGAF is promoted by The Open Group, i.e., it is not an academic project. Its main concern is with the specification of an extensive process model with eight main phases. The documentation includes examples of various diagram types but lacks a specification of modeling languages. ArchiMate [37], also promoted by The Open Group, extends TOGAF with a language to model enterprise architectures. The metamodel is underspecified and leaves room for individual adaptations. ArchiMate modeling tools are freely available.

Taken together, there are a variety of enterprise modeling methods. However, in contrast to MEMO, most of these methods do not include a metamodeling language. Furthermore, most of them lack comparably elaborate specifications of DSMLs.

4 Proof of Concept

In this section, we describe the implementation of selected MEMO languages using ADO*xx*. The implemented tool is called MEMO4ADO. We decided to use ADO*xx* especially for two reasons. First, we embrace the idea of creating an "open models" platform. We believe that a movement towards the common development and (reuse) of open models [18, 25] is suited to promote the field of enterprise modeling substantially—both in academia and practice. However, we had to learn that a good idea alone is not sufficient to create a movement. It is important to take action and to build incentives. The joint project that is documented in this volume delivers a wide range of reusable modeling tools that are all based on one platform. Therefore, there is a good chance to integrate the tools and, as a consequence, to integrate the models created with these tools as well. This provides a basis to build an attractive collection of reusable models that may also serve as an incentive for the development of further extensions. Second, we realized that our DSMLs are too extensive for teaching purposes. Nonetheless, we wished to involve students in the development, use, and maintenance of our modeling languages and tools. ADO*xx* seemed to be a good choice for this purpose. Using the ADO*xx* Development and Modeling Toolkits, we estimated that it would not take students too long to become productive. The implementation in ADO*xx* also offered an opportunity to devise a MEMO version specifically tailored for teaching purposes. Finally, the "open models" platform provides an attractive vision for teaching: a laboratory of models and modeling languages that cannot only be navigated and examined by students, but which may also be the subject of continuous evolution through student projects.

4.1 Scope and Objectives of the ADOxx Implementation

The basic purpose of the developed MEMO4ADO tool is to offer an accessible facility to help grasp the idea of multi-perspective enterprise modeling, especially for Bachelor's-level students. In addition, we implemented tool-specific auxiliary functions for which the ADO*xx* environment provided a suitable ground.

The ensuing process by which the modeling languages of MEMO have been implemented was governed by two principal constraints. One concerns the fact that the modeling environment was sought to be usable for teaching purposes. Because the full set of MEMO modeling languages was expected to be too complex for the target group (see Sect. 3), the scope of implementation was reduced. From the whole set of MEMO modeling languages, a subset of three languages were selected for the present implementation: The MEMO OrgML focusing on *organizational structures* [11], the MEMO OrgML focusing on *business processes* [12], and the MEMO GoalML to describe *organizational goal systems* [26]. In the future, selected concepts of other languages will be added, particularly concepts of the MEMO ITML to describe *IT infrastructures* [23, 24]. Taken together, these languages and concepts provide a coherent method subset to aid basic strategic, organizational, and infrastructural analyses (illustrated in Sect. 4.4). But while limited in number, the selected modeling languages are still complex and comprehensive in scope. They needed to be further adjusted for the target group. The consequential narrowing down of the metamodels is described in the following Sect. 4.2.

The second constraint which affected the implementation process is related to the MEMO language architecture. MEMO modeling languages are designed such that a sharp distinction is made between model elements that are instantiated at the type level (M_1) and at the instance level (M_0). To define these relations, the MEMO metamodeling language [13] provides meta-modeling concepts such as *intrinsic features* and *language level types* (see Sect. 2.2). Such metamodeling concepts are not a part of the ADO*xx* meta-metamodel [8, p. 8]. The ADO*xx* meta-metamodel includes concepts to define meta classes, attributes, and relationships at level M_2, which can be instantiated at type level M_1 in the ADO*xx* Modeling Toolkit [8, pp. 6–7]. But ADO*xx* does not offer ways of instantiating and managing instance populations at level M_0 that would represent instantiations of model elements from level M_1. As a result, the selected MEMO metamodels had to be redesigned such that the desired domain aspects could all be modeled at exactly one abstraction level. The criteria which have been considered in this process are described below.

4.2 Preparation of Metamodels

The concepts, abstract syntax, and parts of the semantics of the MEMO modeling languages selected for implementation are specified in the form of metamodels in different publications (see [11, p. 50] [12, p. 55] [26, p. 201]). Each metamodel includes a number of meta types (typically 20–40) plus a range of meta relationships. The metamodels are specified using both common metamodeling concepts such as 'MetaEntity' and 'MetaAttribute' as well as advanced concepts of MEMO MML, including intrinsic features, language level types, and attributes marked as 'derivable' or 'obtainable' (see Sect. 2.1). Additionally, each metamodel is augmented with a set of OCL constraints. The existing MEMO metamodels served as a starting point for the ADO*xx* implementation. However, in view of the two constraints described above (Sect. 4.1), a number of modifications and simplifications had to be made to the original metamodels so that an implementation would become technically feasible and conceptually adequate for the target group. Because the complete list of modifications and resulting metamodels cannot be presented here, the most salient implementation tasks are summarized below and illustrated by means of an example (see Fig. 8).

Reduction of concepts. In order to advance language accessibility, several concepts were omitted for the tool implementation. This mainly concerns concepts for advanced users to describe domain details or concepts that represent less intuitive abstractions. As an example of the former, advanced OrgML control flow concepts such as 'while' or 'repeat' loops were not considered. As an example of the latter, the GoalML concept 'GoalSystem' was not implemented (see Fig. 8). While such a concept can serve to specify and analyze joint properties of goal systems (e.g., the transitivity of goal priorities), we opted not to implement it as we did not see a sufficiently clear way of embedding it in the initial set of diagram types.

Modification of concepts. For several MEMO language concepts, we chose to implement a modified and simplified conceptualization. The redesign mainly centered around the aims of easing language use and enhancing tool usability. For instance, the original GoalML metamodel demands to specify a goal and its components in terms of several distinct concepts, including 'AbstractGoal', 'GoalMatter', 'SituationalAspect', and various relationships (see the upper part of Fig. 8). This conceptualization enables to specify a goal in great detail (e.g., it permits to define a goal whose "substance" is composed of a variety of different real-world aspects). It also contributes to reuse (e.g., the same goal matter 'Revenues' could be referenced by several goals). However, in the ADO*xx* Modeling Toolkit, it might be considered inconvenient to have to create and interlink numerous model elements for the pur-

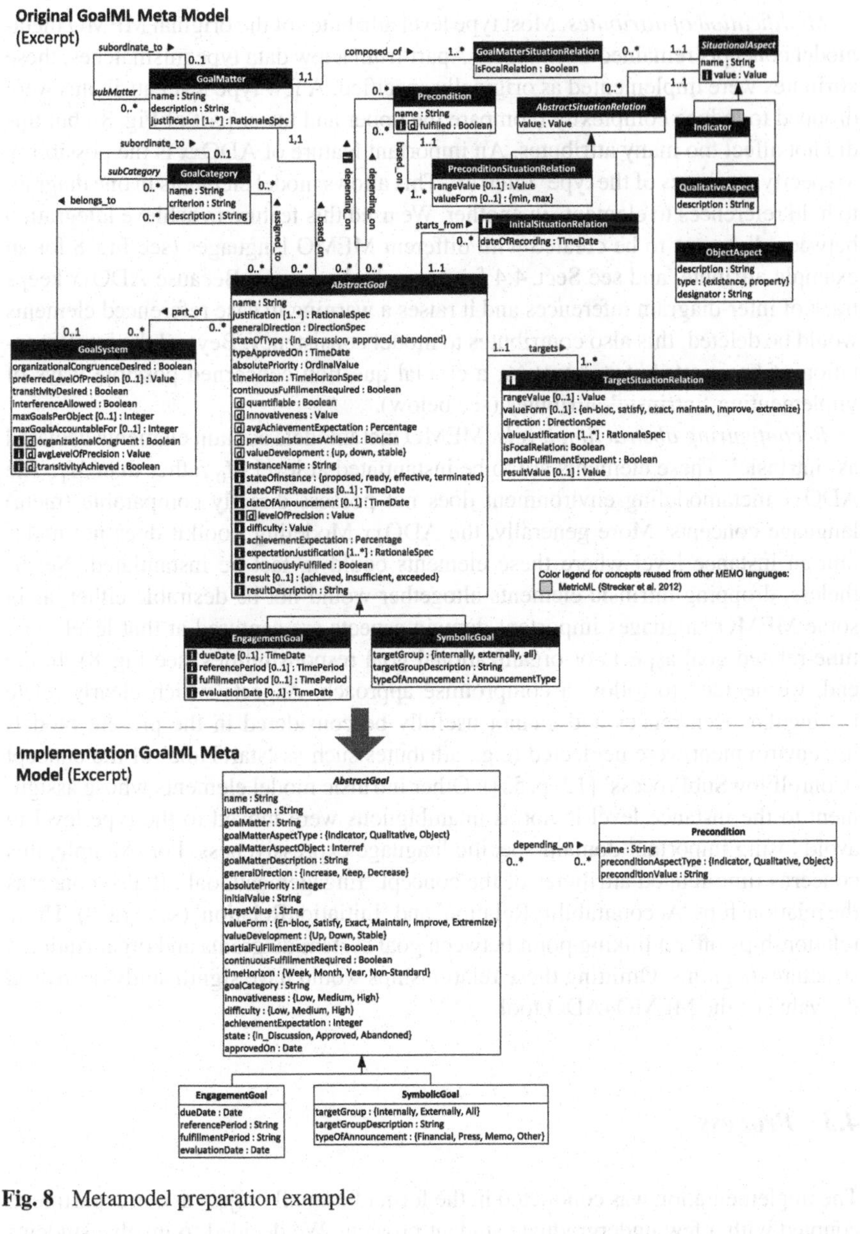

Fig. 8 Metamodel preparation example

pose of creating a single goal. Therefore, we subsumed the formerly distinct goal components in one central concept (see the lower part of Fig. 8). This improves language accessibility—though at the cost of language expressiveness. It remains to be seen which compromise proves useful in the long term.

Modification of attributes. Most type level attributes of the original MEMO metamodel concepts remained unchanged. Apart from a few data type mismatches, these attributes were implemented as originally specified. A few type level attributes were dropped to reduce complexity (compare the upper and lower part of Fig. 8), but this did not affect too many attributes. An important feature of ADO*xx* is the possibility to specify attributes of the type 'Interref'. This allows model elements in one diagram to hold references to elements in another. We used this feature to achieve integration between diagrams to be created with different MEMO languages (see Fig. 8 for an example attribute, and see Sect. 4.4 for example diagrams). Because ADO*xx* keeps track of inter-diagram references and it raises a warning in case referenced elements would be deleted, this also contributes to model consistency. Beyond the implementation of basic attributes, however, a crucial question concerned possible ways of implementing 'intrinsic' attributes (see below).

Reconfiguring abstraction levels. MEMO metamodels contain elements declared as 'intrinsic'. These elements are to be instantiated at level M_0 rather than M_1. The ADO*xx* metamodeling environment does not possess directly comparable (meta) language concepts. More generally, the ADO*xx* Modeling Toolkit does not maintain an instance level where these elements could in fact be instantiated. Nevertheless, dropping intrinsic elements altogether would not be desirable either, as in some MEMO languages important domain aspects are captured at that level (e.g., time-related goal aspects or organizational goal responsibilities, see Fig. 8). In the end, we decided to follow a compromise approach. Aspects which clearly relate to singular occurrences and cannot usefully be considered in the present modeling environment were neglected (e.g., attributes such as 'startTime' of the concept 'ConrolFlowSubProcess' [12, p. 55]). Other intrinsic model elements whose assignment to the instance level is not as unambiguous were moved to the type level to avoid losing important domain-specific language expressiveness. For example, this concerns time-related attributes of the concept 'EngagementGoal'. It also concerns the relationships 'AccountabilityRelation' and 'InitiationRelation' (see Fig. 8). These relationships offer a linking point between goal system diagrams and organizational structure diagrams. Omitting these relationships would have significantly decreased the value of the MEMO4ADO tool.

4.3 Process

The implementation was conducted in the form of a small project at our department, coupled with a few undergraduate student projects. We decided to involve students in the process for two reasons. First, implementing modeling languages addresses skills central to our field—the ability to grasp advanced abstractions (as required in metamodeling), scrutinizing and integrating domain-specific concepts from the field of management studies, and technical proficiency. Second, involving students provided an opportunity to gather first-hand feedback and suggestions on language and tool usability. At our department, a few student assistants supported us in imple-

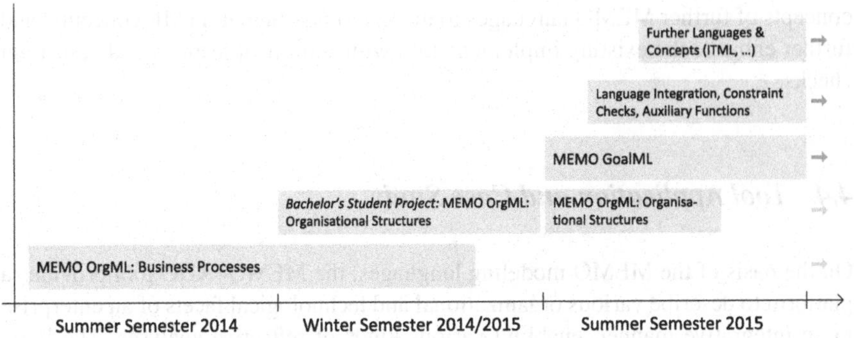

Fig. 9 Implementation milestones

menting the languages.[1] The undergraduate student projects, in turn, were completed by student groups of 3–4 persons. From the conducted students' projects, a project concerned with the OrgML for organizational structures particularly contributed to the present tool.[2] Figure 9 shows a timeline of implementation milestones.

In our experience, the time needed to complete implementation tasks varied greatly between different kinds of tasks. The preparation of metamodels typically took considerable time, as it demanded to reconcile different language architectures (see Sect. 4.2). This task was particularly challenging for undergaduate, Bachelor's-level student groups because most members were not familiar with advanced meta-modeling concepts at the beginning of the process. The following implementation of selected concepts and their attributes could usually be done swiftly, as this is a straightforward exercise in the ADO*xx* Development Toolkit. The same is true for the concrete syntax. Then again, what tended to require great effort was the implementation of additional constraints which accompany all MEMO metamodels. In the MEMO language architecture, these constraints are defined using OCL. In ADO*xx*, such constraints can be implemented in the form of manually invocable or event-triggered routines written in the AdoScript language. However, because OCL is a declarative language and the ADO*xx* script language is an imperative one, the transformation was not trivial. It was also complicated by the fact that several MEMO language constraints are quite complex in nature (see, e.g., [12, pp. 61–63] [26, pp. 203–207]). Consequently, the present tool is capable of evaluating some, but not all MEMO language constraints. The implementation of further constraint checks is an ongoing activity (see Fig. 9). Finally, the time it took to realize additional auxiliary functions (such as different levels of notational details; see Sect. 4.4.2) varied with the nature of the function. In the future, we will continue to add language

[1]In particular, we would like to thank David Becher for his major contributions to the implementation of the OrgML (business processes), the GoalML, and the integration of the languages.

[2]We would like to thank the project members Jeannot Gerth, Jonas Kaiser, Jesse Okpure, and Marijan Srsa for their important contributions to the implementation of the OrgML (organizational structures).

concepts of further MEMO languages to the tool (in particular, ITML concepts) and further enhance the existing implementation with additional features and constraint checks.

4.4 *Tool Application and Case Study*

On the basis of the MEMO modeling languages, the MEMO4ADO tool provides a platform to describe various organizational and technological facets of an enterprise in an integrative manner, enabling various kinds of reflective analyses. The basic way of using the MEMO4ADO tool consists in creating different *core diagrams* that describe selective abstractions of the enterprise in question (i.e., goal systems, organizational structures, and business process control flows) and to subsequently interrelate them by means of additional *integrative diagrams* and *references* between the diagrams. Dependent on the specific MEMO-based method followed, the diagrams may be created in different partial orders (e.g., top–down considerations starting with goal systems, or operational analyses starting with business process control flows; see also Sects. 2.3 and 3.2). However, it is constitutive of MEMO that the models are not to be taken as a single-blow approach to specify and afterwards implement parts of an organization (i.e., to "engineer" an enterprise in a narrow sense). Instead, the models are intended to serve as a means of analyzing, reflecting on, and perhaps rethinking ways of working in iterative, collaborative processes. The full scope of possible application scenarios for the languages cannot be presented here. For details, see the process models and examples in the respective publications [12, 13, 26]. To offer an overview of the modeling tool, we will first present the implemented diagram types and illustrate their basic use by means of an example (Sect. 4.4.1). Subsequently, we will describe auxiliary functions that were implemented to aid language use (Sect. 4.4.2).

4.4.1 Basic Functionality and Diagram Types

Figure 10 shows an overview case of the different diagram types that can be created with the MEMO4ADO tool. The figure also illustrates the interrelations between the different diagram types and exemplifies how model elements defined in one diagram may be referenced in another. The diagram types are described successively below.

Goal System Diagram (core diagram type; top left). This is the essential MEMO GoalML [26, 30] diagram type to establish, investigate, and restructure an organization's goal system. The diagram type enables the user to describe goals, of which the GoalML offers two kinds, and their various possible relationships at a high level of detail. *EngagementGoals* describe goals which are mainly established for specific organizational units and whose attainment can be measured after a given period. *SymbolicGoals* are intended to describe goals that serve broader purposes of motivation and inspiration. Each kind of goal possesses a variety of attributes to

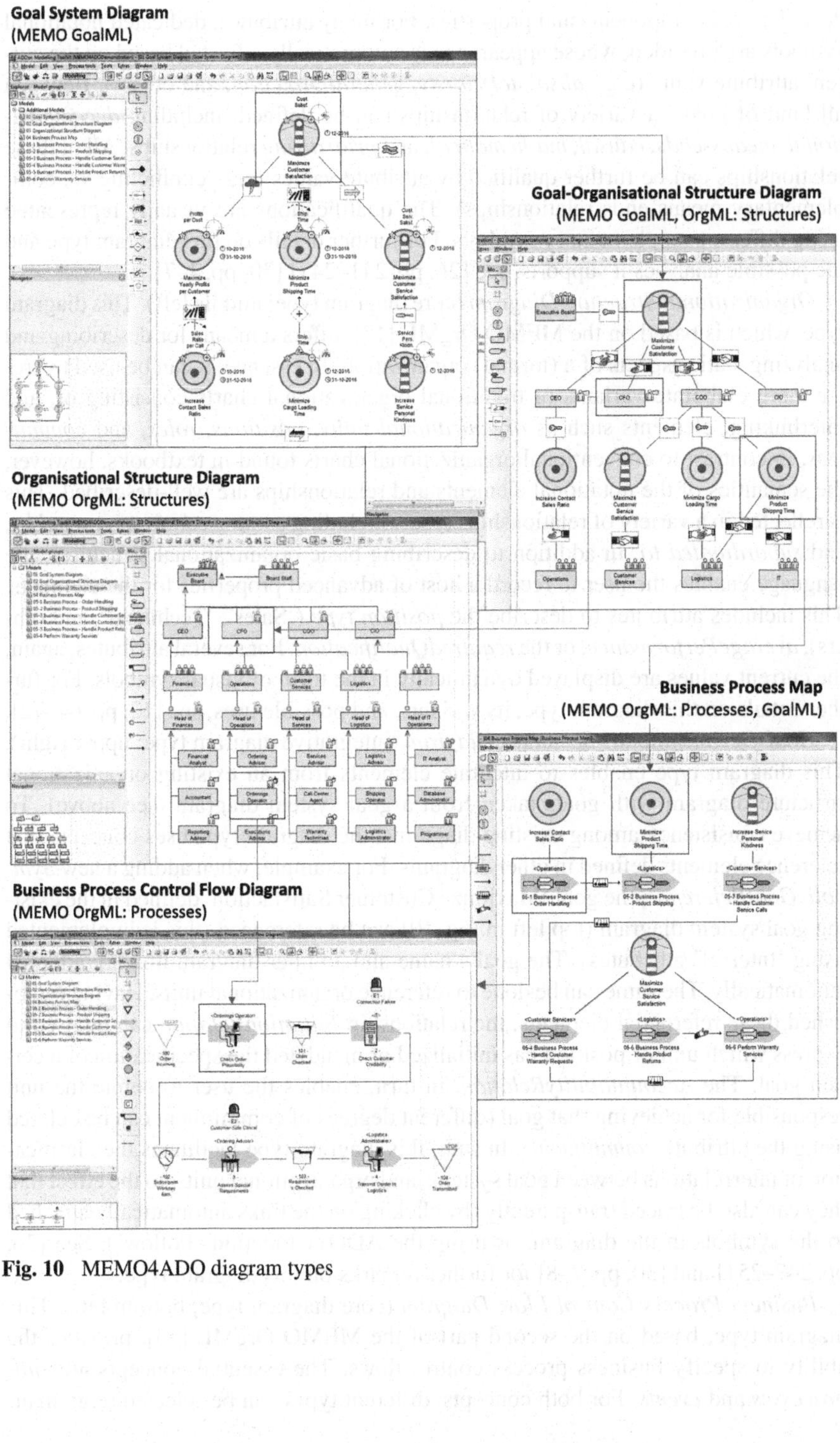
Goal System Diagram
(MEMO GoalML)
Goal-Organisational Structure Diagram
(MEMO GoalML, OrgML: Structures)
Organisational Structure Diagram
(MEMO OrgML: Structures)
Business Process Map
(MEMO OrgML: Processes, GoalML)
Business Process Control Flow Diagram
(MEMO OrgML: Processes)

Fig. 10 MEMO4ADO diagram types

describe goal components and properties. For many attributes, dedicated notational symbols are provided, whose appearance is automatically adjusted based on the current attribute value (e.g., *absolutePriority*, *generalDirection*, and others). Between all kind of goals, a variety of relationships can be defined, including *decompositional*, *means-ends*, *causal*, *mathematical*, and *prioritizing* relationships. All of these relationships can be further qualified by attribute values (e.g., conflicting vs. complementary means-ends relationships). The qualifications are visually represented using different supplementary symbols. For further details on this diagram type and the possible analyses it supports, see [26, pp. 241–247] [30, pp. 4–7].

Organizational Structure Diagram (core diagram type; middle left). This diagram type, which is based on the MEMO OrgML [12], offers a means for describing and analyzing static aspects of a (formal) organization. In essence, it can be used to create more elaborate variants of traditional organizational charts consisting of, and interlinking, elements such as *organizational units*, *positions*, *roles*, and *committees*. In contrast to conventional organizational charts found in textbooks, however, the semantics of the notational elements and relationships are well-described. This is reflected in a variety of relationships types, including *composed of*, *supervised by*, and *subordinated to*. In addition to describing basic organizational structures, the language enables the user to record a host of advanced properties for the elements. This includes attributes to describe the *position type* ('Sales', 'Technical', and others), *averagePerformance*, or the *requiredQualification*. For several attributes, again, the current values are displayed dynamically in the form of visual symbols. For further details on this diagram type, its variants, and possible uses, see [12, pp. 64–72].

Goal-Organisational-Structure Diagram (integrative diagram type; upper right). This diagram type enables to integrate elements from an existing organizational structure diagram with goals taken from a goal system diagram (see above). To achieve consistency among existing diagrams, the diagram type uses concepts that reference elements defined in other diagrams. For example, when adding a new *SymbolicGoalReference*, the goal 'Maximize Customer Satisfaction' defined in the existing goal system diagram (top left in Fig. 10) can be referenced (this is implemented using 'Interref' attributes). The goal's name and an inter-diagram link are adopted automatically. The same can be done to reference organizational units. Having established these referential elements, the relationship *InitiationRelation* can be used to express which unit or position has initialized or mandated the specification of a certain goal. The *AccountabilityRelation*, in turn, enables the user to define the unit responsible for achieving that goal (different degrees of commitment can be defined using the attribute *commitment*). In sum, this diagram type facilitates the clarification of interrelations between goal systems and organizational units, to the effect that they can also be traced transparently (by clicking on the links automatically attached to the symbols in the diagram, or using the ADO*xx* function 'Follow'). See [26, pp. 247–251] and [30, pp. 7–8] for further remarks on this diagram type.

Business Process Control Flow Diagram (core diagram type; bottom left). This diagram type, based on the second part of the MEMO OrgML [13], provides the ability to specify business process control flows. The essential concepts are *subprocesses* and *events*. For both concepts, different types can be selected (e.g., manual, IT-supported, and fully automated subprocesses; and time-triggered, message-triggered, or generic change-triggered events). Again, changes of these and other attribute values are signified visually. The organizational units or positions which are responsible for fulfilling a given subprocess can be specified using the *in charge of* attribute, representing another inter-diagram relationship (see Fig. 10). Subprocesses and events have to be related alternately by means of the central *subsequent* relationship. More complex control flow structures can be defined using parallelization (concept *Fork*) or exclusive path decision points (concept *Decision*). For further details and examples regarding this diagram type, see [13, pp. 89–95].

Business Process Map (integrative diagram type; lower right). This diagram type distinguishes itself from control flow diagrams in that it provides an overview of different business process types in an enterprise rather than describing one business process type in detail. The central concept, *business process*, offers a reference attribute which enables the user to link it to a control flow diagram. As a result, business process maps can be used as a starting point to navigate to richer descriptions of particular business process types. Business processes may also be related on a macro-level, such as by means of the relationships *supports*, *may trigger*, and *similar to*. Finally, because business processes may also be taken as reference objects of organizational goals, this diagram type enables to add references from business processes to existing goals (using the same concepts as in goal-organizational-structure diagrams). For example, the organizational goal 'Minimize Product Shipping Time' might refer to the business process type 'Product Shipping' (middle of the business process map in Fig. 10). Again, the elements in the diagram contain clickable links to directly navigate to the source diagrams. See [13, p. 89] for further notes on business process maps and [26, p. 253] for general remarks on goal reference object diagrams.

Taken together, the above diagram types are a coherent and tightly integrated subset of MEMO diagrams. Using the capabilities of the ADO*xx* environment, interrelationships between different areas of an enterprise can be recorded and explored dynamically. Possible application scenarios, which could only be indicated here, range from strategic goal planning processes to organizational restructuring efforts to process bottleneck analyses. For more details on these and further capabilities of the languages, refer to the cited language documentations.

4.4.2 Auxiliary Functions and Support in Language Use

While the basic diagram types offer a ground for creating and interlinking various diagrams, building and using comprehensive enterprise models is still a challenging task. In order to ease language use and to improve model versatility and interpretability for different target groups, we are continuously adding auxiliary functions to the environment. Three of these are briefly outlined below.

Constraint Checks. The MEMO metamodels are accompanied by a number of constraints to prevent semantically inconsistent or nonsensical models. We implemented a subset of these constraints. There are two kinds of constraints (see [13, pp. 57–63]). Ad hoc constraints can be recognized as soon as an invalid model part is created. For instance, it is not possible that two positions are the superior of each other at the same time. When trying to define such a relation, an error message containing an explanation is shown. Other constraints can be checked only once a model is considered complete. For example, a complete business process control flow model needs to include a start and a stop event. For these kinds of constraints, we implemented the feature 'Check Model Validity' (found in the menu). When calling this function, a model is evaluated and possible errors and confirmation messages are displayed in the form of a user dialog. Please note that while we intend to further extend the scope of constraint checks, the tool does not check the full set of constraints of the MEMO languages.

Different Levels of Notational Detail. When considering MEMO diagrams such as those shown in Fig. 10, one may find that these diagrams exhibit a level of notational detail which might be overly complicated for some purposes. To improve diagram legibility and clarity for these scenarios, we implemented a function that allows switching between different levels of detail. This feature is currently available for the GoalML and perhaps will be added for other languages in the future. The function is found in the menu. Figure 11 (left-hand side) illustrates a goal system diagram with a high level of detail as compared to one with a lower level of detail.

Auxiliary Overview Textboxes. Attribute values of model elements can be specified and investigated using the ADO*xx* notebook dialog. Sometimes, it may also be considered helpful to see values of attributes at a glance while interpreting a diagram. For this purpose, we implemented various additional text box views for each language. These views attach a basic text box to each model element in which the values for selected attributes are listed textually. Some modes focus on general overview attributes, whereas others focus on special topics such as financial aspects. Figure 11 (right-hand side) shows an example.

Building on the underlying diagram types, the auxiliary functions are meant to additionally enhance the usability and convenience of the MEMO4ADO tool. Further enhancing the scope of these functions, as well as adding further modes of accommodating tool use are ongoing tasks on our agenda.

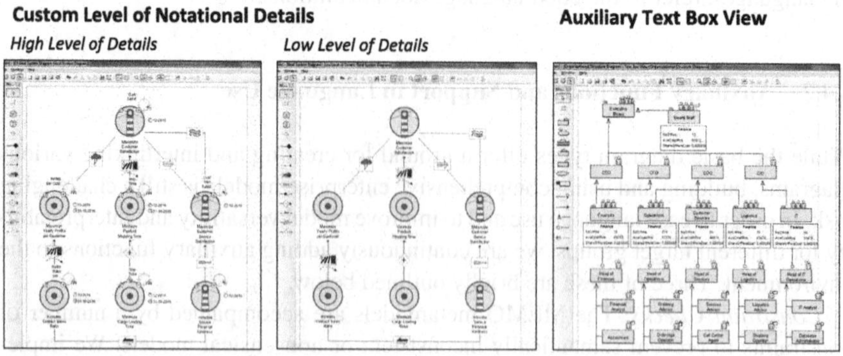

Fig. 11 Auxiliary function examples

5 Conclusion

MEMO is an enterprise modeling method whose development was initiated as early as two decades ago and which continues to be a subject of active research. Studies into ways of modeling organizational action systems and information systems have resulted in an integrated and still growing set of comprehensive modeling languages. ADO*xx* is a valuable addition to the modeling environments that have been used in the history of MEMO. First, ADO*xx* is highly accessible, both for language users and metamodelers. For language users, the ADO*xx* Modeling Toolkit offers a clear user interface which hides many unnecessary technical (meta) modeling details. Initial application in Bachelor's-level modeling courses indicate that students swiftly learn how to use the MEMO4ADO tool, and that they appreciate the modeling support it offers. Compared to our Ecore- and Eclipse-based tools, we have the impression that ADO*xx* is regarded as more intuitive and ergonomic. We also see that ADO*xx* facilitates the developer's task, as the pre-defined meta-level concepts provided in the Development Toolkit are a convenient basis to develop modeling languages for two-level language architectures. We furthermore argue that ADO*xx* is a stable and mature environment. Finally, ADO*xx* provides a basis for implementing a host of additional features, drawing on its capabilities for model analysis and the incorporated ADOScript language. The benefits of these features are exemplified in this and the other contributions in this volume.

At the same time, investigations into the nature of reconstructing professional languages by means of conceptual (meta) models have led us to conclude that traditional two-level language architectures do not suffice to satisfy advanced modeling requirements. These insights have, as a first step, stimulated the development of advanced metamodeling concepts for three-level language architectures (e.g., "intrinsic features", discussed in this contribution). These concepts could not directly be translated to the ADO*xx* language architecture. Furthermore, our work on the specification of modeling languages confirmed the assumption that a flexible number of classification levels promote reusability and flexibility of models and languages. In addition, the simultaneous use of a programming language that also features an arbitrary number of classification levels allows the common representation of models and code. Because an account of an arbitrary number of classification levels is beyond the scope of most current modeling tools, including ADO*xx*, we are now working on an XMF-based tool that in fact provides the ability to create multilevel models and multilevel software systems that share the same representation [16]. The further development of this tool as well as the reconstruction of existing MEMO languages for a corresponding architecture is where our future research is heading.

The MEMO4ADO tool presented in this chapter is meant to provide a platform to dynamically create and explore enterprise models on a coherent, limited scope. The tool focuses mainly on concepts to model aspects of organizational action systems (e.g., goals, structures, and processes). The capabilities of ADO*xx* enable the user to recognize and trace links between different areas of an enterprise. We intend to use the tool in the context of a Bachelor's-level modeling course as a laboratory in which students are asked to investigate an existing multi-perspective enterprise model and to extend it with further partial models, such as new business processes. Future development of MEMO4ADO will include the implementation of further auxiliary functions and the integration of additional concepts from other MEMO languages. For example, we wish to add concepts from MEMO ITML [23] to provide the ability to describe information systems infrastructures and to enable additional diagram types in which IT concepts can be interrelated with elements of the organizational action system.

Tool Download http://www.omilab.org/memo4ado.

References

1. Atkinson, C., Kühne, T.: Reducing accidental complexity in domain models. Softw. Syst. Model. **7**(3), 345–359 (2008)
2. Bock, A.: Beyond narrow decision models: toward integrative models of organizational decision processes. In: Aveiro, D., Frank, U., Lin, K.J., Tribolet, J. (eds.) Proceedings of the 17th IEEE Conference on Business Informatics (CBI 2015). IEEE Press, Los Alamitos (2015)
3. CIMOSA: Open system architecture for CIM. Springer, Berlin, Heidelberg, New York (1993)
4. Clark, T., Sammut, P., Willans, J.: Applied Metamodelling: A Foundation for Language Driven Development, 2nd edn. Ceteva (2008). http://www.eis.mdx.ac.uk/staffpages/tonyclark/Papers/Applied%20Metamodelling%20%28Second%20Edition%29.pdf
5. Clark, T., Willans, J.: Software language engineering with XMF and XModeler. In: Mernik, M. (ed.) Formal and Practical Aspects of Domain-Specific Languages, pp. 311–340. Information Science Reference (2012)
6. Dietz, J.L.G.: Enterprise Ontology: Theory and Methodology. Springer, Berlin (2006)
7. Ferstl, O.K., Sinz, E.J.: Modeling of business systems using SOM. In: Bernus, P., Mertins, K., Schmidt, G. (eds.) Handbook on Architectures of Information Systems, pp. 347–367. Springer, Berlin (2006)
8. Fill, H.G., Karagiannis, D.: On the conceptualisation of modelling methods using the ADOxx meta modelling platform. Enterp. Model. Inf. Syst. Archit. **8**(1), 4–25 (2013)
9. Frank, U.: Multiperspektivische Unternehmensmodellierung: Theoretischer Hintergrund und Entwurf einer objektorientierten Entwicklungsumgebung. Oldenbourg, München (1994)
10. Frank, U.: The MEMO Meta-Metamodel. Research Report of the Institute for Business Informatics 9, University of Koblenz, Koblenz (1998)
11. Frank, U.: MEMO Organisation Modelling Language (1): Focus on Organisational Structure. ICB Research Report 48, University of Duisburg-Essen, Essen (2011)
12. Frank, U.: MEMO Organisation Modelling Language (2): Focus on Business Processes. ICB Research Report 49, University of Duisburg-Essen, Essen (2011)
13. Frank, U.: The MEMO Meta Modelling Language (MML) and Language Architecture: 2nd edn. ICB Research Report 43, University of Duisburg-Essen, Essen (2011)
14. Frank, U.: Domain-specific modeling languages—requirements analysis and design guidelines. In: Reinhartz-Berger, I., Sturm, A., Clark, T., Wand, Y., Cohen, S., Bettin, J. (eds.) Domain Engineering: Product Lines, Conceptual Models, and Languages, pp. 133–157. Springer (2013)
15. Frank, U.: Multi-perspective enterprise modeling: foundational concepts, prospects and future research challenges. Softw. Syst. Model. **13**(3), 941–962 (2014)
16. Frank, U.: Multilevel modeling: toward a new paradigm of conceptual modeling and information systems design. Bus. Inf. Syst. Eng. **6**(6), 319–337 (2014)

17. Frank, U.: Power-modelling: Toward a more versatile approach to creating and using conceptual models. In: Proceedings of the Fourth International Symposium on Business Modelling and Software Design, pp. 9–19 (2014)
18. Frank, U., Strecker, S.: Open reference models—community-driven collaboration to promote development and dissemination of reference models. Enterp. Model. Inf. Syst. Archit. **2**(2), 32–41 (2007)
19. Frank, U., Strecker, S.: Beyond ERP Systems: An Outline of Self-Referential Enterprise Systems. ICB Research Report 31, University of Duisburg-Essen, Essen (2009)
20. Goldstein, A., Frank, U.: Components of a multi-perspective modeling method for designing and managing it security systems. Information Systems and e-Business Management (2015)
21. Gronback, R.C.: Eclipse Modeling Project: A Domain-Specific Language (DSL) Toolkit. Addison-Wesley, Amsterdam (2009)
22. Gulden, J., Frank, U.: MEMOCenterNG—a full-featured modeling environment for organisation modeling and model-driven software development. In: Proceedings of the 2nd International Workshop on Future Trends of Model-Driven Development (FTMDD 2010) (2010)
23. Heise, D.: Unternehmensmodell-basiertes IT-Kostenmanagement als Bestandteil eines integrativen IT-Controllings. Logos, Berlin (2013)
24. Kirchner, L.: Eine Methode zur Unterstützung des IT-Managements im Rahmen der Unternehmensmodellierung. Logos, Berlin (2008)
25. Koch, S., Strecker, S., Frank, U.: Conceptual modelling as a new entry in the bazaar: The open model approach. In: Damiani, E., Fitzgerald, B., Scacchi, W., Scotto, M., Succi, G. (eds.) Open Source Systems, pp. 9–20. Springer, New York (2006)
26. Köhling, C.A.: Entwurf einer konzeptuellen Modellierungsmethode zur Unterstützung rationaler Zielplanungsprozesse in Unternehmen. Cuvillier, Göttingen (2013)
27. Object Management Group: Meta Object Facility (MOF) Core Specification: Version 2.0 (2006). http://www.omg.org/spec/MOF/2.0/
28. Object Management Group: Object constraint language: Version 2.2 (2010). http://www.omg.org/spec/OCL/2.2/
29. Odell, J.J.: Power types. J. Object Oriented Program. **7**(2), 8–12 (1994)
30. Overbeek, S., Frank, U., Köhling, C.A.: A language for multi-perspective goal modelling: challenges, requirements and solutions. Comput. Stand. Interfaces **38**, 1–16 (2015)
31. Sandkuhl, K.: Enterprise Modeling: Tackling Business Challenges with the 4EM Method. The Enterprise Engineering Series. Springer, Berlin (2014)
32. Schauer, H.: Unternehmensmodellierung für das Wissensmanagement: Eine multiperspektivische Methode zur ganzheitlichen Analyse und Planung. VDM, Saarbrücken (2009)
33. Scheer, A.W.: Architecture of Integrated Information Systems: Foundations of Enterprise Modelling. Springer, Berlin (1992)
34. Steinberg, D., Budinsky, F., Paternostro, M., Merks, E.: EMF: Eclipse Modeling Framework, 2nd edn. Addison-Wesley, Upper Saddle River (2009)
35. Strecker, S., Frank, U., Heise, D., Kattenstroth, H.: MetricM: a modeling method in support of the reflective design and use of performance measurement systems. Inf. Syst. e-Bus. Manag. **10**(2), 241–276 (2012)
36. The Open Group: TOGAF Version 9. The Open Group Series. Van Haren, Zaltbommel (2009)
37. The Open Group: ArchiMate 2.0 Specification: Open Group Standard. The Open Group Series. Van Haren, Zaltbommel (2012)
38. Zachman, J.A.: A framework for information systems architecture. IBM Syst. J. **26**(3), 276–292 (1987)

Holistic Conceptual and Logical Database Structure Modeling with ADO*xx*

Frank Kramer and Bernhard Thalheim

Abstract Conceptual database modeling is supported by many languages, e.g., the higher order entity-relationship modeling (HERM) language. The model should be the basis for a logical and later a physical realization. There are many tools that provide a graphical support. There are, however, rather few tools that provide a direct translation of the conceptual model into a logical one. Moreover, most of the translators follow an interpreter approach and oblige the modeler to later correction, normalization and optimization of the translated model. We show that the schemata developed in the HERM language on the basis of ADO*xx* can be properly translated into a relational logical language. Therefore, the database structuring can evolve, be maintained and integrated through the conceptual model instead of recoding.

Keywords Conceptual database modeling · Database schema development · Metamodel · Schema transformation and compiler translation

1 Introduction

Building an information system includes the development of a database model on the physical level. Creating a conceptual database model is the first step towards obtaining a physical model. The conceptual database model represents an abstraction of the real database model and concentrates on the elements of the database and their relations with each other. It is used to understand, discuss and document the structure of a database. If a good conceptual model is created, it can be translated into the corresponding logical representation and from there into the final physical representation. Thereby, the conceptual model could not be created on the basis of the physical model. This is because physical models cannot include all design decisions that are made for the database structure and so, there is no unambiguous translation from a physical into a conceptual database model. Creating the logical model as a translation of the conceptual model has also the advantage that later changes can

F. Kramer · B. Thalheim (✉)
Christian-Albrechts-University Kiel, Computer Science Institute, 24098 Kiel, Germany
e-mail: thalheim@is.informatik.uni-kiel.de

D. Karagiannis et al. (eds.), *Domain-Specific Conceptual Modeling*,
DOI 10.1007/978-3-319-39417-6_12

be easily made on the conceptual model. The translation of the evolved model then results in a better logical model.

As modeling language, normally an entity-relationship modeling language is used. Entity-relationship models follow a global-as-design principle, i.e., the model represents the global structure of the database and local viewpoints of users are represented over views of the schema. One version of the entity-relationship languages is the higher order entity-relationship modeling language (HERM) [13]. HERM has a generic algebra and logic, i.e., the fragment of predicate logic and the algebra of derivable operations may be derived from the HERM algebra whenever the structure of the database is given. Using HERM for database development has two important advantages over other extended entity-relationship models. First, the language is well-suited for the modeling of huge schemata and second, paths can be found through the schema which shows which data belong together. Yet, one disadvantage of HERM is that it is not suitable for pixel schemata. Pixel schemata means a schema that consists of a large set of entity types with a small set of attributes and a few tuples inside the entity classes.

To create a graphical HERM schema, a tool is needed that enables an automatic translation into a logical model after the modeling. There are, however, rather few tools that provide a direct translation of the conceptual model to a logical one. But normally this tool uses an interpreter approach to create the logical model. Eventhough an interpreter has its disadvantages, for example, a missing normalization and optimization, a later correction of the result and that design decisions and different translation options are often not taken into consideration. A better approach for the translation is a compiler approach. Here, preprocessing allows defining the compiler directives, which subsequently facilitates a translation based on the design information of the designer. These directives are used to create a schema that is normalized, optimized and prepared for evolution of the schema.

In this paper, we demonstrate how a graphical modeling tool based on ADO*xx* [1] can be created. This tool allows a translation based on directives which represent a first step on a compiler approach translation. Thereby, we implemented a first prototype using the ADO*xx* metamodeling platform and ADO*xx* ADOScripts for the development. This prototype is currently revised and extended with additional features. In this revision process, we will switch to a Java implementation where ADO*xx* will be embedded as modeling tool with a Java-based compiler translation of the designed HERM model. To demonstrate the creation of our tool, we first describe the HER modeling language and the associated metamodel that is used in ADO*xx* in Sect. 2. Section 3 then explains the compiler approach that is used for the translation into the logical model. On this basis, Sect. 4 describes the development of an ADO*xx* prototype. We use the example of a hotel booking system to show how a conceptual model can be built and translated based on directives. Finally, Sect. 5 concludes the paper and gives a brief outlook to future work regarding our tool development.

1.1 Related Work

There are different tools that provide a solution for conceptual modeling and transformation. One of the tools that can be used is the commercial tool ERWin [6]. ERWin allows the user to create extended entity-relationship schemata. The representation of the elements is conform to the known representation. For the representation of cardinality constraints, the crow's food notation is used. Furthermore, ERWin provides the possibility to translate the schema into its SQL representation by an interpreter. For the modeling of HERM schemata, the tool is suitable only to a limited extent. Cluster types, complex attributes and higher order relationship types are not really representable and there are no transformation rules for these elements.

Another tool is Visual Paradigm [11] which can be used for entity-relationship modeling and translation. Like ERWin, it is a commercial tool. Here, the representation of relationship types is done by round rectangles. Apart from that, all other elements are displayed as known. For the representation of cardinality constraints, the participation semantic is used. Also Visual Paradigm gives the possibility to translate the schema into its SQL representation by an interpreter. For the modeling of HERM schemata, Visual Paradigm is partly suitable. Creating higher order relationship types is possible and also the translation of the types is good. Yet, in Visual Paradigm the modeling and translation of cluster types and complex attributes are not suitable.

A suitable solution for modeling and transforming of HERM schemata can be found in the commercial tool DB-Main [3]. DB-Main also allows the modeling of entity-relationship schemata. The cardinality constraints are represented in the participation semantic. Furthermore, you can create complex attributes and also cluster types without any problems. Only the higher order relationship types must be constructed with the usage of groups and inclusion constraints. This turns out as time-consuming and not very obvious modeling that can make a schema complex and confusing. But overall DB-Main is one of the few tools that allows to model a HERM schema with all its elements. DB-Main also provides a translation of the schema into its SQL representation by an interpreter. Thereby, the HERM transformation is only semi-automatic because some translation rules for the HERM are not translated correctly and must be corrected by a user manually. For larger schema this could be a time-consuming task.

2 Higher Order Entity-Relationship Modeling Language

To define the structure and behavior of the database, we will use the Higher Order Entity-Relationship Modeling Language (HERM). This modeling language was introduced by Thalheim in [13]. We will now give a short introduction to the important elements that are used in a HER-Model. Thereby, we describe the formal definition of the HERM elements as well as their graphical representation. After this, we will present the HERM metamodel that will be used for our modeling tool. The description of the HERM elements concentrates on the introduction of attributes, entity types, relationship types and cluster types. For a closer description of these elements and the integrity constraints in such a model, we refer to [13] or [14].

2.1 Formal Definition of HERM Elements

The first element of a HERM schema are attributes. Attributes can be distinguished into basic and complex attributes. Basic attributes are defined as A::B with an attribute name A, a base type B, like integer or datetime and an association :: that associates a name with a base type. Complex attributes are constructed on base attributes and by a recursive type equality $t = B | t \times \cdots \times t | < t > | [t] | \{t\} | \{ | t | \} | : t$ over a set of basic data types B, a set of labels L and constructors for tuple (product), list, optional, set and bag. For example, the complex attribute name could be represented as name::(< FirstName >, LastName, [{|AcadTitles|}]). Based on this an entity type E is characterized by its attributes and its integrity constraints. The set of integrity constraints Σ_E contains the key denoted as id(K) and other integrity constraints. A key is a set of attributes of E that identifies one element of an entity type E clear over all other elements in E. So an entity type E can be defined as E = (attr(E), Σ_E) with a set of attributes attr(E), a subset id(E) $\subseteq$ attr(E) and a set of integrity constraints Σ_E.

In a HERM schema, a cluster type is used to represent the generalization of different types. This is a disjoint union of types that are domain compatible on their identification type. Domain compatible means that types are subtypes of a common more general type. Since identification must be secured, the union must be disjoint. Otherwise, an element of the cluster cannot be related to the associated component. Based on this, a cluster C is defined as $C = l_1 : R_1 \cup l_2 : R_2 \cup \cdots \cup l_k : R_k$ with a disjoint union of labelled types $R_1, \ldots, R_k$. A graphical representation for cluster types is displayed in Fig. 1(b). Associations between entity types or clusters of entity types are defined as first-order relationship types. In the HERM schema, relationship types can also be defined on the basis of already defined relationship types. As a restriction, such types cannot be cyclic and must be inductive. Therefore, an order is introduced for relationship types. A relationship type can only be defined by all types that have a lower order than the relationship type. So a relationship type of order i is defined as an association between entity types or relationship types with an order less than i. Furthermore, it is required that at least one type in that association has an order of $i - 1$ if $i > 1$. The graphical representation of higher order relationship types is displayed in Fig. 1(a). Relationship types can have a set of attributes. In a HERM schema, a subset of these attributes can be used to extend or redefine the key that exists through the association of the types. Additionally, relationship types can be used to define a specialization if only a association to one type exists. To provide an understanding of a connection between a relationship and the type, a connection can get a label that describes the role of this connection. So formally, a

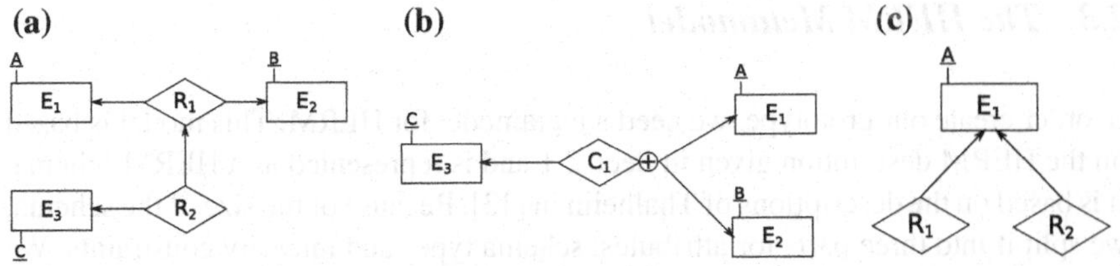

Fig. 1 Special HER-Model elements. **a** Higher-order relationship type, **b** Cluster type, **c** IsA specialization

relationship type with name R can be defined as R = $(compon(R), attr(R), \Sigma_R)$ with a set of labelled components compon(R), a set of attributes attr(R) and a set Σ_R of integrity constraints. Thereby Σ_R includes the identification of the relationship type by a subset id(R) of $compon(R) \cup attr(R)$.

A database schema S = $(\mathfrak{S}_1, \ldots, \mathfrak{S}_m, \Sigma_G)$ is now given by a set of database types $\mathfrak{S}_1, \ldots, \mathfrak{S}_m$ and a set of global integrity constraints Σ_G. Thereby, the database types are based on a set of global base types which are used as value types for attribute types. A database type $\mathfrak{S}$ is defined $\mathfrak{S}$ = (S, Op, Σ) with a structure S that could be an attribute, entity, cluster or relationship type, a set of operations Op and a set of static integrity constraints Σ.

2.2 *Graphical Representation of HERM Elements*

In a HERM schema, entity types are represented as rectangles and relationship types as diamonds. Attribute types are associated to the corresponding relationship or entity types. If a set of attributes identifies an entity type, these attributes are underlined. For a relationship type, a set of underlined attributes stands for a key extension and a set of overlined attributes stands for a key redefinition. Arrows are used to describe the order that must exist between the elements in a HER-Model. Thereby, the arrows point from the element of higher order to the element of lower order. The cluster type is represented as a diamond with a circle and a plus within the circle.[1]

To represent the cardinality between a relationship and the associated types, participation semantic is used. In the model, the (min, max) representation is used to represent this semantic. Figure 1 shows how the special elements for higher order types, cluster and specialization are represented. Elements like entity types, relationship types, attributes and keys are also displayed.

[1]We give the formal definition of higher order entity-relationship types and cluster types in Sect. 2.1. The IsA specialization of extended entity-relationship models is displayed in HERM as a unary relationship type that represents the specialized type.

2.3 The HERM Metamodel

In order create our prototype, we need a metamodel for HERM. This model is based on the HERM description given in Sect. 2.1 and is represented as a HERM schema. It is based on the descriptions of Thalheim in [13]. Because of the size of the schema, we split it into three parts for attributes, schema types and integrity constraints. We start with the attribute metamodel that is shown in Fig. 2. Thus, an attribute type can be an atomic or complex attribute. The atomic attribute has exactly one domain that represents the basic type. For a domain we can express cast functions to allow a representation of one domain in another. With the 1- and n-construct, the operations that are applicable to the attributes are described. Thereby, the 1-constructs are linked on their domain type to sets, bags and collections like union. Similar to the 1-constructs, the n-constructs are linked on their domain type to the cartesian product, lists, multi lists, union and disjoint union. The role and label of the attribute is described with the component clusters. For an n-construct operation, there can be more than one attribute involved, so the labels are keys and we need a sequence position for the operation.

The metamodel for a HERM Schema is shown in Fig. 3. The connection to the attribute metamodel can be established with the attribute type cluster that can also be found in Fig. 2. A schema type in HERM can be an attribute type, an entity type, a relationship type or a cluster type. Furthermore, there is an identification facility

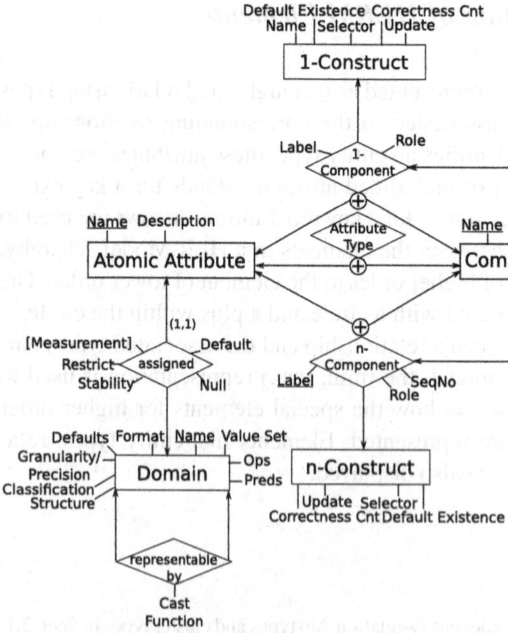

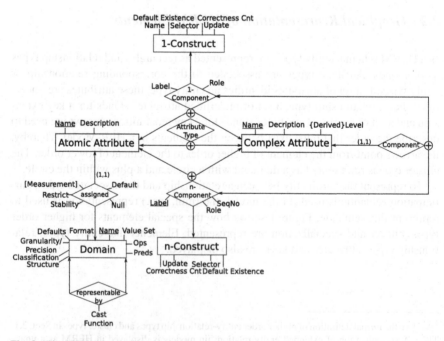

Fig. 2 The HERM Attribute Metamodel

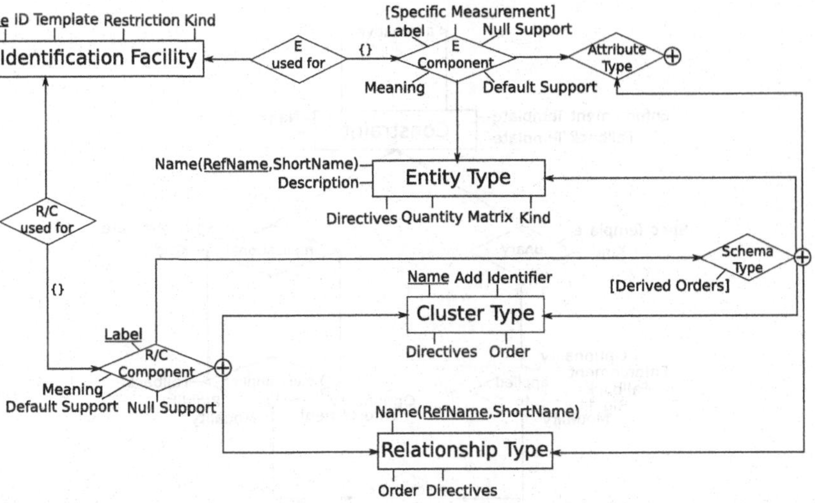

Fig. 3 The HERM Schema Metamodel

that defines the keys for the elements. This facility is connected to the entity components and the relationship/cluster (R/C) components to describe the keys for these elements. The kind of attribute within the facility defines the kind of access, for example, if it is a primary or secondary access. Furthermore, the entity, relationship and cluster types get a directives attribute. This attribute stores directives for the translation into a relational representation. In Sect. 3.4 we describe the usage of directives in our compiler approach.

For a schema element, we need the integrity constraints that are defined for the element. To describe the integrity constraints, we use the metamodel that is shown in Fig. 4. The model can be connected to the schema model in Fig. 3 with the schema type cluster type. Every constraint has an enforcement and fallback template that can be used. Furthermore, there can be alternatives if the constraint cannot be used. Every constraint can be specialized into a unary or an implication constraint with its own specified template and kind of constraint. The constraint can then be applied to the schema element whereby some options can be defined like an enforcement of the constraint or the optionality.

3 Translation of Conceptual Database Schemata

This section presents a compiler approach for translating a conceptual entity-relationship schema into a logical representation. For the translation, there are some basics that must be taken into consideration for every translation approach. In the area of entity-relationship modeling, there are a lot of different extended entity-

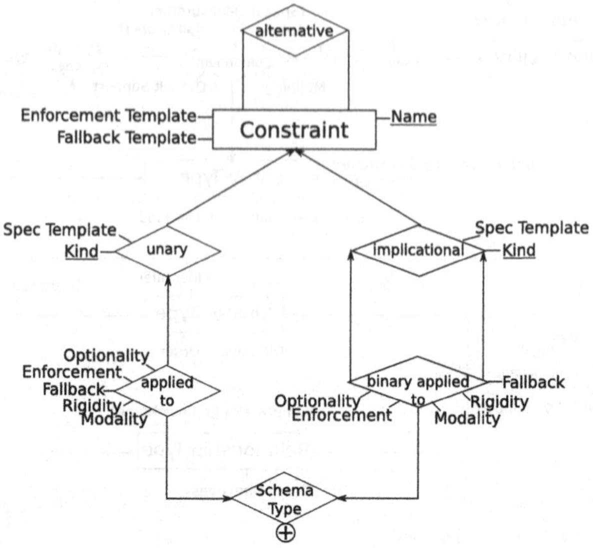

Fig. 4 The HERM Integrity Constraint Metamodel

relationship models. Most of them are only an extension of the classical model that was developed by Chen [2]. However, all these models have their own translation rules which have an impact on the translation process. Integrity constraints must also be taken into consideration for the translation process. Often, only a part of the existing explicit and implicit constraints are translated. Another point is the process support that is enabled through some extended entity-relationship models. Such models allow the explicit modeling of processes like transactions that must be supported by a possible translation. Furthermore, there are translation techniques which are non-deterministic and allow a direct interaction with the developer of the schema to get a better translation. Often a translation has requirements that must be fulfilled before the translation process can start. This could be a specific normal form for the schema or meta-assumptions like a unique name assumption. The preservation of the design information for the translation into a logical model should also be possible. However, a translation into a physical model is usually not supported so that the physical model must renounce the design information. Finally, the target schema should have a high quality. For this purpose, there is a series of approaches to create a minimal, normalized or non-redundant schema for a different start schema.

With these basics in mind, we demonstrate a compiler approach for the translation of extended entity-relationship models. For this, we first present the classical interpreter approach and describe where the disadvantages are of this approach. After this, we describe our compiler approach that eliminates most of the disadvantages of the interpreter approach.

3.1 Interpreter Approach

The interpreter approach is described in many books about the foundations of database system as for example from Elmasri and Navathe in [4]. During the interpretation of the schema, the types of the schema are translated in a specific order into their relational representation. Thereby, such an interpreter carries out a translation of a schema in the following steps:

1. Transform the complex attributes of the schema into first normal form attributes.
2. Translate every entity type into a single relation.
3. For every weak type, translated it in layers whereby the attribute set is extended by the key of the identifying entity type.
4. Hierarchical types are translated.
5. Translate binary relationship types that are 1:1 connected.
6. Translate n-ary relationship types that are 1:1 connected.
7. Translate binary relationship types that are 1:n connected.
8. Translate n-ary relationship types that are 1:n connected.
9. Translate relationship types that are n:m connected.
10. Recursive relationship types are translated.
11. Translate is a relationship types.
12. Translate cluster types.

Some of these steps, such as the translation of specialized types or binary 1:1 relationships allow a different translation. For example, a hierarchical type has four transformation options, namely event-nonseparation, event-separation, union or weak universal relation. Depending on the realization of the interpreter, one of these options is chosen. The interpreter approach has the advantage that it is solid. It produces a solution for every schema that could be used within an application. But there are also some disadvantages. First, the interpretation of large schemata becomes very slow and inefficient; this is because, so as to create a translation order, the interpreter must pass the schema multiple times to create the right order. Furthermore, the translation is often not of good quality. Many decisions for the translation depend on the application and the information a developer has about the environment. In the interpreter approach, there is no chance to bring these decisions into the translation, because the interpreter does not include them into the translation.

3.2 Compiler Approach

For the translation of a conceptual database model into a logical representation, a compiler approach offers an alternative to the interpreter approach. A first step to such a compiler can be found in Embley and Mok in [5, 10]. They describe a rule-based transformation of the type system depending on the language that is used for the conceptual model. Therefore, the conceptual model is transformed into an intermediate language. The transformation rules are defined for every element of the entity-relationship model. There can be different rules for the same element that represents different translation options, like the choice for hierarchical types. A controller is then used to ensure that the right rule is used for the transformation. Yet, to obtain a good transformation, two things must be done. First, the basic assumptions for the controller must be described, so that the controller can ensure the translation. Second, the schema must be normalized before or after the mapping. For the normalization, the complex attributes must be transformed, for integrity constraints that have no key on the left-hand side new entity types must be created, reducible n-ary relationship types must be handled and cycles must be reduced.

The compiler approach for translating schemata based on the higher order entity-relationship modeling language was inspired by this rule-based approach, the classical compiler theory [12] and works about transformation of entity-relationship model transformation [7–9]. Like a compiler for programming languages, the compiler for HERM schemata performs a lexical, syntactical analysis on the schema. After this, the optimization and preparations are done. In the end, the schema is translated into the target language. So, during the compilation of a schema the following concrete steps are performed:

1. Compiler configuration to DBMS.
2. Lexical analysis.
3. Syntactical analysis.
4. Derivation of intermediate schema.
5. Preparation for optimization.
6. Schema tuning.
7. Injection of controlled redundancy.
8. Redefinition and revision of schema types.
9. Big or huge database optimization.
10. Preparation for evolution and changes.
11. Service derivation.
12. Derivation of the finalized schema in the target language.

Hence, the first step performs a preprocessing for the translation. The defined preprocessing directives describe how the schema has to be translated. The next step transforms the schema into a canonical representation, creates a constraint environment and a token forest. After this, the types are combined into units and the defined directives are integrated. Next, the schema passes a correctness test based on a semantic analysis. If the schema is correct, the support structures, a pre-schema, views, indices, procedural components and triggers are created. To optimize the intermediate schema, the compiler prepares the elements by a post normalization, view optimization, materialization, separation into database phases, hints, kernel types, platform adaptation and enforcement rules. Then, the schema is tuned by an operational optimization that uses application scenarios and statistics, analyze critical components and tune the access and manipulation processes. After optimization and tuning, the compiler inserts controlled redundancy to the schema using copies and replication, derivable data, repeating groups, abstract terms, object copies and outer joins. When the redundancy is injected, the schema types can be redefined and revised. Therefore, the compiler analyses the storage intensive types, performs a key revision, eliminates and contracts types and duplicates, combines or segments types. In the next step, the optimization for the database management system is done. For this, the compiler analyses and adjusts the throughput, the retrieval performance, the processes for insert, update and delete. Moreover, checkpoints and recovery strategies are created and the administration and scheduling is checked. After this, policies for changes are introduced to enable evolution on the schema. Next, the compiler creates information and features for the user as service. In a last step, the final schema is derived into the target language and the compiling process ends.

The compiler approach has some advantages over the interpreter approach. First, the compiler creates not only a simple translation that depends only on the schema. The compiler also takes the environment into consideration, optimizes the structures and prepares for evolution. In contrast to the interpreter, the compiler integrates the developer of the schema to the translation process by creating translation directives based on the developers choice. Furthermore, the compiler not only creates the target schema. In addition, integrity constraints are created with the usage of views, triggers and procedures. These components are not created with the interpreter. A good preprocessing is needed in order to enable this advanced translation. Therefore, the next part takes a closer look at what must be done during the preprocessing for conceptual database schemata.

3.3 *Preprocessing of Conceptual Database Schemata*

The preprocessing of a compiler for conceptual database schemata enables an environment where the translation of conceptual database schemata can be managed as needed for the application. Therefore, nine special preprocessing rules should be enforced, namely

1. Look at database management system parameters.
2. Perform a database system profiling.
3. Derive directives for compiling.
4. Derive abbreviations and synonyms.
5. Extract all implicit constraints to explicit constraints.
6. Eliminate weak entity types.
7. Perform a compactification for hierarchies and multiple relationship associations.
8. Perform an orthonormalization of the schema.
9. Check of the schema.

The first rule states that the database management system parameters must be examined. This includes the type of the database, the structuring mechanisms, overlay structures, the architecture of the system, support for integrity maintenance and enforcement, the kind of type system and show type support. With the second rule, a database system profile is developed. The profile includes the database schema, functionality, support schemata, information about access, modification, performance and the adornment of complex attributes, roles for relationship and cluster types that cannot be distinguished in the schema. As the result of the third rule, a set of directives for the translation process is created. This is one of the most important rules and we will give a closer description of compiler directives in Sect. 3.4. The fourth rule says that, in a schema where the unique name assumption is not valid, a synset for each type that has not a unique name must be added. For example, the attribute name can be extended with to person.name, employee.person.name and so on. With rule five, explicit constraints are extracted that are implicitly coded into the type definition. This includes inclusion dependencies for all components of types of order ≥ 1, component construction constraints, constraint references, domain constraints, set constraints and exclusion constraints for surrogates of different types. With rule six, all weak entity types are eliminated that exist within the schema. Thereby, every weak type is replaced by the identification type construction. With rule seven, the hierarchies within a schema are categorized into specialization and generalization, and transformations are performed with an additional creation of explicit subtype constraints. Furthermore, the relationship associations pass a compactification with rule eight. Therefore, multiple relationship types between the same set of components may either be represented by a bulk schema with a separator attribute and remain as such in the case that semantics are not homogenisable. The component types could be injected into the relationship types as an exceptional decision. With the eighth rule, the schema is orthonormalized. For this, the schema is checked if it is not well-formed. If the check is positive, it will be orthonormalized. Furthermore, redundancy for derivable aspects are reduced and pivotisation is applied whenever it can be semantically based. Rule nine states check of the schema. Hence, the compliance is checked to best practice and the coherence of integrity constraints, satisfiability and enforcement schema like diamond problems are checked. All these rules create an environment that allows the compiler to translate the schema into the best possible logical model. For this translation, the directives play an important role. Therefore, the next section takes a closer look at the derivation of directives during the preprocessing.

3.4 Compiler Directives

During the preprocessing, the compiler creates general information that supports the compilation of the schema. As a result, a set of compiler directives is created. Compiler directives represent the choice of the developer for the best translation options depending on the application and the environment. This could be general translation decisions like the treatment of NULL markers or specific decisions of element options like the translations style of a concrete cluster type within the schema. Generally, the user must create directives as general descriptions for

- realization styles and tactics
- configuration parameter like the coding or the policies
- generic operations
- hint for realization of the database
- performance expectations
- constraint enforcement policies
- support features for the system realization

These directives are then used during the whole compilation to create a highly specialized schema that represents all design information the developer enters during schema creation. To support the designer by creating the directives, a modeling tool can suggest default translation options to the developer during schema creation. Furthermore, the compiler must ask the developer if important directives are missing during compilation. Therefore, the developer can again get default suggestions for the choices.

Take for example a cluster type within a HERM schema. For the translation of such a type there are five different approaches. First, a cluster type can be translated with a combination approach. For this, the identification of the participating types are used for the cluster type if the identification is compatible. Otherwise, an explicit separator like an attribute named kind is introduced that shows an abbreviation of the path to the corresponding abbreviation. For the separation approach, the cluster type is decomposed into new types that relate the cluster to its components. The cluster itself is represented as a potentially disjoint union view on the separated types. If the surrogate approach is used, a cluster type with a surrogate key is introduced. The corresponding types can then participate in the cluster partially over the component with subtypes, partially over the component with NULL reference or fully over the component. This could be useful if the identification of the participating elements is different. For the view approach, the cluster is represented as a view that represents an expression of the cluster. Finally, for the union approach, the cluster type is extended by a surrogate key and by all identifiers of the participating types with an NULL-existence constraint where only one of the identifiers cannot be NULL. Obviously, all these approaches are different and result in a different translation. A directive can now represent the best choice for the translation of a cluster in the given situation rate by a designer.

4 Proof of Concept

Our concept of a modeling and translation tool is developed as a library for ADO*xx* called HERMxx. This library allows a user to create a HERM schema and translate it into its SQL representation. This section presents our prototype of the HERMxx library. For this, we have chosen to use a hotel reservation application as our case study to create a HERM schema and the associated translation.

4.1 A Hotel Reservation Application

For our case study, we have chosen a hotel reservation application. In basic terms, a client can book one or more rooms in a hotel during a period of time. Therefore, we have to handle the information about the hotels, their rooms and the booking by a user. We now take a closer look at the information that is given in our scenario.

4.1.1 Hotel Information

A hotel is situated in a certain location in one country. The location is identified by the city and street and has a postcode. For the country, we know the country code that identifies it, the name and the currency of the country. Furthermore, a hotel belongs to a hotel chain and has a star rating. For the chain its name is given and a url where a client can access the information about the chain. With the star-rating system, a statement about the quality of the hotel is given. For example, a four-star-rated hotel is of a higher quality than a two-star-rated hotel. To access information about the hotel, a url is given that can be used by a client. If a client has questions about the hotel, the email and contact information such as the phone number are also provided. Last, a hotel can have a specific characterization with special conditions during a period of time. For example, there can be a gym that can be used by premium guest during the winter.

4.1.2 Room Information

Every hotel has a set of rooms that belongs to a room type. Every room type gets a standard rate that must be paid if such a type is booked. For every room, the floor and the room number are given and an actual rate is given that depends on the details in the room like a double bed and whether smoking is allowed in the room. But the rate of a room depends not only on the type, the room details and the smoking information. Also the period of booking is relevant for the rate. For example, a room during the height of the season is much more expensive than in the low season. Furthermore, there can be discounts on the rate if there is a special offer such as a Christmas special or long term booking of the room.

4.1.3 Booking Information

The booking is done by a client. Thereby, a client can be a travel agent or a guest of the hotel. We know the travel agent's name, the contract he contracted with the hotel and a history. A guest must specify his name and address as well as the information if there is a membership to the hotel chain, special requirements that must be known like a food allergy, past records and other details like the date of birth. For every booking, a booking number is created that identifies the booking process. A client can only book a certain amount of rooms of a room type in a hotel for a period of time. For example, a guest can book two rooms of the type double room. The concrete room for the booking is occupied by the hotel. The booking is recorded by a staff person. From this person we know the social security number (SSN), name, nickname and the service. Furthermore, the current state of the booking must be known. For example, a booking can be cancelled, accepted or pending with all consequences depending on the state. Last, the booking date is stored for documentation.

4.2 The HERMxx Prototype

To create a HERM schema and translate it into a logical form for our hotel case study, we used our prototype for ADO*xx* called HERMxx. For this, the prototype can be divided into two parts. The first part is for modeling a database structure as a HERM schema and the second part is for translating this model into the logical database structure based on SQL. We start with the creation of a HERM schema using the modeling view that is shown in Figs. 5 and 6. Thereby, the whole HERM schema displayed here is based on the metamodel we describe in Sect. 2.3. Every HERM schema is syntactically checked against this model. As a result, every model created with the HERMxx tool is a syntactically correct model. The individual parts of the modeling tool are described below.

The first one is the modeling toolbar of HERMxx in Fig. 5. Point 1 shows the ADO*xx* model group where the model is stored. Thereby, the name of a model that has not saved changes is represented in red characters. Point 2 shows the model bar. All the possible elements that can be used for developing a HERM schema are shown here. We describe the possible elements in Sect. 2. If a user selects one of the elements, like the entity type, he can place this object on the drawing area. An overview of the existing model is shown in the left down side in point 3. This overview is helpful to keep track on larger models and to navigate fast to a certain point of the model. The important new elements of the HERM are complex attributes, higher order relationship types and the cluster type for generalization. All these three elements can be represented with our modeling tool.

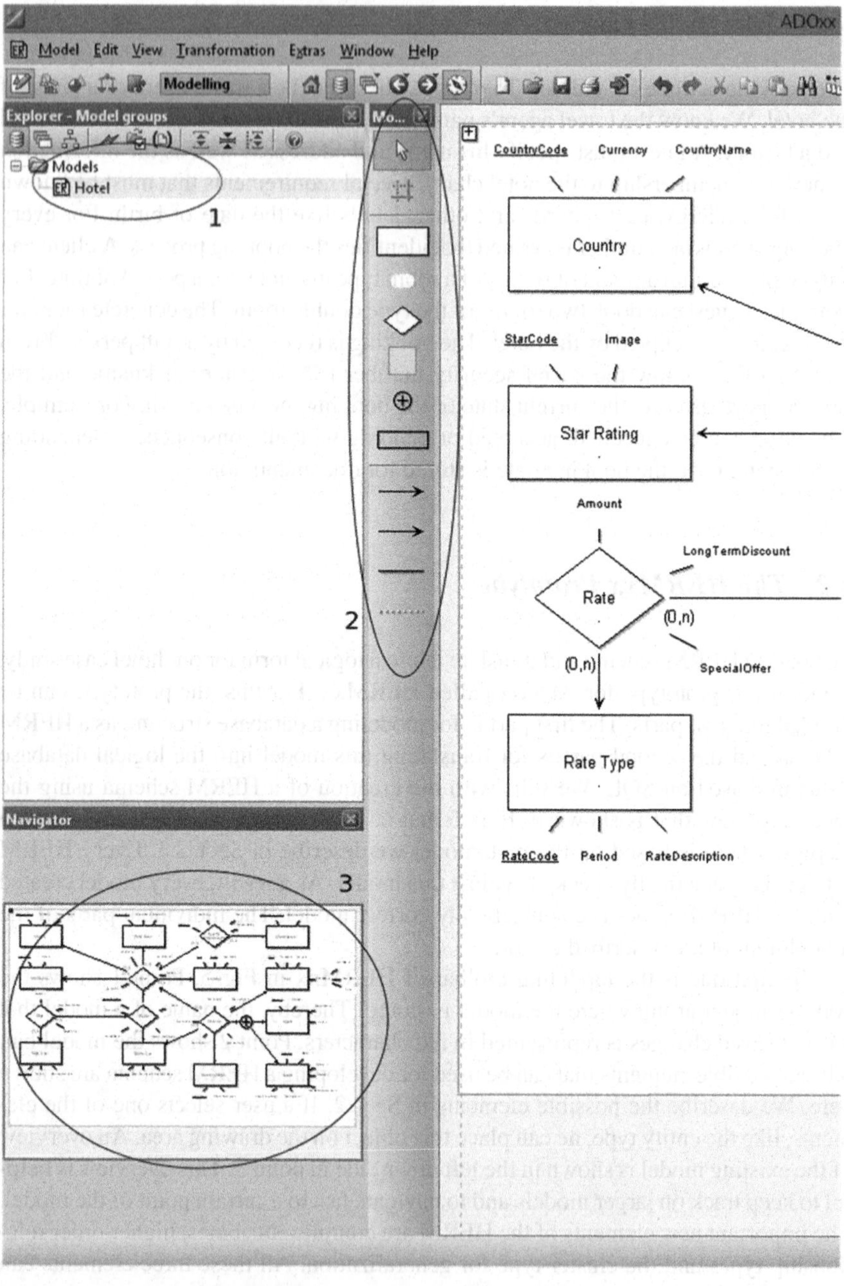

Fig. 5 HERMxx modeling toolbar

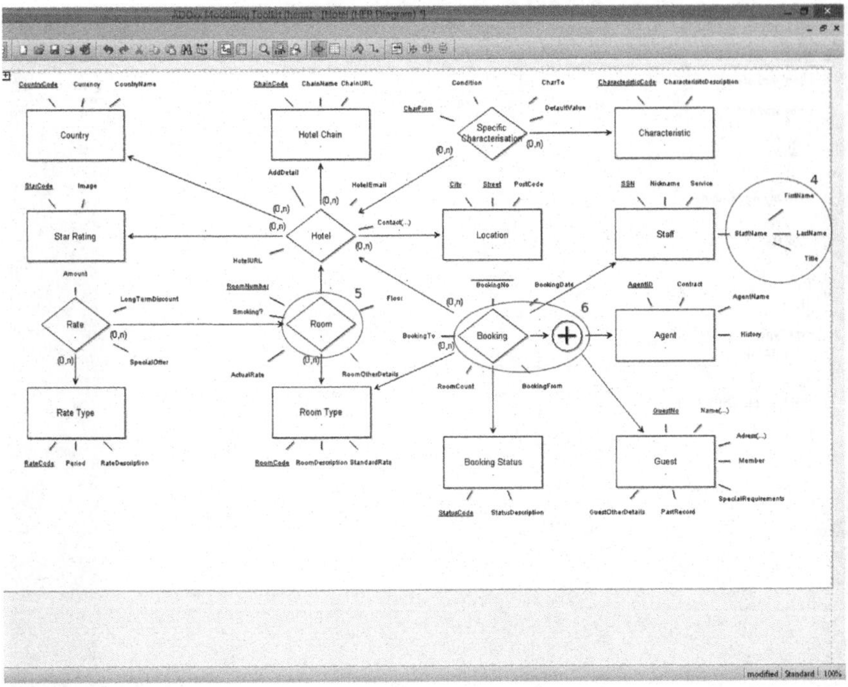

Fig. 6 Example HER-Model in HERMxx

Figure 6 shows a HERM diagram created with the modeling tool. Point 4 shows how a complex attribute, in our example the name, can be realized. Because of the required hierarchical structure, the complex attribute can be represented in such a tree structure. Higher order relationship types can be simply represented as shown in point 5. A higher order relationship type can be easily connected with a lower order type by connecting an arrow between the two types. The cluster type element can be represented as a circle with a plus or union inside it that represents the different cluster options. A relationship type is then connected to the circle to represent a cluster type. Point 6 shows the representation within the drawing area.

Another important advantage of HERMxx is the possibility to define the data types for the attributes during the modeling phase. Their definitions are used as a directive in the translation to create the right SQL data types for the attributes. Figure 7 shows how the data type definition of an attribute works. Suppose we want to define the BookingDate attribute. Therefore, we can first assign a name to the attribute and determine if it is a key attribute for this element. Then, we have the choice to define if it is a normal, complex or multi-valued attribute. For normal attributes, we can then define a SQL data type, in our example timestamp and give examples and a description for the data type. The examples and the description are relevant for documentation and for the understanding of the attributes in the model.

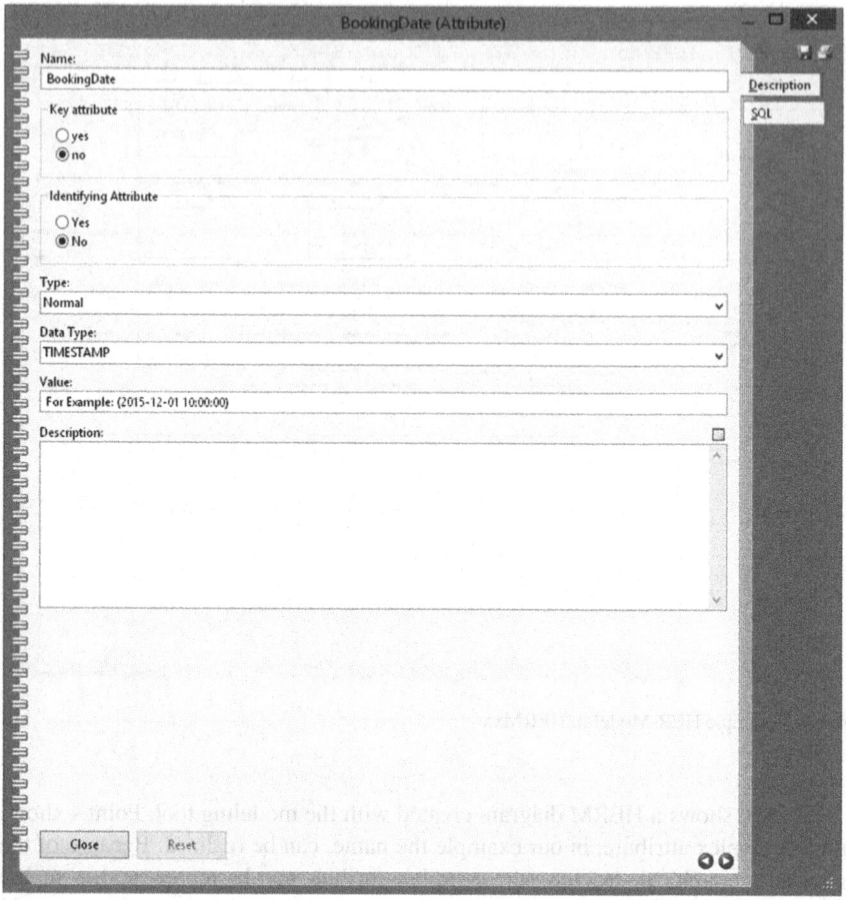

Fig. 7 Attribute View in HERMxx

In the second step, we now want to translate this model into SQL to use it as logical database structure. To demonstrate how this translation works, we only show how the cluster type booking is translated. Showing the whole translation would exceed the length of this chapter. The implementation of the translation is based on our concept of a compiler approach described in Sect. 3. For our prototype, we developed the directives that are used to describe the developer's choices for the translation, like the attribute type information or descriptions of strong connected types with a one to one cardinality. Moreover, for our cluster type example, there are different approaches to the translation. For a cluster type, a developer can choose between a combination, separation, surrogate, view or union approach. So, in the case that such a translation decision is needed, the developer has to make this choice during the modeling. When a directive is missing during the translation of an element the tool will ask the developer for a decision. The Listing 1 shows the cluster translation as pseudo-code that is used in the HERMxx library.

```
...
if(type = 'cluster'){
  if(no directive known){
    ask user for directive;
    directive = developer decision;
  }
  if(directive = 'combination'){
     use identification directly;
     introduce an explicit separator;
  }
  else if (directive = 'separation'){
     decompose cluster type into new types;
     create disjoint union view on the separated types;
  }
  else if (directive = 'surrogate'){
    introduce surrogate key for the cluster;
    build subtypes depending on the surrogate key;
  }
  else if (directive = 'view'){
     represent the cluster by a view;
  }
  else if (directive = 'union'){
     extend cluster type by a surrogate key;
     set identifiers of components NULL except one;
  }
}
...
```

Listing 1 Cluster translation

Thus, it is first checked if there is a directive for the translation defined by the developer. If there is no directive, the system asks the developer which directive should be performed for the element. To support a developer, the system shows a default translation directive the developer can choose. Based on the chosen directive, the translation process begins. The result is executable SQL code that a developer can execute on his database management system. In our example, we use the separation directive to get the translation into the relational representation shown below. Thereby, we also demonstrate some of the other tables that are needed for the foreign key constraints. We only show here the relational representation because the SQL representation would, like the translation algorithms, exceed the length of this chapter.

```
(Hotel, {ChainCode, City, Street,
            CountryCode, StarCode,...}),
Staff({SSN, StaffName,
            Nickname, Service}),
Agent({AgentID, Contract,
            AgentName, History}),
Guest({GuestNo, Name(...), Address(...),
            SpecialRequirements, ...}),
BookingStatus({StatusCode, StatusDescripiton})
RoomType({RoomCode, RoomDescripition, StandardRate})
BookingAgent({BookingNo, ChainCode, City, Street,
            AgentID, StatusCode, RoomCode, SSN,
            BookingDate, ...}),
BookingGuest({BookingNo, ChainCode, City, Street,
            GuestNo, StatusCode, RoomCode,
            SSN, BookingDate, ...}),
}

Hotel[ChainCode]⊆HotelChain[ChainCode],
Hotel[City,Street]⊆Location[City,Street],
Hotel[CountryCode]⊆Country[ContryCode],
Hotel[StarCode]⊆StarRating[StarCode],
BookingAgent[ChainCode,City,Street]⊆
            Hotel[ChainCode,City,Street],
BookingAgent[AgentID]⊆Agent[AgentID],
BookingAgent[StatusCode]⊆BookingStatus[StatusCode],
BookingAgent[RoomCode]⊆RoomType[RoomCode],
BookingAgent[SSN]⊆Staff[SSN],
BookingGuest[ChainCode,City,Street]⊆
            Hotel[ChainCode,City,Street],
BookingGuest[GuestNo]⊆Guest[GuestNo],
BookingGuest[StatusCode]⊆BookingStatus[StatusCode],
BookingGuest[RoomCode]⊆RoomType[RoomCode],
BookingGuest[SSN]⊆Staff[SSN],
BookingAgent[BookingNo] || BookingGuest[BookingNo]
...
BookingAgent.BookingDate::timestamp,
BookingAgent.SSN::integer,
BookingAgent.AgentID::varchar(25),
BookingAgent.BookingNo::integer,
BookingAgent.ChainCode::varchar(10),
BookingAgent.City::varchar(58),
BookingAgent.Street::varchar(70),
BookingAgent.StatusCode::varchar(10),
BookingAgent.RoomCode::varchar(20),
...
```

As shown above, the entity types Staff, Agent, Guest, BookingStatus and RoomType are translated into single relations with the underlined attributes as primary key. The hotel relation depends on the HotelChain, Location, Country and StarRating whereby the primary key is composed of the hotel chain and the location as a chain can only own one hotel at one location. Based on the separation approach, for every element that is involved in the cluster a single relation is created. In our booking example, the system creates the relations BookingAgent and BookingGuest. In these relations, the only difference lies in the foreign key to AgentID receptively GuestNo. All other attributes and foreign keys are the same. To express that the BookingID is unique for both relations the constraint BookingAgent[BookingNo] || BookingGuest[BookingNo] is introduced which means that BookingID can be either in BookingAgent or in BookingGuest. Furthermore, to express that our data types are translated into this representation there are some examples for data type definitions like BookingAgent.BookingDate : : timestamp or BookingAgent.City : : varchar(58).

5 Conclusion

This paper demonstrates how the modeling and translation of HERM schemata can be performed using ADO*xx*. Thereby, we described a metamodel of HERM that can be used within the tool to create graphical HERM schemata. These schemata can then in a next step be translated into a logical representation. Therefore, we described a compiler-based approach that uses designer defined directives to get a normalized, optimized and evolution save translation of the schema. To show how our approach works, we created the ADO*xx* library HERMxx. With the example of a hotel booking application, we display how a HERM schema can be created. Furthermore, we show by way of example of a cluster type element how a translation into a logical database model based on directives could be used after modeling.

Yet, our approach is only a first prototype. In a subsequent step, we must finish our modeling tool for HERM first by fixing the bugs in the modeling interface. Moreover, the compiler is not finished yet. We have implemented the possibility to define directives for the choice of translation options on HERM elements. These directives must be extended by other areas like global design decisions or configuration parameters. Furthermore, we want to create all steps of the compiler approach for schema translation using ADO*xx*.

Tool Download http://www.omilab.org/hermxx.

References

1. ADOxx website. https://www.adoxx.org/live/home
2. Chen, P.P.S.: The entity-relationship model—toward a unified view of data. ACM Trans. Database Syst. (1976)
3. DB-Main. http://www.db-main.eu/
4. Elmasri, R., Navathe, S.: Grundlagen von Datenbanksystemen. Pearson Studium (2002)
5. Embley, D.W., Mok, W.Y.: Mapping conceptual models to database schemas, Chap. 5, pp. 123–163. Springer, Berlin (2011)

6. ERWin. http://erwin.com/
7. Kolp, M., Zimányi, E.: Enhanced ER to relational mapping and interrelational normalization. Inf. Softw. Technol. (2000)
8. Lockemann, P.C., Moerkotte, G., Neufeld, A., Radermacher, K., Runge, N.: Database design with user-definable modelling concepts. Data Knowl. Eng. (1993)
9. Markowitz, V.M., Shoshani, A.: Representing extended entity-relationship structures in relational databases: a modular approach. ACM TODS (1992)
10. Mok, W.Y., Embley, D.W.: Transforming conceptual models to object-oriented database designs: practicalities, properties, and peculiarities. In: Conceptual Modeling—ER'96, 15th International Conference on Conceptual Modeling, Cottbus, Germany, 7–10 Oct 1996, Proceedings (1996)
11. Paradigm, V.: http://www.visual-paradigm.com/
12. Pittman, T., Peters, J.: The Art of Compiler Design: Theory and Practice. Prentice Hall (1992)
13. Thalheim, B.: Entity-Relationship Modeling. Springer, Berlin (2000)
14. Thalheim, B.: Encyclopedia of Database Theory, Technology and Systems, chapter Section or subsection. Springer (2009)

Tool Support for the Semantic Object Model

Otto K. Ferstl, Elmar J. Sinz and Dominik Bork

Abstract This chapter introduces tool support for the semantic object model (SOM). The conceptual design of a multi-view modeling tool is presented after describing the core concepts of the SOM method and laying the corresponding methodological foundation. The chapter foremost addresses the modeling enthusiast, interested in how to utilize the SOM method with the ADO*xx* modeling tool.

Keywords Semantic object model • Multi-view modeling tool • ADO*xx*

1 Introduction

The semantic object model (SOM)[1] is a comprehensive methodology for modeling business systems [1–4, 194ff]. SOM is fully object-oriented and designed to capture business semantics explicitly. The general bases of the SOM methodology are concepts of systems theory as well as organizational theory.

SOM supports the core phases of business engineering such as analysis, design and redesign of a business system. A business system is an open, goal-oriented, socio-technical system. Thus, the analysis of a business system focuses on the interaction with its environment, goal-pursuing business processes, and resources. Moreover, the dynamic behavior of a business system requires investigation of properties such as stability, flexibility and complexity [5].

[1]This section is based on [1].

O.K. Ferstl · E.J. Sinz (✉)
University of Bamberg, 96045 Bamberg, Germany
e-mail: elmar.sinz@uni-bamberg.de

O.K. Ferstl
e-mail: otto.ferstl@uni-bamberg.de

D. Bork
University of Vienna, 1090 Vienna, Austria
e-mail: dominik.bork@univie.ac.at

D. Karagiannis et al. (eds.), *Domain-Specific Conceptual Modeling*,
DOI 10.1007/978-3-319-39417-6_13

The backbone of the SOM methodology is an enterprise architecture which uses different perspectives on a business system via a set of models. These models are grouped into three model layers referred to as business plan, business process models and resource models. Each layer describes the business system as a whole, but with respect to the specific perspective on the model. In order to reduce complexity, each model layer is subdivided into several views, each focusing on specific aspects of a model layer. On the meta level, the modeling language of each layer is defined by a metamodel and derivated view definitions. Thus, the enterprise architecture provides a modeling framework which helps to define the specific semantics and to manage the complexity of the model [6]. In this chapter, we outline the methodological framework of SOM, its modeling language as well as the conceptualization of an SOM modeling tool based on the ADO*xx* metamodeling platform.

In terms of systems theory, a business system is an open, goal-oriented, socio-technical system [7]. It is open because it interacts with customers, suppliers, and other business partners transferring goods and services. The business system and its goods/services are part of a value chain which in general comprises several consecutive business systems. A corresponding flow of finance runs opposite the flow of goods and services.

The behavior of a business system is aimed at business goals and objectives. Goals specify the goods and services to be provided by the system. Objectives (e.g., profit and turnover) are defined levels against which business performance can be measured.

Actors of a business system are humans and machines. Human actors are persons in different roles. Machine actors, in general, are plants, production machines, vehicles, computer systems, etc. SOM pays specific attention to application systems which are the machine actors of the information processing subsystem of a business system (information system). An application system consists of computer and communication systems running application software. The degree of automation of an information system is the ratio of tasks carried out by application systems to all tasks of the information system.

The notion of a business system as open and goal-oriented reflects a perspective from outside the system. An inside perspective shows a distributed system of autonomous, loosely coupled components which cooperate in pursuing the system's goals and objectives. The autonomous components are business processes [4, 8] which produce goods and services and deliver them to other business processes.

The cooperation of business processes is coordinated primarily through process-specific objectives which are derived from the overall objectives of a business system. This is done by the business system's management. Within the degrees of freedom defined by the process-specific objectives, a secondary coordination is done by negotiation between the business processes.

Inside a business process, there are components which also cooperate and have to be coordinated. This coordination is done by an intra-process management which controls the activities of the process components by sending instructions to them and supervising their behavior. In contrast to the coordination between business

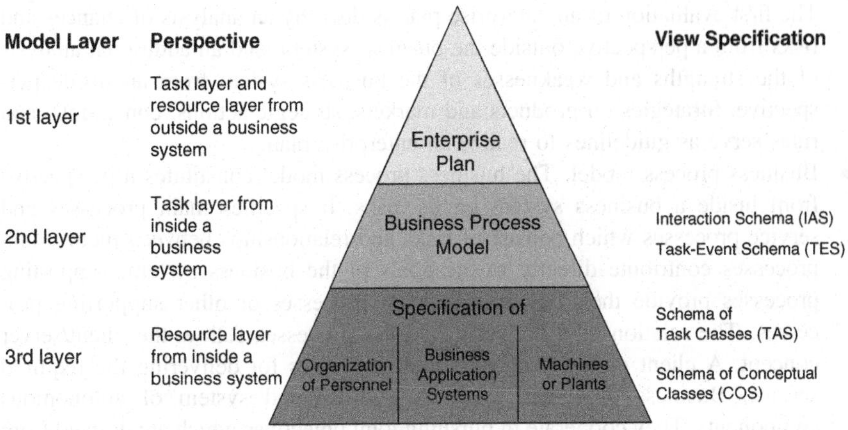

Fig. 1 Enterprise architecture [4]

processes, the components of a business process are guided closely by the process management.

The components of a business process as well as the business processes as a whole take care of functions which are essential to every business system. The following classification of these functions helps to identify business processes and their components: (1) input-output-function to implement the characteristic of openness, e.g., a production system, (2) supply function to provide material resources and energy, (3) maintenance function to keep the system running, (4) sensory function to register disturbances or defects inside or outside the system, (5) managing function to coordinate the subsystems [9].

2 The SOM Enterprise Modeling Method

The SOM methodology[2] utilizes an enterprise architecture which consists of three layers (Fig. 1) [4].

- Enterprise plan: The enterprise plan constitutes a perspective from outside a business system. It focuses on the global task and the resources of the business system. The specification of the global task includes the universe of discourse, the goals and objectives to be pursued, as well as the goods and services to be delivered. Requirements on resources are derived from the global task and have to be cross-checked to the capabilities of available resources. Hence, both global task and resources determine themselves mutually.

[2]This section is based on [1].

The first evaluation of an enterprise plan is done by an analysis of chances and risks from a perspective outside the business system, and an additional analysis of the strengths and weaknesses of the business system from an inside perspective. Strategies on products and markets, strategic actions, constraints, and rules serve as guidelines to realize an enterprise plan.

- Business process model: The business process model constitutes a perspective from inside a business system on its tasks. It specifies main processes and service processes which consist of tasks and relationships between them. Main processes contribute directly to the goals of the business system; supporting processes provide their outcome to main processes or other supporting processes. The relationships between business processes follow the client/server concept. A client process engages other processes for delivering the required service. Business processes establish a distributed system of autonomous components. They cooperate in pursuing joint objectives which are derived from the overall objectives of a business system.
- Specification of resources: In general, personnel, application systems as well as machines or plants are resources for carrying out the tasks of business processes. In the following, we focus on information processing tasks and, therefore, omit machines and plants. Tasks of the information system are assigned to persons or to application systems classifying a task as non-automated or fully-automated. A partly-automated task has to be split into sub-tasks which are non-automated or fully-automated. The assignment of persons or application systems is aimed at the optimal synergy of person–computer cooperation.

The different layers of the enterprise architecture help to build business systems in a flexible and manageable way. They cover specific aspects of an overall model which are outside perspective (enterprise plan), inside perspective (business process model) and resources. The relationships between the layers are specified explicitly. Each layer establishes a distributed system of autonomous, loosely coupled components. In contrast to a single-layered monolithic model, the multi-layered system of three models allows local changes without affecting the overall architecture. For example, it is possible to improve a business process model (inside perspective) yet retain goals and objectives (outside perspective) or replace actors of one type by other ones.

Following an outside-in approach, it is advisable to build the three model layers top down the enterprise architecture. However, the architecture does not force this direction. There may be good reasons to start from this guideline, e.g., when analyzing existing business systems. Here it is sometimes difficult to find an elaborated enterprise plan so modeling starts at the business process layer focusing on the inside perspective. The enterprise plan may be completed when the other layers are fully understood. In each case, the effects on other layers have to be balanced and approved.

The enterprise architecture implies that functionality and architecture of the business application systems are derived from the business process model. The relationships between both layers are formaliszd to a high degree. Design decisions and results at the business process layer are translated automatically into the layer of application systems. The architecture of the layer of application systems uses the concept of object-integration to combine conceptual and task classes [10]. Alternatively, it is possible to link a business process model to an existing, traditional application system which follows the traditional concepts of function integration or data integration. In this case, tasks to be automated are linked to functional units of the application system.

3 Conceptualization of the SOM Modeling Method

In this section, the language for SOM business process[3] models is defined. The language is specified by a metamodel (Sect. 3.1) and a set of decomposition rules (Sect. 3.2). Finally, Sect. 3.3 briefly introduces SOM resource modeling.

3.1 The Metamodel for Business Process Modeling

The metamodel for business process modeling shows notions and relationships between notions (Fig. 2). It is specified as a binary entity-relationship schema. Relationships between notions are associated with a role name as well as two cardinalities to denote how many instances of the one notion can be connected to one instance of the other notion, at least and at most. Within the metamodel, the notions are represented by entities. Each entity also contains the symbols used for representation within a business process model.

As introduced in Sect. 2, a business process model specifies a set of business processes with client/server relationships among each other. A business process pursues its own goals and objectives which are prescribed and tuned by the management of a business system. Cooperation between processes is a matter of negotiation. The term business process denotes a compound building block within a business process model and, therefore, it is not a basic notion of the language. A business process consists of at least one business object and one or more business transactions.

At the initial level of a business process model, a business object (object in short) produces goods and services and delivers them to customer business processes. Each business object belongs exclusively to a business process of the universe of discourse or to the environment of a business system. A business transaction (transaction in short) transmits a good or service to a customer business process or receives a good or service from a supplier business process. A transaction connecting different business processes belongs to both processes.

[3]This section is based on [1].

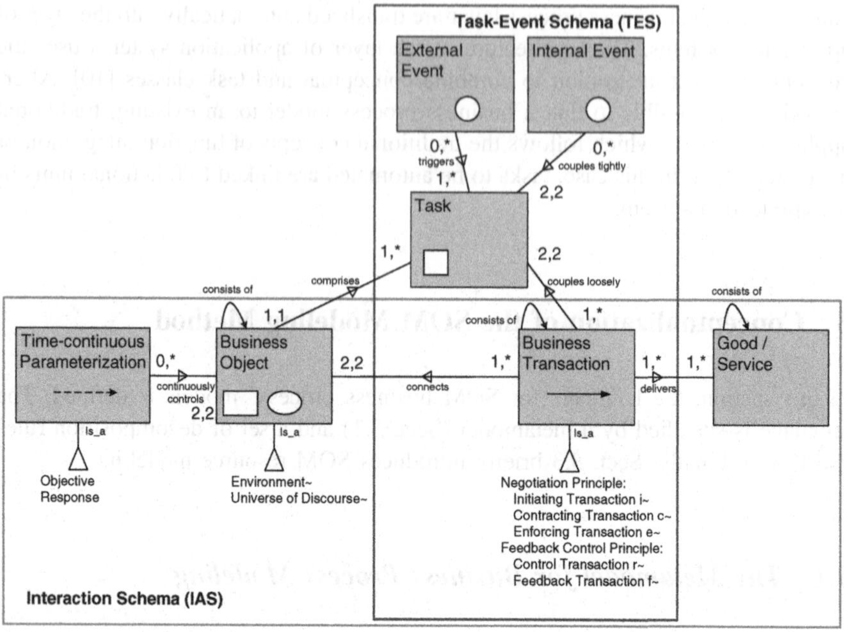

Fig. 2 Metamodel for SOM business process models [1, p. 344; 11, p. 219]

A business process may be refined using the decomposition rules given below in Sect. 3.2. At a more detailed level of a business process model, each business object appears in one of two different roles: an operational object contributes directly to producing and delivering a good/service, while a management object contributes to managing one or more operational objects using messages. A business transaction transmits a good/service or a message between two operational objects or a message between two management objects or between a management object and an operational object.

A business transaction connects two business objects. Conversely, a business object is connected with one to many ("*") in-going or out-going business transactions. From a structural viewpoint, a transaction denotes an interaction channel forwarding goods, services, or messages. From a behavioral viewpoint, a transaction means an event which is associated with the transmission of a specific good, a service package, or a message.

A business object comprises one to many tasks, each of them driving one to many transactions. A transaction is driven by exactly two tasks belonging to different business objects. The tasks of an object share common states and are encapsulated by the object. These tasks pursue joint goals and objectives which are attributes of the tasks.

The SOM methodology uses two different concepts of coupling tasks (Fig. 3, top): loosely coupled tasks belong to different objects and, therefore, operate in

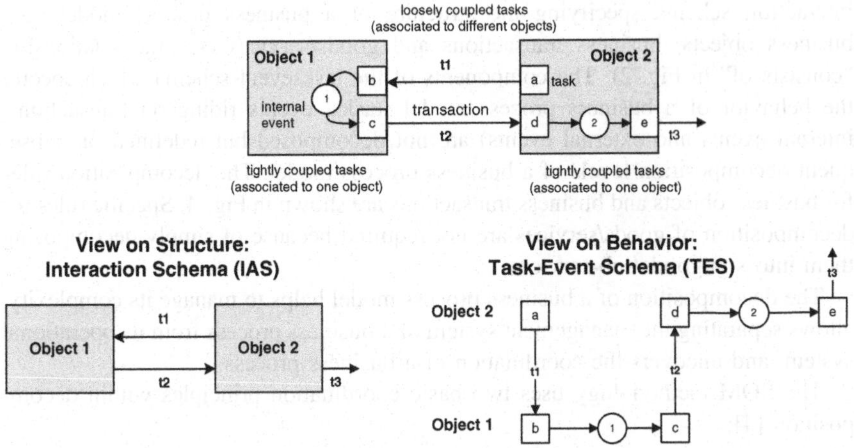

Fig. 3 Representation of structure and behavior in an SOM business process model

different states. The tasks are connected by a transaction which serves as an interaction channel for passing states from one task to the other. A task triggers the execution of another task by an event (good, service package, or message) riding on the interaction channel. Tightly coupled tasks belong to the same object and operate on the same states. The tasks are connected by an internal event which is sent from one task to trigger the execution of the other. The concept of encapsulating tightly coupled tasks by an object and loosely coupling the tasks of different objects via transactions is a key feature of the object-oriented characteristic of the SOM methodology.

The third type of event is the external event. An external event denotes the occurrence of an event like "the first day of a month" which is not bound to a transaction.

Because of its complexity, a business process model is represented in two different views (Fig. 3 bottom and Fig. 2): The interaction schema is the view of the structure. It shows business objects which are connected by business transactions. The task-event schema is the view on behavior. It shows tasks which are connected by events (transactions, internal events, or external events). These two views are complemented by hierarchical decompositions of business transactions and business objects. These additional views specify the relationships between the interaction schemas showing a varying level of detail.

3.2 Decomposition Rules

The SOM methodology allows a business process model to be decomposed by stepwise refinement. Decomposition takes place with the components of the interaction schema specifying the structure of a business process model, i.e., business objects, business transactions and goods/services (see the relationship "consists of" in Fig. 2). The components of the task-event schema which specify the behavior of a business process model (tasks, events riding on transactions, internal events and external events) are not decomposed but redefined on subsequent decomposition levels of a business process model. The decomposition rules for business objects and business transactions are shown in Fig. 4. Specific rules for decomposition of goods/services are not required because of simply decomposing them into sub-goods/sub-services.

The decomposition of a business process model helps to manage its complexity, allows separating the management system of a business process from its operational system, and uncovers the coordination of a business process.

The SOM methodology uses two basic coordination principles within decomposition [4]:

- Applying the feedback control principle (rule 1), a business object is decomposed into two sub-objects and two transactions: a management object O' and an operational object O'' as well as a control transaction T_r from O' to O'' and a feedback transaction T_f in opposite direction. These components establish a feedback control loop. The management object prescribes objectives or sends control messages to the operational object via the control transaction. Conversely, the operational object reports to the management object via the feedback transaction.

Rule Nr.	***Decomposition rules for business objects:***
(1)	O ::= { O', O", T_r(O', O"), [T_f(O", O')] }
(2)	O ::= { O', O", [T(O', O")] }
(3)	O ::= { spec O' }$^+$
(4)	O' $\mid$ O" ::= O
(5)	O ::= { O', { O", P_o(O', O"), [P_R(O", O')] }$^+$ }
	Decomposition rules for business transactions:
(6)	T(O, O') ::= [[T_i(O,O') seq] T_c(O', O) seq] T_e(O, O')
(7)	T_x ::= T'_x { seq T''_x }$^+$ $\mid$ T'_x { par T''_x }$^+$ (x = i, c, e, r, f)
(8)	T_x ::= { spec T'_x }$^+$ (x = i, c, e, r, f)
(9)	$T_i \mid T_c \mid T_e$ ::= T

Fig. 4 Decomposition rules for business objects and business transactions (::=replacement, { } set, { }+list of repeated elements, [] option, ∣ alternative, seq sequential order, par parallel order, spec specialization)

- Applying the negotiation principle (rule 5), a transaction is decomposed into three successive transactions: (1) an initiating transaction T_i, where a server object and its client learn to know each other and exchange information on deliverable goods/services, (2) a contracting transaction T_c, where both objects agree to a contract on the delivery of goods/services, and (3) an enforcing transaction T_e, where the objects transfer the goods/services.

The types of transactions resulting from the decomposition are shown in the metamodel (Fig. 2) as specialized transactions.

Figure 5 illustrates the application of the coordination principles for the decomposition of SOM business process models. The decomposition of the first level into the second level is done by applying the negotiation principle. Applying the feedback control principle leads to the third level.

In addition to the coordination principles given above, a transaction may be decomposed into sub-transactions of the same type which are executed in sequence or in parallel (rule 6). Correspondingly, a business object may be decomposed into sub-objects of the same type (management object or operational object) which may be connected by transactions (rule 2). Objects, as well as transactions, may be specialized within the same type (rules 3 and 7). The other rules (4, 8, and 9) are used for replacement within successive decompositions.

It is important to state that successive decomposition levels of a business process model do not establish new, different models. They belong to exactly one model and are subject to the consistency rules defined in the metamodel.

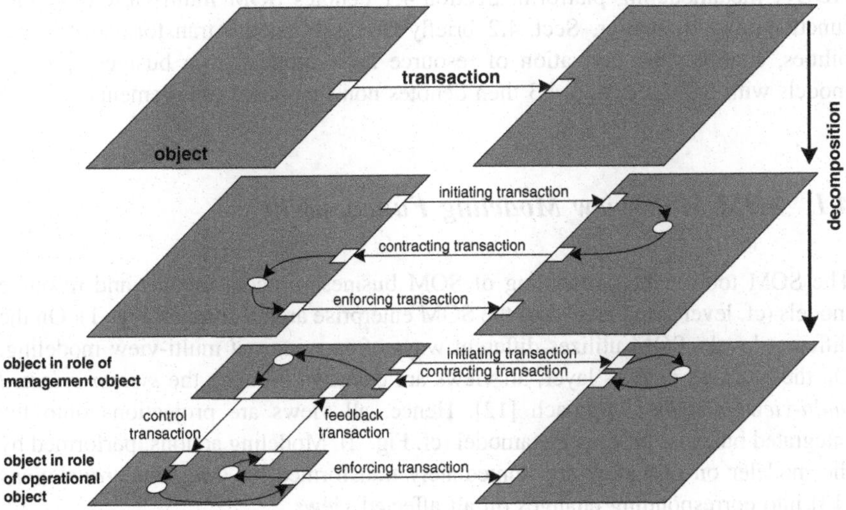

Fig. 5 Decomposition of SOM business process models

3.3 Resource Modeling

Tasks which are fully or partly automated and hence are executed by application systems have to be specified on the resource layer. The creation of the corresponding schemas is initially done by a model-driven approach. As this approach cannot be described here in detail, only a short synopsis is given. For a detailed description see [11].

Following the organizational foundation of the SOM method, the focus is on the concept of task. Tasks at the business process layer are embraced by means of a common object. These objects are modeled by (object-specific) classes at the resource layer. Transactions between objects are mapped to (transaction-specific) classes as well as relationships between classes. Both types of classes result in a schema of conceptual classes (COS). The tasks at the business process layer are modeled by (task-specific) classes at the resource layer, leading to the schema of task classes (TAS).

A task-specific class orchestrates the corresponding sub-schema of conceptual classes. Task-specific classes at the same level are coordinated by choreography.

4 The SOM Modeling Tool

This section discusses the conceptualization of the theoretical foundation introduced above towards a modeling tool for the SOM method. The tool is based on the ADO*xx* metamodeling platform. Section 4.1 denotes SOM multi-view modeling functionality. Thereafter, Sect. 4.2 briefly discusses model transformation capabilities, enabling the derivation of resource layer models from business process models with SOM. Section 4.3 then denotes non-functional requirements.

4.1 SOM Multi-view Modeling Functionality

The SOM tool enables modeling of SOM business process models and resource models (cf. level 2 and level 3 of the SOM enterprise architecture on Fig. 1). On the different levels, SOM utilizes different ways of carrying out multi-view modeling. On the business process layer, all views are created following the *system-oriented multi-view modeling* approach [12]. Hence, all views are projections onto the integrated business process metamodel (cf. Fig. 2). Modeling actions, performed by the modeler on one view are immediately transformed by *transition translations* [13] into corresponding changes on all affected views.

On the resource level, both modeling views are kept isolated from each other. Modeling on this layer follows the *diagram-oriented multi-view modeling* approach [12]. However, considering the creation of the resource views, the SOM method specifies *state translations* [13] that transform complete business process models into semantically equivalent schema of task classes and schema of conceptual class models. These state translations are specified as metamodel mappings. Notions of the business process metamodel are mapped to notions of the resource layer metamodel (see Sect. 4.2 for the metamodel mapping and an example model transformation).

The SOM tool is special when it comes to the way modelers interact with the tool. Generally, conventional drag and drop modeling is prohibited at most times. This comes not only from the way multi-view modeling is performed, it is also a requirement that comes from the formalized specification of the modeling procedure [cf. 14] by means of the decomposition rules (cf. Fig. 4). In order to increase the utility of the tool, zooming operators were introduced, allowing modellers to immediately switch between already defined decomposition levels of a business process. Applying the zooming operator causes only changes on the visualized SOM views. The integrated model is not affected. Table 1 provides an overview of the constituents of the multiple SOM modeling views (realized as ADO*xx* model types) and aligns the most important tool functionality to them.

Table 1 SOM views realized as ADO*xx* model types and corresponding tool functionality

SOM view (ADO*xx* model type)	Modeling concept	Tool functionality
Interaction schema	Business object	Increase business process level
	Business transaction	Decrease business process level
		Auto-layout/smooth edges
Task-event schema	Task	Define process behavior
	Business transaction-internal/external event	Increase business process level
		Decrease business process level
Object decomposition schema	Business object	Decompose object/Transaction
	Business transaction	revoke decomposition
Transaction decomposition schema	Decomposition relationship	Zoom on selected level
		Add/Remove environmental object
		Add/Remove enforcing transaction

4.2 SOM Model Transformation Functionality

The SOM methodology not only specifies the business process and resource modeling on the second and third layer of the enterprise architecture, respectively. Moreover, SOM also defines a metamodel-based model transformation of comprehensively specified business process models into initial business application systems models (i.e., the schema of task classes and the schema of conceptual classes).

The SOM modeling tool provides the modeler the functionality to automatically apply these transformations. The hereby created business application systems models can be further processed with the tool, e.g., combining classes that have significant functionality and/or data overlaps, normalization or generalization of classes.

Figure 6 illustrates the metamodel mapping between the business process layer and the resource layer (cf. the SOM enterprise architecture in Fig. 1). Tasks are transformed into task-specific classes (rule 1), business objects into object-specific classes (rule 2), business transactions into transaction-specific classes and interacts_with relationships (rule 3), goods/services are transformed into service-specific classes, and internal/external events are transformed into interacts_with relationships.

In Fig. 7, this mapping is exemplified by a simple SOM business process, consisting of a distributor and a customer that are coordinated by three business transactions. This model is transformed into a schema of conceptual classes (Fig. 7 bottom left) and a schema of task classes for the customer business object (Fig. 7 bottom

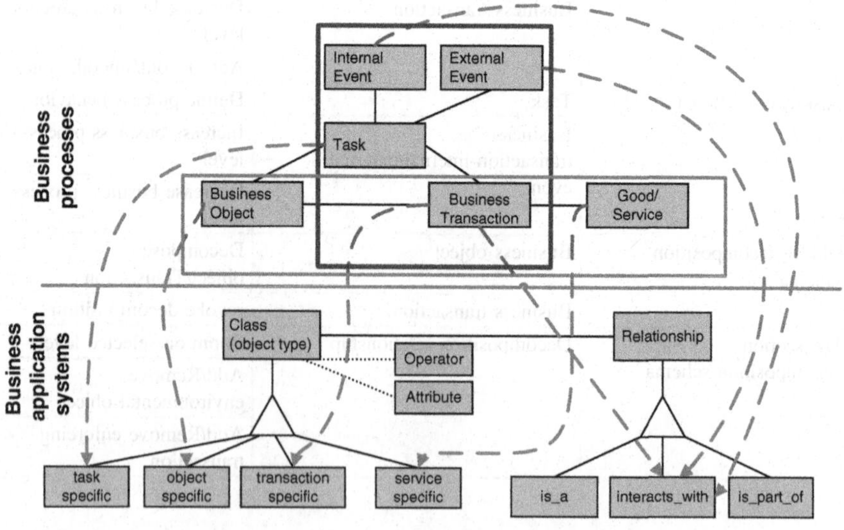

Fig. 6 Transforming SOM business processes into SOM business application systems

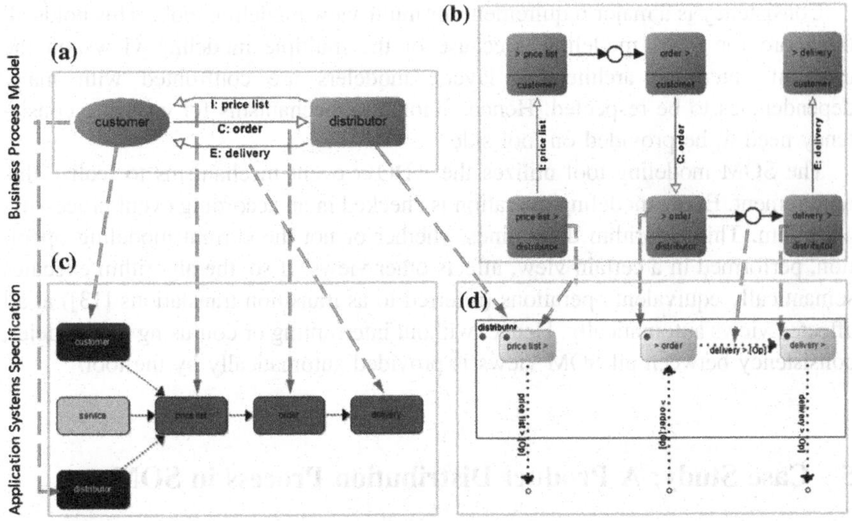

Fig. 7 Interaction schema (**a**), task-event schema (**b**) and the transformed schema of conceptual classes (**c**) and schema of task classes (**d**)

right). The dashed arrows indicate some of the transformation rules applied to the business process model. Because of the limited space available here, the resource layer and the corresponding transformation rules cannot be discussed in more detail. However, the interested reader is referred to [11, p. 222ff] for an overarching specification of both, the resource layer of SOM and the transformation rules.

4.3 Non-functional Tool Requirements

From the very beginning, the conceptual design of the SOM modeling tool was aiming at the best usability, i.e., how to support the modeler in processing multiple views simultaneously and applying the decomposition rules. In [15], the authors emphasized the importance of:

- Decoupling the decomposition of business objects and business transactions from the definition of new business process levels by means of specifying the relationships between the decomposed objects and transactions;
- providing visual support in the reconfiguration of relationships between business objects in different decomposition levels;
- enabling zooming in and out of already defined business process levels; and
- realizing layout algorithms, e.g., "auto-layout" and "smooth-edges" that automatically adjust the visualization of the SOM business process model in its multiple views after a modeling action has been executed.

Consistency is a major requirement for multi-view modeling tools. This holds all the more for SOM modeling. Because of the multiple modeling views on the different enterprise architecture layers, modelers are confronted with many dependencies to be respected. Hence, automatic mechanisms for ensuring consistency need to be provided on tool side.

The SOM modeling tool utilizes the ADO*xx* event mechanisms to realize this requirement. Every modeling operation is checked in an according event processing algorithm. This algorithm determines whether or not the current modeling operation, performed in a certain view, affects other views. If so, the algorithm executes semantically equivalent operations (referred to as transition translations [13]) at all affected views automatically. Hence, without interrupting or confusing the modeler, consistency between all SOM views is provided automatically by the tool.

5 Case Study: A Product Distribution Process in SOM

In the following section, the application of the SOM modeling tool is demonstrated by means of a case study, showing the different modeling steps to be applied in order to transform an initial SOM business process into a precise description of a distribution of goods/services between a distributor and a customer. One focus of the SOM method is on business process modeling. Because of the limited space available here, the following case study will, therefore, concentrate on modeling of SOM business processes.

For example, Fig. 8 introduces the business process distribution of a trading company visualized as a screen shot of the SOM modeling tool. At the initial level, the interaction schema view (bottom left model type) consists of three components, (1) the business object distributor which provides a service, (2) the transaction service which delivers the service to the customer (visualized in the transaction decomposition view on the upper right), and (3) the business object customer itself. Distributor is an internal object belonging to the universe of discourse while customer is an external object belonging to the environment. All business objects are visualized in the upper right view, the object decomposition view. At this level, the entire cooperation and coordination between the two business objects is specified by the transaction service.

Figure 8 (bottom right) shows the corresponding sequence of tasks which is very simple. The task names in the task-event schema are derived from the name of the transaction. Here, the task *service* > (say "send service") of distributor produces and delivers the service, the task > *service* (say "receive service") of customer receives it. The arrow service here defines the sequence of the two tasks belonging to the transaction service which is represented in the interaction schema by an arrow, too.

Transactions like services connect business objects inside the universe of discourse and link business objects to the environment. When modeling a value chain, the business process model of a trading company includes a second business

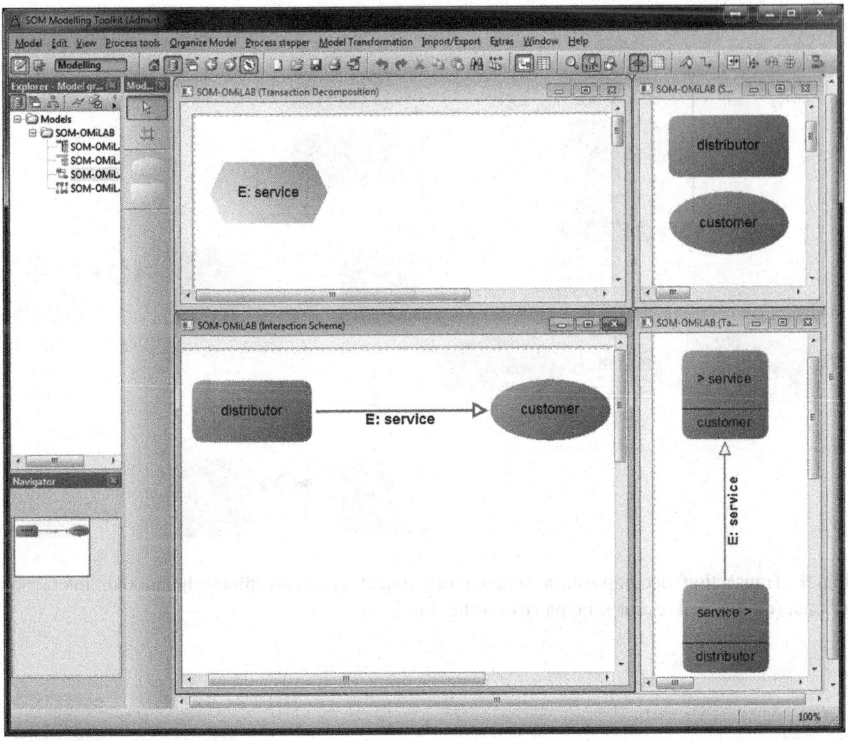

Fig. 8 Initial level of the business process distribution process

process procurement, which receives services from a business object supplier, belonging to the environment, and delivers services to a distributor.

Example (Fig. 8) will be continued now. For readability reasons, the figures concentrate on selected views in the following. The surrounding text will describe the modeling steps performed in all views. As customer and distributor negotiate about the delivery of a service, the service transaction is decomposed according to the *negotiation principle* into the sub-transactions *i: price list* (initiating), c: *order* (contracting), and e: *service* (enforcing transaction); visualized in the transaction decomposition schema in Fig. 9a. The corresponding task-event schema (Fig. 9d) is determined implicitly because the sub-transactions are executed in sequence (as defined by the negotiation decomposition rule in Fig. 4). The tasks of each business object are connected by object-internal events.

After this initial step, the resulting business transactions and business objects need to be further decomposed to more precisely depict the actual distribution of goods and services:

First, the e: service transaction is decomposed into the sequence *e:(seq.) delivery* and *e:(seq.) cash up*. The cash up transaction is further decomposed according to the *negotiation principle* into the sequence *c: invoice* and *e: payment* (see Fig. 10a).

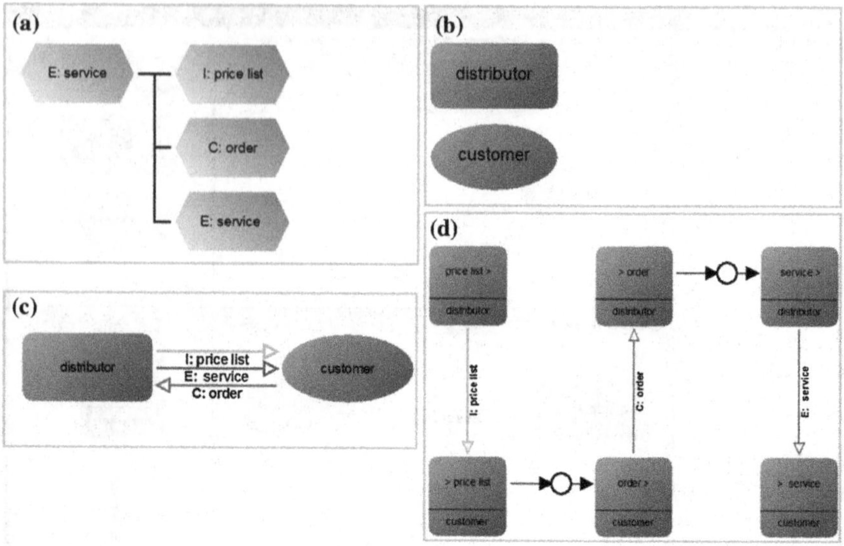

Fig. 9 Transaction decomposition schema (**a**), object decomposition schema (**b**), interaction schema (**c**), and task-event schema (**d**) on the 2nd level

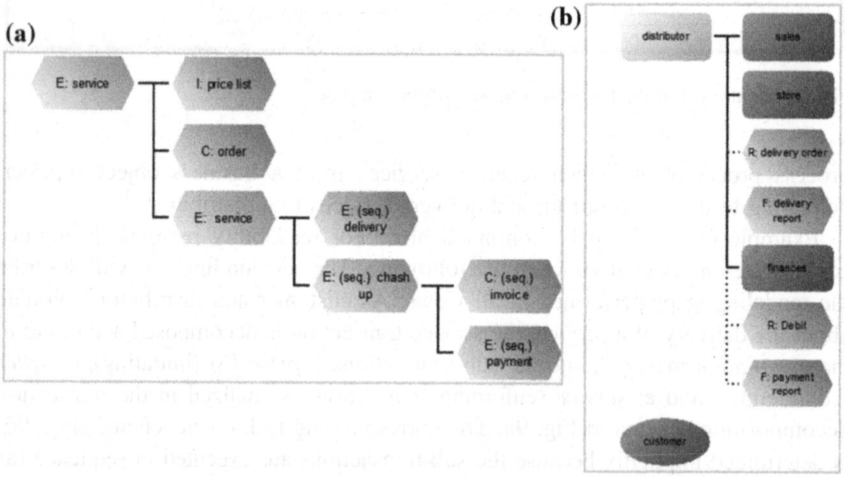

Fig. 10 Transaction decomposition schema (**a**) and object decomposition schema (**b**) on the 3rd level

The initiating transaction is omitted because the business objects already know each other. The contract of the invoice transaction refers to amount and date of payment, not to the obligation to pay in principle which is part of the transaction c: order.

Second, the feedback control principle is applied two times to distributor to (i) uncover the internal management of the business object, and (ii) derive at a homogeneous mapping between business transactions and business objects. Following the feedback control principle (cf. Fig. 4), this leads to the sub-objects sales (management object), *store* (operational object) and *finances* (operational object). Sales and store are coordinated by the transactions r: *delivery order* (control transaction) and f: *delivery report* (feedback transaction). Sales and finances are coordinated by the transactions r: *debit* and f: *payment report* (see Fig. 10b).

Figure 11 shows the interaction schema of the third business process level. The sales sub-object deals with *price list, (seq.) invoice* and *order,* the store sub-object is responsible for delivery. Consequently, the finances sub-object takes care of the *(seq.) payment.*

The last step in this case study is to define the behavior of the business process on its final decomposition level. Because of the different decomposition rules applied, the sequence of transactions cannot be derived automatically for the final process. Hence, the modeler is required to define the process behavior in the task-event schema by utilizing the internal event relationship and consecutively clicking on the outgoing and incoming task an internal event shall connect. Figure 12 shows the final task-event schema.

The business process is still initiated by the sales object sending a price list to the customer. The customer then sends an order back to sales. This initiates a control transaction delivery order to the store that actually delivers the good or service to the customer and responds with a feedback transaction (delivery report). After the report is processed, the sales object initiates two transactions: The sales object sends an invoice to the customer and it requests a debit to be handled by the finances. On receiving the customer's payment, the finances reports by means of a feedback transaction the payment report back to sales. This concludes the distribution process.

The complete case study with illustrations of all decomposition levels and views is available online at the Open Models Laboratory (OMiLAB) project page of

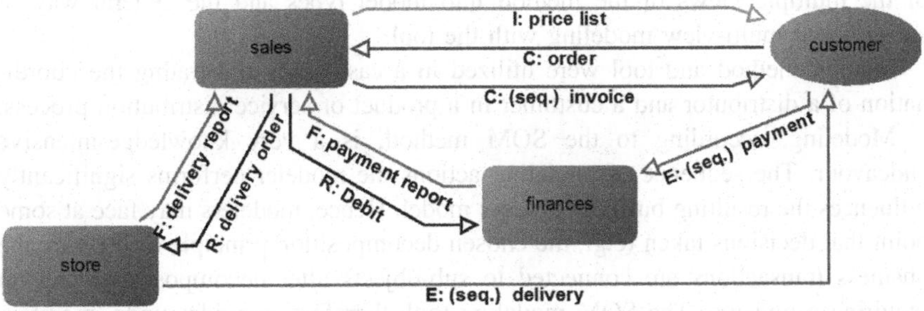

Fig. 11 Interaction schema on the 3rd level

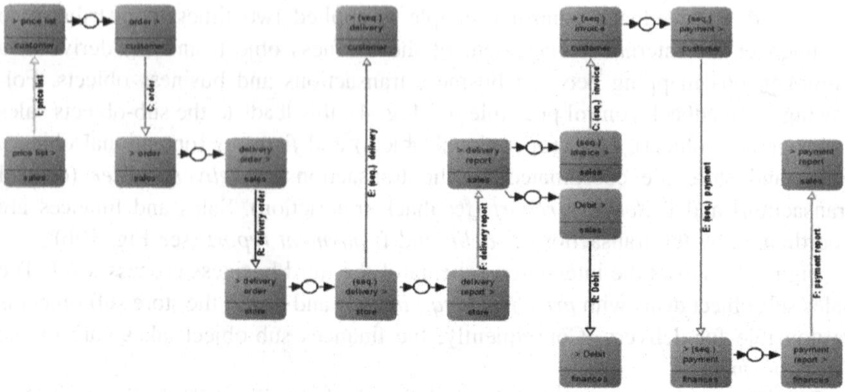

Fig. 12 Task-event schema on the 3rd level

SOM.[4] It also features the transformation of the final distribution business process into initial (i) schema of task classes, (ii) schema of conceptual classes and (iii) business process modeling and notation (BPMN) (cf. [16]). A comprehensive discussion on the conceptualization of the SOM method towards a multi-view modeling tool can be found in [17].

6 Conclusion

The previous sections gave a brief introduction to the SOM methodology for business systems modeling. A comprehensive enterprise model consists of sub-models for each layer of the enterprise architecture (see Fig. 1). The sub-models are balanced carefully within the architectural framework.

Consequently, the conceptualization of these characteristics towards the ADO*xx*-based SOM modeling tool was described. An emphasis was on the transformation of the multiple views of the method into model types and the general way of carrying out multi-view modeling with the tool.

Finally, method and tool were utilized in a case study illustrating the coordination of a distributor and a customer in a product or service distribution process.

Modeling, according to the SOM method, is a very knowledge-intensive endeavour. The sequence of modeling actions the modeler performs significantly influences the resulting business process model. Hence, modelers may face at some point that decisions taken (e.g., the chosen decomposition principle or the way the business transactions are connected to sub-objects after decomposition) end up requiring a revision. The SOM modeling tool, therefore, provides undo-operators

[4]The complete distribution business process case study, http://www.omilab.org/web/som/tutorial, [online] last access: 23.10.2015.

for almost any modeling action. With "revoke decomposition", the modeler is enabled to discard an already performed decomposition completely from all views in order to revise the decomposition. Moreover, relationships between business objects and business transactions can be revised independently from the decomposition itself by applying the "decrease business process level" operator (cf. Sect. 4.3).

Using the modeling tool in university courses at the University of Bamberg revealed that besides solid knowledge on the theoretical foundation of the SOM method, an introduction of the modeling tool is also required. Once students have this knowledge, the feedback gained after using the tool for solving modeling case studies was throughout positive. Future work will, therefore, focus on extending the SOM modeling tool project page[5] within the OMiLAB homepage with further tutorials, videos, a handbook and further FAQ's answered by the developers. The SOM modeling tool is freely available on the OMiLAB webpage.[6]

Tool Download http://www.omilab.org/som.

References

1. Ferstl, O.K., Sinz, E.J.: Modeling of business systems using SOM. In: Bernus, P., Mertins, K., Schmidt, G. (eds.) Handbook on Architectures of Information Systems. International Handbook on Information Systems, vol. 1, pp. 347–367, 2nd edn. Springer (2005)
2. Ferstl, O.K., Sinz, E.J.: Objektmodellierung betrieblicher Informationssysteme im Semantischen Objektmodell (SOM). WIRTSCHAFTSINFORMATIK **32**(6), 566–581 (1990)
3. Ferstl, O.K., Sinz, E.J.: Ein Vorgehensmodell zur Objektmodellierung betrieblicher Informationssysteme im Semantischen Objektmodell (SOM). WIRTSCHAFTSINFORMATIK **33**(6), 477–491 (1991)
4. Ferstl, O.K., Sinz, E.J.: Der Ansatz des Semantischen Objektmodells (SOM) zur Modellierung von Geschäftsprozessen. WIRTSCHAFTSINFORMATIK **37**(3), 209–220 (1995)
5. Bahrami, H.: The emerging flexible organization: perspectives from silicon valley. Calif. Manage. Rev. 33–52 (1992)
6. Sinz, E.J.: Architektur betrieblicher Informationssysteme. In: Rechenberg, P., Pomberger, G. (eds.) Informatik-Handbuch, pp. 875–887. Hanser-Verlag, München (1997)
7. Ferstl, O.K., Sinz, E.J.: Grundlagen der Wirtschaftsinformatik. Band 1, 3rd edn. Oldenbourg, München (1998)
8. Ferstl, O.K., Sinz, E.J.: Geschäftsprozeßmodellierung. WIRTSCHAFTSINFORMATIK **35**(6) 589–592 (1993)
9. Beer, S.: The Brain of the Firm, 2nd edn. Wiley, Chichester (1981)
10. Ferstl, O.K.: Integrationskonzepte betrieblicher Anwendungssysteme. Fachbericht Informatik 1/92. Universität Koblenz-Landau (1992)
11. Ferstl, O.K., Sinz, E.J.: Grundlagen der Wirtschaftsinformatik, Band 1, 7th edn. Oldenbourg, München (2013)

[5]OMiLAB project page of SOM, http://www.omilab.org/web/som, [online] last access: 23.10. 2015.

[6]Download the SOM modeling tool, http://www.omilab.org/web/som/download, [online] last access: 23.10.2015.

12. Bork, D., Sinz, E.J.: Bridging the gap from a multi-view modelling method to the design of a multi-view modeling tool. Enterp. Model. Inf. Syst. Archit. (EMISA) **8**(2) 25–41 (2013)
13. Bork, D., Buchmann, R., Karagiannis, D.: Preserving multi-view consistency in diagrammatic knowledge representation. In: Zhang, et al. (eds.) Proceedings of the 8th International Conference on Knowledge Science, Engineering and Management. LNAI vol. 9403, pp. 1–6 (2015)
14. Bork, D., Fill, H.-G.: Formal aspects of enterprise modeling methods: a comparison framework. In: Sprague, R.H.J. (ed.) Proceedings of the 47th Hawaii International Conference on System Sciences, pp. 3400–3409. IEEE Computer Society Press, Big Island, Hawaii, USA (2014)
15. Bork, D., Sinz, E.J.: Design of a SOM business process modelling tool based on the ADOxx meta-modelling platform. In: Lara, et al. (eds.) Pre-Proceedings of the 4th International Workshop on Graph-Based Tools, University of Twente, Enschede, pp. 90–101 (2010)
16. Puetz, C., Sinz, E.J.: Model-driven derivation of BPMN workflow schemata from SOM business process models. In: Enterp. Model. Inf. Syst. Archit. **5**(2), 57–72 (2010)
17. Bork, D.: A development method for the conceptual design of multi-view modeling tools with an emphasis on consistency requirements. Ph.D. thesis, University of Bamberg (2015)

Part VI
Enterprise Strategic Management

Evaluation Chains for Controlling the Evolution of Enterprise Models

Frank Wolff

Abstract In many circumstances, enterprise management requires diverse information which concerns distinct domains like company strategy, business processes and IT-systems. Enterprise models provide management with essential information, and, therefore, they are considered almost indispensable. However, the creation and maintenance of an encompassing enterprise model have proven to be a challenging task. Fundamental are the diversity of influencing factors, coupled with the long time required both for creating and using such a model. Therefore, a dedicated framework to control enterprise modeling was developed based on the concept of evaluation chains. As the assessment involves a number of people and the controlling process spans over a number of years, a modeling tool was implemented in the ADO*xx* metamodeling platform to ease the practical usage of evaluation chains in organizational settings.

Keywords Economic assessment • Modeling management • Goal alignment • Utilization perspectives

1 Challenges of Enterprise Modeling Management

Successful enterprise management requires considerable amounts of information. If this information is related to the structure of the company, it often cannot be easily attained, and sometimes mutual understanding between different stakeholders is hindered by misinterpretations because of the complex interrelationships in the company, e.g., in its business processes or in the IT-systems and their applications. Conceptual models offer an appropriate means to provide vital information and by that to support the tasks of enterprise management. For this purpose, a number of generic and more dedicated modeling methods have been proposed (e.g., [1–3] or

F. Wolff (✉)
Baden-Wuerttemberg Cooperative State University,
68163 Mannheim, Germany
e-mail: frank.wolff@dhbw-mannheim.de

D. Karagiannis et al. (eds.), *Domain-Specific Conceptual Modeling*,
DOI 10.1007/978-3-319-39417-6_14

[4]). Although the different modeling methods are similar in some aspects, they vary widely in others. Most notably are differences between the object types contained and the symbols used for representing them.

While good enterprise models appear to be simple and intelligible, their creation and actualization are quite baffling. The different groups involved are one major challenge. This is because of many cognitive, political and organizational issues [5]. Another aspect is the distribution of changes of an enterprise in time and through its entities. The effort for data collection for organizational and IT-issues can be very high and the respective data quality is often rather low [6].

All these characteristics call for active management of enterprise modeling processes [7, 8]. One main duty of the governance would be to ensure that pending updates for models activate the relevant triggers. Besides organizational arrangements, also, technical coupling is an important force for up-to-date and correct enterprise models [9]. This applies very much to the automatic conversion of systems data into models and vice versa. Moreover, the connection between different spheres of modeling often is a challenge in practice (e.g., business processes and IT-infrastructure).

Besides practical issues and methodological divergences, there has frequently been an open dispute between the proponents of enterprise modeling and its opponents. The latter often refer to experiences with enterprise data models which practically had little impact because they were not completed or were up-to-date only for a short time. Similar problems are also reported from current practice with encompassing enterprise process and architecture models in companies [10, 11]. Some organizations are using them successfully, but many others have problems after the initial application of their enterprise models. Either modeling ceased completely in these organizations, or a long-term practice was only established for restricted (minor) areas.

Based on extensive practical experiences and numerous discussions with other practitioners, the author concluded that a major hindrance for a wider successful application of enterprise models originates from the inadequate adaptation of the modeling activities to the particular conditions and requirements of the companies.

A technically and economically well-balanced adaptation to these conditions and requirements is not easy because of the diversity of factors influencing the modeling process. Some of the factors are very prominent like the methods and tools for modeling. Other factors are not so obvious, more difficult to assess and to influence, like the culture of information sharing, the modeling management or the effects of business and organizational change. As the effort for a thorough analysis from scratch is likely to be quite high, a method for supporting a rational evaluation appears to be indispensable.

The description of the method and its development will start with an overview of the main elements and steps of the method in Chap. 2. This part also includes a general specification of major concepts employed for the assessment. In Chap. 3, this will be complemented with the definition of respective metamodels for a domain-specific modeling language to support the evaluation. Chapter 4 provides insights into the implementation of the metamodel in ADO*xx* (compare [12]). In

Chap. 5, the application of the method is presented based on an example case. The conclusion and outlook follow in the final chapter.[1]

2 Evaluation Chains to Uncover Interdependencies in Enterprise Modeling

Because of the challenges described in the preceding section, the author developed a systematic framework to support an evaluation of enterprise modeling in close cooperation with other researchers and practitioners. The method is intended to ease the effort required for a systematic improvement and adaptation of enterprise modeling in large organizations to changing requirements and circumstances. An important foundation for the method was the collection and compilation of existing knowledge on different factors influencing costs and benefits of enterprise modeling [7]. The method also comprises some assumptions on the underlying pattern of its economic dependencies in enterprise modeling and its assessment

- A long-term perspective is essential considering the extent of the activities and the distribution of costs and benefits for enterprise architecture modeling.
- Cooperation of different specialists is required to account for the complexity of the subject.
- Focusing on benefits to business provides for an appropriate guidance to modeling activities and illustrates advantages to management whose backing is indispensable in most cases [13].
- For clear communication between the different participants, a dedicated modeling method is required. This modeling method must be comprehensible for collaborators of different spheres of a company, e.g., from management, IT and services.

2.1 *Systematic Evaluation of Enterprise Modeling in an Organization*

Figure 1 depicts an overview of the developed systematic approach to evaluating enterprise modeling. The first step of the evaluation is the investigation of the information required by the *Business perspective*. It is the basis for identifying the specific modeling goals of an organization and for partitioning the evaluation into separate *Utilization perspectives*. The *Utilization perspectives* are an instrument to subdivide the usually complex evaluation of enterprise modeling into manageable entities. This is crucial in all organizations, except for the very small ones.

[1]The author acknowledges very valuable remarks for improvements to this paper by Alexander Bock and Ulrich Frank from the University of Duisburg-Essen.

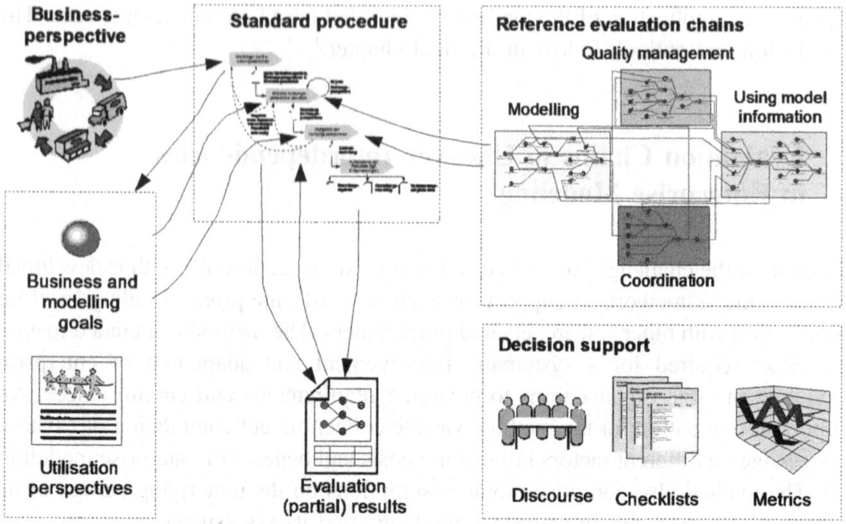

Fig. 1 Overview of a systematic approach to the evaluation of enterprise modeling

The advance of the evaluation and necessary decisions are directed by the *Standard procedure*. It covers the required steps of the assessment and guides ruling on important structural options for the evaluation. The *Reference evaluation chains* are dedicated Evaluation chains which reflect the interdependencies of influencing factors in enterprise modeling processes. These reference models offer factual guidance and a basis for documenting the specific valuations of various influences in the examined organization. The three methods of *Decision support* have different purposes [14]. The *Discourse* defines rules for cooperation and exchange of subjective valuations among the participants in major evaluations [15]. The *Checklists* support the *Discourse* and the *Metrics* ease a continual routine control of modeling processes.

The results will be integrated after the separate evaluation of individual utilization perspectives. This often reveals helpful synergies, but may also uncover conflicting interests which must be settled to realise effective modeling processes [14]. Besides structuring the evaluation process, the utilization perspectives also provide an adequate means of defining areas of responsibility [16]. They considerably facilitate planning and control of the evolution of comprehensive enterprise models.

2.2 *Evaluation Chains*

The evaluation of enterprise modeling processes in a company is a complex activity requiring the involvement of different specialists. To facilitate the work, the method incorporates evaluation chains as a visual language to guide the participants by highlighting the crucial content of the evaluation. In the following paragraphs, the underlying concepts will be presented in more detail.

The analysis of the literature and experiences from practice revealed fundamental similarities between major influences in the modeling process with their respective dependencies for crucial domains ([2, 17–19] et al.). These influencing factors range from the modeling language over the required tools to the work of different participants in the modeling processes. The identified elements were compiled in the reference evaluation chains which contain essential topics for evaluations of enterprise modeling.

More details are incorporated in the evaluation by the discourse of relevant specialist and further knowledge is infused into the valuations by checklists. The checklists comprise some general questions such as, "Have all relevant alternatives for … (e.g., the modelling tool) been considered?" and more specific questions, such as "Is modelling support available/Can modelling support be guaranteed when it is called for?".

The complete reference evaluation chain, which represents the crucial factors of the modeling processes, overall is in many cases too large for one diagram. Therefore, the whole reference evaluation chain has been divided into four aspects: (a) *Modeling*, (b) *Quality management*, (c) *Coordination* and (d) *Using model information*, which reflect major issues of the overall process. In this article, only the aspect of coordination will be presented. All four aspects are displayed and described in [7, 9].

2.2.1 Roots of the Evaluation Chain Concept

The concept of evaluation chains was developed based on a close analysis of contemporary generic methods to support decisions in business. The challenges were documented in [14] and an early version in [20].

For the evaluation of modeling, the following two major problems were identified in the initial analysis: (a) the complexity of the topic and (b) the practical necessity for evaluations during different phases of the 'life-cycle' of an enterprise model. The latter is reinforced by the uncertainty inherent in the assessment of many influential factors. This also recommends a long-term approach, including learning and adaptation activities. It is ideal if systematic evaluations start with the design of the modeling framework. Then they should be continued as a concurrent control activity during the evolution and use of the enterprise models. But the approach is also easily adaptable to start with subsequent phases in the life cycle of an enterprise model.

The analysis of generic evaluation methods revealed important deficiencies in respect of the intended usage in the modeling domain (see also [21]). Classical methods of economic decision poorly support a systematic inclusion of long-term factors and interdependencies [7]. Most appropriate were the methods based on causal relationship diagrams of decision theory [22], system dynamics [23] and balanced scorecards [24]. But they also only partly fulfilled the requirements. For this reason, the concept of evaluation chains was developed. It is a fusion of the methods mentioned beforehand. Additionally, evaluation chains also integrate distinctions for representing the influences in productive processes common in German business administration theory [25].

2.2.2 Elements of Evaluation Chains

An evaluation chain is based on three primary element types: (a) *Goal*, (b) *Factor* used in the process or influencing it, and (c) *Result*. Goals are reflecting a desired state in business. To reach a goal usually one or more factors must be employed. The employment of a factor often incurs some costs. Typical examples for factors in modeling processes are the work of modelers, the modeling tool, but also general influences like the rate of change in the business.

Another differentiation of the elements is due to the significant difference between goals and results which originate (a) in business (*Business goal* and *Result*) and (b) those which are part of the modeling activities (*Modeling Goal* and *Modeling intermediate result*). The former have a direct link to potential benefits for business. The latter are closely linked to enterprise modeling (in different circumstances other instrumental activities are also possible). The elements are represented in Fig. 2.

The distinction between business and modeling for goals (and results) emphasises business goals. It is intended to direct modeling in a way that it provides real benefits to the business. A modeling goal reflects a required or aspired state which is necessary for the modeling processes, e.g., high level of knowledge of the modelers. As business goals can be attained in different ways, modeling goals often have a higher degree of variability compared with directly specified business goals.

To depict the relations between elements, only one type of relation is used, the type *influences*. It is sufficient for a discursive evaluation. If necessary, it can be classified more specifically through annotations. (See, e.g., [26, 27]).

Figure 3 sketches the principle of an evaluation chain. It reflects the most important elements for an evaluation. It starts with a business goal. To reach this goal some dedicated modeling goal is aspired. A factor must be employed to realise

Fig. 2 Core elements of an evaluation chain

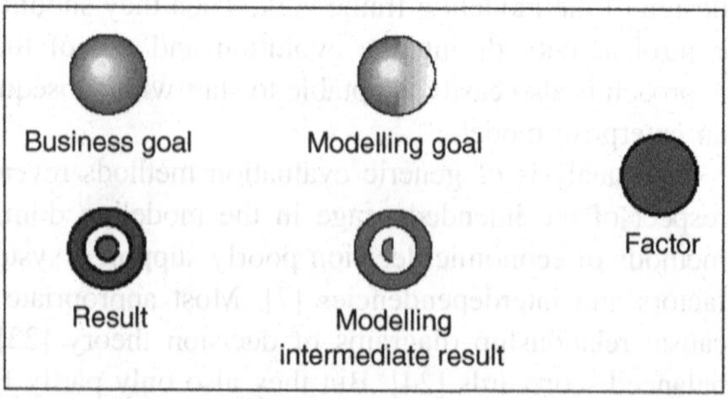

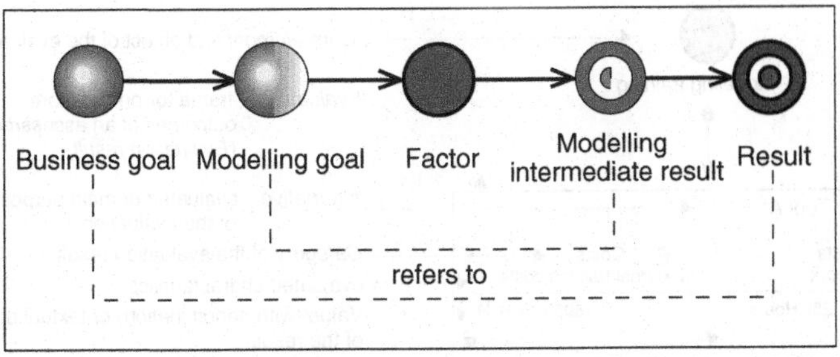

Fig. 3 Principle of an evaluation chain

it. This factor produces a modeling intermediate result which refers to the modeling goal. The modeling intermediate result influences a (final) result which satisfies a business goal.

Some auxiliary elements are provided for evaluation chains. The elements are (a) *Referenced factor*, (b) *Referenced intermediate result* and (c)*Aggregate intermediate result*. They are displayed in Fig. 4 and derive their semantics from their base elements: factor or intermediate result. Their purpose is to simplify the graphical diagram of extended evaluation chains by allowing links that are not visualized in the diagram.

Evaluation chains are used in different situations in combination with other methods particularly discourse or measurement. In all these assessments, the findings of the probe must be recorded. For an often distributed discourse of experts, the documentation of single findings is of high importance as many detailed evaluations are determined by interdependencies of a number of factors and intermediate results in the enterprise modeling processes. Therefore, the evaluation findings of different aspects must regularly be balanced in later stages.

Depending on the nature of the analyzed element, the available knowledge and the purpose of the evaluation, different types of values are required to describe the findings of an assessed element. As quite distinct kinds of elements are influential in enterprise modeling processes, e.g., modeling tool, available models and work of modelers, also different types of value are required. The evaluation chain provides for: (a) numeric values, with definable dimensions (including money), (b) enumerations, and (c) qualitative descriptions. In Fig. 5, this is illustrated directly in an example for the element of *Modeling training* and its associated cost which has been evaluated for an alternative "Tool A". Costs are expressed in two dimensions:

Fig. 4 Elements to simplify complex evaluation chains

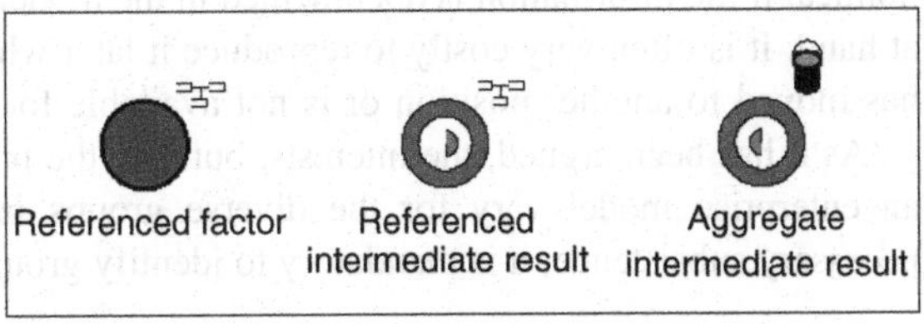

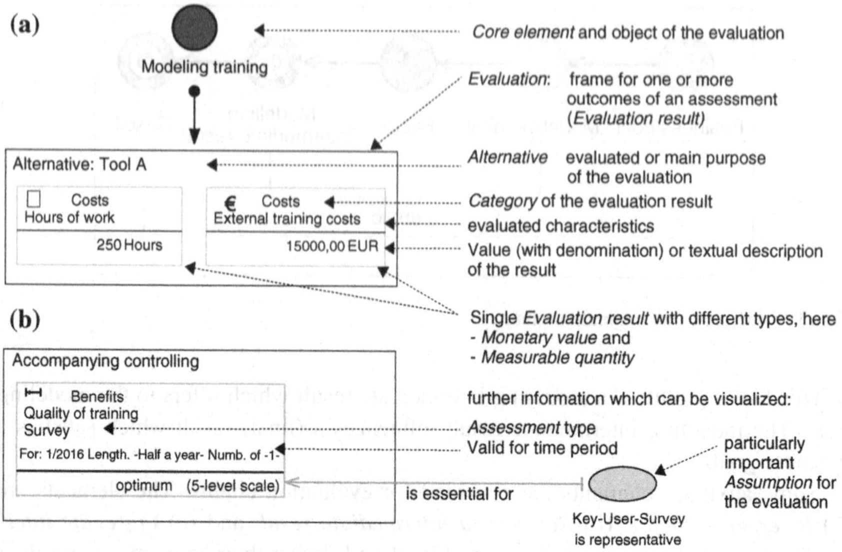

Fig. 5 Representation examples of evaluations for the factor of *Modeling training* focussed on (a) *Costs* (on *top*) and (b) *Benefits* of the *Quality of training* (*below*)

hours of work and money. Below the first evaluation, another evaluation on the perceived benefits of the quality of training result is depicted. (Please note, in the evaluation chain this evaluation would also be connected to the evaluated element.) In the second evaluation, the α-Element documents the important assumption for this evaluation that the *Key-User-Survey is representative*.

2.2.3 Partitioning of the Evaluation into Utilization Perspectives

Many obstacles to a smooth modeling process originate in the diverse participants required for a broad company modeling effort (see [28]). This is related to the wide variance in specific knowledge for the different domains and the perspectives of people who create models or are otherwise involved in enterprise modeling. For example, management has more sophisticated demands on the visual design of symbols used in models than the IT-personnel [29]. The IT experts again will emphasise precision and detail of information [17].

Another aspect for a company is that it is usually much easier and more economical if the information is documented in the model while the information is well at hand. It is often very costly to reproduce it later when the knowledgeable person has moved to another position or is not available for other reasons.

As it has been argued, the interests, but also the problems, to create the parts of an enterprise model vary for the diverse groups involved. In order to prepare necessary subsistence, it is mandatory to identify groups with similar characteristics and interests. The term *Utilization perspective* was selected in order to emphasise the prospective benefits of modeling for those groups. Figure 6 presents the criteria used for distributing the groups involved in modeling appropriately into groups.

The distribution is based on two basic perspectives (a) the overall *Business perspective* and (b) the *Modeling perspective*. The business perspective determines the *Goals for using models* and thereby modeling. The modeling perspective is rooted in the basic domain of the model. It is related to the typical *Knowledge* of the people working in a domain. The business and the modeling perspectives are important for the *Context of work*. The elements of the context of work may stem initially from the generic characteristics of modeling context and the business goals. It should also be noted that, in many cases, other conditions impact upon the interest and cognition of participants, e.g., the type of education, nature of work, geographical or cultural traits. By clustering groups of people along their context of work and their typical modeling knowledge, important stakeholder groups can be identified in regard of enterprise models.

The individual characteristics and goals of the stakeholders are identified as the foundation. Then, the similarities of goals and stakeholder characteristics are used to discover common perspectives. This analysis is balanced by considering an appropriate number of utilization perspectives for an enterprise. This number depends on the size and the strategic importance of enterprise modeling for the company. Besides basic utilization perspectives which cover one subject area of a company, e.g., the production of a major product line, other perspectives, such as engineering or IT, are allowed for. If model information from different perspectives is required for an additional purpose, interrelated utilization perspectives are created.

The utilization perspectives help an organization to (a) discover conflicts of interest between participants and/or company goals, and subsequently to resolve them, (b) control the current required update of an enterprise architecture model and

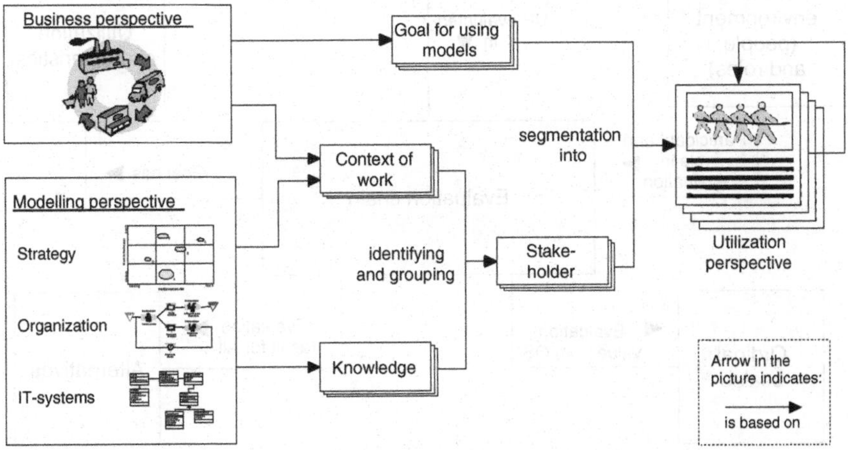

Fig. 6 Criteria for distributing enterprise modeling into utilization perspectives

(c) make up a more realistic assessment of options to model its enterprise [7, 30]. An appropriately adopted organization was identified to have high influence on the prospects of reaping the benefits from an enterprise model [31].

3 Underlying Meta-Concepts of the Evaluation Chain Method

An evaluation of enterprise modeling is based on a number of different kinds of information. Additionally, it is partitioned in different areas, the Utilization perspectives. To better represent this information in models, separate types of models are required. They are represented in Fig. 7. At the top, there is the *Overview on the utilization perspectives*. The *Evaluation chain* is at the centre and at the sides there are several supporting models which are used to standardize terms or describe the environment. Particularly important is (a) the *Working environment* which specifies the groups and the roles of the persons involved in the modeling processes. Besides, there are models for the definition of (b) *Ordinal scales*, (c) standard types of goals, perspectives and model content categories *Utilization characteristics* and (d) the *Alternatives* considered in the evaluation.

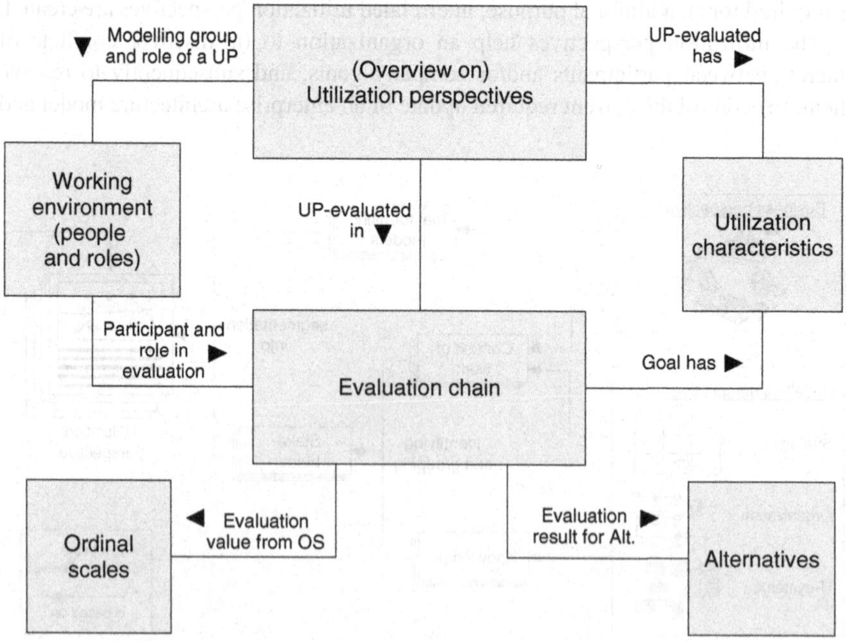

Fig. 7 Overview on the model types of the evaluation chain method

The principle of the evaluation chain was depicted in Fig. 3. The presented graphics of the symbols, but also the boxed textual descriptions of the outcomes of specific evaluations are defined in the metamodel of the evaluation chain. In this paper, two detailed views of the metamodel will be presented: (a) on the core Evaluation chain and (b) on the Utilization perspectives. For a view on the metamodel for the evaluation results, one can refer to [7].

The metamodel of the core Evaluation chain in Fig. 8 is based on the general abstract *Core evaluation element*. The common base reflects a homogenous characteristic of these elements; they can exert influence on one other. In classical system theoretic diagrams, they are represented by the same general type. As argued before, for greater clarity the *Core evaluation element* is specialized in three classes: *Goal* (abstract), *Factor* and *Result* (abstract). The Goal is specialized into a leading *Business goal* and dependent *Modeling goal*. In most cases, in order to reach a goal some means must be employed. These means are defined as *Factors* in an Evaluation chain (Figs. 8 and 10).

A factor has some characteristics which assist the judgement on alternative paths of action. Most important is the *kind of factor* which is shown at the top on the left side with a Factor. Values are: (a) V = variable, (b) R = resource (c) E = external (comp. Fig. 11). This distinction serves as an indicator of how easily a factor can be changed. While external factors cannot be controlled directly, the variable factors can be controlled and changed deliberately. Resources can be directly affected by management, but the typical cost distribution normally objects swift changes in these factors.

The general classification in V, R and E is complemented with further attributes on the character of the factor and its respective economic perception. The Boolean choices for the monetary, the qualitative and the investment character of the Factor

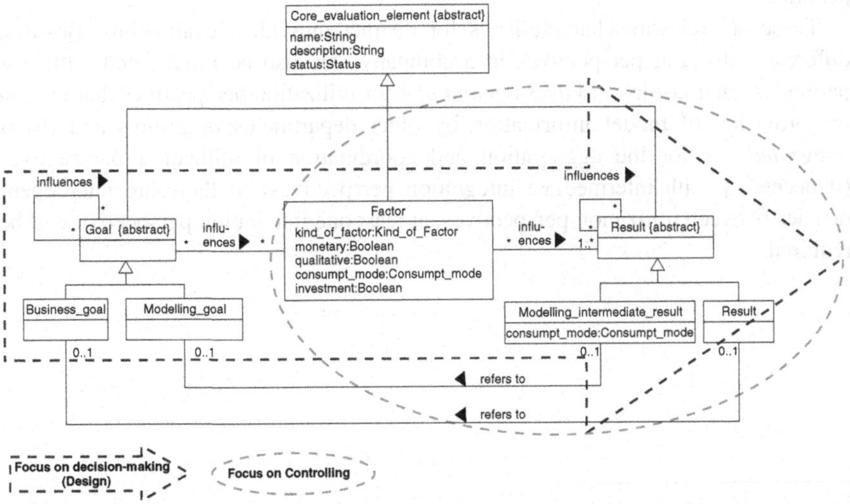

Fig. 8 Metamodel of the core evaluation chain

are common economic concepts. The consumption mode (consumpt-mode) takes into account the standard economic conception and particular notions of information economics [16]. While normal factors are completely consumed or depreciated when used, information or knowledge does not wear off when used.

The abstract class *Result_abstract* is specialized into a *Modeling intermediate result* and a business *Result.* This mirrors the Business goal and the Modeling goal. When comparing different approaches of economic evaluation two main types have been identified: (a) decision oriented and (b) controlling focused.

In decision-oriented concepts, the dependencies are conceptualized the same way as in evaluation chains. They start with general goals; they are translated into specific action goals which then are substantiated in some factors or resources. Consequently, the results of the action and the consumption of resources are compared with related goals.

The controlling focus fuses the goals with values for the resource consumption of factors or the results pursued and measured. If all goals have a corresponding result value, then both views can be incorporated into homogenous Evaluation chains. In this method, this can be found in the reference evaluation chains which also were modeled in a composite controlling view where the goals are implicitly contained in the aspired states of the business and modeling results.[2]

Utilization perspectives help to segment evaluations in larger organizations, especially, if they pursue different kinds of usage for their models, in other words have more goals. In Fig. 9, this is described in the second part of the metamodel. Besides the structural composition of individual evaluation chains for utilization perspectives, it also contains the shaping group or groups, and the pursued goals. The goal itself can be attributed with generic *Usage goals*, a *Category of content* and a *Perspective.* The group involved is characterized by its *Modeling role* or roles, its *Model-related knowledge* and if required by assigning the acting *Person* or persons.

These are relevant characteristics for distinct individual evaluations. Besides, different utilization perspectives in a company can also be interrelated with two particular relationships: (a) *uses content of*—for utilization perspectives that rely on the provision of model information by other departments or groups and (b) *is integrated in*—for the aggregation and coordination of utilization perspectives (if necessary with intermediate integration perspectives). If there are interdependencies between utilization perspectives, at least one integration perspective will be required.

[2]Anyway, it should be noted that this is a preliminary simplification, which must be validated with the importance of a distinctive handling and analysis of the goal structures in organizations.

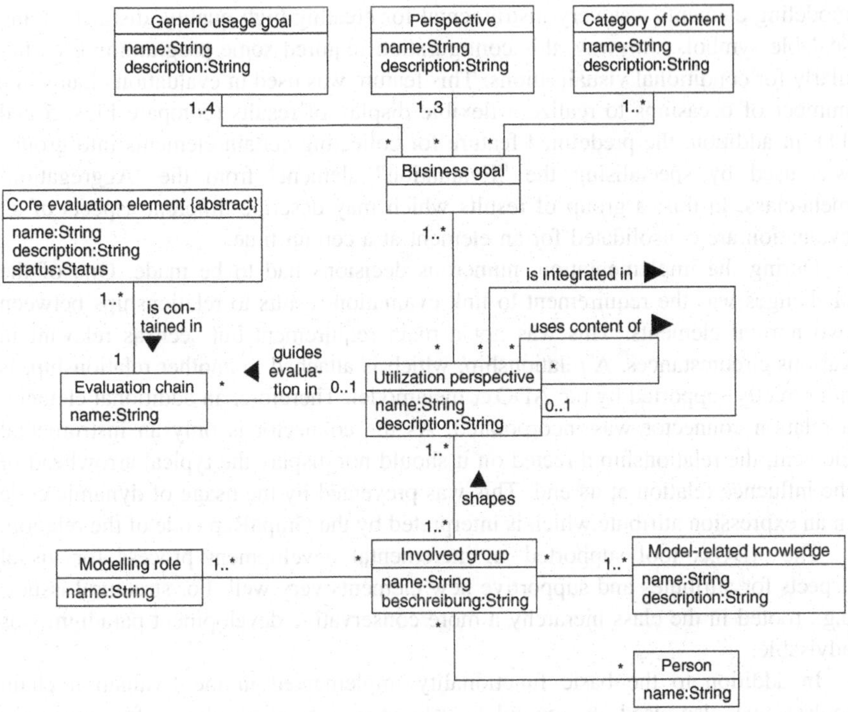

Fig. 9 Metamodel of utilization perspectives

4 Implementation of Evaluation Chains in ADO*xx*

The design and implementation of the Evaluation chains in ADO*xx* and its predecessors had two main iterations: First, a principal study of the configuration options and the capabilities of the metamodeling toolset combined with an experimental design of first elements and interdependencies.[3] Second, the systematized concepts of evaluation chains were implemented after an intensive study of related scientific work. In the second phase, many graphics were reused from the first configuration, but the structure of the metamodel changed substantially. In the implementation, the structure was focused by introducing groups of elements according to their usage of different model types and the direct inheritance of classes, e.g., for the core evaluation elements.

The rich functionality of ADO*xx* offered many options in the implementation (comp [12]). Especially the GraphRep language for designing the symbols of the

[3]The term 'Bewertungskette', in English, Evaluation Chain, was suggested in the discussion of the first prototype in ADONIS at the Department of Knowledge Engineering (DKE) by Prof. Dimitris Karagiannis.

modeling elements was very instrumental for creating high quality, distinctive and scalable symbols. Anyway, this configuration required some programming particularly for conditional visualisations. This feature was used in evaluation chains in a number of occasions to realize a flexible display of results (compare Figs. 5 and 11). In addition, the predefined feature for collecting certain elements into groups was used by specialising the "Evaluation" element[4] from the 'Aggregation' meta-class. In this, a group of results which may describe different aspects of an evaluation are consolidated for an element at a certain time.

During the implementation, numerous decisions had to be made. One of the challenges was the requirement to link evaluation results to relationships between two normal elements. This was not a main requirement but seen as relevant in various circumstances. A relationship, which is attached to another relationship, is not directly supported by the ADO*xx* metamodel. Therefore, an additional element, a relation connector was incorporated. As the connector is only an instrumental element, the relationship directed on it should not display the typical arrowhead of the influence relation at its end. This was prevented by the usage of dynamic code in an expression attribute which is interpreted by the GraphRep code of the relation.

The ADO*xx* tool supported an incremental development process for visual aspects for attributes and supportive new elements very well. For structural issues, e.g., rooted in the class hierarchy a more conservative development paradigm was advisable.

In addition to the basic functionality implemented in the Evaluation chain toolset, we also used the complete reference evaluation chains for enterprise modeling [9] and some further examples to ease the start of new users.

5 Applying Evaluation Chains to Manage the Enterprise Modeling Process

This section presents an illustrative example of a mechanical supplier company. Outline of the example: The mechanics company has two major divisions; one is working for the aviation industry, and the other is manufacturing a wide range of basic mechanical parts for other non-regulated industrial customers. Some subsidiaries have been founded abroad for improving business in other countries. The subsidiaries often also profit from lower wages or material prices. Due to their success, more foreign affiliations are planned.

The separation of utilization perspectives for the example mechanical company is presented in Fig. 10. It differentiates five main utilization perspectives: (a) Production improvement and relocation perspective of the standard parts business, (b) Aviation certificate perspective, (c) IT-perspective, (d) Preparing decisions and

[4]The metamodel for the evaluation elements could not be included in this article. It is presented in [7].

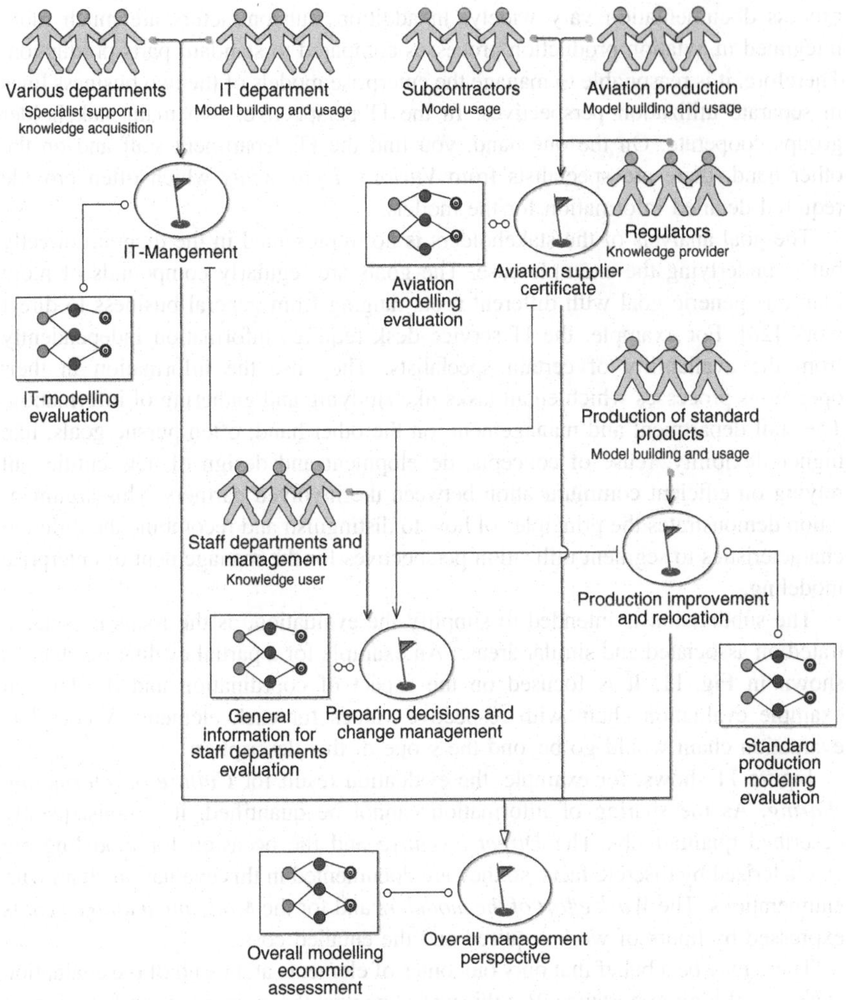

Fig. 10 Example for a typical distribution of utilization perspectives in a company

change management perspective. The base business perspectives for the enterprise model directly create models of, for example, business processes. They are depicted on the right side of the diagram (a&b). The IT-perspective is on the left side at the top. At the centre, there is the perspective of staff for general decision-making which does not provide its own models but relies on other models and is very valuable for the company. At the bottom, there is the (e) integration perspective which is required to harmonize and integrate all partial evaluations.

The two base business perspectives are structurally very similar and only differentiated by the additional stakeholder group of regulators and subcontractors. This may seem to be only a small variance, but the respective requirements for process documentation vary widely. In addition, subcontractors are much more integrated in aviation production processes compared to standard parts production. Therefore, it is reasonable to manage the enterprise models of the two business lines in separate utilization perspectives. In the IT-perspective, two main stakeholder groups cooperate. On the one hand, you find the IT-department staff and on the other hand, there are specialists from *Various departments* which often provide required detailed information for the models.

The goal analysis of the stakeholders is not represented in the diagram directly but is underlying the example case. The goals are regularly compounds of more than one generic goal with different roots ranging from general business to direct work [28]. For example, the IT-service desk requires information independently from the availability of certain specialists. They use the information in their operations processes which entail tasks like studying and gathering of information. The staff department and management, on the other hand, often pursue goals, like higher flexibility, reuse of concepts, development and design of new entities all relying on efficient communication between the involved partners. This argumentation demonstrates the principles of how to distinguish and recombine the different characteristics to segment utilization perspectives for the management of enterprise modeling.

The subdivision is intended to simplify the evaluation, as the focus is concentrated on associated and similar areas.[5] An example for a partial evaluation chain is shown in Fig. 11. It is focused on the aspect of coordination and displays an example evaluation chain with respective values for each element. A complete evaluation chain would go beyond the scope of this description.

Figure 11 shows, for example, the evaluation result for *Culture of information sharing*. As the sharing of information cannot be quantified, it is consequently described qualitatively. The *Direct incentive* and the occasion for modeling are characterized by discrete facts, so they are documented in this evaluation chain with enumerations. The *Work effort of the modelers* and for the *Modeling management* is expressed by hours of work required and the entailed costs.

There may be a belief that only outcomes of elements at the end of the evaluation chain are of high importance. But this would neglect the main intention for using an instrument like the evaluation chain. Factors and intermediate results in the initial steps of the modeling process are supportive and indispensable for the later steps. So the input and values realized in these stages often point to potential problems quite early, when their correction or avoidance is possible at low costs [23, 26].

The evaluation chains are also intended to assist concurrent control. In this context, the evaluation results will not be determined in a discourse. Controlling should be based on metrics which correspond to the elements in the evaluation chains. These are metrics from modeling processes, e.g., number of support calls,

---

[5]Legend: a) Oval with a flag = Utilisation perspective (UP), b) Persons = Involved group, c) Connected bullets = Evaluation chain, d) Big arrow between UPs = is integrated, e) Open arrow between UPs = uses content of.

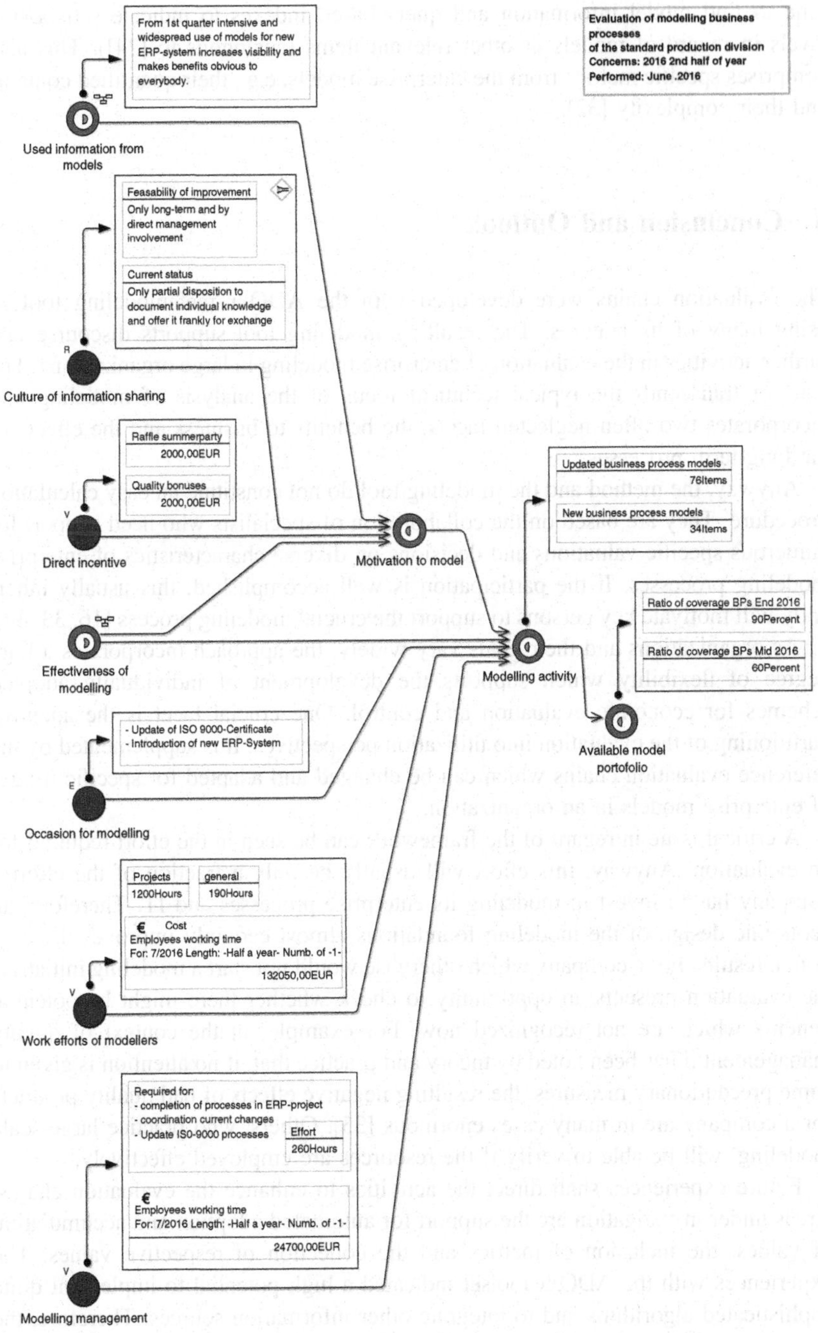

Fig. 11 Example evaluation of the coordination aspect

time to find model information and query-based indexes to indicate satisfaction levels in regard of models or other relevant items (analogous to [24]). This also comprises specific metrics from the enterprise models, e.g., their quantified contents and their complexity [32].

6 Conclusion and Outlook

The evaluation chains were developed with the ADO*xx* metamodeling toolset, using many of its features. The resulting modeling tool supports discourse and further activities in the evaluation of enterprise modeling in large organizations. The concept transcends the typical technical focus of the analysis of modeling and incorporates two often neglected facets, the benefits to business and the effects of the long-term processes.

Anyway, the method and the modeling tool do not constitute an easy calculation procedure. They are based on the collaboration of specialists who need support for numerous specific valuations and decisions on diverse characteristics of enterprise modeling processes. If the participation is well accomplished, this usually inherently will motivate key persons to support the crucial modeling process [16, 33, 34].

As organizations and their goals vary widely, the approach incorporates a high degree of flexibility which supports the development of individually adopted schemes for economic evaluation and control. One crucial facet is the adaptive partitioning of the evaluation into utilization perspectives. It is supplemented by the reference evaluation chains which can be changed and adapted for specific usages of enterprise models in an organization.

A critical issue in regard of the framework can be seen in the effort required for an evaluation. Anyway, this effort will usually be only a fraction of the effort a company has to invest in modeling its enterprise processes and IT. Therefore, an economic design of the modeling foundations almost certainly improves the economic results. For a company which otherwise would not start a modeling initiative, the evaluation presents an opportunity to check whether there might be potential benefits which are not recognized now. For example, in the context of quality management it has been noted by theory and practice that, if no attention is given to some precautionary measures, the resulting negative effects of bad quality products for a company are in many cases enormous [35]. Others, who practice large-scale modeling, will be able to verify if the resources are employed effectively.

Future experiences shall direct the activities to enhance the evaluation chains. Areas under investigation are the support for automated adoption and accumulation of values, the inclusion of metrics and the collection of respective values. The experiences with the ADO*xx* toolset indicated a high potential to implement quite sophisticated algorithms and to integrate other information sources. Therefore, the author is looking forward to a further enhancement of the Evaluation chain toolset.

Tool Download http://www.omilab.org/evaluationchains.

References

1. Braun, C., Winter, R.: A Comprehensive enterprise architecture metamodel. In: Desel, J., Frank, U. (eds.) Enterprise Modelling and Information Systems Architectures, Proceedings of the Workshop in Klagenfurt 2005. GI LNI P- 75, pp. 64–79. Bonn (2005)
2. Lankhorst, M., et al.: Enterprise architecture at work—modelling, communication and analysis, 3rd edn. Springer, Berlin (2013)
3. Frank, U.: Multi-perspective enterprise modeling: foundational concepts, prospects and future research challenges. Softw. Syst. Model. **13**, 941–962 (2014)
4. Scheer, A.: ARIS: business process modelling, 3rd edn. Springer, Berlin (2000)
5. Seppanen, V., Heikkila, J., Liimatainen, K.: Key issues in EA-implementation: case study of two finnish government agencies. In: Proceedings of the 2009 IEEE Conference on Commerce and Enterprise Computing, IEEE Computer Society, pp. 114–120 (2009)
6. Roth, S., Hauder, M., Farwick, M., Matthes, F., Breu, R.: Enterprise architecture documentation: current practices and future directions. In: 11th International Conference on Wirtschaftsinformatik (WI). Leipzig, Germany (2013)
7. Wolff, F.: Ökonomie multiperspektivischer Unternehmensmodellierung. Gabler, Wiesbaden (2008)
8. Franz, P., Kirchmer, M.: Value-driven Business Process Management—The Value Switch for Lasting Competitive Advantage. McGraw-Hill (2012)
9. Wolff, F.: An evaluation framework for enterprise architecture modelling. Enterp. Model. Inf. Syst. Architect. **3**(1), 48–61 (2008)
10. Stirna, J.: The influence of intentional and situational factors on enterprise modelling tool aquisition in organizations. Dissertation, University of Stockholm (2001)
11. Keller, W.: IT-Unternehmensarchitektur: Von der Geschäftsstrategie zur optimalen IT-Unterstützung. dpunkt-Verlag, Heidelberg (2007)
12. Fill, H.-G., Karagiannis, D.: On the conceptualisation of modelling methods using the ADOxx metamodelling platform. Enterp. Model. Inf. Syst. Architect. **8**(1), 4–25 (2013)
13. Checkland, P., Scholes, J.: Soft Systems Methodology in Action. Wiley, Chichester (1990)
14. Wolff, F., Frank, U.: A multiperspective framework for evaluating conceptual models in organisational change. In: Bartmann, D., et al. (eds.) ECIS 2005—13th European Conference on Information Systems: Information Systems in a Rapidly Changing Economy, pp. 1–12. Association for Information Systems, Regensburg (2005)
15. Renn, O.: The role of scientific input and public participation for technology assessment. In: Decker, M. (ed.) Interdisciplinary Technology Assessment, pp. 123–143. Springer, Berlin (2003)
16. Wigand, T.R., Picot, A., Reichwald, R.: Information, Organization and Management: Expanding Markets and Corporate Boundaries. Wiley, Chichester (1997)
17. Persson, A.: Enterprise modelling in practice: situational factors and their influence on adopting a participative approach. Dissertation, University of Stockholm (2001)
18. Frank, U.: Multiperspektivische Unternehmensmodellierung. Oldenbourg, München (1994)
19. Schütte, R.: Grundsätze ordnungsmäßiger Referenzmodellierung. Gabler, Wiesbaden (1998)
20. Wolff, F.: Evaluation chains for an integrated economic assessment of knowledge-based processes: study in the context of software reuse. In: Althoff, K., et al. (eds.) 3rd Conference on Professional Knowledge Management—Experiences and Visions: WM 2005. DFKI Kaiserslautern, pp. 237–240 (2005)
21. Walter, S.G., Spitta, T.: Approaches to the Ex-ante evaluation of investments into information systems. Wirtschaftsinformatik **46**(3), 171–180 (2004)
22. Eisenführ, F., Weber, M.: Rationales Entscheiden, 3rd edn. Springer, Berlin (1999)
23. Sterman, J.D.: Business Dynamics: Systems Thinking and Modelling for a Complex World. McGraw-Hill Companies, Boston (2000)
24. Kaplan, R.S., Norton, D.P.: The Balanced Scorecard: Translating Strategy into Action. Harvard Business School Press, Boston (MA) (1996)

25. Wöhe, G., Döring, U.: Einführung in die Allgemeine Betriebswirtschaftslehre, 22nd edn. Vahlen, München (2005)
26. Ulrich, H., Probst, G.: Anleitung zum ganzheitlichen Denken und Handeln, 2nd edn. Paul Haupt, Bern (1990)
27. Senge, P.M.: The Fifth Discipline: The Art and Practice of the Learning Organization. Doubleday Books, New York (1990)
28. Wolff, F.: Better Segmentation of Enterprise Modelling Governance through Usage Perspectives. The Practice of Enterprise Modeling, Proceedings PoEM 2014, LNBIP 197, pp 224–234. Springer (2014)
29. Pook, K.: Wissen im Fluß: Prozeßorientierung im Wissensmanagement unter Verwendung grafischer Modelle. Tenea, Berlin (2003)
30. Morello, F.: Creating incentive-driven tasks to improve knowledge management in sales chain relationships. In: Karagiannis, D., Reimer, U. (eds.) Proceedings of PAKM 2002, Vienna, Austria, pp. 87–96. Springer, Berlin (2002)
31. Foorthuis, R.M., van Steenbergen, M., Mushkudiani, N., Bruls, W., Brinkkemper, S., Bos, R.: On Course, but not there yet: enterprise architecture conformance and benefits in systems development. In: Proceedings of 31st ICIS 2010 (2010)
32. Van Belle, J.: Evaluation of Selected Enterprise Reference Models. In: Fettke, P., Loos, P. (eds.) Reference Modeling for Business Systems Analysis, pp. 266–286. Idea Group, Hershey (PA) (2007)
33. Ciborra, C.: Reframing the role of computers in organizations: the transaction costs approach. Off. Technol. People **3**(1), 17–38 (1987)
34. Davis, R.: Business Process Modelling with ARIS. Springer, London (2001)
35. Crosby, P.B.: Quality without Tears. McGraw-Hill Companies, Singapore (1984)

Part VII
Internet of Things/Future Internet

Algebraic Method to Model Secure IoT

Yeongbok Choe and Moonkun Lee

Abstract Process algebra can be considered to be one of the best methods to model IoT systems since it can represent the main properties of things in the systems: communication, movements, deadlines, etc. The best known algebras are *π-calculus* and *mobile ambient*. However, there are some limitations to model the different types of movements of the things with secure requirements. π-calculus passes the name of ports for indirect movements unrealistically, and mobile ambient uses ambient to synchronize asynchronous movements forcefully and unnaturally. This paper presents new process algebra, called *δ-calculus*, to model the different types of such synchronous movements for the things in IoT over some target geographical space. A process can be nested in another process, and their configuration will be changed by these movements. Any violation of the secure movements can be detected and prevented by the properties of the movements: synchrony, priority and deadline. To demonstrate the feasibility, a tool, called SAVE, was developed on the ADO*xx* metamodeling platform with an emergency medical system, which is one of the best suitable application domains for IoT.

Keywords Process algebra • δ-calculus • Modeling • Verification

1 Introduction

Internet of Things (IoT) is one of the most promising IT domains supported by smart devices: it consists of things connected together by Internet in order to provide users with intelligent services over some geographical area [1]. Since it deals with human lives and assets, as well as environment, it must provide them with complete security and privacy, namely *secure requirements* [2], to meet

Y. Choe · M. Lee (✉)
Chonbuk National University, Jeonbuk 561-756, Republic of Korea
e-mail: moonkun@jbnu.ac.kr

Y. Choe
e-mail: cyb0612@gmail.com

D. Karagiannis et al. (eds.), *Domain-Specific Conceptual Modeling*,
DOI 10.1007/978-3-319-39417-6_15

stakeholders' security needs. Any violation of the requirements may cost human lives and assets as well as destruction of environment. Therefore, it is critical to specify and verify all the requirements at the time of modeling the IoT systems with formal methods, as recommended by a number of international standards organizations (IoT-GSI).

Generally, formal methods can be classified into the following three mathematical structures: Logic, state machine and process algebra [3]. Among these, process algebra can be more suitable than other types to model the behavior of the IoT systems due to formal representation of things as processes, movements as interactions, and time and priority as IoT-related properties, with the support of algebraic equivalences for analysis of behaviors. The most well-known process algebras are *π-Calculus* [4] and *Mobile Ambient* [5] with their evolved versions [6].

π-calculus is designed by Robin Milner by extending the basic notion of CCS [7] to model the movement of processes based on the notion of value passing. Instead of representing the actual movements of a process (actor) from one process (source) to another process (target), the name of a port of the actor is passed from the source to the target to represent the movement of the actor. It can be considered as the imaginary indirect representation of the actual direct movements.

Mobile Ambient is designed by Luca Cardelli and Andrew D. Gordon with the new notion of ambient, which assists the movements of processes synchronously. Ambient provides a means for controlling asynchronous movements in synchronous manner, but it increases the complexity of specification with the additional dimension of the ambient. Consequently, the specification and verification of the movements become very complex and complicated. Moreover, some processes can fall into some deadlock state since no movement is possible for nested ambient.

These algebras and their evolved ones have the limitations to represent additional properties of IoT, such as geographical space of IoT, different types of movements of the things with different modes in time with priority, etc. In order to overcome the limitations, this paper introduces new process algebra, namely, *δ-calculus* [8], with the notion of the following geographical space and the distinctive properties of the movements:

- Geographical space: A geographical space can be defined as a system space, where all of its processes will be both processes and their child processes
- Movement types: There are two types of movements: *In* and *out*. The *in* is an interaction for one process to move into another process; the *out* is an interaction for one process to move out of its parent process.
- Movement modes: There are two modes of movements: *active* and *passive*. The *active* is an autonomous movement of a process to move in its sibling process or to move out of its parent process. The *passive* is a heteronomous movement for a process to be moved into its sibling process or to be moved out of its parent process.
- Time: The temporal properties of the movements are *ready time*, *interaction time*, *execution time* and *deadline*. In addition, the proper actions for the violations of deadlines can be specified.

- Priority: A discrete level of priority can be assigned to each process. Therefore, it is possible to control the accessibility of a process to another process.

These properties will provide the basic features to model the behavior of IoT on a specific geographical space.

The steps of modeling IoT are as follows:

- Specification: The first step is to specify IoT with δ-calculus. All the things in IoT will be specified on a geographical space with the detailed actions, especially, the movement actions with time and priority.
- Execution: The next step is to generate the execution tree for the specification. It shows all possible execution paths for the specification.
- Simulation: The next step is to simulate each execution path from the execution tree. It generates a *Geo-Temporal Space* (GTS) diagram for the simulation of each path.
- Verification: The last step is to verify all the secure requirements by model-checking [9] on all the simulation diagrams.

The secure requirements in the last step include dependencies among processes/things and their actions, especially prioritized temporal movements. They describe under what restrictions things or processes in IoT should behave.

The modeling approach based on δ-calculus can be considered as one of the most suitable methods to model IoT and verify its secure requirements. In order to demonstrate the justification and feasibility of the approach, a tool, called SAVE [10], was implemented on ADO*xx* [11].

The organization of the paper is as follows. Section 2 introduces the basic notions of δ-calculus, including syntax, semantics and algebraic laws with a simple example. Section 3 represents the models for the calculus: specification, execution and simulation models. Section 4 presents the SAVE tool on ADO*xx* and demonstrates feasibility of the approach with an IoT example. Finally, the conclusions are presented in Sect. 5.

2 Method Description: δ-Calculus

δ-calculus is a process algebra to model the behavior of processes by defining distribution of processes on a geographical space and their actions, especially movements in time and with priority.

2.1 Syntax

The syntax of δ-calculus is shown in Fig. 1. The description of each construct is as follows:

Fig. 1 Syntax of δ-calculus

$$
\begin{array}{|l|}
\hline
P ::= nil \mid A \mid P_{(n)} \mid P[Q] \mid P\langle r_t \rangle \mid P+Q \mid P|Q \mid A \bullet P \\
A ::= \varnothing \mid r_t(\overline{msg}) \mid r_t(msg) \mid M \\
M ::= m_t^p(k)\ P \mid P\ m(k)_t^p \\
m ::= in \mid out \mid get \mid put \\
\hline
\end{array}
$$

- Inaction (*nil*): No action for a process.
- Action (*A*): Actions performed by a process, such as empty, communication and movements.
- Priority ($P_{(n)}$): The priority of the process *P* represented by a natural number $n \geq 0$. The higher number represents the higher priority.
- Nesting (*P*[*Q*]): *P* contains *Q*.
- Channel ($P\langle r \rangle$): A channel *r* of *P* to communicate with other processes.
- Choice (*P* + *Q*): Only one of *P* and *Q* will be selected non-deterministically for execution if their priorities are similar. If the priorities are different, the process with the higher one will be selected.
- Parallel ($P|Q$): Both *P* and *Q* are running concurrently.
- Sequence ($A \cdot P$): P follows after action *A*.
- Empty action (∅): Do nothing for 1 unit time.
- Communication (*r*(*msg*); $r(\overline{msg})$): *P* communicates with other process connected with the channel *r* to pass the message *msg*. The mode of passing is indicated by $\overline{msg}$ for sending and *msg* for receiving.
- Movement request ($m_t^p(k)P$): A request for a movement to or from a target process with a key. Here *t*, *p* and *k* represent the time, priority and the password for the movement, respectively. The timing properties are described in detail in Sect. 2.4.
- Movement permission ($P\,m_t^p(k)$): The permission for the movement from the above request. The timing properties are described in detail in Sect. 2.4.

Basically, the movements are synchronous: The request to enter or move out requires permission from its target process in the autonomous case, and, similarly, the request to make another process to enter into or move out of itself has to require permission from the target process in the heteronomous case, too.

For example, the *Producer-Buffer-Consumer* (*PBC*) system with three main processes *Producer* (*P*), *Buffer* (*B*) and *Consumer* (*C*) with an additional process *Resource* (*R*) can be represented, in δ-calculus, in order to pass *R* to *C* through *B*, as follows:

$$
\begin{aligned}
PBC1 :&= P[R] \| B \| C;\\
P :&= PB(\overline{send}) \cdot put\, R \cdot exit;\\
B :&= PB(send) \cdot get\, R \cdot CB(need) \cdot put\, R \cdot exit;\\
C :&= CB(\overline{need}) \cdot get\, R \cdot exit;\\
R :&= P\, put \cdot B\, get \cdot B\, put \cdot C\, get \cdot exit;
\end{aligned}
$$

In *PBC*, *P* sends the *send* message to *B* through the *PB* channel to inform *B* to *put R*, and *puts R* out of its space. After receiving the message, *B gets R* and waits for the *need* message from *C* before *putting R*. After receiving the message, *B puts R* out of its space. C sends the *need* message to *C* to *get R*. If *C* receives the message, *C gets R*. *R* has been properly transported to *C* through *B*.

2.2 Semantics: Transition Rules

The semantics of δ-calculus are defined in Tables 1 and 2 as transition rules. The description of each rules in Table 1 are as follows:

- Action: It is a transition rule for the execution of a communication action *r*(*a*) on a channel *r* with a message *a*. It does not require any premise for the transition, after which *P* will has executed next.
- Choice: *ChoiceL* and *ChoiceR* transition rules can be equally chosen under the same premise. *ChoiceP* rule is determined by priority.
- Parallel: The transition of a process in *ParlL* and *ParlR* rules does not influence its parallel process. But *ParCom* rule requires that two parallel processes must synchronously interact with each other in order to make their corresponding transitions to be occurred.

The descriptions of each rule in Table 2 are as follows:

- Movement: *In*, *Out*, *Get* and *Put* transition rules represent the general synchronous movements. Each movement must have its corresponding co-movement. Similarly, *InP*, *OutP*, *GetP*, *PutP* rules are for the movements with priority.

Table 1 Communication semantics of δ-calculus

Action	$\frac{-}{r(a) \cdot P \xrightarrow{r(a)} P}$	ChoiceL	$\frac{P \xrightarrow{A} P'}{P+Q \xrightarrow{A} P'}$
ChoiceR	$\frac{Q \xrightarrow{A} Q'}{P+Q \xrightarrow{A} Q'}$	ParlL	$\frac{P \xrightarrow{A} P'}{P \mid Q \xrightarrow{A} P' \mid Q}$
ParlR	$\frac{Q \xrightarrow{A} Q'}{P \mid Q \xrightarrow{A} P \mid Q'}$	ParCom	$\frac{P \xrightarrow{A} P', Q \xrightarrow{A} Q'}{P \mid Q \xrightarrow{\tau} P' \mid Q'}$
NestO	$\frac{P \xrightarrow{A} P'}{P[Q] \xrightarrow{A} P'[Q]}$	NestI	$\frac{Q \xrightarrow{A} Q'}{P[Q] \xrightarrow{A} P[Q']}$
NestCom	$\frac{P \xrightarrow{A} P', Q \xrightarrow{A} Q'}{P[Q] \xrightarrow{\tau} P'[Q']}$		

Table 2 Movement semantics of δ-calculus

In	$\dfrac{P \xrightarrow{in\ Q} P',\ Q \xrightarrow{P\ in} Q'}{P \vert Q \xrightarrow{\delta} Q'[P']}$	Out	$\dfrac{P \xrightarrow{out\ Q} P',\ Q \xrightarrow{Q\ out} Q'}{Q[P] \xrightarrow{\delta} P' \vert Q'}$
Get	$\dfrac{P \xrightarrow{get\ Q} P',\ Q \xrightarrow{P\ get} Q'}{P \vert Q \xrightarrow{\delta} P'[Q']}$	Put	$\dfrac{P \xrightarrow{put\ Q} P',\ Q \xrightarrow{Q\ put} Q'}{P[Q] \xrightarrow{\delta} P' \vert Q'}$
InP	$\dfrac{P_{(n)} \xrightarrow{in^P\ Q} P'_{(n)}}{P_{(n)} \vert Q_{(m)} \xrightarrow{in^P\ Q} Q_{(m)}[P'_{(n)}]}(n>m)$		
OutP	$\dfrac{P_{(n)} \xrightarrow{out^P\ Q} P'_{(n)}}{Q_{(m)}[P_{(n)}] \xrightarrow{out^P\ Q} P'_{(n)} \vert Q_{(m)}}(n>m)$		
GetP	$\dfrac{P_{(n)} \xrightarrow{get^P\ Q} P'_{(n)}}{P_{(n)} \vert Q_{(m)} \xrightarrow{get^P\ Q} P'_{(n)}[Q_{(m)}]}(n>m)$		
PutP	$\dfrac{P_{(n)} \xrightarrow{put^P\ Q} P'_{(n)}}{P_{(n)}[Q_{(m)}] \xrightarrow{out^P\ Q} P'_{(n)} \vert Q_{(m)}}(n>m)$		
InN	$\dfrac{P \xrightarrow{in\ Q} P',\ Q \xrightarrow{P\ in} Q'}{P \vert Q[R] \xrightarrow{\delta} Q'[P' \vert R]}$	GetN	$\dfrac{P \xrightarrow{get\ Q} P',\ Q \xrightarrow{P\ get} Q'}{P[R] \vert Q \xrightarrow{\delta} P'[R \vert Q']}$

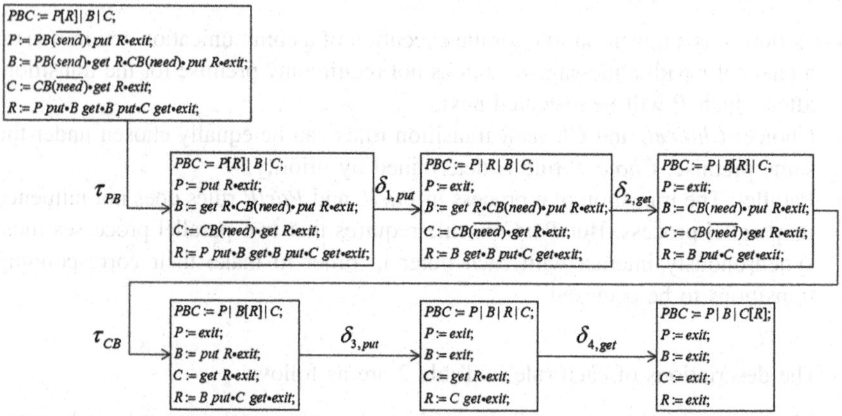

Fig. 2 A sequence of transitions for PBC example based on semantics

The timing requirements for the movement transition rules are described in detail in Sect. 2.4.

For example, Fig. 2 shows the execution of the *PBC* example by the transition rules of the communication (τ) in Table 1 and the movements (δ) in Table 2 as follows:

1. τ_{PB}: The communication between $P{:}\ PB(\overline{send})$ and $B{:}\ PB(send)$.
2. $\delta_{1,put}$: The *put* movement between $P{:}\ put\ R$ and $R{:}\ P\ put$.
3. $\delta_{2,get}$: The *get* movement between $B{:}\ get\ R$ and $R{:}\ B\ get$.

4. τ_{CB}: The communication between $C{:}\,CB(\overline{need})$ and $B{:}\,CB(need)$.
5. $\delta_{3,put}$: The *put* movement between $B{:}\,put\,R$ and $R{:}\,B\,put$.
6. $\delta_{4,get}$: The *get* movement between $C{:}\,get\,R$ and $R{:}\,C\,get$.

2.3 Laws

The algebraic laws are defined in Table 3. These laws are used to restructure the textual configuration of processes in a system or to reduce synchronous binary interactions, that is, communication and movements, between two interactive processes as a means of execution.

For example, the execution of the *PBC* example is supported by these algebraic laws as follows. Note that ':' implies 'of', such that $P{:}\,PB(\overline{send})$ implies the $PB(\overline{send})$ action of P:

$$
\begin{aligned}
PBC &= P[R] \| C|B \\
&= P[R] \| (C|B) && \text{(by associative law on|)} \\
&= (P[R] \| B)|C && \text{(by commutative and associative law on|)} \\
&= (P{:}\,PB(\overline{send})|B{:}\,PB(send))|C && \text{(by binary communication operation)} \\
&= (P{:}\,put\,R[R{:}\,P\,put]\|B)|C && \text{(by binary } put \text{ movement Operation)} \\
&= P|(R{:}\,B\,get|B{:}\,get\,R)|C && \text{(by associative laws and } get \text{ operation)} \\
&= P|(B{:}\,CB(need)[R]\|C{:}\,CB(\overline{need})) && \text{(by binary communication operation)} \\
&= (P|B{:}\,put\,R[R{:}\,B\,put])|C && \text{(by binary } put \text{ movement Operation)} \\
&= P|B|(R{:}\,B\,get|C{:}\,get\,R) && \text{(by associative laws and } get \text{ operation)} \\
&= P|B|C[R]
\end{aligned}
$$

Table 3 Laws of δ-calculus

Choice(1)	$P+P \equiv P$	Choice(2)	$P+Q \equiv Q+P$
Choice(3)	$(P+Q)+R$ $\equiv P+(Q+R)$	Parallel(1)	$P\|nil \equiv P$
Parallel(2)	$P\|Q \equiv Q\|P$	Parallel(3)	$(P\|Q)\|R \equiv P\|(Q\|R)$
Nesting(1)	$P[nil] \equiv P$	Nesting(2)	$R[P]+R[Q] \equiv R[P+Q]$
Distributive (1)	$P\|(Q+R)$ $\equiv (P\|Q)+(P\|R)$	Distributive (2)	$(A_1+A_2).P$ $\equiv A_1.P+A_2.P$

2.4 Time Property

There are four types of timing specifications in δ-calculus: system, process, communication and movements, as follows:

- System: The time properties for S are defined as a tuple (r, e, d) in the form of subscript to S, that is, $S_{(r,e,d)}$, where r, e and d imply *ready time*, *execution time* and *deadline* for S, respectively. Restrictions are $r \leq e$, $e \leq d$, and $r + e \leq d$. Note that all numbers are natural.
- Process: The properties for P are defined as $P_{(r,e,d)}$, same as those of S.
- Communication (τ): It is a synchronous interaction with a *send* action and its *receive* action. The time properties for both actions are as follows:
  - Send: The properties are defined as $send_{([l_s,u_s],e_s,d_s)}$, where $[l_s, u_s]$, e_s and d_s imply *time period* for synchronization, *execution time* and *deadline*, respectively. Restrictions are $l \leq u$, $(u-l) \leq e$ and $l + e \leq d$.
  - Receive: The properties are defined as $receive_{([l_r,u_r],e_r,d_r)}$, same as those of *send*.
- Movements (δ): Since it is a synchronous interaction as communication, the specifications are the same as those of *send*, for the movement actions that request movements (*requester*), and *receive*, for the movement actions that permit the request (*permitter*). The additional time for the movement is defined as $move_{([l,u],[e,e_m],d_s)}$, where e_m is the execution time for the movement. It is only applicable to the process that actually moves, namely, *mover*.

For example, the following is a *PBC* example with timing properties. There are the timing specifications for system, processes and actions. Note that the actual time for the movement of R is 8 in total, which is less than the execution time 10 of R.

$$PBC1_{[0,15,25]} = P_{[0,10,20]}[R_{[0,10,15]}] \| B_{[0,15,20]} | C_{[0,10,20]};$$

$$P_{[0,10,20]} = PB(\overline{send})_{([0,2],1,-)} \cdot put\,R_{([0,2],1,-)} \cdot exit;$$

$$B_{[0,15,20]} = PB(send)_{([1,3],1,-)} \cdot get\,R_{([0,2],1,-)} \cdot CB(need)_{([1,3],1,-)} \cdot put\,R_{([0,2],1,-)} \cdot exit;$$

$$C_{[0,10,20]} = CB(\overline{need})_{([0,2],1,-)} \cdot get\,R_{([0,2],1,-)} \cdot exit;$$

$$R_{[0,10,15]} = P\,put_{([0,2],[1,2],4)} \cdot B\,get_{([0,2],[1,2],4)} \cdot B\,put_{([0,2],[1,2],4)} \cdot C\,get_{([0,2],[1,2],4)} \cdot exit;$$

3 Method Conceptualization: Models for δ-Calculus

There are three different types of models for δ-calculus: specification, execution and simulation.

3.1 Specification Model: System and Process

A system model is defined as the following tuple: $S = (P, C, I, T)$, where P is a set of processes described by δ–calculus, C is a set of channels between processes, I is the set of inclusion relations among the processes in P, and T is the global clock. The graphical icons for System View are shown in Table 4, with its metamodeling definition.

System View is the view with processes interacting with each other over some geographical space. In the view, a process will be represented as a node and a channel as an edge between nodes. A node can be nested in another node. Any movement can be represented as a movement edge, and it changes the configuration of the view.

A process model is defined as a sequence of actions: $P = (a_1 \cdot a_2 \cdot \cdots \cdot a_n, t)$, where a_i's are the actions in order defined in δ–calculus and t is a local clock. The graphical icons for process view are shown in Table 5, with its metamodeling definition.

As stated, system and process views represent graphically a system and its processes, respectively. For the complete specification of a system, there should be 1–1 correspondence between each node in system view and its process view. Further for each interaction, there should be 1–1 correspondence between a synchronizing action of a synchronizer and the synchronized action of its synchronisee. These correspondences guarantee the proper structural condition for syntactical completeness. If not, the proper execution of the system cannot be performed due to syntactic inconsistence.

Process View shows the detailed actions of each process in System View. There is 1–1 correspondence between each action of process in δ-calculus and Process View icon, except *start* and *end* icons.

Table 4 Process modeling definition with icons

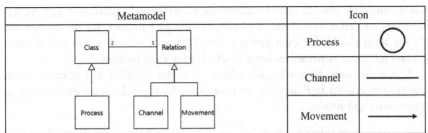

Metamodel	Icon	
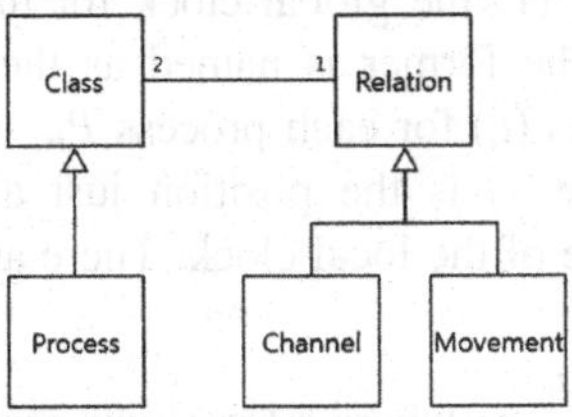	Process	
	Channel	
	Movement	

Table 5 Process model definition with icons

Metamodel

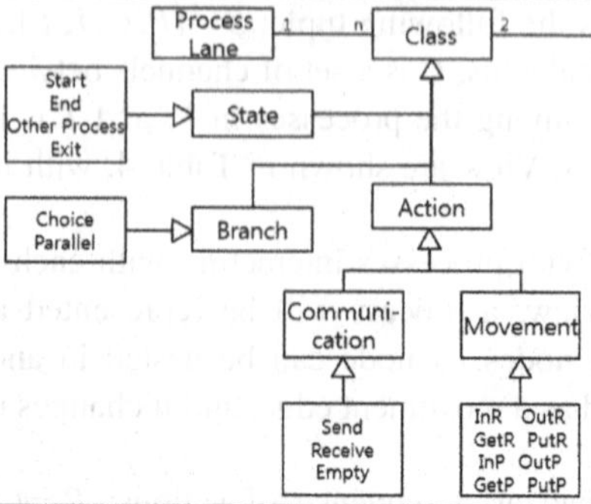

Icon

Process Lane		Start		End		Other Process	
Exit		Choice		Parallel		Send	
Receive		Empty		In R		Out R	
Get R		Put R		In P		Out P	
Get P		Put P		Sequence			

3.2 Execution Model: Labelled Transition System

The execution model for the system is based on the notion of system state and its transition. Since the system consists of processes, its state is defined as a set of states of its processes with the two additional state variables: a set of inclusion relations among processes and a global clock. The inclusion relations are due to the changes of the system configuration as a result of the movement actions, and every action consumes time. In order to control such a temporal synchrony of actions, it is necessary to define two types of clocks: (1) the global clock for the system and (2) the local clocks for each process. The former is named as the global clock (T) and the latter is named as local clocks (t_i) for each process P_i.

A *process state* is $p_i = (\cdot_i, t_i)$, where $\cdot_i$ is the position just after a_i in the sequence of actions in P and t_i is the time of the local clock. There are two special states: *start* and *final*.

A *system state transition* is $p_{j-1} \xrightarrow{a_j^t = (a_j, t_j)} p_j$, where a transition occurs from p_{j-1} to p_j by an action a_j, which takes the time t_i.

The transition is based on the rules defined in the semantics of δ-calculus. For example, if $p_0 = (0, 0)$ and the first action of sending a message on the channel c in P occurs in the time 2, then $p_1 = (1, 2)$ by $p_0 \xrightarrow{c(\bar{m}), 2} p_1$.

The *execution model* for processes in δ-calculus is $p_0 \xrightarrow{a_1^{t_1}} p_1 \xrightarrow{a_2^{t_2}} p_2 \rightarrow \cdots \rightarrow p_f$, where each p_i is a process state, which is transited to the next state after performing an action a_i in the time t_i. There are two special states, s_0 and s_f, for the *start* and *final* states, respectively.

It is possible not only to have multiple transitions from one process state, but also to one process state. Moreover, it is possible not only to have no *final* state, but also to have multiple *final* states. However, there should be a single *start* state.

A *system state* is $s_i = ((p_{1,i}, p_{2,i}, \cdots, p_{n,i}), I_i, C_i, T_i)$, where each $p_{j,i}$, I_i, C_i and t_i represent the state of each process P_i, a set of the inclusion relations among processes, a set of channels and the global time, respectively.

A *system state transition* between one system state to another state is $s_j \xrightarrow{i_j^t} s_{j+1}$, where $i_j = \left((P_a{:}\,a, P_{\bar{a}}{:}\,\bar{a}), t_j\right)$. Here s_j and s_{j+1} are system states, i_j^t is a synchronous interaction between processes P_a and $P_{\bar{a}}$ with the action a of P_a and the action $\bar{a}$ of $P_{\bar{a}}$ in the time t_j. The transition is based on the rules defined in the semantics of δ-calculus.

The system execution model for δ-calculus is the labelled transition system: $s_0 \xrightarrow{i_1} s_1 \xrightarrow{i_2} s_2 \rightarrow \cdots \rightarrow s_f$. Each s_j represents a system state, and i_k does a system state transition. There are two special states, s_0 and s_f, for *first* and *final* states, respectively.

It is possible not only to have multiple transitions from one system state, but also to one system state. Moreover, it is possible not only to have no *final* state, but also to have multiple *final* states. However, there should be a single *start* state.

The graphical icons for Execution View are shown in Table 6, with its metamodeling definition. The view is represented as *Execution Tree* (ET).

Table 6 Execution model definition with icons

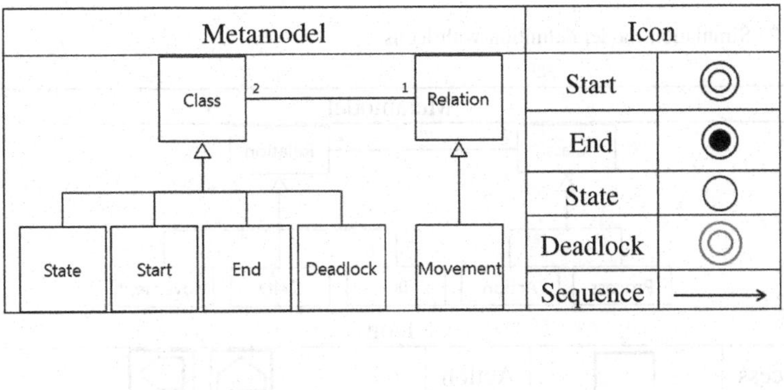

3.3 Simulation Model: GTS Diagram

The *simulation model* for system S is represented by the following tuple: $\mathbf{S}=(\mathbf{P},\mathbf{I})$, where $\mathbf{P}=\{\mathbf{P}_1,\ldots,\mathbf{P}_n\}$ with $\mathbf{P}_i$ for each process P_i in the system S, and $\mathbf{I}=\{\mathbf{i}_1^{t_1},\ldots,\mathbf{i}_m^{t_m}\}$ with $\mathbf{i}_j^{t_j}$ for each interaction in the system transitions. Further each $\mathbf{P}_i$ is represented by the following sequence: $\mathbf{P}_i=\langle \mathbf{a}_{j,1}^{t_{j,1}},\cdots,\mathbf{a}_{j,j_n}^{t_{j,jn}}\rangle$, where each $\mathbf{a}_i$ is the simulated action in the time t_i.

The graphical icons for simulation view are shown in Table 7, with its metamodeling definition. The view is represented as *Geo-Temporal Space* (GTS) diagram, where all the processes, their actions and the interactions among them are represented as GTS blocks with the following restrictions:

- Syntactic restriction:
  - Action blocks in P_i cannot be overlapped in any space at any time in the GTS block of P_i, that is, $\mathbf{P}_i$.
  - If $P|Q$, there is no overlap in their GTS blocks, but an overlap in time.
  - If $P[Q]$, there is an overlap of the Q GTS block over the P GTS block during the period of time for inclusion.
- Semantics restrictions for communication:
  - The sender P GTS block and the receiver Q GTS block must be in the same time period in their GTS blocks.
- Semantic restriction for movements:
  - For the active *in* movement, the mover Q GTS block must be in the same space with the target P GTS block at the same period of time.
  - For the active *out* movement, the mover Q GTS block must be in the target P GTS block at the same period of time.

Table 7 Simulation model definition with icons

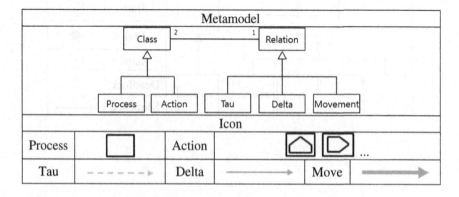

Metamodel					
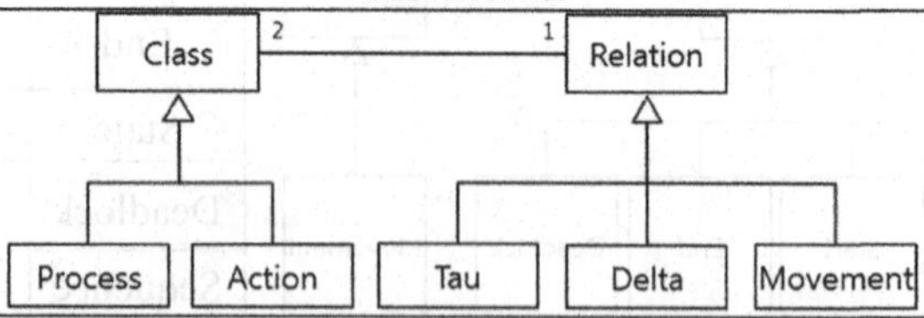					
Icon					
Process		Action	 ...		
Tau		Delta		Move	

- For the passive *get* movement, the mover *Q* GTS block must be in the same space with the target *P* GTS block at the same period of time.
- For the passive *put* movement, the mover *Q* GTS block must be in the target *P* GTS block at the same period of time.

4 Proof of Concept

4.1 SAVE Tool

A tool, called SAVE (*Specification, Analysis, Verification Environment*), for δ-calculus was developed on ADO*xx* [11], as shown in Fig. 3. It consists of four basic components as follows:

- Modeler: It provides capability to specify system and process views.
- EM Generator: It generates an execution model, in *Execution Tree* (ET), for the views and makes each path of the model to be selected for simulation.
- Simulator: It generates a model for the selected simulation, in a GTS diagram.
- Verifier: It verifies the secure requirements of the system by model-checking on the diagrams.

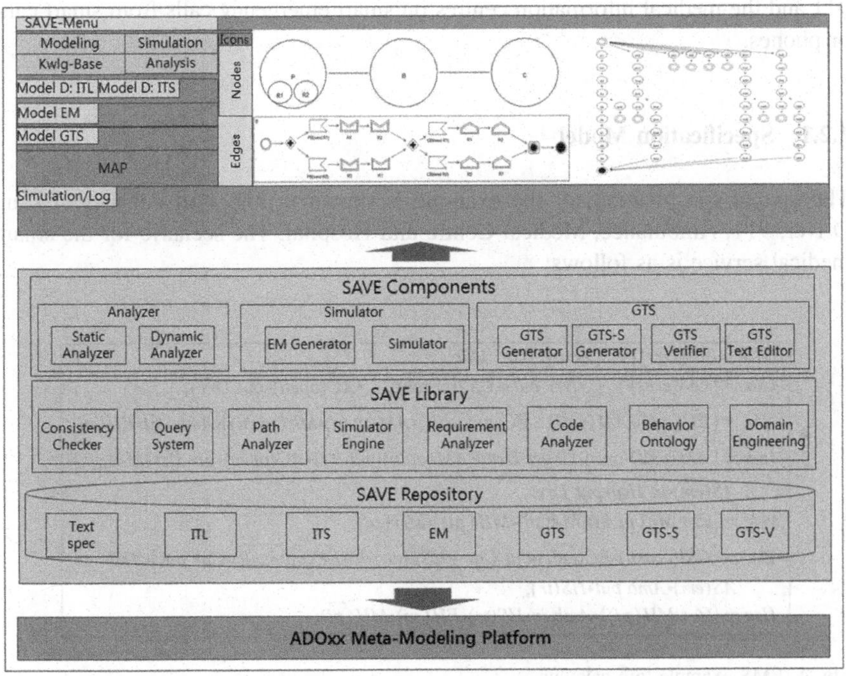

Fig. 3 SAVE architecture

The graphical representations of the models in SAVE are designed by the ADO*xx* Development Tool, and the procedures of its components are built from the ADO*xx* libraries. The detailed logics of the procedures are programmed in the AdoScript language. ADO*xx* provides three layers to implement mechanisms and algorithms for SAVE:

- First layer: The pre-defined functionality, a basic set of features most commonly used by modeling tools.
- Second Layer: Approximately, 400 APIs for the generation of objects, editing of their properties, etc.
- Third layer: Ways of interaction to outside of ADO*xx*. The simple interaction is by exporting and importing XML files.

SAVE uses the functionalities of the first layer to implement the graphical elements and attributes of the graphic models, and it uses those of the second layer to implement Modeler, EM Generator, Simulator, and Verifier.

4.2 *IoT Application: EMS Example*

Emergency medical system (EMS) is one of the best applications for IoT [1]. The system provides drivers with smart emergency medical services at the time of accidents. The services are realized by integrated intelligent systems between the 911 and the medical information centres on smart emergency calls from smart cars or phones.

4.2.1 Specification Model

The textual specification for the example is shown in Fig. 4. It consists of Car, Driver, 911, Ambulance, Medical Centre and Hospital. The scenario for the smart medical service is as follows:

$$
\begin{aligned}
EMS &:= Car[Drv] \mid 911[Amb] \mid Hsp \mid Mdc; \\
Car &:= \left(CS1(\overline{crash})_{[0,60]} \bullet Drv\ out + CS2(\overline{crash})_{[61,-]} \bullet AC(open) \bullet put\ Drv \right); \\
911 &:= \left(EC(call) \bullet AM(\overline{call}) + EC(autocall) \bullet AM(\overline{auto}) \bullet ME(\overline{pi,hi}) \right) \bullet Amb\ out \bullet EH(pi); \\
Amb &:= \left(AM(call) \bullet out\ 911 \bullet get\ Drv + AM(auto) \bullet out\ 911 \bullet AC(\overline{open}) \bullet get\ Drv \bullet MA(pi) \right) \bullet \\
&\quad AS(\overline{em}) \bullet in\ Hsp \bullet put\ Drv; \\
Mdc &:= \left(\varnothing + ME(pi,hi) \bullet MA(\overline{pi}) \bullet MH(\overline{pi}) \right) \bullet MH(pi); \\
Drv &:= \left(CS1(crash) \bullet EC(\overline{call}) \bullet out\ Car + CS2(crash) \bullet EC(\overline{autocall}) \bullet Car\ put \right) \bullet Amb\ get \bullet \\
&\quad AS(em) \bullet Amb\ put \bullet HS(tr); \\
Hsp &:= (\varnothing + MH(pi)) \bullet Amb\ in \bullet HS(\overline{tr}) \bullet EH(\overline{pi}) \bullet MH(\overline{pi});
\end{aligned}
$$

Fig. 4 EMS example in δ-calculus

1. At the time of an accident, Car calls Driver.
2. If Driver receives the call in 60 unit times, Driver makes an emergency call *manually* to 911 to inform the accident and moves out of the car. If not, Driver makes the call *automatically* and will be moved out of car later by Ambulance.
3. When 911 receives a call from Driver, it informs Ambulance to go to the location of the accident to handle the 'manual' or 'automatic' call cases. In case of the automatic call, additionally, it sends Driver ID, with Hospital ID, to Medical Centre to get the medical information of Driver.
4. Ambulance goes to Car and handles the situation. For the manual case, Driver takes on Ambulance and gets the first aid treatment. For the automatic case, Ambulance takes Driver on, gets Driver's medical information requested by 911, makes the information-based first aid treatment, and informs Medical Centre of the treatment. After the treatment, it takes Driver to Hospital for the further medical treatment.
5. Medical Centre receives the ID's of Driver and Hospital, it sends Driver's medical information to Ambulance and Hospital. And later, it will get Driver's medical status from Hospital after the medical treatment.
6. Hospital receives Driver's medical information from Medical centre and treats Driver based on the information at the time of Driver's arrival by Ambulance. After the treatment, it informs both 911 and Medical Centre of Driver's medical status.

Figure 5 shows System View for EMS in SAVE on ADO*xx*. This is the first configuration of EMS before the accident. There are four main processes, that is, Car with Driver, 911 with Ambulance, Hospital and Medical Centre.

Figure 6 shows Process Views for EMS in SAVE on ADO*xx*. There are 6 processes. Each corresponds to each process in System View. There is 1–1 correspondence between each action of process in the EMS code and the node of the action in its Process View, except *start* and *final* nodes.

4.2.2 Execution Model

Figure 7 shows the execution tree for EMS example. Each path in the tree represents one possible execution path for the example. There are total 32 possible execution paths in the tree. It is due to six choice operators from each process in composition with two complemented alternatives, which means that there is no need to make composition of their respective choices: $2^{6-1} = 2^5 = 32$ case of the composition.

Further it shows that there are only two possible cases for normal termination: one for the manual call case on the left-most side of the figure and another for the automatic call case on the right-most. The rest of cases between the sides are deadlock.

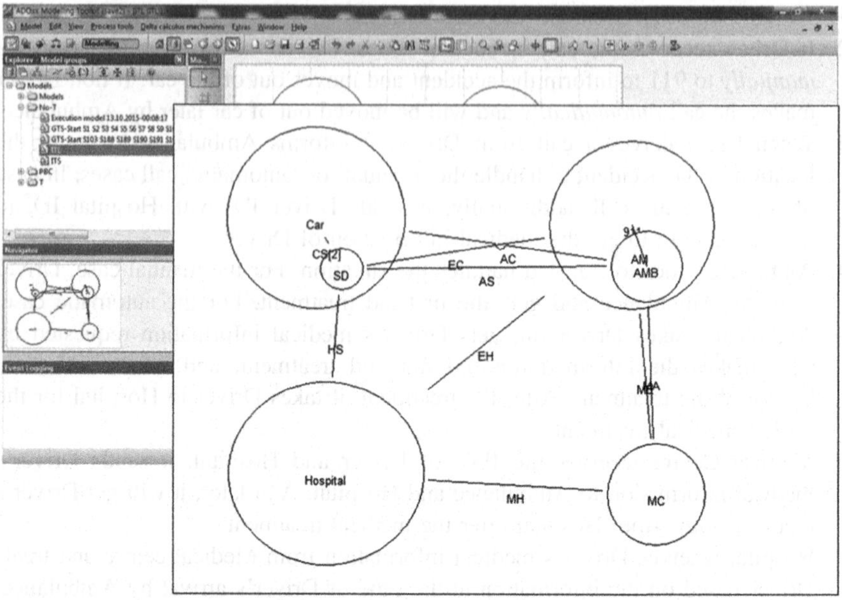

Fig. 5 System view for EMS example

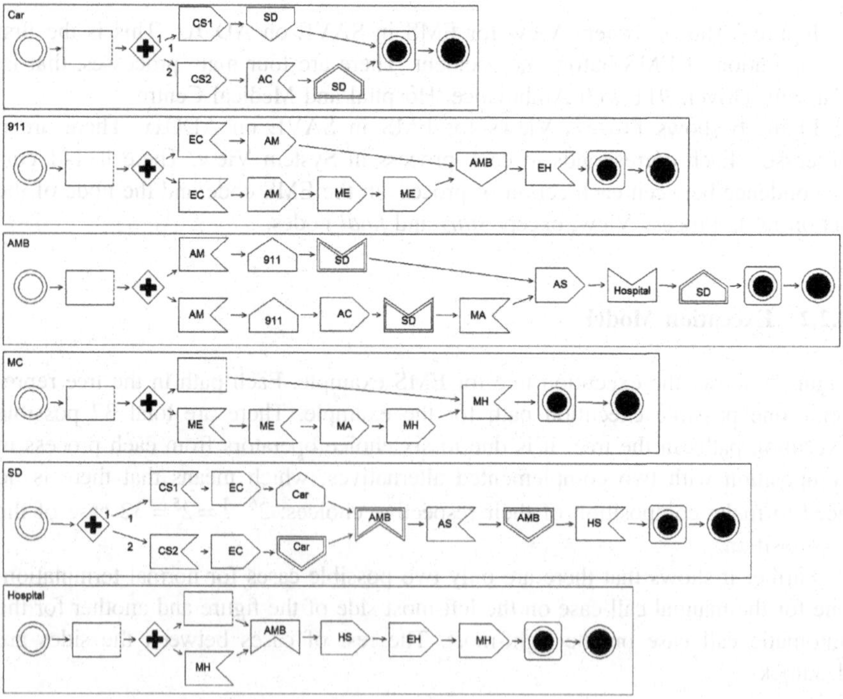

Fig. 6 Process views for EMS example

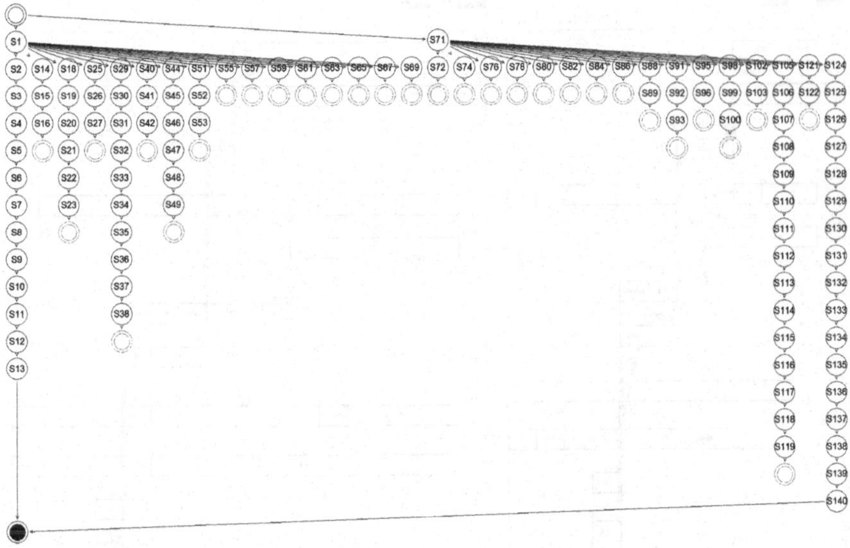

Fig. 7 Execution tree for EMS example

4.2.3 Simulation Model

Figure 8 shows the simulation data, in GTS diagrams, generated for two execution paths of the normal termination from the execution tree, based on the interactions listed in Table 8. The one on the right is for the manual call case and the one on the left is for the automatic call case. The communication and movement interactions in the table are represented as interaction edges between action blocks and their co-action blocks in the diagrams.

Both diagrams show that Ambulance moves from 911 to Car to take Driver on and transports Driver to Hospital in time. Both also show that the pre-defined calls are conducted among 911, Ambulance, Hospital and Medical Centre in order to automate the smart EMS service.

4.3 Verification

The last step of modeling process is to verify the secure requirements of the EMS example by model-checking the simulation data in the GTS diagrams for the requirements. There can be a number of dependencies among interactions to be considered as the requirements. Some of the secure requirements for the example can be summarized as follows:

- R1: Accident must be notified to 911 before Ambulance leaves 911.
- R2: Type of Accident must be known before Ambulance arrives at the scene.

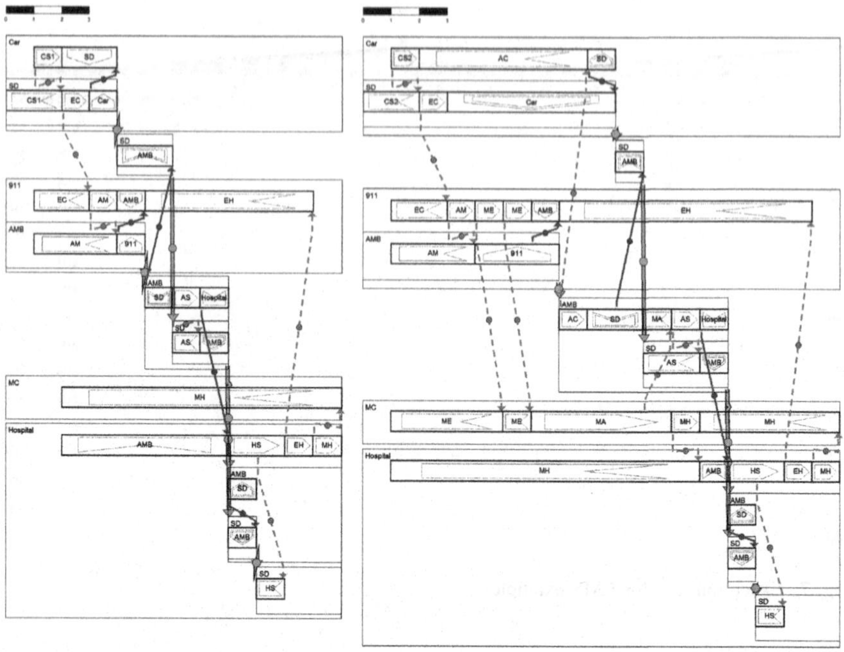

Fig. 8 Simulation data for 2 normal execution paths in EMS example

Table 8 List of interactions from simulations for Path 1 and 32 in execution tree

Simulation for Path 1	Simulation for Path 32
$\tau_1 = ((Car\colon CS1(\overline{crash}), Drv\colon CS1(crash)), 1)$	$\tau_1 = ((Car\colon CS2(\overline{crash}), Drv\colon CS2(crash)), 1)$
$\tau_2 = ((Drv\colon EC(\overline{call}), 911\colon EC(call)), 2)$	$\tau_2 = ((Drv\colon EC(\overline{autocall}), 911\colon EC(autocall)), 2)$
$\delta_1 = ((Drv\colon out\,Car, Car\colon Drv\,out), 3)$	$\tau_3 = ((911\colon AM(\overline{auto}), Amb\colon AM(auto)), 3)$
$\tau_3 = ((911\colon AM(\overline{call}), Amb\colon AM(call)), 3)$	$\tau_4 = ((911\colon ME(\overline{pi,hi}), Mdc\colon ME(pi,hi)), 4)$
$\delta_2 = ((911\colon Amb\,out, Amb\colon out\,911), 4)$	$\delta_1 = ((Amb\colon out\,911, 911\colon Amb\,out), 6)$
$\delta_3 = ((Amb\colon get\,Drv, Drv\colon 911\,get), 5)$	$\tau_7 = ((Amb\colon AC(\overline{open}), Car\colon AC(open)), 7)$
$\tau_4 = ((Amb\colon AS(\overline{em}), Drv\colon AS(em)), 6)$	$\delta_2 = ((Car\colon put\,Drv, Drv\colon Car\,put), 8)$
$\delta_4 = ((Amb\colon in\,Hsp, Hsp\colon 911\,in), 7)$	$\delta_3 = ((Amb\colon get\,Drv, Drv\colon Amb\,get), 9)$
$\delta_5 = ((Amb\colon put\,Drv, Drv\colon 911\,put), 8)$	$\tau_5 = ((Mdc\colon MA(\overline{pi}), Mdc\colon MA(pi)), 10)$
$\tau_5 = ((Hsp\colon HS(\overline{tr}), Drv\colon HS(tr)), 9)$	$\tau_6 = ((Mdc\colon MH(\overline{pi}), Mdc\colon MH(pi)), 11)$
$\tau_6 = ((Hsp\colon EH(\overline{pi}), 911\colon EH(pi)), 10)$	$\tau_8 = ((Amb\colon AS(\overline{em}), Drv\colon SA(em)), 11)$
$\tau_7 = ((Hsp\colon MH(\overline{pi}), Mdc\colon MH(pi)), 11)$	$\delta_4 = ((Amb\colon in\,Hsp, Hsp\colon 911\,in), 12)$
	$\delta_5 = ((Amb\colon put\,Drv, Drv\colon 911\,put), 13)$
	$\tau_9 = ((Hsp\colon HS(\overline{tr}), Drv\colon HS(tr)), 14)$
	$\tau_{10} = ((Hsp\colon EH(\overline{pi}), 911\colon EH(pi)), 15)$
	$\tau_{11} = ((Hsp\colon MH(\overline{pi}), Mdc\colon MH(pi)), 16)$

Table 9 Secure requirements for simulations 1 and 2

Requirements	Simulation of Path 1	Simulation of Path 32
R1	$\tau_2 < \delta_2$	$\tau_2 < \delta_1$
R2	$\tau_2 < \delta_2$	$\tau_2 < \delta_1$
R3	$\tau_2 \rightarrow (T \rightarrow \tau_5)$	N/A
R4	N/A	$\tau_2 \rightarrow (\tau_5 \rightarrow \tau_8)$
R5	$\tau_4 < \delta_5$	$\tau_8 < \delta_5$
R6	$\tau_2 \rightarrow (T \rightarrow \tau_5)$	N/A
R7	N/A	$\tau_2 \rightarrow (\tau_5 \rightarrow \delta_5)$
R8	$\tau_5 < (\tau_6 \wedge \tau_7)$	$\tau_9 < (\tau_{10} \wedge \tau_{11})$
R9	$((T(\tau_4) - (T(\tau_1)) \leq 15$	$((T(\tau_8) - (T(\tau_1)) \leq 15$
R10	$((T(\delta_5) - (T(\tau_1)) \leq 30$	$((T(\delta_5) - (T(\tau_1)) \leq 30$

- R3: In case of the manual call, no driver's medical information is needed for first aid treatment by Ambulance.
- R4: In case of the automatic call, driver's medical information is needed for first aid treatment by Ambulance.
- R5: Driver should be treated at first by Ambulance before being arrived at Hospital.
- R6: In case of the manual call, no driver's medical information is needed for treatment at Hospital.
- R7: In case of the automatic call, driver's medical information is needed for treatment at Hospital.
- R8: After the treatment at Hospital, Hospital must inform the results to both 911 and Medical Centre.
- R9: Driver must be treated first in 15 unit times by Ambulance.
- R10: Driver must be transported to Hospital in 30 unit times by Ambulance for the further medical treatment.

These requirements can be represented as the dependency relations among the interactions in Table 8 for both simulations, as shown in Table 9.

By checking the simulation data for each case, it can be verified if all the requirements in Table 9 are satisfied by the relations among the interactions and their timing properties in Table 8.

Finally, it can be concluded that the secure requirements for the example is valid for the specification in δ-calculus.

5 Conclusion

This paper presented a formal method to specify the IoT systems in a process algebra, called δ-calculus, and verify the secure requirements by generating all the possible execution paths from the execution tree for the specification, simulating all the cases of the executions from the tree and model-checking the results of all the cases to verify the secure requirements.

In order to develop the method, a tool, called SAVE, was developed on the ADO*xx* metamodeling platform and the approach in the method was demonstrated with an EMS example in SAVE. SAVE consists of four components: modeler, EM generator, simulator and verifier. For example, modeler allows to specify system view for EMS and Process Views for each processes in EMS. After specification, EM generator produces an execution tree for EMS, which consists of 32 possible execution paths: 30 abnormal cases as deadlock and Two cases for normal termination. From the tree, the two normal cases were selected for the simulation and generated the GTS diagrams as a result of the simulation. Finally, Verifier verified the secure requirements for EMS by model-checking the diagrams to see whether the requirements are satisfied or not in the diagrams.

Recently, the case study for a more complex EMS example was reported in [12] to demonstrate capability of reducing a considerable amount of execution paths in the execution tree with complement and conjunctive choices, from 15,823 paths to 6 paths. It will be a challenging work to apply the reduction method to the real industrial examples.

δ-calculus can be one of the best suitable methods to model IoT systems and SAVE can be one of the practical tools to realize the method in practice.

Acknowledgments This work was supported by Basic Science Research Programs through the National Research Foundation of Korea (NRF) funded by the Ministry of Education (2010-0023787), and the MISP (Ministry of Science, ICT and Future Planning), Korea, under the ITRC (Information Technology Research Centre) support program (IITP-2015-H8501-15-1012) supervised by the IITP (Institute for Information & Communications Technology Promotion), and Space Core Technology Development Program through the NRF (National Research Foundation of Korea) funded by the Ministry of Science, ICT and Future Planning (NRF-2014M1A3-A3A02034792), and Basic Science Research Program through the National Research Foundation of Korea (NRF) funded by the Ministry of Education (NRF-2015R1D1A3A01019282).

Tool Download http://www.omilab.org/save.

References

1. Whitmore, A., Agarwal, A., Xu, L.D.: The internet of things—a survey of topics and trends. Inf. Syst. Front. **17**(2), 261–274 (2015)
2. Larcom, B.: Secure Requirement. https://www.frisc.no/arrangementer/finse-winter-school-2014/ (2014)
3. Heitmeyer, C., Mandrioli, D.: Formal Methods for Real-Time Computing: An Overview, Formal Methods for Real-Time Computing, pp. 1–32. Wiley (1996)
4. Milner, R., Parrow, J., Walker, D.: A calculus of mobile processes (i-ii). Inf. Comput. **100**, 1–77 (1992)
5. Cardelli, L., Gordon, A.: Mobile ambients. In: Nivat, M. (ed.) ETAPS 1998 and FOSSACS 1998, LNCS, vol. 1378, pp. 140–155. Springer, Heidelberg (1998)

6. Lin, H.: Predicate μ-calculus for mobile ambients. J. Comput. Sci. Technol. **20**(1), 95–104 (2005)
7. Milner, R.: A Calculus of Communicating Systems. Springer, New York (1982)
8. Choe, Y., Lee, M.: δ-calculus: process algebra to model secure movements of distributed mobile processes in real-time business application. In: 23rd European Conference on Information Systems (2015)
9. Clarke, E.M., Emerson, E.A.: Design and synthesis of synchronization skeletons using branching-time temporal logic. In: Kozen, D. (ed.) Proceedings of the Workshop on Logic of Programs, Yorktown Heights, vol. 131 of Lecture Notes in Computer Science, pp. 52–71. Springer (1981)
10. Choe, Y., Choi, W., Jeon, G., Lee, M.: A Tool for Visual Specification and Verification for Secure Process Movements, eChallenges e-2015, Nov 2015
11. Fill, H., Karagiannis, D.: On the conceptualisation of modelling methods using the ADOxx meta modelling platform. Enterp. Modell. Inf. Syst. Arch. **8**(1), 4–25 (2013)
12. Choi, W., Choe, Y., Lee, M.: A reduction method for process and system complexity with conjunctive and complement choices in a process algebra. In: IEEE 39th Annual International Computer, Software and Applications Conference (2015)

Security Requirements Engineering for Cloud Computing: The Secure Tropos Approach

Haralambos Mouratidis, Nikolaos Argyropoulos and Shaun Shei

Abstract Security is considered an important aspect of software systems, especially in the context of cloud computing. Nevertheless, current practices towards securing software systems fail to take into account security issues during the early development stages and also cannot properly address the unique characteristics and needs of the cloud environment. To address such issues, Secure Tropos was developed as a security-oriented requirements engineering approach, offering a modeling language and sets of diagrams which facilitate the elicitation and elaboration of security features for software systems. In this work, we introduce Secure Tropos by discussing its main concepts, their relations and the main diagrams used to capture the different aspects of a software system. SecTro, a CASE tool developed specifically for the creation and analysis of Secure Tropos diagrams, is used to model a case study as an illustrative example. Finally, future work on expanding the functionalities offered by Secure Tropos is discussed.

Keywords Information Security · Cloud computing · Security requirements engineering · Security modeling · Secure Tropos

1 Introduction

It is widely recognized that security is an important aspect of any software system that stores and/or handles sensitive and confidential information. It is therefore expected that software system developers are able to develop and deploy very

H. Mouratidis (✉) · N. Argyropoulos · S. Shei
Secure and Dependable Software Systems (Sense), Research Cluster,
University of Brighton, Brighton BN2 4GJ, UK
e-mail: H.Mouratidis@brighton.ac.uk

N. Argyropoulos
e-mail: N.Argyropoulos@brighton.ac.uk

S. Shei
e-mail: S.Shei@brighton.ac.uk

D. Karagiannis et al. (eds.), *Domain-Specific Conceptual Modeling*,
DOI 10.1007/978-3-319-39417-6_16

secure systems. However, this is not always the case. One of the main reasons for that is that software system developers, lacking a strong background in computer security, are asked to develop secure software systems without appropriate modeling languages and methodologies to guide them during the development process. As a result, security is usually considered as an afterthought, meaning that security enforcement mechanisms have to be fitted into a pre-existing design. This often leads to the resulting information systems being afflicted with security vulnerabilities, which are often the major cause of system security disasters and require costly readjustments.

The emergence of cloud computing for the provision of number of services (e.g., email, data storage and web content management) further amplifies the issue of problematic security implementations. As a result, some organizations are still hesitant to fully commit to this technology because of the negative publicity regarding data-breaches [1, 2], security leaks [3] as well as interoperability and compatibility issues when migrating towards cloud environments [4–6]. Moreover, through the extension of existing technologies to fit the context of cloud computing, we also inherit the security issues and vulnerabilities of each [7]. This creates a complicated scenario where we need to consider security from multiple perspectives.

This problematic situation is mainly caused by the current lack of standardized modeling languages and approaches to holistically capture computing environments, both traditional and cloud-based, in the context of software security. Therefore, the development of secure software systems is in need of a holistic modeling language that captures both the customer requirements and cloud services in the context of security [7]. Moreover such requirements, along with potential security issues have to be identified and elaborated early in the development process.

It is therefore essential for security to be considered from the early stages and throughout the software development lifecycle, especially in the security-critical environment of cloud computing. Nevertheless, to follow such paradigm, sound software engineering methodologies and practices need to be developed that support the simultaneous analysis of both security and software requirements; they also need to be transformed into an appropriate design and the implementation of that design. Additionally, in order to support the design of secure cloud solutions, it is important to introduce techniques that will be based on appropriate modeling languages which will enable modeling of concepts that are unique in the context of the cloud.

We argue that by modeling software systems based on security requirements, we are able to capture and address security issues which would otherwise impact the system after implementation. In this work, we will test this hypothesis through a running example of a healthcare system. As illustrated in Fig. 1 the investigated system aims to support the creation and storage of electronic prescriptions the medical personnel depends on for the provision of treatment to patients. Because of the sensitive nature of the information required for the creation of such prescription documents (e.g., patient information), a number of critical security issues arise which need to be addressed, preferably during the design of the system.

In order to achieve that, the Secure Tropos methodology will be used, as it provides a structured approach for goal-oriented security requirements, applicable to

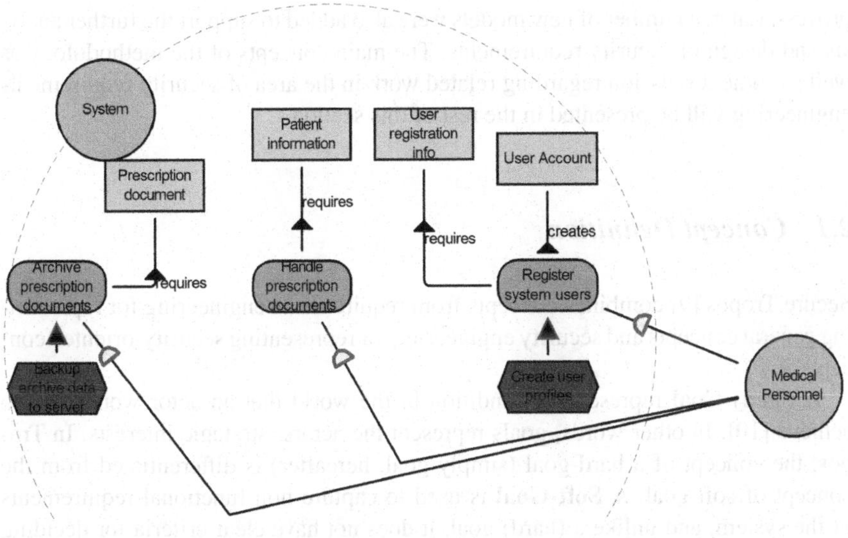

Fig. 1 An overview of the e-prescription system

traditional software systems and cloud computing environments. The Secure Tropos methodology provides a modeling language that represents security requirements through security constraints, allowing developers to model multi-agent, software systems and their organizational environment by using actors, goals and relational links such as dependencies. The novelties introduced by this approach are the following:

- Allowing developers not only to model but also to reason about the technical as well as the social issues of security.
- Allowing developers to represent security concerns at different levels of software description.
- Allowing developers to verify in the design stage, whether the developed solution satisfies the security requirements of the system.
- Supporting reasoning of different cloud deployment models based on the relevant security requirements.
- Supporting the selection of a cloud provider based on the satisfiability of the service provider to the relevant security requirements.

2 Method Description

The main motivation behind the creation of Secure Tropos was the lack of a methodology to support the capturing, analysis and reasoning of security requirements from the early stages of the development process. In order to achieve that, it was decided to extend the Tropos methodology [8] into two directions: concepts/language and process. Later, a number of new models were also added to support the further analysis and design of security requirements. The main concepts of the methodology as well as some discussion regarding related work in the area of security requirements engineering will be presented in the rest of this section.

2.1 Concept Definition

Secure Tropos [9] combines concepts from requirements engineering for representing general concepts and security engineering for representing security-oriented concepts.

A (hard) **Goal** represents a condition in the world that an actor would like to achieve [10]. In other words, goals represent the actors' strategic interests. In Tropos, the concept of a hard-goal (simply goal, hereafter) is differentiated from the concept of soft-goal. A **Soft-Goal** is used to capture non-functional requirements of the system, and unlike a (hard) goal, it does not have clear criteria for deciding whether it is satisfied or not and, therefore, it is subject to interpretation [10]. For instance, an example of a soft-goal is "the system should be scalable". According to Chung et al. [11], the difference between a goal and a soft-goal is underlined by saying that goals are satisfied, whereas soft-goals are satisfied.

An **Actor** represents an entity that has intentionality and strategic goals within the multi-agent system or within its organizational setting [10]. An actor can be human, a system, or an organization.

In the context of cloud computing, we also define a special class of an actor, a **Cloud Actor**. A cloud actor is an actor that demonstrates two unique characteristics, it provides a deployment model and it supports a service model. It is worth stating that as an actor, a cloud actor also inherits all the attributes and associations of the actor, for example it has goals, capabilities and it requires resources [12].

We also differentiate a special class of an actor, a **Malicious Actor**. A malicious actor's intention is to introduce threats to the system, which exploit vulnerabilities [12].

A **Plan** represents, at an abstract level, a way of doing something [8]. The fulfilment of a task can be a means for satisfying a goal, or for contributing towards satisfying a soft-goal. In Tropos developers model different (alternative) tasks, which actors might employ to achieve their goals. Therefore, developers can reason about the different ways in which actors can achieve their goals and decide for the best possible way.

A **Resource** presents a physical or informational entity that one of the actors requires [8]. The main concern when dealing with resources is whether the resource is available and who is responsible for its delivery.

A **Dependency** between two actors refers to the fact that one actor depends on the other to attain some goal, execute a task, or deliver a resource [10]. The depending actor is called the depender and the actor who is depended upon is called the dependee. The type of the dependency describes the nature of an agreement (called dependum) between dependee and depender. Goal dependencies represent delegation of responsibility for fulfilling a goal. Soft-goal dependencies are similar to goal dependencies, but their fulfilment cannot be defined precisely, whereas task dependencies are used in situations where the dependee is required to perform a given activity. Resource dependencies require the dependee to provide a resource to the depender. By depending on the dependee for the dependum, the depender is able to achieve goals that it is otherwise unable to achieve on its own, or it is not able to achieve them as easily or as well as with the help of a dependee [10]. On the other hand, the depender becomes vulnerable, since if the dependee fails to deliver the dependum, the depender is affected in their aim to achieve its goals.

A **Secure Dependency** introduces one or more Security Constraint(s) that must be fulfilled for the dependency to be valid [12]. In the Secure Tropos methodology, we distinguish among three types of secure dependencies: dependee secure dependency, depender secure dependency and double secure dependency. In terms of the modeling language, different Secure Dependency types are defined using depender and dependee attributes of Security Constraints.

A **Security Constraint** is the main concept introduced by Secure Tropos. Security Constraints are used, in the Secure Tropos methodology, to represent security requirements [13]. A Security Constraint is a specialisation of the concept of constraint. In the context of software engineering, a constraint is usually defined as a restriction that can influence the analysis and design of a software system under development by restricting some alternative design solutions, by conflicting with some of the requirements of the system, or by refining some of the system's objectives. In other words, constraints can represent a set of restrictions that do not permit specific actions to be taken or prevent certain objectives from being achieved. Often, constraints are integrated in the specification of existing textual descriptions. However, this approach can often lead to misunderstandings and an unclear definition of a constraint and its role in the development process. Consequently, this results in errors in the very early development stages that propagate to the later stages of the development process causing many problems when discovered; if they are discovered. Therefore, in the Secure Tropos modeling language, we define security constraints, as a separate concept. To this end, the concept of security constraint was defined within the context of Secure Tropos as: *A security condition imposed to an actor that restricts achievement of an actor's goals, execution of plans or availability of resources*. Security constraints are outside the control of an actor. This means that, in contrast to goals, security constraints are not conditions that an actor wishes to introduce, but conditions it is forced to introduce.

Security Objectives are a set of principles or rules that contribute towards the achievement of the system's security [13]. These principles identify possible solutions to the security problems and, usually, they can be found in the form of the security policy of the organization. Examples of such objectives are authorisation, integrity and availability.

A **Vulnerability** is defined as a weakness or flaw, in terms of security and privacy that exists from a resource, an actor and/or a goal [12]. Vulnerabilities are exploited by threats, as an attack or incident within a specific context.

A **Threat** refers to the circumstances that have the potential to cause loss; or a problem that can put in danger the security features of the system [12]. Threats can be operationalised by different attack methods, each exploiting a number of system vulnerabilities.

An **Attack Method** in Secure Tropos is an action aiming to cause a potential violation of security in the system [13].

Security Mechanisms are standard security methods which help meet the security objectives [13]. Some of these methods are able to prevent security attacks, whereas others are able only to detect security breaches. It must be noted that further analysis of some security mechanisms is required to allow developers to identify possible security sub-mechanisms. A security sub-mechanism is a specific way of achieving a security mechanism. For instance, authentication is a security mechanism for the fulfilment of a protection objective such as authorisation. However, authentication can be achieved by sub-mechanisms such as passwords, digital signatures and biometrics.

2.2 Related Work

The literature provides quite a few examples of research that focus on the identification and analysis of security properties during the various stages of the software systems development process.

Anton et al. [14] propose a set of general taxonomies for security and privacy to be used as a general knowledge repository for a (security) goal refinement process. Schumacher and Roedig [15] apply the pattern approach to the security problem by proposing a set of patterns, called security patterns, which contribute to the overall process of security engineering. Although useful, these approaches lack the definition of a structured process for considering security. A well defined and structured process is of paramount importance when considering security during the development stages of software systems. On the other hand, a number of researchers model security by taking into account the behavior of potential attackers. Van Lamsweerde and Letier [16] use the concept of security goals and anti-goals. Anti-goals are malicious obstacles set up by attackers to threaten the security goals of a system. Crook et al. [17] introduce the notion of anti-requirements to represent the requirements of malicious attackers. Anti-requirements are expressed in terms of the problem domain phenomena and are satisfied when the security threats imposed by the attacker are realized in any one instance of the problem. Similarly, Lin et al. [18], incorporate anti-requirements into abuse frames. The purpose of abuse frames is to represent security threats and to facilitate the analysis of the conditions in the system in which a security violation occurs. An important limitation of all these approaches is that security is considered as a vague goal to be satisfied, whereas a precise description and enumeration of specific security properties is still missing.

On the contrary, another "school of thinking" indicates the development of methods for analyzing and reasoning about security which are based on the relationships between actors (such as users, stakeholders and attackers) and the system. Liu et al. [19] analyze security requirements as relationships amongst strategic actors by proposing different kinds of analysis techniques to model potential threats and security measures. Although a relationship-based analysis is suitable for reasoning about security, an important limitation of existing approaches is that each of them only guides the way security can be handled within a certain stage of the software development process.

Another direction of work is based on the extension of use cases and the Unified modeling Language (UML). In particular, McDermott and Fox [20] adapt use cases to capture and analyze security requirements, and they call the adaption an abuse case model. An abuse case is defined as a specification of a type of complete interaction between a system and one or more actors, where the results of the interaction are harmful to the system, one of the actors, or one of the stakeholders of the system. Similarly, Sindre and Opdahl [21] define the concept of misuse case, the inverse of use case, which describes a function that the system should not allow. They also define the concept of mis-actor as someone who intentionally or accidentally initiates a misuse case and whom the system should not support in doing so. Jurjens proposes UMLsec [22], an extension of the Unified modeling Language (UML), to include modeling of security-related features, such as confidentiality and access control. Lodderstedt et al. [23] also extend UML to model security. In their work, they present a security modeling language called SecureUML. They describe how UML can be used to specify information related to access control in the overall design of an application and how this information can be used to automatically generate complete access control infrastructures. An important limitation of all the usecase and/or UML related approaches is that they do not support the modeling and analysis of security requirements at a social level but they treat security in system-oriented terms. In other words, they lack models that focus on high-level security requirements, meaning models that do not force the designer to immediately go down to security requirements.

Mouratidis and Giorgini [24] propose Secure Tropos, an extension of the Tropos methodology. The approach is based on the concept of security constraint to analyze security requirements from the early stages of the development process. Similarly, Giorgini et al. [25] extended the i*/Tropos requirements engineering framework to deal with security requirements. Mellado et al. [26] introduced the security requirements engineering process (SREP), which is based on several common criteria constructs, i.e., security functional components, protection profile and security assurance components to elicit and analyze security requirements. The security quality requirement engineering methodology (SQUARE) is another security requirements engineering approach similar to SREP [27]. Both SREP and SQUARE are asset-based and risk-driven methods that follow a number of steps, for eliciting, categorizing and prioritizing security requirements. However, SREP integrates knowledge and experience from the Common Criteria and Information Security Standards, such as ISO/IEC 27001, while eliciting security requirements. Houmb et al. [28] introduce the SecReq approach to elicit, analyze and trace security requirements from the requirements engineering phase to design. Pavlidis et al. [29] use trust-based concepts such as resolution, trust, trust relationship and entailment to support analysis and modeling of security. Rosado et al. [30] demonstrate an activity for elicitation, analysis and modeling of security and functional requirements, where Security is considered as subfactor of software quality. The work systematically uses SPEM 2.0 to define the tasks and integrate the artefacts for the security analysis.

3 Method Conceptualization

3.1 Secure Tropos Notation

Secure Tropos is a requirements engineering methodology aimed at fully capturing the properties of software systems and the organizational environment, focusing on modeling security [24]. The language extends the concepts of (social) actor, goal, task, resource and social dependency from the i* modeling language and redefines existing concepts introduced in the Tropos language and development process [31]. The Secure Tropos methodology closely follows the software development lifecycle with emphasis on security and privacy requirements, allowing the developer to incrementally create and refine models of the system-to-be during the analysis and design stage.

The Secure Tropos notation is fully defined in [24]. Figure 2 shows the metamodel of the Secure Tropos methodology. The white boxes indicate different elements in the modeling language. The grey boxes indicate the relationships that link different elements together. The concrete notation is presented within *views* over the next subsections, where each view denotes a specific phase of activity in the modeling process. The Secure Tropos Views will be discussed below.

3.1.1 Organizational View

The diagram in Fig. 3 illustrates the main nodes of an organizational view of Secure Tropos. It depicts a node-link diagram enclosed in a bounding rectangle. The nodes in the node-link diagram vary in shape according to the type of Secure Tropos element they depict. The links similarly vary.

(1) Actor: The circular node depicts an *actor*. An example actor labelled "Actor 1" can be seen in Fig. 3.

(2) Goal: The semi-oval node depicts a *goal*. Goals can be decomposed into subgoals and combined using Boolean operations. An example goal labelled "Goal 1" can be seen in Fig. 3. Goals are linked through a *Dependency* link, depicted by one semi-circles on each side of the goal element.

(3) Dependency: A *Dependency* link indicates that an actor depends on another actor in order to achieve some goal/plan or to obtain a resource, where the direction the semi-circle is pointing towards denotes the dependee. An example dependency

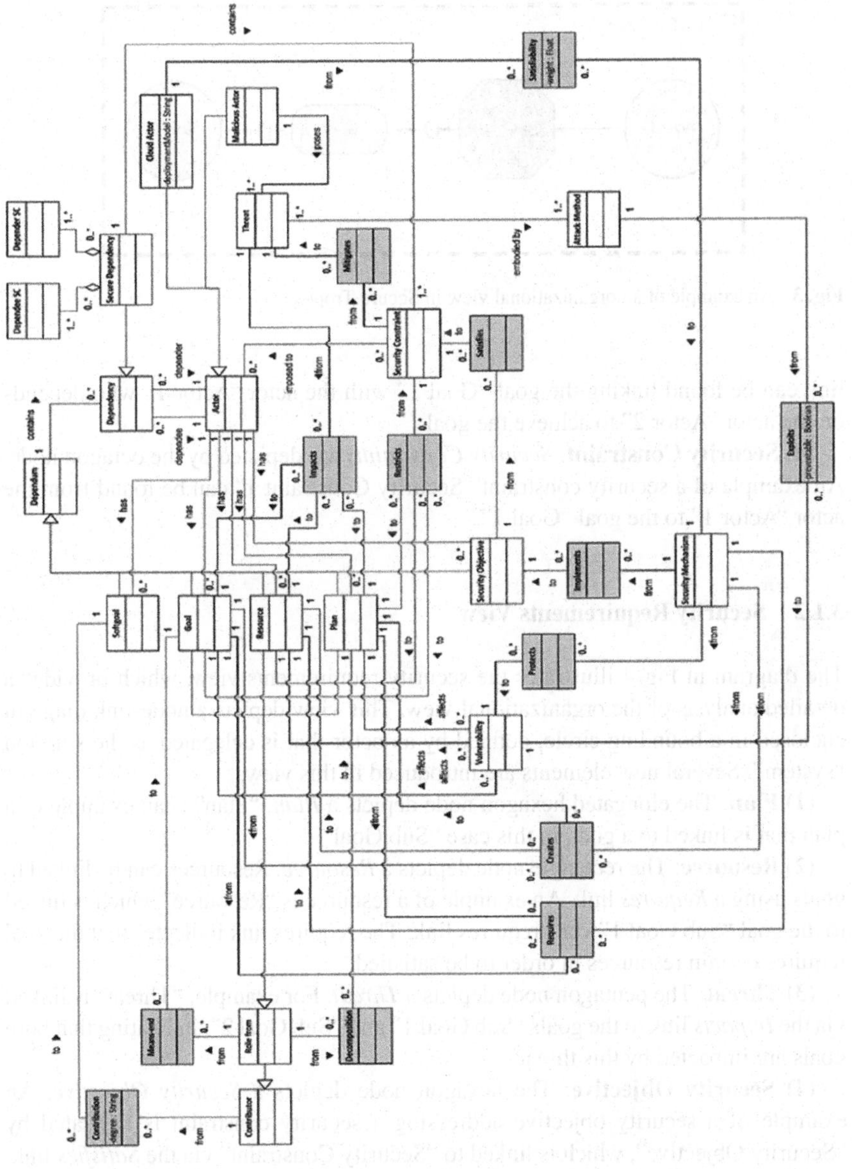

Fig. 2 The MetaModel of the Secure Tropos methodology

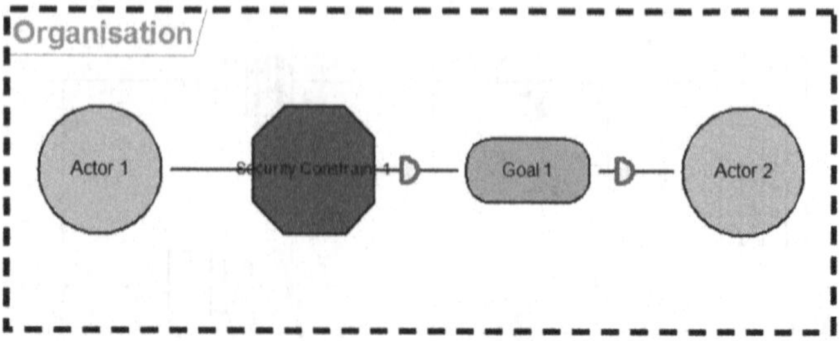

Fig. 3 An example of an organizational view in Secure Tropos

link can be found linking the goal "Goal 1" with the actor "Actor 1" who depends on the actor "Actor 2" to achieve the goal.

(4) Security Constraint: *Security Constraints* are depicted by the octagon node. An example of a security constraint "Security Constraint 1" can be found from the actor "Actor 1" to the goal "Goal 1".

3.1.2 Security Requirements View

The diagram in Fig. 4 illustrates the security requirements view, which provides a detailed analysis of the organizational view. This view depicts a node-link diagram enclosed in a bounding circle, defined by an actor that is delegated as the solution "system". Several new elements are introduced in this view.

(1) Plan: The elongated hexagon node depicts a *Plan*. "Plan" is an example of a plan that is linked to a goal, in this case "Sub Goal 1".

(2) Resource: The rectangle node depicts a *Resource*. Resources can be linked to goals using a *Requires* link. An example of a resource is "Resource" which is linked to the goal "Sub Goal 1" via a requires link. The requires link indicates that the goal requires certain resources in order to be satisfied.

(3) Threat: The pentagon node depicts a *Threat*. For example, "Threat" is linked via the *Impacts* link to the goals "Sub Goal 1" and "Sub Goal 2", indicating that both goals are impacted by this threat.

(4) Security Objective: The hexagon node depicts a *Security Objective*. An example of a security objective addressing a security constraint is indicated by "Security Objective", which is linked to "Security Constraint" via the *Satisfies* link. The *Security Mechanism* "Security Mechanism 1" and "Security Mechanism 2" fulfils the *Security Objective*, which is indicated by the *Implements* link.

(5) Security Mechanism: The hexagon node with two parallel horizontal lines depicts a *Security Mechanism*.

(6) Restricts: The *Restricts* link shows that the security constraint places a restriction upon a goal, for example "Security Constraint" which restricts the goal "Sub Goal 2".

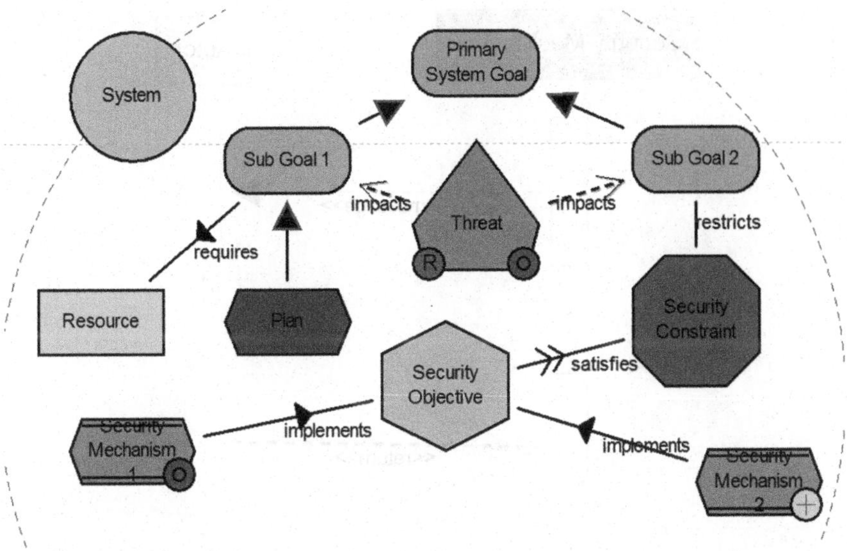

Fig. 4 An example of a security requirements view in Secure Tropos

(7) Service Identification: As part of the ongoing work towards modeling and analyzing cloud-based security, we proposed a **Goal-Plan-Resource** pattern for identifying services based on the existing notations found in Secure Tropos [32]. We are then able to build around the services to generate an infrastructural view of a cloud deployment, thus allowing us to identify threats and vulnerabilities on the cloud level.

3.1.3 Security Components View

The diagram in Fig. 5 illustrates an example of a security components view, describing the exchange of messages between actors and security mechanisms.

(1) Message: The *Message* link indicates the passing of data from one element to another, in this case from "Security Mechanism" to "Actor".

(2) Return: The *Return* link indicates the response from one element to another, in this case from "Actor" to "Security Mechanism".

3.1.4 Security Attacks View

The security attacks view shown in Fig. 6 allows the refinement of threats by modeling attackers and ways to mitigate attacks on vulnerabilities. Table 1 shows the relationship of each threat and the components involved.

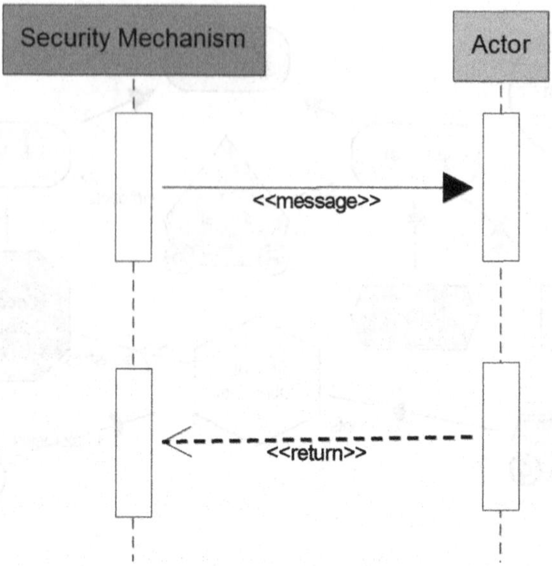

Fig. 5 An example of an security components view in Secure Tropos

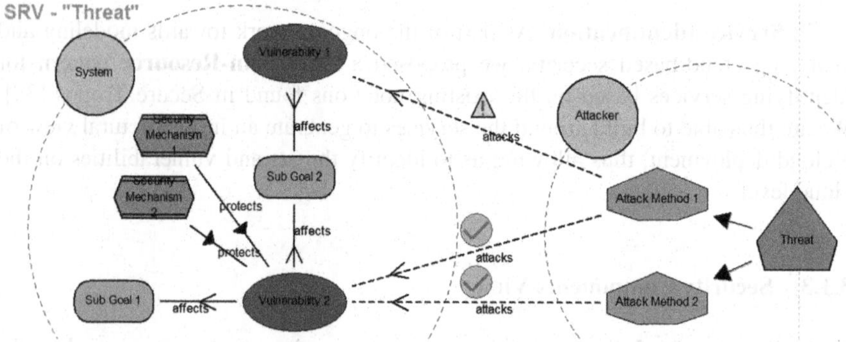

Fig. 6 An example of a security attacks view in Secure Tropos

(1) Attack Method: The Heptagon node describes the method of attack that is performed by Threat nodes on Vulnerability nodes. In this case, "Attack Method 1" attacks "Vulnerability 1", which is not protected by *Security Mechanisms* thus generating an alert about an unaddressed attack.

(2) Vulnerability: The oval node indicates a *Vulnerability*, which can *affect* goals and is *protected* by *Security Mechanisms*. For example "Vulnerability 2" affects both "Sub Goal 1" and "Sub Goal 2", while it is protected by "Security Mechanism 1" and "Security Mechanism 2"

Table 1 An example of concept relationships in the security attacks view

Threat	Attack method	Vulnerability	Security mechanism
Threat 1	Attack Method 1	Vulnerability 1	$<>$
		Vulnerability 2	$< Sec.Mech1, Sec.Mech.2 >$
	Attack method 2	Vulnerability 2	$< Sec.Mech1, Sec.Mech.2 >$

3.1.5 Cloud Infrastructure View

Building upon the proposed pattern for identifying services, we propose the Cloud Infrastructure View to conceptually capture properties defining cloud infrastructure through two conceptual categories [33]. Based on the security requirements obtained from previous views, we are able to create and refine cloud attributes defining the application layer and physical components which make up the envisioned cloud system (Fig. 7).

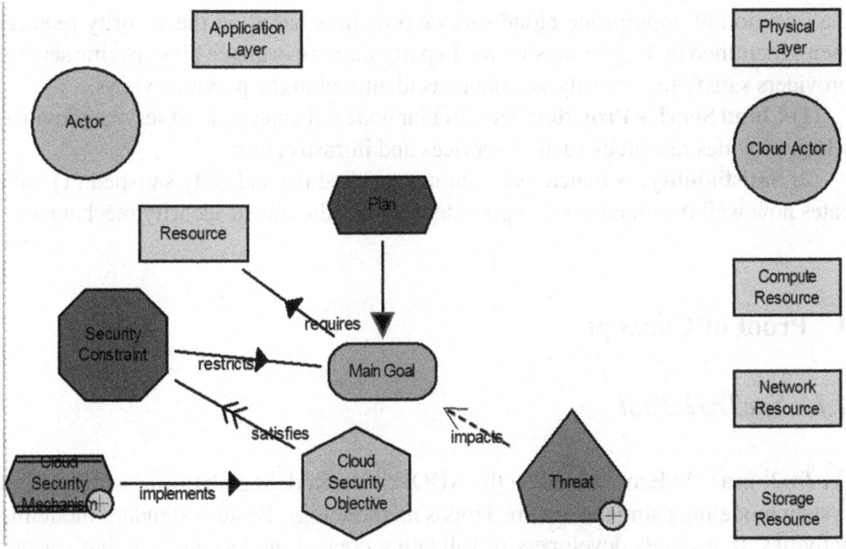

Fig. 7 A proposed example of a cloud infrastructure view in Secure Tropos

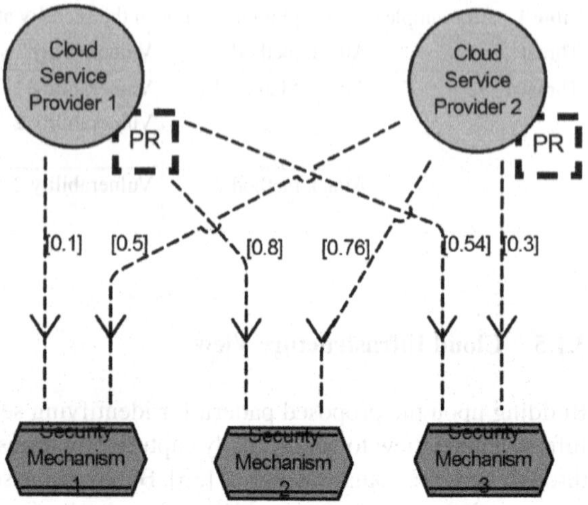

Fig. 8 An example of a cloud analysis view in Secure Tropos

3.1.6 Cloud Analysis View

In the cloud analysis view shown in Fig. 8, we provide a visual indication to facilitate the selection of appropriate cloud service providers based on the security requirements identified in the previous views. In particular, we evaluate how specific service providers satisfy the security mechanisms identified in the previous views.

(1) Cloud Service Provider: The circular node indicates a cloud service provider, which provides resources such as services and infrastructure.

(2) Satisfiability: A metric between not satisfied (0) and fully satisfied (1) indicates how well the cloud service provider satisfies the linked security mechanism.

4 Proof of Concept

4.1 SecTro2 Tool

SecTro2[1] is a CASE tool based on the ADO*xx* metamodeling platform, which allows system modeling using the Secure Tropos methodology. Besides standard modeling activities, it also aids developers in validating created models and running various analyzes against them. SecTro2 supports generating graphical images as well as producing Word and PDF reports of the created models and their features.

SecTros workspace consists of the drawing canvas in the centre, on the top there is a series of tabs for showing the developed diagrams for each stage of Secure Tropos and on the left a toolbox containing the graphical representations of all the concepts

[1] Available at: http://www.omilab.org/web/secure-tropos/.

of Secure Tropos [34]. The different supported views along with their notation, which were introduced in the previous section, will be utilized in a case study to demonstrate their applicability in the design of a real life system.

4.2 Case Study

In order to exhibit the applicability of Secure Tropos and the supporting SecTro tool, this section describes their application to a real life case study of the established Greek national e-prescription system [35]. This is a cloud-based system, which is currently used by Greek health care professionals to handle patients' electronic medication and clinical tests prescriptions.

Medical practitioners can create an electronic prescription document, which can then be fulfilled, by using the same platform, by any pharmacist or clinic staff. The healthcare professionals access the e-prescription system via an online portal. The back-end of the system was created, and it is also maintained, by a non-profit organization, which is in charge of the e-governance infrastructure of the Greek Ministry of Health.

Next, some of the system's main functionalities will be modelled. Using the different modeling views supported by the SecTro tool, security-related features of the system will be analyzed from a variety of perspectives.

4.2.1 Organizational View

The main goals of the system are modelled in the organizational view of the e-prescription system. As illustrated in Fig. 9 the "Medical Practitioners" depend on the system to achieve a number of goals. For the purposes of this illustrative example, we selected three of their most important goals, namely "Register system users", "Handle prescription documents" and "Archive prescription documents". The security constraints limiting the interactions of the users with the system in order to achieve each goal, are derived from the legal framework binding this system [35].

In particular, the security constraint "Authorized access only" aims to ensure that only registered users access and operate the system. Similarly, the security constrain "Correct data received and stored" restricts the creation, fulfilment of and access to prescription documents, aiming to ensure the integrity of the information stored in the system. "Confidentiality of personal information" requires that the sensitive and personal patient information contained in a prescription document be accessed only by authorized system users. Finally, the security constraint "System always available" ensures the uninterrupted functionality of the e-prescription system.

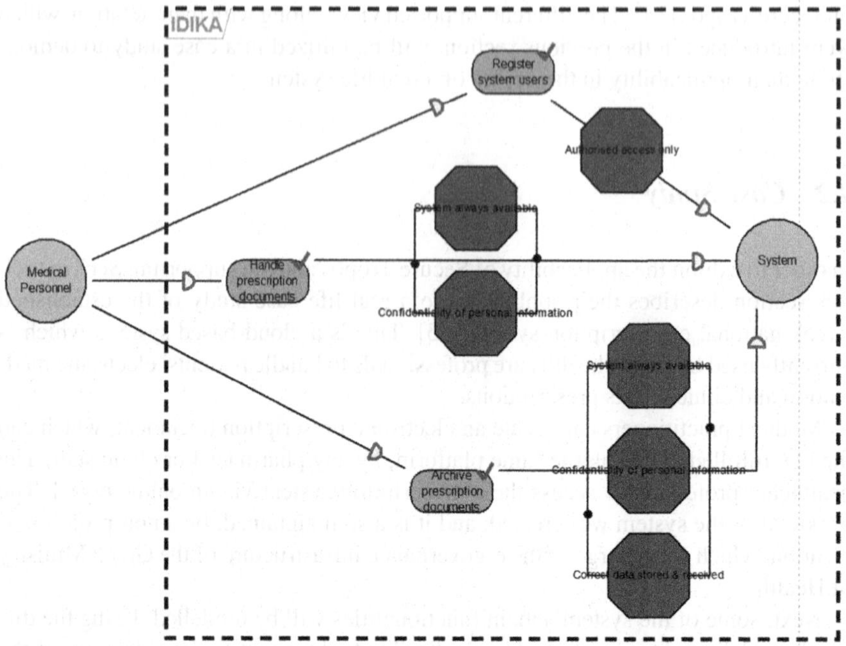

Fig. 9 The organizational view of the e-prescription system in Secure Tropos

4.2.2 Security Requirements View

The security requirements view of the e-prescription system, illustrated in Fig. 10, provides a more detailed representation of the security aspects of the system. Table 2 describes the relationship between the threat, attacks expected and mitigation mechanisms for the "User Impersonation" threat. A number of resources are introduced which represent various assets that are either created from or required for the achievement of each of the modelled goals. In our case, such resources include "User Accounts", "User registration information", "Patient information" and "Prescription documents". Plans are included in this model to indicate activities required for the achievement of certain system goals. For instance, the plan "Backup archive data to server" is needed for the achievement of the "Archive prescription documents" and the plan "Create user profile" is required for the goal "Register system users".

Threats can also be modeled in this view of the system, impacting different goals and resources. In our example, we introduce the threats of "Reduced system availability", "Data Leakage" and "User Impersonation", each linked to the goals and resources it can potentially impact. The security constraints introduced in the organizational view of the system are satisfied through the implementation of security objectives. For example, the security constraint "Authorized access only" is satisfied by the security objectives "Authentication" and "User Authorization". Such secu-

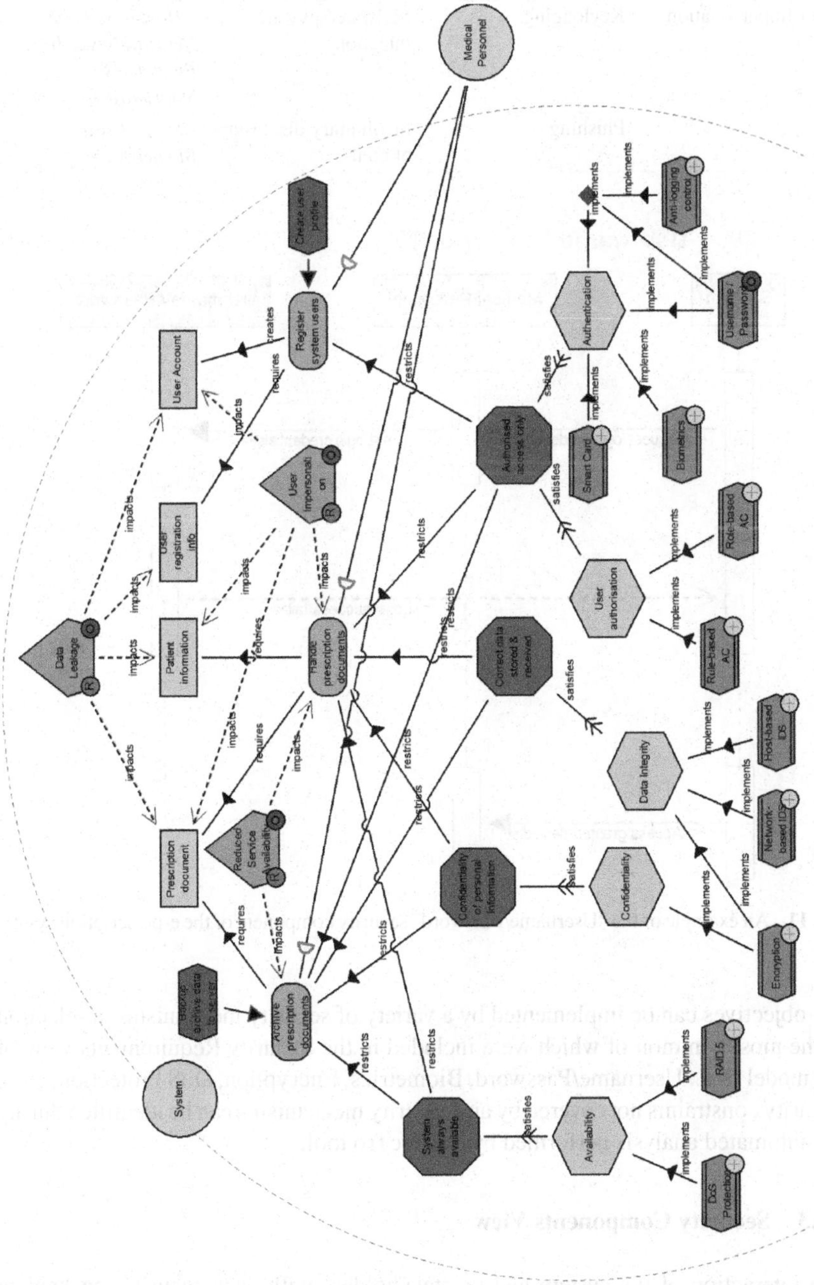

Fig. 10 The security requirements view of the e-prescription system in Secure Tropos

Table 2 Concept relationships for the "User Impersonation" threat

Threat	Attack method	Vulnerability	Security mechanism
User Impersonation	Keylogging	Malware/spyware infection	*<Host-based IDS, Network-based IDS, Biometrics, Smartcard>*
	Phishing	Involuntary disclosure of cred	*<Smart Card, Biometrics>*

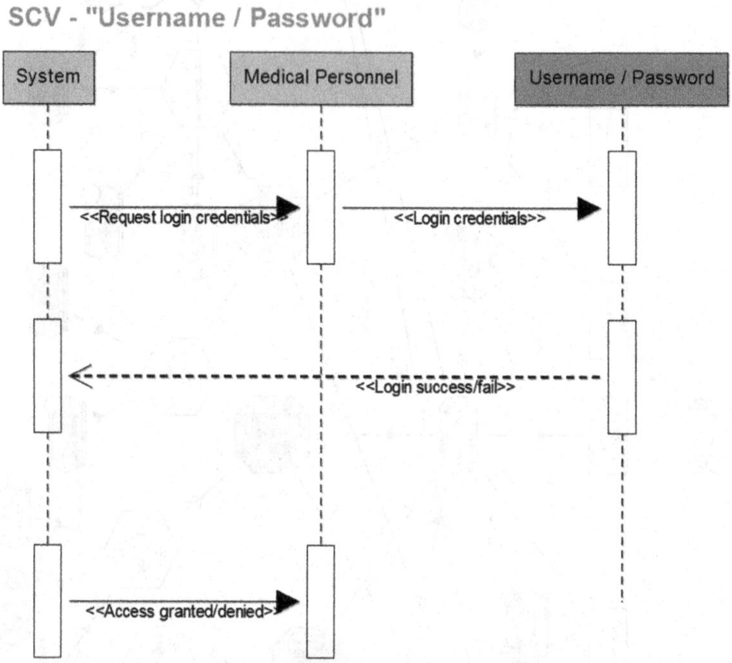

Fig. 11 An example of the "Username/Password" security component of the e-prescription system

rity objectives can be implemented by a variety of security mechanisms, a selection of the most common of which were included in the Security Requirements view of our model (e.g., Username/Password, Biometrics, Encryption, DoS Protection, etc.). Security constraints not covered by any security mechanisms can be identified during the automated analysis performed by the SecTro tool.

4.2.3 Security Components View

The interaction of the system and its stakeholders with each security mechanism is modelled in the security components view. For the purpose of our example, the "Username/Password login" mechanism is illustrated in Fig. 11. In this view, the

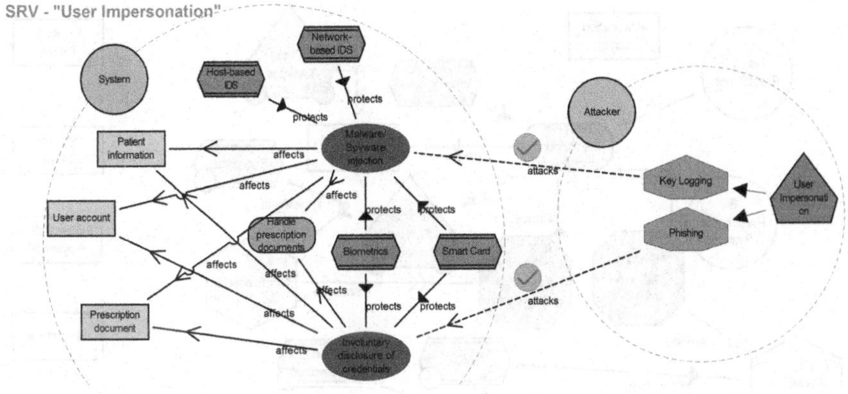

Fig. 12 Security attacks view for the "User Impersonation" threat of the e-prescription system

exchange of messages between the system, its users and the security mechanism indicates the sequence of steps necessary for the achievement of user authorisation via the "Username/Password" security mechanism.

4.2.4 Security Attacks View

The security attacks view, illustrated in Fig. 12, demonstrates how the "User Impersonation" threat can impact the system. This threat can utilize a number of attack methods to manifest itself, which for our example can be "Key Logging" and "Phishing". Such methods exploit certain vulnerabilities of the system such as "Malware/Spyware infection" and "Involuntary disclosure of credentials" by the system users, which can affect a number of system resources and goals, as illustrated in our model. The security mechanisms introduced at the security requirements view of the model can protect the system against each of the identified vulnerabilities. The automated analysis function offered by the SecTro tool can indicate if any of the vulnerabilities is left untreated.

4.2.5 Cloud Infrastructure View

The cloud infrastructure view captures predefined or identified services and decomposes them down further into detailed components. In the example shown in Fig. 13, we focus on a subset of the e-prescription system and define the properties through the identification of a service. Then we populate the envisioned components in light of the identified service, in order to provide more detail in the cloud service provider analysis stage. The application layer conceptually captures the logic and structure of the system, where we can further analyze threats on the cloud level. By linking the application layer to the physical layer, we are able to indicate and cross-reference dependencies between different components and thus identify potential vulnerabilities.

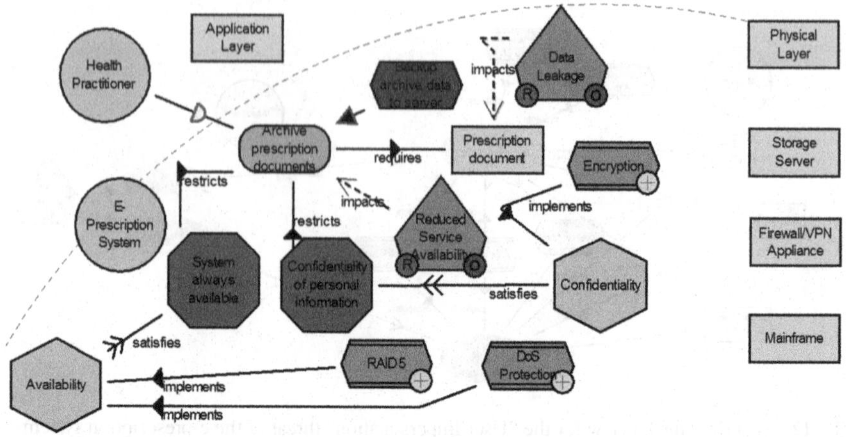

Fig. 13 The cloud infrastructure view for the e-prescription system

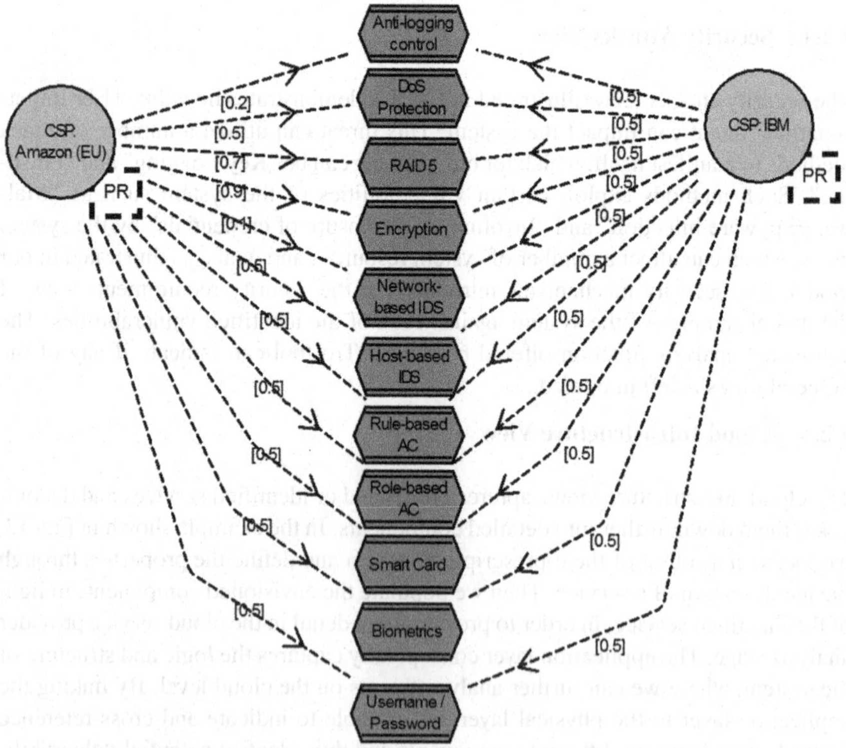

Fig. 14 The cloud analysis view for the e-prescription system

4.2.6 Cloud Analysis View

The cloud analysis view of the system facilitates the selection of a cloud provider which can better satisfy the system's security needs. For our example, Fig. 14 illustrates the degree of satisfiability, from zero (0) to one (1), of each security mechanism by two different cloud providers, namely Amazon and IBM. The automated analysis function offered by the SecTro tool can then calculate the provider with the highest degree of satisfiability. The security mechanisms listed depend on the previous activities in eliciting and modeling organizational structure and security requirements.

5 Conclusion

Security is an important non-functional aspect that needs to be considered during the development of software systems. As discussed above in this chapter, a number of research attempts have focused on the elicitation and implementation of security requirements during the software development lifecycle. In this work, we presented Secure Tropos, a goal-oriented security requirements engineering method. Secure Tropos demonstrates a number of novel features, such as allowing developers not only to model but also to reason about the technical as well as the social issues of security; allowing developers to represent security concerns at different levels of software description; and allowing developers to verify at the design stage, whether the developed solution satisfies the security requirements of the system [13]. The SecTro tool [34] is a CASE tool developed to support the creation and analysis of Secure Tropos models.

Current research focuses on the integration of security features captured via Secure Tropos in business processes. The introduction of security to business processes requires structured and flexible approaches, able to encapsulate the rationale behind security choices, align it with high-level organizational objectives and facilitate well-informed and risk-aware decisions. To that end, a transformation method was proposed in [36], as part of a wider framework, for the derivation of secure BPMN business process designs from organizational Secure Tropos goal models via intermediate, security-annotated, process skeletons. In [37], an algorithmic approach is introduced for the transformation of legacy business process models to Secure Tropos goal models. Secure Tropos offers the means for capturing the security-related aspects of the redesigned system (e.g., security constraints, mechanisms and threats), which can then be incorporated back into the process model via a set of goal-to-process transformation rules. As a result, security choices of the system's stakeholders can be operationalised by the redesigned business processes.

The current Secure Tropos framework considers the organizational ecosystem and security requirements around software systems. However, to fully capture security requirements at the cloud level, the cloud properties need to be well defined and context-sensitive. Initial steps were taken to analyze cloud providers based on their offerings in terms of services and infrastructure. The cloud analysis view decomposes the providers' offerings down to specific security mechanisms and shows how suitable these are against stakeholder requirements. The next step would be modeling cloud computing systems in terms of the services, physical infrastructure and stakeholders involved. This would allow in-depth analysis of threats and vulnerabilities dependent on context, such as in scenarios involving services deployed to multiple service providers. In [32], a pattern is defined for service identification based on grouping the concepts of goal, plans and resources in software systems. An initial description of properties required by services when migrated to cloud environments is also given. In [33] a view to capture properties residing in cloud infrastructures is proposed. This abstract view conceptually captures the cloud infrastructure by defining components from the application and physical layer. The application layer hosts the logic behind the cloud system through services, cloud services and applications. Each service represents specific goals that should be satisfied in order to fulfil some system requirements, which are then migrated towards the cloud environment. The physical layer captures the infrastructure of providers by defining three subcategories; network, compute and storage. This allows the concrete definition for properties such as geographical location of data-centres, tracking data-flow and defining context-sensitive vulnerabilities.

Tool Download http://www.omilab.org/sectro.

References

1. Depot, T.H.: The home depot reports findings in payment data breach investigation. http://krebsonsecurity.com/2014/09/home-depot-hit-by-same-malware-as-target/ (2014). Accessed 13 Oct 15
2. Pavel, A.: Amazon.com server said to have been used in Sony attack. http://www.bloomberg.com/news/articles/2011-05-13/sony-network-said-to-have-been-invaded-by-hackers-using-amazon-com-server (2011). Accessed 13 Oct 15
3. Cloud Security Alliance: Security research alliance to promote network security. Netw. Secur. **1999**(2), 3–4 (1999)
4. Bergmayr, A., Brunelière, H., Izquierdo, J.L.C., Gorroñogoitia, J., Kousiouris, G., Kyriazis, D., Langer, P., Menychtas, A., Orue-Echevarria, L., Pezuela, C., Wimmer, M.: Migrating legacy software to the cloud with ARTIST. In: European Conference on Software Maintenance and Reengineering, CSMR, pp. 465–468 (2013)
5. Ferry, N., Rossini, A., Chauvel, F., Morin, B., Solberg, A.: Towards model-driven provisioning, deployment, monitoring, and adaptation of multicloud systems. In: 6th International Conference on Cloud Computing, pp. 887–894. IEEE Press (2013)
6. Frey, S., Hasselbring, W.: The cloudmig approach: Model-based migration of software systems to cloud-optimized applications. Int. J. Adv. Softw. **4**(3–4), 342–353 (2011)
7. Armbrust, M., Fox, O., Griffith, R., Joseph, A.D., Katz, Y., Konwinski, A., et al.: Above the clouds: A Berkeley view of cloud computing. Technical report, pp. 07–013. University of California, Berkeley (2009)
8. Bresciani, P., Perini, A., Giorgini, P., Giunchiglia, F., Mylopoulos, J.: Tropos: an agent-oriented software development methodology. Auton. Agent. Multi-Agent Syst. **8**(3), 203–236 (2004)
9. Mouratidis, H.: A security oriented approach in the development of multiagent bsystems: applied to the management of the health and social care needs of older people in England. Ph.D. Thesis, University of Sheffields, UK (2004)

10. Yu, E.: Modelling strategic relationships for process reengineering. Ph.D. thesis, Department of Computer Science, University of Toronto, Canada (1995)
11. Chung, L., Nixon B.: Dealing with non-functional requirements: three experimental studies of a process-oriented approach. In: 17th International Conference on Software Engineering, pp. 25–37. ACM (1995)
12. Mouratidis, H., Islam, S., Kalloniatis, C., Gritzalis, S.: A framework to support selection of cloud providers based on security and privacy requirements. J. Syst. Softw. **86**(9), 2276–2293 (2013)
13. Mouratidis, H.: Secure software systems engineering: the secure tropos approach. J. Softw. **6**(3), 331–339 (2011)
14. Anton, A.I., Earp, J.B.: A requirements taxonomy for reducing web site privacy vulnerabilities. Requir. Eng. **9**(3), 169–185 (2004)
15. Schumacher, M., Roedig, U.: Security engineering with patterns. In: 8th Conference on Pattern Languages for Programs (PLoP), Illinois, USA (2001)
16. van Lamsweerde, A., Letier, E.: Handling obstacles in goal-oriented requirements engineering. Trans. Softw. Eng. **26**(10), 978–1005 (2000)
17. Crook, R., Ince, D., Lin, L.C., Nuseibeh, B.: Security requirements engineering: when anti-requirements hit the fan. In: 10th International Requirements Engineering Conference, pp. 203–205. IEEE Press (2002)
18. Lin, L.C., Nuseibeh, B., Ince, D., Jackson, M., Moffett, J.: Analysing security threats and vulnerabilities using abuse frames. Technical report 2003/10, The Open University (2003)
19. Liu, L., Yu, E., Mylopoulos, J.: Security and privacy requirements analysis within a social setting. In: 11th International Requirements Engineering Conference, pp. 151–161. IEEE Press (2003)
20. McDermott, J., Fox, C.: Using abuse care models for security requirements analysis. In: 15th Annual Computer Security Applications Conference, pp. 55–64. IEEE Press (1999)
21. Sindre, G., Opdahl, A.L.: Eliciting security requirements with misuse cases. Requir. Eng. **10**(1), 34–44 (2005)
22. Jurjens, J.: Secure Systems Development with UML. Springer (2005)
23. Lodderstedt, T., Basin, D., Doser, J.: SecureUML: a UML based modelling language for model-driven security. In: UML 2002 The Unified Modeling Language, pp. 426–441. Springer (2002)
24. Mouratidis, H., Giorgini, P.: Secure tropos: a security-oriented extension of the tropos methodology. Int. J. Softw. Eng. Knowl. Eng. **17**(2), 285–309 (2007)
25. Giorgini, P., Massacci, F., Mylopoulos, J.: Requirement engineering meets security: a case study on modelling secure electronic transactions by VISA and Mastercard. In: 22nd International Conference On Conceptual Modeling (ER 2003), pp. 263-276. Springer (2003)
26. Mellado, D., Fernández-Medina, E., Piattini, M.: A common criterion based security requirements engineering process for the development of secure information system. Comput. Stan. Interfaces **29**, 244–253 (2007)
27. Mead, N.R., Steheny, T.: Security quality requirements engineering (SQUARE) methodology. SIGSOFT Softw. Eng. Notes **30**(4), 1–7 (2005)
28. Houmb, S.H., Islam, S., Knauss, E., Jrjens, J., Schneider, K.: Eliciting security requirements and tracing them to design: an integration of common criteria, heuristics, and UMLsec. Requirements. Eng. J. **15**(1), 63–93 (2010)
29. Pavlidis, M., Mouratidis, H., Islam, S.: Modelling security using trust based concepts. Int. J. Secure Softw. Eng. **3**(2), 36–53 (2012)
30. Rosado, D.G., Fernández-Medina, E., López, J., Piattini, M.: Analysis of secure mobile grid systems: a systematic approach. Inf. Softw. Technol. **52**(5), 517–536 (2010)
31. Bandara, Arosha, Shinpei, H., Jurjens, J., Kaiya, H., Kubo, A., Laney, R., Mouratidis, H., et al.: Security patterns: comparing modeling approaches. In: Software Engineering for Secure Systems: Industrial and Research Perspectives: Industrial and Research Perspectives, p. 75 (2010)
32. Shei, S., Delaney, A., Kapetanakis, S., Mouratidis, H.: Visually Mapping Requirements Models to Cloud Services

33. Shei, S., Márquez Alcañiz, L., Mouratidis, H., Delaney, A., Rosado, D.G., Fernández-Medina, E.: Modelling secure cloud systems based on system requirements. In: Proceedings of ESPRE, pp. 19–24 (2015)
34. Pavlidis, M., Islam, S., Mouratidis, H.: A CASE tool to support automated modelling and analysis of security requirements. In: Nurcan, S., (eds.) IS Olympics: Information Systems in a Diverse World, pp. 95–109. Springer (2012)
35. Greek Parliament: Act 3892: Electronic registration and fulfilment of medical prescriptions and clinical test referrals. FEK **189**(1), 4225–4232 (2010). [In Greek]
36. Argyropoulos, N., Mouratidis, H., Fish, A.: Towards the derivation of secure business process designs. In: 2nd International Workshop on Conceptual Modelling in Requirements and Business Analysis (MReBA) in Conjunction with the 34th International Conference on Conceptual Modeling (ER'15), Stockholm, Sweden, pp. 1–11. Springer (2015)
37. Argyropoulos, N., Márquez Alcañiz, L., Mouratidis, H., Fish, A., Rosado, D.G., De Guzmán, I.G.R., Fernández-Medina, E.: Eliciting security requirements for business processes of legacy systems. In: 8th IFIP WG 8.1 Working Conference on the Practice of Enterprise Modelling, Valencia, Spain. Springer (2015)

Part VIII
Knowledge Engineering

MELCA—Customizing Visualizations for Design Thinking

Igor Titus Hawryszkiewycz and Christoph Prackwieser

Abstract This chapter describes the ways to use ADO*xx* in addressing complex issues in wicked environments. Solutions here usually begin with gathering stakeholders' stories from different perspectives to make sense of the emerging stories and then identify major themes of concern to the stakeholders. These themes are often stated in terms of frames or perspectives, which are then used to identify specific problems and propose solutions. Melca provides ways to develop models to support the frames commonly used in addressing problems in complex environments. This paper describes the generic concepts used to define these frames and illustrates with examples.

Keywords Wicked problems · Design thinking · Visualization

1 Introduction

Melca addresses problems that are now found in complex environments. It focuses on visualizations to be used to promote a better understanding of systems in complex environments and to generate new ideas that lead to innovative solutions. Solutions to systems in complex environments cannot be predefined and addressed using structured methods. Experience has shown that agile methods are needed to generate solutions from ideas arising from collaboration between stakeholders. Systems emerge gradually in ways that are often referred to as agile but can sometimes be chaotic. Solutions often require a creative approach as innovative ideas are often needed to address unexpected problems arising in wicked environments. Solutions are often holistic and require ideas and inputs from interdis-

I.T. Hawryszkiewycz (✉)
University of Technology, Sydney NSW 2007, Australia
e-mail: igor.hawryszkiewycz@uts.edu.au

C. Prackwieser
University of Vienna, 1090 Vienna, Austria
e-mail: Christoph.Prackwieser@dke.univie.ac.at

D. Karagiannis et al. (eds.), *Domain-Specific Conceptual Modeling*,
DOI 10.1007/978-3-319-39417-6_17

ciplinary sources and a large variety of stakeholders. Visualizations must allow experimentation so that designers can easily respond to questions by illustrating alternatives.

One challenging issue in creating agile solutions is that most environments are complex, sometimes called wicked, and solutions are not often very clear, and problems cannot be precisely defined. Design in such environments often require making sense of what is going on, organizing issues and stories into themes. Designers then often use visualizations to identify problems to be solved in each theme and to create innovative solutions. Such visualizations are often free-form and enable designers to build models from a number of perspectives. It calls for open modeling where people see a problem from a number of perspectives and discuss options that through brainstorming lead to innovative solutions.

2 What Are Wicked Problems?

The term wicked problem is often used to describe these kinds of problems. In wicked problems

- There is no definite specific formulation or specification of the problem; there are just general goals such as increased sales in a new market or increasing tourism in some region or increased food security.
- Solutions are not true or false, but better or worse, there is no test of whether a solution will work as any solution can result in unpredictable behaviors of users and stakeholders.
- The environment here is one of increased social networking where many issues are resolved by collaborative engagements between stakeholders where trade-offs are made in the light of deep engagements intended to arrive at mutually acceptable solutions.
- The solutions are made more difficult as they often lead to changes in behavior, which requires a further change to the solutions.

Typical examples include

- Managing recovery during and after an emergency such as flood,
- Urbanization even increasing trends of younger underemployed young people,
- Managing global supply chains subject to disruption, or
- Managing global teams in dynamic environments.

These trends have a number of common features. They require collaboration between people in the systems and access to information systems that can maintain dynamic changes to collaborative work arrangements [3]. Such collaboration is not only applicable to what is often referred to as social problems but is increasingly relevant to the industry where there is greater dependence on social relationships. There is also the emergence of new collaborative systems. One example is managing complex problems in global environments where a new collaboration can emerge in planning an extension to a system. Others include socio-technical innovations such as the transportation infrastructure, but also institutional innovations such a changing ways of work or providing educational services.

The general consensus is that greater agility is needed for systems to evolve. Agility thus requires a framework to ensure consistency between the various directions often followed in complex environments. It also requires a method that integrates innovation into the development process. Design thinking has been seen as a way to create innovative solutions. It creates the environment for creativity [1] through creating a social environment supported by creativity centred processes to generate ideas in particular domains. There are many examples of its use including creating public–private partnerships [5] or in technology innovation [4] on ways to get business value from emerging technologies. Another important characteristic is also illustrated in Fig. 2. This is that a collaborative team needs to access all tools continuously as each provides a different dimension of the problem and changes in one affect the others.

3 Design Thinking Tools and Methods

Design thinking is now increasingly used to generate solutions in such environments. It promises a systematic rather than chaotic approach. Figure 1 illustrates the general idea behind design thinking.

The original version of Fig. 1 was first published by Martin [8] to illustrate the application of design thinking in the business context, and it presents wicked problems as a mystery. There are many things happening but it is hard to focus on any specific one. Hence, the goal here is that rather than starting with a problem to solve, the question is how to identify the problem whose solution will provide the stakeholders with the maximum value. Design teams must thus focus on developing a good understanding of stakeholder needs in the environment and identify solutions that satisfy these needs in the best possible way. Gradually, we develop a focus on what is to be addressed—a theme for design, such as the answer to questions like how are customer preferences changing and **what** is needed to address this change? Here, we collect stories and put them together in a sensible way.

Then we develop ideas of **how** to address what is needed. Here, we find what people want and what they see as important. We also look for solutions that are **holistic and multidisciplinary**. We then brainstorm for ideas of how to provide solutions and release them gradually starting with a minimal value product (MVP).

Design thinking is a collaborative process. It uses a large variety of tools to encourage brainstorming and creativity. Figure 2 shows that design thinking is not only a collaborative process. The important activities here are understanding and empathizing with stakeholders, making sense of what is discovered and identify issues that needed to be addressed, and then experimenting with ideas that provide solutions that address the issues. Frameworks that guide solutions can be based on

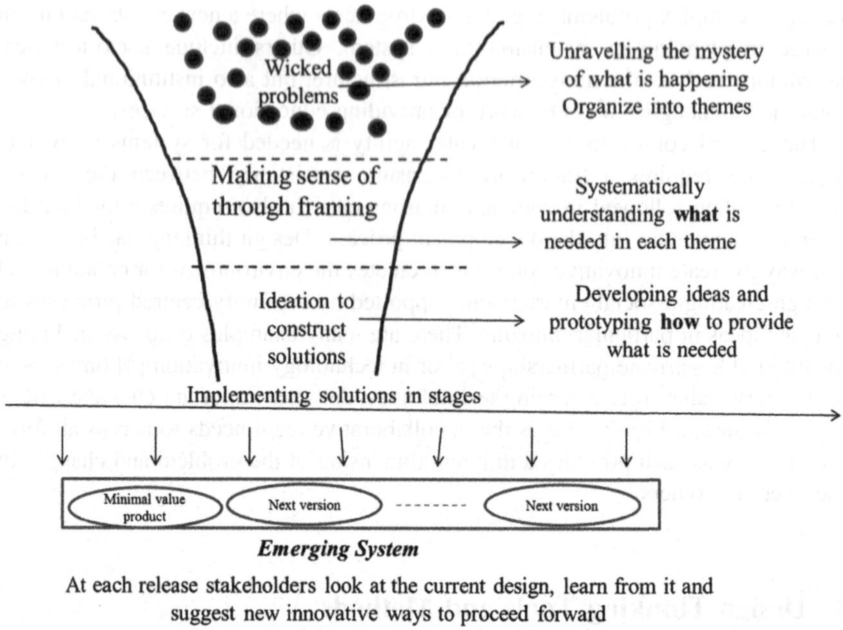

Fig. 1 Design thinking

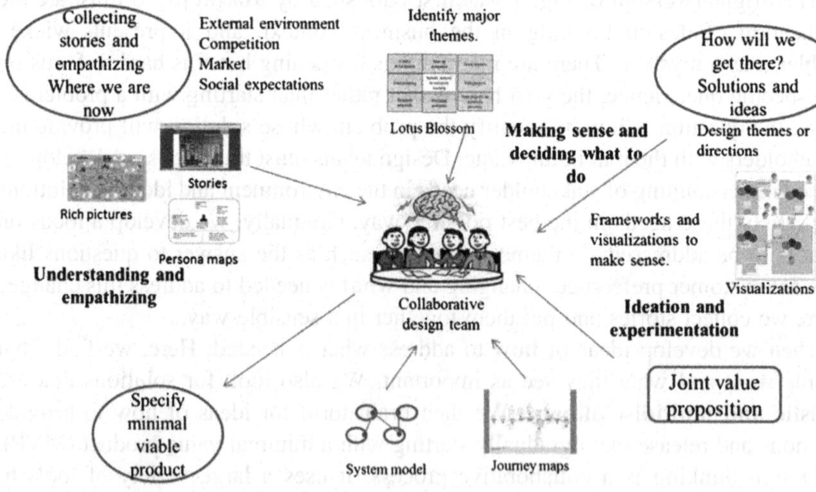

Fig. 2 Design thinking as a collaborative process

Table 1 Tools used in design thinking

Tool	Suggested use	Melca status
Storytelling	The most frequently used tool for divergence and for gathering information and ideas. Focus on connections and relationships	Not supported
Stakeholder maps	To identify who will participate in the design team and their needs and points of view	Show stakeholder responsibilities
Rich pictures	An informal visualization of the objects within the system and relationships between them	Partially supported using existing Melca concepts and needs an easy way to create new concepts
Personas to describe people's values and needs	Describes the needs of stakeholders	Not directly supported but can be improvised through concept properties
Developing joint value proposition	Almost essential in all projects and evolves as design proceeds. Selecting and defining the best ideas	Illustrate the joint value proposition through models of how it will work
Ideation	Designers suggest idea for solutions and describe them using visualizations	Supported through visualizations from different perspectives. Can be improved by showing relationships between models
Journey mapping	Describes the processes to be followed by stakeholders in the system	Partially supported
Lotus blossom to identify design themes	Focuses on divergence or how to break an issue into a number of design themes. Finding and defining problems	Not yet implemented
Mind mapping	Similar to Lotus blossom	Not yet implemented
Business building blocks	Primarily an associative tool for externalizing ideas	Not yet implemented

complexity, which provides a basis for sense making to better understand the environment and learn how to cope with unexpected events. One extension of [1] is the tools to support creativity centred processes. A typical set of tools are described in Table 1.

4 How Does Melca Assist Design Thinking?

In evaluating Melca, the main challenge is that it provides the needed flexibility to encourage innovation through visualizations adapted to selected perspectives. In this respect, Melca provides a variety of concepts that can be combined in unconstrained ways to easily create options. Ultimately, to assist in implementation,

Name	Graphical Visualisation	Description
Class: Role		A responsibility in an organisation; a public persona
Class: Organisational Unit		Any collection of object is with a goal or mission
Class: Artefact		An object in the organisation
Relation: Work relationship		How roles are connected
Relation: Business relationship		
Relation: Exchange knowledge		
Class: Participant (or Person)		An individual in the organisation
Class: Knowledge	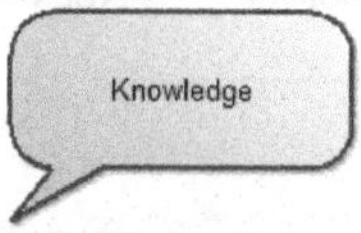	What a person knows
Class: Activity (Business Activity	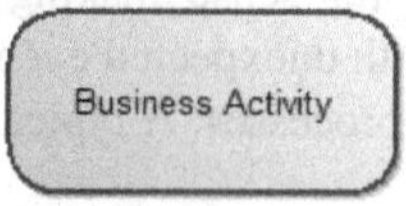	Combination of objects that lead to some outcome
Relation: Social relation-		
ship		
Relation: Data flow		

Fig. 3 Melca concepts

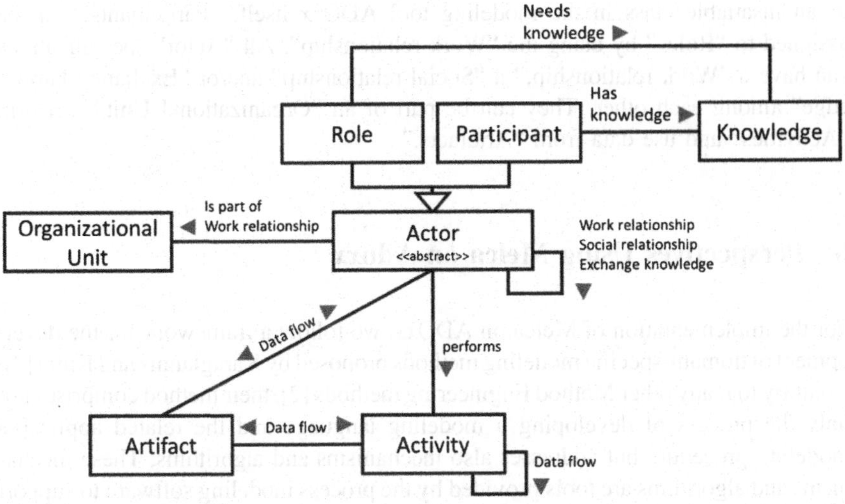

Fig. 4 Melca metamodel—organizational perspective

any model must be reduced into a form that leads to a practical implementation. Hence, we provide ways to customize any model into visualizations. In this paper, we illustrate through empirical examples that Melca can provide a range of visualizations. We define a set of basic concepts and show how they are combined to construct visualization to support different perspectives.

Concepts for Creating Perspectives Fig. 3 provides a description of objects and relations used to create visualizations while Fig. 4 shows the organizational perspective of Melca.

5 Proof of Concept

The paper illustrates how the concepts were used to create a range of visualizations. These include:

- Social networking—here the only objects are roles and individuals together with collaborative activities.
- Knowledge sharing—focuses on individuals or participants and the tacit knowledge they possess and combined with artefacts that store explicit knowledge
- organizational structure—focuses on the organizational location of individuals and their responsibilities in maintaining coordination between their organizational units.

Metamodel In the Melca metamodel, the classes "Role" and "Participant" are both a specialization of the abstract class "Actor." The abstract class is not available as an insatiable class in the modeling tool ADO*xx* itself. "Participants" can be assigned to "Roles" by using the "Work relationship". All "Actor" specializations can have a "Work relationship," a "Social relationship" and/or "Exchange knowledge" among each other. They can be part of an "Organizational Unit," perform "Activities" and use data from "Artefacts."

6 Perspectives Using Melca on Ado*xx*

For the implementation of Melca on ADO*xx*, we follow a framework for the development of domain-specific modeling methods proposed by Karagiannis and Kühn [7]. Contrary to many other Method Engineering methods [2], their method comprises not only the process of developing a modeling language and the related applicable modeling procedure but addresses also mechanisms and algorithms. These mechanisms and algorithms are tools provided by the process modeling software to support the user in efficiently mapping consistent models and to enable additional analysis and reporting functionalities which extend the application field of a modeling method.

Modeling Language Requirements Implementing a method for design thinking poses the challenge to provide a solution which is on the one hand flexible enough to depict a wide range of possible models and, on the other hand, supports the user with guidance and means for delivering consistent and correct models.

The models developed with Melca should be easily understandable by users and, at the same time, meaningful enough to form the basis for instructions for humans and in the future IT systems.

As defined, Melca supports the visualization of the following perspectives of a system:

- Social networking
- Knowledge sharing
- Organizational structure

Melca has to provide the concepts Organization, Role, Person, Artefact, Knowledge, Activities, and Relationships in between these concepts which follow the defined constraints.

The metamodel depicted in Fig. 5 provides all the concepts (classes and relations) supported in the Melca modeling method and is used to create organizational models to map the "Organizational structure." "Social networking" and "Knowledge sharing" models do not need all the concepts provided in this metamodel. Figure 2 shows the subset of required concepts for each type of model.

In order to develop these two additional perspectives in ADO*xx*, there are basically two alternatives.

1. Implement a class and relation-specific filter which can be applied to an organizational model and, if applied, just shows the objects and relations relevant for this perspective. The advantage of this alternative is that all objects and their

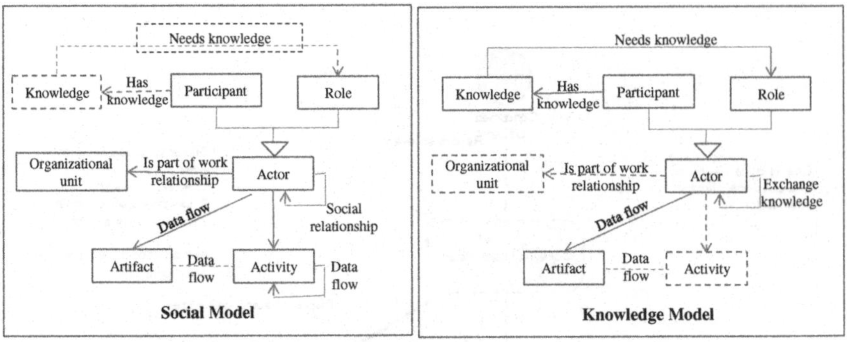

Fig. 5 Metamodels for social and knowledge perspectives

relations have to be mapped just once and in one model but on the other side the model can get quite big and difficult to understand.

2. Reuse objects, as roles and artefacts, in multiple models which can be of different types. A "Model type" in ADO*xx* implements a specific subset of the metamodel. The reuse of objects in different models is supported in the current version of ADO*xx* by a reference mechanism which can transfer selected attribute values across the referenced objects. This mechanism allows for the creation of multiple interlinked models and yet supports analysis and reporting functionalities provided by ADO*xx*.

As the second alternative is far more flexible, we decided to implement Melca using this approach.

Figure 6 illustrates an example of how such concepts can be combined to illustrate a design. The goal here is to collect messages from concerned citizens reporting an incident and plot them on a map. It shows concerned citizens reporting incidents whose impact needs to be assessed. These are collected and then analyzed by a message analyst for plotting on a visualization of a disaster area. At the same time, different citizens may be authorized to directly plot on the map.

Organizational Perspectives Here, the emphasis is on organizational units and how they interact. The organizational perspective is illustrated in Fig. 7. It shows a proposed organization structure for project planning. Figure 5 shows organizational units involved in planning social housing.

Another visualization of organizing is shown in Fig. 8. Here, organizations are not necessarily business units but they refer to how people organize themselves to achieve some purpose. There are a number of workshops organized to capture ideas and work on them. The analysis workshop captures the viewpoints which are then used in a solutions workshop to summarize those that might be of interest to stakeholders. This is then considered by a solution workshop. The solutions are then evaluated by a decision workshop to select one.

Social Perspective The social perspective is becoming increasingly important as business processes to achieve efficiencies are becoming increasingly social. It intends to provide organization leaders to plan how the collaboration and social

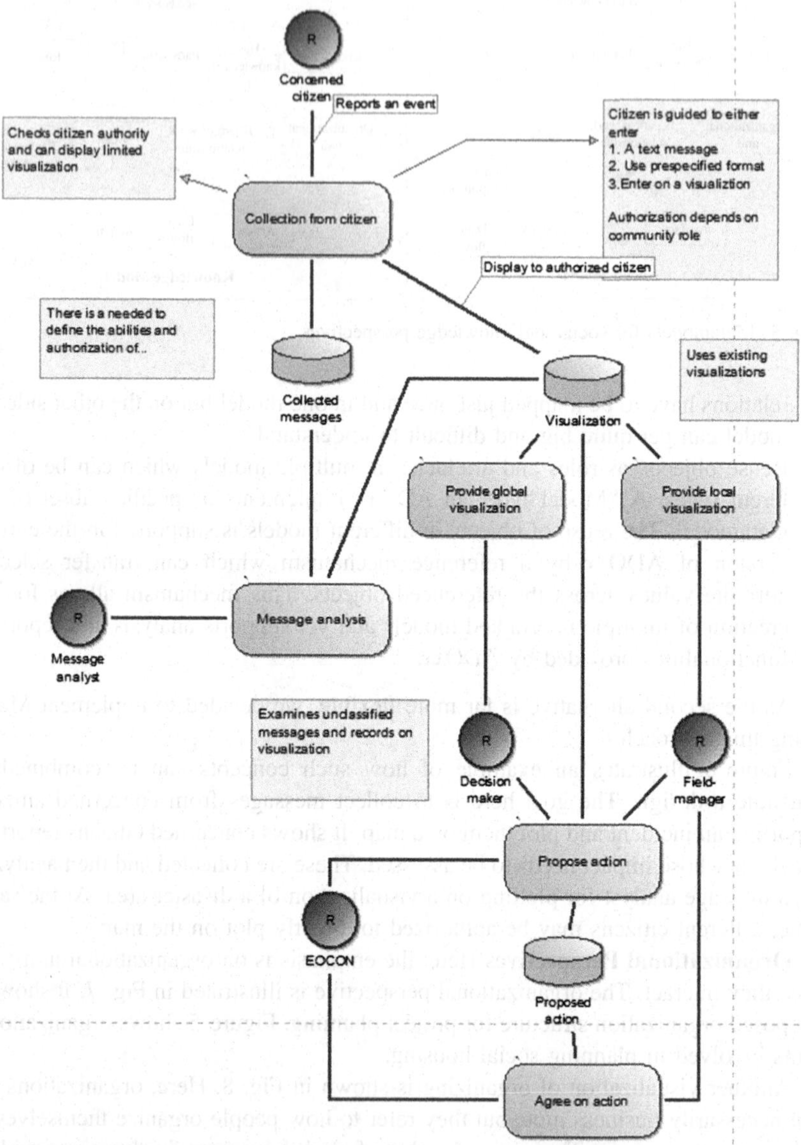

Fig. 6 Ways to capture and filter messages

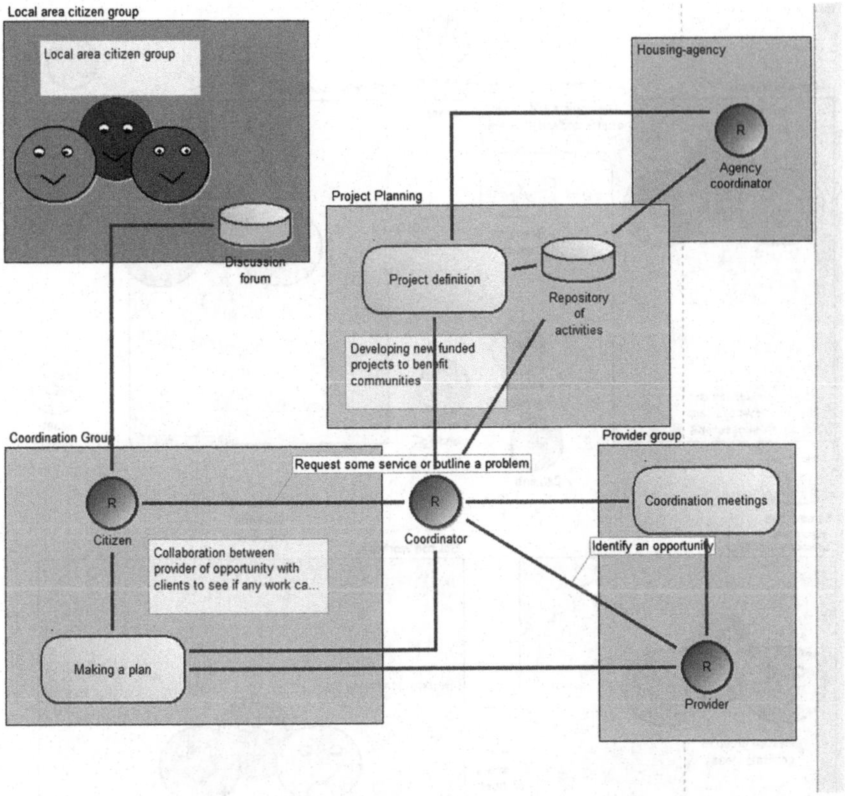

Fig. 7 Organizational perspective for creating a plan

interactions occur between different boundaries of the organization. One way to generate ideas is by showing visualizations from different perspectives. The perspectives that we have identified are the social, business activity, process, and knowledge perspectives [6]. These were described earlier [9] and this paper gives an idea of the visualizations using the social perspective (Fig. 9).

The social perspective, shown in Fig. 4, displays the interaction between the different roles. For example, project managers interact with each professional unit to improve the design and procedure of the projects; for instance, a project manager faced with the environmental issue of removing a heritage listed tree for building social housing within a given timeframe. As well as the PMO (project management office), the delivery manager consults the technical service manager to allocate professional resources for all projects. It indicates the different roles and collaborators' interactions where the social network will be created and where it can be useful for adapting changes effectively in the unanticipated events. Therefore, the social perspective is important for collaboration and participants agreed that

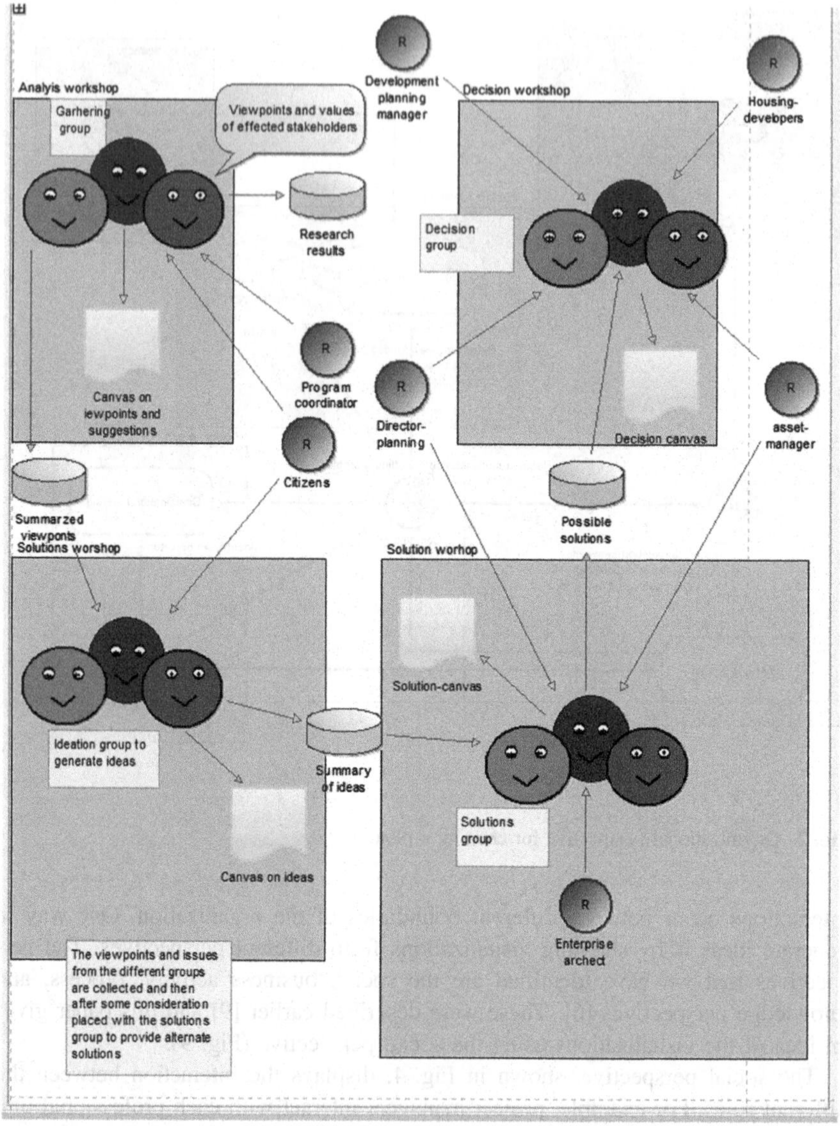

Fig. 8 Collaborative groups

organizations must recognize the formal and informal social behaviors in order to work together effectively.

Using Visualizations generated by Melca We used the visualizations to assist developing a better understanding in complex environments. One example is the completion of the thesis by Paul Yoo published in ICIS 2013 in Milan. Figure 6 is another example showing the use of crowdsourcing in disaster recovery situations.

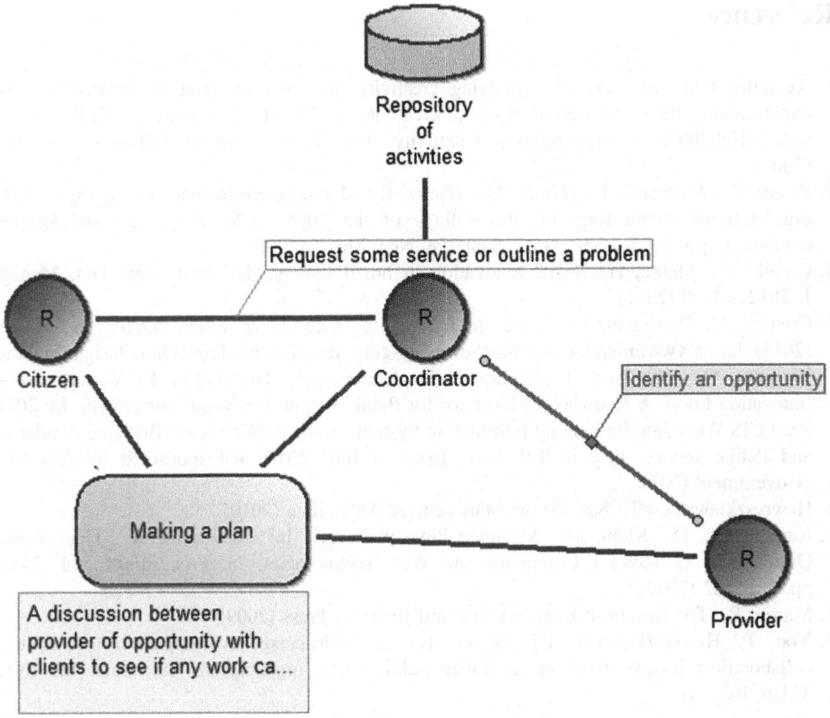

Fig. 9 A visualization from the social perspectives

7 Future Work

What support does Melca on ADO*xx* provide now in design thinking? Within the design thinking process shown in Fig. 2, Melca predominantly facilitates ideation by providing the ability to see systems from different perspectives during the ideation stage. Future work focuses on increasing support for the other tools in Table 1, in order to enhance the ideation stage and go beyond it. Another important aspect here is cross-checking between the different visualizations. The possibilities are

- Adding stories as a class, at least, the important stories could be recorded against each theme,
- Persona maps,
- Easily creating new classes for extending rich pictures to include any class, and
- Including journey maps.

One other important functionality is to maintain traceability between the different visualizations so that a change made in one visualization is immediately reflected in others.

Tool Download http://www.omilab.org/melca.

References

1. Amabile, T.M., Mueller, J.S.: Studying creativity, its processes, and its antecedents: An exploration of the componential theory of creativity. In: Chapter 2 in Zhou, J., Shalley, C. E. (eds.), Handbook of Organisational Creativity. New York: Lawrence Erlbaum Associates (2008)
2. Braun, C., Wortmann, F., Hafner, M., Winter, R.: Method construction—a core approach to organisational engineering. In: Proceedings of the 2005 ACM symposium on Applied computing, pp. 1295–1299. ACM, Santa Fe, New Mexico (2005)
3. Cipolla, C., Moura, H.: Social innovation in brazil through design strategy. Des. Manag. J. **2012**, 40–50 (2012)
4. Courage, C.: Reweaving Corporate dna by weaving a culture of design thinking in CITRIX (2013). http://www.mixprize.org/story/reweving-corporate-dna-building-culturedesign-thinking
5. Forsgren, O., Johansson, T., Albinsson, L., Hartman, T., Gustafsson, T.: Vasterbotten—Innovation Loop: A Knowledge Generator for Public-Private Innovation for growth. In: 2014 Pre-ECIS Workshop Rethinking Information Systems in the Public Sector: Bridging Academia and Public service, held in Tel Aviv, Israel, 8 June 2014, and sponsored by AIS SIG eGovernment (2014)
6. Hawryszkiewycz, I.T.: Knowledge Management. Macmillan (2010)
7. Karagiannis, D., Kühn, H.: Metamodelling platforms. In: Bauknecht, K., Tjoa, A.M., Quirchmayr, G. (eds.) E-Commerce and Web Technologies. In: Proceedings, vol. 2455, pp. 182–182 (2002)
8. Martin, R.: The Design of Business. Harvard Business Press (2009)
9. Yoo, P. Hawryszkiewycz, I.T., Kang, K.: A Multi-perspective approach to facilitate collaboration: a case study on Australian public sector organisations. Int. Conf. Inf. Syst. Milan, Italy (2013)

Business Process Flexibility and Decision-Aware Modeling—The Knowledge Work Designer

Knut Hinkelmann

Abstract This chapter describes the Knowledge Work Designer, a modeling method for knowledge work. It is based on two principles: (1) the separation of business logic and process logic and (2) the support of both structures and unstructured knowledge. Process logic can be represented in a structured way in BPMN and in a nonstructured way with CMMN. For real processes there is no strict separation between structured processes and cases. Therefore, the Knowledge Work Designer offers a deep integration of BPMN and CMMN. Business logic can be represented in a structured way using decision tables. Unstructured business logic can be represented in documents. The separation of business logic and process logic allows for simpler process model and easier maintenance.

Keywords Knowledge work • Business process management • Case management • Decision modeling

1 Introduction

Peter Drucker [1] coined the term knowledge work in 1969. He distinguished between knowledge workers and manual worker. He insisted that new industries will employ mostly knowledge workers. Nowadays, we can see that many workers are knowledge workers. Rosen [2] even regards every worker as a knowledge worker. For Davenport [3], knowledge workers are the key to innovation and growth in today's organization.

K. Hinkelmann (✉)
FHNW University of Applied Sciences and Arts Northwestern Switzerland, 4600 Olten, Switzerland
e-mail: knut.hinkelmann@fhnw.ch

D. Karagiannis et al. (eds.), *Domain-Specific Conceptual Modeling*,
DOI 10.1007/978-3-319-39417-6_18

The objective of the Knowledge Work Designer is to model business processes that cover a broad spectrum of knowledge work. It is based on the following two principles:

- Balance between process logic and business logic
- Support of knowledge work with different degrees of structure

1.1 Balance Between Process Logic and Business Logic

In a business process, we distinguish between process logic and business logic (see Fig. 1).

- Process logic is the knowledge *about* the process, in particular, the process flow with events and activities, the involved participants and resources. The process logic is typically represented in a business process diagram.
- The business logic is the knowledge *in* the process. It corresponds to the practice aspect of [3, 4] and is about how the work is actually done. Understanding business logic means to understand how individual workers or applications respond to the real world of work and accomplish their assigned tasks.

The balance between process logic and business logic is an important consideration for anyone attempting to address knowledge work [3]. Business process modeling tools focus on the process flow. Decision criteria are typically represented as gateways leading to unnecessary complex process models. The Knowledge

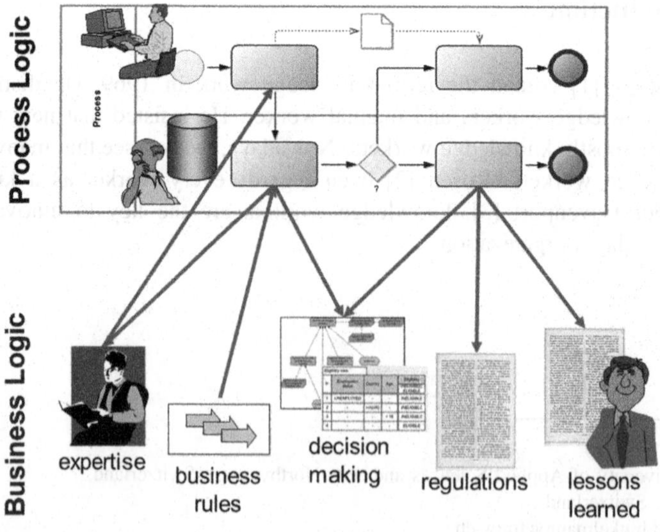

Fig. 1 Distinguishing process logic and business logic

Work Designer, however, contains model types for both process logic and business logic. This allows to model decision-aware business processes as introduced by [5]. A decision-aware business process is a process "that is designed to distinguish between tasks that perform work (i.e., process tasks) and tasks that come to conclusions based on business logic (i.e., decision tasks)" [5].

1.2 Degree of Structure

According to a survey, about 60 % of a knowledge worker's day is spent in unstructured and often unpredictable work patterns, while only about 40 % is structured, predictable, and automatable [6]. The different degree of structure is a characteristic of both business logic and process logic.

Davenport [3] distinguishes four types of knowledge work (see Fig. 2). The distinction is based on two dimensions: level of interdependence and complexity of work. Process logic determines the way of collaboration while business logic corresponds to the knowledge work of individual actors. The Knowledge Work Designer offers modeling languages for both structure and nonstructured knowledge work on individual and collaborative level.

Gadatsch [7] distinguishes three instead of two types of processes with respect to their degree of structure (Fig. 3).

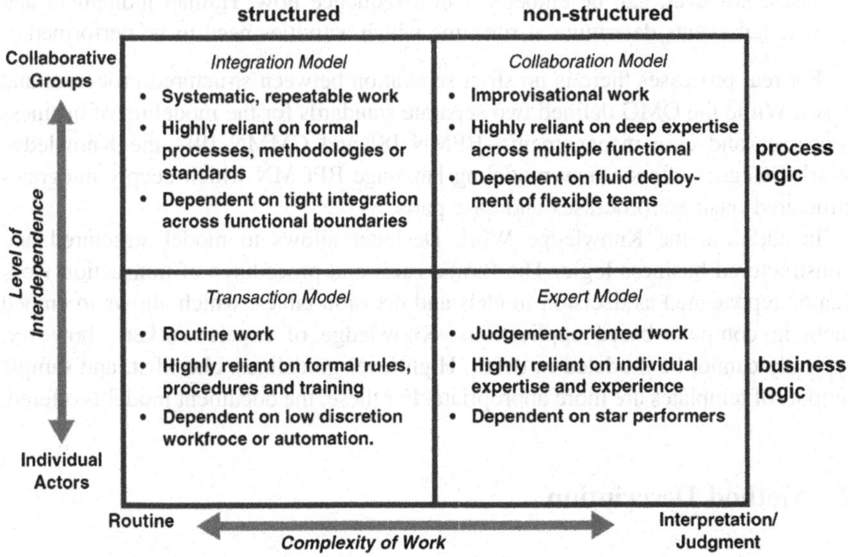

Fig. 2 Four approaches to knowledge work, from [3]

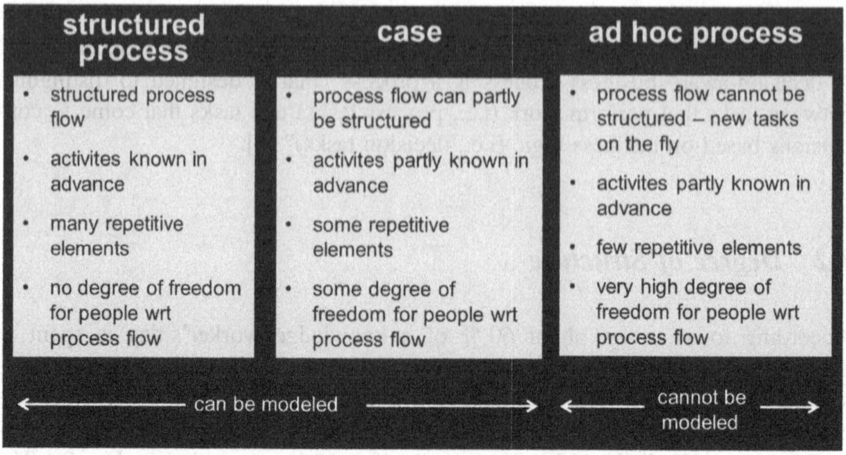
structured process
case
ad hoc process
structured process flow
activites known in advance
many repetitive elements
no degree of freedom for people wrt process flow
process flow can partly be structured
activites partly known in advance
some repetitive elements
some degree of freedom for people wrt process flow
process flow cannot be structured – new tasks on the fly
activites partly known in advance
few repetitive elements
very high degree of freedom for people wrt process flow
can be modeled
cannot be modeled

Fig. 3 Distinguishing processes by their degree of structure—translated from [7]

- For structured processes the activities and the conditions for their execution are known in advance.
- Ad hoc processes consist of activities, not all of which are known in advance. New tasks can be added on the fly and the people have a lot of freedom when to do which tasks. This means that the process flow cannot be modeled.
- Case processes contain both structured and ad hoc parts. There are tasks for which the conditions for their execution can be specified in advance. Not all tasks, however, can be embedded in a sequence flow. Human judgement and external events determine at run-time which activities need to be performed.

For real processes there is no strict separation between structured processes and cases. While the OMG defined two separate standards for the modeling of business processes and case management—BPMN [8] and CMMN [9]—the Knowledge Work Designer offers a new modeling language BPCMN which deeply integrates structured business processes and case parts.

In addition, the Knowledge Work Designer allows to model structured and nonstructured business logic. The formal rules and procedures of transaction work can be represented as decision models and decision tables, which allows to embed them in computer-based applications. Knowledge of expert workers, however, typically cannot be modeled in detail. High-level guidelines, checklist, and sample outputs of templates are more appropriate. For these, the document model is offered.

2 Method Description

The Knowledge Work Designer comprises standard modeling techniques for business processes (BPMN), case management (CMMN) and decisions (DMN). These modeling approaches, however, are not sufficient to model knowledge work appropriately. Therefore, the Knowledge Work Designer makes extensions and modifications on several aspects of the modeling technique:

- Modeling language:
  - In order to be able to model any degree of process structure, an integration of business process modeling and case modeling is provided. The new modeling language is called Business Process and Case Management Notation (BPCMN).
  - A document model type is used, which serves two purposes: It can be used to represent the context of a case and it serves to model unstructured aspects of business logic.
- Modeling procedure:
  - The concept of decision-aware business processes separates process logic and decision logic.

2.1 *Business Process Modeling*

For structured business processes, all possible paths are defined in advance. Control flows from one activity to the next. There is an incoming sequence flow and an outgoing sequence flow relation for every activity. The control flow is explicitly represented and visualized using events and gateways. The Knowledge Work Designer uses the Business Process Model and Notation BPMN 2.0 [8] to model business processes.

2.2 *Case Management Modeling*

Adaptive Case Management (ACM) was proposed as an alternative approach for the management of unstructured and often unpredictable work patterns [6]. Case management processes are not predefined or repeatable, but instead, depend on evolving circumstances and decisions regarding a particular situation. Human judgment is required in determining how to proceed [10]. Depending on their individual knowledge and skills, people approach the same problems differently. Therefore, it must be possible to plan tasks at run-time.

The OMG published the new Case Management Model and Notation (CMMN), a modeling language specific for case management [9]. A case plan model contains plan item tasks and discretionary tasks. Plan item tasks are part of predefined segments; they correspond to the structured part of a case. Discretionary tasks are available to the Case worker, to be applied in addition. They can be added to the plan of the case instance at run-time (see Fig. 4). The execution of the discretionary

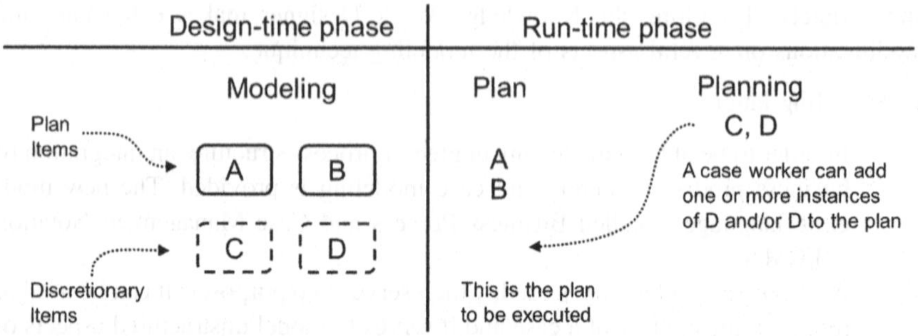

Fig. 4 Design-time modeling and run-time planning with discretionary tasks [9]

tasks depends on the context as well as the skills, experiences and preferences of the individual worker. This is how human judgment is supported by CMMN.

2.3 Document Modeling for Representing Case Files

Case execution is driven by events, context, and content. While activities occur, information is created and added to the case. This information together with the context around it determines the state of a case. Thus, a case evolves over time toward achieving a goal. It requires the ability to jump forward and backward or to repeat activities depending on the circumstances of the case (see Fig. 5).

All information that is required as context for managing a case is defined by a case file. The state of the case is determined by the content within the case file. The case file is not a single file but a kind of virtual folder with references to information in different formats and media: text documents, spreadsheets, emails, reports, databases, systems of records, voice mail, etc.

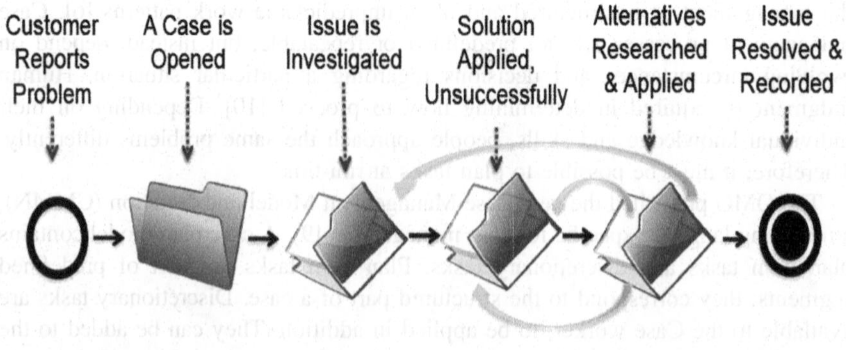

Fig. 5 Evolvement of case execution depending on information in case file [6]

The Knowledge Work Designer uses the document model to represent the case file. A document in a document model can refer to any kind of structured and nonstructured information sources.

2.4 Business Process and Case Modeling

While case management is often considered as different from conventional business process management [6], in reality they cannot be strictly separated. A structured business process can contain parts which deal with nonroutine cases requiring additional investigation by different people. Silver [11] gives the example of dispute resolution as part of a structured payment process. When a customer disputes a charge or demands a refund, case management is usually required. Another example is underwriting, which is part of a structured process, but might require dealing with exceptions or requiring additional input.

On the other hand, there can be situations where a case management process contains structured elements. Project management is a typical example. Although it is composed of unanticipated tasks, it can contain structured process parts like financial reporting.

The only connection between process modeling and case management that is supported by the BPMN and CMMN standards is by referencing. CMMN has a special process tasks which can be used to call a business process. In a similar way, BPMN can be extended to call a CMMN case as a subprocess. This is done in the Knowledge Work Designer as shown in Fig. 6.

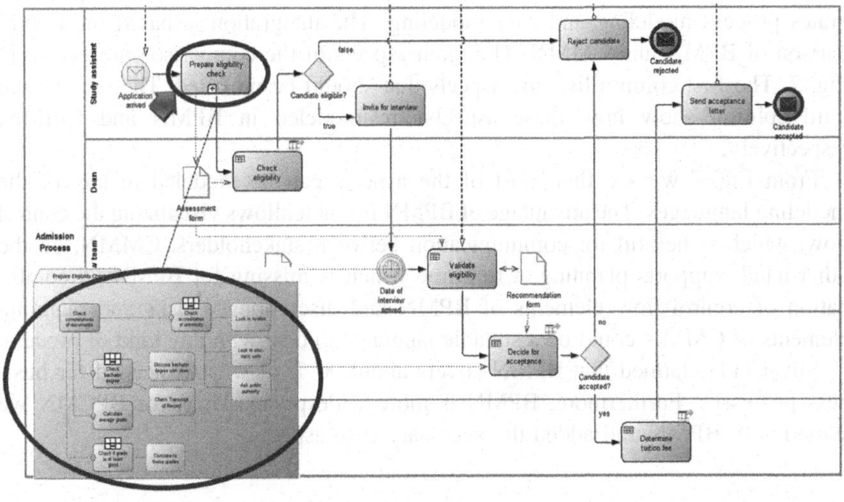

Fig. 6 A CMMN case as a subprocess of a BPMN model

	BPMN	CMMN
Tasks	Tasks	Tasks
Process hierarchy	Subprocesses, Call Activities	Process Tasks, Case Tasks
Events	Events: start – intermediate – end catching – throwing	Event Listeners, implicit Events, Milestones
Control Flow	Gateways/Events	Sentries
	Sequence Flow	Sentry with empty condition
Planning	--	Discretionary Tasks
Responsibilities	Lanes	Role attribute
Process Container	Pool	Folder

Fig. 7 Contrasting elements of BPMN and CMMN

This referencing, however, has some drawbacks. A process has to be broken into small fragments, which then are modeled using either BPMN or CMMN, depending on the level of structure. This makes sense, if there are larger parts, which can be isolated. In real processes, however, there are situations, in which there are discretionary tasks just for single activities in a structured process. On the other hand, even for case models it can make sense to make the control flow between some tasks explicit.

This is why the Knowledge Work Designer contains a new model type called BPCMN (Business Process and Case Management Notation), which deeply integrates process modeling and case modeling. The integration is based on a comparison of BPMN and CMMN. The main aspects of the comparison are shown in Fig. 7. The first column lists the aspects that should be modeled. The second and third column show how these aspects are modeled in BPMN and CMMN, respectively.

From Fig. 7 we see that most of the aspects can be modeled in any of the modeling languages. The advantage of BPMN is that it allows visualizing the control flow, which is helpful for communication between stakeholders. CMMN, on the other hand, supports planning at run-time which is missing for BPMN. A combination of control flow elements of BPMN and discretionary tasks and planning elements of CMMN could be a suitable language to deal with any kind of process.

Silver [11] claimed that BPMN covers about 90 % of what is needed for business processes. Furthermore, BPMN is more widespread. Thus, for BPCMN we started with BPMN and added the necessary case aspects.

2.5 Decision-Aware Business Processes

The term "decision-aware business process" was coined by [5]. They define a decision-aware business process as process that is designed to distinguish between process tasks and decision tasks. A basic idea behind this distinction is to separate the modeling of business logic from the modeling of decision logic, the latter being a special kind of business logic.

Separating business decisions from business process tasks simplifies the business process model and allows managing business logic in a declarative form.

- A business process model is a *procedural* solution because it prescribes a set of tasks that are carried out in a particular sequence.
- A decision table is an example of a *declarative* solution consisting of a set of typically unordered rules. A declarative solution only specifies what needs to be done, with no details as to how, in a step-by-step manner, it is to be carried out, because sequence is irrelevant to arriving at the correct result [5].

By separating business logic from business process logic, the process model becomes much simpler. Figure 8 shows on the left side a business process where decision logic about discount calculation is modeled with gateways. On the right side, the same process is shown as a decision-aware process. The rules for the discount calculation are described in a separate decision model. From the point of view of the business process, the decision logic is a black box evaluating conditions and reaching a conclusion. It can be viewed, managed, and executed independent from the process.

The separated modeling of business logic and process logic improves agility by making changes easier. It permits changes in the decision model without changing the business process model and vice versa. Furthermore, the decision model or individual decision tables and rules can be easily reused in several business processes.

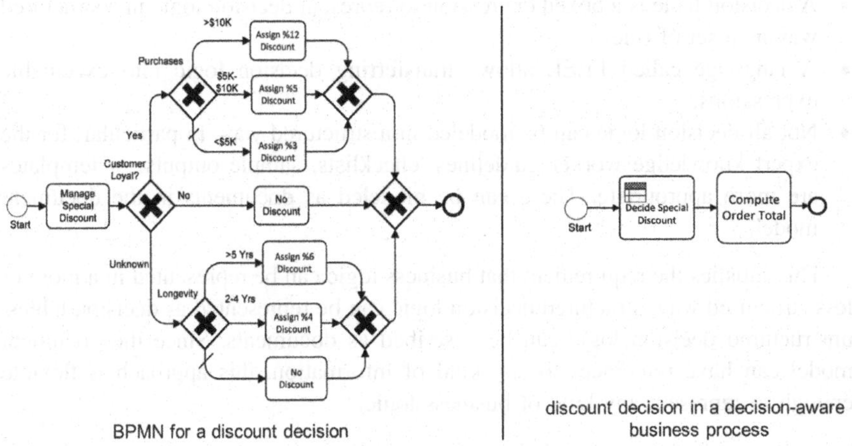

Fig. 8 Discount decision in BPMN and as a decision-aware business process [13]

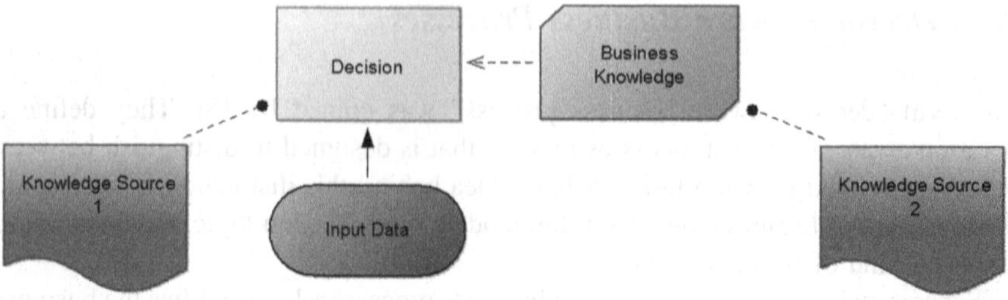

Fig. 9 DMN elements and requirements in a decision requirements graph [12]

2.6 Modeling Business Logic

To model business logic, the Knowledge Work Designer has a focus on decision modeling. The primary modeling method is the Decision Model and Notation (DMN) from the [12]. A DMN model consists of the Decision Requirements Diagram and the decision logic.

The Decision Requirements Diagram consists of four elements: Decision, Business Knowledge, Knowledge Source, and Input Data.

Figure 9 illustrates the elements and the requirements. The key element is the Decision. The Decision invokes a Business Knowledge model, which contains the decision logic. The Knowledge Sources represents the authority for a decision or business knowledge. An example for a knowledge source can be a regulation which determines the rationale for the decisions. The link between the business knowledge and its source provides traceability and a way for impact analysis.

The Decision and the Business Knowledge contain references to the decision logic. The Knowledge Work Designer supports three ways to represent decision logic

- A decision table is a boxed expression to represent decision logic in a structured way as a set of rules.
- A language called FEEL allows transferring decision logic into executable expressions.
- Not all decision logic can be modeled in a structured way. In particular, for the expert knowledge worker guidelines, checklists, sample outputs, or templates are more appropriate. These can be modeled as documents in the document model.

This satisfies the requirement that business logic can be represented in a more or less structured way: structured decision logic can be represented as decision tables; unstructured decision logic can be described as documents. Since the document model can have references to any kind of information, this approach is flexible enough to represent any kind of business logic.

3 Method Conceptualization

The model types of the Knowledge Work Designer are shown in Fig. 10. There are model types for both process logic and business logic. For both of them, there are model types for different degrees of structure.

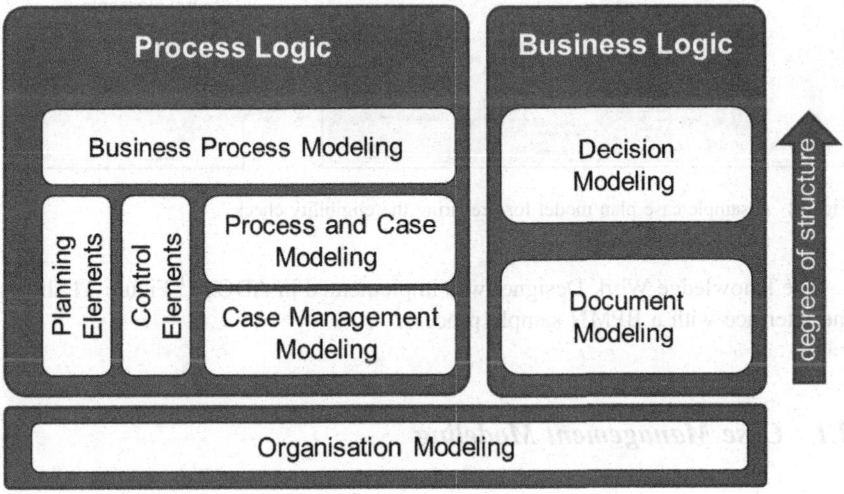

Fig. 10 Model types of the Knowledge Work Designer

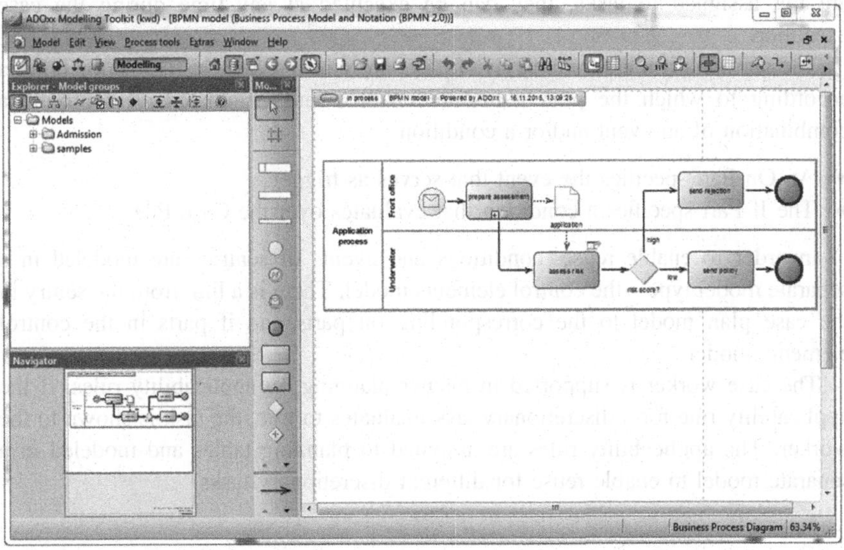

Fig. 11 Screenshot of a business process model in the Knowledge Work Designer

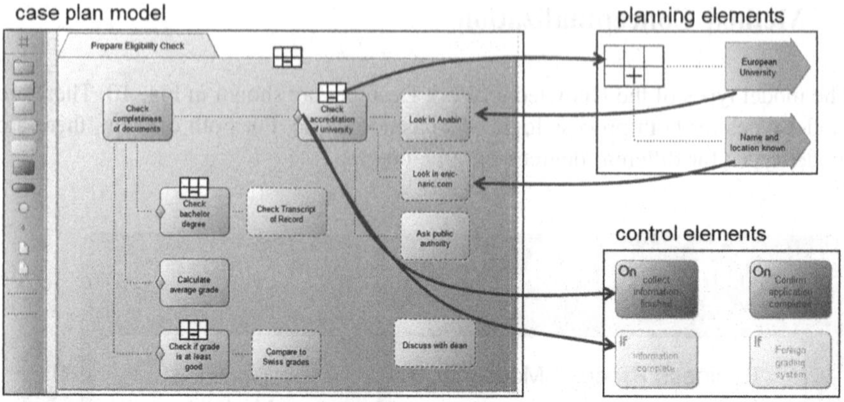

Fig. 12 A sample case plan model for preparing the eligibility check

The Knowledge Work Designer was implemented in ADO*xx*.[1] Figure 11 shows the interface with a BPMN sample process.

3.1 Case Management Modeling

Figure 12 shows an example of a case management model. The modeling language implements CMMN 1.0. It allows modeling both tasks and discretionary tasks. The latter are modeled with dashed borders. They can either be assigned to tasks. If they are not assigned to tasks, they can be executed at any time during the case execution.

The diamonds on the boundaries of tasks are sentries. Sentries define the criteria according to which the plan items are enabled and terminated. A sentry is a combination of an event and/or a condition.

- An On-Part specifies the event that serves as trigger.
- The If-Part specifies a condition that evaluates over the Case File.

In order to enable reuse, conditions and events of sentries are modeled in a separate model type—the control elements model. There is a link from the sentry in the case plan model to the corresponding on parts and if parts in the control elements model.

The case worker is supported in his/her planning by applicability rules. If the applicability rule for a discretionary task evaluates to true, the task is shown to the worker. The applicability rules are assigned to planning tables and modeled in a separate model to enable reuse for different discretionary tasks.

[1]ADOxx.ORG, http://www.adoxx.org, last visit on 08.03.2016.

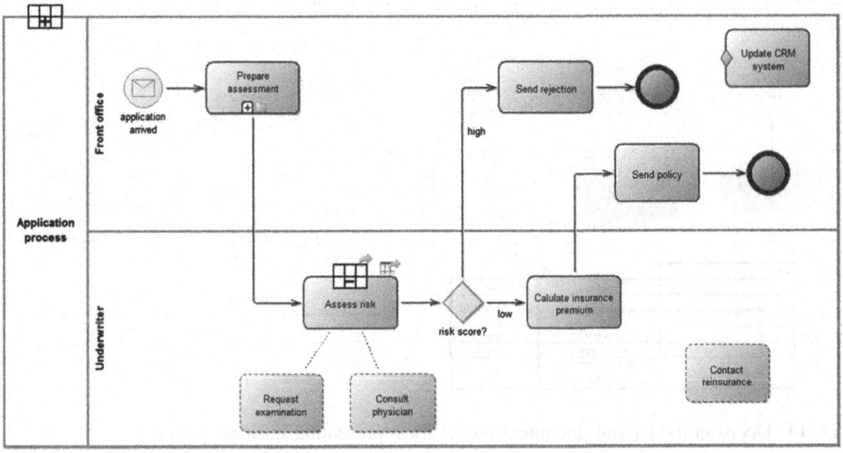

Fig. 13 Example of a BPCMN model

3.2 *Business Process and Case Modeling*

The Business Process and Case Modeling Notation BPCMN extends business process modeling with features of case management modeling. Figure 13 shows an example of a BPCMN model.

The process contains a structured part consisting of activities which are connected via sequence flow relationships as well as unstructured elements.

- The task "Assess risk" has two discretionary tasks associated to it—and a planning table which refers to applicability rules.
- The task "Update CRM" system is not embedded in the sequence flow. Its execution is determined by the sentry that is connected to it.
- There is a discretionary task "Contact reinsurance" which is not associated to a task and thus can be executed at any time. The planning table for this task is attached to the pool, which is the container of the process.
- The subprocess "Prepare assessment" calls a case model—as indicated by the small folder icon at the bottom of the element.
- The task "Assess risk" is a business rules tasks. It has a reference to a decision model. Thus, this is an example of a decision-aware business process.

3.3 *Modeling Business Logic*

As explained in Sect. 2.6, business logic can be represented in a structured and nonstructured way. The left part of Fig. 14 shows a decision model for the risk assessment of an insurance. The decision uses the data from the application as input

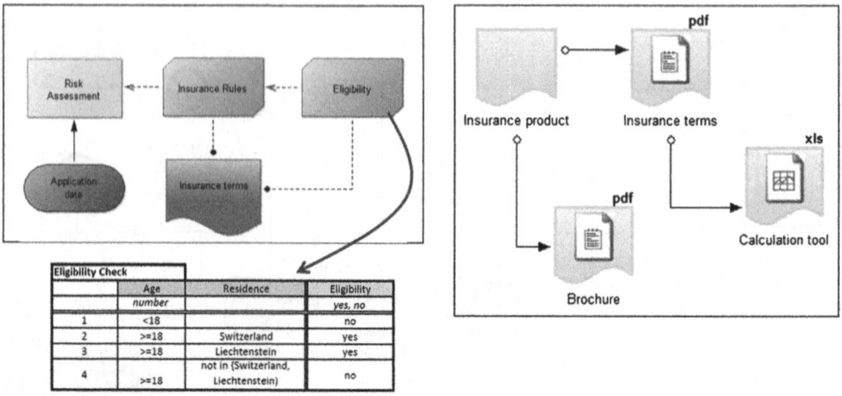

Fig. 14 Decision model and document model for representing business logic

and determines a risk score. The decision logic is assigned to the business knowledge element "Insurance Rules". They are based on the Insurance terms which are a reference to an element in the document model.

The insurance rules can be represented in many different ways. A decision table is a formal representation, which can be interpreted by humans and can be translated into code for a rule engine. The document model can be used to represent nonstructured business logic, knowledge sources and documents of a case file.

4 Proof of Concept

The Knowledge Work Designer was applied to the admission process of the Master of Science study programs at School of Business FHNW. This is a description of the process

- The process starts when we receive the application from a candidate. First, the study assistant prepares the eligibility check of the candidate. The study assistant makes sure that all information is available to assess eligibility.
- It is ascertained that the bachelor degree is regarded as equivalent to Information Systems, Information Technology, or Business Administration. The study assistant may check the transcript of record if he/she is unsure.
- It is ascertained that the university from which the candidate got the bachelor degree is accredited. If the university is unknown to the study assistant, the study assistant typically looks in the Anabin database or on www.enic-naric.net www.enic-naric.net. The study assistant can also ask public authorities to confirm the status of the university.

- It is ascertained that the average grade is at least "good". If the average grade is not mentioned in the transcript, it is calculated by the study assistant. For unknown grading systems one has to find out how it compares to the Swiss grades.
- The study assistant can discuss with the dean at any time.
- The candidate is registered in the administration system.
- When all information is available, the dean checks the eligibility of the candidate.
- Candidates who are obviously not eligible are rejected.
- The other candidates are invited for an interview, which is made by the interview team. The output of the interview is a recommendation which is then input for the admission committee.
- The admission committee decides whether the candidate is accepted.
- For accepted candidates the administration determines the tuition fee.
- The study assistant informs the candidate about acceptance and tuition fee.

A first analysis showed that neither BPMN, nor CMMN alone are appropriate to model the process. The process is structured but it contains tasks, whose execution depends on the individual worker. For example, a university might be unknown to one study assistant, while another study assistant might know it. Thus, the check in the database only depends on the individual worker and the time when the assessment is made. The same is true for the translation of foreign grades.

A first solution was to identify those tasks which need human judgment and model them as a CMMN subprocess, while the main process in modeled in BPMN. The resulting model is shown in Fig. 6. The CMMN subprocess is shown in Fig. 12.

The disadvantage of this model is that for the CMMN subprocess the control flow is not visible. Furthermore, there is no visualization of the roles of the participants who are involved in the CMMN subprocess. These disadvantages can be overcome with the BPCMN model as shown in Fig. 15.

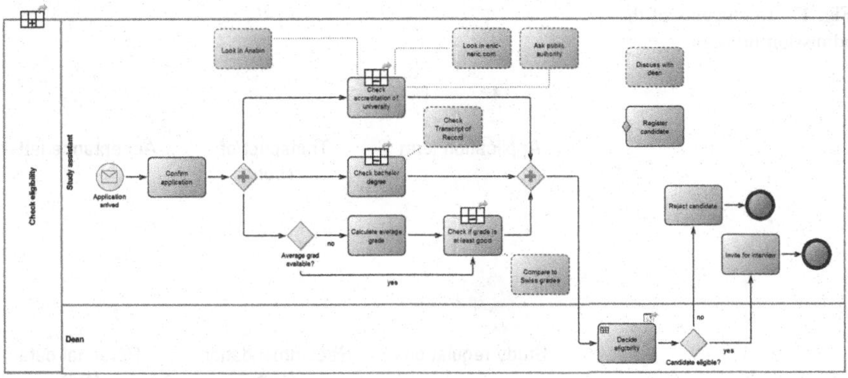

Fig. 15 A BPCMN model for eligibility check

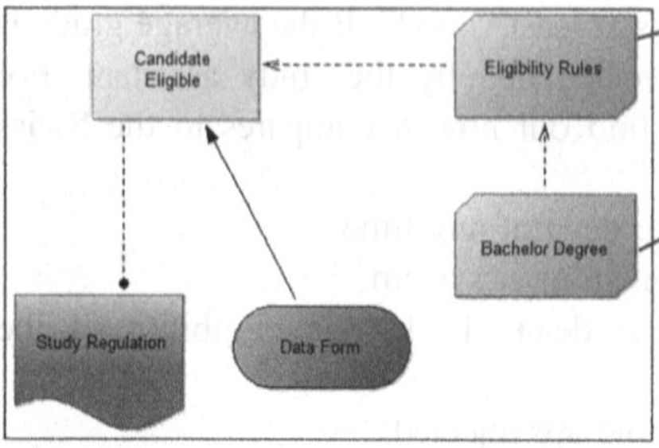

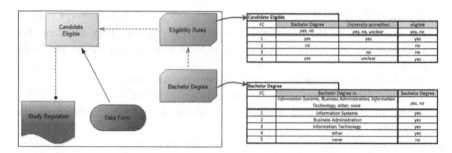

Candidate Eligible

FC	Bachelor Degree	University accredited	eligible
	yes, no	*yes, no, unclear*	*yes, no*
1	yes	yes	yes
2	no		no
3		no	no
4	yes	unclear	yes

Bachelor Degree

FC	Bachelor Degree in	Bachelor Degree
	Information Systems, Business Administration, Information Technology, other, none	*yes, no*
1	Information Systems	yes
2	Business Administration	yes
3	Information Technology	yes
4	other	yes
5	none	no

Fig. 16 Decision model for the eligibility check

In the model of Fig. 15, the control flow of the process is visualized. It can easily be seen that there are three parallel paths, but the task "Calculate average grade" is executed only if the average grade is not available. In the corresponding CMMN model in Fig. 12 the control flow is hidden in the conditions of the sentries. This declarative representation allows to model any level of complexity. In reality, however, people are used to think about process flow.

Flexibility of process execution is represented by

- the discretionary tasks, whose execution depends on the judgment of the individual participant.
- the task "Register candidate", which is not part of the sequence flow and is executed as soon as its sentry evaluates to true.

The gateways in the process model determine the process flow but do not refer to any business logic. The business logic for the eligibility of the candidate is modeled separately in a DMN model (see Fig. 16).

The decision model contains the structured part of the business logic. The Study regulation refers to the corresponding document in the document model (Fig. 17).

Fig. 17 Documents of the admission process

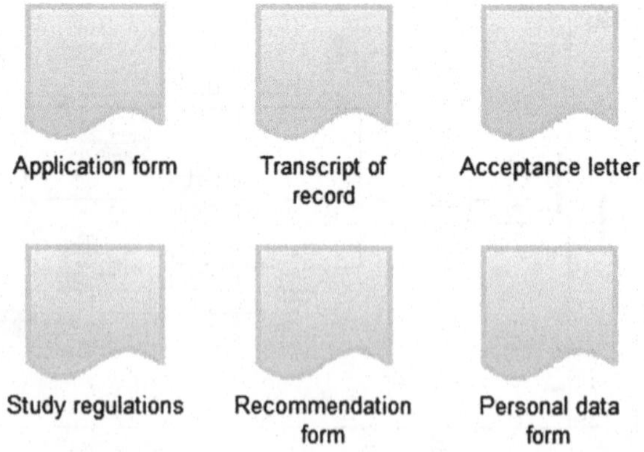

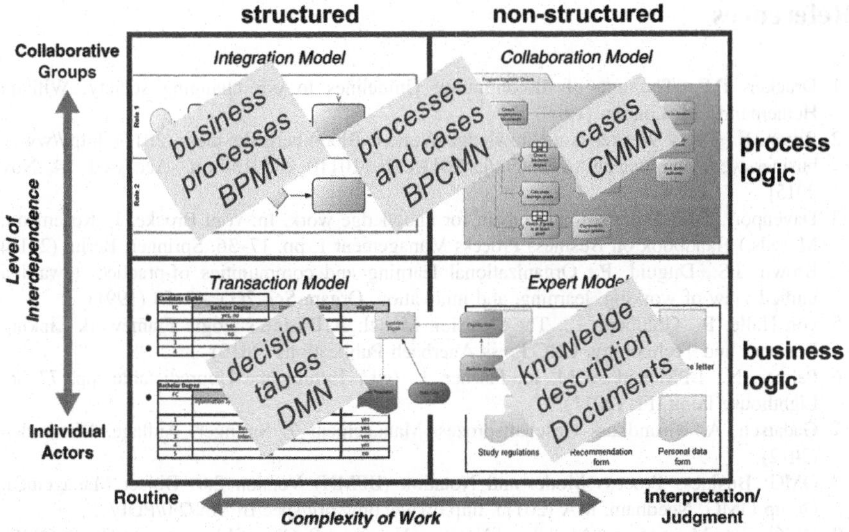

Fig. 18 Knowledge models and model types in the Knowledge Work Designer

The document model not only contains the unstructured business logic but also documents and data which determine the state of the process execution.

5 Conclusion

The Knowledge Work Designer is a modeling tool for flexible, decision-aware business processes. It includes a *combination* of modeling languages for both structured and nonstructured process logic and business logic as well as a new *integration* of business process and case modeling (see Fig. 18).

Process logic can be represented as a structured business process using BPMN, as a nonstructured case plan in CMMN or as a combination of both called BPCMN. The document model allows referencing any information, be it structured data or any kind of documents. Decision tables of DMN are currently the only representation formalism for structured business logic. Any other business logic can be stored in a file and referenced via the document model.

Future versions of the Knowledge Work Designer will include support for other types of visual knowledge representation like class diagrams, semantic networks, or ontologies.

Acknowledgments I thank Arianna Pierfranceschi who implemented the BPCMN model type. She put a lot of effort in the attractive design of the model elements and the scripts, which make modeling in the Knowledge Work Designer enjoyable.

Tool Download http://www.omilab.org/kwd.

References

1. Drucker, P.F.: The age of discontinuity: Guidelines to our changing society. William Heinemann Ltd, London (1969)
2. Rosen, E.: Every Worker Is a Knowledge Worker. Bloomberg Business (2011). http://www.businessweek.com/managing/content/jan2011/ca20110110_985915.htm. Accessed 14 Nov 2015]
3. Davenport, T.H.: Process management for knowledge work. In: vom Brocke, J., Rosemann, M. (eds.) Handbook on Business Process Management 1, pp. 17–36. Springer, Berlin (2010)
4. Brown, J.S., Duguid, P.: Organizational learning and communities of-practice: toward a unified view of working, learning, and innovation. Organ. Sci. **2**(1), 40–58 (1991)
5. von Halle, B., Goldberg, L.: The Decision Model: A Business Logic Framework Linking Business and Technology. CRC Press Auerbach Publications (2010)
6. Palmer, N.: BPM and ACM. In: Fischer, L. (ed.) Taming the Unpredictable, pp. 77–86. Lighthouse Point, FL (2011)
7. Gadatsch, A.: Grundkurs Geschäftsprozess-Management 7. Springer, Auflage, Wiesbaden (2012)
8. OMG: Business Process Model and Notation (BPMN) Version 2.0. Object Management Group OMG, Needham, MA (2011). http://www.omg.org/spec/BPMN/2.0/PDF/
9. OMG: Case Management Model and Notation Version 1.0. Object Management Group OMG, Needham, MA (2014). http://www.omg.org/spec/CMMN/1.0/PDF
10. McCauley, D.: Achieving agility. In: Fischer, L. (ed.) Mastering the Unpredictable: How Adaptive Case Management Will Revolutionize the Way That Knowledge Workers Get Things Done. Future Strategies Inc. (2010)
11. Silver, B.: Case management: addressing unique BPM requirements. In: Fischer, L. (ed.) Taming the Unpredictable, pp. 87–98. Lighthouse Point, FL, Future Strategies (2011)
12. OMG: Decision Model and Notation Version 1.0. Object Management Group OMG, Needham, MA (2015). http://www.omg.org/spec/DMN/1.0/PDF
13. Debevoise, T., Taylor, J.: The Microguide to Process and Decision Modelling in BPMN/DMN. Booksurge, North Charleston SC (2014)
14. Silver, B.: Sudden Impact: IBM Merges Case into BPM (2014). http://brsilver.com/sudden-impact-ibm-merges-case-bpm-forgets-announce/. Accessed 15 Nov 2015

Part IX
Production Management Systems

Modeling Product-Service Systems for the Internet of Things: The ComVantage Method

Robert Andrei Buchmann

Abstract This chapter provides an overview on the current state of the ComVantage modeling method implementation. The method addresses the domain of product-service systems that must run in an Internet of Things environment. This specificity manifests in several aspects: (i) the underlying business model is based on the provision of products, services or a mix of these (e.g., maintenance services attached to products with embedded systems); (ii) collaborative business processes must be supported by mobile apps that consume Linked Data; (iii) model contents must be available to model-aware run-time systems running in a Linked Data environment; (iv) modeling concepts must be linked to IoT resources and their properties, in order to provide a mash-up back-end knowledge base to Internet of Things applications. The method was initiated in a European FP7 research project, therefore project context will also be highlighted, to better outline the motivational frame.

Keywords Linked data • Mobile maintenance • Requirements modeling • Product-service systems

1 Introduction

The goal of the chapter is to describe the approach that the ComVantage method takes to model product-service systems (PSS) that raise requirements for running in an "Internet of Things" (IoT) environment, where resources are addressable and accessible through means established by the Linked Data technological space—that is the RDF data model [29], SPARQL queries [31], HTTP-based protocols for

R.A. Buchmann (✉)
Business Information Systems Department, Babes-Bolyai University,
400591 Cluj-Napoca, Romania
e-mail: robert.buchmann@econ.ubbcluj.ro

D. Karagiannis et al. (eds.), *Domain-Specific Conceptual Modeling*,
DOI 10.1007/978-3-319-39417-6_19

remote querying [30] and the middleware necessary to expose legacy data sources to the Internet of Things. The overall method specification is available in ([15]—deliverables D312, D822) and an academic proof of concept is hosted by the Open Model Laboratory (OMiLAB)—remote access and ABL source are available at [24], the source must be run on the ADO*xx* metamodeling platform [5]. The proof of concept implements only a fragment of the overall method specification, to be analyzed in this paper, whereas the overall specification includes extensions for a wider enterprise modeling scope, designed for possible productisation in project follow-up activities.

The method was initially envisioned as a SCOR-inspired supply-chain modeling method, with an early stage iteration described previously in [11]. The method and its OMiLAB proof of concept further evolved by gradually incorporating various domain-specificity aspects pertaining both to (a) the application areas to be modeled (i.e., collaborative production and maintenance systems) and (b) the application environment (mobile apps at the front-end, Linked Data [16] at the back-end). The targeted application environment is present both in the way of first class modeling concepts (e.g., mobile app requirements) and in the way of run-time enablers (e.g., the serialisation of models for linking and querying in the Internet of Things). To assimilate domain-specificity, the method has been evolving according to practices established by the Agile Modeling Method Engineering (AMME) framework [20], with OMiLAB as an instance environment to run AMME. In the remainder of this introduction, we outline some motivational aspects that are generalized beyond the project context and will serve as a basis for the concluding SWOT analysis.

Although originating in different paradigms (RFID networks and knowledge representation, respectively), the Internet of Things and the Semantic Web have converging concerns on the common foundation established by the Linked Data technological space, which enables cross-organizational federation of data that is exposed explicitly (via URIs) or implicitly (via reasoning) by various types of resources. To stimulate this convergence, adapters have been developed for different kinds of data sources:

- Adapters that lift legacy systems' repositories to the Web of Data—e.g., D2RQ for relational databases [3], XLWrap for spreadsheets [21], Any23 for distilling RDF from Web documents [2];
- Middleware that exposes IoT sensors as addressable resources [27], making their properties remotely query-able (over HTTP or related protocols).

The work at hand adds to these a third source, which has the potential of providing a "semantic glue" between data graphs derived from the two types of sources. As Fig. 1 shows, this new source of semantics is a domain-specific modeling tool—that is, an implementation of a PSS modeling method that prescribes mechanisms for linking domain-specific model elements to existing URIs and for exporting the semantics described in diagrammatic form in a format compatible with Linked Data. The output has the potential of establishing, even in the absence of ontologies, a semantic bridge between execution-time data derived

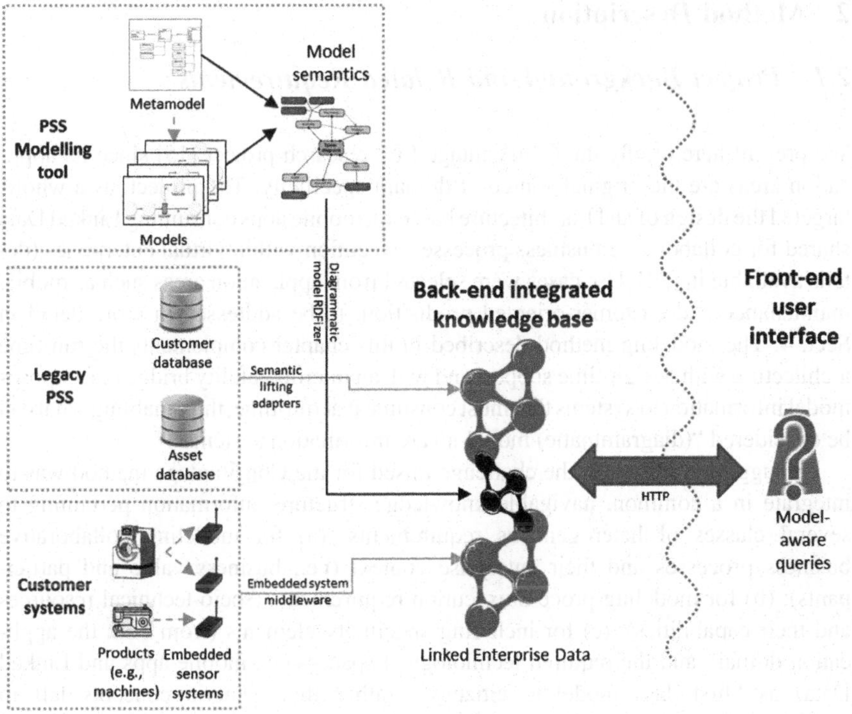

Fig. 1 Application environment for the ComVantage modeling method

from different sources and to support, at the same-time, design-time requirements (e.g., decision support) and run-time requirements raised during the management of a PSS. *Domain-specificity* is a characteristic of essential importance, since it ensures that relevant semantics are machine-readable and accessible by queries that cross over the three sources and information. This means that model elements should not be generic objects with domain-specific interpretation provided by users (as it is the case with general purpose languages) but rather that concepts with prescribed domain-specific properties and relations are first class symbols of the language.

In order to create a comprehensive overview, the remainder of the paper is structured as follows: Sect. 2 explains the method development context—i.e., the originating project background, enablers and a discussion of benefits relative to the state of the art. Section 3 discusses design aspects and design decisions with respect to the modeling method building blocks. Section 4 highlights the proof of concept implementation illustrated by application cases. The paper ends with a concluding SWOT analysis.

2 Method Description

2.1 Project Background and Related Requirements

We present here briefly the ComVantage FP7 research project [15] since its application areas are the original source of domain-specificity. The project, as a whole, targeted the design of an IT architecture based on mobile apps consuming Linked Data shared for collaborative business processes execution within virtual enterprises (details available in [22]. Use cases were selected from application areas such as mobile maintenance and customer-oriented production, to be addressed in more detail in Sect. 4. The modeling method described in this chapter complements the run-time architecture with design-time support and with an interoperability bridge that exposes model information to systems that must consume it at run-time, thus enabling what can be considered “(diagrammatic) model-aware information systems”.

As suggested in Fig. 2, the challenge raised for the ComVantage method was to integrate in a common, navigable knowledge structure, information pertaining to several classes of heterogeneous requirements: (a) for modeling collaborative business processes and their enterprise context (i.e., business value and participants); (b) for modeling process execution requirements (socio-technical resources and their capabilities); (c) for including specificity elements (from both the application domain and the required technological space—i.e., mobile apps and Linked Data) as “first-class modeling citizens” (rather than generic concepts left to domain-specific interpretation); (d) for ensuring usability and understandability through notational customization; (e) for ensuring interoperability with run-time software components, regardless of how the model semantics evolve through different method iterations. In addition to these, a horizontal requirement emerged, to

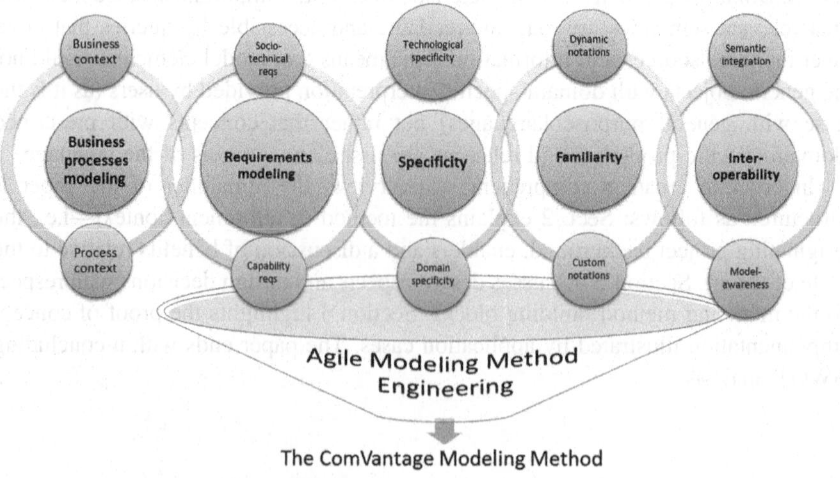

Fig. 2 Classes of modeling requirements

avoid a "take-all or leave-all" approach, thus allowing the modeler to tackle aspects relevant to different scopes; therefore, a hybrid modular language developed with an agile metamodeling approach was of essence.

The method was developed in an iterative cycle, using the OMiLAB resources and laboratory (which also hosts the academic prototype). For fast prototyping, the ADO*xx* metamodeling platform [5] was employed, as it provides built-in support for addressing some of the mentioned requirements. Its foundational meta^{2}model provided the semantic skeleton for an RDF vocabulary designed for the export of models as Linked Data named graphs in several serialisation syntaxes (e.g., TriG [4]).

On a conceptual level, the work is rooted in the notion of a *modeling method* provided in [19]. In order to separate concerns and achieve modularity, the modeling language was partitioned in *model types* capturing different views or facets of the system under study. The modeling procedure was documented in ([15]—deliverable 352) and will only briefly be covered in Sect. 4, for selected use cases, in order to highlight the model links that can expose cross-model semantics to the Web of Data. An overview of the method mechanisms was provided in [13]—here we will only focus on the model serialisation mechanism that exports domain-specific semantics to the Internet of Things, where it can enrich queries in the absence of domain ontologies.

From a methodological perspective, the iterative Agile Modeling Method Engineering (AMME) approach was followed, whose framework and enablers was discussed in detail in [20]. Three high-level methodological phases were involved:

- *Phase 1 (Bottom-up integration)* started with the acquisition of knowledge from use case scenarios and the design of early model mock-ups serving different application domains [9, 14];
- *Phase 2 (Ontological refinement)* dealt with an analysis of the acquired concepts and the identification of recurring semantics. Foundational relations and classes were identified, from which all other concepts can be specialized (e.g., "part-of" relations as a basis for both organizational decomposition—in an organigram, and sub-process decomposition—in a business process model). This led to a multi-abstraction layering and tighter integration of the modeling stack, with a gradual incorporation of domain-specificity;
- *Phase 3 (Top-down separation of concerns)* redesigned the modeling language in different types of diagrammatic models, aiming for a balance between visual cluttering (i.e., too many weakly related concepts in the same model type) and excessive fragmentation (i.e., too many model types forcing the user to frequently navigate between them).

The designed model types were organized in a stack across different vertical enterprise "facets":

- The *Motivators* facet describes the object of the enterprise activity, typically value models that incorporate both product features and associated services. For the mobile maintenance scenarios, these are maintenance services attached to leased machines;

- The *Participants* facet includes resources that may be involved in process execution: *liable entities* (i.e., business entities, individual roles or employees), *assets* (i.e., mobile apps, data sources), *capabilities* (i.e., the business value provided by partners, employee skills, app requirements);
- The *Tasks* facet describes the work to be performed, typically in procedural fashion (modeled as control flows with some notational customization which will be noticeable in the running examples).

Horizontally, different modeling scopes enable the modeler to work on different layers of detail, each one using different domain-specific interpretations on the three facets—e.g., in the *supply chain scope* control flows are used to describe collaborative production processes, while in the *app execution scope* they describe the steps of interaction performed by a user on an abstract app UI. Different types of models serve these different facets and scopes, as described in the overall method specification in ([15]—deliverables D312, D822) and cannot fit the space of this paper. Several scopes will be covered by the use case discussions in Sect. 4.

2.2 Related Work and Proposed Benefits

Product-service systems emerged from combining goals of manufacturing enterprises with those of service enterprises. Modeling for PSS has been traditionally concerned with simulation and statistical modeling for decision support [1, 26]. However, valuable support may also come from the field of enterprise modeling, where different methods have emerged at the intersection of conceptual modeling and software engineering, with the aim of supporting communication, evaluation and analysis of the structure and behavior of enterprises, typically to achieve alignment between the business and its underlying information systems. Enterprises have been described with fully fledged modeling methods aiming for global adoption—see Archimate [25]. Alternatively, enterprises have been described in terms of supply chains [6] or through holistic business process management frameworks [7]. With respect to model interoperability, model serialisation mechanisms have been built as XML vocabularies: BPEL [23], XPDL [32], typically to enable some degree of process automation or code generation. The ComVantage method distinguishes from such predecessors by several characteristics to be highlighted throughout this paper:

- It addresses the paradigm of product-service systems from the direction of enterprise modeling, considering model analysis requirements and connectivity within the Internet of Things. *Interoperability* with the Internet of Things is based on a multi-abstraction RDF Schema for exporting and linking model information. Therefore, instead of aiming for code generation, the method treats models as a domain-specific knowledge base that can support semantic queries and reasoning, as well as the possibility of establishing a semantic bridge between model elements and resources relevant to product-service systems. Simulation may also be supported, if domain-specific parameters present in the models are populated and the simulation engine is able to query them across the Web of Data;

- It is a *non-standard* method, as it does not aim to bring all its users on the same level of detail. The work aimed for a trade-off between (i) the level of generality (reuse across domains) and (ii) the depth of domain-specificity captured in various aspects, in order to expose domain semantics to both design-time users and run-time domain-aware systems. Consequently, the modular nature of the ComVantage method incorporates fragments (model types) of varying specificity, which can be used together or independently (depending on the semantic richness necessary to answer model queries);
- It is an *evolving method*, being driven by changing requirements, therefore it employs the OMiLAB to manage this evolution. Just as the discipline of software engineering has shifted from rigid development models (e.g., waterfall) to agile methodologies after recognising the inherent evolution of requirements, the discipline of modeling method engineering must achieve similar flexibility with respect to modeling goals.

3 Method Conceptualization

3.1 Syntactic and Semantic Specificity

Domain-specificity manifests both in the syntactic and semantic aspects of the modeling method. On functionality level, this specificity is preserved by the RDF export component, since its modular vocabulary contains an abstraction layer that is synchronized at export time with changes in the language metamodel, as it will be explained in Sect. 3.2. Figure 3 shows examples of how domain-specificity manifests at syntactic and semantic level:

- *On semantic level*, each modeling symbol is attached to a non-ambiguous machine-readable meaning in the form of editable properties and semantic links that were prescribed at metamodel level. In the figure, a machine defect is defined by its annotations with diagnosing sensor levels and with the skills/knowledge required for a maintenance intervention, as well as with hyperlinks that allow navigation (hence improved usability) across related models;
- *On syntactic level*, the semantic specificity determines notational dynamics: in the figure, a maintenance activity symbol is enriched (based on the presence of semantic links) with hotspots that act on two levels (i) as visual cues on semantics (the fact that the activity requires app support, a performer and is described in more detail in a subprocess) and (ii) as functional hyperlinks that contribute to model navigability, hence usability and understandability.

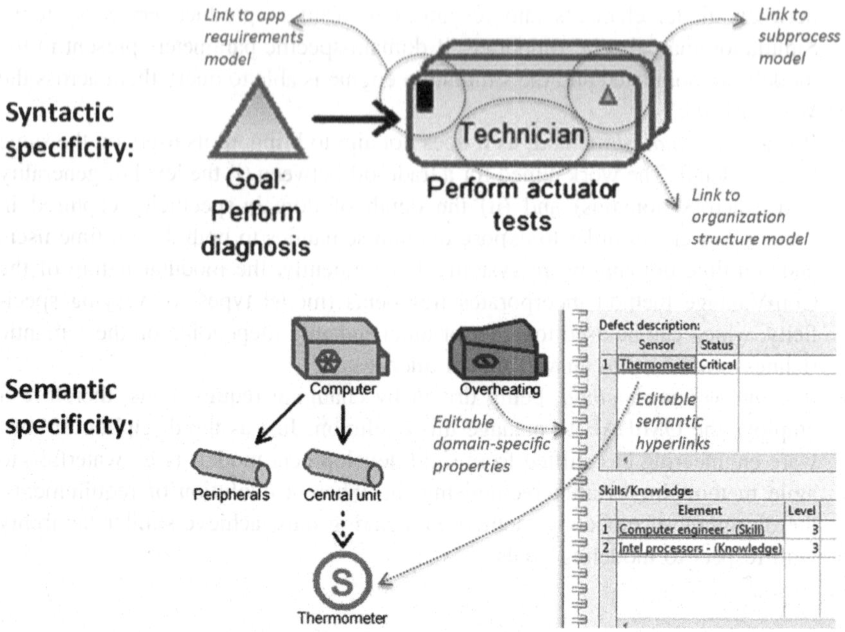

Fig. 3 Manifestations of domain-specificity in the ComVantage modeling proof of concept

The semantic links across different types of models are overviewed by the metamodel representation in Fig. 4, where containers designate different types of models and the concepts that are bound to them by metalevel constraints. Modeling relations manifest both as visual connectors (if inside a model type) or as semantic links/hyperlinks across different models (and also between objects of the same model, to avoid visual cluttering). Examples of such links will be highlighted for different scenarios, in relation to the proof of concept demonstrator, in Sect. 4.

3.2 *Model Serialisation Mechanism*

The presented metamodel is also the semantic backbone of the model serialisation output, which spreads across three abstraction layers with different degrees of flexibility, as suggested by Fig. 5:

1. On the *meta*^{2} *layer*, foundational concepts (e.g., the classes of all models, all model elements, all connectors, all inter-model hyperlinks, all editable properties) are specialized from primitive RDF Schema concepts (i.e., rdfs:class, rdf: property);
2. On the *metalayer*, further specializations are generated from the language concepts, hence it evolves in synchronization with the metamodel changes;

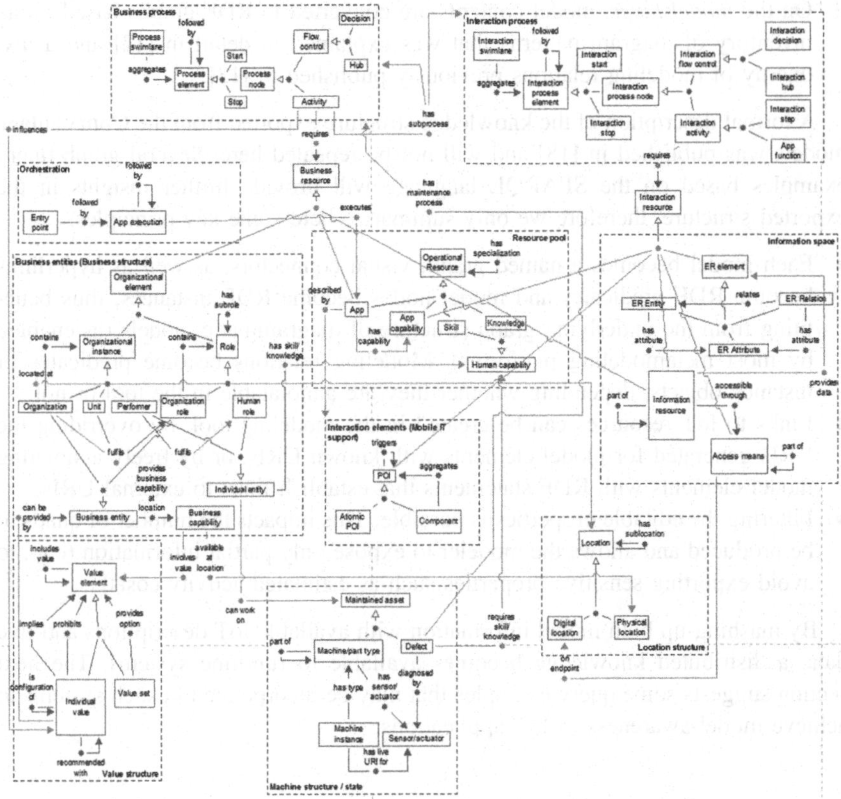

Fig. 4 The core metamodel of the OMiLAB ComVantage modeling proof of concept

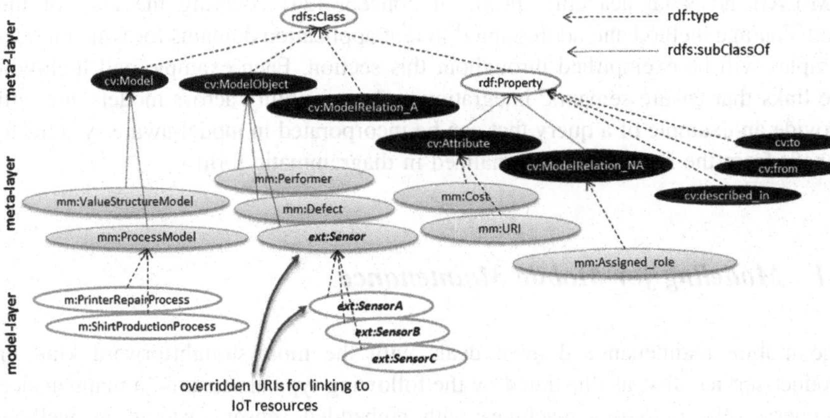

Fig. 5 The model serialization vocabulary and model linking levels

3. On the *model layer*, model contents are converted to RDF graphs based on an inventory of diagram patterns that was explained in detail in [12] and a taxonomy of modeling relations previously published in [13].

A formal description of the knowledge structure exported from the ComVantage models was published in [18] and will not be repeated here. Several graph query examples based on the SPARQL language will provide further insights in the exported structure, therefore we only summarize here some key principles:

- Each model becomes a named graph; visual connectors, as well as hyperlinks become RDF predicates and model nodes become RDF instances, thus benefiting from the underlying graph structure of diagrammatic models (as enabled by most metamodeling platforms). Modeling relations become predicates or instance objects, depending whether they are annotatable in the tool or not;
- Links to IoT resources can be created in the modeling tool, by overriding the URIs generated for model elements with known URIs, or by freely annotating model elements with RDF statements that establish links to external URIs;
- Filtering the editable properties is possible. This impacts the number of quads to be produced and allows the modeler to expose only partial information (e.g., to avoid exporting sensitive properties such as estimated activity costs).

By mashing-up both model information with available IoT descriptions and live data, a distributed knowledge becomes available to run-time systems. The next section suggests some query examples that may be incorporated in such systems to achieve model-awareness in IoT applications.

4 Proof of Concept and Use Cases

OMiLAB hosts an academic proof of concept [24] covering the core of the ComVantage method and addressing different application domains for which model samples will be exemplified throughout this section. Each example will highlight the links that ensure semantic integration and navigability across models and will provide an example of a query that can be incorporated in model-aware systems to benefit from the knowledge externalized in diagrammatic form.

4.1 Modeling for Mobile Maintenance

The mobile maintenance domain deals with the most straightforward kind of product-service mix, as illustrated by the following typical scenario: a maintenance company sells or leases machines with embedded sensor systems, as well as maintenance services associated with those machines. The embedded sensors are polled across IoT and, upon the detection of critical levels for a relevant combination of sensors, maintenance processes are initiated (if a service level agreement was established). The services are delivered in the form of preventive or corrective repair processes prepared for different types of defects described in terms of sensor value combinations (relative to some thresholds). Based on experience, for each machine, a repository of defect descriptions and associated repair processes is accumulated as a portfolio which can become a knowledge base for future queries and knowledge management systems. The maintenance process involves experts of different skills, who must be selected and notified based on the machine and defect characteristics.

Figure 6 shows model samples that can describe such a scenario and highlights the links that are prescribed at metamodel level for this domain. The links manifest as hyperlinks in the modeling tool (therefore allowing model navigation), and will generate semantic links (RDF predicates) once the models are exported as Linked Data (therefore allowing queries across models of different types, as well as queries that cross between model elements and external, existing IoT resources). Some link examples are hereby discussed:

- A machine type is described as a partonomy of components, with sensors and actuators attached to them on any decomposition level. Foreseen defects for that

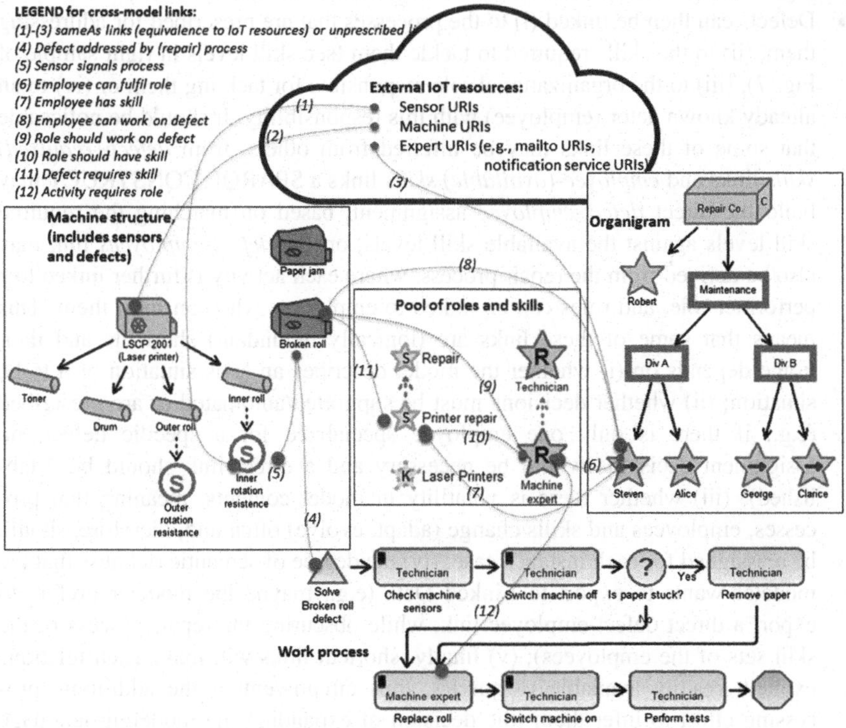

Fig. 6 Explicit links that can be queried for the mobile maintenance domain

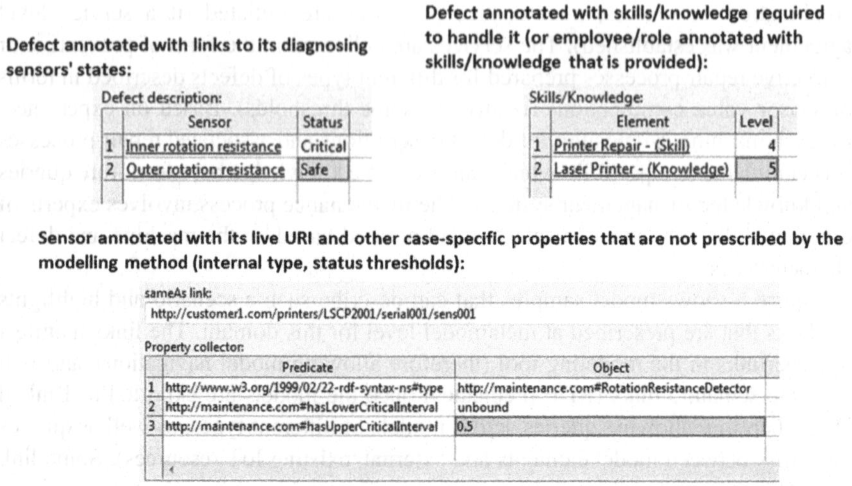

Fig. 7 Annotations relevant at query-time

type of machine are described as sets of its sensors' levels (see the left sample in Fig. 7 where defect-sensor links are annotated with sensor levels);

- Defects can then be linked (i) to the processes that are prescribed for addressing them, (ii) to the skills required to tackle them (see skill levels in right sample of Fig. 7), (iii) to the organizational role responsible for tackling them or (iv) to an already known actor (employee) with this responsibility. It should be noticeable that some of these links may be inferred from others: from *defect-(required) skills* links and *employee-(available) skills* links a SPARQL CONSTRUCT may build the direct *defect-employee* assignment, based on matching the required skill levels against the available skill levels; or, the *defect-employees* link may also be derived from the repair process, where each activity is further linked to a performer role, and roles can be linked to employees who can fulfil them. This means that some of these links are (logically redundant) shortcuts and their usage depends on (i) whether the model describes an as-is situation or a to-be situation; (ii) whether decisions must be supported/automated or are prescribed (e.g., if there is only one employee specialized for a specific defect, no assignment decisions would be necessary and a direct link should be established); (iii) whether there is volatility in model contents, meaning that processes, employees and skills change (adapt, evolve) often and, therefore, should be reassigned for each instance case; (iv) the degree of semantic richness that the modeler wants to export to Linked Data (e.g., maybe the modeler prefers to export a direct defect-employee link, while obscuring the repair process or the skill sets of the employees); (v) finally, shortcut links will make such relations explicit, readily available to queries, thus circumventing the additional processing effort to infer them (the decision of expanding the modeling language with such shortcuts must be based on the foreseen queries and how run-time systems are intended to use models);

- The "sameAs" links are equivalences established between model elements and existing IoT resources (e.g., live sensors which can be read at a known URI, see the bottom sample in Fig. 7). Once such a link is established, the resource URI will override the URI that would otherwise be generated quasi-arbitrarily by the RDFizer. Sameness links will allow queries to cross between sensor descriptions and IoT live values, as well as reasoning based on these relations. A second possibility of linking to external resources is the "property collector" table which annotates model elements with arbitrary statements, unconstrained by the modeling language. In Fig. 7 (bottom sample), a sensor was annotated with its real live URI, a type (according to some external vocabulary) and concrete value intervals for its "Critical" state. These could be used in SPARQL queries to reason on the relation between the model-level sensor description and its run-time counterpart. These linking mechanisms are available for all use cases (actually for all modeling concepts) and will not be mentioned again in the subsequent sections, although the opened potential for integration with run-time resources must be kept in mind.

A SPARQL query example is provided here to retrieve the names and phone numbers of employees whose skill lists include a direct shortcut link to defects signalled by the sensor named "Inner rotation resistance" (prefix declarations are omitted—we assume that the cv: prefix was defined by the modeler during the model export). Notice the rdf:rest/rdf:list pattern that is used to export the tabular link annotations (top of Fig. 7) as ordered lists of records. An exception from this general table serialisation approach is the property collector (bottom of Fig. 7), which will provide straightforward RDF triples with the annotated element acting as subject. Additional comments on this use case and in relation to the Internet of Things are published in [10].

```
SELECT ?nm ?ph WHERE
#first the defects signalled by the specified sensor are identified in a subquery on the machine structure graph
{SELECT ?def WHERE
{GRAPH :machineStructure
{?def cv:DefectDescription ?sensList.
?sensList rdf:rest*/rdf:first ?sense. ?sense cv:Sensor "Inner rotation resistance"; cv:Status "Critical"}}
#then the employees having direct links to those defects are retrieved from the organigram graph
GRAPH :organigram
{?x  cv:SkillsKnowledge ?skillList; cv:Name ?nm; cv:Phone ?ph. ?skillList rdf:rest*/rdf:first ?def}
```

4.2 Modeling for Customer-Oriented Production

The customer-oriented production area deals with a typical virtual enterprise scenario: a company provides a customizable class of products. The customization options may include different features of different types, including associated services. Once an order is created, the customization options are selected and a production process is triggered, involving suppliers and service providers from an existing collaboration network, based on their declared capabilities in relation with the features that have been selected for the product-service mix.

Figure 8 depicts model samples designed for such a scenario and their navigable/queryable links:

- A configurable product class is designed in a fashion inspired by feature-oriented modeling [17], as a decomposition of different kinds of contributing "values" (features, parts, associated services) including their associated costs (which can then be aggregated through queries in order to support analysis of different configurations). Notational cues indicate which of the features are optional (e.g., embroidery on a shirt), which are mixed-in services (e.g., an annual shirt replacement service for an additional fee) and which customization options can be selected by the customer (e.g., sleeve type, color). In the same model type, a portfolio of product configurations may be created, by fixing some of the optional/selectable features and possibly prohibiting others (e.g., the embroidered white shirt implies embroidery but cannot be applied on blue color);

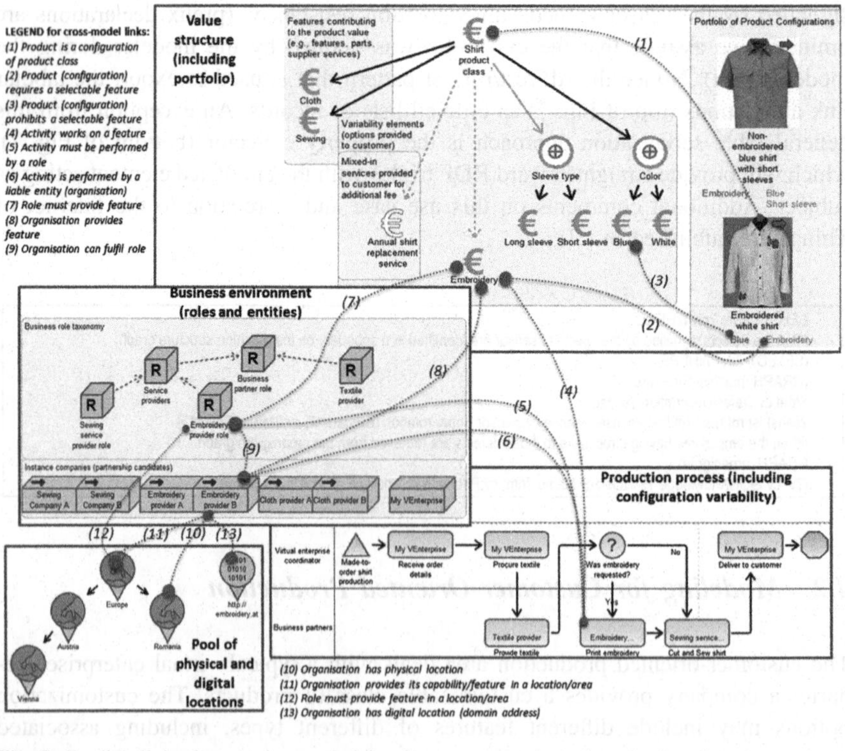

Fig. 8 Explicit links that can be queried for the customer-oriented production domain

- A production process for this product class is designed, including paths for the different possible configurations. Certain activities are linked to the features that they act upon, as well as to the business roles/entities that are responsible for them. Just like in the previous use case, shortcut links may also be established if certain relations are fixed and rigid (e.g., directly from the embroidery feature to the company embroidery provider A);
- Concrete business partners may also be linked to their physical and digital (URL) locations, as well as to the physical area where they can provide their value. Roles are considered "requirements" (a business role is required to provide a capability/feature in a certain area/location), which is quite similar, but for a different domain-specificity, to the skill requirements matching in Sect. 4.1.

A SPARQL query example is provided here to trace all business roles (or entities, if available) involved in the production activities for the features of some given product configuration. Prefix declarations are omitted.

```
SELECT ?feature ?act ?role ?entity
WHERE {
# the ?feature variable should be bound to all features required in the product configuration
 VALUES ?feature {
  <http://www.comvantage.eu/example#Value-447250-Sewing>
  <http://www.comvantage.eu/example#Value-447260-Embroidery>
  <http://www.comvantage.eu/example#Value-446989-Cloth>}
GRAPH ?proc {
 # the activities that influence each feature are retrieved
  ?inf cv:Value ?feature .
  ?inflist rdf:rest*/rdf:first ?inf .
  ?act cv:influences ?inflist .
 # the responsibles assigned to those activities are retrieved
  ?act cv:Assigned_role ?ass .
  ?ass cv:described_in ?busstruct}
 GRAPH ?busstruct {
# If the assigned responsible was a role, look further for business entities who are linked to it
  {?ass a cv:Business_role .
   BIND (?ass AS ?role)
   OPTIONAL {?entity cv:fulfils ?role}
  } UNION {
# If the assigned responsible is a business entity, retrieve it
   ?ass a cv:Business_entity .
   BIND (?ass AS ?entity)}}}}
```

4.3 *Modeling Process-Centric Requirements*

Both of the previously discussed use cases can be extended with an underlying case of capturing requirements for the technological specificity of the ComVantage project—that is, mobile apps consuming Linked Data. This section will exemplify it as an extension for mobile maintenance although the approach is equally applicable to customer-oriented production. The approach was described in more detail in [13].

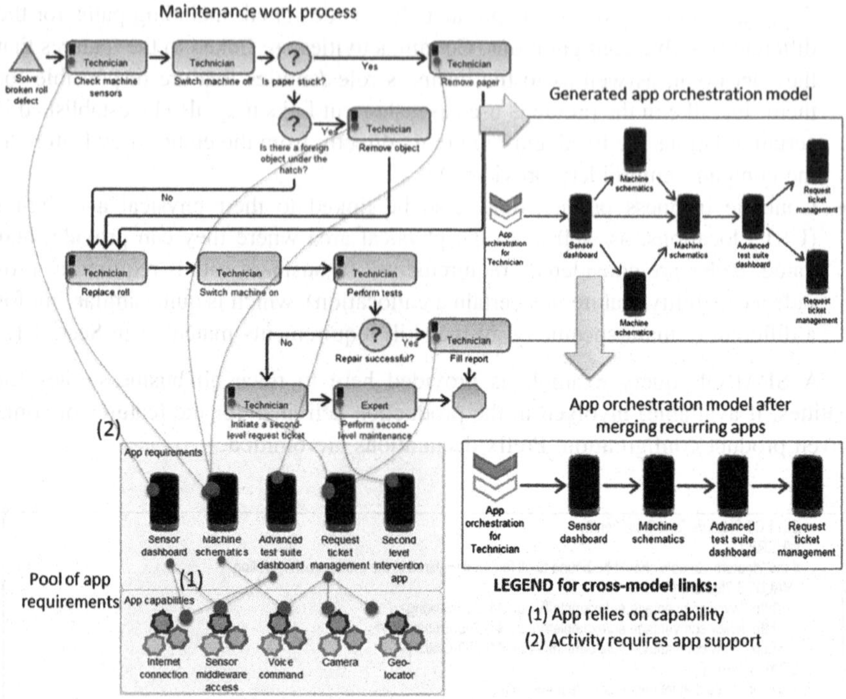

Fig. 9 Automated generation of app orchestration models from the business flow

Figure 9 extends the work process in Fig. 6 with links to the app features and capabilities required to support the technician in some of the tasks. These links become the basis for the automated generation of app orchestration models—that is, the app usage precedence dictated by the flow of the work process. In ComVantage this type of models were queried by an orchestration engine in order to deploy mobile apps chained according to the business flow [33], to guide or train employees with respect to the available app support.

Figure 10 provides further details on app requirements in terms of user-app interactions. Existing approaches to interaction modeling were based on discourse modeling [8] or task trees [28]. However, ComVantage describes interactions as domain-specific sub-processes, with each task having a fixed interpretation given by its links: a task is a user action on the app UI, supported by some abstract user interface element and possibly involving some data requirements.

Finally, the last layer of requirements modeling is concerned with data requirements and data access means. These are further linked as resources to the interaction models, as shown in Fig. 11. Certain interaction steps may be alternated with functions where some back-end data is accessed. These steps can be linked to (i) an information resource lacking granularity (e.g., retrieval of maintenance ticket information requires ticket information), (ii) granular elements of a rudimentary ER diagram (e.g., retrieval of maintenance ticket information requires access to ticket

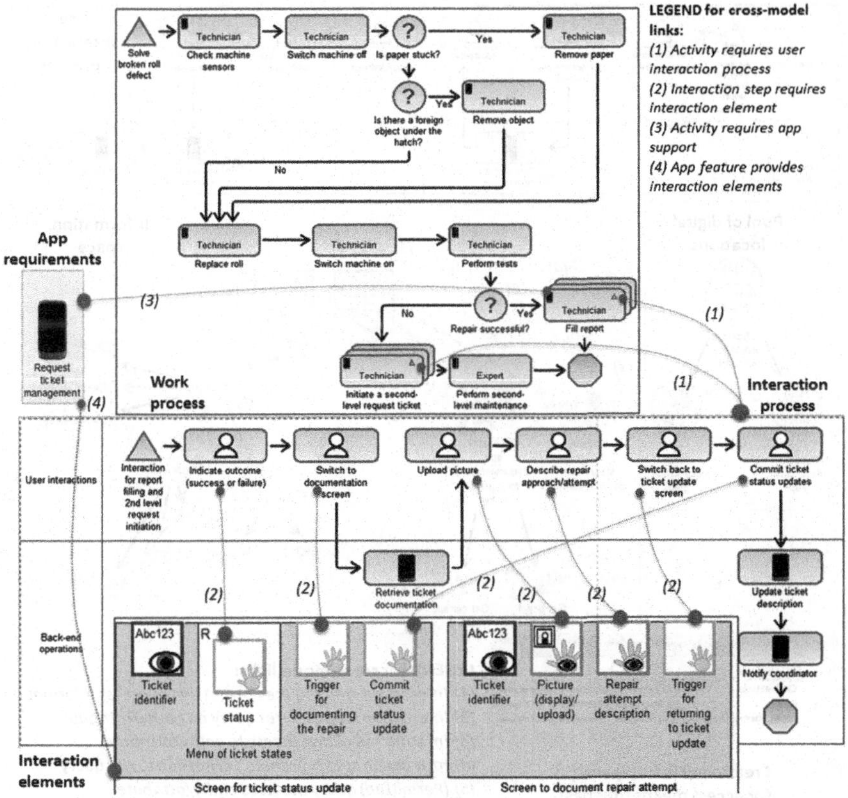

Fig. 10 Explicit links for modeling user-app interaction

status and last repair attempt description), (iii) queries that have been prepared to support the function; queries may be further annotated with the actual SPARQL query, with the SPARQL endpoint (a digital location) and/or the data entity properties on which it acts. Therefore, queries are access means implemented for the required information resources; they can be further decomposed in subqueries for further analysis.

The proposed modeling approach to requirements representation was designed for collaborative work between business stakeholders and app designers who exchange models of different precision and granularity, while agilely mixing requirements representations and early design decisions in a traceable manner: a rich semantic network can be exported from such a model set, and a client-side model-aware tool can consume it for requirements tracking. A simplified example of a SPARQL query is provided here, to retrieve the location of the company whose employee requires a particular ER attribute ("CurrentStatus").

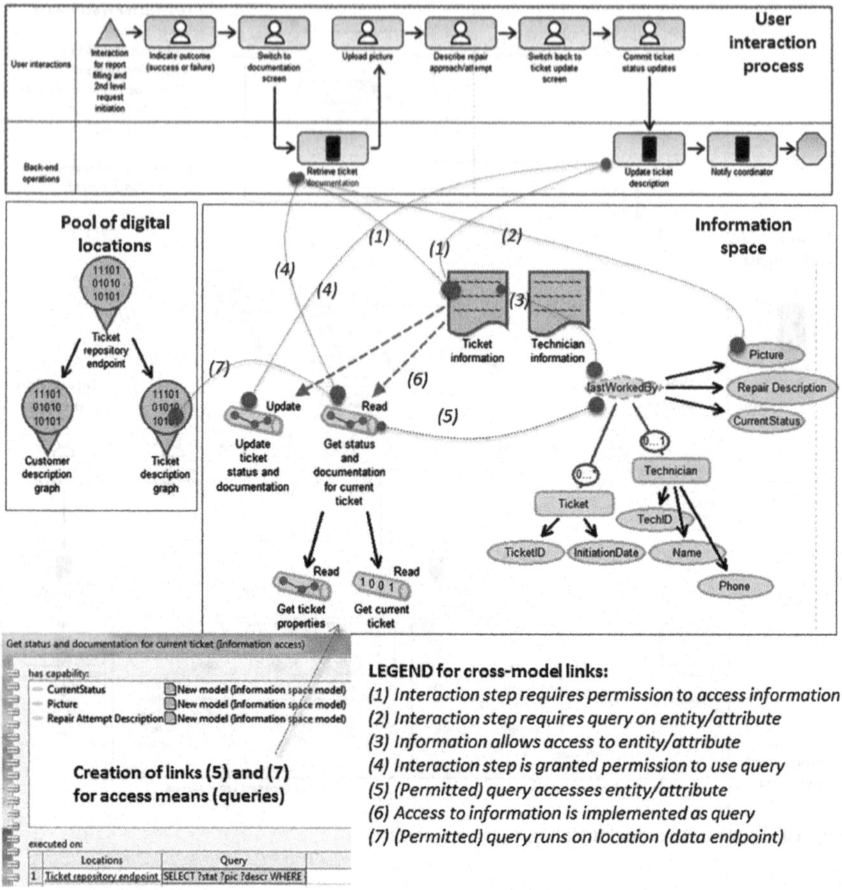

Fig. 11 Explicit links for modeling data requirements and access means

```
SELECT ?location
WHERE {
GRAPH :informationSpace {?infres cv:hasCapability/cv:decomposition/cv:Name "CurrentStatus"}
GRAPH ?interactionProcess {?interactionStep cv:Requires ?infres}
GRAPH :workProcess {?activity cv:ReferencedProcess ?interactionProcess; cv:Assigned_role ?employee}
GRAPH :organigram {?organizationRole cv:decomposition+ ?employee; cv:Address ?location}}
```

5 Conclusion

The ComVantage method was designed to expose a semantically rich enterprise description for querying and reasoning within an Internet of Things based on the Web of Data. Its domain-specificity covers product-service systems, with instance use cases hereby discussed from several application areas, each with a different domain-specificity. Relative to the discussed cases, various additional scenarios can be envisioned, where "model-aware" run-time systems would benefit from linking models to IoT resources: (i) in the mobile maintenance scenario, live sensor URIs can be linked to their representative model elements to automate technician assignment and initiation of maintenance processes; (ii) in the customer-oriented production scenario, value URIs and production step URIs may be used to mark different production stages for an order tracking system; or, a product costing system may query across the decomposition and variability of a product-service mix (and associated costs); (iii) in the requirements modeling scenario, a requirements tracking system can ensure semantic traceability from the high-level enterprise context elements (roles, organizations, products) down to low-level IT support (data endpoints and queries). Based on the presented proof of concept, the following conclusions were derived in the form of a SWOT analysis:

- *Strengths*: The ComVantage method advocates the notion of agility in metamodeling, as model semantics must evolve based on (i) requirements for design-time decision support, as well as (ii) requirements propagating from run-time systems that must consume model information. The method is hybrid in the sense that it adapts and integrates a variety of modeling approaches that evolved from disparate concerns towards the common ground of enterprise modeling: business process modeling (based on control flows), feature modeling (for product-service mixed value descriptions), ER modeling (for data requirements), interaction modeling, requirements modeling. Elements of domain-specificity are mixed with generic concepts to avoid a "take-all-or-leave-all" approach, allowing modelers to separate concerns and to describe different facets of a "ComVantage enterprise" (some more specific than others). The model RDFizer mechanism provides a novel approach to model interoperability, by exposing multi-faceted enterprise models in the form of an RDF knowledge base that can be linked to existing IoT resources—consequently, a diagram-data mash-up establishes richer back-end for run-time components that must support the management and tracking of PSSs;
- *Weaknesses*: Currently the OMiLAB implementation includes experimental extensions with deeper concept specialisations designed for the ComVantage project, which are less relevant outside the project scope. This will be cleaned up in future iterations to improve reusability across different projects and to stabilize the degree of domain-specificity;
- *Opportunities*: The modeling method opens potential for answering questions on the modeling level regarding the opportunity of employing Linked Data as support technology for PSS collaboration networks. Integration with sensor ontologies is another direction to be pursued, towards enabling a model-driven Internet of Things;
- *Threats*: Standard methods and languages are generally preferred in enterprise modeling, since they bring all users on the same level of abstraction and encourage global adoption. Therefore, the generalized relevance of the work at

hand depends on the desired trade-off between reusability and domain specialisation, as well as on the uptake of model-aware information systems, whose evolving requirements are an inherent cause for gradually evolving the specificity of modeling languages.

Acknowledgments The research leading to these results was funded by the European Community's Seventh Framework Programme under grant agreement no. FP7-284928 ComVantage.

Tool Download http://www.omilab.org/comvantage.

References

1. Alix, T., Zacharewicz, G.: Product-service systems modelling and simulation as a strategic diagnosis tool. In: Emmanouilidis, C., Taisch, M., Kiritsis, D. (eds.) IFIP Advances in Information and Communication Technology, vol. 398, pp. 361–368. Springer, Heidelberg (2013)
2. Apache Software Foundation: The Any23 project—official website, http://any23.apache.org (2015). Accessed 1 Oct 2015
3. Bizer, C., Cyganiak, R.: The D2RQ project—official website, http://d2rq.org (2015a). Accessed 1 Oct 2015
4. Bizer, C., Cyganiak, R.: The TriG syntax specification—official website, http://wifo5-03.informatik.uni-mannheim.de/bizer/trig (2015b). Accessed 1 Oct 2015
5. BOC GmbH: ADOxx—official website, https://www.adoxx.org/live/home (2015a). Accessed 1 Oct 2015
6. BOC GmbH: ADOLog—official website, https://uk.boc-group.com/adolog (2015b). Accessed 1 Oct 2015
7. BOC GmbH: ADONIS—official website, https://uk.boc-group.com/adonis (2015c). Accessed 1 Oct 2015
8. Bogdan, C., Falb, J., Kaindl, H., Kavaldjian, S., Popp, R., Horacek, H., Arnautovic, E., Szep, A.: Generating an abstract user interface from a discourse model inspired by human communication. In: Jr, Sprague R.H. (ed.) Proceedings of HICSS 2008, p. 36. Hawaii, USA, IEEE (2008)
9. Buchmann, R.A.: Conceptual modeling for mobile maintenance: the comvantage case. In: Jr, Sprague R.H. (ed.) Proceedings of HICSS 2014, pp. 3390–3399. Hawaii, USA, IEEE (2014)
10. Buchmann, R.A., Karagiannis, D.: Enterprise modeling for the Internet of Things: the ComVantage method. In: Kim, K.J., Noukov, J. (eds.) Proceedings of ICISA 2016, pp. 1283–1293. Springer, Saigon, Vietnam (2016)
11. Buchmann, R.A., Karagiannis, D.: Modelling collaborative-driven supply chains: the ComVantage method. In: Bakhtadze, N, Chernyshov, K., Dolgui, A., Lototsky, V. (eds.) Proceedings of IFAC MIM 2013, St. Petersburg, Russia, part 1, vol. 7, pp. 567–572. Elsevier, Amsterdam (2013)
12. Buchmann, R.A., Karagiannis, D.: Pattern-based transformation of diagrammatic conceptual models for semantic enrichment in the Web of Data. In: Ding, L., Pang, C., Kew, L.M., Jain, L.C., Howlett, R.J. (eds.) Proceedings of KES 2015, Singapore, Procedia Computer Science 60, pp. 150–159. Elsevier, Amsterdam (2015)
13. Buchmann, R.A., Karagiannis, D.: Modelling mobile app requirements for semantic traceability. J. Requirements Eng. (2015). doi:10.1007/s00766-015-0235-1

14. Buchmann, R.A., Karagiannis, D., Visic, N.: Requirements definition for domain specific modelling languages: the Comvantage case. In: Kobylinski, A., Sobczak, A. (eds.) Proceedings of BIR 2013, pp. 19–33. Warszaw, Poland, Springer, Heidelberg (2013)
15. ComVantage Consortium: Project public deliverables. http://www.comvantage.eu/results-publications/public-deriverables (2015). Accessed 1 Oct 2015
16. Heath, T., Bizer, C.: Linked data: evolving the web into a global data space, 1st edn. Morgan & Claypool, San Rafael, USA (2011)
17. Kang, K., Cohen, S., Hess, J., Novak, W., Peterson, A.: Feature-oriented domain analysis (FODA) feasibility study. Software Engineering Institute, Technical Report CMU/SEI-90-TR-021 (1990)
18. Karagiannis, D., Buchmann, R.A.: Linked open models: extending linked open data with conceptual model information. Inf. Syst. **56**, 174–197 (2016)
19. Karagiannis, D., Kühn, H.: Metamodelling platforms. In: Bauknecht, K., Tjoa, AM., Quirchmayr, G. (eds.) Proceedings of the Third International Conference EC-Web 2002—DEXA 2002, Aix-en-Provence, France. LNCS, vol. 2455. Springer, Heidelberg (2002)
20. Karagiannis, D.: Agile modeling method engineering. In: Karanikolas, N., Akoumianakis, D., Nikolaidou, M., Vergados, D., Xenos, M. (eds.) Proceedings of PCI 2015, pp. 5–10. Athens, Greece. ACM, New York (2015)
21. Langegger, A., Wöß, W.: XLWrap—Querying and integrating arbitrary spreadsheets with SPARQL. In: Bernstein, A., Karger, D.R., Heath, T., Feigenbaum, L., Maynard, D., Motta, E., Thirunarayan, K. (eds.) Proceedings of ISWC 2009. LNCS, vol. 5823, pp. 359–374. Springer, Heidelberg (2009)
22. Münch, T., Buchmann, R., Pfeffer, J., Ortiz, P., Christl, C., Hladik, J., Ziegler, J., Lazaro, O., Karagiannis, D., Urbas, L.: An innovative virtual enterprise approach to agile micro and SME-based collaboration networks. In: Camarinha-Matos, L.M., Scherer, R.J. (eds.) Proceedings of 14th IFIP Conference on Virtual Enterprises, Dresden, Germany, pp 121–128. Springer, Heidelberg (2013)
23. OASIS: BPEL—official website, https://www.oasis-open.org/committees/tc_home.php?wg_abbrev=wsbpel (2015). Accessed 1 Oct 2015
24. OMiLAB: The metamodelling site for the ComVantage project. http://www.omilab.org/web/comvantage/home (2015). Accessed 1 Oct 2015
25. Open Group (2015) The ArchiMate® 2.1 Specification—official website, http://www.opengroup.org/archimate/. Accessed 1 Oct 2015
26. Phumbua, S., Tjahjono, B.: Towards product-service systems modelling: a quest for dynamic behaviour and model parameters. Int. J. Product. Res. **50**(2), 425–442 (2012)
27. RST and K&A: Data Harmonisation Middleware adapter. http://www.comvantage.eu/prepare-your-data/dhm-middleware-adapter (2015). Accessed 1 Oct 2015
28. W3C: ConcurTaskTrees—official website, http://www.w3.org/2012/02/ctt/ (2012). Accessed 1 Oct 2015
29. W3C: RDF—official website, http://www.w3.org/RDF/ (2015c). Accessed 1 Oct 2015
30. W3C: SPARQL Graph Store HTTP protocol specification—official website, http://www.w3.org/TR/sparql11-http-rdf-update (2015b). Accessed 1 Oct 2015
31. W3C: SPARQL Query Language specification—official website, http://www.w3.org/TR/sparql11-query/ (2015a). Accessed 1 Oct 2015
32. WfMC: XPDL specification—official website, http://www.xpdl.org (2015). Accessed 1 Oct 2015
33. Ziegler, J., Graube, M., Pfeffer, J., Urbas, L.: Beyond app-chaining—mobile app orchestration for efficient model driven software generation. In: Proceedings of the 17th IEEE International Conference on Emerging Technologies and Factory Automation, Krakow, Poland, pp. 1–8. IEEE (2012)

User Story Mapping-Based Method for Domain Semantic Modeling

Dimitris Kiritsis, Ana Milicic and Apostolos Perdikakis

Abstract User story mapping (USM) for domain modeling is a method derived from the software functionality definition domain, which puts the end-user and his perspective in focus. The domain of interest is defined through the collection of user activities, which indirectly gathers all actors, resources, processes and overall dynamics of the domain. USM is a manual procedure that is conducted between the semantics expert and the domain expert, and can sometimes require a number of time-consuming iterations. The ADO*xx* metamodeling platform facilitated the development of a USM digital tool which provides enhanced performance and visual environment.

Keywords Metamodeling · Ontology · User story mapping

1 Introduction

The problem of identifying and representing, analyzing and managing information and knowledge is crucial to achieve business goals in an efficient and flexible way. An emergent challenge consists in providing a context-driven access to federated information and knowledge and fostering their cross-disciplinary reuse. We propose a bottom-up approach based on the User Story Mapping method (USM). This method is user-centric and leads to the definition of expected exploitation scenarios. Common concepts and viewpoints are derived by the generalization and merging of defined roles, activities, and usages sequences. Combined with appropriate tools and methods, it results in the definition of the knowledge domain and therefore

D. Kiritsis (✉) · A. Milicic · A. Perdikakis
École polytechnique fédérale de Lausanne, 1015 Lausanne, Switzerland
e-mail: dimitris.kiritsis@epfl.ch

A. Milicic
e-mail: ana.milicic@epfl.ch

A. Perdikakis
e-mail: apostolos.perdikakis@epfl.ch

D. Karagiannis et al. (eds.), *Domain-Specific Conceptual Modeling*,
DOI 10.1007/978-3-319-39417-6_20

improves capabilities for sharing and reusing this knowledge in the collaborative product development.

Innovation is the application of knowledge to produce new knowledge [3]. It requires systematic efforts and a high degree of organization. As we enter the knowledge society, the ownership of knowledge and information as a source of competitive advantage is becoming increasingly important. In other words, organizations depend more on the development, use, and distribution of knowledge-based competencies. This is particularly relevant in knowledge-intensive processes such as product innovation. Consequently, research and development (R&D) organizations are paying more attention to the concept of managing their knowledge base and tools in order to increase competitive advantage, through effective decision making and increased innovation [2, 9, 14]. Knowledge is a key resource that must be managed if improvement efforts are to succeed and businesses are to remain competitive in a networked environment [5]. In particular, the two major challenges that organizations must face are: (a) ensuring that they have the knowledge to support their operations and (b) ensuring that they optimize the knowledge resources available to them. Managing knowledge is about creating an environment that fosters the continuous creation, aggregation, use and reuse of both organizational and personal knowledge in the pursuit of new business value. In short, the overriding purpose of enterprise knowledge management is to make knowledge accessible and reusable cross disciplinary and independently of time and location.

Capturing domain specific knowledge is one of the main challenges in the field of Knowledge-Based Engineering (KBE). Several methodologies have been elaborated to guide knowledge acquisition activities and thus avoid omitting essential knowledge [11], but they usually require time-consuming collection and analysis of (often implicit) knowledge about the product and its design process, respectively. Thus, most approaches to designing KBE-Tools address especially repetitive engineering tasks, since the potential to reduce time and cost by means of such approaches has to be balanced against the effort needed to gather and formalize the required knowledge in a scheme (e.g., an ontology) [7].

The process of capturing the knowledge generated in the implicit form, over a period of organizations operations, requires methodical communication and exchange of information between a number of different actors. Deep understanding and a common vocabulary have to be established between KBE experts and domain experts, since the domain experts can often fail to recognize some of personal experience as a valuable knowledge component. On the other hand, KBE experts have to gain deep understanding of the domain, to be able to recognize and formalize all the relevant relations and dependencies within operations performed in an organization. The domain can be highly complex, containing a number of operations and functionalities of many different organization departments and KBE experts have to be able to grasp the overall structure in one model or schema. This may involve issues such as non-harmonized terminology or unclear hierarchy model within the organization. Addressing every relevant actor within the organization individually allows KBE engineers to detect inconsistency in terminology or cause-effect relations between different departments and generate a model that spans the entire domain and imposes mutual understanding.

The User Story Mapping method appears to be a promising approach to address the previously stated challenges by providing an efficient, time saving and bottom-up requirements analysis for the design of KBE-Tools. It is a user-centric method, which enables software designers to learn what future users expect from this KBE-Tool, as well as it helps the users to express their overall functionality demands. Although initially designed for the purpose of software product requirement definition [10], it can be equally efficiently applied to knowledge domain definition.

The study presented in this chapter results not only in the application of USM method for KBE-Tools requirements, but also provides a form of template schema covering the functionalities of most manufacturing organizations. The template, i.e., an abstract, reusable schema, was created in previous work [8] by generalizing schemas from several organizations in various domains. This template, simplifies the application of USM in every future organization, as the KBE experts can use it as the guideline for communication with domain experts, making it easier to recognize relevant actors and key-functionalities of the given organization.

2 Method Description

We hereby propose an approach derived from agile software development, termed User Story Mapping (USM) [10], for knowledge domain definition. When a new software product is being developed, one of the first steps of the process is to document the idea. This usually results in a description of key features that the developed product will have, optionally including a short abstract, called the "elevator pitch" that will be used to advertise the product and show its value to the customer. After shortly documenting the idea, the next step is to develop a concrete list of action items or tasks, also called backlog, that need to be implemented in order to transform the idea into a concrete product. Unfortunately, such backlogs, event arranged in a priority order are usually flat structures. They help the team members to understand what needs to be done next, but unfortunately do not explain why it needs to be done and what the whole system or product does. Such approach can be compared with having the puzzle pieces, but not knowing what the whole picture should look like, not knowing what the final goal is.

2.1 State of the Art in Knowledge Domain Definition

Knowledge is an elusive concept and therefore it is important to define it in context in order to understand it. The term is used in several different ways in the literature. For example, Nonaka and Takuechi in [9], two of the early researchers in this field, adopt a philosophical angle and define knowledge as "justified true belief". In this view, knowledge is an opinion, idea or theory that has been verified empirically and agreed upon by a community. Stewart [12] also considers knowledge in terms of intellectual capital. On the other hand, Bohn [1] examines knowledge in terms of a company's processes. He believes that an organization's knowledge about its processes may range from total ignorance about how they work to very complex and formal mathematical models. According to Davenport et al. [2], knowledge is information combined with experience, context, interpretation and reflection. It is a high value form of information that is ready to be applied to decisions and actions. Simply put, knowledge can be defined as the integration of ideas, experience, intuition, assertions, skills and lessons learned that have the potential to create value for a business by informing decisions and improving performance. In this view, knowledge is a key enabler to organizational success. However, in order for knowledge to be useful it must be available, accurate, effective and accessible.

Application of knowledge engineering in PLM context required that the format used for representing the knowledge be understandable by both humans and machines. For this reason, a number of methods have been developed, including relational diagrams and linked tables but eventually ontologies have emerged as the preferable choice. In theory, an ontology is a "formal, explicit specification of a shared conceptualization" [4]. An ontology renders shared vocabulary and taxonomy which models a domain with the definition of objects and/or concepts and their properties and relations. In other words, in computer science and information science, an ontology formally represents knowledge as a set of concepts within a domain, and the relationships between those concepts. It can be used to reason about the entities within that domain and may be used to describe the domain. This schematic representation of knowledge makes it very intuitively understandable for humans. It is a common language between different actors and a bridge for knowledge exchange. On the other hand, ontological tools require every concept and relation to be semantically defined and structured, which makes ontology machine-understandable. If populated, ontologies prove to be very convenient for organizing and storing the data. This enables automatic reasoning and inference which means that besides the knowledge gathered at the time when the ontology is being modeled, additional relations will be automatically build up in time. In the perspective of selecting an ontology as knowledge representation method, capturing domain knowledge needs to lead to definition of the domain concepts. Precisely, the USM-based approach is the first step of this process.

Specification and conceptualization of ontologies lean on the identification of the relevant concepts of a particular domain, their type and the constraints on their use. However, existing methodologies (Diligent, Methontholgy, On-To-Knowledge) lack detailed and clear guidelines for building the concepts. It is important to emphasize that, the process of concepts definition represents a key issue for knowledge gathering, as it has to cover in an optimal way the whole domain. On the other hand, several knowledge resources may exist and their concepts reuse can be of a key importance.

The NeOn Methdology [13] comes to deal with the aforementioned issues and provides some methodological guidelines for performing the ontology requirements specification activity, to obtain the requirements that the ontology should fulfil. Particularly, it consists of elaborating an ORSD (Ontology Requirements Specification Document) which aims to list, among others, the intended uses, the end-users and a set of questions describing the requirements that the ontology should fulfil.

Nevertheless, this approach of listing intended uses and questions that the ontology should respond to may appear as a flat structure, in the sense that it does not lead to study and analyze the domain mainly in terms of interactions that link the end-users and usages, before going deep into the questions that the concepts should be able to answer. The research conducted in this chapter focuses on the first phase of concepts definition as it represents the main basis for knowledge definition and conceptualization. The following sections discusses the proposed approach for dealing with concepts definition based on one of the agile methods, called the User Story Mapping.

2.2 User Story Method Contribution

Downsides with software development can be also transferred to challenges in domain knowledge definition. Interviewing actors of the organization will give pieces of domain knowledge, without knowing what the whole picture is, and even with some of the pieces missing.

USM is a method for creating a good backlog of user stories, where actors receive guidance on how to formulate the description of their activities and functions, reducing the risk of misunderstanding because of different terminologies. Important novelty to notice is that while system functionality requirements gathering procedure requires interviews only with future users of a software product, USM for the purpose of domain definition requires that employees of all roles tell the story of their activities. Even though not all of them will be defined as actors of the domain scenario, some of them might be a relevant source of information.

USM is a method for structuring the backlog so that every requirement is precisely positioned in the structured system functionality. Last but not the least, it is a visual aid for KBE experts who can thus obtain an overview of an entire domain. As such, it is a communication bridge not only between KBE experts and actors but also among the actors themselves.

Obtaining lists of concepts, which will be part of a domain ontology, from user stories, is not trivial and it always reflects the personal style and the previous experiences of the semantic expert. There are a number of attempts to standardize the structure and the terminology but because of the complexity and number of different domains, none has emerged as dominant. Nevertheless, existing ontologies and knowledge bases are always a relevant part in the extraction of the lists of concepts.

3 Method Conceptualization

A user story map is a user-centric approach and organizes the backlog along scenarios and users. It answers the question: how does a user use the product? It is important to clarify that, here, the product is a KBE platform. Defining the usage by all relevant users thus defines the domain knowledge, the existing one, the needed one and the produced one. In this manner, the method for software functionality requirements definition is transformed into a method for domain knowledge definition. The backlog consists of several structure blocks as shown in Fig. 1:

- Usage dimension—It describes how a user would use the product. It shows the sequence of steps that a user would perform when using the product. It is very important that usage steps cover the whole scope of the product usage.
- User dimension—This dimension defines the types of users that will use the developed product. This dimension helps to identify different users and the aspects of the product that will be interesting for those users.
- Backbone—This section describes the activities that a user performs in a usage step. The backbone describes the activities that a user performs using the developed product. This section is called backbone as it often represents the essentials of the product and fits as a guideline for the definition of the user stories, which are actually a refinement of the backbone.
- User stories as backlog items—This is the actual placeholder for the user stories. The user stories are ordered vertically under each activity and represent a refined

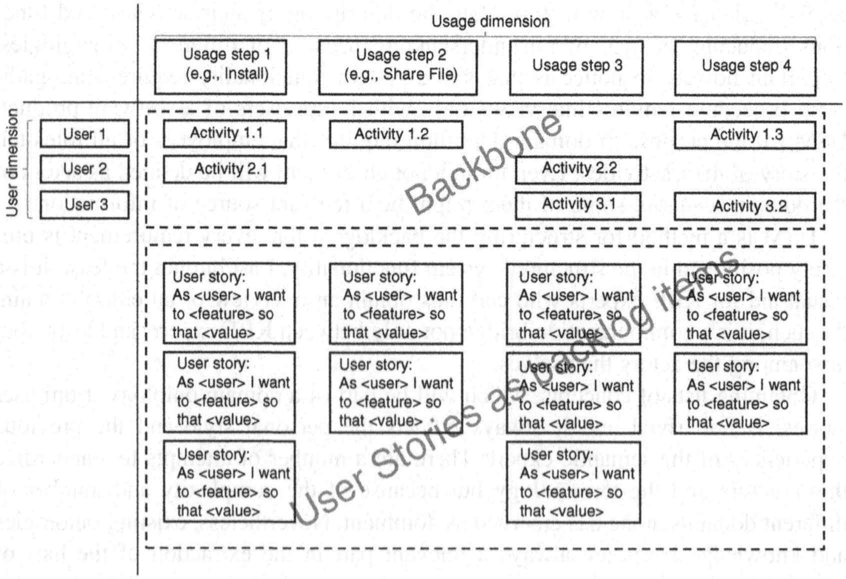

Fig. 1 User story map

version of an activity. It is recommended that user stories follow the pattern "As < user > I want to < feature > so that < value >'. After all user stories have been defined, they also need to be prioritized, taking into account the value that this user story brings, the technical risk of implementing it and the effort that will be needed to implement the story.

Although the USM method was originally proposed and used in the area of agile software development, it is a generic method for structuring and sharing information about a product. It visualizes in a simple way several aspects of a product looking from the user perspective. It is both means of communication and means of documenting knowledge in PLM.

If we consider the USM to be the first step of gathering information regarding the domain of interest, the following steps can be defined as translating functional needs into a list of concepts. As explained above, if we select ontology as a knowledge representation tool, modeling it requires that all relevant objects and factors are defined as concepts. After USM, we have a detail and structured information about knowledge present in the domain, how it is exploited and exchanged between actors. Creating concepts requires recognizing leading objects and factors that will be translated directly into concepts. For example, in a manufacturing company, the term "machine" will be present in a number of user stories, so it is clear that the ontology will contain the concept "Machine". This concept will model all the knowledge about one machine, as well as its usage and functionalities.

Beside users' activities and experiences, valuable sources of knowledge are industrial standards and experiences from previous projects and organizations. The same procedure of recognizing key aspects for the purpose of concepts definition can be applied here. One of the most useful sources of guidelines is the existing abstract ontologies that can be used as templates or reference schemas [8]. An example of such ontology which will be used as proof of a concept in this work is given in Fig. 2. The idea is that every specific concept, extracted through user story analysis can be identified as sub-concepts of one of the abstract "Upper" concepts and thus leading to an automatic tree structure design.

Finally, all these concepts have to be organized into a network covering the entire domain. A key for structuring it can also be found in USM. Relations between concepts can be recognized as "cause-effect" dependencies between concepts, as information flow connections, as co-operation between concepts, as "parent-child" set-up, etc. These relations will tie domain concepts according to the functionality of the organization, thus modeling knowledge about the dynamics involved.

Based on this, we can create a simple algorithm for building a complete and structured knowledge base (Fig. 3):

- Step 1: apply the USM method
- Step 2: gather other sources of information (standards, templates, past experience, etc.)
- Step 3: create a unique list of concepts that covers entire domain

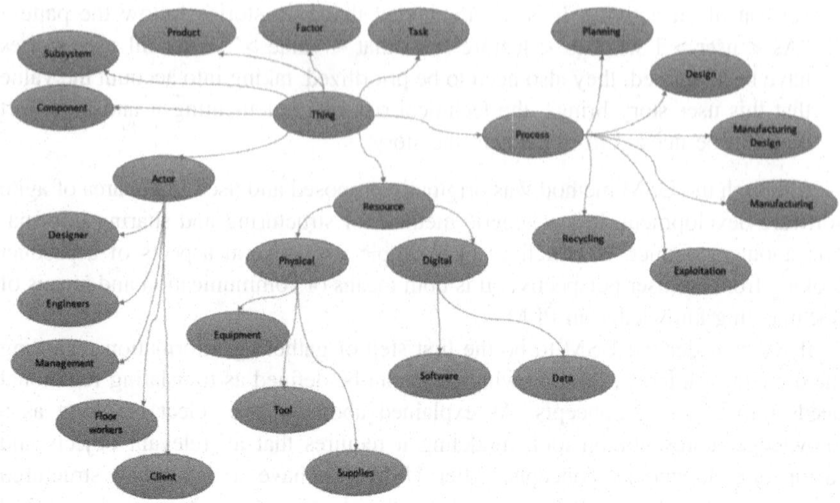

Fig. 2 Upper Ontology as reusable resource

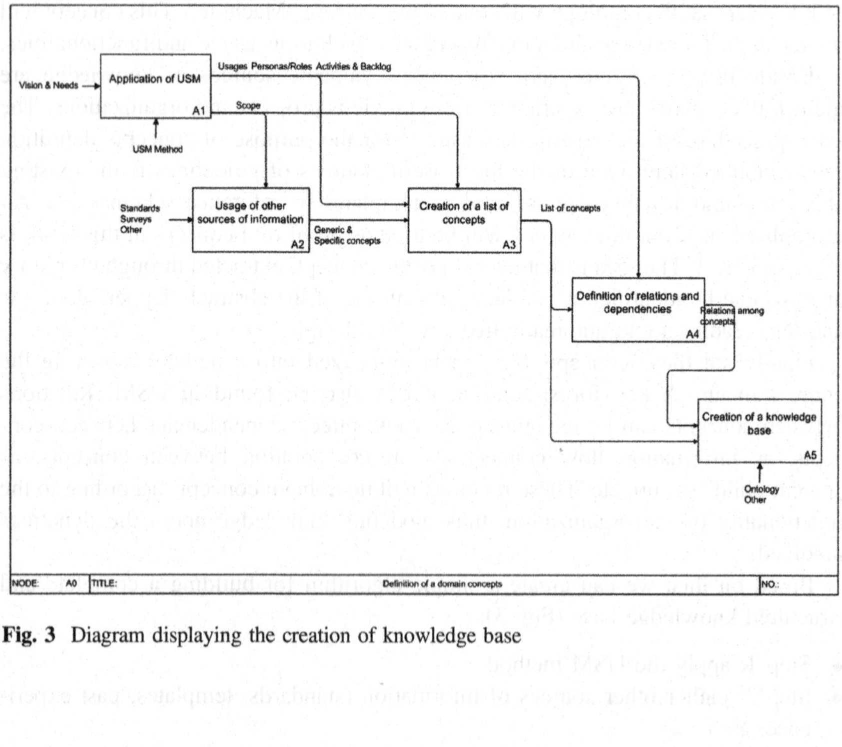

Fig. 3 Diagram displaying the creation of knowledge base

- Step 4: define relations and dependencies among these concepts
- Step 5: create a dynamic knowledge base covering the domain, expressed in some of the standard formats like relational database, ontology, semantic model, etc.

Obviously, in this scenario, the USM is a vital part as it will create a base view of the domain in question. Switching from USM to the list of concepts is a relatively straightforward step. Functionalities required by user stories are described in the form of sets of functional modules and each module is translated into a concept of the domain such as resources, other actors or target goals. Next, the list is extended with additional concepts coming from other sources of information like industrial standards or similar projects. Finally, the concepts are described using relations and expressed in some of the usual knowledge base formats. The conceptual metamodel is given in Fig. 4. Each item of the backlog is one user story, defined by one

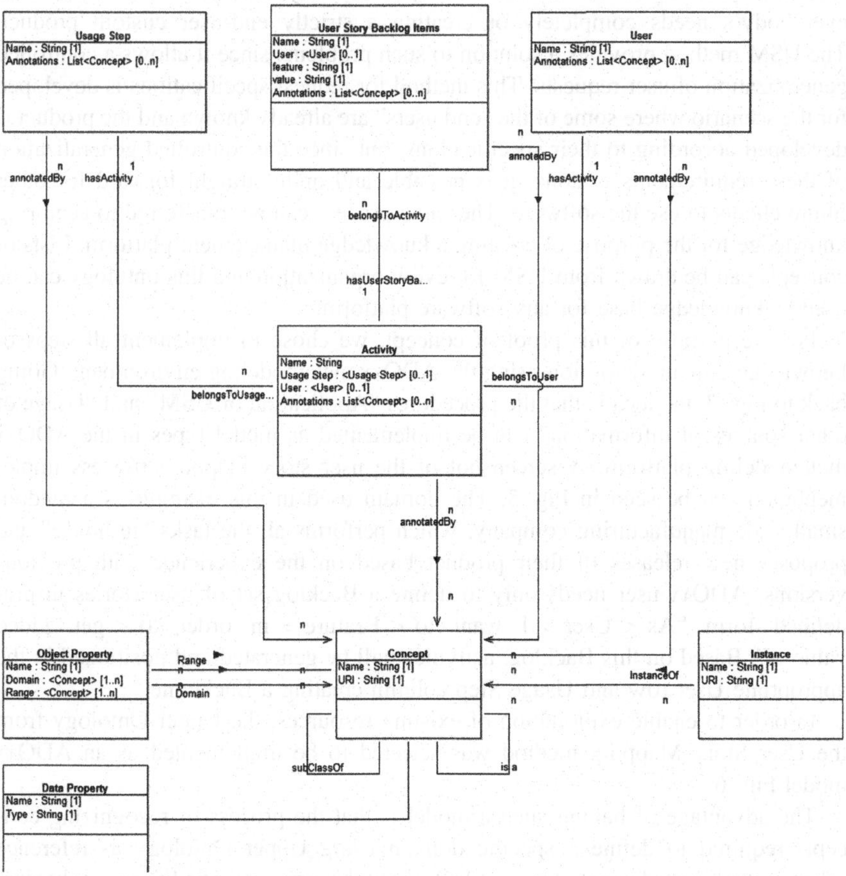

Fig. 4 Conceptual metamodel of USM

specific user and one specific activity belonging to one specific usage step (usage of the knowledge base). Each activity will thus contain specific examples of the concept Actor (user), the concept Resources (required for the activity) and the Product/Part (which are the topic of knowledge base usage). The concepts gathered in this manner are described with names, data properties (which are the attributes of the real-life object modeled through the concept), object properties (describing the interaction between different objects) and instances as real-life examples of the given concept.

4 Proof of Concept

USM method gives a great approach on "end user" request specification. In real-life scenarios, when creating new software, there is always a dilemma between creating a generic product which can be used by everybody, but does not really cover everybody's needs completely or creating a strictly end-user custom product. The USM method provides a solution to such problems since it allows a controlled generalization of user requests. This method for request specifications is developed for the scenario where some of the "end users" are already known and the product is developed according to their specifications, but since the controlled generalization of these requirements is done, it is possible and quite straight forward for other future clients to use the software. The same process can be transferred to acquiring knowledge for the purpose of creating a knowledge management platform. Lists of concepts can be drawn from USM for every organization and this ontology can be used as knowledge base for any software platform.

For the purpose of this proof of concept, we chose to implement all steps of knowledge domain definition using the ADO*xx* metamodeling environment. Going back to Fig. 3, the idea is that the procedures "Application of USM" and "Usage of other sources of information" can be implemented as model types in the ADO*xx* metamodeling platform. A screenshot of the user story mapping process implementation can be seen in Fig. 5. The domain used in this example is a random small-scale manufacturing company, which performs all the tasks "in-house" and proposes new releases of their product based on the experience with previous versions. ADO*xx* user needs only to define a Backlog set of user stories in predefined form "As < User > I want to < Feature > in order to < get added value >". Based on this Backlog, activities will be generated and positioned in the appropriate User row and Usage Step column creating a Backbone.

In order to enable exploitation of existing resources, the Upper Ontology from the User Story Mapping method was selected to be implemented as an ADO*xx* model Fig. 6.

The advantage of having such a model is that the process of recognizing concepts required to define a specific domain using Upper Ontology as reference schema, can be implemented as an ADO*xx* tool through semantic lifting mechanism [6]. The semantic lifting is an advanced option of ADO*xx* as it allows extension of

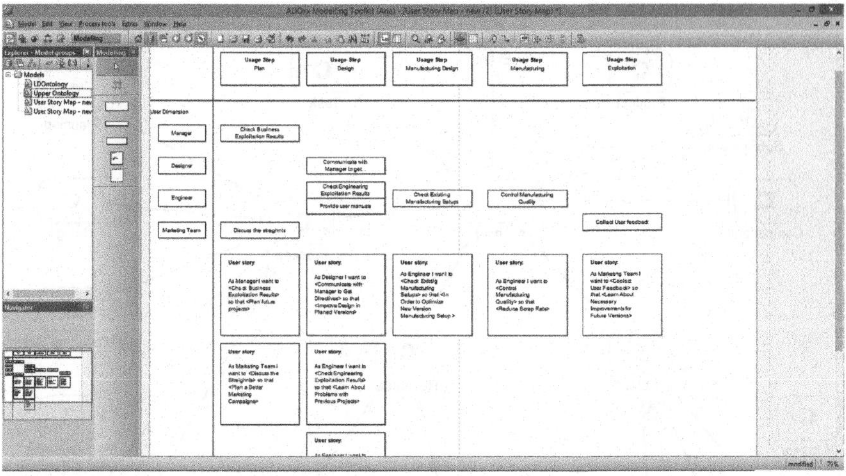

Fig. 5 Example of the ADO*xx* model type of USM

modeling language with existing semantic models that will be used for semantic annotation, as shown in Fig. 7.

Using mechanism & algorithms capabilities of the ADO*xx* metamodeling platform, the third step that is "Creating list of concepts" is implemented by enabling the ADO*xx* user to annotate Activities from Backbone with concepts from the Upper Ontology. In the case that Upper Ontology concepts are too generic, the ADO*xx* user is enabled to define his own concepts, as sub-concepts of the Upper Ontology. For example, the Activity "Check Business Exploitation Results", needs to be annotated as "Data"- > "Digital"- > "Resource" but it still remains a very generic annotation. The ADO*xx* user is then allowed to create the additional concept "User Feedback" that will be the sub-concept of the Upper Ontology, "User Feedback"- > "Data"- > "Digital"- > "Resource", as shown in Fig. 8. These new concepts can be further used to annotate Activities. By annotating the entire Backbone of activities, the list of concepts is created by merging all concepts that were used in the annotation process, those from the Upper Ontology together with the newly added. The ADO*xx* model will generate this list automatically and create a visualization.

The next step is "Definition of relations", as step number four. The challenge with definition of relations (or object properties, according to ontological terminology) is that some level of interaction can be usually found for every two concepts and only a small portion of them is relevant and useful for domain description. That is, it is not the issue of finding the relation between two concepts, it is the issue of selecting the ones that are worth defining as object properties. The recommendation system for this challenge was created by using the ADO*xx* metamodeling platform, relaying again on the Activity Backbone. The reasoning is that if one Activity was annotated with two or more concepts, then it is reasonable to assume

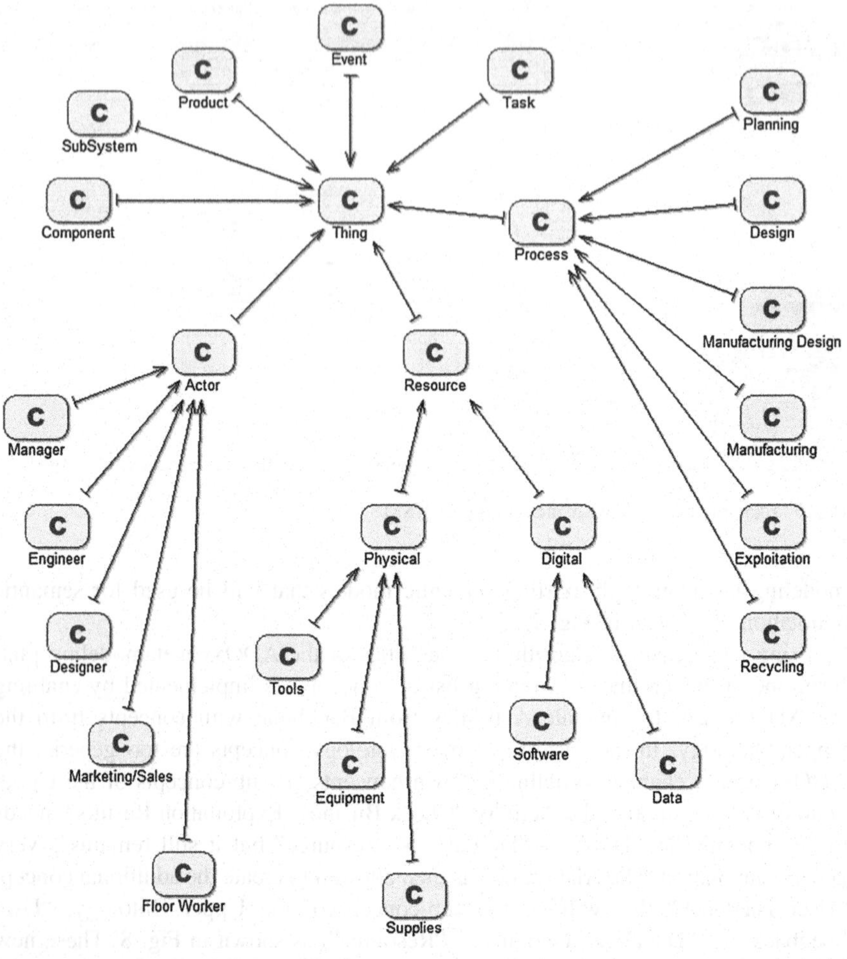

Fig. 6 Upper Ontology as ADO*xx* model

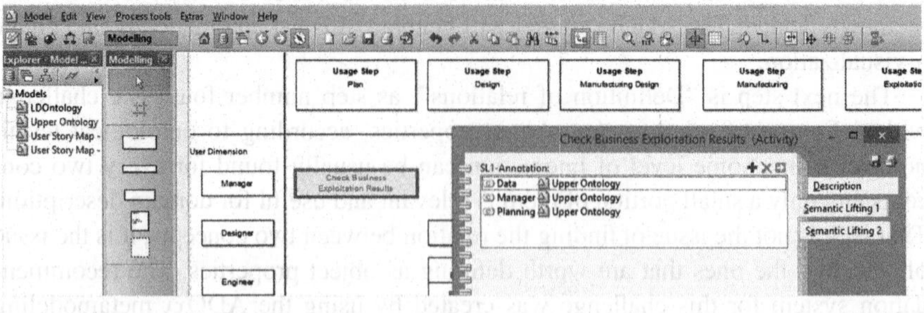

Fig. 7 Semantic annotation in ADO*xx*

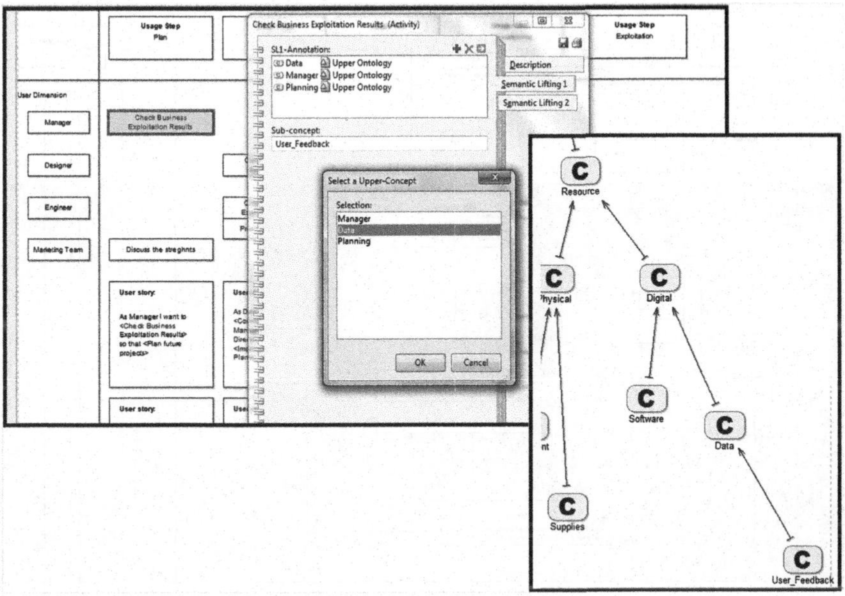

Fig. 8 Addition of new sub-concepts in ADO*xx*

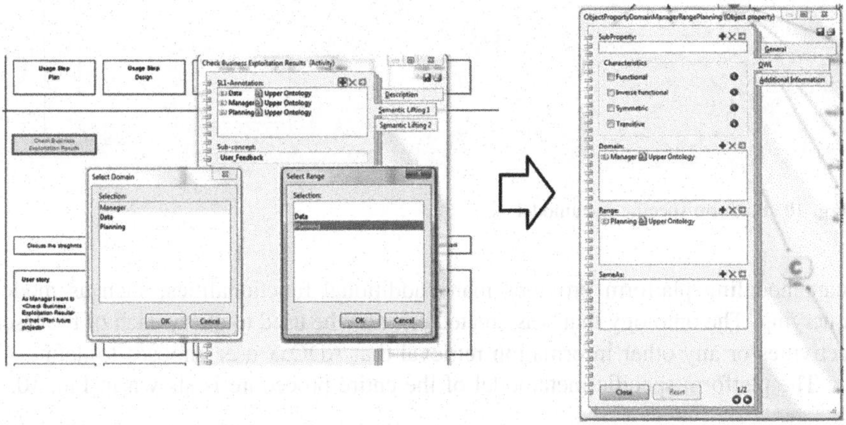

Fig. 9 Object property definition in ADO*xx*

that those two concepts should have an object property connecting them. The tool is implemented as a recommendation system, meaning that the ADO*xx* user is presented with an option to create an object property which he can freely accept or decline, as shown in Fig. 9.

Finally, combining the final lists of concepts and object properties leads to the ADO*xx* enhanced User Story Mapping for ontology design in Step 5. The ADO*xx*

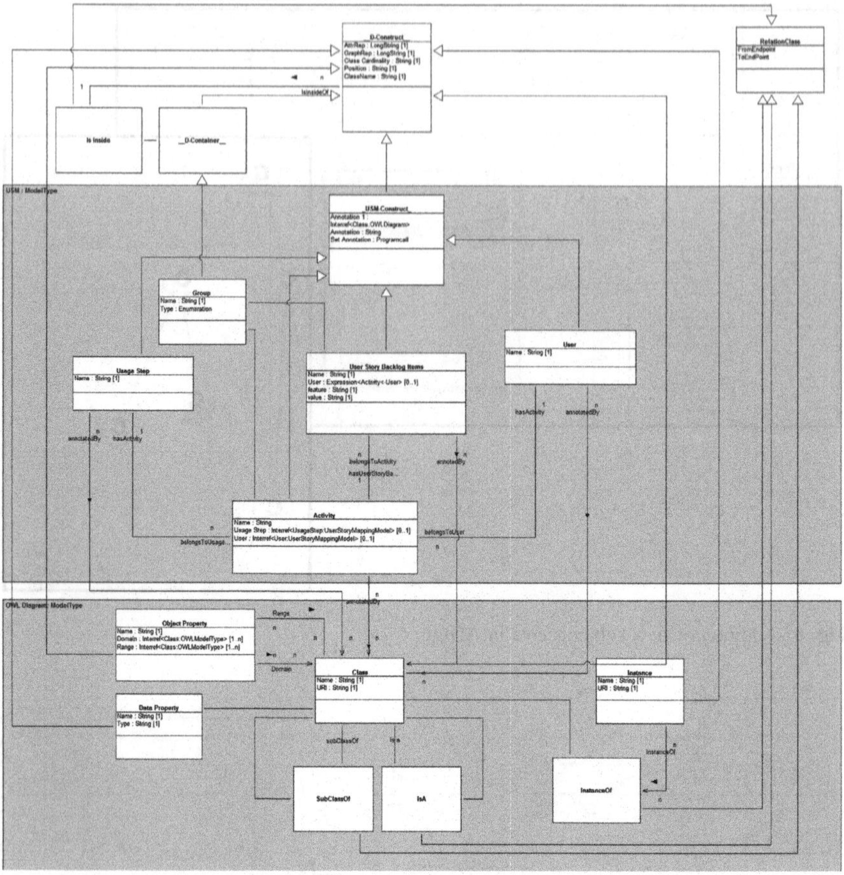

Fig. 10 Platform specific metamodel

metamodeling platform provides many additional functionalities, such as model querying. The ontology that was created can now be used to query each of the User activities or any other information retrieval that ADO*xx* user chooses to define.

The platform specific metamodel of the entire procedure is shown in Fig. 10.

5 Conclusion

The identification and representation of knowledge in a product related domain is still a great challenge. In this contribution, we propose the USM method for knowledge extraction as well as a formal guideline for applying this method. On the use-case, we showed that it is convenient, efficient, and successful in giving the expected results. The USM method gives us a tool which can directly translate raw data into a list of relevant concepts that covers the entire functional profile of the software in question and thus it gives us a detailed image of the domain this software operates on. It is simple, straightforward and it enables end-users to express their descriptions of the domain in a common, everyday language, rather than using technical terms, which is more probable to lead to gathering of more detailed information. Beside formalization of the information, it proves to be an excellent tool for the generalization of "end-user" requests and a vital step toward the creation of the knowledge base. Further on, we showed how the domains dynamics is represented using the ontology relation, thus giving the full semantic model of the manufacturing domain.

By implementing USM methodology on the ADO*xx* metamodeling platform, the entire procedure is enhanced through automatisation of deterministic steps and strategic procedure conduction. Each step can be performed independently and repeatedly, if needed. Each step is documented and can be revisited or discussed in the future.

The ADO*xx* platform opens a field of opportunities for future work that are out of scope of USM as an ontology modeling methodology. The ADO*xx* system enables the user to export models as RDF or XML structures, making them available for other software tools. On the other hand, the current export mechanism enables the user to export models while the procedures and algorithms defined on those models are not available outside ADO*xx*. One potential direction of future work is designing a mechanism that will translate existing mechanisms into SWRL syntax. Using this approach, ontology in RDF could be enriched with ontological rules in SWRL providing enhanced ADO*xx* model export capabilities and thus improving interoperability.

Tool Download http://www.omilab.org/usm.

References

1. Bohn, R.: Measuring and managing technological knowledge. In: The Economic Impact of Knowledge. Butterworth (1998)
2. Davenport, T., De Long, D., Beers, M.: Successful knowledge management projects. Sloan Manage. Rev. **39**(2), 43– +. (1998)
3. Drucker, P.F., Drucker, P.F.: Post-Capitalist Society. Routledge. http://books.google.com/books?hl=en&lr=&id=IYVBmM5z69cC&pgis=1 (1994)
4. Gruber, T.R.: A translation approach to portable ontology specifications. Knowl. Acquisition **5** (2), 199–220 (1993). doi:10.1006/knac.1993.1008
5. Gunasekaran, A.: Agile manufacturing: a framework for research and development. Int. J. Prod. Econ. **62**(1–2), 87–105 (1999). doi:10.1016/S0925-5273(98)00222-9
6. Hrgovcic, V.: Conceptual modeling of the organisational aspects for distributed applications: the semantic lifting approach. Comput. Softw. Appl. http://ieeexplore.ieee.org/xpls/abs_all.jsp?arnumber=6605780 (2013)
7. Kiritsis, D.: Semantic technologies for engineering asset life cycle management. Int. J. Prod. Res. **51**(23–24), 7345–7371 (2013). doi:10.1080/00207543.2012.761364

8. Milicic, A., Perdikakis, A., Kadiri, S.El.: Towards the definition of domain concepts and knowledge through the application of the user story mapping method. Prod. Lifecycle Manage. http://link.springer.com/chapter/10.1007/978-3-642-35758-9_6 (2012)
9. Nonaka, I., Takeuchi, H.: The Knowledge-creating Company: How Japanese Companies Create the Dynamics of Innovation. Oxford University Press. http://books.google.com/books?hl=en&lr=&id=B-qxrPaU1-MC&pgis=1 (1995)
10. Patton, J., Economy, P.: User story mapping: discover the whole story, build the right product. (2014)
11. Skarka, W.: Application of MOKA methodology in generative model creation using CATIA. Eng. Appl. Artif. Intell. **20**(5), 677–690 (2007). doi:10.1016/j.engappai.2006.11.019
12. Stewart, T., Ruckdeschel, C.: Intellectual capital: the new wealth of organisations. Perform. Improv. **37**(7), 56–59 (1998). doi:10.1002/pfi.4140370713
13. Suárez-Figueroa, M.C.: NeOn Methodology for Building Ontology Networks: Specification, Scheduling and Reuse. Facultad de Informática (UPM). http://oa.upm.es/3879/2/MARIA_DEL-_CARMEN_SUAREZ_DE_FIGUEROA_BAONZA.pdf. Accessed 25 June 2010
14. Sveiby, K.E.: The New Organizational Wealth: Managing & Measuring Knowledge-based Assets. Berrett-Koehler Publishers. http://books.google.com/books?hl=en&lr=&id=xKNXlgaeCjAC&pgis=1 (1997)

Product-Service-System Modeling Method

Xavier Boucher, Khaled Medini and Hans-Georg Fill

Abstract This paper addresses enterprise modeling needs, in a specific field of industrial management: the design and management of industrial product-service-systems. During the last decade, the industrial sector has undergone a change of the business model, through an increasing internalisation of service activities in manufacturing companies. The objective of this chapter is to develop a generic metamodel, which could be used to further develop IT support solutions for the design and lifecycle management of product-service-systems. The specification of this metamodel together with the associated modeling method are explained then illustrated on an industrial case study.

Keywords Metamodeling · Modeling method · Product-service systems · Scenarios of product-service-systems · Manufacturing servitisation

1 Enterprise Modeling Needs, in the Field of Product-Service-Systems

The need for a modeling method dedicated to the so-called product-service-systems (PSS) has been directly pushed by changes in the industrial business. During the last decade, the manufacturing industry has undergone a paradigm shift through the development and spread of servitisation and PSS concepts. From the point of view

X. Boucher (✉) · K. Medini
Ecole Nationale Supérieure des Mines de Saint-Etienne,
42023 Saint-Etienne Cedex 2, France
e-mail: boucher@emse.fr

K. Medini
e-mail: khaled.medini@emse.fr

H.-G. Fill
Research Group Knowledge Engineering, University of Vienna,
1090 Vienna, Austria
e-mail: hans-georg.fill@univie.ac.at

D. Karagiannis et al. (eds.), *Domain-Specific Conceptual Modeling*,
DOI 10.1007/978-3-319-39417-6_21

of industrial managers, the transition towards PSS has to be managed as a change of business model, where PSS are implemented as an innovation strategy, shifting from developing and selling physical products to developing and selling the use of a system of products and services capable of adapting easily to the personalized demands of the clients. Coupling, or even integrating, industrial production and service delivering poses many innovative challenges for the manufacturing industry at the technological, organizational and even human levels.

The notion of PSS has been progressively refined and formalized through the scientific literature. Several authors, such as [8, 13, 18, 21] proposed definitions for product-service-systems or even industrial product-service-systems [17]. A rather consensual definition considers PSS as "a value proposition that consists of a mix of tangible product and intangible service designed and combined so that they jointly are capable of fulfilling final customers' needs" [21]. As a general understanding of the notion of product-service-systems, the key structuring aspects can be highlighted:

- The change of economic model, based on the fact that PSS are based on selling the use of a product (product sold as a service) and not selling the product itself. Economically, this is a deep transformation both for the provider and for the customer, since this represents a switch from a so-called transactional economic model where the product possession is transferred from the provider to the client, towards a relational economic model, where the product remains in possession of the provider and the client only pays for its usage (made accessible through a service offer).
- The constant innovation of PSS on the 'value proposition'. PSS put the focus on being able to ensure a constant engineering and re-engineering of the value proposition lifecycle, and to deliver several complementary forms of value to the client through innovative channels.
- The transformation of industrial processes, notably characterized by the high collaborative level required that value be delivered. PSS value creation chains generally required to involve a network of partnerships within the PSS delivering process coordinating heterogeneous industrial processes (service- or manufacturing-oriented) and highlights strong needs to collaborate with the customers and several stakeholders during the design and industrialisation of PSS offers.

Some concrete examples will easier illustrate the notion of 'Product-Service-Systems' for non-specialists. For easy understanding, we will take examples from a very common field of the industrial economy: the transport systems. In every-day life, usual customers are used to buying a car as an individual solution for personal transport. In that case, customers and producers are situated in the traditional economy: buying a car is a transaction where the vehicle changes of the owner. A PSS solution consists in providing a full solution to the need of mobility of the customer. The question is no more to sell a product and make a sufficient margin during the sale, but the issue is to provide a full 'function' or 'solution to a global problem', which creates several forms of added value both for the customer and eventually for other stakeholders (reduction of ecological impact, for instance). The industrialization of this global PSS solution for mobility can take several distinct forms, which we can explain by means of a basic PSS typology. Complementary to previous definitions, several authors developed PSS typologies to better describe the full scope of such businesses. [11, 13, 20] or, more recently, [3] progressively converged towards a widely accepted classification based on the nature of the PSS offer:

- *Product-Oriented PSS*: the product is sent with a traditional economic model, but the sales contract includes services deployed along the product lifecycle. Such after-sales services will help in guaranteeing functionality and durability of the product owned by the customer. Referring to the example of transportation vehicles, a product-oriented PSS would only be maintenance contracts sold together with the traditional sale of the vehicle.
- *Use-Oriented PSS*: there is a change towards a relational economic model based on the sale of use. The provider only contracts some access or utilization of a system, without product purchase for the customer. In such cases, the PSS provider can increase its own motivation in extending the lifespan of the system, so as optimizing its potential use. If we develop again the mobility example, you can find today in several cities easy solutions to use an urban car while paying only the availability and the effective use. The car is shared among all its users and remains in possession of the provider. The provider has to create and maintain a full-service delivery solution to make the car easily and attractively usable.
- *Result-Oriented PSS*: independently of any pre-defined product, the provider guarantees to answer specific customer needs, with a contracted engagement on the final result/performance. In this case, the customer only pays for the provision of the results specified in the agreement. The level of risk for the providers is higher. To end with the mobility example, in the result-oriented PSS, the customer does not look for the availability and usage of a specific vehicle. He just looks for a global solution to its mobility problem: the PSS provider will build an ad hoc customized solution, which can be based on different types of vehicles and services, adapted to each context. The whole solution will be sold as a service contract.

Of course, the application extent of PSS is very large, and not all specifically oriented on transportation of logistic solutions. On the contrary, the entire economy is affected by this transformation, concerning Business to Business economic relationships as well as Business to Customer. Section 4 of this chapter will present a completely different example. This large applicative area, thus concerning small and medium size enterprises as well as large companies, induced strong needs of business process and business model change management, where advanced enterprise modeling methodologies should play a key role.

Based on the synthetic description of PSS and the industrial transition towards this innovative business model, the requirements for advanced enterprise engineering and modeling environments can be better understood. These requirements are driven by the decision needs of industrial managers. For industrial managers, changing from a traditional industrial economy, centred on manufacturing and sales processes with a philosophy of mass production, towards a functionality-oriented economy focusing on customized integrated solutions mixing products and services, is a deep, drastic and generally rather a progressive transformation of their Business Models. This situation of Business Models transformation for industrial companies generates strong needs of decision support systems linked to system modeling and engineering [14]. Key issues currently underlined by the academic literature focus on:

1. strong necessity of supporting tools for the engineering of PSS offers and for the configuration of multi-actor value creation networks;
2. requirements to manage enterprise transformation programs and assess alternative PSS transition scenarios;
3. operational management of PSS, with the requirements for advanced PSS life-cycle management solutions.

All these needs linked to PSS decision-making are directly linked to enterprise models, considered as support for various aspects of virtual enterprise design and engineering: **the specification of generic reusable and customizable PSS-oriented enterprise models has become a keystone of research in this area**.

One of the objectives of this book chapter is to make a concrete and consistent contribution to this field of research by structuring a generic framework for PSS modeling and analysis. The modeling concept proposed, based on several concrete past experiences of PSS modeling, aims at covering in a generic manner the various viewpoints required for PSS engineering. This model proposal is not considered as closed, but on the contrary, fully open to future development and improvement. In its current version, the modeling construct explained below intends to cover several important areas: the PSS offer (linked to product, services, as well as market); the multi-actor organizational capabilities and performances characterising PSS delivery processes; the alternative scenarios of the value creation network corresponding to distinct business models.

This chapter was structured as follows: Sect. 2 introduces the main concepts of the modeling methods and puts forth the overall structure of the models; Sect. 3 describes which modeling procedure should be followed for their application; an industrial case study illustrates the method in Sect. 4, before opening further perspectives in Sect. 5.

2 Method Conceptualization and Metamodel Proposal

2.1 PSS Modeling Requirements

The paper is the result of an explorative research methodology combining requirements from the PSS literature and requirements from practical use cases. The literature suggests that traditional modeling methods do not allow a clear representation of PSS because of the complexity induced by coupling physical products with

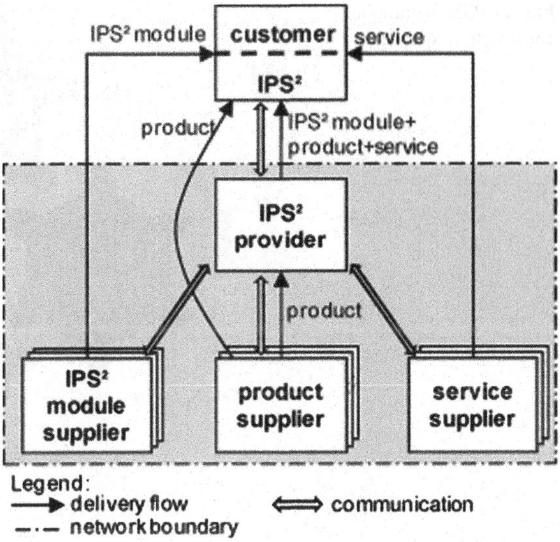

Fig. 1 IPSS network organization [17]

services in one offer and the strong linkages between the PSS offer and its value network. The value is generated out of collaborative processes throughout the PSS value network, thus, the definition of the offer should take into account the organization of the actors (firms), business processes, etc. involved in the network (Fig. 1).

As a matter of fact, PSS conceptualization has been a major concern in the scientific literature of the recent years. However, little attention was given to operational solutions which could implement the requirements identified at the conceptual level [2, 4]. Among the most important issues that need to be dealt with, is the impact of servitisation on the various actors of value creation networks. PSS design, as a key element of the industry servitisation process, induces organizational changes in terms of the actors' responsibilities (e.g., final PSS customer, supplier, intermediary, etc.). From the very beginning of the PSS design process, the interaction between the PSS offer and the organizational network in charge to deliver it has to be taken into account. Thus, it is important to involve PSS actors in the design of the offer and in the configuration of its value network. For instance, this allows coping with their different expectations when defining the PSS solution space and when choosing performance indicators to assess alternative PSS scenarios [16].

These requirements were used as guidelines throughout the development of the modeling method presented in this chapter. This modeling method was developed following an iterative metamodeling procedure shown in Fig. 2. Of course, literature input on PSS modeling was used as a starting point to develop the metamodel; moreover, the iterative metamodeling procedure utilized several PSS modeling use cases from different manufacturing sectors as very concrete complementary requirements. More specifically, the available knowledge about a given use case was translated into a metamodel describing the way a PSS scenario could (not should be!) be modeled. This process results in an initial use case based metamodel

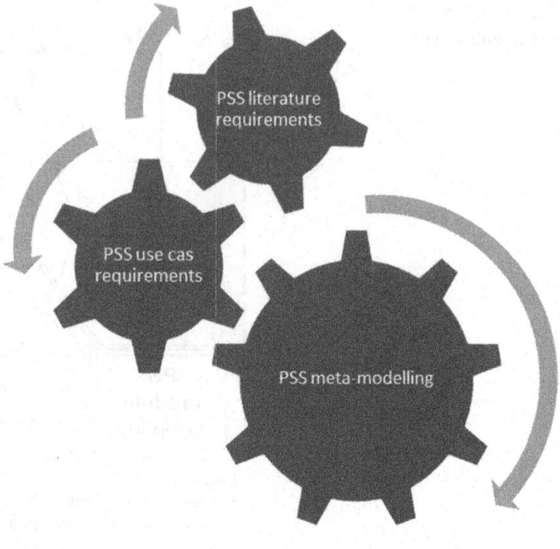

Fig. 2 PSS metamodel construction approach

that was refined, in a second step, based on the PSS modeling and metamodeling requirements. In other words, this second step consisted in replacing the context-dependent constructs and relationships of the metamodel by more generic ones (Fig. 2).

The metamodel resulting from applying this metamodeling approach is finally composed of two main parts corresponding to two complementary characteristics of product-service-systems: the structural versus behavioral characteristics of the PSS (Fig. 3). The structural part of the metamodel ('*PSS structure*') gathers the modeling constructs necessary to formalize the architecture of the PSS offer together with its value creation network. It is composed of three modeling perspectives corresponding to various aspects of the PSS structure, namely 'Product', 'Service' and 'Organization'. The second part of the metamodel (PSS dynamics) corresponds to the behavioral dimension of the PSS, including the market behaviors linked to the offer as well as performance factors associated with the organizational capabilities. It is composed of three additional modeling perspectives, namely 'Offer', 'Scenario' and 'Performance'.

All these modeling perspectives support decision-making at different stages of the PSS design process. These six perspectives are briefly introduced below:

- The *Organization perspective* aims at modeling the capabilities of the actors (firms) involved in the PSS network to take in charge PSS value creation activities. We consider here the notion of *Activity* as a delimited set of operations, organized in a more or less structured way, to produce some specific output.
- The *Product perspective* has the objective to represent the overall structure of manufactured or purchased physical components or products embedded in the material part of the PSS.

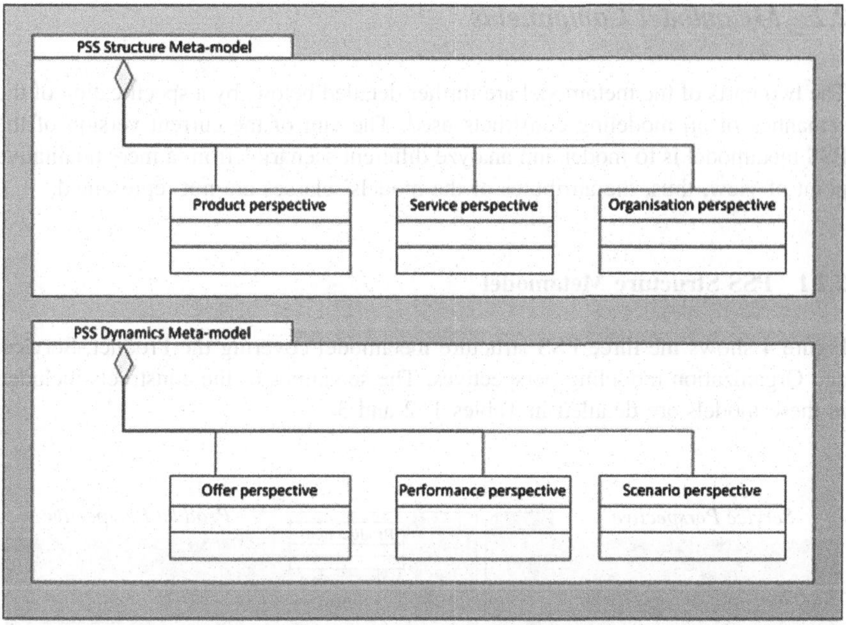

Fig. 3 Overall structure of the metamodel with 6 model types

- The *Service perspective* aims at modeling intangible activities or added-values delivered to the customer, in the form of services associated with the lifecycle of the PSS offer. This intangible component of the PSS involves interactions with the customer [12, 17].
- The *Offer perspective* makes it possible to specify (i) the way combinations of products and services are offered on the market to achieve an overall functionality required by the customer, as well as (ii) the dynamics of the demand characterizing the market. Such structured information on demand and offer is necessary for dynamic analyses of PSS value chains.
- The *Scenario perspective*: as a general definition, a scenario can be understood as a description of a possible future that reflects different perspectives on the past, the present and the future [10, 22]. In the current context, a scenario is a description of a potential configuration of the PSS value creation chain, supporting a prospective analysis and which can be associated with a quantitative assessment model.
- The *Performance perspective* defines the set of selected *Indicators* for evaluating the scenarios from the different actors' points of view. An *Indicator* can be defined as an index of business activities: a financial or non-financial measurement, either tactical or strategic, which is linked to specific strategic goals and objectives [1]. The indicator's value differs according to business drivers [19].

The next sections provide a more detailed specification of the PSS structure and dynamics, respectively.

2.2 Metamodel Components

The two parts of the metamodel are further detailed below, by a specification of the semantics of all modeling constructs used. The aim of the current version of the PSS metamodel is to model and analyze different scenarios from a mere qualitative point of view, thus, the attributes of the models' classes are not represented.

2.2.1 PSS Structure Metamodel

Figure 4 shows the three PSS structure metamodel covering the Product, Service, and Organization modeling perspectives. The semantics of the constructs included in these models are detailed in Tables 1, 2 and 3.

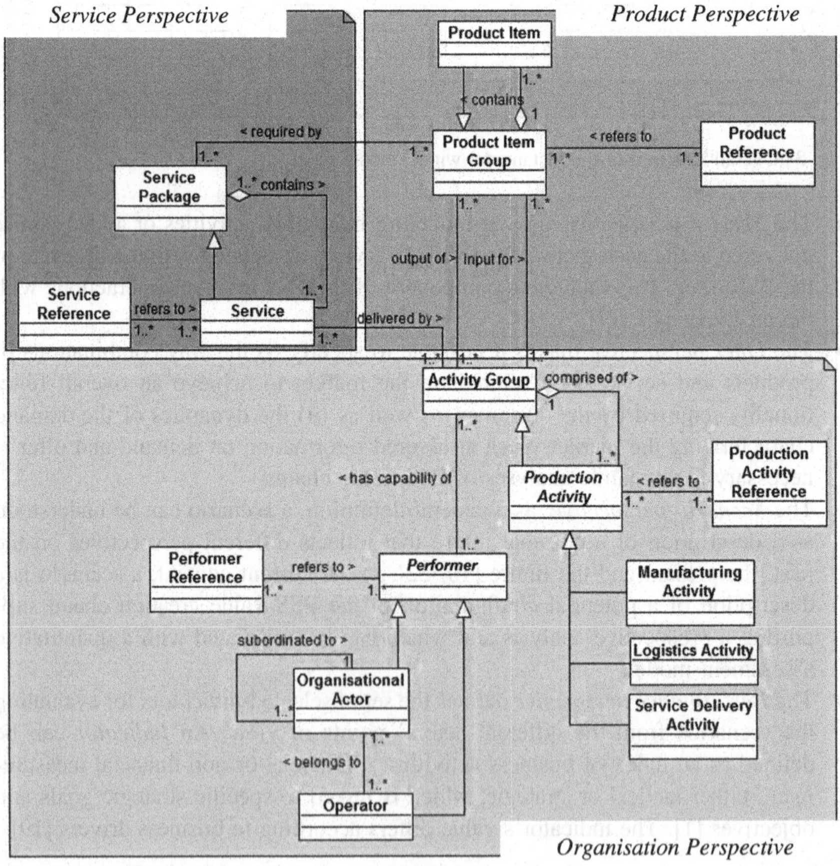

Fig. 4 PSS structure metamodel

Table 1 Product perspective semantics

Construct	Informal semantics	Graphical notation
Product Item	A manufactured or purchased physical component or product, embedded in the material part of the PSS	
Product Item Group	A group of Product Items sharing common features	*Product Item Group name*
Product Reference	Reference object making possible to refer to one or more *Product Items*, within other metamodel than the "PSS Structure Metamodel"	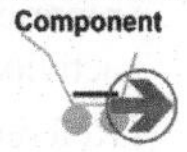

Table 2 Service perspective semantics

Construct	Informal semantics	Graphical notation
Service package	A specific and consistent set of services, presenting common but also complementary features and which are designed to be included within the same PSS offer	*Service Package name*
Service	Intangible added value delivered to a customer, as part of a PSS offer	**Service** *Service name*
	A service is defined here as the "The intangible result of activities realized by some actor(s) with the intention to create and deliver value for some other actor(s), resulting in a change of state for this (these) actor(s)."	
Service Reference	Reference object making possible to refer to one or more *Service*, within another metamodel than the "PSS Structure Metamodel"	

Please note also, in Fig. 4, four abstract classes named 'Product Reference', 'Service Reference', 'Production Activity Reference' and 'Performer Reference'. These four classes are not used as PSS modeling constructs: they only make possible a clear interconnection between the structural and behavioral parts of the metamodel. Concretely, they will be reused in Sect. 2.2.2, to present more easily the PSS Dynamics Metamodel.

The *Product* and *Service* modeling perspectives are the backbones of the PSS offering and they need to be clearly represented in order to ease the subsequent design steps. For the decision-making requirements of PSS offer design and engineering, a rather simple product model is useful, to represent basically the bill of materials for the technical devices of the PSS offer. The Service *perspective* offers the possibility to specify services and organize them into alternative 'service packages' associated to product lifecycle. The services offered have to be linked to organizational capabilities, through the notion of 'Service delivery activity'.

Table 3 Organization perspective semantics

Construct	Informal semantics	Graphical notation
Production Activity	Represents any type of production activity required in the PSS delivery process	
	Production activities can be further specialized into the 3 subtypes: '*Manufacturing activity*' required for the production of PSS '*Product Items*'; '*Logistic activity*' required for the physical delivery within the PSS offer; 'S*ervice delivery activity*' representing any other type of service production activity	
Production Activity Reference	Reference object making possible to refer to one or more *Production Activity*, within another metamodel than the "PSS Structure Metamodel"	
Organizational Actor	Refers to an organizational unit (e.g., company, production unit, subsidy, etc.) involved in the PSS delivery network, and in charge of some '*Production activities*'	
Operator	Refers to any individual operator belonging to some of the PSS network organizational actors, and directly in charge of some '*Production activities*'	
Performer	An abstract class referring to the Organizational Actor or Operator and in capacity and responsibility to perform a given '*Production activity*' require in the value creation network	–
Performer Reference	Reference object making possible to refer either to one or more *Operator **or** Organizational Actor*, within another metamodel than the "PSS Structure Metamodel"	

Additionally, regulating the collaboration among the actors (firms) involved in the PSS design is a prerequisite for the design process itself. The *Organization perspective* includes the actors and the value creation activities contributing to PSS delivery. These activities are paramount to subsequent PSS design steps, in particular, scenarios configuration. They structure the organizational model: any group of activities (construct 'Activity group') is linked to a product item, and can be taken in charge by a performer, either a collective performer ('Organizational actor' construct) or an individual one ('Operator' construct).

2.2.2 PSS Dynamics Metamodel

Figure 5 shows the three PSS dynamics modeling perspectives namely Offer, Scenario and Performance. The semantics of the modeling constructs are detailed in Tables 4, 5 and 6.

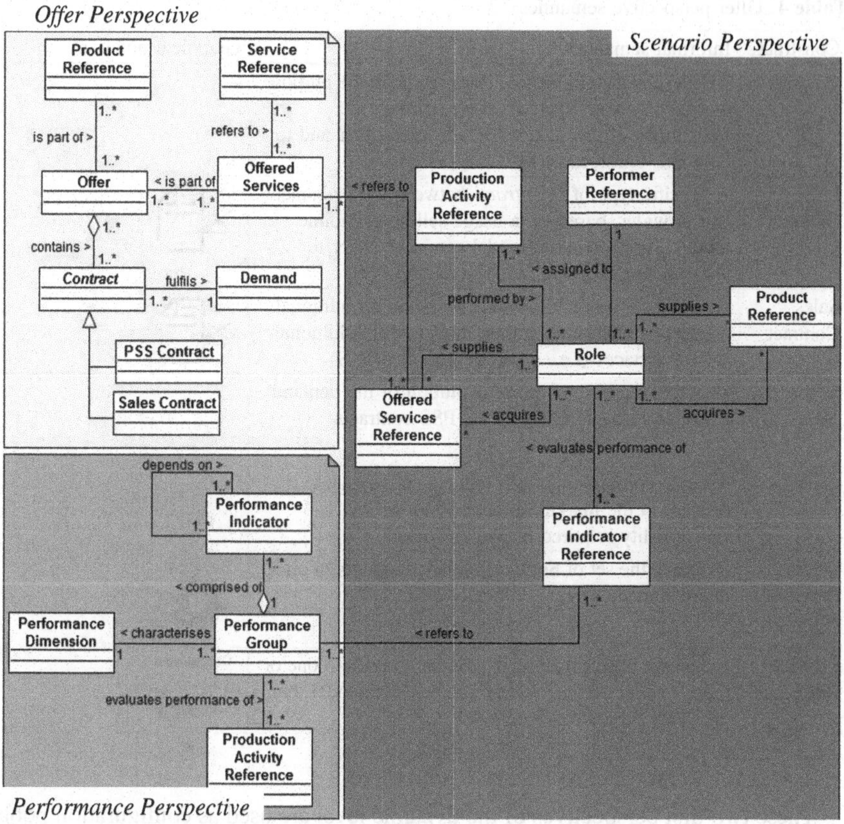

Fig. 5 PSS dynamics metamodel

The first requirement for the dynamic analysis of PSS value creation networks, the *Offer* modeling perspective structures the market-oriented data concerning demands and offers. Available product and services are combined into different PSS offerings. Then, these PSS offerings are structured into *Contracts* corresponding to agreements, elaborated to mitigate risks by defining the obligations of the distinct stakeholders to one other, including customers [9, 17]. Each *Contract* can be characterized by the temporal evolution of the demand during the lifecycle considered.

Secondly, the *Performance* modeling perspective structures the performance dimensions and indicators that will be used to measure value creation performance. The performance dimensions selected as pertinent for the assessment of PSS scenarios (e.g., Economic, Ecological, Industrial dimensions) are specified by sets of indicators ('Performance Groups'). These indicators can be then assigned to production activities as well as organizational roles.

Table 4 Offer perspective semantics

Construct	Informal semantics	Graphical notation
Contract	Refers to a customer-provider agreement, the purpose of which is to mitigate risks by defining the obligations of the stakeholders to each other and to have this enforceable by law [9, 17]	–
PSS Contract	A specific type of '*Contract*' between the customer and provider, based on a usage-selling economic model. This economic model can refer either to usage-oriented or availability-oriented PSS	
Sales Contract	A specific type of '*Contract*' based on a traditional product selling an economic model, with additional sale of services (i.e., a product-oriented PSS)	
Demand	Characterizes the temporal evolution of the demand expected to be fulfilled by the PSS contracts	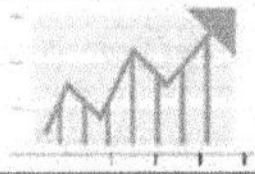
Offer	Specific combinations of products and services offered on the market, to achieve an overall functionality required by the customer	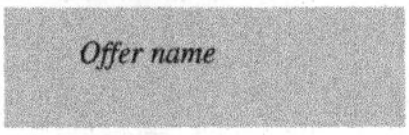
Offered Services	Refers to the set of Services included in a given offer, then contract	
Product Reference	Reference object making it possible to refer to one or more *Product Items*, within another metamodel than the "PSS Structure Metamodel"	

These two first perspectives of the dynamic level are used as configuration pools in order to specify alternative configurations of the way the PSS solution could be delivered to the customer. These configurations correspond to organizational scenarios: the third modeling perspective, the *Scenario*, is the central component of the metamodel. The key construct is, here, the notion of 'Role', which defined the responsibility of any 'Performer' of the collaborative network with regards to '*Product Items*', '*Services*' and '*Production Activities*'. A scenario is a specific configuration of the PSS value creation network, together with the definition of the performance system selected for evaluation. As such, the association of a 'Scenario Model' together with an 'Offer Model' and 'Performance Model' finally provides a well-structured specification of decision-aid required for PSS design, in the form of performance-based comparison of alternative organizational scenarios.

Table 5 Scenario perspective semantics

Construct	Informal semantics	Graphical notation
Role	Represents the set of responsibilities for '*Production Activities*', assigned to any '*Performer*' which contributes to the PSS value creation network. These '*Production Activities*' responsibilities can concern either service or product production and delivery	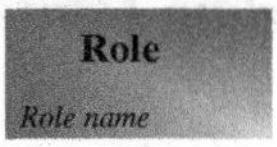
Performer Reference	Reference object making it possible to refer either to one or more *Operator or Organizational Actor*, within another metamodel than the "PSS Structure Metamodel"	
Performance Indicators Reference	Reference object to one or more Performance Indicators (cf. '*Performance Indicator*' definition)	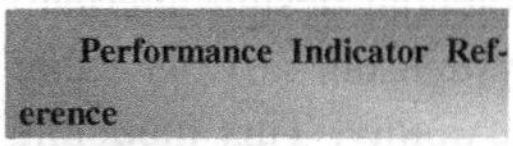
Production Activity Reference	Reference object making it possible to refer to one or more *Production Activity*, within another metamodel than the "PSS Structure Metamodel"	
Service Reference	Reference object making it possible to refer to one or more *Service*, within another metamodel than the "PSS Structure Metamodel"	
Product Reference	Reference object to one or more Products (cf. '*Product Item*' construct)	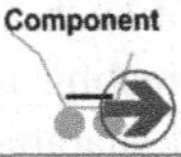

Table 6 Performance perspective semantics

Construct	Informal semantics	Graphical notation
Performance dimension	Specifies a specific performance area (e.g., Economical, Ecological, Industrial dimensions…) which can be selected for PSS scenario assessment	
Performance indicator	Refers to an index characterizing industrial and business activities: a financial or non-financial measurement, either tactical or strategic, which is linked to specific strategic goals and objectives [1]. The indicator's value differs according to business drivers [19]	
Performance Group	Refers to a delimited set of *Performance Indicators,* all of them related to the same '*Performance Dimension*' and gathered for a consistent purpose	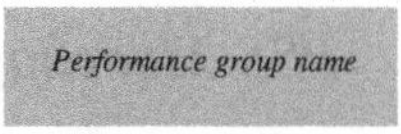
Production Activity Reference	Reference object making it possible to refer to one or more *Production Activity*, within another metamodel than the "PSS Structure Metamodel"	

3 PSS Modeling Method: Context and Procedure

3.1 Modeling Context

The general objective of the metamodel developed is to provide the generic concepts required to build a structured qualitative description of all the components of a PSS offer under design. This qualitative description should also serve as a repository of quantitative knowledge, expected to be reused afterwards to implement specific decision support systems. As explained in the introduction of the chapter, the design of integrated Product-Service-Systems suffers from a high complexity because of (i) the interaction between product and service which opens lots of potential design alternatives but also (ii) the necessity of designing not only the system but also its value creation network, here again with large possibilities of flexibility. This modeling approach is proposed to be integrated as a support for PSS Design. In its current state of development, it mainly aims at supporting a phase of definition of the general architecture of the PSS offer: the specification of all the material and immaterial components of the offer, together with the value creation network required to deliver it.

The PSS designers will follow this modeling approach in order to make explicit some PSS design they are working on. The structure of the models and the associated modeling procedure will help them in providing a consistent description of all the elements of such a complex design. The qualitative models generated constitute a first interesting result to support the design process, by capitalising in a very reusable and sharable manner a large diversity of knowledge concerning the PSS offer. More specifically, the metamodel helps in clearly identifying the various organizational scenarios which appear as pertinent to concretely implement the PSS offer on the market.

However, this modeling procedure is also proposed to answer some additional further goals. Medini and Boucher [14] emphasize that, at the time of designing the overall architecture of PSS solutions, decision-makers clearly lack methodological and technical solutions to evaluate the economic viability of a PSS-oriented business model and to assess the practical implications of alternative configurations of the PSS value networks. The modeling library presented in this chapter also aims at serving as a knowledge repository used as a starting point for developing a simulation-based evaluation of the various organizational scenarios resulting from the approach.

3.2 PSS Modeling Procedure

The goal of the modeling is to provide a visual representation of the PSS organizational scenario and a starting point for analyzing and discussing them. One should note that this PSS scenario modeling work is part of a deeper process of PSS design: the descriptive knowledge structured within the models evolves a long time during all the PSS design process. Until now, the modeling procedure (Fig. 6) has been applied based on the intervention of a modeling expert, in charge of collecting the knowledge from PSS designer. Data collection is performed through a set of structured interviews, complemented when necessary with structured questioners to obtain specific pieces of information. The organization of this information collection procedure is contextualized in every specific case study. The models also constitute a cognitive support, helping designers to make their creativity explicit, then offering the possibility to further develop specific decision-aids.

If the final objective underlined above is to analyze the potential value creation networks required for a PSS design, a prerequisite task is to make explicit the content of the offer itself. In order to start the interaction with PSS designers, the first modeling objective is thus to structure the available knowledge on the PSS offer, covering two key aspects: the content of the offer together with the market characteristics. These two aspects have to be modeled quite interactively because the structure of the PSS offer remains of course very dependent on the requirements of customer usage and markets which are aimed to be fulfilled. In this stage, the 'Product models' are used to represent the key physical items of the offer and the 'Service Model' to specify progressively the basic services which can be delivered along the product lifecycle. In parallel, the markets characteristics have to be structured within the 'Offer Model': different potential usages will lead to consider several offers (consistent package of services and product items) and their associated contracts. Since these models are used within a non-stabilized design process, 'Offer Model' and 'Service Model' are progressively created with several iterations, which contribute to refining the PSS specification.

When these first three models are available, the modeling procedure can go further towards formalising the organizational aspects. The final objective is to generate a clear specification of organizational scenarios which could be later evaluated quantitatively to provide a useful decision-aid (out of the scope of the chapter). First, the Organizational Model has to be created. By specifying the different types of *'Production Activities'*, all the basic components of the PSS delivery process are identified. As a complement, the concrete actors (individual or collective) considered in the analysis are identified and characterized by their capabilities to take in charge some of these *'Production Activities'*. Then the 'Performance Model' is created: it intends to define the performance system which could be used to evaluate the distinct organizational scenarios. The performance model is also intended to cope with the different expectations of the PSS actors, with the possibility to assign personalized *'Performance Group'* for each of them, reflecting its proper point of view. The final modeling step, i.e., the backbone of the modeling approach, is building the scenarios. This step is based on a combination of objects from the other model types which enables a quite straightforward configuration process of the scenario; product, service, offer, organization, and performance models will be used as tools for building PSS value network scenarios.

Fig. 6 Modeling procedure

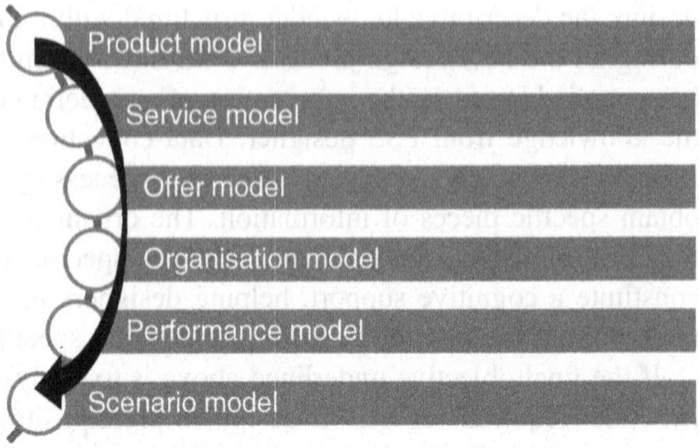

As a result of the modeling procedure, the PSS designers made explicit all the components of the PSS offer and lifecycle, a structured sufficient knowledge to make possible a rigorous assessment of the various alternatives of economic models and value creation networks.

4 Implementation of the Modeling Environment and Industrial Application

4.1 The Industrial Context of the Experimentation

The industrial context is linked to the end-of-life process of treated steel sludge, generated as a waste from the manufacturing industry. In Fig. 7a, most of the time, machining sludge generated by steel manufacturers is sent for incineration. This involves additional costs and of course a strong impact on resources consumption and thus depletion with a high ecological cost.

In order to mitigate the economic and environmental impact in the particular machining sludge sector, a project consortium was created and aims to design a PSS-oriented offering, involving different stakeholders. The idea of the project calls for a fundamental shift away from getting rid of the sludge towards making money out of it and saving natural resources. The traditional (a) and suggested (b) sludge treatments are represented in Fig. 7.

The PSS offer is thus based on a technological innovation: a so-called briquetting machine which transforms industrial sludge, through a compression process, to generate metal-bricks which can then be reused, by selling them to a smelting company. Ecologically, the process is clearly interesting and is a direct example of circular economy. The PSS offer is structured around the briquetting machine. Several different services could be offered along the lifecycle of this machine: the service offers can cover different levels of maintenance, but also different steps of transportation either for the sludge (raw material to be transformed) or for the produced metal-bricks, and could even cover the offer of full ‘usage service

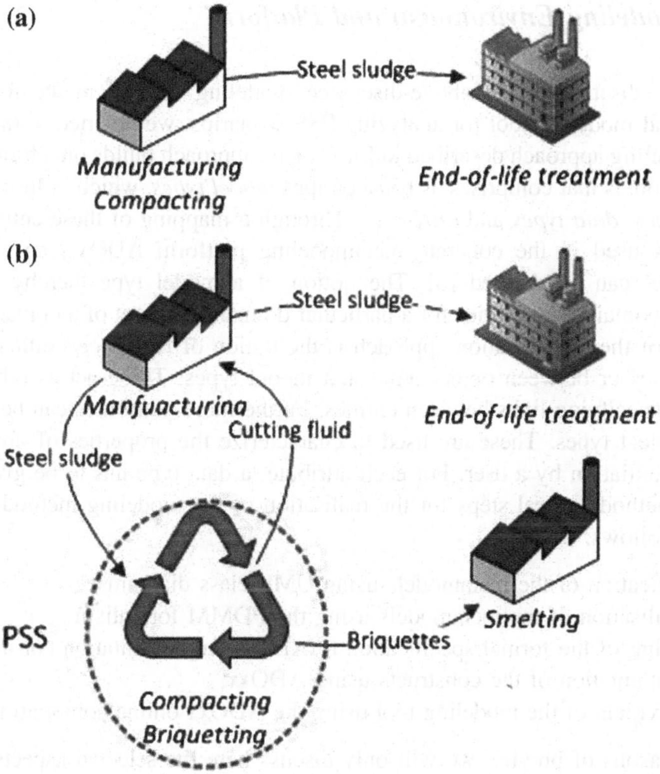

Fig. 7 Traditional (**a**) and innovative (**b**) configurations

contracts' instead of selling the machine to the manufacturing company. All these potential services, introduce a rather large variety of offer configurations which could be launched on the market. Associated with these configurations, several alternative economic models could be envisioned and several alternative business actors (covering different types of industrial and service activities) could be involved in the value creation chain.

This service-oriented context clearly shows that there is a high complexity of decision-making to analyze jointly the configuration of the offer and variety levels, with the balancing of the economic model and coherently with the distribution of responsibilities within the multi-actor value network. The PSS-oriented modeling environment presented above aims at managing this complexity, by proposing a structured way to make explicit all the alternatives of these value creation schemas and to capitalize the pieces of knowledge necessary for decision-making. The application of the modeling procedure will make explicit all the components of this PSS design and clarify the organizational scenarios to be further analyzed.

4.2 Modeling Environment and Platform

For the realisation of the above-discussed modeling method in the form of an operational modeling tool for analyzing PSS scenarios, we reverted to the FDMM metamodeling approach described in [5, 7]. This approach builds on a formalisation of metamodels that comprises as basic entities *model types*, which in turn comprise *object types*, *data types* and *attributes*. Through a mapping of these entities to the constructs used in the concrete metamodeling platform ADO*xx*, an executable metamodel can be derived [6]. The notion of a model type thereby acts as a semantic container of entities for a particular domain or subset of a domain. A core property of the formalisation approach is the notion of *references*, either between object types or between object types and model types. These act as relations for formally specifying links between entities. Furthermore, attributes can be specified for all object types. These are used to characterize the properties of object types upon instantiation by a user. For each attribute, a data type has to be given.

The methodological steps for the realisation of the modeling method as a tool were as follows:

1. Specification of the metamodels using UML class diagrams;
2. Formalisation of the metamodels using the FDMM formalism;
3. Mapping of the formal specification to ADO*xx* implementation constructs;
4. Implementation of the constructs using ADO*xx*;
5. Deployment of the modeling tool using the ADO*xx* online compilation service.

For reasons of brevity, we will only discuss here the selected aspects of these steps. From the UML metamodels derived in the previous sections, we specified six model types according to the FDMM approach. The reasons for this were twofold. On the one hand, the FDMM formalism prescribes the use of model types, as this occurs later in the implementation step. On the other hand, the pragmatic aspects of usability have to be taken into account. As it would not be feasible for a user to deal with all defined modeling constructs in one large model, the grouping of constructs that semantically belong to a more restrained field of knowledge is reasonable. This greatly helps a user to maintain a good overview of all parts of the knowledge made explicit. Six model types were finally derived, corresponding to the six perspectives presented in the metamodel.

In addition, during the implementation step, graphical representations were specified for all derived constructs. In particular, several symbols were elaborated in a bachelor thesis project conducted by Veronika Lomasow at the University of Vienna. Thereby the symbols were designed using the OMiLAB GraphRep Generator that provides a visual editor for generating GraphRep code.[1]

The current status of the implementation as developed in ADO*xx* is shown in the figure below (Fig. 8).

[1]See http://www.omilab.org/web/guest/graphrep-generator last accessed 02-10-2015.

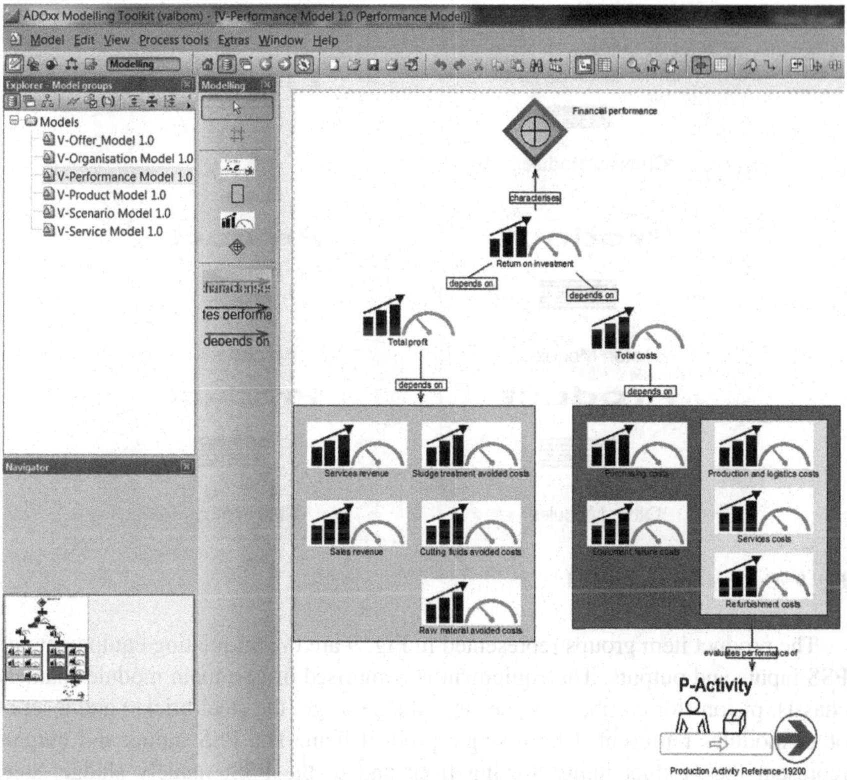

Fig. 8 View of the implemented modeling tool on the ADO*xx* platform. The view puts forth the 'Performance model type', corresponding to the 'Performance perspective' in Fig. 5

4.3 Application of the Modeling Procedure

The suggested PSS solution is built around the briquette-making equipment which facilitates the compacting and briquetting, and makes the sludge reusable. The compacting and briquetting results in two reusable products, (i) metal-bricks, which can be sold to and used by smelters, and (ii) cutting fluid extracted from the sludge, which can be used by the manufacturers themselves. As mentioned above, the services offered can bring added-value, such as installation of the machine, training for the employees, machine performance traceability and maintenance, transportation of several goods, and sale of use contracts. The composition of product and service components in the PSS offer, then its links with economic and organizational models are described in detail below.

Step 1—Specification of product and service components of the PSS offer The PSS offering includes the equipment for compacting and briquetting the machining sludge and a set of services (e.g., maintenance, transportation, installation, etc.). Figures 9 and 10 show the product and service models, respectively.

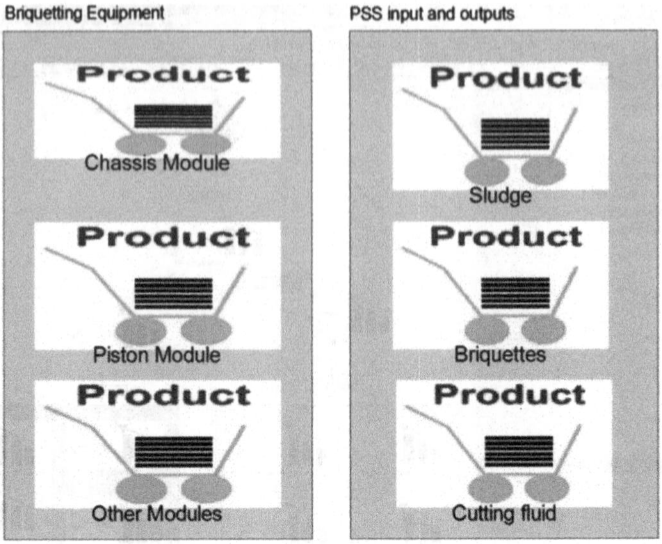

Fig. 9 Use case product model

The product item groups represented in Fig. 9 are the briquetting equipment and PSS inputs and outputs. The equipment is comprised of two main modules namely chassis, piston (for compacting the steel sludge to get the steel bricks) and a set of other modules represented by a single product item. The PSS inputs and outputs represent the product items flowing from and to the PSS, namely sludge, steel bricks and cutting fluid. Steel sludge is the raw material to produce steel bricks out of the compacting and briquetting processes. The cutting fluid is a secondary output of these processes. In fact, a technological innovation in the equipment allows recovering around 90 % of the liquid embedded in the steel sludge. 10 % of the recovered liquid is a valuable cutting fluid.

Figure 10 depicts two examples of service packages which can be included in the offer: basic and extended packages. The basic package includes maintenance and is assumed to be inevitable in both cases: sales and renting contracts. Extended packages include additional services such as traceability (e.g., information about equipment performance), quality control (e.g., steel bricks robustness, non-compliance rate), steel sludge treatment (in case of problems with the equipment), and operator availability (if the PSS customer is not ready to manage the compacting process himself). The service packages represent an answer to specific customers' needs. Having various packages makes it possible to meet as many customers' requirements as possible.

Step 2—Specification of the Offer model Figure 11 shows the offer model including the service packages which can be assigned to the contracts through the "Offered Services" attributes (as illustrated in Fig. 12, which states that the equipment sales contract includes the basic service package). For the case study, the figure underlines one contract with the type 'Sales Contract' and 3 'PSS Contract'

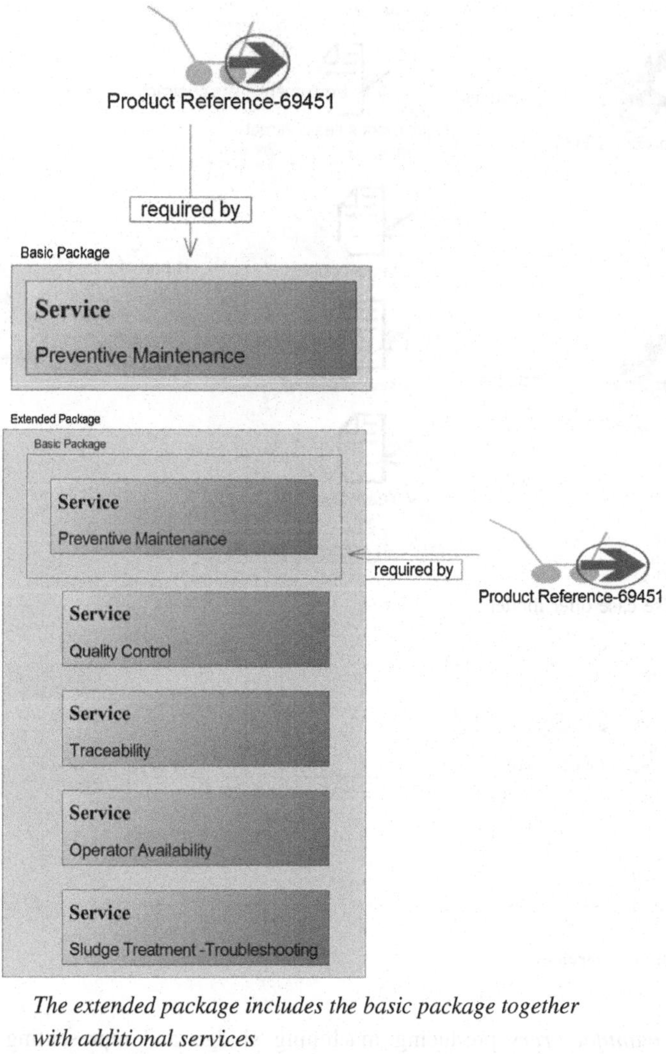

Fig. 10 Use case of service model (2 service packages), *The extended package includes the basic package together, with additional services*

according to variable contract durations. The demand characterising each contract can be distinct.

Step 3—Organization model The actors involved in the PSS value network are as follows:

- *Equipment provider* qualified for manufacturing and refurbishing the briquette-making equipment, he has also the capability of compacting and briquetting.

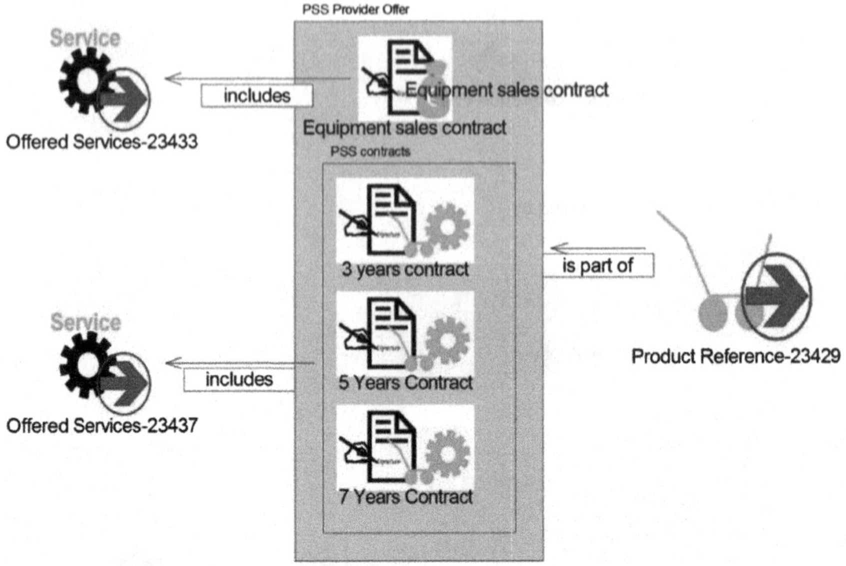

Fig. 11 Use case offer model

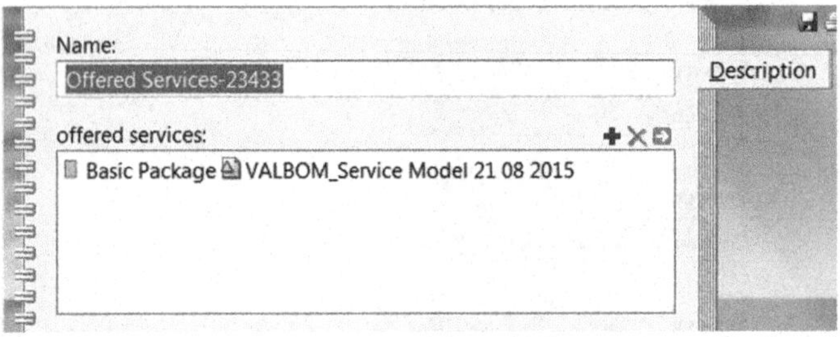

Fig. 12 Offered services

- *Steel manufacturers* producing machining sludge and representing potential customers of the envisioned PSS offering. The steel manufacturer has also the capability of compacting and briquetting as well as all logistics activities.
- *An intermediary* who may be involved in the PSS network by taking over the logistics activities.
- *Smelters* using electric arc furnaces for melting steel scrap and other metals. The smelters are potential customers for the produced steel bricks (cf. Fig. 13).

For confidentiality reasons, specific information about the case companies and institutions will not be disclosed. The organization model depicts the PSS value network and activities and specifies the capabilities of each of the organizational actors with regards to the activities. However, the assignment of organizational actors to given sets of activities is performed only during scenario definition (cf.

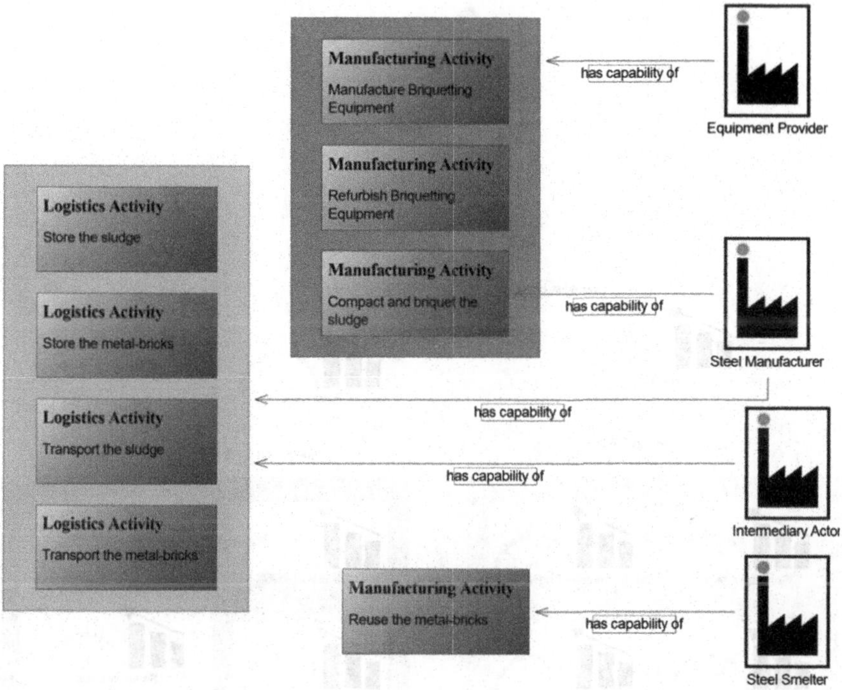

Fig. 13 Use case organization model

scenario model). Thus, by linking the actors to the activities, the organizational model specifies the various industrial-or service-oriented capability sets for each actor, as a required step before the scenario definition.

Step 4—Performance Models The tasks that are supported by this modeling step consist in selecting or developing performance measures consistently with the firm's objectives behind the PSS implementation. More specifically, this step aims to define the performance indicators for each organizational actor involved, then identify physical and financial flows that should be modeled in order to enable indicators calculation by use of simulation. Then, questionnaires are built upon these models and are used for data collection. Indicators should comply with the multi-actor perspective, meaning that the final set of performance measures should accommodate the points of view of all the actors of the PSS value network [16]. In the current use case, the selection of proper performance indicators was straightforward since the main concerns of the stakeholders (i.e., equipment provider, manufacturer and smelter) relate basically to costs and benefits. Figure 14 shows the performance indicators and their dependencies for the current use case.

Indicators selection is paramount to the scenarios evaluation. In the original methodology reported on in [16], the indicators are used for quantitative analysis: the indicators are calculated using a simulation algorithm, which in turn, uses data coming from the components structured in the model types above. The model is implemented

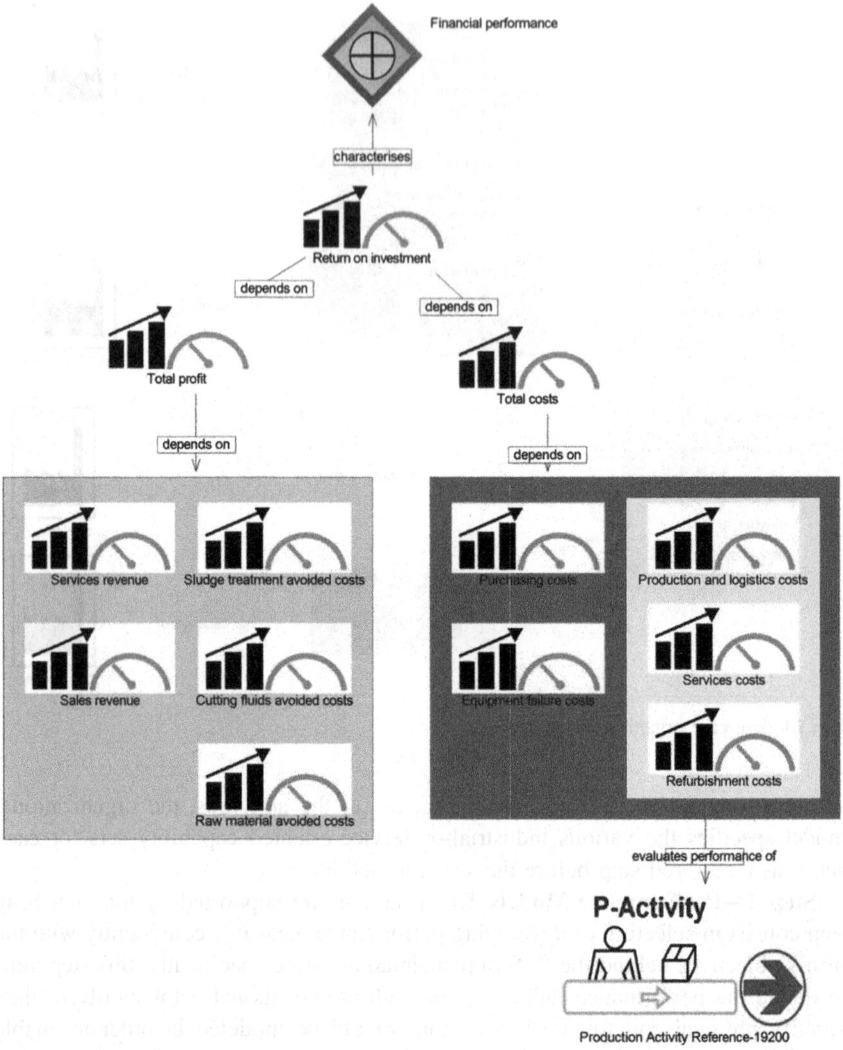

Fig. 14 Use case performance model

in an IT environment in order to provide a useful decision-making support to the PSS organizational actors based on quantitative measures. The rationale of this support is to get informed a priori of the spinoffs of the various scenarios and have some insights into the potential trade-offs ensuring a profitable PSS for all of the actors. The quantitative analysis, however, is out of the scope of the current paper.

Step 5—Scenario Models Scenarios identification relies on semi-structured interviews and intensive meetings involving all the PSS network actors. Basically, the scenarios correspond to alternative business models which appear as technically viable, in order to deliver the PSS on the market. Each scenario is characterized mainly by (i) specific economic model options and (ii) specific assignments of organizational actors to the set of production activities of the PSS Value Chain. The scenarios are intended to be compared among themselves in order to select the more pertinent (generally, the scenarios entailing the lowest amount of risk are the preferred ones).

Scenarios identification relies on an intensive collaboration with the value network actors (i.e., steel manufacturers, equipment manufacturers, smelters). For the case study, the collaboration process (typically, using interviews and questionnaires) resulted in the identification of 18 alternative organizational scenarios. These scenarios were filtered by the industrial decision-makers according to (i) compliance to regulations, (ii) added value for the value network actors themselves but also for the PSS customers [15]. The subsequent scenarios list includes four main scenarios, each of which has specific answers to the two following questions: ***Where is the equipment located?*** and ***Who is the owner of the equipment?***

A typical representation of an organizational scenario is given in Fig. 15. Within the metamodel proposed, PSS actors are decoupled from the value chain activities.

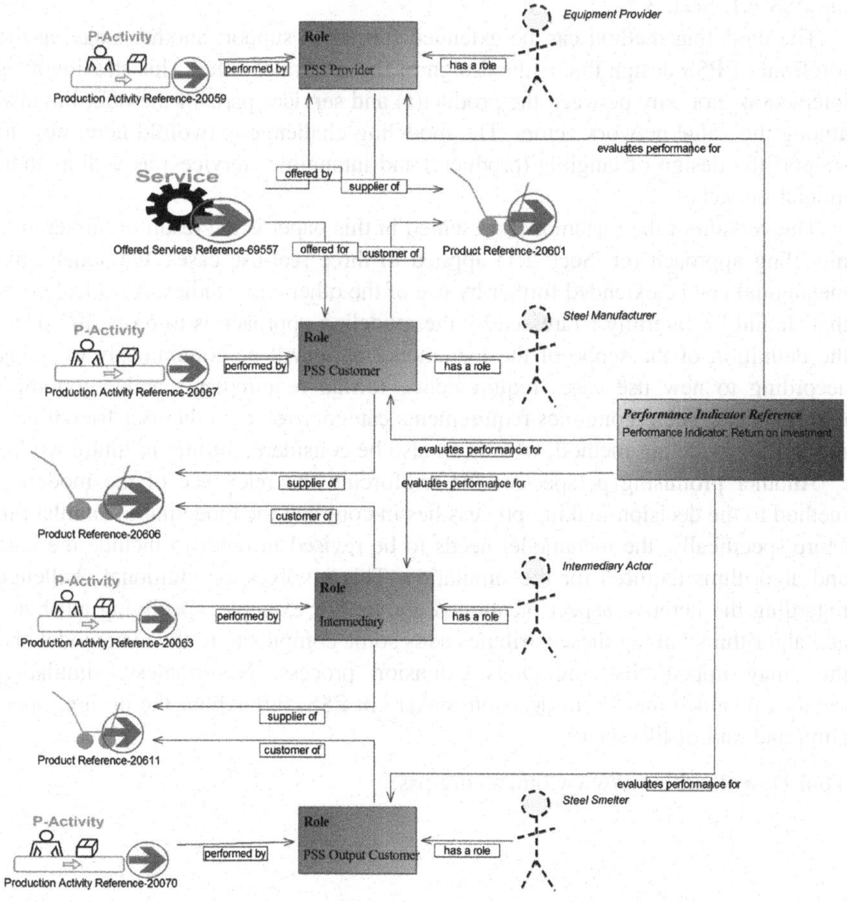

Fig. 15 Use case typical scenario model

Based on this decoupling the '*Role*' construct supports the flexible configuration of the PSS value network, as it broadens the space of feasible combinations of the actors and activities.

5 Conclusion and Perspectives

The proposed modeling method supports the decision-making process in the PSS domain at different design stages. First, product, service and offer models support the early stages where the question to be dealt with is what to offer to the PSS customer. Second, the organization, performance and scenarios models contribute to answering another relevant question, i.e., how to deliver the PSS offer to the customer. More specifically, two major added values can be identified: (i) providing a common understanding of the PSS offers and organizational scenarios and (ii) guiding the designers throughout a well-structured and progressive modeling of the PSS (cf. Sect. 3.2).

The modeling method can be extended further to support another stage, at the forefront of PSS design that is the design of the integrated offer. This step involves interactions not only between the product(s) and services parts of the offer but also among the value network actors. The modeling challenge is twofold here: how to support the design of tangible (products) and intangible (services) as well as their mutual impacts.

The version of the metamodel presented in this paper is the result of an iterative modeling approach (cf. Sect. 2.1) applied to three real-use cases. Obviously, the metamodel can be extended further by use of the other case studies. A critical point that should be carefully addressed by the modeling approach is to properly update the definition of the scope of the metamodel as it will be continuously evolving according to new use cases requirements, formal requirements and ergonomics requirements. The ergonomics requirements category refers to the user-friendliness of the PSS modeling method, which can also be considered further in future works.

Another promising perspective for reinforcing the relevance of the modeling method to the decision-making process lies in coupling the modeling to simulation. More specifically, the metamodel needs to be revised in order to include the data and algorithms required for the simulation. This involves an additional challenge regarding the iterative aspect mentioned above. For example, specifying attributes and algorithms linking these attributes adds some complexity to the metamodel and thus may impede its continuous extension process. Nevertheless, simulation remains of much interest to decision makers in PSS, throughout the design, operation and end-of-life stages.

Tool Download http://www.omilab.org/pss.

References

1. APICS: APICS Dictionary (2013). http://www.apics.org/dictionary. Accessed 31 Oct 2014
2. Aurich, J.C., Mannweiler, C., Schweitzer, E.: How to design and offer services successfully. CIRP J. Manuf. Sci. Technol. **2**(3), 136–143 (2013)
3. Baines, T.S., Lightfoot, H.W., Evans, S., Neely, A., Greenough, R., Peppard, J., Roy, R., et al.: State-of-the-art in product-service systems. Proc. Inst. Mech. Eng. Part B-J. Eng. Manuf. **221**(10), 1543–1552 (2007). doi:10.1243/09544054JEM858
4. Beuren, F.H., Gomes Ferreira, M.G., Cauchick Miguel, P.A.: Product-service systems: a literature review on integrated products and services. J. Clean. Prod. **47**, 222–231 (2013)
5. Fill, Hans-Georg, Karagiannis, Dimitris: On the conceptualisation of modelling methods using the ADOxx meta modelling platform. Enterp. Modell. Inf. Syst. Arch.—Int. J. **8**(1), 4–25 (2013)
6. Fill, H.-G., Redmond, T., Karagiannis, D.: Formalizing meta models with FDMM: the ADOxx case. In: Cordeiro, J., Maciaszek, L., Filipe, J. (eds.) Enterprise Information Systems, LNBIP, vol. 141, pp. 429–451. Springerlink (2013)
7. Fill, H.-G., Redmond, T., Karagiannis, D.: FDMM: A formalism for describing ADOxx meta models and models. In: Maciaszek, L, Cuzzocrea, A., Cordeiro, J. (eds.) Proceedings of ICEIS 2012—14th International Conference on Enterprise Information Systems, vol. 3, pp. 133–144. SciTePress (2012)
8. Goedkoop, M.J.: Product service systems, ecological and economic basics. Ministry of Housing, Spatial Planning and the Environment, Communications Directorate (1999)
9. Herring, C., Milosevic, Z.: Implementing B2B contracts using BizTalk. In: Proceedings of the 34th Hawaii International Conference on System Sciences, Hawaii, USA (2001)
10. Lelah, A., Boucher, X., Moreau, V., Zwolinski, P.: Scenarios as a tool for transition towards sustainable PSS. Procedia CIRP **16**, 122–127 (2014)
11. Hockerts, K.: Innovation of eco-efficient services: increasing the efficiency of products and services. In: Greener Marketing: A Global Perspective on Greening Marketing Practice, vol. 95, pp. 95–108. Greenleaf Publishing in Association with GSE Research (1999)
12. MacDonald, M., Payne, A.: Marketing Plans for Service Businesses. A Complete Guide, 2nd edn. Butterworth Heinemann Publications, Oxford (2006)
13. Manzini, E., Vezzoli, C.: A strategic design approach to develop sustainable product service systems: examples taken from the 'environmentally friendly innovation' Italian prize. J. Clean. Prod. **11**(8), 851–857 (2003)
14. Medini, K., Boucher, X.: Value chain configuration for PSS delivery—evidence from an innovative sector for sludge treatment. CIRP J. Manuf. Sci. Technol. (2015)
15. Medini, K., Boucher, X., Peillon, S., Matos, C.D.: Product service systems value chain configuration—a simulation based approach. In: Proceedings of the CIRP IPSS Conference (IPSS 2015), Saint-Etienne, France (2015a)
16. Medini, K., Peillon, S., Boucher, X., Vaillant, H.: Performance measurement for the design of product-service systems. In: Proceedings of 15th Working Conference on Virtual Enterprises (PRO-VE 2014), Albi, France (2015b)
17. Meier, H., Völker, O., Funke, B.: Industrial Product-Service Systems (IPS2). Int. J. Adv. Manuf. Technol. **52**(9–12), 1175–1191 (2011)
18. Mont, O.: Product-service systems: panacea or myth? Doctoral dissertation, International Institute for Industrial Environmental Economics, Lund University, Sweden (2004)
19. Taisch, M., Heydaria, M.R., Carosi, A., Zanetti, C.: Service performance monitoring and control toolset. Procedia CIRP **16**, 62–67 (2014)
20. Tukker, A.: Eight types of product-service system: eight ways to sustainability experiences from SusProNet. Bus. Strategy Environ. **13**(4), 246–260 (2004). doi:10.1002/bse.414

21. Tukker, A., Tischner, U.: Product-services as a research field: past, present and future. Reflections from a decade of research. J. Clean. Prod. **14**(17), 1552–1556 (2006). doi:10.1016/j.jclepro.2006.01.022
22. Van Notten, P.W.F., Rotmans, J., van Asselt, M.B.A., Rothman, D.S.: An updated scenario typology. Futures **35**(5), 423–443 (2003)

Part X
Requirements Engineering

The *i** Framework for Goal-Oriented Modeling

Xavier Franch, Lidia López, Carlos Cares and Daniel Colomer

Abstract *i** is a widespread framework in the software engineering field that supports goal-oriented modeling of socio-technical systems and organizations. At its heart lies a language offering concepts such as actor, dependency, goal and decomposition. *i** models resemble a network of interconnected, autonomous, collaborative and dependable strategic actors. Around this language, several analysis techniques have emerged, e.g., goal satisfaction analysis and metrics computation. In this work, we present a consolidated version of the *i** language based on the most adopted versions of the language. We define the main constructs of the language and we articulate them in the form of a metamodel. Then, we implement this version and a concrete technique, goal satisfaction analysis based on goal propagation, using ADO*xx*. Throughout the chapter, we used an example based on open source software adoption to illustrate the concepts and test the implementation.

Keywords i-Star · *i**—Framework · Goal-oriented modeling · Satisfaction analysis techniques · Goal-oriented requirements engineering

X. Franch (✉) · L. López · D. Colomer
Universitat Politècnica de Catalunya, 08034 Barcelona, Spain
e-mail: franch@essi.upc.edu

L. López
e-mail: llopez@essi.upc.edu

D. Colomer
e-mail: dncolomer32@gmail.com

C. Cares
Universidad de la Frontera, 4780000, Temuco, Chile
e-mail: carlos.cares@ceisufro.cl

D. Karagiannis et al. (eds.), *Domain-Specific Conceptual Modeling*,
DOI 10.1007/978-3-319-39417-6_22

1 Introduction

Goal-oriented methods are well-known in the software engineering field since the early nineties. They are used both in broad areas as requirements engineering [28] and organizational modeling [21], and in more specific scopes as adaptive system modeling [3] and software architecture representation [15].

For instance, if we consider goal-oriented requirements engineering, it is recognized that goals play a crucial role for domain understanding and elicitation of stakeholders' intentions [27]. Goals can be formulated at different levels of abstraction, from strategic concerns to technical issues, and are less volatile than requirements [28]. Therefore, they can be considered as an essential artefact in the early phases of requirements engineering, when still alternatives are considered and stakeholder intentions do need further discussion. Goal-oriented methods allow analyzing consequences of decisions, making interrogative questions and explore solution spaces.

Several goal-oriented approaches include actors in their definition which have their own intentions and goals. The existence of actors in models makes these methods agent-oriented [29]. Agent orientation offers a natural and powerful means of analyzing, designing, and implementing a diverse range of software solutions (Jennings et al. [20]). Agents exhibit properties such as autonomy, reactivity, pro-activeness and social ability, which allow representing, analyzing and designing software solutions for agents and multi-agents systems, but also for all kinds of complex systems that involve cooperation and co-creation of value [29].

The *i** framework [32] is currently one of the most widespread goal-oriented and agent-oriented modeling and reasoning methods in the field. It supports the construction of models that represent an organization or socio-technical system, together with its constituent processes, as an intentional network of actors and dependencies. Reasoning techniques allow checking properties and performing some kind of qualitative [13, 17] and quantitative [9] analysis, or even both [2].

For instance, Horkoff and Yu [16] show how *i** models are adequate to support early domain exploration through iterative inquiry over captured knowledge. This favor early system scoping and decision making. Questions that naturally arise are of the type "what if", "is this possible", "if so, who" and "if not, why not". A semi-automated algorithm will interact with the stakeholder as required in order to pose questions and process answers. All in all, *i** models are an excellent artefact in terms of knowledge discovery.

In this chapter, we will present the *i** method in detail. In Sect. 2, we provide the historical perspective and present the constructs of the language. In Sect. 3, we propose a metamodel, outline some concepts referring to semantics and present some analysis technique. In Sect. 4, we present an implementation of the method in ADO*xx*: the metamodel and an analysis technique. Finally, in Sect. 5 we present the conclusions.

2 Method Description

In this section, we provide a historical view of the *i** framework including some references to related work, and then we develop the main concepts of the language that will be further detailed in the next sections.

2.1 A Tour of the i* Framework Evolution

Figure 1 makes explicit the origins and current state of the *i** framework. There are two approaches that have greatly influenced its shape.

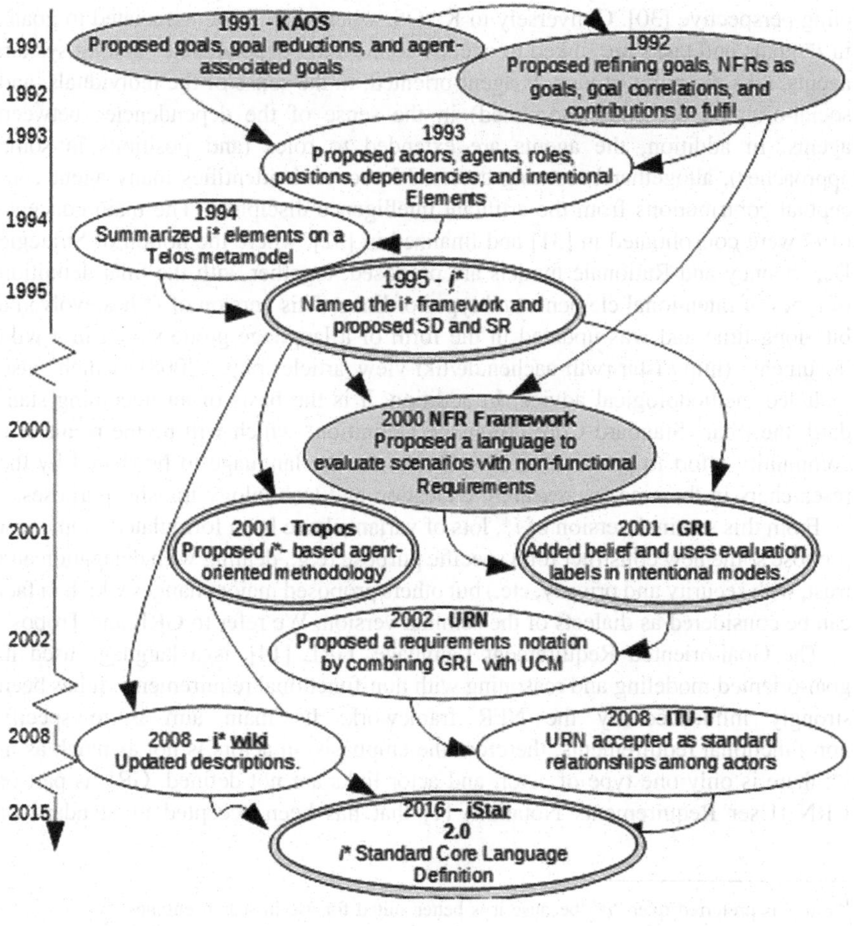

Fig. 1 Genealogy of the i* framework and variants

On the one hand, the KAOS framework [6, 7], which was the first widespread approach to goal-oriented requirements engineering. Its emphasis is on semi-formal and formal reasoning about behavioral goals to derive goal refinements, operationalisations, conflict management and risk analysis. It includes several concepts that appear in *i**: system goal, goal reduction and the notion of linking a goal to agents, which have the responsibility to accomplish the goals.

On the other hand, the Non-Functional Requirements (NFR) Framework [5, 26] introduces the concept of non-functional requirement as a system goal that should be satisfied, expressed with the notion of softgoal. Also, this proposal uses the concept of justification for selection, in which softgoals can contribute positively or negatively to the achievement of other softgoals. The NFR proposal was completed at the year 2000 and since then has experienced a great adoption by the requirements engineering community. Contrary to KAOS, the notion of agent was not included in the language.

With respect to these two antecedents, *i** proposed a simple but relevant modeling perspective [30]. Conversely to KAOS, where agents are associated to goals, in *i** goals and tasks are linked to agents, conforming dependencies among system agents, thus the point of view is agent-oriented, in the sense of the individuals, and social-oriented (or context-oriented) in the sense of the dependencies between agents. In addition, the agents are extended to roles (and positions in some approaches), altogether becoming actors. Moreover, it identifies many agent conceptual contributions from the artificial intelligence discipline. The main concepts of *i** were consolidated in [31] and finalized in [32], where the notion of Strategic Dependency and Rationale models are proposed, together with the final definition of types of intentional elements and types of links. This version of *i** has evolved a bit along time and was updated in the form of a language guide stored in a wiki document (http://istar.rwth-aachen.de/tiki-view_articles.php, 2008) which also included methodological advice. In addition, it is the basis of an upcoming standard, the iStar[1] Standard Core Language Definition[2] which will be the result of a community effort to produce an agreed core for the language to be shared by the researchers in the area for research, education and technology transfer purposes.

From this seminal version of *i**, lots of variants have been formulated. Some just propose some new construct for a specific purpose (e.g., dealing with delegation and trust, with security and privacy, etc.) but others proposed major changes which in fact can be considered as dialects of the seminal version. We refer to GRL and Tropos.

The Goal-oriented Requirement Language, GRL [14], is a language used in goal-oriented modeling and reasoning with non-functional requirements. It has been strongly influenced by the NFR framework. Its main aim is to specify non-functional requirements, therefore the emphasis on actors is not as much as in *i**: there is only one type of actor, and actor links are not defined. GRL is part of URN (User Requirements Notation) [1] that has been accepted as standard of

[1]"iStar" is preferred over "*i**" because it is better suited for use in search engines.

[2]The standard has not still been published at the time of publishing this book.

ITU-T (International Telecommunication Union-Telecommunication Standardization Sector) [19].

Tropos [4] is another variant whose main purpose is to complement the language with methodological guidance. Due to this focus, some simplification on the language was made.

2.2 The *i** Language

As a consequence of this historical evolution, the constructs of the *i** framework modeling language (from now on, the *i** language) are different depending on the variant adopted. We find several situations:

- Core concepts that are included in all the most well-known variants. Among them, we can mention the general concept of actor and the notion of goal.
- Concepts that are present in a great majority of variants although they may slightly vary in some details or in the semantic meaning. As examples, we find types of actors and decomposition links.
- Concepts that are specific of a particular proposal. For instance, the notion of trust and delegation, beliefs, or the declaration of temporal precedencies among tasks.

In this chapter, we are going to focus on the first two types of concepts. As main sources, we will use: the seminal Ph.D. thesis by Yu [32], the wiki version (2008) and the ongoing version of the standard core (2016).

2.2.1 Actors and Actor Links

Actors are active, autonomous entities that aim at achieving their goals by exercising their know-how, in collaboration with other actors (see Sect. 2.2.3). They may be human (e.g., a person, a role played by a person), organizational (e.g., a company, a department, an agency) or technological (e.g., a software agent, cloud system, some device). Actors can appear in an *i** model without any further categorization (i.e., as *general* actors) or can be classified into any of the two following types:

- *Role*: a role represents an abstract characterization of the behavior of a social actor within some specialized context or domain of endeavour. For instance, a project manager or a consultant.
- *Agent*: an agent is an actor with concrete, physical manifestation. Examples are a particular organization or person.

Most often, actors do not appear isolated in an *i** model, instead they may be linked through several *actor links*:

- *plays*: links an agent to a role. An agent plays a role, committing to take on the responsibilities of that role. So, a particular person may play the role of project management for a project.
- *is-part-of*: links actors of the same type. It represents the classical conceptual modeling parthood construct, in which one actor of any type is composed of several other actors of the same type. For instance, the sales department may be part of a given organization.
- *is-a*: links actors of the same type. It represents the typical specialization construct, in which one actor of any type specializes another actor of the same type. E.g., a programmer role may be specialized into junior and senior programmer roles.

2.2.2 Intentional Elements

Intentionality of actors is made explicit by identifying their *intentional elements* inside their *boundary*. The boundary delineates accurately what is under the actor's control; whatever needs that are not inside the boundary, need to be fulfilled in collaboration with other actors through dependencies (see Sect. 2.2.4).

Inside the boundaries, four types of intentional elements can be declared:

- *Goals*: a goal represents a state of the world that is sought to be achieved. The actor only expresses the intention to achieve this goal but not the means to attain it; these means can be identified later through some type of element links (see Sect 2.2.3). For instance, a person may have as goal to travel abroad for holidays.
- *Softgoals*: a softgoal expresses a goal whose fulfilment is not clear-cut; instead, its satisfaction condition is subject of interpretation. This subjectivity is the difference between goals (sometimes called *hard goals* to make it clearer) and softgoals. For this reason, some authors use the term *satisficed* when talking about softgoals satisfaction (although we will not use this term). Intentional elements that help in (or prevent from) attaining a softgoal can be connected to the softgoal using some other type of element link (see Sect 2.2.3). E.g., a service provider may have as softgoal to reduce significantly the service provision time next year, but the concept of "significantly" is not exactly defined.
- *Tasks*: a task represents an activity whose execution is prescribed according to some established procedure. Contrary to goals, then, the actor is expressing a particular way of doing. For example, an open source community may have a task for reporting a bug in an open source component.
- *Resources*: a resource stands for a physical or intentional entity that is produced or provided by the actor. For instance, a project manager may identify a project plan as valuable asset that she produces.

In this book chapter we will consider only these four types of elements. Still, in the literature we may find other types of elements proposed, like beliefs or domain assumptions to express a condition on the world that an actor thinks to be true (see wiki version) and quality constraints to state fit criteria for softgoals [23].

2.2.3 Intentional Element Links

Intentional elements in actors are connected using several types of *intentional element links*. This way, actors are able to express complex intentionality in a structure form, facilitating later analysis.

As happened with types of intentional elements, there is a plethora of proposals of intentional element link types and furthermore, for the universally agreed ones (e.g., means-end), different interpretations or restrictions have been formulated. In this book chapter, we use the following ones:

- *Means-end*: means-end links offer a way to identify alternative means to achieve a goal. Typically, the end will be a goal and the means will be a task. For instance, a traveller may express two different alternatives for the goal of travelling abroad for holidays: organizing the trip himself/herself, or contacting a travel agency.
- *Decomposition*: decomposition links allow decomposing complex elements into simpler ones of the same type with the only exception of resources which are allowed to appear in task decompositions. While means-end links can be viewed as a connection between the problem space (the end) and the solution space (the means), decomposition links do not change the space. Decompositions maybe AND-, OR- or XOR-decompositions. For instance, a task for scheduling a meeting may be AND-decomposed into three subtasks: getting availability from participants, finding a time slot, and communicating the final choice.
- *Contribution*: contribution links express how intentional elements contribute to the satisfaction of a softgoal. Contribution can be positive (supporting) or negative (damaging), and can be an implication or just a connection, yielding to four types of contribution links (*make*, *help*, *break*, *hurt*) as shown in Table 1. As example, if a softgoal is expressing the need of having a secure access control to some software system, we may have as help contribution link a task to perform credential analysis, while a hurt contribution link is to have in the system a backdoor available to some designated users.

Table 1 Types of contribution links

		Strength	
		Implication	Connection
Sign	Positive	Make (a positive contribution strong enough to satisfy a softgoal)	Help (a positive contribution not sufficient by itself to satisfy the softgoal)
	Negative	Break (a negative contribution sufficient enough to deny a softgoal)	Hurt (a negative contribution not sufficient by itself to deny the softgoal)

2.2.4 Dependencies

Besides actor links, *dependencies* also connect actors. A *dependency* is a relationship between two actors: one of them, named *depender*, depends for the accomplishment of some internal intention on a second actor, named *dependee*. For instance, a project manager may depend on a software architect to provide a project effort assessment in order to come up with the project plan. The dependency may be established at the level of actors (an actor depends onto another) or at the level of intentional elements (an intentional element of any kind depends onto another intentional element); mixed combinations are possible.

The dependency is characterized by an intentional element (*dependum*) which represents the reason of dependency. The four types of intentional elements presented in the previous subsection yield to four types of dependencies:

- *Goal dependency*: the dependee shall satisfy the goal, and is free to choose how. For instance, a driver may depend on a car repair service on getting his/her car repaired, without being aware of how the repair is solved.
- *Softgoal dependency*: the dependee shall sufficiently satisfy the softgoal. A softgoal represents a goal that can be partially satisfied, or a goal that requires additional agreement about how it is satisfied. For example, an organization hiring some desk service for providing technical assistance may require timely feedback to customers, where the concept of "timely" may be perceived differently by the involved parties.
- *Task dependency*: the depender requires a dependee to execute a task in a prescribed way. An example could be a project manager asking the project members to declare their time in the project following some available reporting procedure.
- *Resource dependency*: the dependee has to make a resource available to the depender. For instance, a traveller may depend on a travel agency to provide him/her with a flight ticket.

Not all combinations of depender-dependum-dependee types are allowed; see metamodel in the next section for details.

2.2.5 Model Views

The elements presented in the subsections above are articulated to compose an *i** model. It may happen, however, that the resulting model quickly grows and makes it difficult to embrace all the details. Scalability is a well-known problem with *i** models (see [8, 11] for analysis on *i** adoption challenges).

One of the solutions to these problems is the ability to define *model views*. We may mention two popular views proposed by [32]:

- *Strategic dependency* (SD) models. SD models depict a high-level view in which only actors and dependencies appear.
- *Strategic rationale* (SR) models. SR models show the boundary of actors with their intentional elements and links.

Quite often, these two models have been used in a methodological framework that recommends creating first the SD model of the system to be, and then the SR models of the different actors that appear. However, this needs not to be the case.

Other proposals exist to structure the information encoded in *i** models. For instance, [22] proposed Strategic Actor models to show only actors and their actor links (not including dependencies). More generally, [12] presents a proposal for defining arbitrary modules in order to parcel the complexity and then create models as a combination of smaller parts. However, in this chapter, we work only with SD and SR views.

3 Method Conceptualization

This section presents the metamodel that includes the constructs presented in the previous section, and their graphical representation.

3.1 iStar Metamodel

Figure 2 show a UML class diagram representing the *i** language as introduced in Sect. 2.2. Restrictions on the use of the constructs are stated textually as integrity constraints in Table 2.

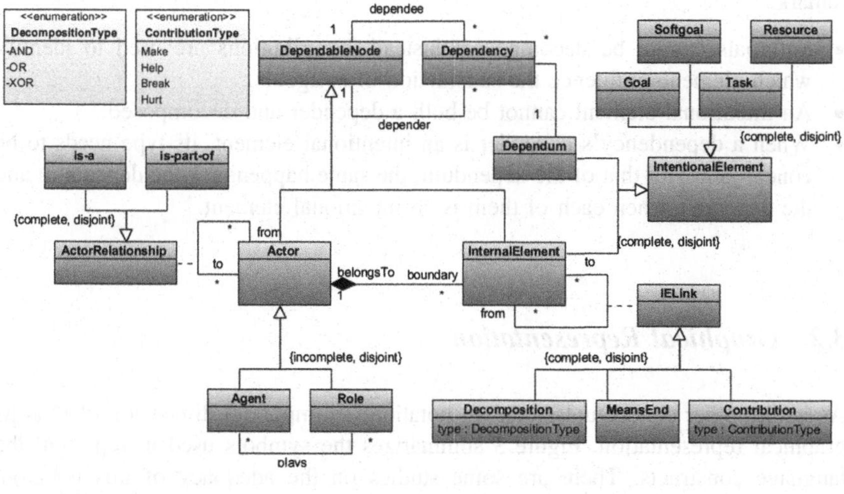

Fig. 2 iStar metamodel

Table 2 Integrity constraints over the iStar language

Actor links (ActorRelationship)	
IC1	The ActorRelationship must connect actors of the same type
IC2	Cycles are not allowed regardless of the ActorRelationship
Intentional Element Links (IELinks)	
IC3	MeansEnd can only have tasks as from and goals as to
IC4	When a Decomposition has a goal as to, it can only have goals as from
IC5	When a Decomposition has a task as to, it can only have tasks or resources as from
IC6	It is not allowed Decomposition with a resource or a softgoal as a to
IC7	Contribution can only have softgoals as to
Dependencies	
IC8	The depender IE cannot be a to in any IELink
IC9	When the depender IE is a goal, the dependum can be a goal or a task
IC10	When the depender IE is a softgoal, the dependum can only be a softgoal
IC11	When the depender IE is a task, the dependum can be a task or a resource
IC12	When the depender IE is a resource, the dependum can only be a resource
IC13	When a dependum is a goal, the dependee IE can be a goal or a task
IC14	When a dependum is a softgoal, the dependee IE can be only a softgoal
IC15	When a dependum is a task, the dependee IE element can be a task or a resource
IC16	When a dependum is a resource, the dependee IE element can be only a resource

The structure of the metamodel shows two fundamental abstract classes. First, *IntentionalElement* which is used both as internal element inside actors and as dependum for dependencies. Second, *DependableNode*, to model the fact that dependers and dependees may be intentional elements or actors. The rest of the metamodel structure is straightforward. Concerning the integrity constraints, we remark:

- Softgoals cannot be decomposed; instead, contributions are used to identify which elements influence the satisfaction of softgoals.
- An intentional element cannot be both a depender and decomposed.
- When a dependency's depender is an intentional element, its type needs to be concordant with that of the dependum; the same happens for the dependum and the dependee when each of them is an intentional element.

3.2 Graphical Representation

As in any other conceptual modeling notation, an important dimension of *i** is its graphical representation. Figure 3 summarizes the symbols used to represent the language constructs. There are some studies on the adequacy of this notation.

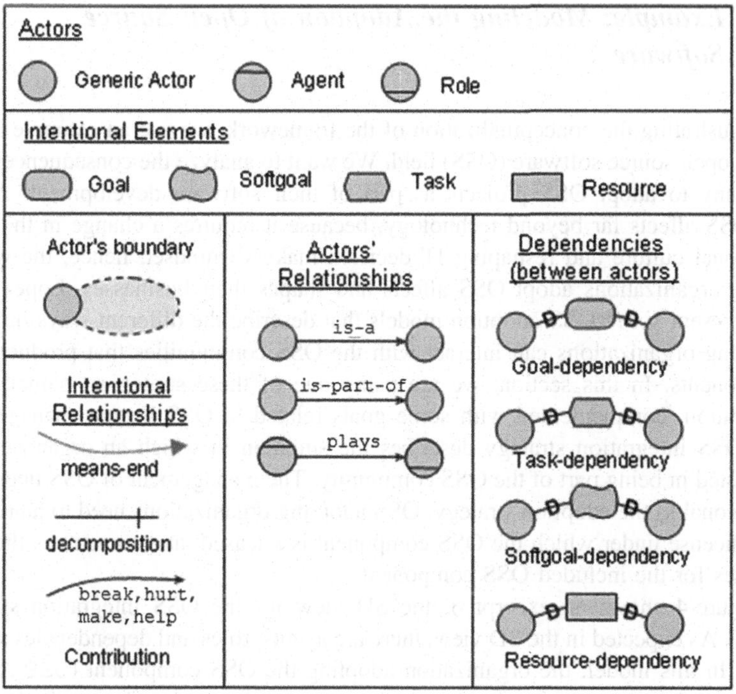

Fig. 3 Graphical representation of *i** constructs

Table 3 Terminological conventions for *i** model elements

Intentional type	Terminological convention	Example
Goal	Object + Passive verb + (non-manner Complement), possibly negated	Information kept safe
Softgoal	Goal syntax + Complement of manner	Data checked quickly
	(Object) + Complement of manner ([element])	Timely [Flight Ticket]
Task	Verb + (Object) + (Complement)	Answer doubts by mail
Resource	(Adjective) + Object + (Qualifier/Modifier)	Bug list

Among them, [25] analyzes the symbols under the lenses of the physics of notation and proposes some changes to comply with its principles. However, today, the graphical representation adopted by the community keeps very close to Yu's original proposal [32].

In addition, some authors have proposed terminological conventions in order to write the different model elements. Among them, we will use in this chapter the proposal by [10] summarized in Table 3.

3.3 Example: Modeling the Adoption of Open Source Software

For illustrating the conceptualization of the framework, we use an example rooted in the open source software (OSS) field. We want to analyze the consequences for a company to adopt OSS projects as part of their software development. Adopting OSS affects far beyond technology, because it requires a change in the organizational culture and reshaping IT decision-makers' mindset, hence, the way in which organizations adopt OSS affects and shapes their businesses. Lopez et al. [24] present six *i** OSS adoption models that describe the different ways in which adopting organizations can interact with the OSS communities that produce OSS components. In this section, we are using one of these strategies, namely OSS integration, complemented with some goals related to OSS license management. The OSS integration strategy describes the situation in which an organization is interested in being part of the OSS community. The management of OSS licenses is orthogonal to the adoption strategy: OSS adopting organizations need to handle the OSS license under which the OSS component is released, and sometimes the OSS licenses for the included OSS components.

Figure 4 shows an excerpt of the SD view for the OSS integration strategy model. As expected in the SD view, there are agents, roles and dependencies among them. In this model, the organization adopting the OSS component (`OSS Adopter`) and the `OSS Community` producing it are represented as *Agents*, in the sense that they are representing a specific physical organization and the group of individuals and organizations that are conforming the community. The model also includes the `Regulator` *Role*, in this case we are interested in the behavior related to make organizations accomplish the law, not including the knowledge about the physical entity that is playing this role.

If we focus on the `OSS Adopter` agent, it is involved in several dependencies of every possible type, either as depender or as dependee:

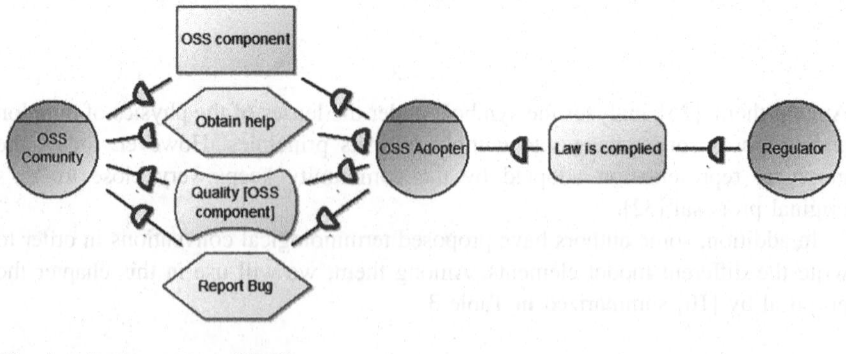

Fig. 4 Adoption strategy: SD View

- *Goal dependency*: Regulator needs that the OSS adopter be compliance with the law (`Law is complied with`). As a goal dependency, the depender does not care about how the dependee is going to fulfil this requirement. In this case, the regulator is not setting the concrete activities that the OSS adopter needs to do for being compliance with the law.
- *Softgoal dependency*: The OSS adopter needs that the quality of the component will be kept in the next releases (`Quality [OSS component]`). This dependency is a softgoal because the organization cannot fix a clear-cut satisfaction criterion for the quality of the produced software.
- *Task dependency*: The OSS community expects that the OSS adopter reports bugs. The way to report bugs in an OSS community is done using specific tools defined by the OSS community. Therefore, the OSS adopter (dependee) needs to follow a specific protocol to fulfil this requirement.
- *Resource dependency*: The `OSS Component` dependency represents the code, which is a physical entity produced by the OSS community.

Figure 5 shows an SR view including part of the rationale of the `OSS Adopter` agent related to the fact of contributing to the community. The OSS adopter decides that they want to take advantage of using OSS components relying part of the maintenance on the OSS community that produces it. This interest is summarized by `Benefit from co-creation significatively taken`, this adoption strategy comes with the commitment of the organization to contribute to the OSS community (`OSS community contributed`).

The `OSS Adopter` rationale contains most kinds of intentional elements and intentional elements links, for example:

- Goal `OSS community contributed`. In this case, as part of the maintenance of its product, the organization needs to contribute the OSS community and there are three different ways to achieve this goal (represented using *Means-end* link), represented by the tasks: `Report bug`, `Develop patches` and `Give support to activities`.
- Some softgoals to identify some goals that do not have well-defined criteria to know when it is fulfilled. For example, the company wants to take benefit from the development provided for the community (`Benefit from co-creation significatively taken`), but this "significatively" does not have a formula to be sure that it has been achieved. Some of the other intentional elements are,
- Task `Commit patch` *AND-decomposed*. This task consists of two subtasks. If the organization is going to contribute to the community by producing code, some of their developers must get the status of committer in the community (`Apply to be a committer`) and adapt their processes to the community practices (`Follow OSS community practices`).
- Contributing positively to this achievement (`Adequate OSS involvement`, `OSS comp. evolved towards desired features`), so *Contribution* links qualified as *Help* are used.

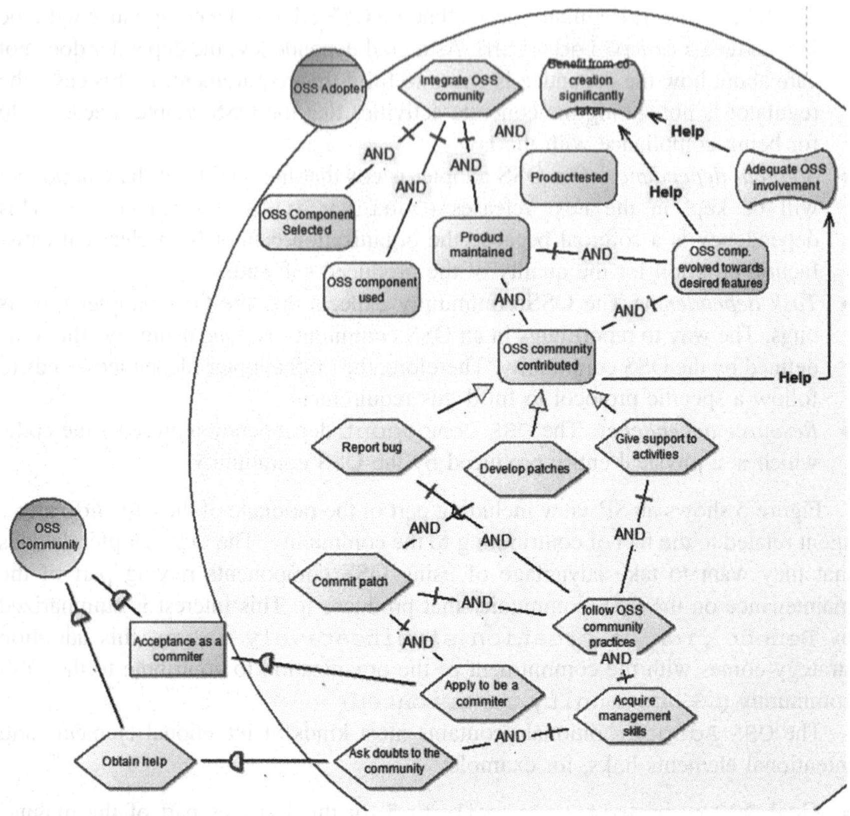

Fig. 5 SR diagram

4 Proof of Concept

4.1 The OMiLAB iStar Tool Metamodel

In order to implement a modeling tool using the ADO*xx* platform, we have adapted the *i** metamodel presented in the previous version into a variant which can be used as an extension of the ADO*xx* metamodel (see Fig. 6).

The metamodel has a main class `__iStar__` that inherits from ADO*xx*'s `__D-contruct__` superclass provided for "graph-based" metamodels. `__iStar__` has two subclasses, namely `__iActor__` and `__iElement__` which further decompose into specific classes that map directly to a graphical representation for actors and intentional elements.

The metamodel also contains four specific classes that represent relation classes. Each of them is mapped into a graphical representation and links to other classes via

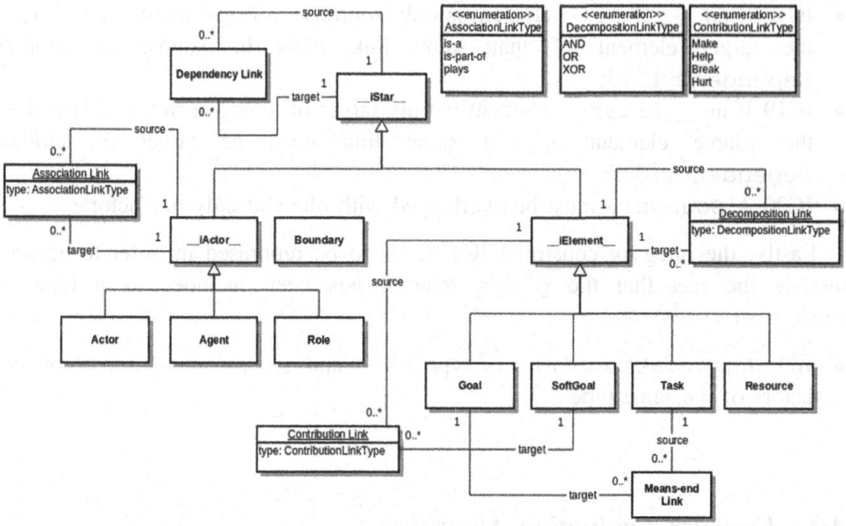

Fig. 6 The *i** metamodel customized for the ADO*xx* platform

the relationships `source` and `target` which will determine the source and target elements that the modeller can use.

We remark that, for the sake of modeling simplicity and tool usability, the concepts of boundary and dependency were reshaped:

- Boundaries are mapped to a separate graphical construct. In order to avoid boundaries without actors, the modeling tool displays a warning message for those boundaries that do not overlap an actor element.
- The explicit concepts of dependum, depender and dependee were abandoned in favor of a `Dependency Link` relation class that has as a source and target any `__iStar__` element. A dependency link element in the adapted metamodel represents only a partial dependency as defined in Fig. 6 such as the relation between a depender and a dependum, or a dependum and a dependee. The constraint regarding the existence of a dependee and a depender is then implemented via external coupling (https://www.adoxx.org/live/external-coupling-adoxx-functionalty).

Finally, it should be mentioned that some of the integrity constraints defined in Table 2 are implicit in the variant of the metamodel used to implement the tool, namely IC3 and IC7. The rest of the constraints are implemented via external coupling using AdoScript (https://www.adoxx.org/live/adoscript-language-constructs). Additionally, we added the following integrity constraints because of the transformation of the shape of the model:

- IC17 `AssociationLinks` of type `plays` must connect and `Agent` (source) and a `Role` (target)

- IC18 If an `__iStar__` element is only source of a `DependencyLink` then the target element of that same link must be source of another `DependencyLink`
- IC19 If an `__iStar__` element is only target of a `DependencyLink` then the source element of that same link must be target of another `DependencyLink`
- IC20 A `Boundary` must be overlapped with one and only one actor

Lastly, the integrity constraint IC1 needs to be rephrased in order to accommodate the fact that the `plays` relation has been included as a type of `AssociationLink`:

- IC1' `AssociationLinks` of type `is-a` and `is-part-of` must connect actors of the same type

4.2 *Forward Evaluation Algorithm*

The reasoning algorithm included in the OMiLAB iStar Tool is an adaptation of the forward evaluation algorithm defined by [18]. This reasoning technique can be used for agent-goal model analysis in early requirements engineering. It is an iterative and interactive process that allows the modellers perform what-if analysis by propagating the satisfaction level through the intentional elements and intentional element links.

The meaning of satisfaction depends on the type of the intentional element:

- goal satisfaction means that the goal attains the desired state;
- task satisfaction means that the task follows the defined procedure;
- resource satisfaction means that the resource is produced or delivered;
- softgoal satisfaction means that the modelled conditions fulfill some agreed fit criterion.

The results of the qualitative evaluation consist of calculating the satisfaction for each intentional in the model, based on an initial set of satisfaction values assigned to some intentional elements. The satisfaction of an intentional element can be qualified as: *Satisfied*, *Partially Satisfied*, *Partially Denied* and *Denied*. According to the propagation algorithm, sometimes the result cannot be qualified as any of the previous values, in this case the result is qualified as a *Conflict*. Figure 7 includes

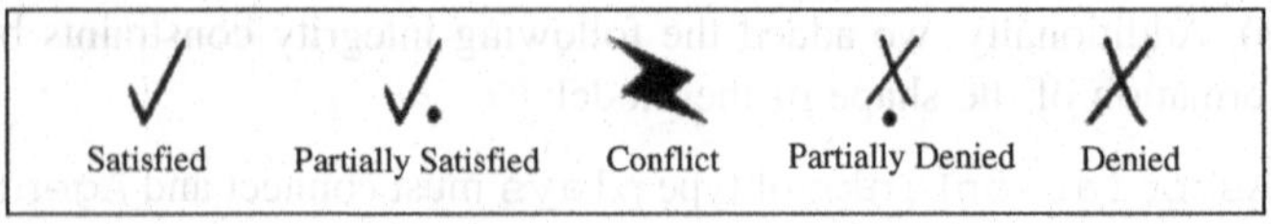

Fig. 7 Qualitative evaluation notation

Fig. 8 Propagation rules for Contribution links (adapted from [18])

Source Label		***Contribution* Link Type**			
	Name	**Make**	**Help**	**Break**	**Hurt**
✓	Satisfied	✓	✓.	✗	✗.
✓.	Partially Satisfied	✓.	✓.	✗.	✗.
↯	Conflict	↯	↯	↯	↯
✗.	Partially Denied	✗.	✗.	✓.	✓.
✗	Denied	✗	✗.	✓.	✓.

the graphical representation for these values. The algorithm is interactive when the results require of the user judgement, concretely when the resulting value is *Conflict* or *Partially Satisfied/Denied.*

The propagation rules are summarized as:

- *Dependency*: The satisfaction value from a dependee intentional element is propagated to the dependum and the satisfaction value from a dependum is propagated to the depender intentional element. Therefore, the dependee satisfaction value is propagated to the depender.
- *AND-Decomposition*: The minimum value from the children intentional element is propagated to the parent intentional element.
- *OR-Decomposition*, *XOR-Decomposition* and *Means-End*: The maximum value from the children intentional element is propagated to the parent intentional element.
- *Contribution*: The satisfaction values are propagated as is shown in Fig. 8.

4.3 An Example of Application

In the example presented in Sect. 3.3 (Fig. 5), the model contains different ways to contribute to the community: reporting bugs, committing patches or giving support to OSS community activities. The organization can decide to contribute in any of these ways; all of them require that the developers follow the OSS community practices (task `Follow OSS community practices`). The *i** models support forward analysis for providing evidence of the goals' satisfaction in some scenarios. For example, considering the situation of an organization that does not have in-house developers with experience in OSS projects. In this case, they need some support from the community to succeed in following the OSS community practices. This need is represented in the model by the `Acquire management skills` task, which is AND-decomposed including the `Ask doubts to the community` subtask, evidencing that the organization needs some help from the OSS

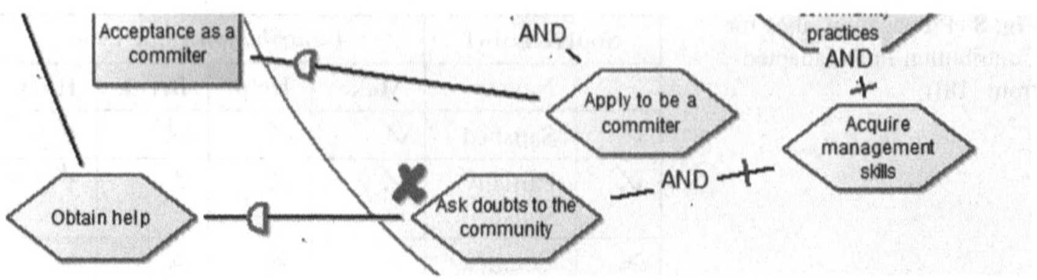

Fig. 9 Scenario: `Ask doubts to the community task` is not satisfied

community (`Obtain help` task dependency). If the OSS community producing the OSS component is not proactive, this means that is not solving the organization doubts. Figure 9 shows how this situation is represented in the model, adding the qualitative label Denied (✗) to the `Ask doubts to the community` task.

Using the forward evaluation algorithm described in Sect. 4.2, the organization realizes that it is not going to be able to contribute to the OSS Community (Fig. 10) because this situation affects to all the available alternatives for contributions (`Report bug`, `Develop patches` and `Give support to activities`

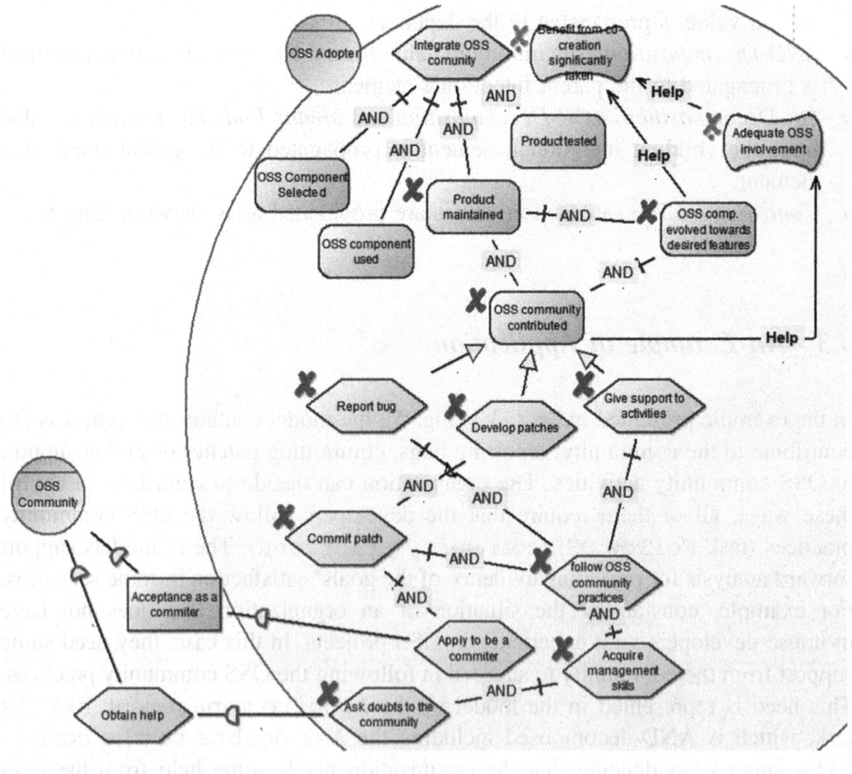

Fig. 10 Forward evaluation results when *`Ask doubts to the community`* is not satisfied

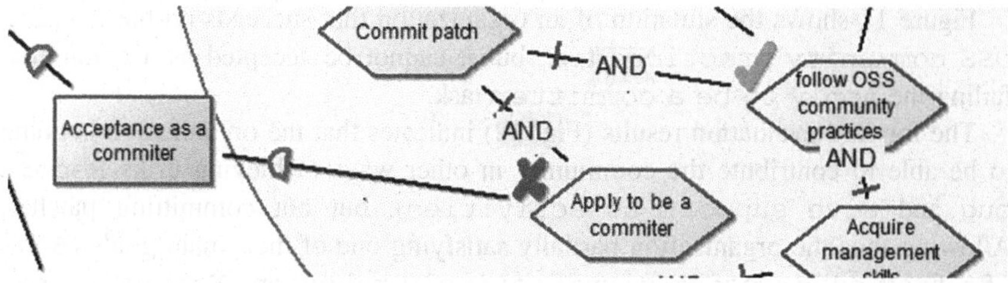

Fig. 11 Failing `Apply to be a committer` task

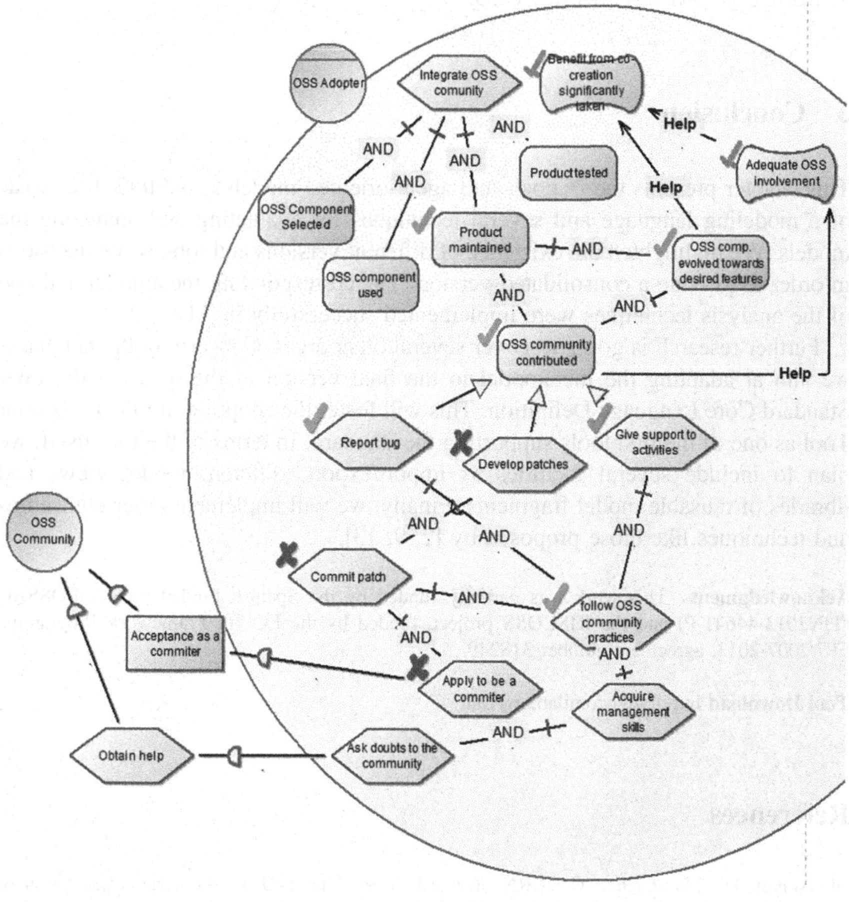

Fig. 12 Forward evaluation results when `Commit patch` is not satisfied

tasks). This result indicates that the organization is going to fail performing the task `Maintain product` and partially failing the softgoal `Benefit from co-creation significatively taken`. Because of this, the organization should not follow this adoption strategy.

Figure 11 shows the situation of an organization that succeeds on the `Follow OSS community practices` task, but it cannot be accepted as a committer, failing the `Apply to be a committer` task.

The forward evaluation results (Fig. 12) indicates that the organization is going to be able to contribute the community in other ways (achieving tasks `Report bug` and `Give support to activities`), but not committing patches. Allowing thus the organization partially satisfying one of their main goals (`Benefit from co-creation significatively taken`) and `Maintain product`, that jointly with the satisfaction of `OSS component selected`, `OSS component used` and `Product tested`, would satisfy the other main goal `Product produced using OSS`.

5 Conclusion

This chapter presents the *i** goal- and agent-oriented modeling method. It consists of a modeling language and several techniques for evaluating and analyzing the models. We highlighted the existence of different versions and took some decisions in order to provide a consolidated version. The corresponding metamodel and one of the analysis techniques were implemented successfully in ADO*xx*.

Further research is going to cover several other areas. Concerning the language, we aim at adapting the metamodel to the final version of the ongoing the iStar Standard Core Language Definition. This will foster the adoption of OMiLAB iStar Tool as one of the first tools supporting the standard. In terms of the tool itself, we plan to include several facilities as import/export, different model views and libraries of reusable model fragments. Finally, we will implement other algorithms and techniques like those proposed by [2, 9, 13].

Acknowledgments This work was partially funded by the Spanish funded project EOSSAC (TIN2013-44641-P) and the RISCOSS project, funded by the EC 7th Framework Programme FP7/2007-2013, agreement number 318249.

Tool Download http://www.omilab.org/istar.

References

1. Amyot, D., Mussbacher, G.: URN: Towards a new standard for the visual description of requirements. In: Proceedings of the 3rd International Workshop on Telecommunications and beyond: the Broader Applicability of SDL and MSC (SAM), LNCS 2599, pp. 21–37. Springer, Berlin (2002)
2. Amyot, D., Ghanavati, S., Horkoff, J., Mussbacher, G., Peyton, L., Yu, E.: Evaluating goal models within the goal-oriented requirement language. Int. J. Intell. Syst. **25**(8), pp. 841–877 Wiley (2010)

3. Bencomo, N., Belaggoun, A.: Supporting decision-making for self-adaptive systems: from goal models to dynamic decision networks. In: Proceedings of the 19th International Working Conference on Requirements Engineering: Foundation for Software Quality (REFSQ), LNCS 7830, pp 221–236. Springer, Berlin (2013)
4. Castro, J., Kolp, M., Mylopoulos, J.: A Requirements-Driven Development Methodology. In: Proceedings of the 13th International Conference on Advanced Information Systems Engineering (CAiSE), pp. 108–123. Springer, Berlin (2001)
5. Chung, L., Nixon, B., Yu, E., Mylopoulos, J.: Non-functional Requirements in Software Engineering. Kluwer Academic Publishing (2000)
6. Dardenne, A., Fickas, S., van Lamswerdee, A.: Goal-directed concept acquisition in requirements elicitation. In: Proceedings of the 6th International Workshop on Software Specification and Design (IWSSD), pp. 14–21. IEEE CS Press, Los Alamitos (1991)
7. Dardenne, A., van Lamsweerde, A., Fickas, S.: Goal-directed requirements acquisition. science of computer programming, vol. 20(1–2), pp. 3—50, Elsevier (1993)
8. Estrada, H., Martínez, A., Pastor, O., Mylopoulos, J.: An empirical evaluation of the i* framework in a model-based software generation environment. In: 18th International Conference on Advanced Information Systems Engineering (CAiSE), LNCS 4001, pp. 513–527. Springer, Berlin (2006)
9. Franch, X.: On the quantitative analysis of agent-oriented models. In: 18th International Conference on Advanced Information Systems Engineering (CAiSE), LNCS 4001, pp. 495—509. Springer, Berlin (2006)
10. Franch, X., Grau, G., Mayol, E., Quer, C., Ayala, C.P., Cares, C., Navarrete, F., Haya, M., Botella, P.: Systematic construction of i* strategic dependency models for socio-technical systems. Int. J. Softw. Eng. Knowl. Eng. **17**(1), pp. 79–106. World Scientific (2007)
11. Franch, X.: Fostering the adoption of i* by practitioners: some challenges and research directions. In Intentional Perspectives on Information Systems Engineering, pp. 177–194. Springer, Berlin (2010)
12. Franch, X.: Incorporating modules into the *i** framework. In: CAiSE 2010. LNCS 6051, pp. 439–454. Springer, Berlin (2010)
13. Giorgini, P., Mylopoulos, J., Nicciarelli, E., Sebastiani, R.: Formal reasoning techniques for goal models. LNCS, vol. 2503, pp. 167–181. Springer, Berlin (2002)
14. GRL: Goal Oriented Requirement Language (2001). http://www.cs.toronto.edu/km/GRL/
15. Grau, G., Franch, X.: On the adequacy of i* models for representing and analyzing software architectures In: Proceedings of ER Workshops, LNCS 4802, pp. 296–305. Springer, Berlin (2007)
16. Horkoff, J., Yu, E.: Finding solutions in goal models: an interactive backward reasoning approach. In: Proceedings of 29th International Conference on Conceptual Modelling (ER), LNCS 6412, pp. 59–75. Springer, Berlin (2010)
17. Horkoff, J., Yu, E.: Analyzing goal models: different approaches and how to choose among them. In: Proceedings of the 2011 ACM Symposium on Applied Computing (SAC), pp. 675–682. ACM, New York (2011)
18. Horkoff, J., Yu, E.: Interactive goal model analysis for early requirements engineering. In: Requirements Engineering, online, Springer, Berlin (2014)
19. ITU-T Recommendation Z.151 (11/08), User Requirements Notation (URN)—Language Definition. http://www.itu.int/rec/T-REC-Z.151/en
20. Jennings, N.R., Sycara, K., Wooldridge, M.: A roadmap of agent research and development. Auton. Agent. Multi-Agent Syst. **1**(1), 7–38 (1998)
21. Kavakli, E.: Modelling organizational goals: Analysis of current methods. 19th ACM Symposium on Applied Computing, pp. 1339–1343. ACM, New York (2004)
22. Leite, J., Werneck, V., Oliveira, A., Cappelli, C., Cerqueira, A., Cunha, H., González-Baixauli, G.: Understanding actor diagram: an exercise of meta modelling. In: Proceedings of the 10yh Workshop on Reuquirements Engineering (WER), pp. 2–12 (2007)
23. Li, F.-L., Horkoff, J., Mylopoulos, J., Guizzardi, R.S.S., Guizzardi, G., Borgida, A., Liu, L.: Non-functional Requirements as Qualities, with a Spice of Ontology. In: Proceedings 22nd

IEEE International Requirements Engineering Conference (RE), pp. 293–302, IEEE CS Press, Los Alamitos (2014)
24. Lopez, L., Costal, D., Ayala, C.P., Franch, X., Annosi, M.C., Glott, R., Haaland, K.: Adoption of OSS components: a goal-oriented approach. In: Data & Knowledge Engineering, vol. 99, pp. 17–38, Elsevier (2015)
25. Moody, D.L., Heymans, P., Matulevicius, R.: Visual syntax does matter: improving the cognitive effectiveness of the i* visual notation. Requirements Engineering, vol. 15(2), pp. 141–175. Springer, Berlin (2010)
26. Mylopoulos, J., Chung, L., Nixon, B.: Representing and using non-functional requirements: a process-oriented approach. IEEE Transactions on Software Engineering, vol. 18 (6), pp. 483–491. IEEE CS Press, Los Alamitos (1992)
27. Mylopoulos, J., Chung, L., Yu, E.: From Object-Oriented to Goal-Oriented Requirements Analysis. Communications of the ACM, vol. 42(1), pp. 31–37. ACM, New York (1999)
28. van Lamsweerde, A.: Goal-oriented requirements engineering: a guided tour. In: 5th IEEE International Symposium on Requirements Engineering, pp. 249. IEEE CS Press, Los Alamitos (2001)
29. Wooldridge, M., Cincarani, P.: Agent-oriented software engineering: the state of the art. First International Workshop on Agent-Oriented Software Engineering (AOSE), LNCS 1957, pp. 1–28. Springer, Berlin (2000)
30. Yu, E.: Modelling organizations for information system requirements engineering. 1st International IEEE Symposium on Requirements Engineering (ISRE), pp. 34–41. IEEE CS Press, Los Alamitos (1993)
31. Yu, E., Mylopoulos, J.: Understanding why in software process modelling, analysis, and design. In: Proceedings of the 16th International Conference on Software Engineering (ICSE), pp. 159–168. IEEE CS Press, Los Alamitos (1994)
32. Yu, E.: Modelling Strategic Relationships for Process Reengineering. Ph.D. Dissertation, University of Toronto (1995)

Part XI
Service Science: Social Implications

Global Service Enhancement for Japanese Creative Services Based on the Early/Late Binding Concepts

Yoshinori Hara and Hisashi Masuda

Abstract Japanese Creative Services (JCS) are defined as high context services affected by contextual factors such as nature, culture, history, and/or lifestyle. They have remarkable aspects of sustainability and scalability because of their strong dependency on the local Japanese context. When considering global service enhancement of such high context services while keeping their unique characteristics, it is important to clarify how communications between a variety of service providers and consumers are supported. The core competence of JCSs is derived from an "Omotenashi" mindset, as the essence of Japanese hospitality that emphasizes utilization of implicit contexts as deliberate preparations. In this chapter, we propose more general characteristics of JCS explicitly, a modeling method where we explicitly distinguish types of service communications as regular and exceptional handling ones and utilize early/late binding concepts in programming. We describe the modeling tool and the application case of a traditional Japanese sushi service (Edomae-Sushi). Analyzing service communication based on this concept, we discuss which part of communication should be supported/trained or replaced by IT/machines more systematically as a value-adding, scalability concept in the global service economy.

Keywords High context • Sustainability • Scalability • Exceptional handling • Late binding

---

Y. Hara (✉)
Kyoto University, Kyoto 606-8501, Japan
e-mail: hara@gsm.kyoto-u.ac.jp

H. Masuda
Japan Advanced Institute of Science and Technology, Ishikawa 923-1292, Japan
e-mail: masuda@jaist.ac.jp

D. Karagiannis et al. (eds.), *Domain-Specific Conceptual Modeling*,
DOI 10.1007/978-3-319-39417-6_23

1 Introduction

1.1 What Are Japanese Creative Services

Japanese Creative Services (JCS) are defined as high context services affected by their contextual factors such as nature, culture, history, and/or lifestyle. Shinise companies, i.e., shops of long standing (usually 100 years or older), often fall into this category such as ryokans (Japanese-style hotels) and fermentation manufacturers/retailers (sake, miso, etc.). Creative services have more added values than those coming only from their primary functional capabilities. For example, an automobile has the primary function to move a person from one place to another. However, the total value of the automobile is not just the primary value. We consider the added values of design, customer experience, story, brand, relationship, etc. in addition to the core service values.

Japan has a traditional way of viewing its four seasons, a unique history and culture, and various languages that affect the way of thinking, so we selected the following four regions as a typical JCS (Fig. 1): Shinise companies, Japanese cuisine services, Japanese cultural activities and Cool Japan.

In an increasingly global and diversified economy, such high context services have issues of sustainability and scalability because their value is strongly dependent on the local context and knowledge. For example, Hall classified Japan as a high context country [2]. Nevertheless, the statistics relating to the productivity of the service sector in Japan is worse than in other developed OECD countries [1]. One of the reasons is that methodologies of productivity improvement, such as standardization and replacement with IT/machines, are not directly applicable to some classes of Japanese services. These are highly human intensive services and include significant amounts of tacit knowledge accumulated over long periods of time. Interestingly, domestic and foreign consumers are often satisfied by the

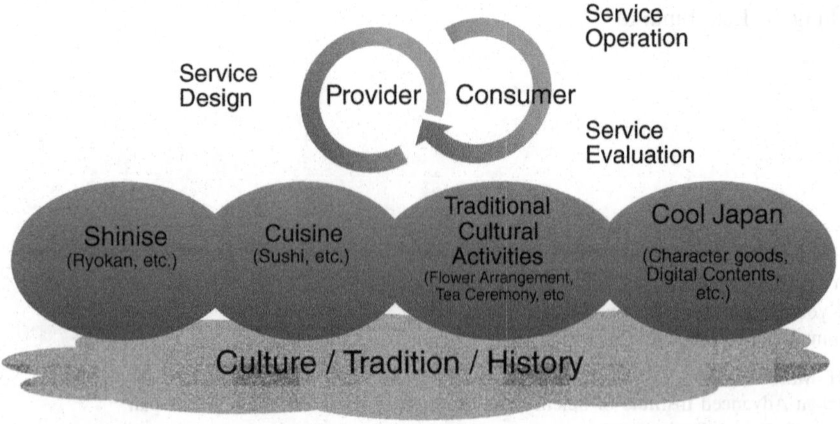

Fig. 1 Fundamentals of Japanese Creative Services

service quality that such Japanese service companies/organizations provide. Some examples of these services are traditional, family-owned, small and medium-sized companies that respect wisdom and creativity to sustain their businesses. This means that the evaluation criteria for the service sector that are currently used may not be adequate to assess this service class in Japan.

Considering global service enhancement of such high context services while keeping their uniqueness, it is important to clarify how to support the communications involved in a wide variety of service providers and consumers. We need to understand which parts are suited for applying normal approaches of standardization and which parts require cautious handling of tacit knowledge that providers/consumers have. There are some challenges in introducing the implementation of IT/machines directly for such implicit communications because the tacit knowledge does not appear clearly in the interaction. This communication requires decision-making by providers and/or consumers themselves on the spot within a dynamic flow.

1.2 Characteristics of Japanese Creative Services

In the case of JCS, the core competence is derived from an "Omotenashi" mindset as the essence of Japanese hospitality, which emphasizes utilization of implicit context through the interaction between service providers and consumers as well as deliberate preparations beforehand. The implicit communications require that service providers and/or consumers understand a kind of template (e.g. "Kata" in JCS) and need to make decisions for performing or consuming it. There is a big differentiation in the results depending on who performs the service, the knowledge of providers/consumers as well as the context on the spot.

Omotenashi is a conceptual word that explains typical Japanese hospitality over the ages. The original meaning of Omotenashi was the attitude of treating guests by the host. It may or may not be a good attitude. However, the current meaning of the word has shifted towards the positive side, which means "to respect others from their points of view", to let them have better experiences.

In order to perform Omotenashi, it is important for a service provider that his intention regarding the service consumer is not recognized. Japanese people have culturally understood this kind of processes as invaluable. We think it is more valuable to sense the context, what others want, and to perform services to fit their ideal rather than to intentionally perform services that are recognized by the service consumer.

This is a quite different mindset compared to the US where the value creation process is intentional in surpassing their consumers' expectations. According to experimental studies [3, 4], Japanese people feel more satisfied by familiarity while US people feel more satisfied by novelty.

Another important aspect of Omotenashi is a two-way awareness process between the service provider and the service consumer. As mentioned above, the service provider performs Omotenashi without any explicit intentions to the consumer. However, this Omotenashi process implicitly presumes awareness of the services by the consumer. Unless the consumer recognizes the service, the value of the service is not revealed. Thus, consumer literacy/ability to recognize such service value is indispensable. Once it is revealed, the value of the service is highly sustainable.

Furthermore, the value of Omotenashi is designed not only for the service consumer but also for the service provider. For example, the value of the traditional tea ceremony is not intended for the guests only, but also for the organizer. As a Japanese proverb states, "70 % of the service value is intended for the tea ceremony master, and the other 30 % is for the guests". Providers feel more comfortable recognizing the situation when their guests have felt the same way towards the tea ceremony. This process to create the value of service is also a unique feature of JCS.

The Omotenashi interaction process is also dependent on time, location, and the people involved. It may be difficult to duplicate such services efficiently since they are labor-intensive and time-consuming. Therefore, the productivity of Japanese service sectors is generally low. However, as a consequence the quality of JCS is high enough to sustain their businesses.

1.3 Sustainability and Scalability in Japanese Creative Services

JCS have relatively high entry barriers for newcomers, i.e., the value is not easily degraded. They are also able to easily sustain their businesses even after they have been widely accepted in a market. On the other hand, it might be difficult to maintain scalability and have large scale businesses because of the requirement of learning the knowledge for providers and/or consumers.

These aspects of JCS can be specified by the unique inheritance process based on a duality structure and template to sustain the business. Japanese traditional cultural activities such as the tea ceremony and flower arrangement are typical examples of JCS. Their unique inheritance mechanism is built on authority and the corresponding inheritance structure of the technology/service competence coexists and can be managed separately. The top level of the authority inheritance structure is called "Iemoto". Usually, the authority rights and related ownership are inherited by the descendant (son, daughter, etc.). In the meantime, the technology/service competence is maintained and inherited with an organization of Deshi (disciples) and Natori, an accredited Deshi (a higher class Deshi).

The advantage of using this inheritance process is the maintenance of sustainability of the JCS for many decades and centuries. An Iemoto of a JCS usually has qualified competence but does not always keep the top quality. Instead, maintaining the legitimacy of the authorisation rights is more important than to keep short-term qualities. On the other hand, people who join the particular JCS are encouraged by the Iemoto to promote their ranks in the Deshi-Natori structure through the various experiences to maintain the technology/service competence. This knowledge accumulation process is advantageous for both the group of Deshi and Iemoto.

Another unique competence to sustain the JCS is the role of "Kata", which is a template and a clue to inherit them. It does not have a rigid framework like typical manuals. The essence of the inheritance is to adjust Kata in accordance with the harmonization of each era. For example, one of the Katas of Noh indicates an appropriate tempo at which a Noh player performs. Recently, the tempo that is specified as a Kata of Noh has been getting slower according to the current social situation. The same goes for the tea ceremony and other JCS. By learning Kata, people can perform the corresponding JCS appropriately and be certified by the community.

Compared with manuals, the advantage of learning Kata is to have the capability to add individual values while performing with Kata for service providers and/or consumers. Kata has the flexibility to perform services and has margins to absorb the differences in each service encounter stage. In other words, the value of Kata is to sustain the JCS by respecting each individual person's creativity.

The Iemoto system which has the duality inheritance structure with Kata templates has been developed since the Edo period (about seventeenth–eighteenth centuries). In particular, after World War II, the system has progressed through housewives' participation in the community of the tea ceremony and flower arrangement. The balance of sustainability and scalability has been well organized. However, due to the change in lifestyles and economic situations, we will have to consider a new framework of balancing for JCS. In particular, in Japan, we need to understand how to apply current IT/machine approaches for handling these issues.

2 Method Description

2.1 Aim

We develop a modeling environment for especially representing service communications of JCS based on early and late binding concepts in programming. To depict such implicit communications like Omotenashi, we need to prepare abstract concepts to represent the templates of JCS, which we call Katas, as exception handling communication against regular handling communications in services. The education for Kata is mainly to share experiences among expert employees and novice ones during a long period. Our approach is to support such training sessions or improve them by applying a process modeling perspective using early/late binding concepts.

We can understand more detailed information related to the relationships of templates and the actual outputs in service communication by analyzing them based on a class/instance structure. For regular handling communications, the metamodeling approach has no use because of the one-for-one structure. But for exception handling, we use the approach for representing these because of the one-to-many structure. In particular, the representation of how to perform using Kata templates in JCS becomes more precise through the application of metamodeling.

In a training scenario, service providers can understand which part is suited to manuals and for which part it is required to understand the context and utilize it beyond manuals. Using this method, we can completely prepare beforehand the process for the regular handling type, which we can write down in a manual precisely applying an early binding concept analogous to static typing. On the other hand, for the process of exception handling, experts can share their knowledge/skills in a reading context using our modeling environment.

2.2 Concepts

For representing regular and exceptional communication in JCS, we introduce the Service Communication Model, which consists of the Service Communication Instance Model (SCIM), Service Communication Class Model (SCCM) and Service Communication Sub-Instance Model (SCSIM) on the ADO*xx* platform. For regular communication handling, we apply an early binding concept that can prepare the process beforehand completely. This is an analogy of static typing in programming. On the other hand, for exceptional ones, we apply a late binding one that requires real-time decision-making by providers and/or consumers. This is an analogy of dynamic typing. The SCIM depicts the actual communication in service directly. The SCCM depicts a sequence of templates of regular/exceptional handling communications between service providers and consumers. The template object has links to each SCSIM. The SCSIM depicts the actual communications partially connected with an adequate template on SCCM. The above approach is developed from our previous activity detailed in [5, 6].

The main characteristic of the regular handling communications is to combine a simulation based on a template beforehand and an actual performance on the spot. These templates can be represented by manuals. On the other hand, exceptional communications do not match the template and the result of actions. There are a wider variety of results than produced by standard ones. For representing these exceptional templates, we need to represent their irregular/uncertainty patterns, especially when they depend on the context.

By representing such communications systematically, we can discuss which parts of high context services should be supported by humans or replaced by IT/machines. In particular, it is important that we understand the results we will get based on each Kata because the templates do not produce one performance. In other words, the templates of Kata are accepted as a proactive attempt of exceptional handling by understanding the implicit context. For improving the added value from, for example, the template or Kata, the late binding concept is useful for the representation as well as the early binding concept for the standard process.

2.3 Advantages

This method contributes to establishing a suitable way for surveying of regular/exception handling communications in services and supports training and/or implementation with IT/machines related to both cases. With respect to surveying the implicit communication, we have to consider how to perform a template (Kata) of a specific service by each provider and/or consumers. Our method enables the definition of performing Kata using a class/instance structure and we can discuss how to utilize result(s) from this analysis based on early/late binding concepts.

Currently, it is difficult to export and globalize high context services, like JCS, into other areas that are distant from the original context. The cost of education for service providers in JCS is very high as well as consumers' expectations based on their local context. Novice employees will share the experience with the experts during a long period of understanding. In other words, this kind of training requires a very long time at the same place for them. If we apply a normal standardization using, for example, manuals to address such problems, the uniqueness of the services will disappear because of the standardized context.

We emphasize another direction to adapt such a situation for producing added value in service with remaining local contexts. The proposed modeling approach aims to contribute a kind of support for training and sharing of experiences for a wide variety of service providers as well as consumers involving high context services. This approach is a new direction of service differentiation with utilizing local contexts against conventional standardization.

3 Method Conceptualization

3.1 Overview of Method Based on Early/Late Binding Concepts

For representing regular/exceptional communications of JCSs, the Service Communication Model, which is our proposed method, consists of the Service Communication Instance Model (SCIM), Service Communication Class Model (SCCM) and Service Communication Sub-Instance Model (SCSIM) (based on the understanding of conceptualization of models in [7–9]).

By the SCIM (Figs. 2 and 3), we depict service communications directly as a format of a sequence of each slide that represents one remark/action by a service provider or a consumer. The slides display image data generated from a list of text data that is written down with one remark/action per line. The beginning of a sequence of slides shows information of date, consumers and service providers. The following slide displays communications between consumers and service providers.

By the SCCM (Fig. 4), we depict the flow of templates of services. Each template has two kinds of links into the SCSIM, in other words, we divide service communications into regular handling and exceptional ones. The characteristic of a

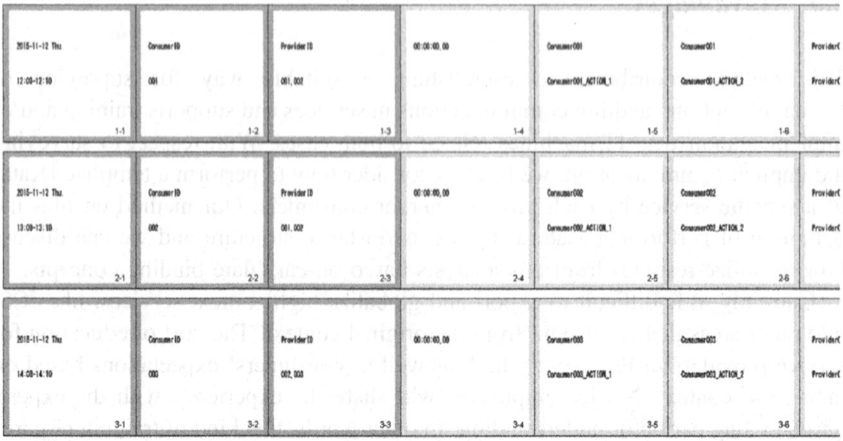

Fig. 2 Overview: Service Communication Instance Model

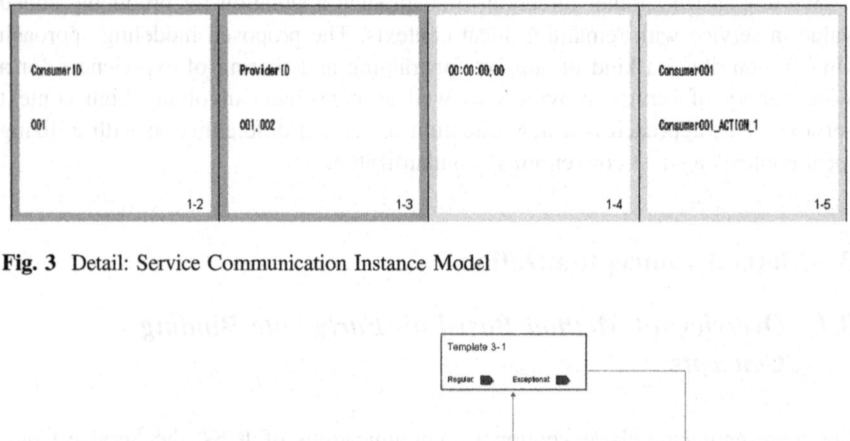

Fig. 3 Detail: Service Communication Instance Model

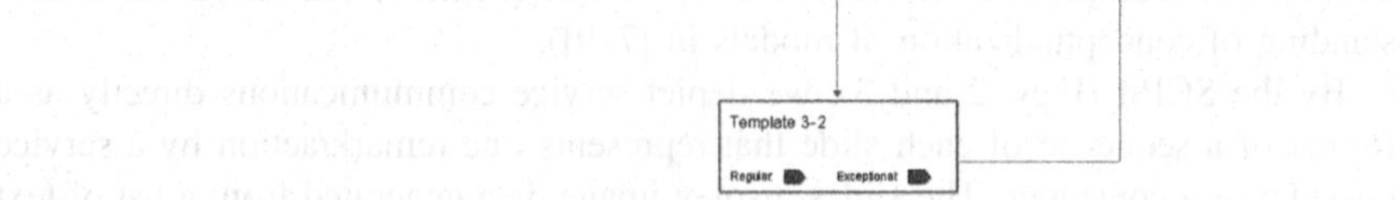

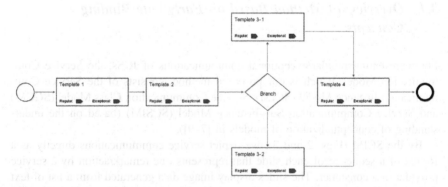

Fig. 4 Service Communication Class Model

regular handling communication is to be able to write down the actions beforehand completely. The exceptional one is that we cannot define the actions beforehand completely because the contexts on the spot affect the performance.

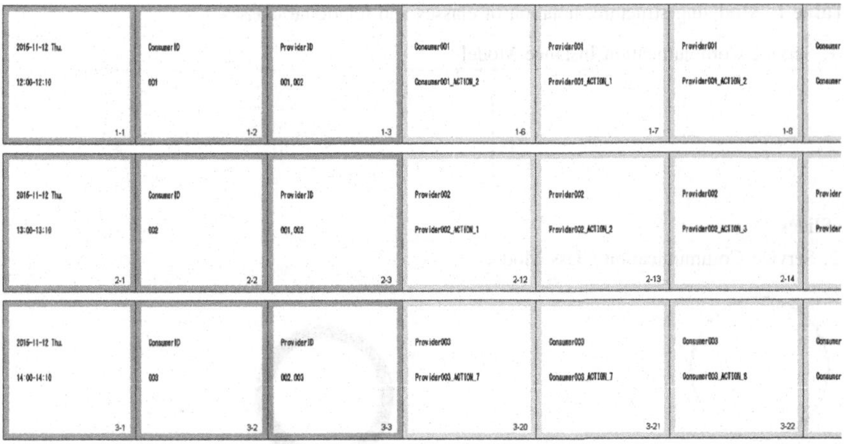

Fig. 5 Overview: Service Communication Sub-Instance Model

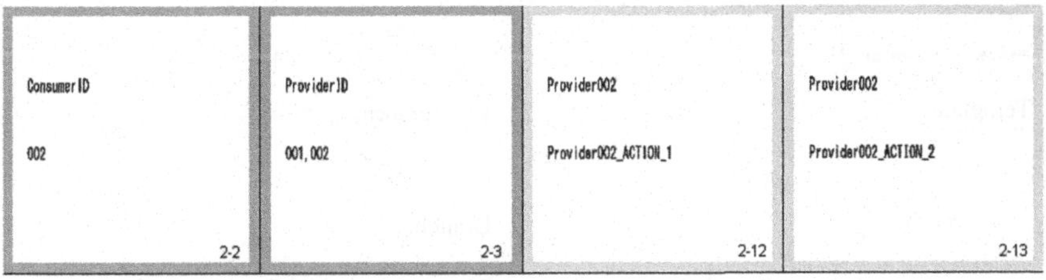

Fig. 6 Detail: Service Communication Sub-Instance Model

By the SCSIM (Figs. 5 and 6), we depict service communications as a format of sequences of each slide that are connected with an adequate template of SCCM. The sequence displays image data generated from a list of text data that is written down one remark/action per line, partially.

3.2 Notation, Syntax and Semantic Requirements

We explain the components of our proposed method with the following table (Table 1), which represents the classes of the ADO*xx* modeling environment and their dependencies as the result of the conceptualization process described in [10].

The SCIM has one class on the ADO*xx* modeling environment: *Slides*. *Slides* display image data as a sequence of actual remarks/actions of the service communications with information of date, consumer(s) and provider(s). The image data is generated from a text file with a list format with one line for one remark or action. Each image file will be set at an adequate directory in the local computer system.

Table 1 Modeling structure: notation of classes and relational classes

1. Service Communication Instance Model	
 Slides	
2. Service Communication Class Model	
 Start	 End
 Template	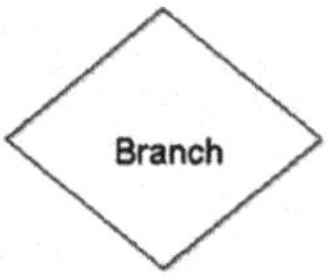 Branch
 Subsequence	
3. Service Communication Sub-Instance Model	
 Sub-Slides	

The SCCM has five classes on the environment: *Start*, *End*, *Template*, *Branch*, *Subsequence* (Relational Class). *Start* represents the beginning of the service communication. *End* represents the end of the service communication. *Template* represents the type of templates of each service communication. Each template has two types of links into SCSIM for regular handling and exceptional handling communications. *Branch* represents the branch for representing a connection of templates. *Subsequence* is a relational class for connecting two objects.

The SCSIM has one class on the ADO*xx* modeling environment: *Sub-Slides*. *Sub-Slides* display image data as a sequence of actual remarks/actions of the service communications with information of date, consumer(s) and provider(s) partially. The image data is generated from a text file with a list format with one line for one remark or action. Each image file will be set at an adequate directory in the local computer system.

4 Proof of Concept

4.1 Tool Prototype

4.1.1 Overview of Tool of Representation for Service Communications

We show the prototype tool of our proposed method and the applicable example of a Japanese traditional sushi service as the epitome of JCSs. There are three perspectives for depicting the models. The first one is the SCIM for representing the actual process of service communications. The second one is the SCCM for representing the template structure of service communications. In particular, each template has two kinds of links into the SCSIM, for regular handling and exceptional communications. Finally, the SCSIM is for representing the actual process of communications partially that are connected with an adequate template of SCCM.

We need to write down a service communication as list data for importing the data into our modeling environment. The data format is made as a text file that has a list of remarks/actions of communications. One line represents one remark/one action in communications. And the top of the lines shows the date and the name/ID of consumers and providers. The separator, which is a ":", works as a break line at the slide of the model. We use it to divide the name of the consumer/provider and their remark/action. We can also include a time stamp like "00:00:00, 00".

For displaying these lines of a text file, we have to transform them into image files (e.g. png). Each image file represents one remark/action of service communication per line in the text file. For generating such image files from a text file, *ImageMagick* may be used. For handling *ImageMagick*, some script languages (e.g. *Perl* and so on) are useful. Please see the help document for the details of this model on the OMiLAB site for this book.

After setting these image files into an adequate directory in the PC/Server, we are able to display them as a sequence of slides in the ADO*xx* modeling environment. First of all, we need to overview the actual service communications using the SCIM. Then, we will make a sequence of the processes as a flow of templates related to them, i.e., we generalize the SCIM using the SCCM. In particular, we can set two types of links into the SCSIM as part of the template object. The first type of links is for regular handling communications. The other is for exceptional ones. Finally, we are able to analyze service communications using the SCSIM, which is for representation of partial processes of service communications connected with each adequate template.

4.1.2 How to Use the Tool

The procedure for using this tool is presented below as a list of instructions. We can divide the procedure into three parts. The first part is for preparation for using this tool in the ADO*xx* environment. The second one is for making three types of models by means of our method. Finally, the third one is for interpreting the results, and we keep on developing the model structure.

- Step. 1 Downloading the abl file of this tool from the JCS page on OMiLAB
- Step. 2 Importing the abl file into your ADO*xx* environment
- Step. 3 Writing down a service communication as a text data (TXT) (one line per time stamp/actor/remark/action)
- Step. 4 Transforming a text file into images files (PNG) Step. 5 Setting the image files into an adequate directory Step. 6 Surveying the structure using the SCIM
- Step. 7 Making a sequence of templates on the SCCM
- Step. 8 Dividing communications in terms of each template on the SCSIM Step. 9 Connecting between SCCM and SCSIM with a link
- Updating this structure continuously (go to Step. 3)

The first part of this procedure is for preparation of this method in the ADO*xx* modelling environment. The abl file of this tool is uploaded on the JCS page on OMiLAB. It can be downloaded from the site. Then, the abl file must be imported into the local ADO*xx* modelling environment. Before making the model, the user must make a list of time stamp/actors/remarks/actions of service communications. The text format is prepared as follows:

- *Line1* Time stamp (DATE)—e.g. 2015-11-26 Thu. etc.
- *Line2* ConsumerID:—e.g. Consumer#1, #2 etc.
- *Line3* ProviderID:—e.g. Provider#1, #2 etc.
- *Line4* Time stamp—e.g. 00:00:00, 00:01:00 etc.
- *Line5* Consumer1: Action1—e.g. (entering) etc.
- *Line6* Consumer1: Remark1—e.g. Hello etc.
- *Line7* Provider1: Remark1—e.g. Hello etc.
- *Line8* Consumer1: Action2—e.g. (reading a menu list) etc.

Then, the user must transform the text file into image files. *ImageMagick* can be used for the transformation. Finally, they need to be set into an adequate place in the system (the default setting is for Windows, C://process-data//1//1//1.png and so on). Please see the help document of this model on the site for this book for the detailed procedure.

The second part is dedicated to the procedure of making a model using this tool. First, we represent the overall service communications using the SCIM. Here, we call the image files prepared in advance as slides. The SCIM will display the slide as a sequence. The user can change the target image files by choosing an adequate directory name on the *Slides* object. The part of the preface can also be emphasized (e.g. Time stamp (DATE), ConsumerID, ProviderID, and so on).

The next step is that we will make a sequence of templates that generate actual service communications, i.e., we generalize the SCIM using the SCCM. The flow of templates can be represented using Class *Start*, *End*, *Template*, *Branch* and *Subsequence*. In particular, we can set two types of links into the SCSIM on the *template* object. The first type of links is for regular handling communications. The other is for exceptional ones.

Finally, we have to prepare the SCSIM in terms of the flow of templates and make each SCSIM that is able to connect with each *template* object by dividing the regular handling and exceptional handling communications. The class *Sub-Slides* is almost the same class as *Slides*, but the start and end process can be changed. A part of the sequence of a communication can also be displayed. After preparing the SCSIM, the user can connect them into an adequate *template* object on the SCCM.

The third part of this procedure is for interpreting models that are made by this tool. It is important to learn how to spruce up the process data that are generated as image files in terms of regular/exceptional handling communications. On the regular handling side, we can handle them based on a kind of a manual. This is to lead the application to the early binding concept. This type of communication can be prepared completely beforehand. In particular, the user might prepare a well-written manual or would replace them with some IT/machines and so on.

On the exceptional handling side, there are various possibilities. This is to lead the application to the late binding concept. Reading the context and responding to the context are crucial. This part is required for decision-making on the spot so that we have to have another training session besides the regular handling ones. In particular, for novice employees in high context services, it is useful to share the experience of expert employees, in other words, the experts can share their experience with novices without sharing actual experiences. Finally, this procedure is an iterative process for updating models, that is, if you store a new service communication data set, this model structure is going to be updated based on the new data.

4.2 Case Study

4.2.1 Background

We represent a Japanese traditional sushi service, i.e., "Edomae-Sushi", using our proposed method. Edomae-Sushi services require highly skilled service providers and a deep knowledge of Japanese traditional sushi services, from both a consumer and provider perspective.

The layout in the restaurants is normally counter style, meaning that, consumers will receive the services in face-to-face communication with the chefs.

There are two types of ordering systems for the Edomae-Sushi service. The first one is a course menu style system called "Omakase", the second one is a free-style ordering approach by consumers themselves called "Okonomi". The order of the

Omakase is decided by the chef. Therefore, consumers do not need to make a selection themselves. To receive the Okonomi, consumers need to have knowledge of the Edomae-Sushi services because the chefs will not explain the system. This is a unique aspect of this service.

The remarkable points of the Edomae-Sushi service are that there is no fixed menu list, that is, the providers will change the daily dishes depending on the market circumstances, and also consider direct responses from consumers on the spot. For example, novice consumers of the Edomae-Sushi service may order a course menu (Omakase). If they want to try the free-style ordering system (Okonomi), consumers need to think what kind of fish is available in that respective season. Some consumers may watch and imitate the orders of others. Consumers are not familiar with each other but the interior of this type of restaurant generates communication between them.

The chefs of Edomae-Sushi services understand the knowledge/experience of consumers in performing their service and are going to change the treatment for consumers depending on the consumers' knowledge as well as the individual context. For novice consumers who are not familiar with such services, providers are going to explain a lot to them, so that they can receive the sushi services. On the other hand, for experienced consumers, there are minimal explanations of the services. The daily ingredients are limited, i.e., there is a rank of the valuable ones. A chef might consider that they try to provide the best ingredient to a consumer who can understand its value. Consumers have a chance to gain the best ingredients by such implicit negotiations.

4.2.2 Application Example for Japanese Traditional Sushi Services

There are three models for representing the Edomae-Sushi service. First of all, the SCIM is for representing actual communications between providers and consumers. The SCCM represents the flow of templates that are performed by service providers, and we are able to set two kinds of links into the following sub-instance model, the first one is for regular handling communication, and the other is for exception handling. Finally, the SCSIM is for representing actual communications between providers and consumers partially connected with adequate templates while considering regular/exception handling.

The data is gained by video/audio recordings in Edomae-Sushi services. We conducted an experiment and had the video/audio data related to Edomae-Sushi performances. There are several consumers. One consumer is quite familiar with and an expert of the Edomae-Sushi service.

The SCIM is for representing the actual communication between providers and consumers (Figs. 7 and 8). The example diagram of Edomae-Sushi is written in Japanese. The slide is able to use any image files so that you can use any languages for this method. The first three boxes in Fig. 7 are for preface information (Date, Consumer ID, Provider ID). The rest is for the service communications.

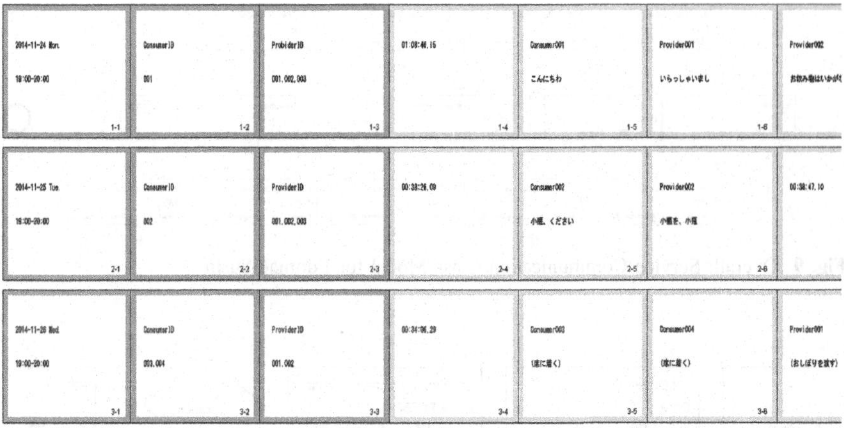

Fig. 7 Overall: Service Communication Instance Model for Edomae-Sushi

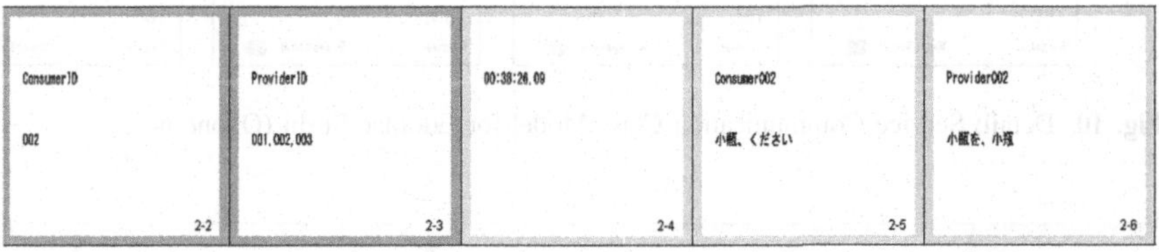

Fig. 8 Detail: Service Communication Instance Model for Edomae-Sushi

On the SCCM, we are able to represent a sequence of templates with two links into regular handling communications and exceptional handling ones (Figs. 9 and 10). Regular handling communications are that we can prepare the communications completely beforehand, there are no ambiguous parts for decision making on the spot, and we can interpret this type of communications as an early binding concept in programming. For Edomae-Sushi service, this type of communications is represented as an "Omakase" ordering system. Exceptional handling communications are that we cannot prepare the communications completely beforehand, there are several points of decision making on the spot by providers or consumers e.g. because of utilizing implicit contexts, and we can interpret this type of communications as a late binding concept in programming. For Edomae-Sushi service, this type of communications is represented as an "Okonomi" ordering system.

Finally, the SCSIM is for partially representing actual communications connected with an adequate template of the SCCM (Figs. 11, 12, 13 and 14). For example, the unique pattern of the Edomae-Sushi begins with a first drink order in both Omakase and Okonomi styles. When they go to the second order, consumers

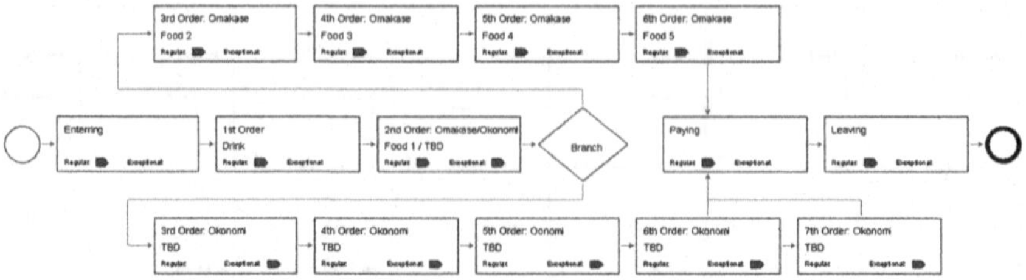

Fig. 9 Overall: Service Communication Class Model for Edomae-Sushi

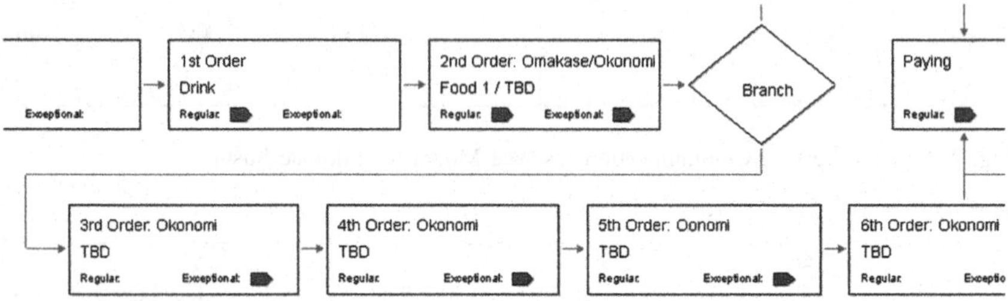

Fig. 10 Detail: Service Communication Class Model for Edomae-Sushi (Okonomi)

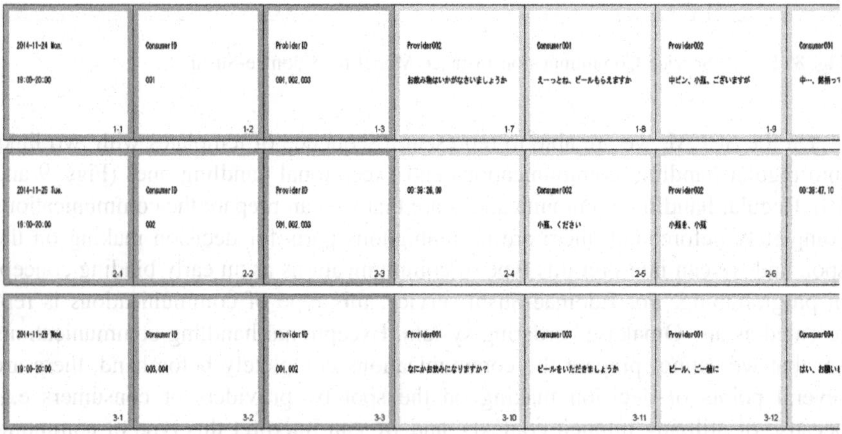

2014-11-24 Mon.
19:00-20:00
ConsumerID
001
ProbiderID
001, 002, 003
Provider002
お飲み物はいかがなさいましょうか
Consumer001
えーっとね、ビールもらえますか
Provider002
Consumer001
2014-11-25 Tue.
19:00-20:00
ConsumerID
002
ProviderID
001, 002, 003
00:38:26.09
Consumer002
Provider002
00:38:47.10
2014-11-26 Wed.
19:00-20:00
ConsumerID
003, 004
ProviderID
001, 002
Provider001
なにかお飲みになりますか？
Consumer003
ビールをいただきましょうか
Provider001
Consumer004

Fig. 11 Overall: Service Communication Sub-Instance Model for Edomae-Sushi—1st Order

decide on Omakase or Okonomi styles. Okonomi style is affected by the characteristics of consumers. Thus, we can interpret the results as exceptional handling communications, and this is definitely different to Omakase style.

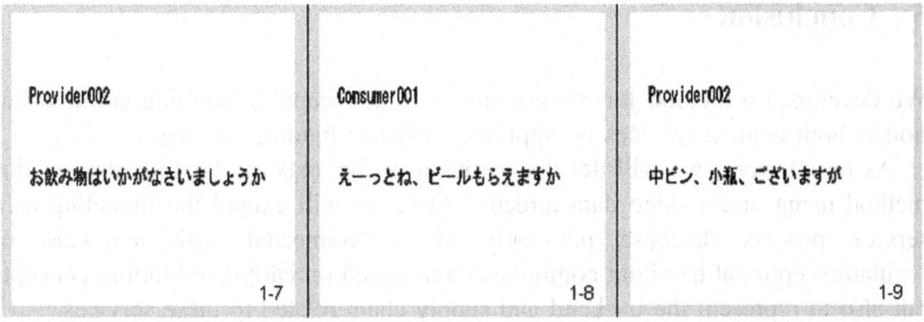

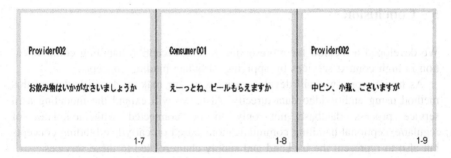

Fig. 12 Detail: Service Communication Sub-Instance Model for Edomae-Sushi—1st Order

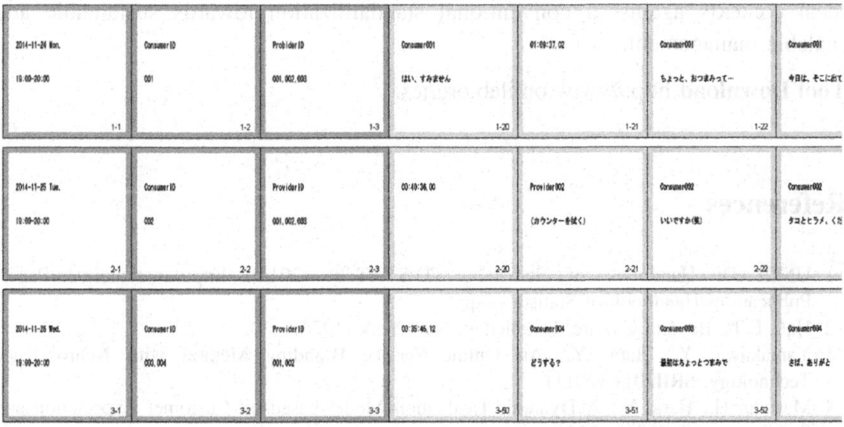

Fig. 13 Overall: Service Communication Sub-Instance Model for Edomae-Sushi—2nd Order

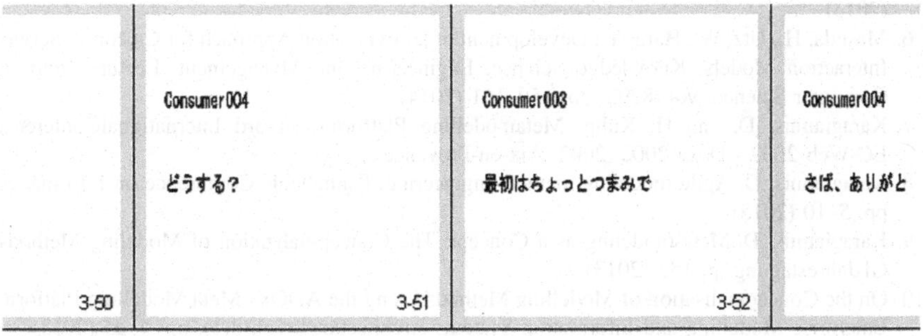

Fig. 14 Detail: Service Communication Sub-Instance Model for Edomae-Sushi—2nd Order

5 Conclusion

We developed a method for representing regular/exception handling communication in high context services by applying early/late binding concepts.

As future work, we will develop easier ways for making the slide data of this method using audio/video data directly. Also, we will extend the modeling as a service process database not only to be connected with templates of regular/exceptional handling communications based on early/late binding concepts but also to represent the backend and supply chain related to these services.

We believe that this kind of approach will contribute to creating new value in the field of service science, in order to be applied to value-added global services. In particular, this approach is a new direction of service differentiation with utilizing local contexts against a conventional standardization towards sustainable and scalable management.

Tool Download http://www.omilab.org/jcs.

References

1. UNCTAD: Handbook of Statistics, TD/STAT.39 (2014). http://unctad.org/en/Pages/Publications/Handbook-of-Statistics.aspx
2. Hall, E.T.: Beyond Culture. Doubleday, New York (1976)
3. Yamakawa, Y., Hara, Y.: An Online Service Branding Method with Neuroscience Technology, SRII2011 (2011)
4. Masuda, H., Hara, Y.: A Dynamic Evaluation Model based on Customer Expectation and Satisfaction, SRII2011 (2011)
5. Masuda, H., Utz, W., Hara, Y.: Context-Free and Context-Dependent Service Models based on "Role Model" Concept for Utilizing Cultural Aspects, Knowledge Science, Engineering and Management Lecture Notes in Computer Science, vol. 8041, pp. 591–601. Springer (2013)
6. Masuda, H., Utz, W., Hara, Y.: Development of an Evaluation Approach for Customer Service Interaction Models, Knowledge Science, Engineering and Management. Lecture Notes in Computer Science, vol. 8793, pp. 150–161 (2014)
7. Karagiannis, D. and H. Kühn. Metamodelling Platforms. in 3rd InternationalConference EC-Web 2002 - Dexa 2002. 2002. Aix-en-Provence,.
8. Karagiannis, D.:Agile modeling method engineering. Panhellenic Conference on Informatics, pp. 5–10 (2015)
9. Karagiannis, D.:Meta-modeling as a Concept: The Conceptualization of Modeling Methods. GI-Jahrestagung, p. 152 (2013)
10. On the Conceptualisation of Modelling Methods Using the ADOxx Meta Modelling Platform. Enterprise Modelling and Information Systems Architectures, vol. 8(1), pp. 4–25 (2013)

HCM-L: Domain-Specific Modeling for Active and Assisted Living

Heinrich C. Mayr, Fadi Al Machot, Judith Michael, Gert Morak, Suneth Ranasinghe, Vladimir Shekhovtsov and Claudia Steinberger

Abstract Modeling and modeling methods are crucial for information systems engineering but are seldom seamlessly integrated into all phases of development and operation: Practitioners challenge the benefits of modeling and complain about the confusing variety of concepts with overlapping semantics, symbols and syntactic rules of today's standardized, "universal" modeling languages. Therefore, domain-specific modeling languages (DSMLs) are gaining increasing popularity: they are lean and convenient, support the productivity of modeling, and help to increase model quality and comprehensibility. There are, however, few approaches to embedding a DSML into a domain-specific modeling method (DSMM) that provides guidelines about how to use a given DSML and to evaluate related models. This chapter aims to make a contribution towards filling that gap by discussing, as an example and proof of concept, a domain-specific modeling method for the human cognitive modeling language HCM-L, a DSML for the domain of active and assisted living. As a modeling language without tool support has no chance to be used in practice, we are conducting that discussion on the basis

H.C. Mayr (✉) · F. Al Machot · J. Michael · G. Morak · S. Ranasinghe
V. Shekhovtsov · C. Steinberger
Application Engineering Research Group, Alpen-Adria-University Klagenfurt, Klagenfurt, Austria
e-mail: heinrich.mayr@aau.at

F. Al Machot
e-mail: fadi.almachot@aau.at

J. Michael
e-mail: judith.michael@aau.at

G. Morak
e-mail: gert.morak@aau.at

S. Ranasinghe
e-mail: suneth.ranasinghe@aau.at

V. Shekhovtsov
e-mail: volodymyr.shekhovtsov@aau.at

C. Steinberger
e-mail: claudia.steinberger@aau.at

D. Karagiannis et al. (eds.), *Domain-Specific Conceptual Modeling*,
DOI 10.1007/978-3-319-39417-6_24

of HCM-L modeler, a tool that was implemented using the metamodeling platform ADO*xx* and can be accessed via OMiLAB, the Open Models Laboratory for modeling method engineering. HCM-L modeler is component of an ambient assistance system for supporting elder persons in mastering their daily life activities.

Keywords DSML design • Active and assisted living (AAL) • Modeling tool • Activity recognition • End user interaction

1 Introduction

Modeling and modeling methods are crucial for information systems sngineering. In practice, however, they are rarely embedded into all phases of development and operation: Practitioners challenge the benefits of modeling and complain about the confusing variety of concepts with overlapping semantics, symbols and syntactic rules of today's standardized, "universal" modeling languages.

Certainly, generic languages are meritorious due to their versatility in arbitrary domains as well as a broad body of experience and knowledge that has emerged from intensive use and research. Nevertheless, such languages tend to follow the "law of logistic growth" [1], being continuously extended up to a complexity and lack of concept orthogonality that affects their transparency and makes them hardly manageable for practical use. Think for example of UML which grew from initially five "diagrams" up to 17 (standard) and 8 additional diagrams in the version 2.0 [2]. Such complexity may lead to misunderstandings and scepticism.

As an alternative, domain-specific modeling languages (DSMLs) are gaining an increasing popularity: they are lean and convenient, support the productivity of modeling, and help to increase model quality and comprehensibility. Moreover, they come with lexical/graphical notations that are familiar and/or easy to understand by the users in that domain.

To increase the use of such DSML in practice, however, it has to be embedded into a domain-specific modeling method (DSMM), which features the procedure of how to apply the language, i.e., a "modeling procedure model" as well as appropriate mechanisms and tools to be used in such a procedure.

Few approaches have been reported so far regarding such efforts. This chapter, therefore, describes our results and experiences when developing a DSML for the domain of ambient and assisted living [3] within the framework of the project HBMS (Human Behavior Monitoring and Support).[1]

The aim of this project is to develop an AAL System, which

1. monitors an individual while carrying out daily life activities,
2. detects abstracts, aggregates and integrates the observed behavior into an individual human cognitive model (HCM), and

[1]This work was funded to a large extent by the Klaus Tschira Stiftung gGmbH, Heidelberg.

3. assists the individual in cases of need via a multimodal interface by retrieving knowledge from the human cognitive model from a case base and from a domain ontology using reasoning algorithms.

Thus, HBMS will facilitate it for elderly people with memory weaknesses to live longer autonomously in their familiar environment.

The chapter is organized as follows: Sect. 2 shows how DSMLs fit into the (meta) model hierarchy and describes current work on DSML creation processes. In Sect. 3, we outline the HBMS approach and present an overall architecture of the system. Section 4 is dedicated to the "Human Cognitive Modeling Language" HCM-L, which was developed within the HBMS framework. In Sect. 5, we discuss the modeling tool "HCM-L Modeler" which was developed using the metamodeling platform ADO*xx*. In Sect. 6, finally, we put the things together and describe the main HBMS functions. The paper concludes with a short outlook on future research.

2 Domain-Specific Modeling

A domain[2]-specific modeling language (DSML) is designed for exclusive use in a certain domain, and for specific purposes. When introducing a new modeling language, however, one should ascertain whether it is really needed or at least justified with respect to the intended application domain. As natural languages evolve over time following social, economic or environmental changes, modeling languages do so, too. They have to meet given challenges as efficiently and adequately as possible. Standardized languages have benefits due to their universal applicability and their wide range of concepts. However, exactly this wide range can be a drawback for the efficient and effective use of such a modeling language, in particular if non-experts—e.g., doctors, engineers or even the end-users themselves—should be able to understand and validate models intuitively. Consequently, in such cases a lean DSML, which comes with only few but appropriate concepts, may be justified.

Using the 4-level model hierarchy (see, e.g., [5–8]) as a basis, a DSML is an extension of M3 and a metamodel for M1 as shown in Fig. 1. That means that the DSML is defined on level M2 using a metamodeling language provided on M3. On level M1, the DSML is used to create concrete models that are instantiated on level M0.

Much work has been published on evaluating modeling languages [9, 10] on how to use a DSML [11, 12], but only few on the process of DSML/DSMM design.

Within the context of developing a DSML for enterprise modeling, [10] suggests a sequence of "macro process steps", namely clarification of scope and purpose, analysis of generic requirements, analysis of specific requirements, language

[2]A more detailed previous version of this section has been published in [4].

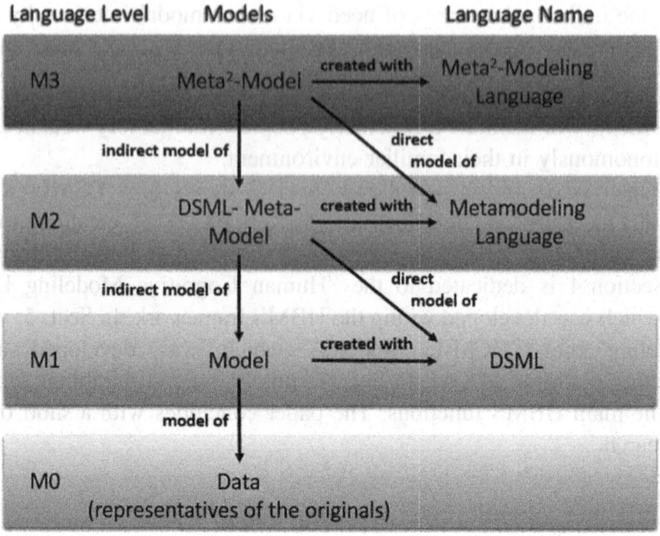

Fig. 1 Modeling hierarchy for a DSML

specification, design of graphical notation, development of modeling tool, evaluation and refinement. For each of these steps, several "micro process steps" are defined. In [11], modeling methods are defined as consisting of, (1) a modeling technique and (2) mechanisms and algorithms which work on the models (level M1). The modeling technique is divided into a modeling language, in our case a DSML, and a modeling procedure, which defines the application of the language. We propose an approach, which is based on this work, but is to some extent more generic than [10], and more reflecting domain-specific aspects than [11].

In particular, we propose to divide the DSML creation process in five main phases (see Fig. 2): *preparation*, *modeling language*, *modeling process, modeling tool* and *evaluation*. Each phase consists of several steps which are inspired by the work of [10] and [11]. These phases are only sketched here; for more details, see [4].

Preparation The preparation phase is to make sure that all relevant facts of the domain in question are known and well defined. We divide this phase in the steps *clarification of* scope and purpose, *requirements analysis* and *context analysis*.

Clarification: The *scope* drives the definition of the modeling concepts to be provided as part of the metamodel, which again determines the models that can be created on level M1. The *purpose* mainly relates to the profile of future user groups of the intended DSML: users of the modeling tool, users who have to understand the models on M1, e.g., doctors in the case of AAL.

Requirements Analysis: The main task here is to reveal the aspects to be modeled. This can be achieved by creating usage scenarios and exemplary diagrams. Another source of knowledge is domain-specific standards and relevant literature,

Fig. 2 The DSMM-creation process

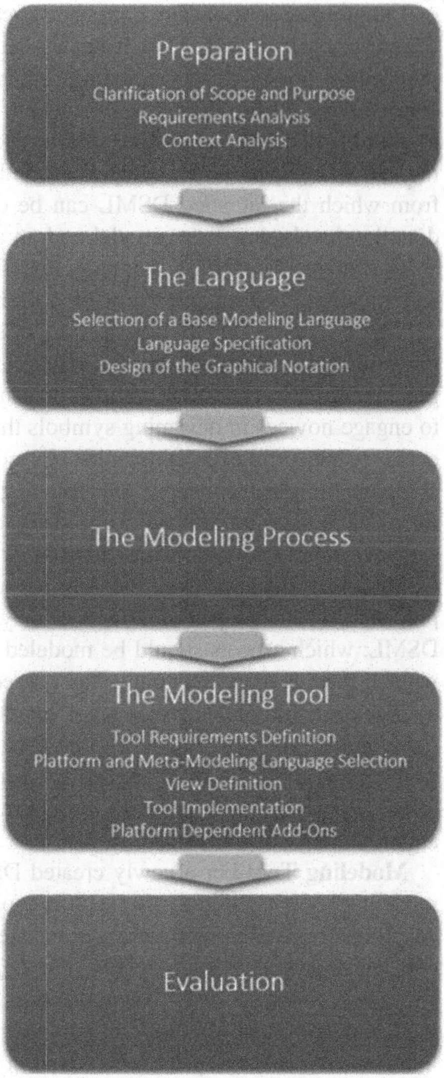

and even more important: stakeholder involvement. Clearly, requirements analysis has to be done iteratively, until a stable specification has been reached.

Context Analysis: Although context analysis elicits requirements too, treating it as a step on its own may lead to a deeper understanding of the given domain. As an example, [13] introduces a context model focusing on a person's surroundings, such as things, services and information accessed by the person, mental and physical information about the person, social aspects like friends or relatives, context about what a person is doing and spatial–temporal information. A comprehensive overview of current context modeling approaches is presented in [14].

Language Creation The Language Creation phase concentrates on the language definition on level M2. First it has to be made clear, based on the results of the preparation phase, which modeling dimensions—structure (statics), function (operations) or behavior (dynamics)—have to be covered by modeling concepts. Also, to simplify the task, it is advisable to evaluate existing universal and/or specific modeling languages with similar scope and purpose, in order to select one as a basis from which the intended DSML can be derived. The language definition then is done by developing a metamodel and an appropriate graphical notation.

In general, a modeling language is defined by specifying its syntax, semantics and notation. For an overview of current approaches to syntax and semantics definition see, e.g., [11]. For specifying the graphical notation, the nine "*principles for designing cognitively effective visual notations*" as presented in [15] represent a good guide. However, also the idea presented in [16] is worth considering, namely to engage novices in designing symbols that are comprehensible to novices, as this could outperform experts' results. As some language constructs might be too complex for graphical representation (e.g., logical conditions), other appropriate forms of representation have to be defined. Again an iterative approach is necessary, informed by experiments involving the relevant stakeholders.

Modeling Process The modeling process definition should provide a stepwise procedure of how a particular model may be systematically built using the given DSML: which aspects should be modeled first, which view a modeler should start with (if there is more than one). The procedure should cover all modeling elements to provide a comprehensive insight for the modeler, and possibly also provide a "style guide" for which pattern to be used in which situation [17]. In Becker [18], some (general) useful rules are provided for creating business information models: to model only relevant parts, to leave irrelevant parts of the UoD, or to take care about naming conventions.

Modeling Tool For a newly created DSML there inherently is no ready-to-use modeling tool. Consequently, such a tool has to be created from scratch or by adapting an existing one. Again, several steps are to be performed in order to end up with an appropriate solution: (1) *tool requirements definition*, (2) *selection of a platform/framework and a metamodeling language*, (3) *view definition*, (4) *tool implementation* and (5) *platform-dependent add-ons*.

A framework for step 1 can be found in [17]. For step 2, we propose an approach opposite to that of [10]: instead of starting with selecting a metamodeling language, for economic reasons we would first select an appropriate framework/platform for tool generation. The decision then includes the choice of the metamodeling language. There are several such frameworks or platforms [11, 19].

As humans have perceptual and cognitive limits, it is important to provide different views on the content (step 3); these should help to reduce the complexity, e.g., by dividing a model into parts or by appropriate abstraction mechanisms focusing on particular aspects; also overall cognitive maps may help the reader to assemble information into a coherent mental representation of the models (see [15]).

The metamodel of the DSML should be formulated using the framework's metamodeling language. Based hereon, the tool implementation (step 4) is generative to the extent supported by the chosen platform.

Step 5 consists in exploiting—along the requirements—platform-specific features, e.g., interfaces or coupling possibilities to external software, components for model checking, simulation, analysis, transformation or generation of documentation.

Evaluation The evaluation has to be carried out in co-operation with the stakeholders against the goals and requirements, which have been determined in the preparation phase. Also, quality aspects on levels M1 and M2 have to be evaluated (for model quality categorization see, e.g., [20, 21]). A promising approach for completeness checks on level 2 is a pattern-based analysis like the one presented in [22] for business process modeling.

3 HBMS System: Architecture and User Roles

With advancing age, there is a tendency towards having an impaired memory and thus forgetting how to overcome the challenges of the daily life: "episodic knowledge" gets lost in parts.

Current forecasts of the global population ageing make clear that cognitive impairments are becoming a major problem in our societies. Thus, in 2050, more than 2 billion people will be over 60 [23], nearly 80 % of them living in the world's poorer countries [24]. This global challenge forces researchers around the world to focus on active and assisted living (AAL) (formerly: ambient assisted living [2, 20]), a subdomain of ambient assistance. AAL aims at developing methods, tools and software systems that enable elderly people, unobtrusively, to stay autonomous in their homes. AAL was pushed substantially in 2004, when it became a strategic support action (SSA) in the 6th Framework Program of the European Union, and since then, large budgets are assigned to the research into AAL and healthy ageing.

The aim of HBMS (human behavior monitoring and support) has been to maintain the personal autonomy of an elderly person as long as possible by supporting her/his individual mental processes. For that purpose, HBMS relies on conceptual behavior modeling, and on reasoning algorithms for deriving optimal support from an integrated model of abilities and episodic knowledge that an individual had (or has, but has temporarily forgotten). Broadly speaking, the HBMS process consists of observing the behavior of a target person (*learning mode*) using available activity recognition infrastructure and systems, and to transform and preserve the observations in a knowledge base, the *human cognitive model (HCM)*.

In *support mode*, the HCM, a case base of concrete observations and a potentially existing domain ontology are exploited to assist the target person, when needed, in taking appropriate actions for reaching her/his current goal (Fig. 3).

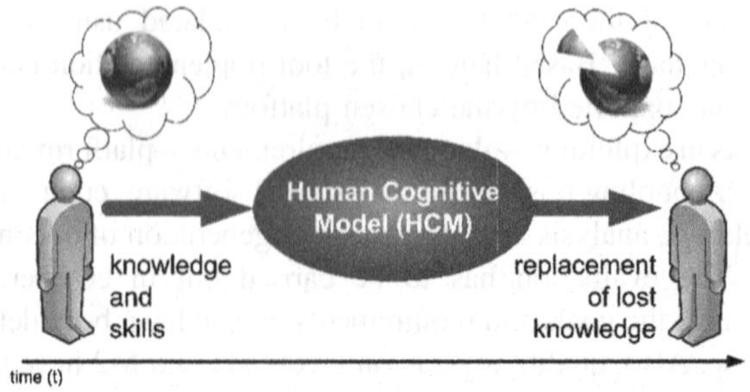

Fig. 3 Human cognitive model, kernel of the HBMS concept

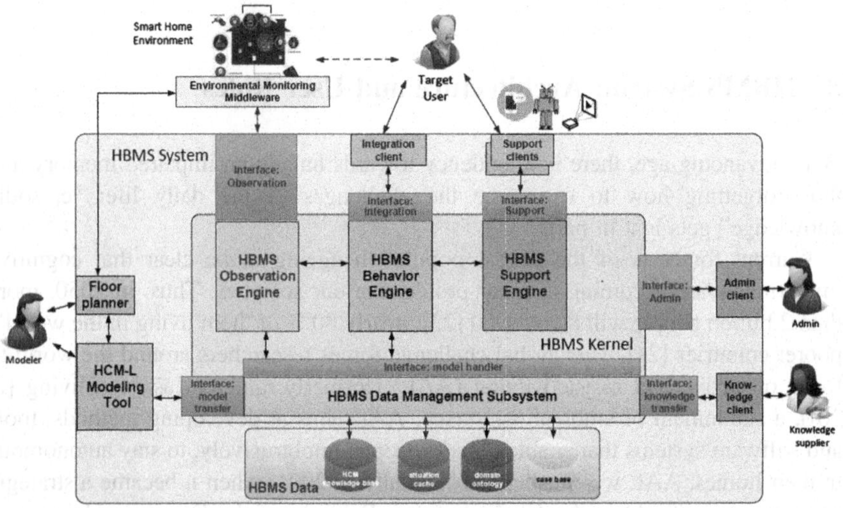

Fig. 4 Simplified HBMS-system architecture

Figure 4 shows a simplified architecture of the HBMS system. Activity monitoring and context acquisition is done outside the HBMS boundaries. We are working at a universal observation interface, which will allow to connect any available activity recognition or environment monitoring system to the HBMS system by automatically transforming their outputs into instances of HCM-L, the modeling language developed within the framework of the HBMS project. In the current stage, Nimbits [http://www.nimbits.com], an open source middleware tool for the Internet of Things, is used for this purpose.

There are four roles a HBMS-system user can take by applying the appropriate HBMS-clients:

Target User The target user resides in a smart home environment. The environmental monitoring middleware monitors his/her behavior using sensors or other activity recognition methodologies. Via the observation interface, the *HBMS-*

observation engine communicates to this environmental monitoring middleware. It listens to the observation data arriving from this component, analyzes and processes this data, and transfers recognized behavior situations to the *HBMS behavior engine*; the HBMS behavior engine handles the behavior situations arriving from the observation engine in context of the current HCM knowledge base. In learning-mode, the behavior engine collects obtained behavior situations to form a behavior sequence and integrates this sequence into the existing HCM. In cases of integration-doubts, the target user (or a deputy) is involved into the behavior integration process via an integration client.

In support mode, the behavior engine retrieves appropriate knowledge from HCM using reasoning mechanisms and transfers suitable knowledge chunks to *HBMS support engine*. The HBMS support engine is responsible for the context-sensitive multimodal assistance of the target user by using an appropriate support client.

Modeler Using the HCM-L modelling tool, the modeler is able to describe the behavior of the target user manually using HCM-L as graphical modeling language without using the learning mode capabilities of the HBMS-system described above. The HCM-L modeling tool is also the means to visualize, analyze, verify and validate HCM knowledge which has been learned while monitoring the target user. As an example, a doctor could also act in this role for diagnosing possible impairments of the target user. The floor planner tool facilitates the modeler to easily describe the environmental context of the target user in the form of graphical floorplans.

Administrator Via the admin client, the current state of the system can be monitored and visualized. Also, all administrative functions like user management or support client configuration can be dealt with using this client.

Knowledge Supplier The knowledge client allows to obtain knowledge from external sources and to integrate this knowledge into HBMS data (e.g., domain knowledge, external behavior knowledge).

In brief, the HBMS system includes the following data sources:

- *HCM*—the complete cognitive model of the target user; it serves as a source for generating situation cache elements,
- *HBMS Situation Cache*—the operational knowledge base in the system: it contains currently relevant and referenced HCM fragments, and state data collected from observations,
- *HBMS Domain Ontology*—an ontology representing domain-specific knowledge, which is referenced from both, HCM and HBMS Situation Cache;
- *HBMS Case Base*—a database of all observed action sequences; it is exploited, e.g., by reasoning algorithms of the support engine for weighting alternatives when determining the most likely next step to be advised.

4 HCM-L, a Modeling Language for the AAL Domain

The Human cognitive modeling language (HCM-L) is a lean modeling language which serves to represent and reproduce episodic knowledge of a certain person without loss. The scope is limited to the episodic knowledge of a person (autobiographical events and contextual information) and is further restricted to activities which were planned to be supported in the HBMS system, like activities of daily live, usage of electronic devices or software and others [25].

The terms *'cognitive modeling'* or *'models of cognition'* originate from cognition psychology and are important concepts for cognition science as well as for Artificial Intelligence (AI) [26]. In psychology and AI, theories of human problem solving are tested using a computer program, which tries to have the same control processes during problem solving as humans are supposed to have (see, e.g., the General Problem Solver in [27]). The main goal of cognitive modeling is to find out the basic principles of human intelligence. Usually, this is done by checking if a given AI-model is able to find solutions for a problem similar to supposed human problem-solving processes; or, in the opposite direction, psychological findings about the human memory are validated by simulation using AI-techniques [28].

Methodical considerations encouraged us to design and apply the method development approach as presented in Sect. 2. Concerning the *preparation phase*, the *clarification of scope and purpose* stemmed from the initial project idea which was motivated by personal experiences of one of the authors within his familiar environment. The *requirements elicitation and analysis* step started with a comprehensive literature analysis about the state of the art in AAL systems, which was followed by elicitation workshops with interested person of different age groups, as well as an analysis of common (generic) modeling languages. The latter revealed that these languages did only partly fulfil the elicited requirements. For the *context analysis* we carried a deep analysis of current AAL projects, research concerning smart homes, pervasive and ubiquitous systems, as well as activity and behavior recognition. As general standards for the domain are under development but rarely used in projects, e.g., universAAL [29], we could not use them as such.

As it was quite clear from requirements analysis that we would need a modeling language integrating dynamic (behavior) and structural (context) aspects, we decided to use previous experiences in conceptual modeling gained with KCPM, the Klagenfurt Conceptual Predesign model [30, 31], a lean, user-centred language for software requirements modeling, and use this as the basis for HCM-L. Consequently, the KCPM concepts were evolved and adapted to cognitive modeling. Thus, we could benefit from adopting the thing concept (a more intuitive way of abstracting from classes and attributes), as well as from the KCPM approach to relate resources and actions.

The HCM-L metamodel was created in several iterative steps using a UML class-diagram-like representation. As our goal was to create an intuitively understandable language, some of the (needed) complexity was displaced to a textual sub-language. For the same reason, it was decided to provide as few graphical elements as possible. Some sample diagrams were created with this first draft set of modeling elements. The elements were revised in several iterations based on feedback of end users, colleagues and because of findings from [15], e.g., icons were added, the color and thickness of different connections was changed for a higher visual distance.

With HCM-L, the resulting “Human Cognitive Modeling Language”, a new variant of the concept of cognitive modeling has been added, which is closer to the meaning of modeling in Informatics: The cognitive model is seen as an abstract extract of the episodic knowledge of a person; as such, it can be used as a knowledge base for services such as support activities, diagnosis, time series analyses and others.

In the realm of HBMS, models are encapsulated units of a certain person’s behavior and of the respective relevant context. As such, HCM-L models form a knowledge base for reasoning services to optimally support a person: they are the core of the HBMS-System, and the central source of knowledge for other system components.

A preceding analysis of common (generic) modeling languages revealed that these only partly fulfilled our requirements [32]. As a consequence, we decided to create a DSML fulfilling the key requirements:

1. to provide models which can be used as a knowledge base in the support system,
2. to focus on human behavior and its context, and
3. to be understood intuitively by the relevant stakeholders in the AAL domain, e.g., people in general and their relatives, caregivers or doctors.

Consistent with the aim of the HBMS project, our DSML development was driven by the focus on conceptualizing human activities of daily life in the private home of one person, e.g., using electronical devices, dressing, cooking, writing an email and so on [4].

Following [11], the HCM-L *syntax* is described by a metamodel (see Fig. 5), the *semantics* by explanation in natural language, and the *notation* by a set of graphical elements (see Fig. 6). HCM-L is grounded in activity theory [33], which describes the nature of human activities in general.

The key modeling concept of HCM-L is *behavioral unit (BU)*; a BU is defined to encapsulate alternative sequences of individual actions a person may perform to reach a particular *goal*. For modeling actions, HCM-L features the concept *operation*; operations are connected by directed *flows*, which allow to represent action sequences and thus the direction of the behavioral process.

Operations may differ in detail (i.e., taking a coffee cup or a tea cup), in particular depending on the effects of a previous one. To describe such detailed functionality, HCM-L offers the concept *instruction*, as an attribute of operation. Basically, an instruction consists of simple additions, modifications and removals of concrete relationships between context elements (see below).

As there might be alternative sequences of actions for reaching the same goal that have one or more actions in common, there might be forks (i.e., several flows

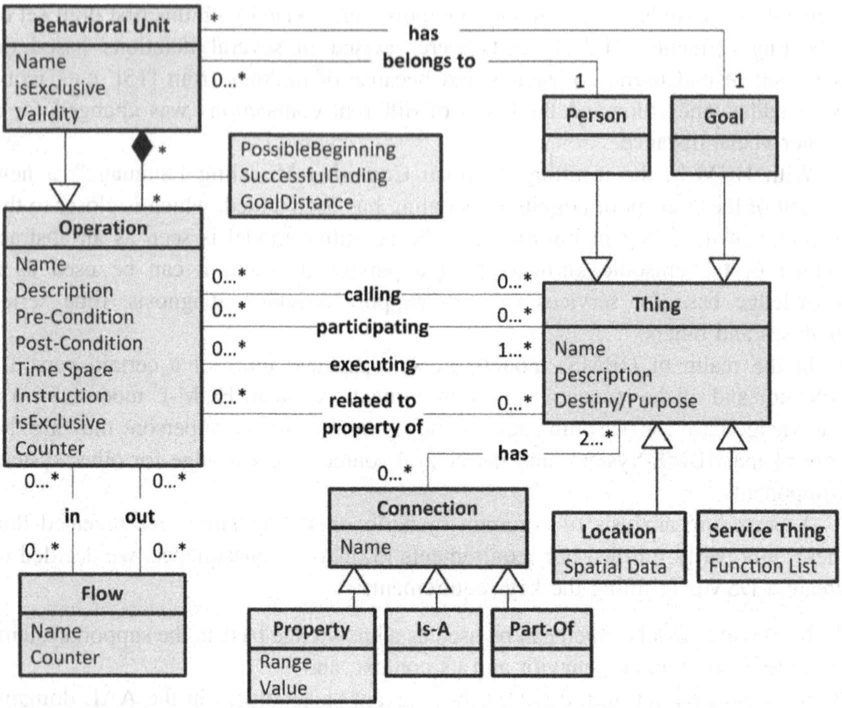

Fig. 5 HCM-L metamodel

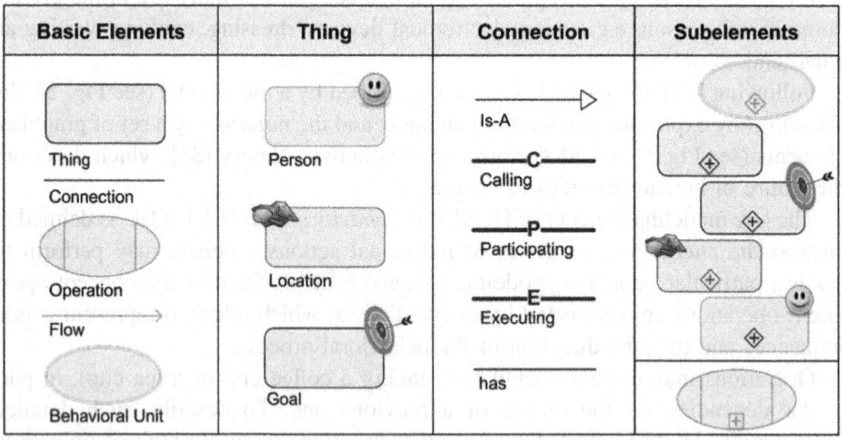

Fig. 6 Graphical notation of the HCM-L

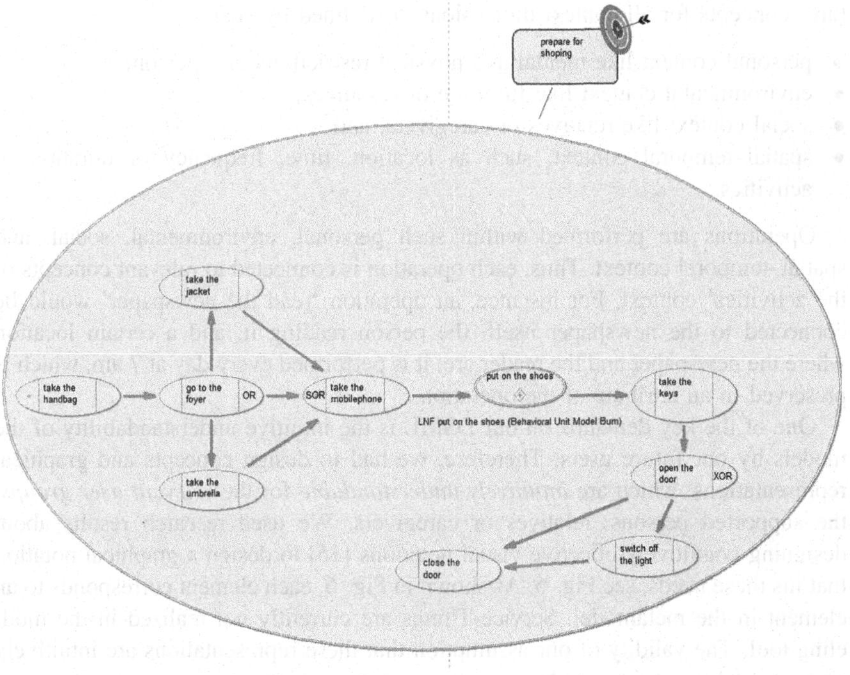

Fig. 7 Behavioral unit "prepare for shopping"

start from the same operation), and merges (i.e., several flows direct to the same operation), see Fig. 7. Consequently, modeling concepts are needed to describe the conditions that control the choice of the outgoing flow (and as such the correct sequencing) as well as the detailed instructions depending on the incoming flow. For this purpose, HCM-L features the concept of *Pre-* and *Post-Conditions*. Pre-Conditions define what conditions should be fulfilled before an operation is executed, and such may also influence the detailed instruction to be performed. Post-conditions define which operation should be executed as a next step, i.e., evaluate to a particular Flow. conditions may refer to values of attributes of things, related operations that have been successfully executed before, time constraints or combinations of all these. Pre- and post-conditions are formulated as logical expressions in infix-notation; except from their leading logical operator—AND, XOR, OR and SOR (synchronized or), see Fig. 7—they are not represented in the main graphical model but in notebooks related to each element and thus also to operations. This design decision reduced the semantic complexity of the graphical model. A formal language for defining more complex conditions and instructions was developed in the meanwhile and will be published separately.

To model the context in which daily human activities take place, HCM-L features concepts for all context dimensions, as defined by [13]:

- personal context like mental and physical restrictions of a person,
- environmental context like furniture or resources,
- social context like relatives or caregivers, and
- spatial–temporal context, such as location, time, frequency or duration of activities.

Operations are performed within such personal, environmental, social, and spatial–temporal context. Thus, each operation is connected to relevant concepts of the activities' context. For instance, an operation 'read the newspaper' would be connected to the newspaper itself, the person reading it, and a certain location where the newspaper and the reader are; it is performed every day at 7 am, which is preserved in an attribute of the operation.

One of the key demands on our DSML is the intuitive understandability of the models by our future users. Therefore, we had to design concepts and graphical representations, which are *intuitively understandable* for the *relevant user groups*: the supported persons, relatives or caregivers. We used research results about designing cognitively effective visual notations [15] to design a graphical notation that fits these needs, see Fig. 6. As shown in Fig. 6, each element corresponds to an element in the metamodel. Service-Things are currently not realized in the modeling tool. The validity of our assumption that these representations are intuitively understandable was proved by several experiments [34].

In accordance with activity theory, HCM-L observes the nature of human activities on different levels: (1) a BU as an overall process (represented by the BU symbol without content), (2) a BU with its operations and flows (represented by the BU symbol with content), and (3) a BU as a subtask, which means that a BU may inherit the properties of an operation (see Fig. 5), and, at the lowest level, (4) operations that realize actions [35]. Thus, it is possible to model the hierarchical structure of activities, which is one of the five principles of activity theory.

The element Operation-Makro (bottom right in Fig. 6) was introduced to summarize a sequence of operations without branches and merges by one model element. This helps in reducing the number of elements in a model and shortens the diagram. Thus, it supports human complexity management. In contrast to the other elements, the operation-Makro has no semantic meaning and no equivalent construct in the metamodel.

A *semantic analysis* of HCM-L [32] based on workflow patterns showed that it is—for the domain of ambient assistance—sufficiently powerful and fits the need of modeling human daily activities of one person better than general-purpose languages like BPMN or UML.

5 HCM-L Modeler, an ADO*xx*-Based Modeling Tool

HCM-L Modeler is a modeling tool for HCM-L including syntax, semantics and consistency support. It was developed using the metamodeling platform ADO*xx*, which implements the upper three layers of the OMG meta object facility (MOF).

ADO*xx* is a platform, which helps to build a full supported, professional and personalized modeling tool within a domain-specific application environment. It provides the possibility to develop syntax, semantic and graphical notations of any modeling concept based on different built-in functionalities. Furthermore, it features a scripting language that can be used to control the modeling elements, reference modes, consistency check, querying and many other functionalities. Additionally, it offers the execution and the coupling of external support modules that might be implemented using different programming languages, e.g., Java, R or C++.

HCM-L Modeler allows users to apply the HCM-L modeling concepts fast and easily. It controls the modeling process such that only syntactically correct models can be created. The models are displayed in such a manner that links to all related contexts proposed in HCM-L may be shown and checked.

HCM-L modeler can be used for different applications in the field of cognitive modeling and human behavior understanding. Figure 8 shows an overview of the HCM-L modeler functionality and file structure when modeling the BU of Fig. 7.

Figure 9 gives an impression of the context modeling screen, in particular "Maria's" context, elements of which are related to the operations in the BU "prepare for shopping" as shown in Fig. 7. We are aware that, given the layout rules for this volume, details are hardly readable.

We now shortly outline the major functionalities supported by HCM-L modeler; for details, see [34] or visit the handbook in [36].

Visualization Support All elements and relation classes can be connected in a flexible way. The breaking lines of elements names can be resized autonomously. This flexibility is an advantage in cases where visibility is required to make the model better readable by humans. Furthermore, the modeling area can be zoomed in and zoomed out, and the model navigator helps to track the location of the element in the drawing area.

Model Stepper The stepper animates the succession of operations (of the active model) and allows a stepwise pass through a behavioral unit based on users' decisions. This functionality is supported to step even within referenced sub-models. Basically, this is achieved by highlighting the visited operation. By tracking the operation flows, the stepper supports model understanding and validation. Currently, the stepper steps autonomously, if the operation has one outgoing flow, otherwise, the user gets a dialogue window which lets him choose the next path.

Autonomous Referencing Essentially, the tool creates reference models autonomously and does not allow redundant reference models. This feature supports consistency by helping users to create models without contradictions. Additionally, the attributes of each model element can be specified easily after clicking twice, using the mouse to explore the particular notebook. Various types of

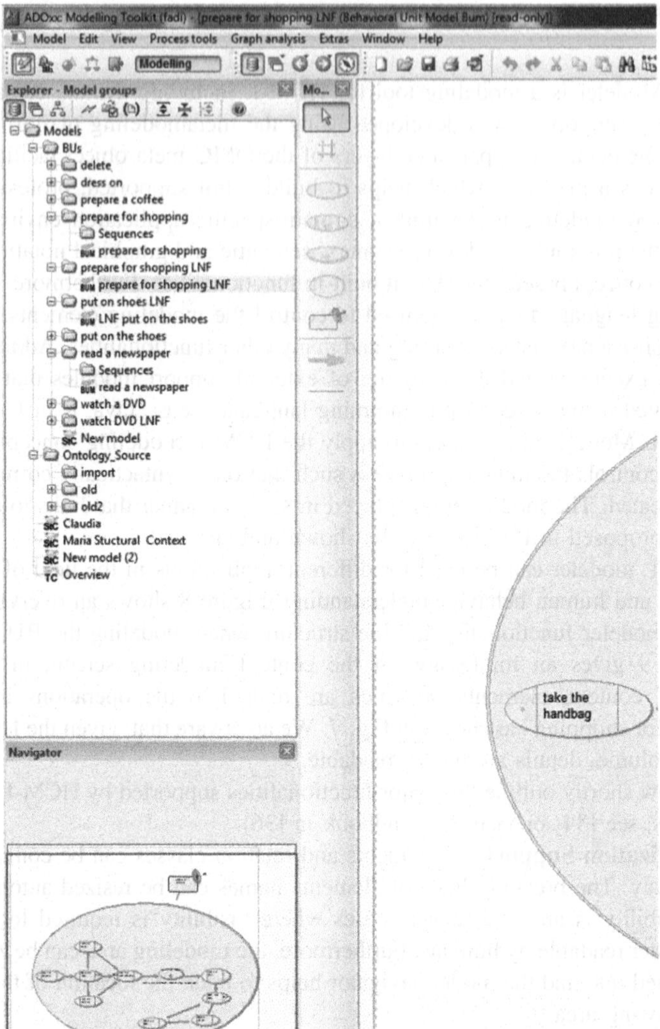

Fig. 8 HCM-L modeler screenshot with BU of Fig. 7

attributes may be added, e.g., enumeration lists, radio buttons, text fields, browse buttons. Autonomous referencing is supported also when adding a relation class, a reference model using the notebook.

Querying The AQL query language is a built-in querying language provided by the ADO*xx* platform. It allows querying models in a style similar to SQL. In ADO*xx*, queries can be pre-defined by the developer or may be formulated manually by a user. The current version of HCM-L modeler does support manual queries as shown in Fig. 10.

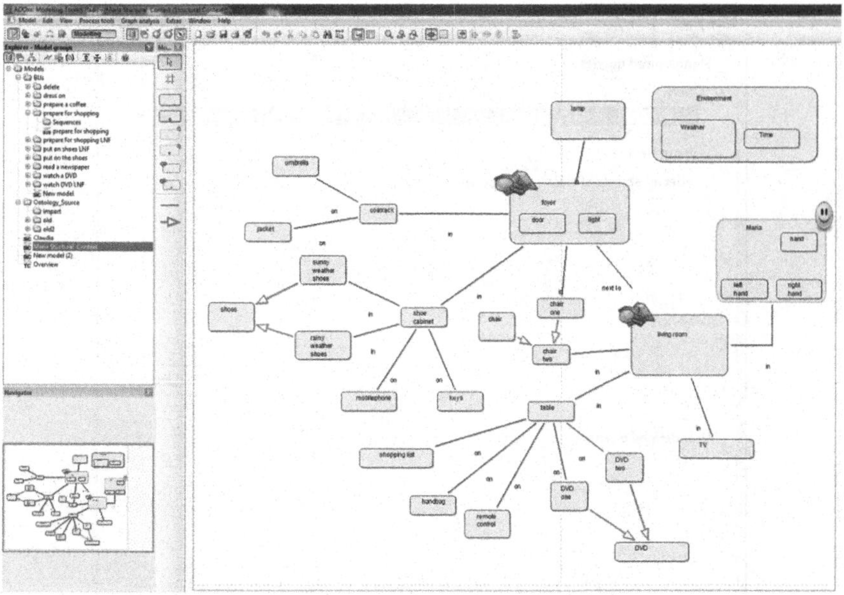

Fig. 9 Context modeling screen

Consistency check The HCM-L modeler is designed to be user-friendly for modelers in order to facilitate the development of correct models: no advanced modeling skills should be needed for creating HCM-L models on level M1. To extend the consistency check feature for particular needs, regular expressions can be added by an expert to control inputs into notebook fields.

Importing and exporting models ADO*xx* offers the possibility to import and export models in a generic XML format. This feature is adopted by HCM-L Modeler in order to allow transforming models to other formats like XML or OWL (implemented within the realm of the HBMS project), as used, for example, by inference or reasoning tools.

Reasoning Support Both model- and rule-based reasoning approaches for behavior modeling require the extraction of different features out of the given overall model. The HCM-L Modeler, among others, offers the possibility to calculate the frequency of specific activities based on the user history: every operation is supported by a percentage value. Furthermore, it delivers for every operation the smallest number of the remaining operations (i.e., operations to be executed) until reaching the current BU's goal, together with all possible paths leading to that goal and under consideration of all subunits.

Media Files HCM-L Modeler offers the possibility to upload media files (video, audio and images files in different formats) into the tool. This feature allows using such files for visualizing complex issues and situations in the support phase.

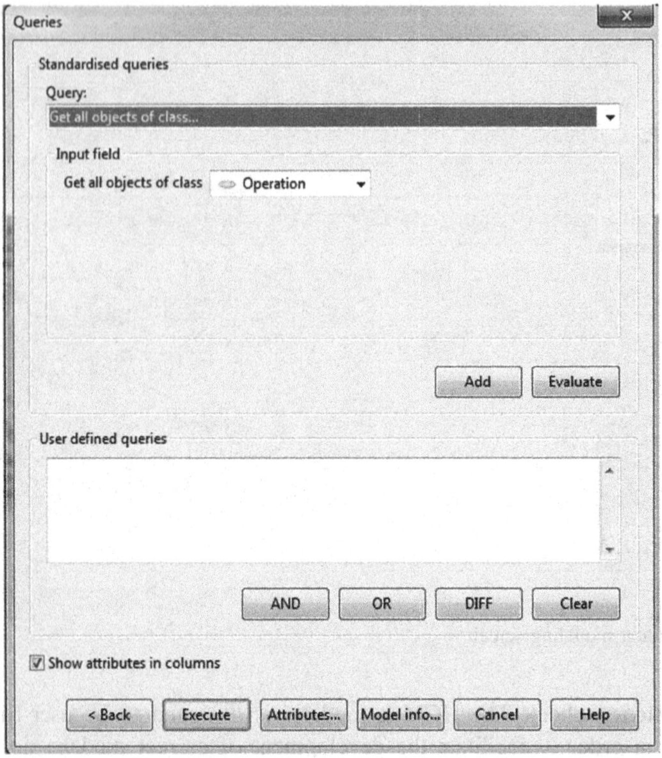

Fig. 10 Querying support in HCM-L modeler

To sum up, ADO*xx* proved to be an appropriate platform for implementing a HCM-L modeling tool. The HCM-L modeler is part of the HBMS system (see Fig. 4), and allows to feed manually created models into the knowledge base, as well as to visualize and analyze models that are automatically generated via activity recognition and the HBMS observation engine.

The next release of HCM-L modeler will provide an advanced rule support dialogue window, which will help the expert user to add rules correctly.

6 Putting Things Together: The HBMS Functionality

6.1 Coupling Activity Recognition Systems

Recent advances in computer science and engineering, electronics and sensor technologies have resulted in a significant progress in the field of designing and implementing activity recognition (AR) systems. Most of these systems are designed to fulfil specific goals, i.e., without the intention of integrating them into more comprehensive ambient assisted living (AAL) environments. Consequently, coupling arbitrary AR systems to HBMS is a challenging task, especially from the point of view of meeting user expectations, and guaranteeing the fulfilment of HBMS functional and non-functional goals continuously during lifetime.

Coupling AR systems, however, would come with many potential advantages [37]:

- Multiple AR systems provide redundancy to guarantee uninterrupted supply of human behavior information, even in case of the failure of one or several AR systems.
- As a rule, a single AR system can only provide a specific subset of observation or context data ("opening a cupboard", "watching TV"); in this case, coupling such AR systems together will enhance the provided coverage of the environment (e.g., spatial and geometrical coverage) as the information hidden from one system can be completed by the others.
- Integrating AR systems would increase the accuracy and confidence of observation by augmenting the observation data coming from one AR with the information obtained by the others, and by validating such data by comparing it to the data coming from other connected AR systems.
- Obtaining the information from coupled AR systems reduces the ambiguity of interpretations, and hence decreases the level of uncertainty in the data. This, in turn, improves object detection.

In general, the AR process consists of several steps: from raw sensor data collection to the activity recognition (Fig. 11). Initially, raw sensor data is collected and passed through the data pre-processing phase to remove the noise and the redundant data from the raw sensor stream. Then, the pre-processed data passes through the segmentation phase to identify the most useful segments of the data. These segmented data are used in the feature extracting phase to extract the main features of the data. The feature extraction phase is followed by a dimensionality reduction process to increase the accuracy of the features and to reduce the computational effort needed for feature classification. Finally, the selected feature sets are used for feature classification and for the recognition process [38].

The traditional activity recognition phases allow for identifying simple human activities. Modern AAL systems, however, require the recognition of more complex activities in order to be able to provide better support. However, identifying complex human activities is challenging. The current approach to solving this problem is augmenting the behavior data with context data of different kind, i.e., environmental, spatial, and temporal data, and trying to predict more complex human behavior patterns based on this integrated data.

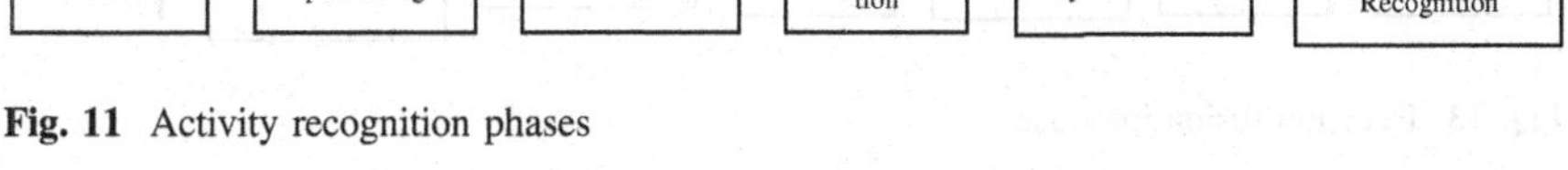

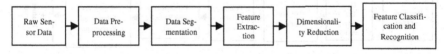

Fig. 11 Activity recognition phases

In order to retrieve more context data, AR systems need to process more sensor data coming from the environment. Most of these sensors provide different kinds of heterogeneous data. Consequently, introducing a common interface for importing and interpreting such data (AR system interface, see Fig. 4) is an essential task. Such interface should be capable of both, handling incoming heterogeneous data and transforming them to units that are processable by the observation engine. Therefore, within the HBMS framework, following the approach introduced in [39], a metamodel for a domain-specific graphical modeling language (AREM-L—Activity Recognition Environment Modeling Language) is under development. The AREM-L generic model and a site-specific AR system configuration are separated by means of an AR system workspace concept, which incorporates both, the generic model and the necessary configuration information.

There are several approaches to implement such AR system interface. First, the interface could be placed before the data pre-processing step, e.g., as a layer which collects raw sensor data from various heterogeneous sensor devices and converts it into a generic homogeneous data format prior to sending for pre-processing.

Second, the interface could be placed at the end of the chain of activity recognition phases (Fig. 12), e.g., as a layer which collects all simple events and context data recognized by the AR systems, and performs a data fusion process to identify complex human behavior activities out of the collected data.

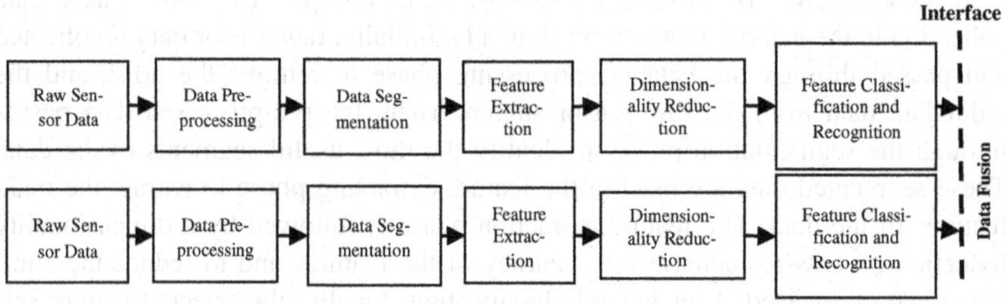

Fig. 12 AR system interface located after the (simple) activity recognition step

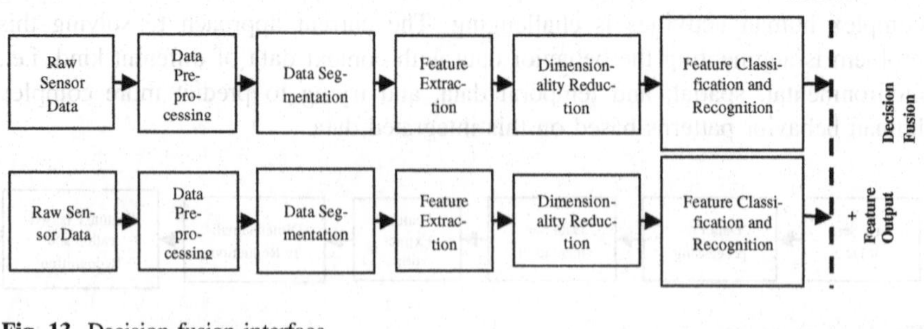

Fig. 13 Decision fusion interface

Third, the final output could be produced by combining several decision support methodologies involving experts (such as voting, fuzzy logic, and statistical methods) to enhance the prediction accuracy (see Fig. 13) [37].

In the HBMS system, we combine the second and the third approach: Coupled AR systems are supplying their pre-processed sensor data; these are transformed in compliance with our AR system integration interface such that both behavior and state context data form HCM-compliant data structures.

6.2 Model-Based Reasoning

Model-based reasoning refers to an inference approach which is applied to a domain-specific model. The major step in model based reasoning is to create first the model, and then, at run-time, run a "smart engine" which combines the knowledge that is provided by the model and the observed sensor data to derive conclusions such as a diagnosis or a prediction.

In the HBMS system, this knowledge and the imported activity recognition data are represented as instances of an HCM-L model. Two reasoning modules work with this data, *prediction module*, and the *rule-based reasoning module*. The *prediction module* is used to find the most likely next operation, when the user stops and does not perform any new operation, or when the currently "running" Behavioral Unit has to be determined. The *rule based reasoning module* is used to find the operation the observed person actually is performing, and to identify the BUs the operation is part of.

The Prediction Module In smart home environments, it is common that different activities share many similar or identical sensors. As an example, the prepare-a-meal and prepare-a-drink activities share simple events like enter the kitchen, open the cupboard and open the fridge. Thus, such situations form a kind of uncertainty which causes poor or bad decisions.

Therefore, the prediction module is needed to predict (1) what the current BU is and/or (2) to predict what the next possible operation is when the model contains more than one possible flow from the current operation.

The key point of our reasoning module is to specify a reasonable window size which is based on the optimal N sensors of the provided environment. Choosing optimal sensors is based on processing the training data using an SVM classifier [40]. In this approach, attributes are ranked by the square of the weight assigned by the SVM. Attribute selection for multiclass problems is processed by ranking attributes for each class separately using a one-vs-all technique and then "dealing" from the top of each pile to give a final ranking [40], i.e., in HBMS: the optimal number of sensors that best characterize this activity.

For (1), after having determined the optimal sensors, the sensor data are collected until the optimal sensors of one activity are activated. As soon as this happens, the following three steps are applied: (a) the assignment of priority levels to sensors, (b) the adjustment of sensors belief and (c) the evidence combination of optimal sensors beliefs using an advanced version of Dempster–Shafer rule that delivers logical results even in the presence of high conflicting data [41]. The evidence combination is performed with respect to the ordered set of sensors priorities that are provided using the optimization capabilities of answer set programming.

For (2) the same mechanism is applied but using the reasoning attributes of the current operation. Thus, we have an optimization problem to be solved based on three priority measures: (1) the importance of performing an operation according to the user history; (2) the cost value of choosing an operation based on the similarity between the current user profile and other users; (3) the time when the operation should be performed [42].

The Rule-based reasoning module Another situation where reasoning is needed is to query the HCM-L model with respect to the logical expressions in the pre- and post-condition slots of each operation. As an example, think of the condition that a specific medicine has to be taken 30 min before breakfast.

SPARQL Inferencing Notation (SPIN) [43] has been selected for being used in HBMS for reasoning in such situations. SPIN supports inferencing over Ontology Web Language (OWL) texts, and as such offers a way to define and to apply constraint checking under closed world semantics and to automatically retrieve the appropriate answer from the sent queries with respect to those constraints. The advantages of SPIN are as follows: (a) it stores SPARQL queries with the model, (b) constraints can be natively executed, (c) it uses a simple form of backward chaining, and (d) it allows for computing sub-queries on demand.

As a result, the HBMS system, by combining optimization and rule-based methods, offers powerful reasoning even under uncertainty.

6.3 End-User Interaction

The main idea of the HBMS project is to support people in performing daily activities when cognitive functions, such as memory, are decreasing. Thus, after having recognized what a person is doing or not, and after having determined whether some advice is necessary, and if so, the best fitting advice has to be communicated to the person. Consequently, the challenge was to select devices (e.g., smart phone, tablet, audio and video devices, others) and to develop user-interfaces that older people can use intuitively and independently.

In a first prototype implementation, Microsoft ASP.NET MVC 3 framework and Microsoft Visual Studio 2013 as IDE was chosen for implementing an interface for tablets and smart phones. In addition to default libraries and packages of ASP.NET MVC 3, many other free and open sources JavaScript libraries such as jQuery

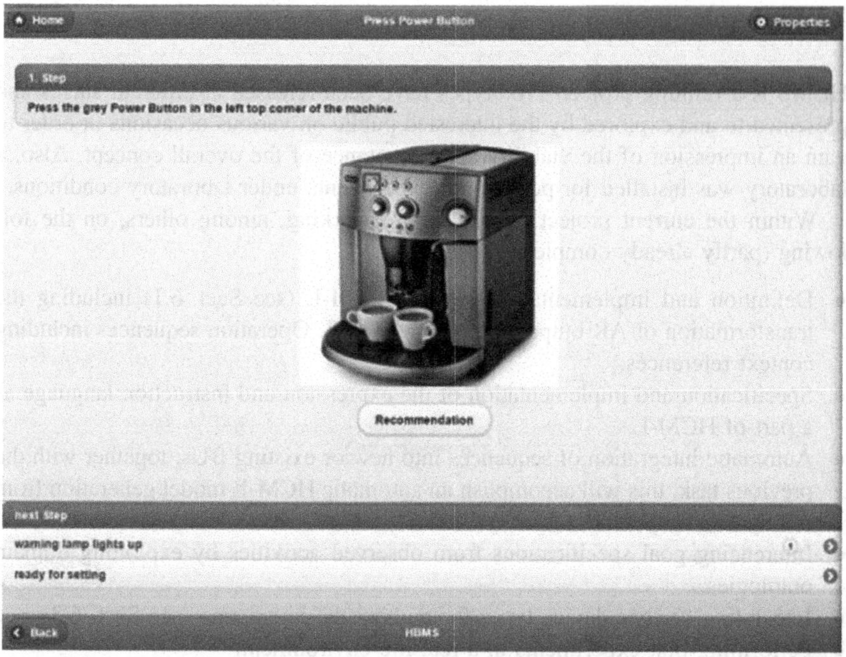

Fig. 14 HBMS interface prototype 1 (obviously, font sizes may be adjusted)

Mobile, jQuery mobile UI [44] and Ajax were used. The main reason for choosing ASP.NET MVC 3 framework was its MVC-based (model-view-controller) pattern and object-oriented aspect of C# programming language, which makes it reasonably easy to build standard and scalable Web applications based on the MVC paradigm. By employing jQuery Mobile components, it was possible to achieve an optimal adjustment to the *"Designing User Interfaces for Older Adults"* challenge, without impacting the functionality. In order to ensure independence from the system environment with regard to databases, the Open Source Persistence ORM Framework NHibernate was used, which is compatible with virtually all relational-database systems. This means that the HBMS-web application can easily be integrated into and used within any relational-system-environment.

Figure 14 shows a typical HBMS prototype support screen. The navigation buttons ("Home", "Back") are located on the top/bottom of the screen. In the middle, a short textual description of the current action with a picture or video is shown. Above the bottom, the possible next steps are listed. When pushing the recommendation button, short pieces of advice are presented in a frame at left-hand side.

In the current project phase, in addition to further development (e.g., improved interaction and multimodal-interface based on Web 2.0) of the existing prototype, we are going to support the output via a voice-command-system, using autonomous robots (e.g., Nao, Pepper [45]), that, in addition, can be used for sending sensor and camera data for activity recognition.

7 Outlook

HBMS is a running project. Prototypes have been released at different stages and presented to and explored by the interested public on various occasions in order to gain an impression of the viability and acceptance of the overall concept. Also, a laboratory was installed for performing experiments under laboratory conditions.

Within the current project phase, we are working, among others, on the following (partly already completed) tasks:

- Definition and implementation of the AREM-L (see Sect. 6.1) including the transformation of AR output streams to HCM-L Operation sequences including context references,
- Specification and implementation of the expression and instruction language as a part of HCM-L,
- Automatic integration of sequences into new or existing BUs; together with the previous task, this will accomplish an automatic HCM-L model generation from AR system outputs,
- Inferencing goal specifications from observed activities by exploiting domain ontologies,
- Integrating various device types for multimodal interaction (see Sect. 6.3),
- Performing first experiments in a real life environment.

We are aware of the fact that there is still a long way to go for having available a HBMS "mass product" which features all necessary means for activity recognition, is easy to roll-out and can be distributed at an affordable price. Nevertheless, we are optimistic and confident that we are on the right track.

Tool Download http://www.omilab.org/hcml.

References

1. Feller, W.: On the logistic law of growth and its empirical verifications in biology. Acta. Biotheor. **5**(2), 51–66 (1940)
2. UML 2.5 Diagrams Overview. http://www.uml-diagrams.org/uml-25-diagrams.html. Accessed 12 Mar 2016
3. ACTIVE AND ASSISTED LIVING PROGRAMME—ICT for ageing well. http://www.aal-europe.eu/. Accessed 12 Mar 2016
4. Michael, J., Mayr, H.C.: Creating a Domain Specific Modelling Method for Ambient Assistance. In: International Conference on Advances in ICT for Emerging Regions (ICTer2015). IEEE (2015)
5. International Organization for Standardization: Information Technology—Information Resource Dictionary System (IRDS) framework. ISO/IEC 10027:1990
6. Object Management Group: Meta Object Facility (MOF) Specification. www.omg.org/cgi-bin/doc/?formal/02-04-03.pdf. Accessed 12 Mar 2016
7. Atkinson, C., Kühne, T.: Model-driven development: a metamodelling foundation. IEEE Softw. **20**(5), 36–41 (2003)

8. Bézivin, J.: On the unification power of models. Softw. Syst. Model., **4**(2), 171–188 (2005)
9. Frank, U.: Domain-specific modelling languages: requirements analysis and design guidelines. In: Reinhartz-Berger, I., Sturm, A., Clark, T., Cohen, S., Bettin, J. (eds.) Domain Engineering, pp. 133–157. Springer (2013)
10. Frank, U.: Outline of a method for designing domain-specific modelling languages. ICB-Research Report 42. University Duisburg-Essen (2010)
11. Karagiannis, D., Kühn, H.: Metamodelling platforms. In: Bauknecht, K., Tjoa, A.M., Quirchmayr, G. (eds.) E-Commerce and Web Technologies. LNCS, pp. 182–197. Springer (2002)
12. Tolvanen, J.-P., Kelly, S.: Defining domain-specific modelling languages to automate product derivation: collected experiences. In: Hutchison, D., et al. (eds.) Software Product Lines, pp. 198–209. Springer (2005)
13. Kofod-Petersen, A., Mikalsen, M.: Context: representation and reasoning. Spec. Issue Rev. d'Intell. Artif. "Appl. Context-Manag." (2005)
14. Bettini, C., Brdiczka, O., Henricksen, K., Indulska, J., Nicklas, D., Ranganathan, A., Riboni, D.: A survey of context modelling and reasoning techniques. Pervasive Mob. Comput. **6**(2), 161–180 (2010)
15. Moody, D.L.: The "physics" of notations: toward a scientific basis for constructing visual notations in software engineering. IEEE Trans. Softw. Eng. **35**(6), 756–779 (2009)
16. Caire, P., Genon, N., Heymans, P., Moody, D.L.: Visual notation design 2.0: towards user comprehensible requirements engineering notations. In: IEEE 21st International Requirements Engineering Conference (RE), pp. 115–124 (2013)
17. Kaschek, R., Mayr, H.C.: A characterization of OOA tools. In: IEEE International Symposium on Assessment of Software Tools, pp. 59–67 (1996)
18. Becker, J.: Die Grundsätze ordnungsmäßiger Modelierung und ihre Einbettung in ein Vorgehensmodel zur Erstellung betrieblicher Informationsmodele. Informationssystem-Architekturen, Rundbrief des Fachausschusses 5.2 der Gesellschaft für Informatik **5**(2), 56–62 (1998)
19. Steinberg, D.: EMF Eclipse Modelling Framework. The Eclipse Series. Addison-Wesley, Upper Saddle River, NJ (2009)
20. Krogstie, J., Lindland, O.I., Sindre, G.: Defining Quality Aspects for Conceptual Models. Chapman & Hall, London (1995)
21. Batini, C., Ceri, S., Navathe, S.B.: Conceptual Database Design. An Entity-Relationship Approach. The Benjamin/Cummings Series in Computer Science. Benjamin/Cummings, Redwood City, Calif (1991)
22. van der Aalst, W., ter Hofstede, A., Kiepuszewski, B., Barros, A.: Workflow patterns. Distrib. Parallel Databases **14**(1), 5–51 (2003)
23. United Nations Population Division, World Population Prospects, the 2012 Revision, Indicator Population 60+, World, medium variant. http://esa.un.org/wpp/unpp/panel_indicators.htm. Accessed 12 Mar 2016
24. United Nations, Department of Economic and Social Affairs, Population Division. World Population Ageing 2013. ST/ESA/SER.A/348 (2013)
25. Michael, J.: Using Cognitive Models for Behavioural Assistance of Humans. In: it—Information Technology, de Gruyter. Accepted 2 Dec 2015
26. Cohen, P.R., Feigenbaum, E.A.: The Handbook of Artificial Intelligence. William Kaufmann, Inc. (1982)
27. Newell, A., Simon, H.A.: Human Problem Solving. Prentice-Hall, Englewood Cliffs, N. J. (1972)
28. Schmalhofer, F.: Constructive Knowledge Acquisition: A Computational Model and Experimental Evaluation, Lawrence Erlbaum Associates (2001)
29. Ferro, E, Girolami, M., Salvi, D., Mayer, C., Gorman, J., Grguric, A., Ram, R., Sadat, R., Giannoutakis, K.M., Stocklöw, C.: The UniversAAL Platform for AAL (Ambient Assisted Living). J. Intell. Syst. (2015)

30. Kop, C., Mayr, H.C.: Conceptual predesign bridging the gap between requirements and conceptual design. In: Proceedings of the 3rd International Conference on Requirements Engineering (ICRE'98), Colorado Springs, April 1998, pp 90–100 (1998)
31. Mayr, H.C., Kop, C.: A user centered approach to requirements modelling. In: Glinz, M., Müller-Luschnat, G. (Hrsg.): Modelierung 2002—Modelierung in der Praxis—Modelierung für die Praxis, pp 75–86 (2002)
32. Mayr, H.C., Michael, J.: Control pattern based analysis of HCM-L, a language for cognitive modelling. In: International Conference on Advances in ICT for Emerging Regions (ICTer2012), pp. 169–175. IEEE (2012)
33. Leont'ev, A.N.: Activity, Consciousness, and Personality. Prentice-Hall, Englewood Cliffs, NJ (1978)
34. Michael, J., Al Machot, F.; Mayr, H.C.: ADOxx based tool support for a behaviour centered modelling approach. In: Proceedings of 8th International Conference on Pervasive Technologies Related to Assistive Environments PETRA 2015. ACM Digital Library Proceedings (2015)
35. Michael, J., Mayr, H.C.: Conceptual modelling for ambient assistance. In: Proceedings of 32nd International Conference on Conceptual Modelling—ER 2013. LNCS, vol. 8217, pp. 403–413. Springer, Berlin/Heidelberg (2013)
36. OMiLAB: HCM-L download. http://www.omilab.org/web/hcm-l/download
37. Raol, J.R.: Multi-Sensor Data Fusion with MATLAB®. CRC Press (2009)
38. Krishnan, N., et al.: Recognition of hand movements using wearable accelerometers. JAISE **1** (2), 143–155 (2009)
39. Shekhovtsov, V.A., Mayr, H.C., Kop, C.: Facilitating effective stakeholder communication in software development processes. In: Nurcan, S., Pimenidis, E. (eds.) Information Systems Engineering in Complex Environments. LNBIP, vol. 204, pp 116–132. Springer (2015)
40. Guyon, I., Weston, J., Barnhill, S., Vapnik, V.: Gene selection for cancer classification using support vector machines. Mach. Learn. **46**(1-3), 389–422 (2002)
41. Ali, T., Dutta, P., Boruah, H.: A new combination rule for conflict problem of Dempster-Shafer evidence theory. Int. J.Energ. Inf. Commun. **3**(1), 35–40 (2010)
42. Al Machot, F., Mayr, H.C., Michael, J.: Behaviour modelling and reasoning for ambient support: HCM-L modeller. In: Modern Advances in Applied Intelligence, pp. 388–397. Springer International Publishing (2014)
43. Fürber, C., Hepp, M.: Using sparql and spin for data quality management on the semantic web. In: Business Information Systems. Springer Berlin Heidelberg (2010)
44. jQuery Mobile UI: https://jquerymobile.com/, accessed December 25, 2015
45. https://www.aldebaran.com/en. Accessed 25 Dec 2015

Part XII
Technology Enhanced Learning

Modeling Learning Data for Feedback and Assessment

Peter Reimann and Wilfrid Utz

Abstract This chapter describes the application of metamodeling concepts to the case of modeling formative assessment methods and their deployment. It builds on Evidence-Centred Assessment Design (ECD) as the approach to conceptualizing the process of assessment design. We describe how we extended ECD by expressing its logic with concepts from metamodeling, and how we developed tool support for the modeling as well as the deployment step in the context of the NEXT-TELL project: the ADVISOR modeling toolkit. To illustrate how this platform-independent approach to assessment design can be utilized to address typical assessment challenges, examples from language learning are provided.

Keywords Assessment • Formative assessment • Assessment design • Metamodeling • e-Learning

1 Introduction

The trend to data-informed decision-making in education has now reached the classroom and lecture room level. Data are no longer entering into the decision-making process only at the level of policy-making—taking the form of research studies and large-scale testing analyses—but are becoming part and parcel of educators' everyday decision-making [1]. On the level of schools, this new use of data takes essentially two forms. First, as a tool in the hand of teachers, data on students' learning are used to provide information on their current learning (feedback) and guide their future learning (feedforward). Second, data on students'

P. Reimann (✉)
Faculty of Education and Social Work, The University of Sydney,
Sydney, NSW 2006, Australia

W. Utz
Research Group Knowledge Engineering, University of Vienna,
1090 Vienna, Austria
e-mail: wilfrid.utz@univie.ac.at

D. Karagiannis et al. (eds.), *Domain-Specific Conceptual Modeling*,
DOI 10.1007/978-3-319-39417-6_25

learning, and more generally on their experience and well-being, are getting used to inform school management about where their school as a whole stands with respect to reaching its goals [2]. Relevant research areas for these two kinds of data are research on formative assessment and data-driven decision making, respectively.

Formative assessment is a vital element of the pedagogical repertoire for preparing twenty-first century students. Shute [3] argues that, in formative assessment, the results of a learner's activities are frequently evaluated with the aim of adjusting or improving instruction (teacher) and learning (student). Hence, formative assessment requires an authentic context, data collected from multiple sources (such as portfolios, self-appraisals, presentations, etc.), and global and specific diagnosis aimed at providing helpful feedback Cowie and Bell, [4] define formative assessment as a bidirectional process between teacher and student to enhance, recognize, and respond to the learning. Formative assessment is considered a promising approach to enable twenty-first century teaching since it potentially promotes self-reflection and self-directed learning processes and, more importantly, it facilitates the integration of new subject-specific knowledge into the student's existing knowledge network. It also helps the teacher adapt the educational processes to the individual needs and, therefore, making formal education more effective and also more enjoyable.

Data-driven decision making (DDDM) pertains to the "systematic collection, analysis, examination, and interpretation of data to inform practice and policy in educational settings" [5]. As such, it includes summative and formative assessment and testing, and other forms of achievement data, but goes beyond achievement data by including in principle all data available to the educational system, such as attendance records, information on socioeconomic background, and all data on students' learning, such as log files from learning management systems [6]. DDDM is not a new concept, since teachers have always used observations on students' behavior and their performance on assignments to inform their decision-making, and policy makers and educators have been debating the use of high-stakes testing data for decades [7]. What is new, predominantly for schools, is that now data—all kinds of data—can be systematically gathered, and that now a good part of the process can be automatized.

The trend to data use in schools was propelled in the US by The No Child Left Behind Act [8], which required schools to provide stringent evidence for their students' achievement in key curriculum areas. While this was largely a compliance measure, with a focus on high-stakes testing for achievement standards, over the years a fundamental shift has been taking place, from data for compliance to the principle of data for continuous improvement. Following this principle, "...data would be used to stimulate and inform continuous improvement, providing a foundation for educators to examine multiple sources of data and align appropriate instructional strategies with the needs of individual students" [5].

The goal to make data useful for individual students necessitates a greater awareness of teachers regarding the potentials and limitations of specific data types in the educational process, and requires new organizational capacities for training teachers [9] and for creating and maintaining the right kind of data [10], with data

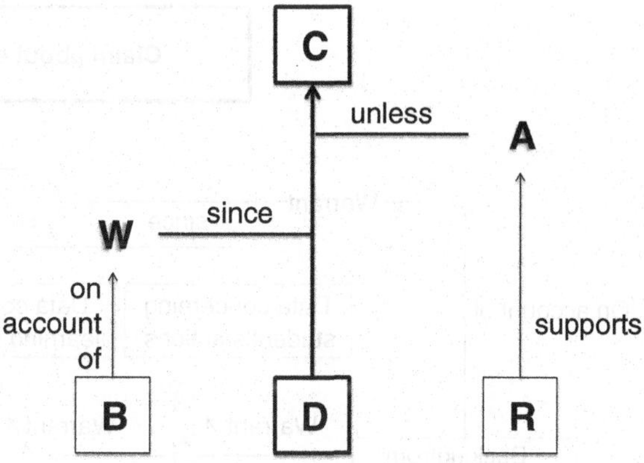

Fig. 1 Toulmin's structure of arguments

for formative assessment playing a key role [11]. This chapter contributes to solutions for these two challenges by suggesting a general method for developing school- and classroom-level diagnostic tools that capture students' learning. The next section will delineate the method, followed by a description of a prototype technical realization based on principles of metamodeling [12], further refined and elaborated in [13].

2 Method Description: ECAAD

ECAAD stands for Evidence-Centred Assessment and Activity Design. It is a method for evidentiary reasoning with educational data that builds on and generalizes the Evidence-Centred Design method suggested in [14]. The development from Evidence-Centred Assessment Design (ECD) to ECAAD was part of the EU-funded project NEXT-TELL[1] [15, 16].

2.1 Evolution of ECAAD

Like ECD, ECAAD takes the Toulmin model of evidentiary argumentation as fundamental. This model can be applied not only to educational assessment, but to reasoning with data in general [17]. In this model (see Fig. 1), reasoning flows from data (D) to claims (C) via justification of a warrant (W), which is in turn supported by a backing (B). The inference from data, or evidence, to claims, may need to be

[1]Project details available online at www.next-tell.eu.

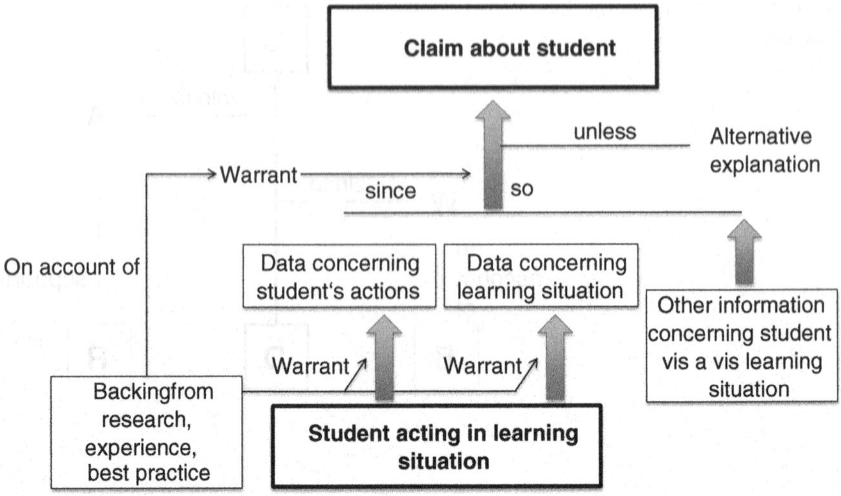

Fig. 2 Assessment as evidentiary argumentation

qualified by alternative explanations (A), which may be based on rebuttal evidence (R) to support them.

Arguments are important for any kind of data analysis since they turns information into knowledge. Data consist of observations of aspects of the world. Observations may be accurate or inaccurate, useful or useless, helpful or unhelpful. To make such qualifications, and to move from observation to action, data need to be turned into knowledge, by making them part of an argument.

It is important to keep in mind that statistical methods alone can never conclusively establish the validity of a claim. Hence, conclusions are never fully justified by "the facts" (evidence) alone. While statistical methods can help us identify which relations exist in a body of data, and how likely those are to be due to chance, more is needed to make the point that these relations have any bearing on the claim. Establishing the warrant is, therefore, essential, but goes beyond mathematical data analysis. This step requires judgment, and consideration for what is known in addition to the data under study, such as former/other research findings.

ECAAD is primarily concerned with applying this argumentation model to assessment, and more generally to diagnostic inferences. Assessment arguments[2] take the form of claims about students' knowledge, skills, competences, aptitudes, etc., grounded in observations on students' behavior, warranted by theories of learning, development, motivation, etc. [14], see Fig. 2. Evidence takes the form of systematic observations on students' performance (e.g., when playing an

[2]From here on, we use "assessment" in a broad sense, and make no distinction to "diagnosis". While diagnosis is the more accurate term, we will not use it because we want to avoid any connotations with 'disease'.

instrument) and work products (e.g., problem solutions, essays, sketches, media artefacts), while warrants provide justifications for drawing inferences (claims) from such observations. A warrant can take for example the form of a research study that has established a relation between particular performance and particular skills (the latent construct; assessment claims are typically about latent constructs: skills, knowledge, aptitudes, motivational dispositions, learning styles, etc.).

Applied to assessment, the general processes of getting from observations on students (test) performance to claims about their knowledge, skills, and abilities (KSAs) requires from the assessment designer to specify (a) a task model (what the student will do), (b) an evidence model (what aspects of the student performance are relevant for assessment), and (c) a student model (how the evidence is to be transformed and combined to yield a value for a KSA element). As shown in Fig. 3, while the assessment planning task progresses from information needs (what do we need to know about the student?) to the task model level, the assessment process itself works in the reverse direction.

Based on this general idea, ECD has been further developed [18, 19] into a model for producing assessment tasks in a systematic manner, making explicit all the steps from domain analysis to the specification of values in the student model. This methodology comprises four steps and is supported by a number of artefact types (domain analysis map, design patterns, task templates, as shown in Fig. 4). We will now shortly introduce the main model types that ECD comprises: domain model, student, evidence and task model, and finally the delivery model.

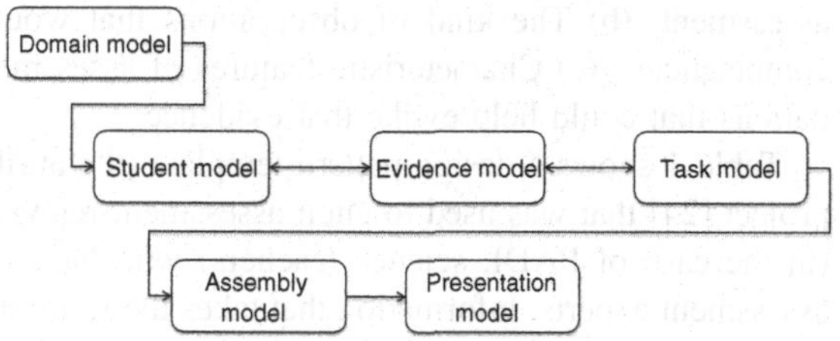

Fig. 3 Models and steps in assessment design

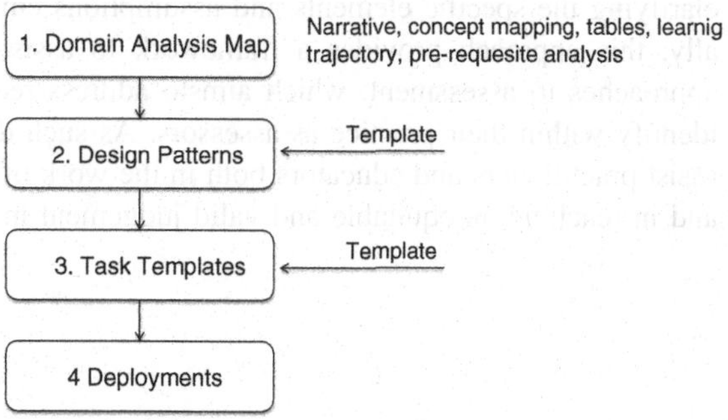

Fig. 4 The ECD assessment development process

2.2 Domain Modeling

Domain modeling comprises the analysis of the learning domain and the articulation of the assessment argument structure [19]. The result of these two steps is the domain model, which can be expressed for instance in the form of design patterns. With domain modeling, the goal is to identify the psychological structure of the competences that are targeted for assessment. As such, domain analysis is similar to instructional analysis, or task analysis, because a clear description of competences is also important when planning instruction [20].

Domain modeling in ECD means essentially to build the assessment argument as visualized in Fig. 2. One way to represent the information in the assessment argument is to formulate this as a design pattern.

Design patterns have received much interest in instructional design circles [21] as a means to extract and represent practitioners' solutions to problems arising in their area of practice. As first suggested in architecture [22], a pattern describes an effective solution to a recurrent problem embedded in a specific context. In education, where the solution takes the form of an instructional (or pedagogical) design, we speak of design patterns. A design pattern is a specifically structured document, usually kept in digital format.

In the context of assessment design, design patterns can be used to lay out the chain of reasoning from evidence to inference of students' professional capacities; they function as "assessment stories", linking together the three most important elements of the assessment argument [23]: (a) The competencies (perhaps further broken down into knowledge, skills, and abilities - KSAs) that are the focus of the assessment; (b) The kind of observations that would provide evidence of those competencies; (c) Characteristic features of assessment strategies and types of situations that could help evoke that evidence.

Table 1 shows a design pattern template (the attributes) developed in the PADI project [24] that was used to elicit assessment-relevant information from educators (in the case of PADI, science teachers) who have domain expertize, but are not assessment experts. Information that takes the form of such a pattern can be used by professional assessment developers to move to a description of the assessment in the form of models as mentioned above, and to implementations.

Design Pattern work can guide analysis of existing assessment practices by clarifying the specific elements and assumptions embedded in practice. Additionally, this approach provides a framework to assist in the development of new approaches to assessment, which aimsto address recurrent problems practitioners identify within their practice as assessors. As such design patterns can potentially assist practitioners and educators both in the work of guiding professional learning and in reaching an equitable and valid judgement in specific assessment contexts.

Table 1 Design pattern attributes [after 24]

Attribute	Value(s)
Rationale	Explanation why this component is an important aspect of the competence assessed
Focal knowledge, skills, and abilities	The primary KSAs targeted by the patterns
Additional knowledge, skills, and abilities	Other KSAs that may be required by this pattern
Potential observations	Some possible things one could see students doing that would give evidence about the KSAs
Potential work products	Some possible modes, like a written product or answer, in which students might produce evidence about the KSAs
Characteristic features	Aspects of the assessment situation that are likely to evoke the desired behavior
Variable features	Aspects of assessment situations that can be varied in order to shift difficulty or focus

2.3 Student, Evidence, and Task Modeling

Student model: In the case of dedicated assessment development, the process usually starts from the student model—from the question of what needs assessing and the nature of the constructs to be assessed. Like learning environments, assessment environments should be informed by knowledge about the nature of the knowledge to be acquired, and the nature of learning. Student models can take many forms, from single values to probabilistic representations, rule representations, to mention just a few [14].

Evidence Model: An evidence model describes which behaviors provide diagnostic information for the sought student attributes, and how to transform the information on behavior to "values" in the student model. Creating an evidence model involves answering three questions: (i) What observations we have on students count as evidence? (ii) How to evaluate students' work products? (iii) How to update the student model based on (usually multiple) evaluations? The effort that goes into formulating evidence models for psychometric tests like the GRE is very extensive since it is not "evident" how a high-level latent construct such as "Analytic Writing" can be identified by looking at students' behavior. Hence, the extensive methodological concern for test construction in the psychometric tradition almost exclusively focuses on item construction, i.e., the evidence model [25].

Task Model: The task model describes the concrete student behaviors to record and the context in which these are elicited. For psychometric tests, this is usually a more or less simple rendering of an item, either on paper—or, increasingly, on computer screens—with very limited (re-)action options for the student: Mark/do not mark an option in a multiple choice item, for instance. For authentic assessment, the task environment tends to be considerably more complex, and extensive.

2.4 Delivery: Assembly and Presentation Modeling

While the model types introduced so far are conceptual in nature, the final part of ECD comprises the modeling of assessment delivery. This includes specifying the runtime behavior of a digital assessment environment that can either be a stand-alone component (computer-based assessment tool) or be integrated into a learning management system or virtual learning environment [26].

2.5 ECAAD: Evidence-Centred Activity and Assessment Design

The ECAAD method as developed in NEXT-TELL generalizes the ECD method in a number of ways. The most important generalization is to not limit the method to summative assessment; formative assessment, in order to be rigorous, also needs to be based on an explicated method. In general, any appraisal, including self- and peer-assessment, should be grounded in sound methods. A further generalization concerns the content and form of the student model: it should be open and allow to represent structural qualitative information about a student as well as allow to represent aspects of students besides knowledge and skill: values, epistemic orientations, emotional relations to subject matter for instance. Thirdly, the evidence-based needs to be widened: ECAAD allows incorporating evidence not only from assessment tasks (as ECD does), but relate to learning and work performance and products in a more general sense, thus allowing the inclusion of evidence from e-portfolios (product focus) and log files that capture students' use of learning software/software used for learning (process focus). Fourthly, the generalized method can be applied to learning in areas other than science, namely language (English as a first/as a foreign language) learning. Finally, the ECAAD method can be used as a basis for communication and negotiation with stakeholders and as a basis for teachers' professional learning—learning about students' learning.

3 Method Conceptualization: ECAAD in NEXT-TELL

The conceptualization of the modeling method is based upon the modeling procedure—the way a user of the method applies it, runs through design phases, performs planning tasks and produces result artefacts as a basis for human interpretation/knowledge sharing and machine interpretation, using the artefacts as configuration items for arbitrary learning management systems (LMS).

The method implementation results in the ADVISOR Toolkit, providing IT-support for certain aspects of the modeling procedure. The interaction concept realizes the inclusion of experts from different domains to collaborate seamlessly (see Fig. 5).

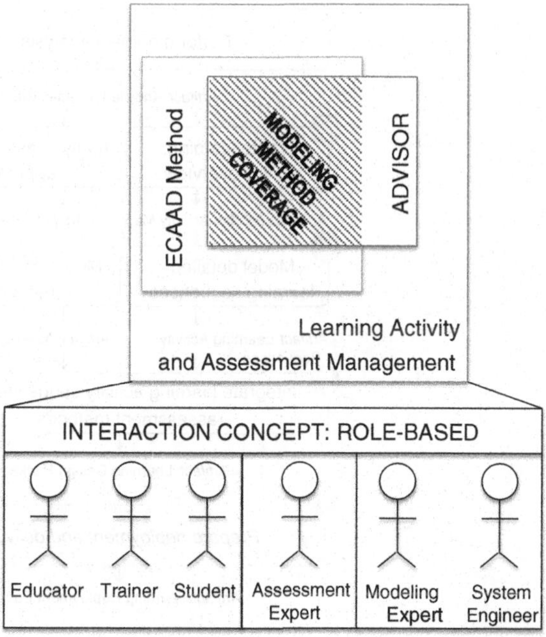

Fig. 5 ECAAD modeling method and ADVISOR tool support

The generic procedure model, as illustrated below in Fig. 6 identifies the main steps and related artefacts to design a course according to ECAAD, starting at the domain/knowledge state analysis to deployable packages as an outcome of the procedure. The method is positioned on the design level, therefore aims to be platform (e.g., LMS) independent as well as (assessment) method independent; applying the method in varying learning settings (school, higher education or organizational) and for different purposes (knowledge externalization, re-use of pedagogical practices rather than learning objects) becomes possible (Fig. 7).

3.1 Modeling Procedure

The tasks and results of the modeling procedure are shown in Fig. 6.

1. **Perform domain analysis**: During domain analysis (conducted by teachers and students alike), learning goals (which would typically come from a curriculum plan) describing student competencies are analyzed and set in relation to prerequisite knowledge, skills, and abilities (KSAs). A domain analysis, thus, yields first an identification of the KSAs that go into the target competencies (learning goals), and second leads to the identification of prerequisite relationships amongst these KSAs. Such a structure can be conveniently represented as a directed graph, a KSA map. Third, and as extension to the typical KSA (prerequisite relations) map, the designer should be supported in specifying not only the correct knowledge but also

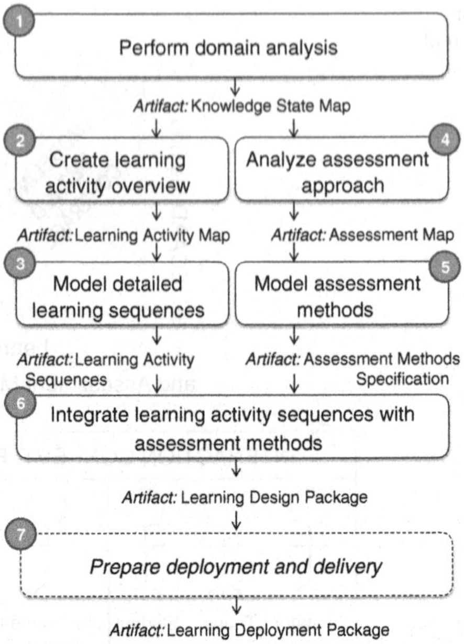

Fig. 6 ECAAD modeling procedure

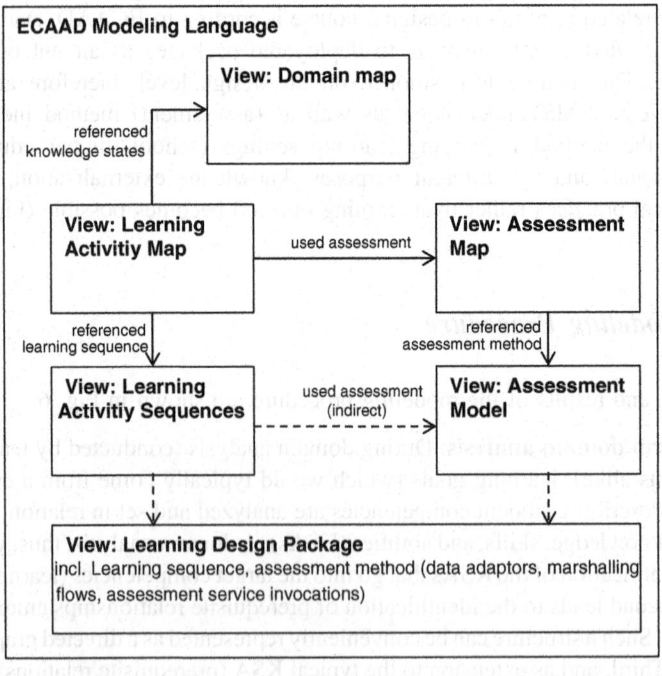

Fig. 7 ECAAD modeling language: abstract model stack

possible misconceptions (for declarative knowledge) and/or "bugs" in procedural knowledge; in other words, there needs to be room for specifying what *can go wrong* with learning, based on knowledge about what frequently goes wrong. Fourth, the domain map should contain information about learning trajectories: likely paths for learning to progress over time, including likely "detours" because of misconceptions and/or buggy procedural knowledge. The resulting artefact is a domain map; these maps construct the input and rationale for further decomposition and analysis in the following steps.

2. **Create the learning activity overview**: The Learning Activity Map (LAM) as an outcome of this step is a high-level description of the teaching/learning sequence students (or a specific student) will undergo to reach the learning goal specified in the Domain Map. The LAM contains information on the general pedagogy (e.g., problem solving, inquiry, knowledge building) with rationale, as well as an outline of the teaching/learning activities, resources involved, and ICTs involved. Furthermore, it does include trigger points for assessment, and a specification of the kind of assessment method required, again with rationales for these decisions. These design rationales correspond to warrants in an argumentative logic; they provide justifications for *why* students should engage in a specific learning activity, and not in others. The learning activity map can also specify alternative learning activities, i.e., activities that would serve the pedagogical purpose as well or nearly as well. A LAM is essentially a skeletal Learning Activity Sequence Model: it contains the most important learning activities, assessment triggers, and assessment methods, partially ordered over time, and including the design rationale. Hence, these maps can be stored in the Learning Activity Sequence Model Repository, appropriately qualified as "maps" rather than fully blown "models".
3. **Model detailed learning sequences**: The artefact generated in this step is a full activity sequence model. Such a model specifies all learning activities related to a specific learning goal. It further contains the resources, materials, and tools/services to be used for deploying the sequence in a learning environment (the classroom, an LMS such as Moodle, in a cloud environment such as Google Docs, etc.) The integration with assessment methods is achieved in a later step (6). Re-use of these sequences is possible through modularization and parameterization within a repository of best-practice sequences.
4. **Analyze assessment approach**: The result of this step is what we call an *Assessment Map*. These are semi-structured descriptions of how to assess a specific knowledge/skill/ability (KSA), including twenty-first century KSAs, using learner performance/product data that come from ICTs. An assessment map is semi-structured in as far as key attributes are pre-specified, the values of which need to be provided as a decomposition.
5. **Model assessment methods**: The specification and design of what to assess and how to assess (the method), is expressed in this step as a process model. An Assessment Model is created building on an Assessment Map, adding all the information necessary to execute the model in a learning environment. The Assessment Model describes in detail (also technically) the elements on how

data for a specific learning activity is collected, filtered, transformed, diagnoses (using assessment categories from the KSA definition), combines and displayed (as feedback to the learner).
6. **Integrate learning activity sequences with assessment methods**: The models created in steps 3 and 5 are combined and integrated and verified for execution. The verification and validation are supported by IT by interactively analyzing the effectiveness of the design for completeness.
7. **Prepare deployment and delivery**: In the final step, the hand-over to the execution environment, i.e., the students' learning environment needs to be achieved. This delivery is made available through specific export interface that translate/re-write the models into an execution language. Candidates for such execution languages are SCORM, DITA, IMS LD, and QTI, but also directly integrating with cloud-based environments such as Google Docs. The main objective is to enable an automatic export and execution functionality, meaning the abstract representation of the model is translated into the execution graph on the fly, by using predefined execution chunks, identified during design time.

3.2 Modeling Language

The modeling language defines the necessary concepts and their interrelations as artefacts resulting from the different steps of the modeling procedure defined above. For the conceptualization, we introduce the term "view" as a composition of concepts, targeting a specific domain of work and/or expertize (see [27, 28] for approaches on conceptualization and formalization). This view concept enables the separation of concerns for a role-based interaction concept in the IT tool.

View: **Domain Map** The domain map view enables the representation of knowledge states and their decomposition. The related model type is called "Knowledge state map". Classification of knowledge states as competence, skills, abilities and learning goals is possible; the representation of negative/inverted KSA is also possible. A decomposition is possible using the "decompose" relation, resulting in a hierarchical representation of knowledge states. Each decomposition result (as a model) is made available in a model repository for re-use and evolution (Fig. 8).

View: **Learning Activity Map/Sequence, Assessment Map/Model** The Learning Activity Map and Learning Activity Sequence view are made available in the modeling language as a single model type with decomposition support of activities and assessments. The modeling approach is sequential, defining a single start and end element per model and the respective sequence of activities and assessments in the model type "Activity and Assessment model"; views are provided by filtering the model accordingly. The view defines the actual activities and assessments and is supported by a library of pre-defined elements; parameterization to the specific context and configuration of elements is performed in the sequence (Fig. 9).

Based on the abstract model stack in Fig. 7, a detailed conceptualization of classes, relation, and their containment in modeltypes was developed as shown in Fig. 10.

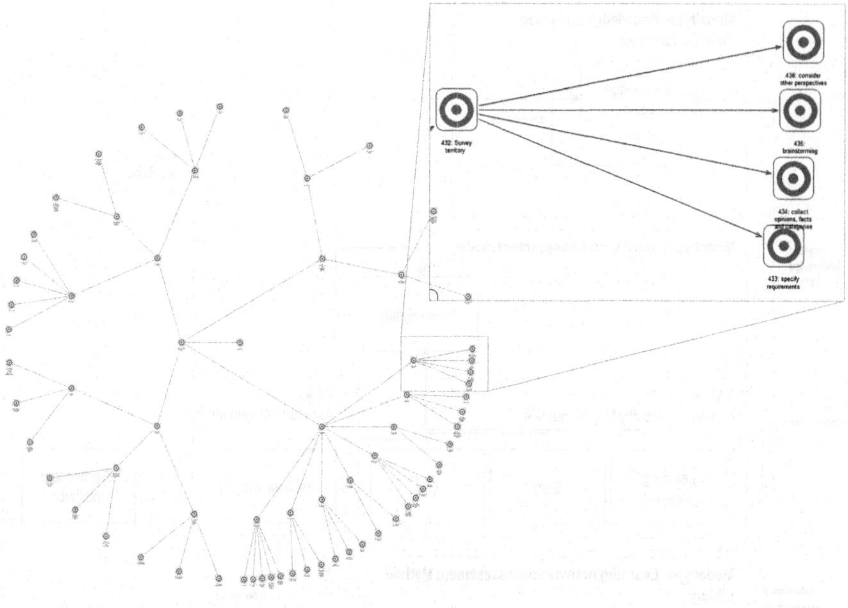

Fig. 8 Example view: knowledge states twenty-first century skills

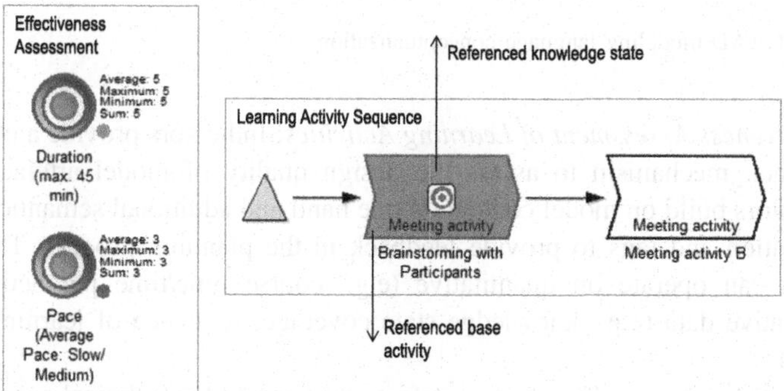

Fig. 9 Example view: draft learning activity sequence

3.3 Mechanisms and Algorithms

Mechanisms and algorithms are defined in ECCAD to support tasks of the modeling procedure. Based on the modeling procedure, the following algorithms/ mechanisms were conceptualized:

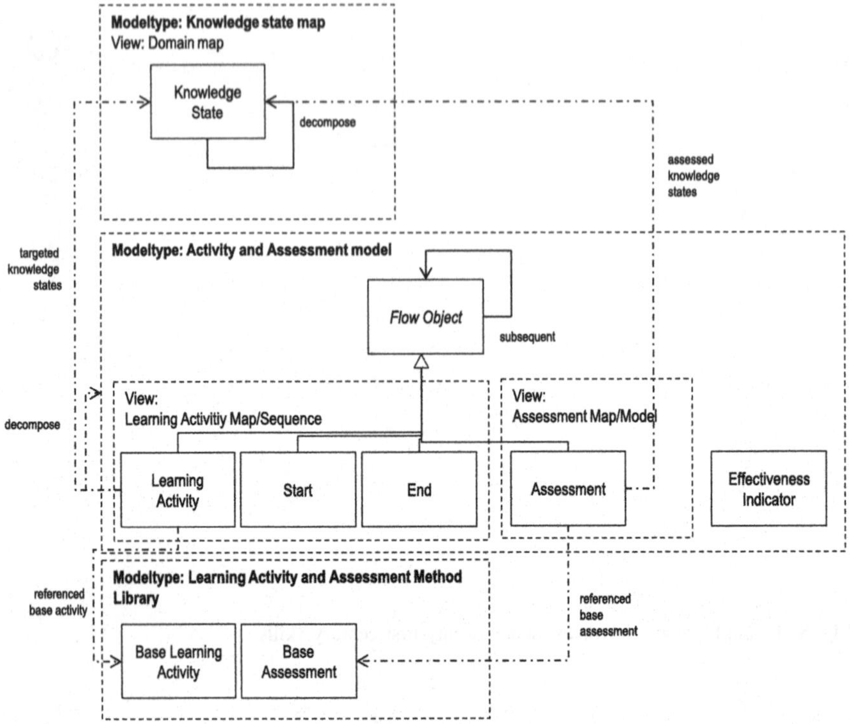

Fig. 10 ECAAD modeling language conceptualization

- *Effectiveness Assessment of Learning Activities*: Indicators provide a continuous feedback mechanism to assess the design quality of model artefacts. These indicators build on model content on one hand and additional semantic/dynamic annotation and tags to provide feedback in the planning process. These indicators can operate on quantitative (e.g., course time/time per activity) and qualitative data (e.g., knowledge state coverage, sequence of learning activity types)
- *Validation support*: The design artefacts are verified for technical execution and validated. Support is provided using cardinalities and rules on one hand, and walkthrough support for user-drive review, on the other. Walkthrough is enabled by the Activity Stepper engine integrated that performs a graph interpretation of the learning activity sequence using a variant of a recursive deep-first search (DFS)
- *Deployment Support*: Applying graph re-writing algorithms, models are transformed for executable usage. Different implementation approaches are foreseen (e.g., file-based interaction, API calls)

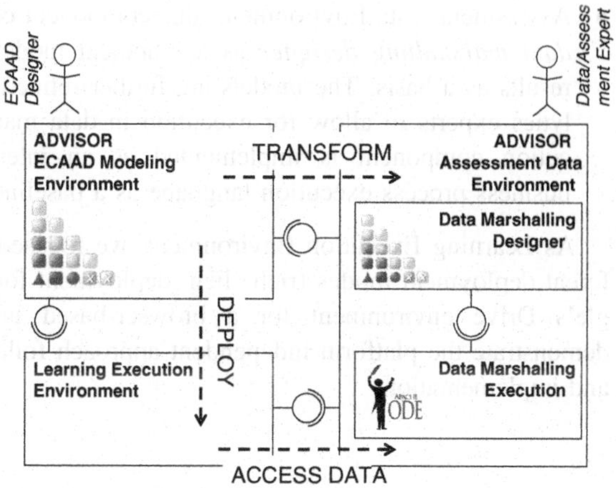

Fig. 11 ADVISOR prototype components

4 Proof of Concept: ADVISOR

The evaluation of the above concept was performed in the context of the NEXT-TELL project by performing a prototypical implementation of the modeling method using the ADO*xx* metamodeling platform.[3]

The prototype was applied by domain experts (teachers, teachers in education) in the context of the project, iteratively refined in 3 cycles to include user experience and refine the method described. The final release was made available as a public demonstration case through NEXT-TELL's dissemination channels targeting on one hand end-users and developers to establish a platform for interaction on domain as well as technical level.

4.1 Prototypical Development

The ADVISOR prototype consists of the following software components, depicted in Fig. 11 graphically:

- *ECAAD Modeling Environment*: This component is developed as a graphical modeling tool, using the conceptualization of the modeling language as described above. The domain expert uses this tool to define learning activities and assessment using a library of pre-defined, community-built artefacts, relate those with knowledge states.

[3]The NEXT-TELL Development Space is available at www.adoxx.org.

- Assessment Data Environment: this component consists of 2 sub-elements, the *data marshalling designer* as a graphical modeling tool, using the ECAAD results as a basis. The models are further refined by assessment and data analytics experts to allow for execution in data marshalling execution. The execution component is implemented as an interpretive workflow using the business process execution language as a baseline.

As Learning Execution Environment, we focused on cloud-based tools in different deployment modes (rich-client deployment for immersive worlds and Google's Drive environment for a browser-based interaction of the learner) to demonstrate the platform independent approach followed in the conceptualization and implementation.

4.2 Case Study Evaluation

Two case studies, used to demonstrate and evaluate the prototype, are presented below. The initial case study targets the design of learning activities and assessment and the hand-over to Google's collaborative word/spreadsheet processing tools as an instance of a cloud-based execution environment. On a technical level, the second case study shows how such a design can be used to derive data marshalling models in the context of learning English as a second language in immersive environments.

Integrating ECAAD with Cloud-Based (Learning) Environments As a base scenario for ADVISOR, this case study was conducted to demonstrate how design artefacts defined in accordance with the modeling method are made available to the learner in cloud-based learning environments. The objective is to enable the domain expert to use the tool to define knowledge states, derive learning activities and assessments, relate them to tools available online and deploy the results.

The models created with ADVISOR act as a user interface/externalization of knowledge of the teacher/student and are also understood as configuration items for the execution environment (setup of users and access rights, import/update, and structure knowledge states, configure learning material and their relation to the states). The case study targets the twenty-first century skills of collaboration in group work, focusing on the aspect of organizing meetings and enabling students to become facilitators in such settings.

The case study is shown in Fig. 12: (a) initially the knowledge state hierarchy is imported from the Open Learner Implementation (acting as the master information system for competences and knowledge states). This step is optional as the knowledge state map can also be directly defined; (b) the domain expert defines the learning sequence (in our case the meeting facilitation process); continuous design evaluation takes place in the tool to make sure the quality of the design meets the criteria defined by the pedagogical setup; (c) the design artefacts are exported and released. ADVISOR takes care to export and create the necessary information in

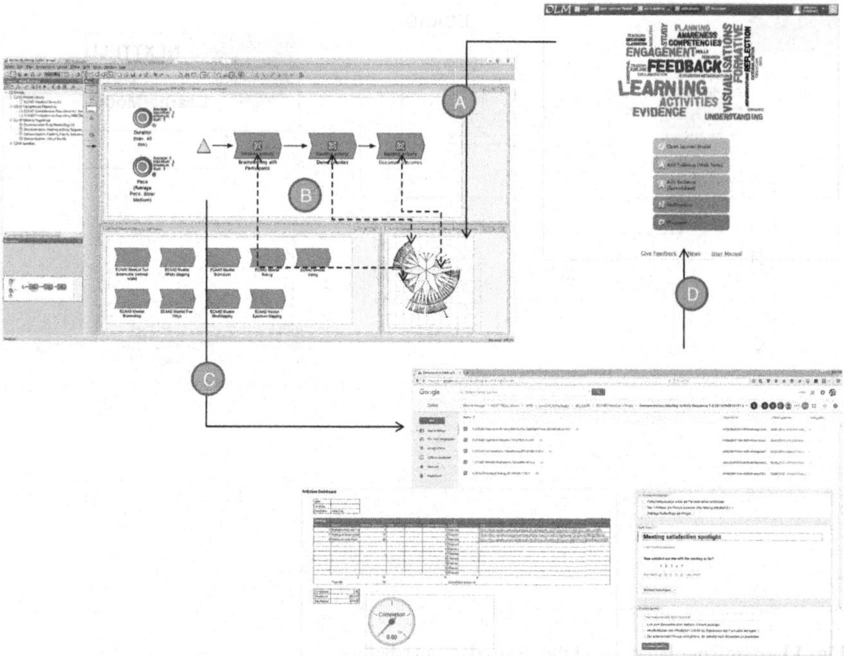

Fig. 12 Meeting facilitation using Google services

Google Drive, adds the students as collaborators. In addition, the necessary adapters are configured.

Data Marshalling for Assessment in Immersive Worlds This case study learning in immersive worlds demonstrates the applicability of ECAAD to establish dynamically data marshalling flows, wiring arbitrary learning execution environment with assessment implementation and knowledge state visualization. The data-driven approach is realized in real-time, enabling a formative assessment for the students. The case developed relates to "Learning English as a Second Language" using virtual/immersive worlds. The language competences of students are evaluated according to the standardized CEFR framework (Common European Framework of Reference for Languages) in a formative way, meaning that evidence created by the student continuously updates the personal/open learner model.

A data marshalling model for evaluating these competences was derived from the ECAAD model using graph-rewriting techniques and manual intervention. This model is executable as it integrates data streams coming live from group discussions between students and facilitators in an OpenSim virtual learning environment, handed over to the PRONIFA student modeling toolkit [29] in a first step. In the second phase, the workflow performs the update of the open learner model using the results returned from the PRONIFA system. Figure 13 shows how (a) the ECAAD-based model is defined in ADVISOR as the applicable learning sequence,

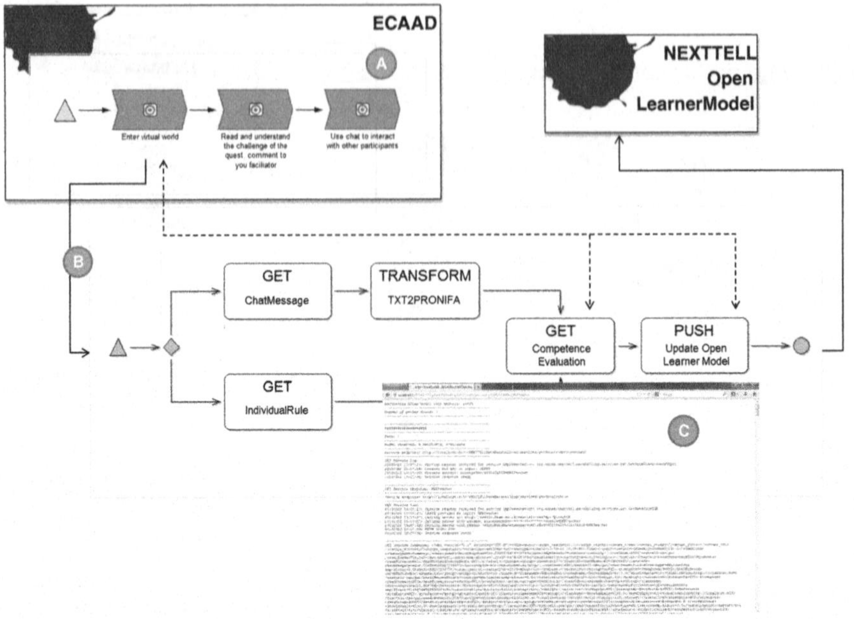

Fig. 13 Assessing language skills using data marshalling

(b) the derived data-marshalling model and its relation to the configuration items as well as tools, and (c) the log message produced by the system to retrieve the chat message, rate it and update the learning model.

As the combination of services is not hard-wired, but dynamically derived from the domain representation in ECAAD, an enhanced integration approach could be developed, resulting in a more effective implementation of time and quality on the one hand and a direct involvement of non-technical experts in the definition of assessment data flows, on the other. Assessment services (represented in Fig. 13 at the bottom as "Competence Evaluation") are interchangeable, therefore providing a high degree of customization to pedagogical approaches.

5 Conclusion

Even though assessment is a key component of teaching, both personal teaching and all forms of computer-supported instruction, the *design* of assessment tasks has received little attention, with the exception of professional test development. Moreover, the reasoning involved in developing summative and formative assessment is rarely considered to be a *design* task. It is rather seen as a question of selecting from a fixed set of alternatives: rubrics and multiple choice item formats, mostly. Informed by modern conceptions of educational assessment, we argue that assessment development, whether summative or formative, is primarily a design task, and that it requires a systematic approach to designing. An example of such an approach is Evidence-Centred Assessment Design, developed by Mislevy and colleagues over the past ten years [18]. We showed how ECD can be further developed by connecting it to concepts of metamodeling, yielding specifications of the method that can be employed to describe assessment methods in a platform-independent (independent from a specific learning management system, for instance) yet formalized environment and close to deployment on particular platforms, such as LMSs. We also reported on the development of tool support for the assessment modeling method and provided examples of modeling and deployment aspects.

The ECD method, in combination with tool support, empowers not only assessment specialists but in principle any educator to design quality assessments. However, the method we described does not automatize assessment design. That is well beyond the state of the art, if possible at all. Our method requires educators who have a strong grasp of the learning domain, and a good understanding of the process of learning in their students. It also requires mastery of at least basic concepts of assessment, including scoring, and knowledge about ICT, in particular, use of computers for knowledge diagnosis and assessment. Therein lies a challenge for the future: since teacher education programs world-wide pay little attention to assessment theory, and provide only basic IT knowledge, only a small minority of teachers at this stage are ready to develop high quality (formative) assessments. This holds for school education and is even worse for Higher Education, where teachers usually have no background in learning sciences, pedagogy, and assessment theory. How to increase assessment and data literacy amongst educators is a question future research needs to answer and future policy development needs to consider.

Tool Download http://www.omilab.org/advisor.

References

1. Wayman, J.C., Stringfield, S., Yakimowski, M.: Software Enabling School Improvement Through Analysis of Student Data (CRESPAR Tech.Rep. No. 67). John Hopkins University, Baltimore (2004)
2. Wayman, J.C., Stringfield, S.: Technology-supported involvement of entire faculties in examination of student data for instructional improvement. Am. J. Edu. **112**, 549–571 (2006)
3. Shute, V.J.: Focus on formative feedback. Rev. Edu. Res. **78**(1), 153–189 (2008)
4. Cowie, B., Bell, B.: A model of formative assessment in science education. Assess. Education **6**, 101–111 (1999)
5. Mandinach, E.B.: A perfect time for data use: using data-driven decision making to inform practice. Edu. Psychol. **47**(2), 71–85 (2012)
6. Kowalski, T.J., Lasley, T.J.H. (eds.): Handbook of Data-based Decision Making in Education. Routledge, New York (2009)

7. Firestone, W.A., Schorr, R.Y., Monfils, L.F. (eds.): The Ambiguity of Teaching to the Test. Erlbaum, Mahwah (2004)
8. No Child Left Behind Act of 2001, U.S.C., Editor (2001)
9. Mandinach, E.B., Gummer, E.S.: A systematic view of implementing data literacy in educator preparation. Edu. Res. **42**, 30–37 (2013)
10. Young, V.M.: Supporting teachers' use of data: the role of organization and policy. In: Mandinach, E.B., Honey, M. (eds.) Data-driven School Improvement, pp. 87–106. Teachers College Press, New York (2008)
11. King, S.P., Amon, C.: Assessment data: a tool for student and teacher growth. In: Mandinach, E.B., Honey, M. (eds.) Data-driven School Improvement, pp. 71–86. Teachers College Press, New York (2008)
12. Karagiannis, D., Kühn, H.: Metamodelling platforms. In: 3rd International Conference EC-Web 2002—Dexa 2002, Aix-en-Provence (2002)
13. Karagiannis, D:Agile modeling method engineering. Panhellenic Conference on Informatics, pp. 5–10 (2015)
14. Mislevy, R.J., Steinberg, L., Almond, R.G.: On the structure of educational assessments. Meas. Interdiscip. Res. Perspect., **1,** 3–67 (2003)
15. Reimann, P., et al.: Specification of ECAAD methodology. Next-Tell Consortium, Graz, Austria (2011)
16. Utz, W., Reimann, P., Karagiannis, D.: Capturing learning activities in heterogeneous environments: a model-based approach for data marshalling. In: IEEE 14th International Conference on 2014 Advanced Learning Technologies (ICALT). IEEE Conference Publications, Athens (2014)
17. Shron, M.: Thinking with Data—How to Turn Information into Insights, p. 93 (2014)
18. Mislevy, R.J., Riscontente, M.M.: Evidence-centred assessment design. In: Downing, S.M., Haladyna, T.M. (eds.) Handbook of Test Development, pp. 61–90. Lawrence Erlbaum, Mahwah (2006)
19. Mislevy, R.J., Riscontente, M.M.: Evidence-centred Assessment Design: Layers, Structures, and Terminology (PADI Technical Report #9). SRI International, Palo Alto (2009)
20. Reigeluth, C.M., (ed.): Instructional-Design Theories and Models. vol. 2. Lawrence Erlbaum Associates, Hillsdale (1999)
21. Goodyear, P., Retalis, S. (eds.): Technology-Enhanced Learning: Design Patterns and Pattern Languages. Sense Publishers, Rotterdam (2010)
22. Alexander, C.: The Timeless Way of Building. Oxford University Press, New York (1979)
23. Mislevy, R.J., et al.: Design Patterns for Assessing Science Inquiry (PADI Technical Report 1). SRI International, Menlo Park (2003)
24. Riscontente, M.M., Mislevy, R.J., Hamel, L.: An introduction to PADI task templates. (Principled assessment designs for inquiry technical report 3). In: Principled Assessment Designs for Inquiry Technical Report 3 (2007)
25. Downing, S.M., Haladyna, T.M. (eds.): Handbook of Test Design, pp. 61–90. Lawrence Erlbaum, Mahwah (2006)
26. Laumer, S., Stetten, A., Eckhardt, A.: E-Assessment. Bus. Inf. Syst. Eng. **1**(3), 263–265 (2009)
27. Fill, H.-G., Redmond, T., Karagiannis, D.: Formalizing meta models with FDMM: the ADOxx case. ICEIS 2012: pp. 429–451 (2012)
28. On the Conceptualisation of Modelling Methods Using the ADOxx Meta Modelling Platform. Enterprise Modelling and Information Systems Architectures **8**(1), 4–25 (2013)
29. Reimann, P., Kickmeier-Rust, M., Albert, D.: Problem solving learning environments and assessment: the knowledge space theory approach. Comput. Educ. **64**, 183–193 (2013)

Modeling for Learning in Public Administrations—The Learn PAd Approach

Guglielmo De Angelis, Alfonso Pierantonio, Andrea Polini, Barbara Re, Barbara Thönssen and Robert Woitsch

Abstract This chapter describes a modeling method that has been conceived to support learning in public administrations. The modeling method foresees the description of both procedures in the public administrations, and the working context of the civil servants. The approach relies on several model types that are used to organize and to relate the knowledge needed by civil servants in order to perform their daily activities. Each model instance describes a view on the concerns expressed by the model type it conforms to. These descriptions intend to provide an easy way for civil servants to retrieve knowledge when they need to learn specific aspects of a procedure, and to make collaboration easier in order to enable the emergence of knowledge related to the procedures themselves. Indeed, the method comes with an infrastructure that allows to automatically set up a wiki-based collaborative platform enabling collaboration and knowledge sharing among the stakeholders involved in the activities of a Public Administration. This chapter mainly reports on the modeling method that was conceived and developed within the FP7 EU research project Learn PAd. Learning aspects, while clearly relevant for the project, will not be directly discussed here.

G. De Angelis
CNR–ISTI and CNR–IASI, Pisa, Italy
e-mail: guglielmo.deangelis@iasi.cnr.it

A. Pierantonio
University of L'Aquila, L'Aquila, Italy
e-mail: alfonso.pierantonio@univaq.it

A. Polini (✉) · B. Re
University of Camerino, Ascoli Piceno, Italy
e-mail: andrea.polini@unicam.it

B. Re
e-mail: barbara.re@unicam.it

B. Thönssen
FHNW, Olten, Switzerland
e-mail: barbara.thoenssen@fhnw.ch

R. Woitsch
BoC, Vienna, Austria
e-mail: robert.woitsch@boc-eu.com

D. Karagiannis et al. (eds.), *Domain-Specific Conceptual Modeling*,
DOI 10.1007/978-3-319-39417-6_26

Keywords Learning · Public administration · Business process management · Case management

1 Introduction

In modern society, public administrations (PAs) are undergoing a transformation of their perceived role from controllers to proactive service providers, and are under pressure to constantly improve their service quality while coping with the quickly changing context (changes in law and regulations, societal globalization, fast technology evolution,) and decreasing budgets. Modern trends in Information and Communication Technologies (ICT), and in particular in relation to the wide usage of social networks, introduce new ways of delivering services to citizens, and often impose profound reorganizations of PA offices. Clearly, a wise introduction of such technologies can drastically improve the reputation of the PA perceived by the citizens, and can also ameliorate the working context for the civil servants. Nonetheless, civil servants are nowadays challenged by these changes, and possible reorganizations of a PA office requires them to understand and put into action novel procedures and rules within tight time constraints.

In such a context, traditional approaches to learning seem to be rather ineffective and need to be complemented with novel learning approaches and solutions. However, Learn PAd[1] EU research project defined a novel learning approach and platform based on the usage of models. In particular, models are used to organize the knowledge needed to perform adequately the activities foreseen by the procedures in which a civil servant acts. Investigations made within the project identified different model types considered particularly relevant to permit the inclusion of all information needed for effective learning. The following model types were identified and included in the approach:

- Business Process (BP) models that allow to represent how activities should be performed in sequence, and the conditions for their execution.
- Case Management (CM) models that allow to represent knowledge-intensive activities in which the flow of tasks is not determined a priori while it results from the knowledge and experience of the civil servant. The relation between CM models and BP models is investigated in Chap. 18.
- Organizational models that allow to represent people, roles, and their responsibilities within the organization.
- Documents and Knowledge Models that, on the one hand allow to represent the structure and objective of documents to be filled, checked, delivered etc., and on the other hand, allow to describe more precisely the knowledge related to the defined models.
- Competency models, that allow to represent the competencies needed to preform some activity and as well as the competencies acquired by a civil servant.

[1] See: http://www.learnpad.eu.

- Business Motivation models that allow to describe business strategies and learning goals of the organizations useful to assess possible improvements in the knowledge of Civil Servants.
- KPI models that allow to represent the learning goals and the KPIs to measure them.

The model types listed above are bound together by the definition of suitable links that, as detailed below, allow to relate concepts in one model to other concepts in other models.

The learning approach devised by the Learn PAd project uses models both to better organize the knowledge and to derive a collaborative space, within a collaborative platform, that can be accessed by the civil servants to create and share knowledge on the activities they have to perform. In particular, the collaborative space is automatically generated from the models and will enable the civil servants to directly refer to knowledge related to the different aspect of the models.

This chapter reports how the approach was defined compare to [9], as well as the metamodels to support the different model types. The resulting modeling environment was made available thanks to the OMiLAB platform.

2 Method Description

The Learn PAd modeling method applies business process management for process-oriented learning, hence the core concepts focus on business process management. As Learn PAd uses the business processes for learning aspects, the idea is to use also the model-based approach for learning related modeling and identify applicable relations between the business processes that represent the object under observation as well as the learning models that describe the Learn PAd approach.

Business processes and learning models are both representatives of conceptual models, hence they have a tight relationship with semantics. Therefore, the integration of the so-called modeling utilities such as ontologies or more human-oriented knowledge acquisition tools seems appropriate.

This results in a hybrid modeling approach combining (a) business process related, (b) learning management related, and (c) the so-called modeling utilities.

Figure 1 depicts the current high level conceptual architecture on the Learn PAd modeling method, highlighting the conceptual elements of the Learn PAd modeling method.

Business Process-Related Modeling: The major aspect in business process-oriented learning is the appropriate representation of a business process. Beside the typical standard approach in using BPMN 2.0 [1] for covering the business process management, Learn PAd additionally requires to specify relevant knowledge and skill profiles. In particular, the business goals, strategies and business motivations, the organizational structure, the document and knowledge models are seen as the context of the business process model in Learn PAd.

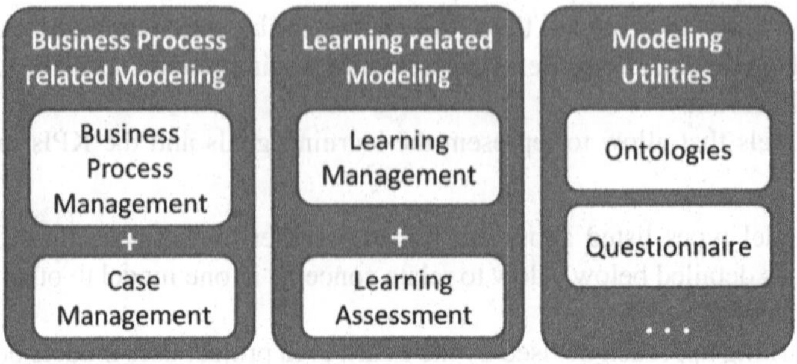

Fig. 1 High level building block of Learn PAd modeling method

The platform includes a Wiki-like infrastructure and, in order to enable collaboration mechanisms for models, the corresponding concepts for collaborative aspects need additionally to be reflected in the business process modeling language.

PAs usually deal with a wide set of business process types: ranging from well-structured processes (e.g. BPMN-like notations), to weakly structured processes (e.g. CM-like notations such as CMMN [2]). Indeed, the Learn PAd modeling method has to cope with hybrid process-oriented modeling notations.

Learning Related Modeling: Learning related modeling deals with the specification of learning goals, definition of the learning content and the teaching path for presenting the content in a personalized way for each individual learner. Typical aspects are learning goals, curricula, skill profiles, teaching content and the packaging towards a learning management platform. The current requirements involve continuously assessing the learning progress, hence combining the teaching path with assessment models that specify the goals that need to be achieved, and the assessment method. Depending on the level of detail, the learning management will be performed using the ECAAD method. Conceptual linkage is foreseen, so that Learn PAd business processes are seen as content packages of the ECAAD method, as well as different business processes models correspond to different phases of the learning process in ECAAD.

Modeling Utilities: Modeling Utilities are modeling concepts that may or may not be used and hence can be flexibly added to the metamodel. Current identified aspects are ontologies for semantically lifted log mining or questionnaire models for a model-driven development of tests.

Although these modeling utilities are not mandatory, the Learn PAd modeling method foresees as possible interaction, such as using the so-called "semantic lifting" approach to integrate ontologies, or to investigate a "graph rewriting" to export and transform relevant parts of the business process to questionnaire models.

Having deeply reflected on the Learn PAd modeling method within its conceptual environment, it is now possible to distinguish between concepts that must be included into the Learn PAd modeling method (e.g. such as BPMN, CMMN, Roles and knowledge), concepts that may be included as nice to have (e.g. such as business motivation, Key Performance Indicators, or skill profiles), and concepts that are not appropriate to be put into the Learn PAd modeling method (e.g. learning goals, learning assessment indicators, questionnaires).

After defining the scope of the Learn PAd metamodel, the next section introduces the method conceptualization in more detail.

3 Method Conceptualization

The Learn PAd project focusses on business process oriented workplace learning. This includes models of organizational structures and procedures, models of resources, models used for the monitoring and assessment of business performance and learners' achievement. To this end, modeling the different facets of a business process is the key for expressing the relations among several model types and model objects and for representing them in a machine understandable way, but cognitively adequate for humans.

One of the main contributions of the project is indeed the possibility to provide precise definitions of almost any aspect of a business process in the context of PAs: enhanced models for business processes which contain additional information about knowledge entities, performance indicators, competencies, organizations, etc. This can be regarded as a dedicated architecture framework [8] for creating, interpreting, analyzing and using business descriptions within the context of Public Administrations. In this respect, a comprehensive metamodel consisting of a *orthographic* [4, 7][2] set of coordinated modeling languages was devised in order to endow typical data and flow descriptions with additional aspects ranging from the specification of the skills necessary for consistently assign a responsibility, to what resources are useful for an administration to achieve its goals.

Figure 2 gives an example of how the Learn PAd models can be structured by Zachman's enterprise architecture framework [14]. The focus is on the *how-aspect* showing the models for the various perspectives, starting on top with a service catalogue defining the services administrations must provide, followed by the conceptual metamodel providing the relevant business concepts. The relations, however, are implicit and hence, the number of a process defined in a service catalogue on the *scope concepts* level, may occur in the process description at the *business concepts* level, but that relation is not formalized and therefore hard to trace. The same holds true for the relation between a process model on the *system logic* layer and the process description. In addition to the *vertical relations*, the *horizontal relations* between *business objects* have to be considered. For the sake of better reading only relations between models on the system logic layer are depicted in Fig. 2.

The consequent holistic view is possible in Learn PAd thanks to a multi-view specification, whose definition is given in terms of metamodels and relationships

[2]The term *orthographic* is intended for denoting a minimal, least coupled set of orthogonal viewpoints.

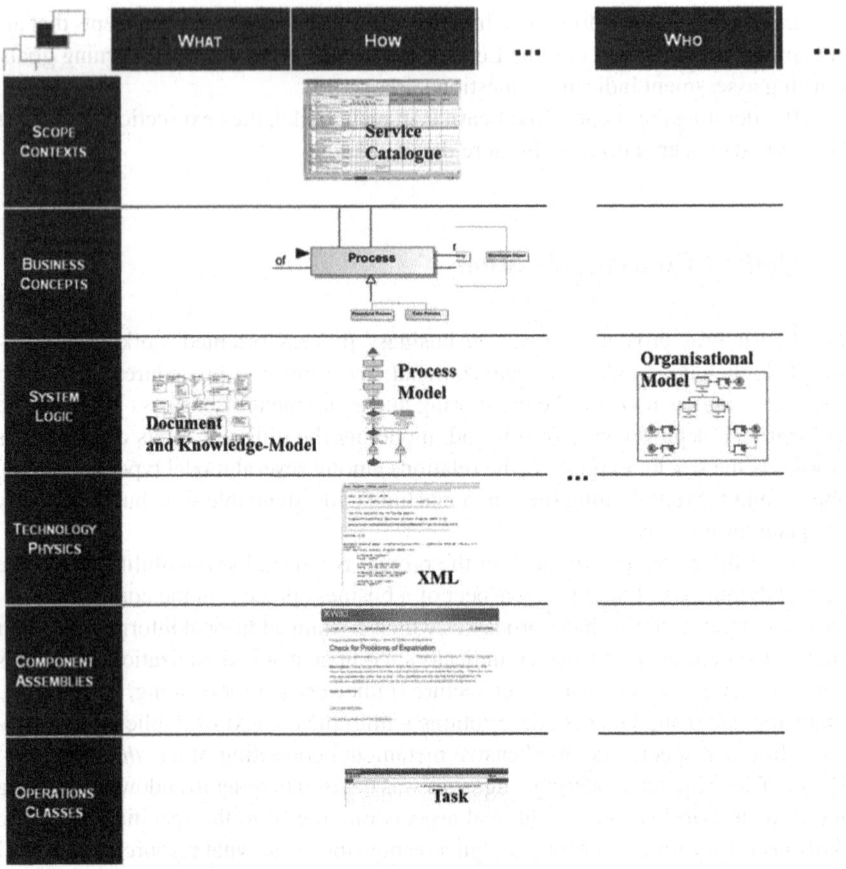

Fig. 2 The Learn PAd models structured by Zachman's matrix

among them as illustrated in Fig. 3. Hence, dependencies between the metamodels become clearly visible and can be utilized for improving collaboration and better supporting workplace learning by increasing transparency. Since in Learn PAd the conceptual model is represented in an ontology knowledge about the interrelations between models, it can be used for actively guiding a learner for example by recommending to access knowledge related to a task it is performing. In particular, each metamodel allows the description of a different viewpoint in the process model. Each viewpoint is then interconnected according to weaving models [5] necessary to maintain the different modeling views consistent. Moreover, they provide a navigation map that facilitates access to any information related to the process, as, for instance the competency profile needed for executing a given activity. Even more importantly, as the weaving models are represented in an ontology, all object types are semantically, and hence unambiguously described. This is of crucial relevance in those cases where the language specification leaves the semantics of given concept open, as for instance the BPMN [1] specification. It presents some ambiguities [12]

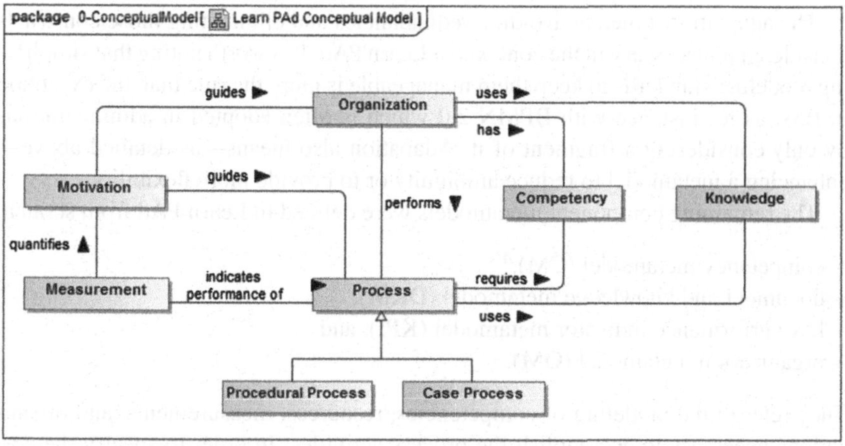

Fig. 3 The Learn PAd metamodel

since the pool and lane concepts can denote various business aspects, for example an organization, a role, or an IT-system.

A process is typically perceived as a sequence of activities that the administration executes in order to produce a service for the end-user. These activities are most of the time knowledge-intensive and require transparency and information tracing. In addition, the responsibility for their enactment is assigned to organizational units within the administrations, which pursue given goals. Therefore, in order to better support the learner, the typical business process modeling was intertwined with additional modeling structures to make knowledge relevant in a given process explicit and to actively recommend context-specific learning material.

Each component metamodel focuses on a different aspect of the business processes. Each cell of the matrix in Fig. 2 shows the provided metamodel. Furthermore, for one model type, several modeling languages are supported. In particular, the business process model type can be expressed in BPMN 2.0 or in CMMN [2]. That is, besides procedural processes also case processes are supported. Learn PAd also enhances BPMN 2.0 by a new object type called knowledge-intensive subprocess which allows for relating to CMMN. Other aspects which are relevant for the Learn PAd objectives are related to the necessity to model business goals and success factors. The way an organization is arranged and how this organizational structure is capable of enacting the process was also considered. The following component metamodels were defined by adapting current industrial standards of modeling languages:

- business motivation metamodel[3] (BMM) [3],
- business process management and notation (BPMN) [1], and
- case management and notation (CMMN) [2].

[3]In order to stress the distinction between model and metamodel, we will use the term metamodel also for denoting standards like OMG's BMM, which we call Business Motivation Metamodel.

The adaptation aimed at avoiding redundancies and eliminating those constructs considered unnecessary in the contexts of Learn PAd. It is worth noting that simplifying modeling standards to keep them manageable is more the rule than the exception in PAs, as for instance with BPMN 2.0 which is often adopted in administrations by only considering a fragment of it. Adapation also means—as detailed above—enhancing a metamodel to reduce ambiguity or to provide more flexibility.

The remaining component metamodels were defined in Learn PAd from scratch:

- competency metamodel (CM),[4]
- document and knowledge metamodel (DKM),
- key performance indicator metamodel (KPI), and
- organization metamodel (OM).

They refer to the modeling of competencies, resources, measurements, and organizations necessary to accomplish the process activities. In order to specify the correspondences across the different model kinds describing the manyfold nature of a process, concepts belonging to two or more metamodels are cross-linked by means of weaving models.

As an example, consider the *lane* concept in Fig. 4. Its semantics is, to some extent, too loose for an accurate enactment of the business process according to the corresponding BPMN specification. In order to restrict its employment just to the intended ones, it can be anchored to the corresponding concepts in the respective metamodels, for example to the organization metamodel as illustrated in Fig. 5, where a lane may accomodate activities whose responsibility belongs to an entire *organizational unit*, to a *performer*, or to a given *role* in the organization. For the sake of clarity, in Fig. 6 a small fragment of the organization metamodel is given where the organization unit is described in terms of its goals and the resource it can rely on. Due to the representation of the metamodels elements in an ontology, concepts become unambiguously defined and machine executable. Furthermore, embedded in a comprehensive enterprise ontology, concepts are refined according the ArchiMate standard [8], as depicted in Fig. 7. To give an example of how the concepts are elaborated in the ontology for the concepts *organization* and *motivation* the refined concepts are depicted. The ontology used in Learn PAd, called ArchiMEO is based on the ArchiMate standard, that is, all concepts and relations defined in ArchiMate 2.1 are formally represented in RDFS 3.0. The ontological representations of the refinements of concepts and relations are considered Learn PAd specific enhancements. The ontology is used for determining context-specific recommendations for learners based both on their level with respect to the European Qualification Framework (EQF), and learning preferences.

[4]The competency metamodel is based on the European Qualifications Framework EQF; https://ec.europa.eu/ploteus/de/node/1440.

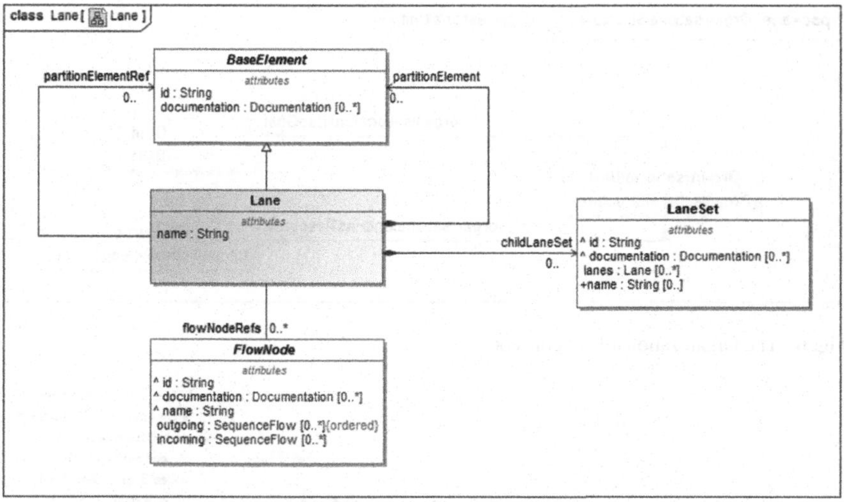

Fig. 4 The Lane concept

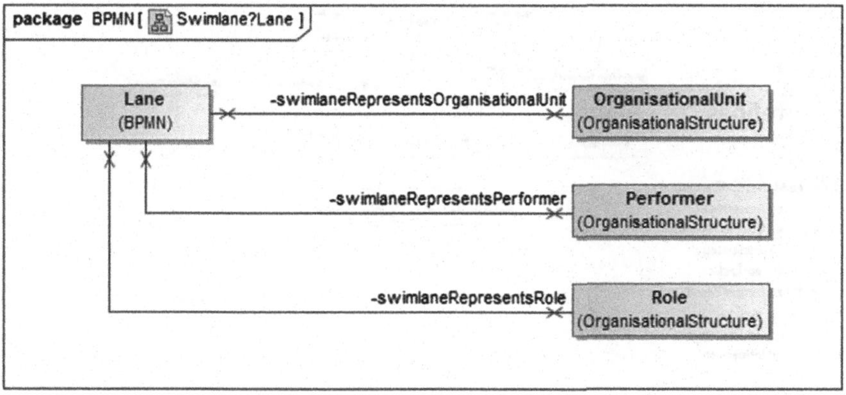

Fig. 5 The Swimlane-Lane weavings

4 Proof of Concept

The modeling approach presented in this chapter was applied to develop the artefacts needed by the demonstrators of the Learn PAd EU research project. Specifically, a set of models were designed by means of a modeling tool prototype that is described in Sect. 4.1. Section 4.2 reports the models derived using the tool considering the case of and Italian PA office in which civil servants have to put in place activities in relation to budget reporting for a financed EU research project.

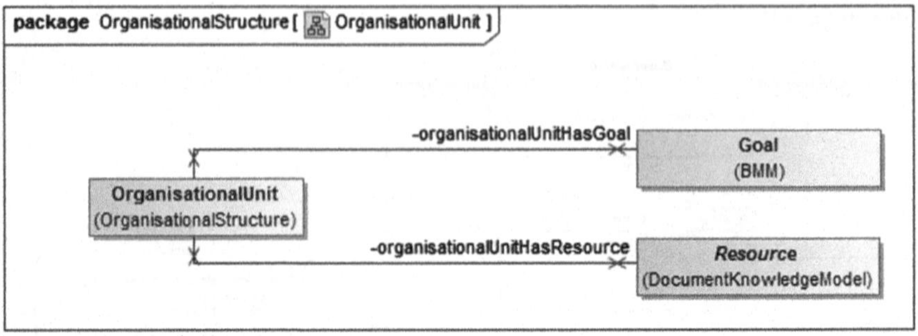

Fig. 6 The Organizational Unit concept

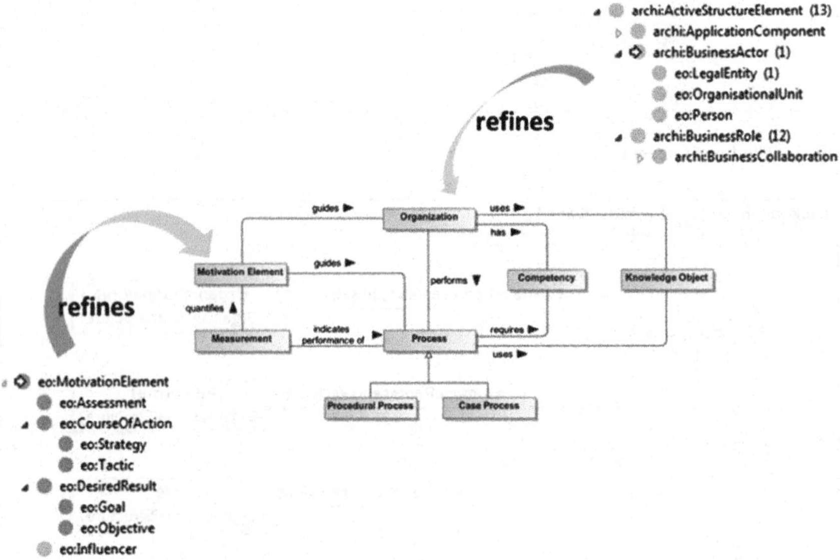

Fig. 7 Example of refinements for concepts

4.1 *Tool Prototype*

The Learn PAd modeling tool was collaboratively developed on the ADOxx.org platform, using ADO*xx* as the metamodel platform [6], and using features and sample scenarios to improve the functionality of the Learn PAd modeler. It can be downloaded from the Learn PAd developer space at: http://www.adoxx.org.[5]

The main goal of the modeling tool is to enable the graphical editing of artefacts conforming to the Learn PAd metamodels. Nevertheless, some scenarios on process-oriented learning revealed additional features generally not directly supported by

[5]See: https://www.adoxx.org/live/web/learnpad-developer-space/learnpad-modeling-environment.

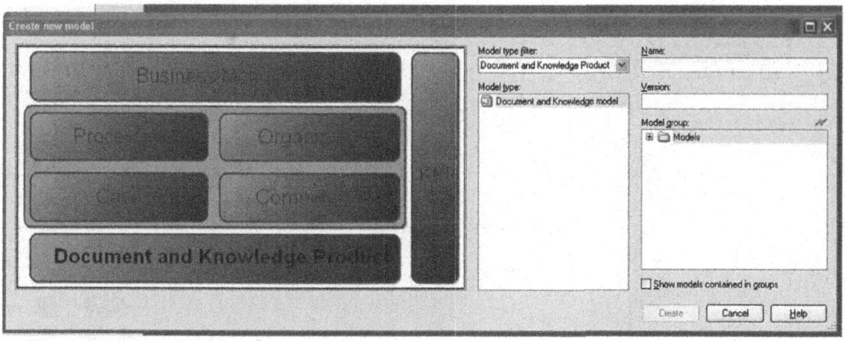

Fig. 8 Graphical representation of model types

modeling environments. In particular, we refer here to mechanisms facilitating collaboration among the various stakeholdes in order to collaboratively develop and enhance the defined business process model.

Model Type Implementation

In addition to the implementation of model types as collections of modeling classes, the model types were grouped in (a) Business Motivation, (b) Processes, (c) Organization, (d) Case Management, (e) Competence Management, (f) Document and Knowledge Products as well as (g) KPI related model types.

Each of the groups contains the relevant modeling types; the user interface introduced in Fig. 8 depicts an intuitive entry point into the complex Learn PAd modeling language. Each of the model types is a collection of modeling classes, hence in the section below, some interesting modeling classes are described.

Modeling Classes Implementation

This section describes the implementation of modeling classes within their corresponding model types. Only the relevant model types are shown below, not the full modeling language, as prototypes; they indicate the core of the process-oriented learning, and the Learn PAd specific additions.

Business Process Model The core of process-oriented learning is the business process as the central object of concern. Although BPMN 2.0 was selected as the current business process modeling notation standards, Learn PAd requires additional attributes and references.

As BPMN is only used for human interpretation in the Learn PAd, only the core set of BPMN 2.0 was used. However, in order to overcome the weaknesses of BPMN that does not deïňĄne the relationship with other modeling aspects, such as the organizational diagram, cases or documents, such references needed to be added to the modeling language.

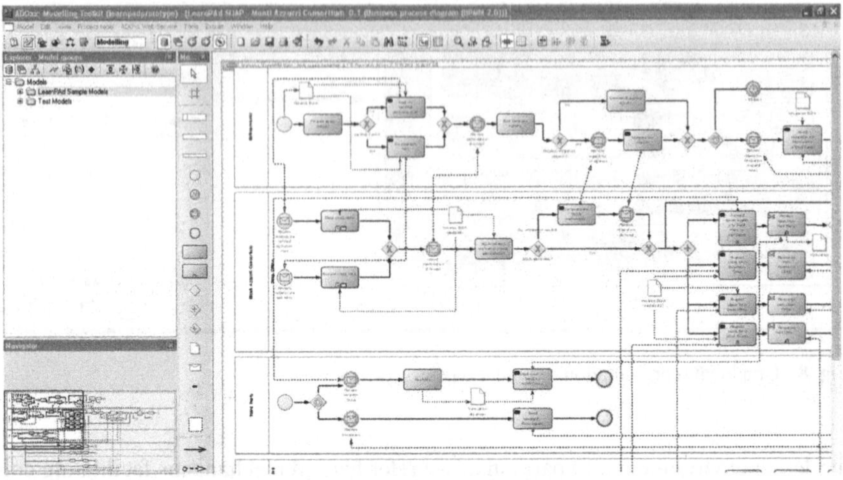

Fig. 9 Business process modeling notation within the prototype

Figure 9 depicts the typical modeling user interface of modeling tools developed on ADOxx. The class representation on the right side is following the graphical notation of the BPMN specification. The menu and icon bar on the top provide the modeling features, the explorer on the left side enables the management of models, whereas the navigator at the left bottom corner supports the modeling in large processes. The model bar in the left centre of the figure provides all necessary BPMN objects, whereas different view modes are filtering the modeling classes and hence provide the relevant set of modeling classes.

Case Management Model Case management can be seen as an alternative to business processes by covering the unstructured or semi-structured parts of the business process. Recently, a CMMN specification was published defining a notation for modeling the so-called cases, which do not necessarily require a sequence, but can be worked out in any order. The relation between business processes and case models was made by a similar concept as the sub-process, where the structured part of the process is represented in the BPMN notation, and the unstructured part is presented in case models as indicated in Fig. 10.

Another interesting implementation is the document and knowledge model, where the modeling class "document" is enriched with the modeling class "knowledge source" and "knowledge resource". This enables the user to describe not only the atomic knowledge representation in form of a document, but also a collection of documents in form of a "knowledge source" as well as the inclusion of implicit knowledge—such as expert knowledge or community opinion—in form of "knowledge resources".

Implementation of the modeling features The basic features in graphical modeling are (a) graphical representation, (b) query, (c) simulation and (d) transformation;

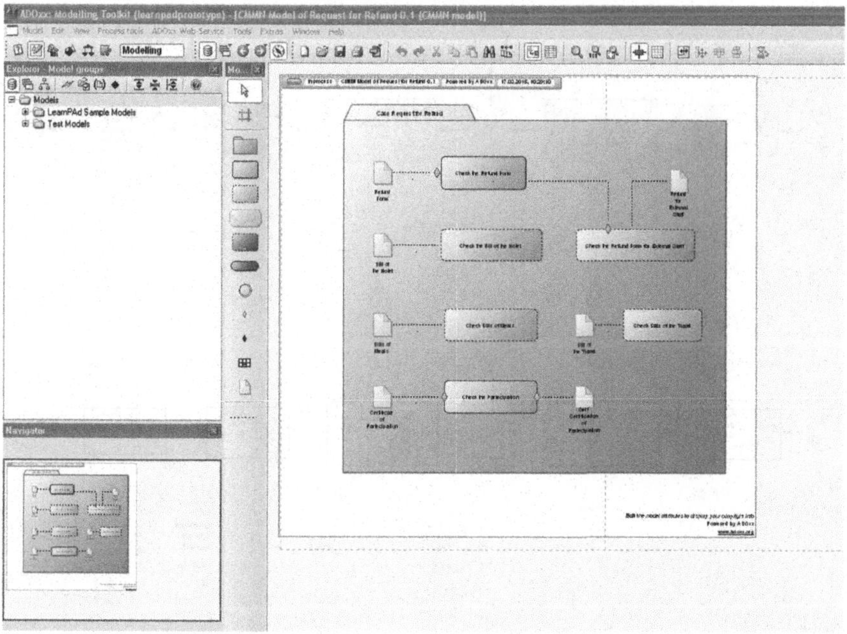

Fig. 10 Case management notation

although Learn PAd uses the basic feature of all of them, there are features that are especially important in the context of human interpretation. In order to support learners with the graphical representation of business processes, the different graphical representation features as well as the collaborative modeling are of high importance. Therefore, the following special features on graphical representation of models are introduced:

- *People-Like View*: to support the graphical representation in a user-friendly way without using typical representation of concept modeling.
- *Bar Display View*: to display all relevant influence factors of the business process with additional bar displays.
- *Comments Sidebar*: to support collaborative changes using comments to objects, like track change comments.

People-Like View The People-Like view allows for an easily interpretable, pictorial representation of tasks within a business process. Having modeled a given business process, the user can toggle the People-Like View to "on", transforming the typical concept model graphical representation into a series of cartoon-like images with a domain specific depiction of the task that needs to be performed. For example, the following chain of tasks is transformed on activation of People-Like View as illustrated in Fig. 11.

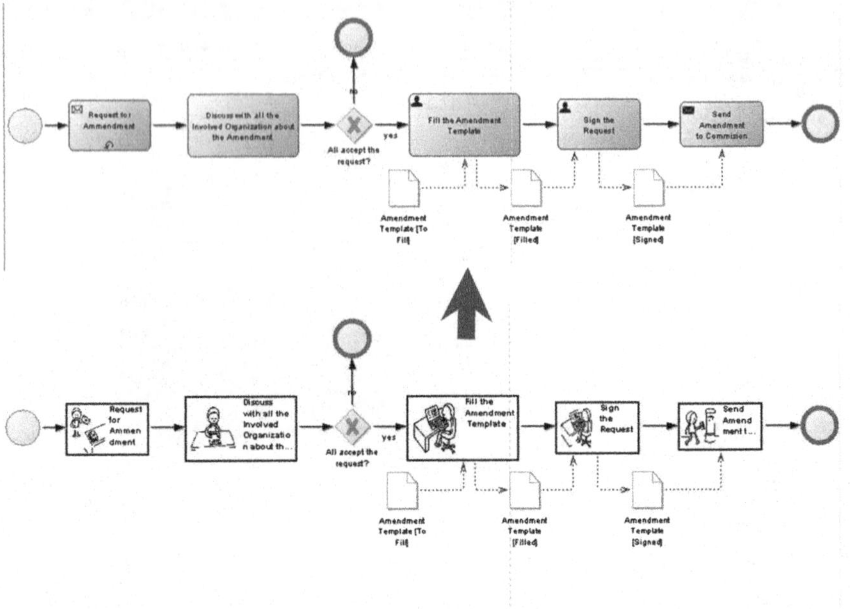

Fig. 11 People-Like View representation of a business process

Comments Sidebar The Comments Sidebar enables the collaborative commenting of modeling objects. On activation of the Commenting Sidebar, the drawing area is divided into an area where modeling is performed and an area where comments for each object are displayed; the bar itself can be placed horizontally—as shown in Fig. 12—or vertically.

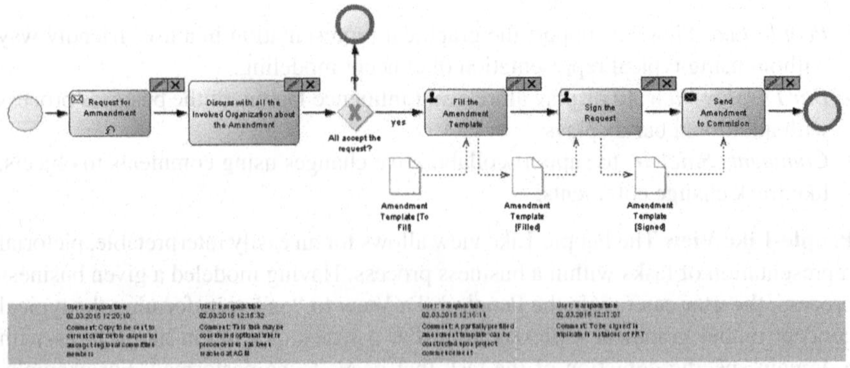

Fig. 12 Commenting Sidebar at a business process

When commenting is enabled, each modeling object receives two tabs at the top-right corner, one in form of a pencil to comment the object and one in form of an "×" to delete the associated comment. Upon entry of a comment, the comment is displayed in the comment bar next to the object, depending on the orientation of the commenting Sidebar. The comment also displays the user that made the comment and the time and date when the comment was made.

In addition to the aforementioned visualization extensions, specific transformation modules were also developed in order to interact with the others *task-specific* software components envisioned by the Learn PAd ecosystem [10]. Any of these interactions is mediated by the so-called Learn PAd Core Platform. Specifically the transformation modules enable to:

- Push New Model Set into Core Platform: This ends the modeling cycles and uploads the business process and all related information into the process-oriented learning platform.
- Retrieve Feedbacks about Model Artefacts from the collaborative platform: this collaboration feature imports comments residing in the wiki component of the learning platform into the modeling environment in form of the aforementioned comment sidebar.

4.2 Case Study

Since 1984, the European Commission (EC) has funded research and innovation in the European Union (EU) through the "*Framework Programmes for Research and Technological Development*" generally referred as FP. The participation in a EU financed project obliges the beneficiary to perform grant management and budget reporting activities as evidence for the tasks of the project. This results in quite a complex scenario so that we considered to validate the proposed modeling and learning solution. We will refer below to the European Project Budget Reporting (EPBR) in relation to the activities that an Italian public research body (in reference to its administrative offices) has to put in place in order to manage the administrative procedures related to the participation in a European research project. Within Public Administrations, it is often the case that the participation in a project requires to involve people from the administrative offices to support the formal reporting of performed activities (i.e., man-months, budget). In particular, we focus here on a more precise scenario, the case when an Italian university takes the role of coordinator for the whole project.

The models shown below were designed applying the storytelling methodology [13]. The methodology expects to involve the stakeholders in describing, using natural language, their daily routine reporting critical activities, and providing possible improvements. The objective is to capture knowledge via stories. With respect to other methodologies that for instance use interviews, the approach has the advantage that it allows a more easily enlightening of details associated with specific working contexts. The team involved in the meeting was composed by one Modeler, five Tellers and one Facilitators. The modeler was a researcher from the University of Camerino with a strong background in BP modeling and software engineering, Tellers were the employees of the university involved in the EPBR, in particular we involved employees from the economical department, the administration department, the IILO office and a couple of researchers from the school of science and technology with previous experience in EU research projects. The Facilitator was a researcher with a strong background in BP modeling and at the same time delegate for budget reporting of some running European and national projects. BP and Learn PAd related models were derived according to the storytelling approach and, finally, in order to validate the appropriateness of the model, a dedicated meeting involving the same stakeholders was arranged. The modeling activity was incremental, it started from a very simple BP and then, according to the discussions and refinement performed during the meeting, the version of the BP presented below was finally released.

The BP is triggered by the reception of the notification acceptance of the project by EU. To continue, the authorization of the involved faculty has to be asked also in order to identify the Principal Investigator. Then, a bank account to manage the budget of the project has to be created; in particular under the Italian law an N-IBA account must be created (standard IBAN is forbidden by law). Each new project has to be added as a new entry to the U-GOV tool that is a software application for the financial management of all the projects in which the university is involved. At this point, the Consortium and the Grant agreement are signed. All the projects of Italian universities have to be approved by the Ministry for Primary Education, Universities and Research (MIUR), then the project must be inserted in the related database, and a specific project-code named CUP has to be requested to the Ministry of Economical Development (MISE). 60 days after signing the Grant agreement, prefinancial funding is provided by the European Community, and then distributed to the project partners according to the project budget plan. At this point, project activities typically start and then the university has to manage the project activities according to the grant agreement that include the need to provide periodic reports, and possibly to make amendments to the contract if differences emerge with respect to the signed contract. At the end of the project, a final project report must be sent to the EU commission. Figure 13 reports the process resulting from the conducted analysis.

The described Business Process uses the following data objects that are described in the corresponding Documents and Knowledge models:

- **Research Project Form**. It is the data object including all the information about the EU project that must be reported to the school council for project approval. The form includes all the information regarding the project, such as the name, code, partner, budget, abstract, etc.
- **Faculty Council Report**. It is the data object reporting the decision taken by the faculty council on an EU project. The decision of the council authorizes, or not, the researchers to take part in the EU funded project.

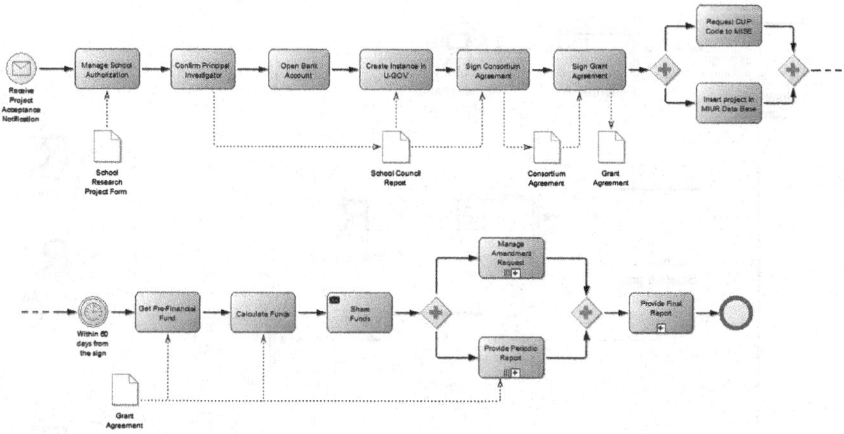

Fig. 13 Grant management process for the project coordinator

- **Consortium Agreement**. It is the data object reporting the legal instrument reflecting the relationship among the partners of the consortium, and should include all the clauses needed for a smooth execution of the project and to possibly solve disputes among partners. It is consistent with the Grant Agreement and it presents preliminary clauses (title, preamble, etc.), technical provisions, financial structure and management structure, Intellectual Property, the dispute resolution system and the final clauses (applicable law termination).
- **Grant Agreement**. It is the data object representing the legal instrument reflecting the relationship between the EU Commission and the project coordinator, acting on behalf of the project partners. The data-object reflects a standard template consolidated by the EU commission and it reports the terms and conditions referring to the accession to the grant agreement of the other beneficiaries, the duration and start date of the project, the reporting period, prefinancing, etc.

With reference to the organizational view, the University of Camerino shows a quite complex structure that includes many different divisions. From the administration point of view, the general regulation of the athenaeum precisely establishes the functional organization of services, divisions and offices. In particular, it details the competence, the attributions and the responsibilities of each office. Few of them are involved in the EU budget reporting activities, as reported in the following and illustrated in Fig. 14. First of all, the Financial and Assets division is delegated to manage the overall budget considering the whole university. Then, the research and technology transfer division is delegated to manage all financial aspects related to the research/technological activities as well as possible outcomes of research and corresponding interactions with external companies. This division includes two subdivisions: (i) the Schools Management division that is responsible for managing all the financial activities, while (ii) the International and Industrial Liaison Office is responsible for promoting the research and the technological activities of the univer-

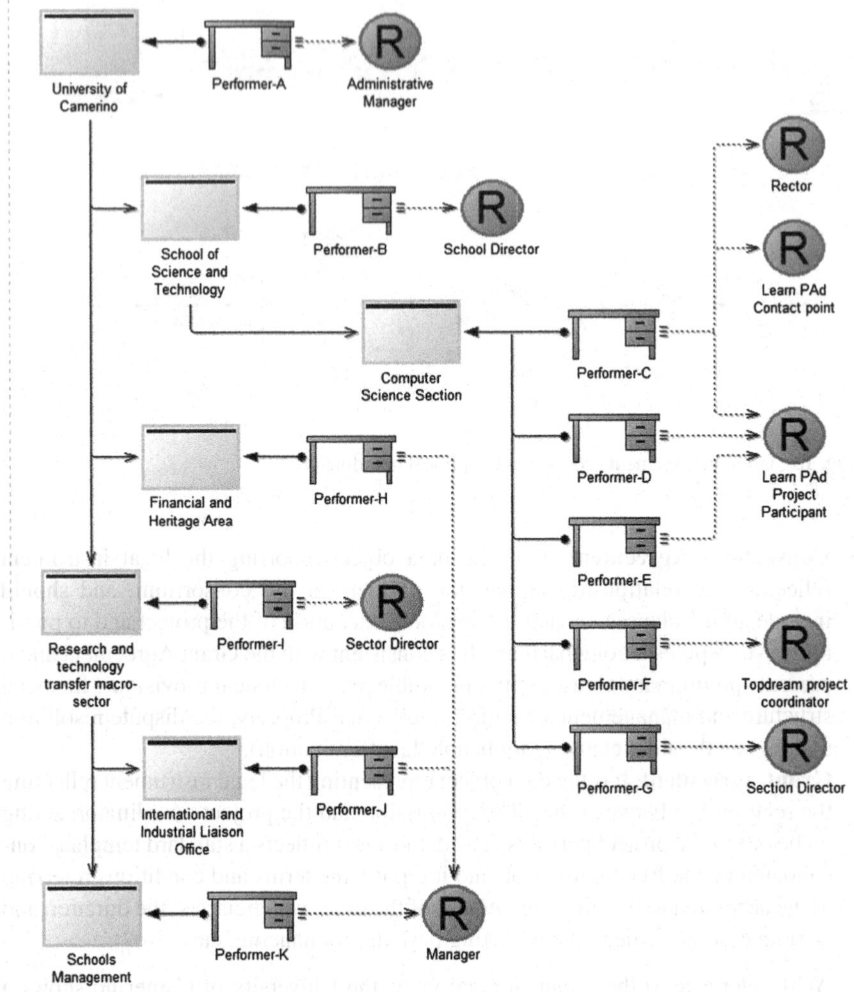

Fig. 14 Excerpt of the Unicam organization chart

sity. It is worth mentioning that, for each division, there is only one person responsible, and other employees playing different or similar roles. Each employee belongs to a single office and has specific competence and expertise as required by her/his role.

For each activity in the process we also defined the needed competences to perform the activity. This work was driven by the classification of skills using three different categories. Therefore, we distinguish between (i) Analytical skills, referring to the selection and gathering of information related to a working activity (i.e., problem finding); (ii) Diagnostic skills, referring to comprehension-evaluation of the working activities to be performed (i.e., problem setting); and (iii) Implementation skills, referring to the final accomplishment of activities and tasks for transformation or achievement of professional results (i.e., problem solving). We also considered the levels of European Qualification Framework (EQF) as it is widely used and adopted, and hence it was used to improve the Learn PAd competence model. The EQF is envisaged as a meta-framework that allows to position and compare learning outcomes/competency levels. Finally, we included learning goals that have to be reached by the civil servant using the platform. These are: proper management of user requests, check regularity/irregularity of the requests, coordination of the administrative procedure in terms of timing and modality provided by the norms, check regularity of data and declarations, and draw up an administrative act. Finally, Key Performance Indicators (KPI) were defined to check if the learning goals are reached. The models derived as a consequence of the described activities are reported in a publicly available deliverable [11]. The models were used to train employees in the Unicam offices and experiments on the effectiveness of the approach are currently running.

5 Conclusions

This chapter described a modeling approach that intends to foster the usage of models for the training of civil servants. The metamodel described in the chapter was implemented on ADO*xx* and the available feature extensions were added to improve the modeling tool for Learn PAd. The tool was developed collaboratively in the development space of ADOxx.org, which enables a transparent and collaborative development from the initial requirement list to the various prototypes, until reaching the current status of the prototype.

The modeling environment was already used to derive the models for the demonstrators foreseen by the Learn PAd research project. This chapter reported some of the models derived in relation to the development of one of the demonstrators foreseen by the Learn PAd project.

Acknowledgments This research has been partially funded by EU project Learn PAd (GA:619583).

Tool Download http://www.omilab.org/learnpad.

References

1. Business Process Model OMG: Notation (BPMN) 2.0. Object Management Group, Needham MA, 2494:34 (2011)
2. OMG: Case Management Model and Notation (CMMN). V 1.0. Technical report, Object Management Group OMG (2013)
3. OMG: Business Motivation Model (BMM). Technical report, Object Management Group OMG (2014)

4. Atkinson, C., Stoll, D.: Orthographic modeling environment. In: Fundamental Approaches to Software Engineering, pp. 93–96. Springer (2008)
5. Del Fabro, M.D., Bézivin, J., Jouault, F., Valduriez, P., et al.: Applying generic model management to data mapping. In: BDA (2005)
6. Dexa, Aix-en-Provence, France, LNCS 2455, Springer-Verlag, Berlin, Heidelberg, pp. 182 (2002)
7. Efendioglu, N., Woitsch, R., Karagiannis, D.: Modelling method design: A model-driven approach, In: iiWAS 15 Proceedings of the 17th International Conference on Information Integration and Web-based Applications and Services, No 59, ACM, NY, USA (2015)
8. Iacob, M.E., Jonkers, H., Lankhorst, M., Proper, E., Quartel, D.A.C.: Archimate 2.0 specification (2012)
9. Karagiannis, D.: Agile modelling method engineering. In: Proceedings of the 19th Panhellenic Conference on Informatics, ACM, New York (2015)
10. Mancinelli, F., De Angelis, G. (eds.): Platform Architectural Description. Number Del. 2.1. The Leand PAd Consortium (2014)
11. Re, B. (ed.): Demonstrators BP and Knowledge Models. Number Del. 8.1. The Learn PAd Consortium (2015)
12. Recker, J., Indulska, M., Rosemann, M., Green, P.: How good is BPMN really? Insights from theory and practice (2006)
13. Santoro, F.M., Borges, M., Pino, J.: Acquiring knowledge on business processes from stakeholders' stories. Adv. Eng. Inf. **24**(2), 138–148 (2010)
14. Zachman, J.A.: Concepts of the Framework for Enterprise Architecture. Los Angels, CA (1996)

Printed in the United States
By Bookmasters

Printed in the United States
By Bookmasters